Text and Tradition in Early Modern North India

Text and Tradition in Early Modern North India

Edited by
Tyler Williams
Anshu Malhotra
John Stratton Hawley

OXFORD
UNIVERSITY PRESS

OXFORD
UNIVERSITY PRESS

Oxford University Press is a department of the University of Oxford. It furthers the University's objective of excellence in research, scholarship, and education by publishing worldwide. Oxford is a registered trademark of Oxford University Press in the UK and in certain other countries.

Published in India by
Oxford University Press
2/11 Ground Floor, Ansari Road, Daryaganj, New Delhi 110 002, India

First Edition published in 2018

ISBN-13 (print edition): 978-0-19-947886-6
ISBN-10 (print edition): 0-19-947886-4

ISBN-13 (eBook): 978-0-19-909167-6
ISBN-10 (eBook): 0-19-909167-6

Typeset in ScalaPro 10/13
by Tranistics Data Technologies, Kolkata 700 091
Printed in India by Replika Press Pvt. Ltd

Contents

Tables

Acknowledgements

The editors wish to thank the Indian Institute of Advanced Study (IIAS), Shimla, India, for graciously hosting the International Conference on Early Modern Literatures in North India in July 2012; the conference brought together scholars of language, literature, religion, and history from around the world to exchange ideas and learn from each other's work. A selection of the papers presented during the conference are presented here in this volume. The conference began in 1979 as the 'International Middle Hindi Bhakti Conference', hosted by the Katholieke Universiteit Leuven, Belgium; it has since met on twelve occasions, each time in a different location and with a different host institution (except for one return to Leuven), but always with an expanding area of linguistic and disciplinary concern, and consequently with an ever-expanding group of scholars. During this particular instantiation of the conference, we were pleased to have the widest representation of languages, regions, and disciplinary perspectives at the conference that had yet occurred; it was also the first time that papers had been presented at the conference in Hindi as well as in English.

This would not have been possible without the intellectual, organizational, and financial collaboration supplied by the IIAS. In particular, the editors would like to thank the former director of the IIAS, Dr Peter Ronald d'Souza, for his intellectual guidance and institutional support, and Dr Rajvinder Singh, for his enthusiastic assistance in every aspect of the conference's planning and implementation. Finally, we would like to thank all those scholars who attended the conference, including those who came from India and from abroad, as well as the fellows in residence at the IIAS itself who participated (including the late and dearly remembered Omprakash Valmiki), for making the conference a resounding success.

Note on Transliteration

The transliteration of non-English terms poses a particularly complex challenge in a volume of this size and scope. Terms and quotations from no fewer than seven languages make their way into the text, and transliteration schemes for different languages can vary quite widely. Not only that, different transliteration schemes are sometimes used by scholars for the same language, depending on the academic context and the needs of a particular audience.

The editors have consequently adopted an approach that attempts to respect the multiplicity and diversity of South Asian languages as well as the variety of scholarly approaches to studying and representing them. Contributors have been encouraged to use the transliteration scheme that most effectively responds to the needs of their own individual situations. In consequence, readers will often encounter differences in the way different languages are represented from one chapter to another. One difference that readers will encounter frequently is the presence or absence of the final 'a' (schwa) of Indic words. The final 'a' has been retained in the context of Sanskrit and in quotations from vernacular verse (where it is pronounced), but has often been omitted from individual terms when they appear in the main text (reflecting common pronunciation in everyday speech). The editors hope that these variations will not be distracting or erect impediments to understanding, and have tried to standardize transliterations and spellings to the greatest extent possible. This has had a particular effect on the names of well-known persons such as Chaitanya or Keshavdas, whom we want to be easily recognizable across chapters. In standardizing their names with these simplified spellings, we create a distance between them and some of the lesser-known figures who appear in the same chapters that they do. We regret these seemingly unavoidable discontinuities.

Conventions adopted by Oxford University Press have also had an effect on the volume, creating regularities of text and formatting that sometimes differ from common academic practices in the field. We flag them here so that readers can anticipate them. First, non-English terms in the body of a given chapter have normally been italicized when they first appear but not on subsequent occasions. There are, however, instances in which terms of non-English origin have become sufficiently common in English speech and writing that they are represented without italics. Indented blocks of text from Indic languages have also been given in roman type, and this is so in the case of text quoted in the notes, as well. In contrast, the titles of books, articles, and similar compositions are given in italics, and the words they contain, if of non-English origin, are presented with diacritics in almost all instances. Some of these conventions may seem strange when first encountered, but we hope that readers will quickly acclimatize themselves and appreciate the effort at standardization that they represent.

Finally, an individual term itself may carry multiple meanings, as in the case of *pad/pada*, which can refer to a unit of prosody, a literary genre, or a musical lyric, depending on the context. We have tried to differentiate and highlight such meanings wherever possible so as not to confuse the reader. The subtle changes in meaning that can occur when a term or concept moves between different languages or traditions can sometimes pose challenges to understanding. Yet challenges such as these, however intricate, are an important part of the collaborative work of scholarship this volume attempts to represent.

TYLER WILLIAMS *AND* ANSHU MALHOTRA

Introduction

The chapters comprising this volume first came together when they were presented in draft form at a conference hosted by the Indian Institute of Advanced Study (IIAS) at Shimla in August 2012. Collectively, they reflect developments in several scholarly disciplines that deal with the literary, historical, and religious heritage of early modern north India, or more appropriately the northern region of South Asia, an area that does not correspond closely to contemporary national boundaries. They touch upon texts, traditions, individuals, and groups that existed in an area that stretches from Kashmir in the north to the northern edge of the Deccan in the south, and from the jungles of Bangladesh in the east to the plains of Pakistani Punjab in the west. The dizzying variety of literary and devotional traditions found across this region and across the chronological space of the 'early modern' period (the contours of which will be discussed later, and which is understood here to extend from the thirteenth through the eighteenth century) makes the material presented in this book both rich and varied. Yet the clear existence of common threads, concerns, processes, and trends across these various traditions makes the act of putting them together a productive enterprise—or at least this is our hope in doing so.

Creating a volume that operates in such a wide geographical and discursive space speaks to the importance of reconstructing multilingual literary histories, a project recently articulated by Francesca

Orsini in regard to the geographical and chronological area of early modern north India and by Sheldon Pollock in regard to the broader history of South Asia in general.[1] The multilingual literary culture that flourished in precolonial South Asia can be seen as having both horizontal and vertical axes: as the process of vernacularization progressed throughout the second millennium, exchanges occurred not only horizontally between the literary cultures of different vernaculars but also vertically between those vernaculars and the superposed cosmopolitan languages of Sanskrit and Persian.[2] Exchanges also occurred horizontally between Sanskrit and Persian—quite likely through the intermediate language of the vernacular—giving additional complexity to this picture.[3] In fact, the matrix of generic, aesthetic, religious, social, and political factors that determined which language was used where and for what purpose is perhaps best characterized by the metaphor of an 'ecology of language' as used by Shantanu Phukan, with its suggestion of a dense interplay between multiple languages, each with its own expressive and ideational role to play in a given culture.[4]

The chapters in this book—covering the linguistic terrain of Sanskrit, Persian, Bengali, Brajbhasha, Avadhi, Urdu, Marwari, and Gujarati[5]—contribute to our understanding of how these languages coexisted, at times sharing a discursive or cultural space (for example, the distinction of being used as a liturgical language), at other times competing for those spaces and the prestige that attended them. Often these languages drew heavily from one another, a fact that a volume of this scope helps us to see. The exchanges that come into view when seen through such a wide-angle lens appear to have occurred not only across languages but also across genres, registers, metrical systems, religious identities, sectarian boundaries, and philosophical traditions.

This is a daunting landscape. In the introduction that follows, we hope to navigate its complexity in ways that will cast light on some of the special contributions made by the chapters that appear here, especially since the working categories to which they have been assigned may not always indicate these cross-cutting contributions. What are those provisional categories? In Part I, we have grouped a set of chapters dedicated to exploring connections between cosmopolitan languages and their vernacular or *bhāṣā* counterparts (more of this immediately below). In Part II, by contrast, we give attention to particular 'poetic genres and personalities', as the title of that section declares—personalities such as Banarsidas, Kabir, Raskhan, and Keshavdas, and genres such as the *pada*, the *savaiyā*, and the *bārahmāsā*. With regard to these genres, metre, *raga*, and religious community emerge as relevant concerns. In Part III, we turn to the matter of writing history—history in the vernacular, and in this instance, the broad vernacular family that came to collectively be called 'Hindi'. Authors of the chapters appearing in this section share the conviction that Hindi language sources for writing history have often not been given the attention they deserve in prior scholarship. In Part IV, finally, we present a set of chapters that examine the formation and preservation of two of the most influential *sampradāys* (traditions of teaching and initiation) that structure the religious lives of people living as far apart as Bengal and Gujarat—those who associate themselves with the founding personalities of Chaitanya and Vallabhacharya.

In this introduction, therefore, we will look at certain themes regarding connection and exchange—themes which connect the chapters of this book across the categories outlined above. The first type of exchange that we will consider occurred between different languages and the literary cultures that developed within them, both 'vernacular' and 'cosmopolitan'. This will naturally lead into an investigation of movements across genre and register, such as drama, travelogue, treatise, bārahmāsā, and *śāstra* (scientific treatise)—thus the second type of exchange. These types of experimentation and modification of genre and register often occurred in the context of dialogue (both collaborative and combative) between different religious and philosophical traditions; such encounters thus constitute the third type of exchange. Having considered these three, we will step back to consider how these various encounters and connections reflect networks of people, texts, and ideas that were 'in motion' during the early modern period. A growing contingent of historians has recently defined the 'early modern' period or ecumene in precisely these terms: as being characterized by an increase in the movement of people and the proliferation of connections between them. We will briefly discuss how the chapters in this volume help us understand ways in which the history of this period is being imagined and written about in the present before turning to consider how early modern poets and chroniclers themselves wrote the history of their times—history 'in the vernacular'. Finally, we will attempt to tie these various strands and stories together by reflecting on the discursive and material conditions in which works and ideas were transmitted and circulated. This discussion of history—material, intellectual, religious, and literary—reflects a growing awareness of how much the disciplines of literature, religious studies, and history have to say to each other. It was an enthusiastic belief in just this type of collaboration that brought scholars of philology, literature, religion, and history together in Shimla.

Exchanges across Languages and Literary Cultures

We begin, in Part I, by emphasizing the manifold connections that existed between and across languages in early modern north India, but our use of the term 'language' suggests that it makes sense to ask what constitutes a distinct language as such. Where, when, and how does the consciousness of an idiom as a distinct and autonomous language (especially a literary language) come to be? In the case of 'Hindi', a term whose exact referent has been debated for the past century and a half, Imre Bangha points us in a provocative and intriguing direction by locating the source of what would later become the literary idioms associated with the Hindi heartland—Brajbhasha, Avadhi, Khari Boli, and so on—in Maru-Gurjar, an idiom originating not in the Gangetic plain but in western India, particularly the lands of modern Gujarat and western Rajasthan. Bangha persuasively argues that it was this literary language, originally cultivated by Jains beginning in the late twelfth century, that eventually spread to the lands known as *madhyadeś*, where in the course of the fourteenth and fifteenth centuries it developed into the forms that we now associate with Brajbhasha and Avadhi. Bangha also reveals that the linguistic and literary evidence for this connection has been apparent for some time, but modern Hindi literary historiography, taking nationalism as its organizing principle and embracing a strict sense of religion as one of the significant boundaries of literary culture, has been largely unable to see it.

Such tight associations between literary idiom and religious or even geographical identity in modern scholarship have also made it difficult to see the lively and productive exchanges that occurred between distinct literary languages in this period. These exchanges and the religious, political, and aesthetic ideas and values that informed them are the subject of the first section of the book, 'Between Cosmopolitan and *Bhāṣā*', which begins with Bangha's historical mapping of how a vernacular language of place (bhāṣā) was gradually transformed into a trans-local literary language capable of doing the ideational and aesthetic work of 'literature' (*kāvya*). As Pollock has argued, this transformation involved the appropriation of elements from the superposed cosmopolitan language and its literature into the vernacular.[6] Arthur Dudney explores this process in the context of Persian and Urdu in his chapter, 'Urdu as Persian: Some Eighteenth-Century Evidence on Vernacular Poetry as Language Planning'. Focusing on the writings of Siraj al-Din ʿAli Khan Arzu (d. 1756), a critic of Persian literature and early theorist of what would come to be known as Urdu, Dudney shows how the sociolinguistic concept of 'language planning' can be used to understand the historical process through which a literary language is delineated and defined as such. He also demonstrates the extent to which individual authors and texts can shape this process—in this case Arzu and a network of authors connected to him that spans a few generations. Defining a new literary idiom involves not only identifying what that idiom *is*, but also specifying what it *is not*. In the writings of Arzu and others, Dudney finds that the concept of *rozmarrah* (colloquial or 'everyday' language) was essential to defining what Urdu was, just as the exclusion of lexical items and forms of speech from Persian and Brajbhasha established what Urdu was not.

The rise of literary vernaculars such as Urdu, Hindi, Bengali, Gujarati, and the like did not, as is sometimes inferred, lead to the total demise of classical, cosmopolitan languages such as Sanskrit and Persian in the early modern period. On the contrary, Sanskrit and Persian continued to inform the development of literature and religious thought in these languages even as vernacular translations, commentaries, and adaptations provided their audiences with a window into the literary, religious, and intellectual world of Sanskrit and Persian. Just this sort of an exchange between Sanskrit and Hindi (Brajbhasha) is the subject of Tyler Williams's essay, 'Commentary as Translation: The *Vairāgya Vṛnd* of Bhagvandas Niranjanī'. Williams examines how the monk-poet Bhagvandas, although ostensibly writing a vernacular commentary (*ṭīkā*) on the Sanskrit *Vairāgya Śataka* (Hundred Verses on Non-Attachment) of Bhartrihari, in fact adapts the genre of the commentary so as to transform Bhartrihari's poetic anthology into a religious treatise. In doing so, Bhagvandas not only gives his audience—the monastic and householder members of the Niranjani Sampraday, as well as members of other devotional sects and even courtly elites—access to the original Sanskrit, but also radically transforms that source text in the process.

The movement of material between Sanskrit and the vernacular was by no means unidirectional, as Samuel Wright demonstrates in his analysis of Radhamohan Thakkur's *Mahābhāvānusāriṇī-ṭīkā*, a Sanskrit commentary on Bengali devotional poetry. In his essay, 'Making Sense of *Bhāṣā* in Sanskrit: Radhamohan Thakkur's *Mahābhāvānusāriṇī-ṭīkā* and Literary Culture in Early Eighteenth-Century Bengal', Wright breaks down the techniques employed by Radhamohan in his exegesis of Gaudiya Vaishnava poetry, particularly his use of Sanskrit lexicon in the glossing of Bengali words and his emphasis on the technique of *śleṣa* (punning). Wright argues that Radhamohan's apposition of Sanskrit and the vernacular through such techniques was not only an attempt to show that Sanskrit poetic theory could be used to explain how vernacular poetry 'works' (that is, achieves its effects), but also to establish that such vernacular poetry worked *as literature*, a distinction previously accorded only to Sanskrit.

Though no longer able to claim a monopoly on literary expression, Sanskrit continued to be an integral part of early modern literary culture, as Luther Obrock demonstrates in his chapter, 'Muslim *Mahākāvyas*: Sanskrit and Translation in the Sultanates', a study of exchanges between the cosmopolitan idioms of Sanskrit and Persian at pre-Mughal Sultanate courts. Obrock introduces us to three remarkable texts: Udayaraja's *Rājavinoda*, an encomium that praises the Muzaffarid Sultan Mahmud Begada of Gujarat using terms adapted from idealized representations of Hindu kingship; Kalyana Malla's *Sulaimaccarita*, a retelling of both the Biblical narrative of David and Bathsheba and the story of the jinn and the fisherman that appears in the *Thousand and One Nights*; and finally Shrivara's *Kathākautuka*, a translation of Jami's *Yūsuf wa Zulaykhā* that effectively transforms the Persian, Sufi-influenced *masnavī* poetic genre into a Sanskrit kāvya of Shaivite devotion. Obrock argues that these works can be understood as sites of cultural and literary encounter where poets and intellectuals experimented creatively to secure Sanskrit's continuing relevance in the changing literary ecology of the regional sultanates.

Moving beyond the first section of the volume, the reader will find that even in chapters that foreground other concerns—theology, history, politics, and aesthetics, among others—the issue of exchange between languages and literary cultures remains clearly visible in the background. For example, Stefania Cavaliere's 'Religious Syncretism and Literary Innovation: New Perspectives on *Bhakti* and *Rasa*s in the *Vijñānagītā* of Keshavdas', engages with a text that is, at least on the face of it, a Hindi translation of a Sanskrit drama—and yet, as Cavaliere shows, the *Vijñānagītā* was so much more than 'just' a translation. Some works from this period reflect influences from multiple languages and literary cultures. In his essay, 'Making the War Come Alive: Ḍiṅgal Poetry and Padmakar's *Himmatbahādurvirudāvalī*', Dalpat Rajpurohit finds in Padmakar's Brajbhasha poetry marked influences from the Ḍiṅgal tradition of western India, Apabhramsha, and Sanskrit. On the other hand, focusing on a single genre can help us connect different languages and traditions. In 'Hindi *Bārahmāsā* Tradition: From Narpati Nalha to Present-Day Folk Songs and Popular Publications', Teiji Sakata compares poems of the bārahmāsā, or 'twelve-month' form, showing us how they form a piece of shared literary heritage between languages that in the modern period have been considered to be quite separate.

The reader will notice in some (though certainly not all) of the chapters collected here that religion—or perhaps construed more broadly, devotion—is often at work in the exchanges between languages and literatures. This is worth noting, as the role of religion in the process of vernacularization in South Asia has been a source of serious research and debate over the past several years. Pollock, in his highly influential model of vernacularization, locates both the drivers of vernacularization and the arena in which it took place in the political sphere, with religion playing a secondary role in terms of both importance and chronology.[7] Some of the chapters in this volume—in particular those by Cort, Wright, and Williams—complicate that picture by showing how authors and texts pursuing explicitly religious projects or concerns could and did contribute to the process of vernacularization. In the time intervening between the conference at Shimla and the publication of this volume, there has been renewed interest in addressing the role of *bhakti* in vernacularization, as in the workshop on '*Bhakti* Literature between the Elite and the Popular' convened at Harvard University in May 2014. The need for further research into the historical particularities of vernacularization in different regions was also addressed at an earlier conference in which Pollock's students and close colleagues celebrated his work.[8] We hope that the current volume helps to enrich this ongoing conversation.

Movement across Genre and Register

The texts and performances described in the pages that follow often cross boundaries not only of language and region, but also of genre and register. This movement of themes, characters, motifs, and symbols not only reveals what was shared between literatures and traditions, but also highlights the factors that distinguished them from one another. Two genres or registers might share common material, but employ it in very different ways—and thus help to define their own boundaries in the course of doing so. To return to the example of the bārahmāsā, Sakata's study surveys several poems composed according to the stylistic conventions of this 'twelve-month' form, yet each one has a distinct narrative, religious, and performative context that informed its reception and shaped its meaning. For example, the bārahmāsā contained within Jayasī's *Padmāvat* dramatizes the emotional states of characters implicated in a longer narrative; the bārahmāsā attributed to the poetess Mirabai is an expression of longing for the Divine in the form of Krishna; the 'folk' versions of the bārahmāsā in Avadhi and Bundeli express more worldly concerns such as longing for a distant beloved or the fear of moneylenders.

Translation and commentary often provided an opportunity for genre-bending. In fact, the multilingual, politically and religiously dynamic world of early modern north India provided a testing ground for all sorts of experimentation along these lines. Such a spirit of experimentation was clearly at work in Keshavdas's *Vijñānagītā*, which, as we saw earlier, was ostensibly a Brajbhasha adaptation of an allegorical Sanskrit drama, the *Prabodhacandrodaya* of Krishna Mishra. Yet, as Cavaliere shows us, the allegorical battle between aspects of the mind becomes in Keshavdas's hands a platform for a much broader discussion of metaphysics, theology, and religious aesthetics, incorporating such diverse influences as the *Yogavāsiṣṭha*, the Purāṇas, the Dharmaśāstras, and the Bhagavad Gītā. In this way, the *Vijñānagītā* reads more like a scientific treatise (śāstra) than a work of allegorical poetry, and reflects Keshavdas's erudition and innovation in weaving together strands of bhakti, Advaita Vedānta, and *rasa* aesthetic theory. Innovation through the manipulation of genre was also at work in the *Vairāgya Vṛnd* of Bhagvandas Niranjani: as mentioned previously, Williams's chapter highlights how this religious poet used the form of the commentary to effectively change a poetic anthology, the *Vairāgya Śataka* of Bhartrihari, into a religious work. As we shall see shortly, Rembert Lutjeharms finds a similar kind of creativity at work in Rupa Goswami's *Padyāvalī*, which assembles verses by multiple poets into a sort of theological treatise. This creativity could also manifest itself across different works by the same poet or scholar, as Shrivatsa Goswami shows us in the case of Gopal Bhatt, who wrote works both in the vein of philosophy and in a style that could be termed a 'code book of conduct'.

In order to see the processes and effects of experimentation in the realms of genre and register, we sometimes have to 'zoom in' on the intricate workings of particular poems and the careers of their individual authors. This is exactly what Hiroko Nagasaki has accomplished in her chapter, 'Duality in the Language and Literary Style of Raskhan's Poetry'. Nagasaki looks closely at the poet Raskhan's signature *chands*, that is, the metrical forms in which he most frequently composed, focusing in particular on the savaiyā. What she finds is a metrical structure that combined Persian and Indic systems of prosody, allowing different methods of scansion and, therefore, different stylistic options. This discovery in turn reveals a connection between Raskhan's poems of Vaishnava bhakti and the highly stylized world of the Persian ghazal, a form heavily influenced by the idiom of Sufi devotion. These insights into stylistic crossover are even more interesting given the hagiographical tradition surrounding Raskhan, which claims he was a Muslim who took up devotion to Krishna at some point in adulthood.

On the other hand, it is sometimes necessary to 'zoom out' to the level of regional political history in order to gain insight into the use of genre and register in a single text. This is the approach Heidi Pauwels takes in 'The Pursuit of Pilgrimage, Pleasure, and Military Alliances: Nagaridas's *Tīrthānand*'. The *Tīrthānand* (1753) is the memoir of a two-year pilgrimage to Braj composed by Nagaridas, also known as Savant Singh, the deposed king of Kishangarh. Pauwels delineates how the 'culturally mediated category' of pilgrimage structures Nagaridas's experience and its narratological reconstruction in the versified memoir; just as pilgrimage itself is a 'polysemous' experience that satisfied multiple goals and needs, the *Tīrthānand* works at multiple levels. As Nagaridas narrates events in the mundane world—visits to temples, devotional singing, religious plays, and the like—he frequently elevates these happenings onto the mythological plane of Radha and Krishna's eternal Braj; at the same time, contemporary political circumstances and errands of royal necessity intrude at critical junctures of the narrative. The *Tīrthānand* is thus a tribute to mythical Braj, a travelogue, and—perhaps, in spite of the wishes of its author—a chronicle of contemporary political and social developments, as will be discussed in further detail later.

The sophisticated blending of historic description, religious imagery, and poetic device is foregrounded in the chapters of Allison Busch, Dalpat Rajpurohit, and William Pinch, all of which explore different aspects of the poet Padmakar Bhatt's *Himmatbahādurvirudāvalī* (1792[?]), an account of the ascetic warlord Anupgir Gosain's victory over the Bundelkhandi prince Arjun Singh Parmar in 1792. The importance of such vernacular chronicles as historical sources will be dealt with shortly; for now, let us note how richly varied the sources and functions of genre and style can be in such a poetic work. As Rajpurohit explains, although Padmakar composed in Brajbhasha, he incorporated metric and stylistic conventions from martial poetry found in multiple traditions—that of the *rāso* and Diṅgal poetry of Rajasthan, to be sure, but also from less expected places such as the *Rāmcaritmānas* of Tulsidas. Describing how these techniques of martial poetry made their way into the Brajbhasha poetry of the seventeenth and eighteenth centuries, Rajpurohit shows how they provided Padmakar with the tools to construct a didactic account of war and present Anupgir in terms of the ideal Kshatriya warrior. Busch takes this analysis further by placing Padmakar and the *Himmatbahādurvirudāvalī* in the context of the literary and political imaginary of the eighteenth century: Padmakar inherits the genre of the *virudāvalī* (itself a multifaceted tradition) from Sanskrit, as well as a rich lexicon from the vernacular, Arabic, and Persian. The form and language of his work thus reflect the changed political and cultural realities of his time. Similarly, the seamless movement between modes of versitic and poetic description in the *Himmatbahādurvirudāvalī* reflects Padmakar's simultaneous function as both historian and poet.

Exchanges between Religious and Philosophical Traditions

Just as a single composition could become a site of movement between and experiments within genres, a particular genre or literary form could often become a site of exchange between different religious or philosophical traditions. Take, for example, the case of the *phaguā*, a type of song associated with the festival of Holi: as John Cort demonstrates in his chapter, '"This Is How We Play Holī": Allegory in North Indian Digambar Jain Holī Songs', the phaguā form—which involved descriptions of spring and the desire for an absent beloved—was shared by various traditions of Jainism and Hinduism alike, but each tradition put it to quite a distinct use. In the case of the Digambar Jains, the antinomian transgressions of the Holi festival presented an ethical problem, and so their poets adapted the sensual and sexualized phaguā into a metaphorical description of various aspects of the 'self' and its struggle for spiritual realization. Digambar poets such as Banarasidas and Dhyanatray 'tamed' Holi by turning its poetic and musical tradition into a didactic dissertation on discipline, even while retaining the narrative elements (such as separated lovers, seasonal fecundity, and so on) that were put to more erotic use in other traditions. On the one hand, they shared in the tradition of phaguā with other groups; on the other, they consciously distanced themselves from other streams of that tradition.

Thus, engaging with a tradition other than one's own could sometimes be a way to establish a meaningful connection with that other tradition while at the same time distinguishing oneself from it; this is the case with the treatment of Vedanta in the Gaudiya Sampraday, as revealed by Rembert Lutjeharms in his chapter, '"Why Do We Still Sift the Husk-Like *Upaniṣads*?" Revisiting Vedānta in Early Chaitanya Vaishnava Theology'. Examining the *Padyāvalī* of the pre-eminent Gaudiya theologian Rupa Goswami, Lutjeharms examines how Rupa creatively arranges both religious and non-religious verses by numerous poets into a dissertation that evinces intimate familiarity with Vedanta (particularly Advaita Vedanta), but ultimately establishes bhakti as being superior to Vedanta's primary object, liberation. Redrawing the lines between Vedanta and Vaishnavism also affords Rupa the opportunity to distinguish Chaitanyaite theology from that of other Vaishnava sects such as the Sri Vaishnava Sampraday, which had also wrestled with Vedanta in its own theological literature.

Exchange between religious and philosophical traditions is also a clear theme in the chapters of Obrock (who deals with the translation and transformation of narratives and tropes from the Bible, Qur'an, and Indian epics at a sultanate court), Cavaliere (who investigates the integration of Vedanta and bhakti in a didactic text for a Mughal patron), Sakata (who surveys the genre of the bārahmāsā across Sufi, romance, and folk traditions), and Williams (who documents the incorporation of Sanskrit poetry on renunciation into the framework of householder bhakti). As these chapters demonstrate, the effect or product of such exchange was not necessarily syncretic—groups and traditions could adopt or incorporate material or practices from other groups while maintaining their own distinct identity.

Networks of Peoples, Texts, and Ideas

All of the themes outlined above involve, in one way or another, exchange, and exchange presupposes some type of connection. Many connections in turn constitute a network, and the chapters in this volume help us to identify what kind of networks—networks of people, places, ideas, and texts—existed in early modern India, and imagine how they worked. Sanjay Subrahmanyam has emphasized that what distinguishes this period in history is the increased contact among different peoples and across greater and greater distances (something we will discuss in greater detail shortly).[9] The task for scholars working on this place and time then is to find these points of contact and the networks they collectively form, and understand not only how they circulated objects and ideas but also how they led to new kinds of community. Jack Hawley, whose study of the decisive role played by Bhatts in the development of Braj and Krishna devotion can be found in this volume, has recently suggested a model for imagining one such aspect of early modern India: the idea of a 'bhakti network'.[10] In Hawley's view, imagining bhakti as a network made of various communities (sectarian and otherwise), institutions, and individuals that moved poems, ideas, motifs, and literary forms across languages, regions, and traditions may help us to make sense of the striking number of shared devotional and literary elements across early modern India, while also recognizing substantial variations in belief and expression. One of the great advantages to such an approach, as opposed to, say, the idea of bhakti as a 'movement', is that it avoids positing a central essence that animates and manifests itself within every instance of bhakti devotion at all places and times, and instead allows the various historical agents crowded under the umbrella of bhakti to tell their own stories of how they obtained an element from one source and developed it in a different direction, passing it on to others.

What might this network have looked like in regard to a single tradition or the poetry of a single author? Jaroslav Strnad gives us some insight into how networks of transmission might have shaped the available Kabir corpus in his chapter, 'Searching for the Source or Mapping the Stream? Some Text-Critical Issues in the Study of Medieval *Bhakti*'. Recognizing that the existing body of Kabir's poetry was produced by the interplay of both oral and written traditions, and analysing the internal structure of individual poems as well as the organizational structure of manuscripts, Strnad suggests how we might trace the growth of this poetry along thematic and stylistic lines, and through the efforts of multiple performers and composers. He consequently argues that the study of poets in this period—many of whose 'original' oeuvres are as elusive as that of Kabir—might be more fruitfully pursued as the mapping of such 'streams' of poetic development, rather than as a hunt for *ur*-texts.

Finally, Emilia Bachrach's chapter, 'Religious Reading and Everyday Lives', shows us how the network of people, ideas, and texts that constitute the world of bhakti continues to produce new devotees, new ideas, and new texts even today. Bachrach paints a vivid ethnographic picture of *vārtā satsaṅg*s in present-day Ahmadabad: meetings in which members of the Vallabha Sampraday, especially women, read and discuss sections of the sampraday's two central hagiographies, the *Caurāsī vaiṣṇavan kī vārtā* and the *Do sau bhāvan vaiṣṇavan kī vārtā*. Showing how these women use the stories of saints' lives to understand and navigate their own social and religious worlds, Bachrach argues that such religious reading practices are an active and productive process, providing a space for debate, interpretation, and exploration of sectarian identity.

The Issue of Early Modernity

We spoke earlier of the need both to zoom in and to zoom out if one hopes to appreciate the full force of changes in register and genre that come into view during the period we have been discussing. But one can and should 'zoom out' even further. Suppose we ask what the chapters collected in this volume contribute to the study of early modern north India as a whole. What then do we see? How do we find ourselves in conversation with the work of major historians in the field?

As we begin this process, we must pause to recognize that the designation 'early modern' remains an embattled category. While some scholars of South Asia have focused exclusively on developments in the eighteenth century, the temporal frame of early modernity for others extends from the fifteenth to the late eighteenth century. Even as the use of the term is becoming a new convention, inasmuch as it is assumed to be self-explanatory, some have questioned its appositeness in the Indian context, citing a lack of self-reflexivity among those imbricated in the processes and institutions of modernization.[11] The scholars who advocate for the conceptual appropriateness of the term speak of the idea of modernity as 'conjunctural' in its origins and development, involving politically, economically, and culturally vibrant societies interacting with one another. In this view, modernity, as a series of historical processes, is understood as transmuting relatively isolated societies into connected entities (as against seeing modernity as Western in its genesis or as an export to other parts of the globe).[12] The dynamics of this period that have been adumbrated—particularly in terms of 'connected histories'—include, among other indicators, growing volumes of trade, both regional and global; communications and a flowering travel literature that was often ethnographic and ethnological in nature; imperial formations with universalist ambitions; and so on.[13] By adopting the 'early modern' in its title, this volume brings to the fore cultural aspects of these connections in the subcontinental north, highlighting some significant ways in which an Indian 'ecumene', to use Christopher Bayly's term, began to shape a public life.[14]

It may be mentioned briefly that the antecedents of the conference on which this volume is based are a series of workshops organized by a group of academics referred to earlier as the 'bhakti group', who produced multiple volumes on *Bhakti in Current Research*. Focusing on bhakti devotional literatures in the vernaculars from the 'medieval period', the group was committed, among other activities, to collecting manuscripts and editing critical editions of the poetry of various saint poets.[15] The change to the rubric of 'early modernity' in the conference in Shimla in 2012 (though the last conference used the rubric, the focus remained firmly on religious literatures), the first of its kind in India, must, therefore, be seen as a self-conscious choice by these academics to acknowledge and include literatures other than those produced within the ambit of bhakti, particularly incorporating the rich legacy of *rīti*, courtly, historical, and Sufi literatures in the period.

More significantly, it indicates a desire to absorb and interact with the exciting new research that is producing the early modern in India as a period of enormous political energy and cultural vibrancy. Thus, the linguistic developments, varied literary efflorescence, historical processes and their representation in literatures, and innovations in the production and transmission of manuscripts and the traditions and communities around them that this volume illuminates are a part of offering new perspectives on the cultures of the time.

The notion of 'connected histories' is an especially evocative descriptor for this volume as it seeks to delve into the complexities of circulation, mobility, and trans-culturation (in the sense of mutual transformation through exchange) in north India. At a time when peoples, with their texts, ideas, cultural habits, and other artefacts, were increasingly on the move, the deepening of older routes and circuits was visible, as was the establishing of new networks. First under the Mughal imperium and later under the new and flourishing regional powers and local courts, individuals and communities, particular places and sacred spaces, languages and manuscripts emerged as agents and locations of pulsating change. At the same time, it needs to be underlined that change, however dynamic, was not always towards a more radical or inclusive order, despite the incorporative predilections of the bhakti *sant*s or Sufi *pīr*s.[16] An emerging ecumene that drew more and more people and places into its ambit could also be hierarchical, marking out differences and institutionalizing the modes of exercise and display of power and privilege. Thus, along with bhakti devotion, or of Sufi expansiveness, caste exclusivity and the assertion of elite authority were also visible. This volume, in highlighting the complexities of the period, illuminates a few areas of particular interest.

Writing Vernacular History

A number of chapters in the volume address the issue of writing history in the vernacular in the early modern period, underscoring the multiple genres in which it was written and the complex sensibilities that suffused it. The difficult question that the chapters tackle is the intransigent one of how we, as academia-based scholars with a commitment to writing 'scientific' history with its modern protocols of sources, verification, and authentication, can receive and appreciate 'histories' that have come to us in other forms that have their own conventions.

The debate on the writing of history in the early modern period can be approached from at least two ends. On one end are a set of historians and literary scholars such as Sanjay Subrahmanyam, David Shulman, and Velcheru Narayana Rao, who have in recent years demonstrated the emergence of 'secular' histories in the vernacular of states in south India, specifically the *nīti* texts that focus on the 'pragmatics' and 'politics' of 'statecraft'.[17] They write of the emergence of a literate class of people with specialized scribal and poetic skills, the *karnams*, who practice polyglossia (their counterpart being the *munshis* of north India) and who are mobile and take their talent and prowess to where it is required. The 'histories' produced in this period, they assert, may be written in the dominant genres of the time, whether kāvya or the purāṇa. However, these texts were written with a sense of causality and with a delineation of events that was secular in its understanding and very worldly in orientation. While the historical in these narratives may sometimes exist alongside, or even be overlaid by, the mythical, these texts also possess what Subrahmnayam, Shulman, and Rao term 'texture', or a manner of transactional relationship between the teller of the tale and the audience through which the author's language and literary and lexical signifiers help the audience distinguish between the fictional and the factual. A number of chapters in this volume show how the historical was self-consciously embedded in the poetic, reflecting some aspects of the 'secular histories' model outlined by Subrahmanyam, Shulman, and Rao; other chapters suggest instances in which this was not the case, reminding us of Partha Chatterjee's point that the wider applicability of this model will have to be demonstrated for the various regions of India, rather than assumed.[18]

On the other end, we can attempt to recuperate the significance of the narrative as it unfolds in a poetic form from the now well-established postmodernist perspective—following Hayden White—that emphasizes the rhetorical and linguistic strategies that are necessarily imbricated in apparently factual historical presentations. While the 'conditions of plausibility', as Chatterjee writes, remain entirely different in the writing of history and of fiction in our times (in terms of the technical apparatus deployed by the historian in the selection and verification of sources), the postmodernist approach illuminates and stresses the narratological skill required to write history, howsoever banal and factual it may seem in content.[19] To put it another way, history written in the present offers a narrative of the past, and so represents the past. The historian's craft involves not only a technical soundness in the collation of data around an event, but also uses an interpretive frame to present the account. In this understanding of the historian as involved in a hermeneutical process, as representing and interpreting events, the poets writing panegyrics in adoration of their princes and patrons, praising their prowess at war, or their honour in defeat were particularly well placed to write history in poetry, or—to borrow a term from Allison Busch's chapter in this volume—to write 'history in Hindī', referring to the 'cosmopolitan vernacular' language in her analysis.[20]

At least four chapters here (Busch, Pinch, Rajpurohit, and Chandan) bring the focus onto the exceptional skill of poets writing verse and recording the important historical events that they were witness to, especially battles as seminal affairs of the state. Each of these chapters has underscored the importance of historical poetry in the vernacular, whether in Brajbhasha, Ḍiṅgal, or Urdu, and has also shown its significance in highlighting either local and regional histories or the delicate and multifarious relationship between local powers and the Mughal state.

The poets in question—and it is worth underlining that they were primarily poets—were important agents not only as witnesses to events, but also in promoting and representing their patrons, and so were historical players themselves. For example, Busch shows that as poets they were inheritors of multiple and diverse traditions, and deployed different registers, tones, and linguistic inflections to convey a range of emotions and events, whether bequeathed from classical Sanskrit kāvya, from Perso-Arabic vocabulary, or from rīti poetics. As all these chapters show, though conscious of historical time and of events—in specific references to dates, the naming of warriors, or in places a tone of reportage—these poets did not necessarily write in the 'realistic' mould. In fact, the more historically important the event, the greater the social standing of the characters involved, and the greater the gravity of the situation to be conveyed, the more recourse they took to mythology, encomiums, and a didactic tone. As William Pinch asks, should this occasional subordination of historical facts to genre and politics worry us? Or is realism not necessarily the best mode to represent the enormity of an occurrence, the polysemous and elusive 'truth' of the matter? Dalpat Rajpurohit and Busch both emphasize the performativity of the poetry in Ḍiṅgal, with its linguistic quality lending itself to relating, among other things, a palpable cacophony of war. The written kāvya, when performed orally, thus gave a sense of the 'reality' of the war as perceived by the poet. The 'realistic' tone, as Subrahmanyam and others have shown in relation to the 'historical' *Rājataraṅgiṇī*, may be as much the product of a poet's imagination as poetic excess in an encomium.[21] Such imaginative poetics undoubtedly accomplished much more than just relate an event: they incited heroic action, proffered moral dictums, and legitimized social churning or indeed affirmed continuing hierarchical statuses, as our chapters show. But they also did perform a historical function, insofar as they represented in their poetry events that they witnessed or were contemporaneous with, for future generations. The changing 'texture' of the poetry at various places, its nuanced atmospherics, allowed for complex receptions of the text, among them an understanding of the historical event.

The poet-historians as witnesses to events and as historical actors (whose paeans could at times play a crucial role in shaping events as much as their understanding of events could shape perceptions) were also deeply implicated in the social institutions and power structures of the society and the polity of which they were a part. This could amount to the perpetuation or defence of an existing social order, or equally to the legitimation of change. All our chapters emphasize how the poet-historians were embedded in the politics they commented on, even if they observed those politics from a corner (albeit a privileged one). Shreekant Chandan, for example, shows how the poet Alam projected Prince Muazzam as a rightful heir to Aurangzeb by borrowing notions of ideal kingship from *akhlāqī* discourses current at the time. In a similar vein, Rajpurohit, Busch, and Pinch comment on the poetry of Padmakar who, towards the end of the eighteenth century, found a way to praise both the defeated Rajput prince Arjun Singh of Bundelkhand as the upholder of Kshatriya dharma and the Brahman Gosain usurper Anupgir, his new patron. This was not just a matter of literary flourish, but also one of political acumen, a realpolitik that took cognizance of the changing politico-social reality. Did this locus as a 'participant-observer', in a manner of speaking, diminish the value of our poet's oeuvre or enhance it? As Pinch posits, truth-telling is more than mere attention to factual detail and, one might add, to an 'objective' commentary on them. In his chapter, he outlines how political theory and sociological transformation are implicit in the complex political and moral manoeuvres in the poetics of his two poet-historians.

Are these examples of *aitihāsik kāvya* (historical poetry) then important only because we can abstract historical facts from them? The distilling of 'facts' from texts that were meant to 'do' other things—entertain, recall genealogical descent, give philosophical elucidation, define ideal political conduct—was after all the purpose to which the British intellectuals of colonial India assigned them. In so doing, as is well known, they commented on the Indians' lack of a historical sense until at least the advent of the political chronicle in the Islamicate cultural setting. The question may be posed in another way: are these examples of poetic accomplishment then merely to serve as 'sources' for modern historians using sophisticated and academe-approved methods? The case of the autobiographical musings of Nagaridas, the *Tīrthānand*, in the mid-eighteenth century, as discussed by Heidi Pauwels, is particularly instructive in this regard. Autobiography, mostly seen as a literary gift of the West and of modernity,[22] is invariably perceived as having a sociological interest (customs, traditions, and private observations of people on private or public life) and granted a 'vernacular', popular status, outside the academic realm of 'proper' history.[23] Its value in the case discussed by Pauwels in illuminating the complex politics of the Mughal, Maratha, and Afghan participants in this period in north India is undoubtedly immense. However, as suggested earlier, in Nagaridas's account the geography and topography of Braj emerge almost as protagonists in their own right. What are we to make of the peregrinations and musings of this remarkable prince? Is this text then no more than a 'source' for the late Mughal politics in which it obliquely participates, or for the light it sheds on bhakti devotion, or whatever else? Or is there something specific to be said about Nagaridas's mental world, his own peculiar structuring of his world, his travel account, and indeed his politics?

There is no doubt that historians will use these texts—whether poetry or the autobiography—as sources whereby they may be able to piece together a sequence of events or sift through historical information that helps in putting a period in perspective. Such a relationship with 'vernacular histories' is an established one, and, one may add, a relationship in which hierarchies of academic location and training come into play. But the case being made here is that these texts have to be also seen for their own merit and traditions, their own truth-telling, and the wholeness of their world view. The poetry written in the various regional courts of the eighteenth century examined here or the autobiographical whimsies of one such as Nagaridas (and there are other examples from the premodern world) have a strong element of writing for posterity, of passing on 'real' stories, traditions, to the coming generations. When at a contemporary moment the past is passed on to the future, history is indubitably transmitted.[24]

A Second Look at Networks: The Dynamics of Transmission

South Asia, as Sheldon Pollock observes, might be a region where orality is 'hyper valued', but where the written had an authority and stature all its own.[25] Making a similar point about precolonial India, Bayly notes that though it was not a highly literate society, it was one acutely aware of literacy, and where many sects fetishized the written word of their spiritual gurus.[26] The dynamic intermeshing of orality and literacy—of the oral and its inscription, of the written word and its oral performance, of texts and their circulation, of the transforming semantic and semiotic valence as these processes proceed—are themes that animate almost all the chapters in this volume.

A parallel development in the early modern period that needs to be tracked is that of looking at the communities that produce, preserve, and perpetuate the written word. The role of the polyglot scribal gentry, the karnams and the munshis, which grew in numbers and importance as the administrative and economic activity of the state expanded and as the use of paper increased, has already been noted.[27] Historians such as Rosalind O'Hanlon and David Washbrook have shown that the scribes and service gentry of this period from the Sanskritic tradition came partly from the class of religious and ritual specialists such as the Brahmans and the pandits already held in high esteem for their sacerdotal status, and also from the 'ambiguous' castes such as the Kayasthas and the Khatris, upwardly mobile and registering newer anxieties about their social status and place in the *varna* hierarchy.[28] The chapters in this volume point to the significance not just of literati serving the state, but also of learned persons who were associated with various bhakti sects of north India in the early modern period. They emphasize their role in the dissemination and circulation of the ideas of the sants, and in many ways making their songs and sayings accessible to a wider public, 'translating' their ideas, as it were, for wider consumption. Some chapters show the simultaneous engagement of members of this class with intellectual labour that would enhance the status of an oral oeuvre not only by producing anthologies of songs, but also by classicizing such songs and thereby increasing their symbolic capital. This concurrent production and participation in the emerging ecumene, giving it its specific character, is importantly placed in the foreground of this volume.

Emphasizing the circulatory role of manuscripts, the reason for their production, Imre Bangha notes their centrality in the emergence of literary cultures, or of 'literarization', in the context of the Jain monks associated with the earliest form of Madhyadeśī, the Maru-Gurjari. While Bangha's attempt is to delineate the diverse lingual and dialectical histories of the modern umbrella language 'Hindi', Jaroslav Strnad is interested in looking at the emergence of manuscript traditions themselves in the context of the *sant dhārā* (nirguṇ saint tradition) of north India, giving attention to the impact of the oral and the performative in the construction of the written and the textual. Underscoring the peculiarity of manuscripts as material artefacts, where scribes kept empty spaces to be filled later, where more padas on similar themes could be inscribed, and as core poems developed into larger traditions, Strnad elaborates on the interaction between singers and memorization, scribes and their social contexts in creating the major traditions around charismatic sants like Kabir.[29] This privileging of 'routes' rather than 'roots', as Finbarr Flood has recently said in highlighting James Clifford's emphasis on exchange and networks, shows the importance of the circulation of abstract ideas and of material artefacts in society. Both cross boundaries and barriers that are normally seen to inhibit communication.[30]

Drawing attention to precisely these circuits of exchange, Tyler Williams speaks about 'translation' as an activity that was much more than a transparent equivalence between languages, a near impossibility on its own. Rather, translation indicates for Williams a broad set of practices that allowed for ideas to move between languages, traditions, and ideological systems, setting up, one may say, the circulatory capillaries of a society in motion. This was not a 'cultural translation' in the sense in which anthropologists use the term, aware as they are of the power implicit in different languages, or power structures through which one culture is 'interpreted' for another.[31] Here notions of cultural amplification, even of recursiveness—as ideas spread, are taken up and reworked, and passed on—are perhaps more appropriate. Williams shows how over time the local community of the Niranjanis in the Marwar region began to interact with trans-local and cosmopolitan literary and aesthetic traditions, even as the followers of the sect came from different castes including the Brahmins (the founder Haridas was from a mixed Jat–Rajput background). The resultant 'transculturation' and 'transcreation'—the metamorphosis of an oral and a non-literary tradition into a sophisticated literary one—indicated the multidirectional and reciprocal nature of cultural exchange transforming the entities involved, and in which the role of the scribal networks was central.

Writing was also central in the interaction between the vernacular Bengali and the cosmopolitan Sanskrit in the eighteenth century, highlighted by Samuel Wright in his analysis of Radhamohan Thakkur's attempt to anthologize the oral *pada*s of his sect. As mentioned earlier, Thakkur attempted to raise the literary prestige of the oral songs not only by providing a Sanskrit commentary on them, but also by rendering them 'literary', as he applied the established literary tropes of the vernacular and the cosmopolitan languages. Wright's observation that Thakkur's commentary provided a Sanskrit reader with the necessary tools to make sense of the songs opens up a world where a complex interaction was taking place between the oral bhakti repertoires of songs gaining greater popularity and prestige on the one hand, and a simultaneous appropriation of the popular for prestigious intellectual activity on the other.

Another example of such intellectual exchange and mutual enrichment is provided by Lutjeharms in his study of Rupa Goswami's *Padyāvalī*, a work that creates a new discourse through anthologization. Lutjeharms shows how the oppositional juxtaposition of the two paths to liberation in fact encompassed histories of dialogue and accommodation via amorous secular Sanskrit poetry. Indeed in the early modern period, as Christopher Minkowski has argued recently, Advaita Vedanta, in combating the challenge from the Dvaitins, emerged as something like a 'large tent' theology, a metadiscourse of Indian philosophy. This trend was further enhanced in the colonial period.[32] Such ideational exchanges, translations, accommodations, and appropriations were an important aspect of the cultural life of the early modern period.

What the growing pace of such interactions did, against the background of growing opportunities for mobility and patronage, was to create new tensions about social status, as O'Hanlon and Washbrook have postulated. In the context of state service for castes who derived their learning from Sanskritic heritage, these historians have pointed to anxieties that stemmed from high castes serving the Muslim state, and with regard to the new skilled entrants and competitors whose social status had to be reworked within the varna hierarchy. O'Hanlon especially has shown the growing prestige of the Maratha Brahmins in Banaras as the Mughal state came to rely on them to clarify legal and theological matters with regard to its Hindu subjects as well as the anxieties that the presence and success of Maratha Kayasthas created in the Deccan.[33] Some of Jack Hawley's recent work, including his chapter in this volume, can be read in tandem with this new research on social perturbations. Examining the history of the southern Bhatts in Braj and their role in establishing and institutionalizing some popular devotional movements, Hawley gives us a sense of their mobility and success in this period. Additionally, he points towards the apprehensions that accompanied mobility from the south to the north, residing in Muslim-ruled states, and the various strategies they engaged in so 'they could reclaim a fuller measure of their Brahminness'. These included, as Swapna Sharma's chapter also depicts, maintaining ritual practice, keeping in touch with their roots in Karnataka, and being aware of each other's Sanskrit writings. Elsewhere, Hawley has also elaborated on why the southern Brahmins in the north maintained contact with the south, and through a reading of popular myths, what prestige was derived from such contact, including the factually mistaken notion of a pristine Hindu rule.[34]

Collectively what these histories suggest is a society energized by broader politico-economic changes than those that had existed before. New opportunities for patronage and mobility set people and ideas in motion, and the acquisition of reading and writing skills became means to gather honour and reputation. The emerging ecumene of the early modern period—characterized by growing communication and exchange, by creative and complex interactions between the oral and the written and between the vernacular and the cosmopolitan, and by new debates on the aesthetic and the acceptable—created a society in the throes of complex cultural changes.[35] The world of devotional bhakti underwent very significant changes at this time. As the oral culture of popular devotion travelled, it acquired larger repertoires and the performative came to animate the textual and the literary in important new ways. So also the social classes that associated themselves with, appropriated, and in turn popularized the bhakti corpus of songs and poems came from varied social backgrounds, including from among the highest castes. Social churning meant new apprehensions about place and status in society. If for some people social unmooring meant new opportunities, for others it could mean a desire for firmer anchorage within a more traditionally recognizable world of prestige and respectability. These are immense transformations—the heart and soul of 'early modernity'—and the literary artefacts introduced in the pages just ahead display them admirably.

Notes

1. Francesca Orsini, 'How to Do Multilingual Literary History? Lessons from Fifteenth- and Sixteenth-Century North India', *The Indian Economic and Social History Review* 49, no. 2 (2012): 225–46; Sheldon Pollock, *Literary Cultures in History: Reconstructions from South Asia* (New Delhi: Oxford University Press, 2003), see in particular his introduction, 1–36; and Sheldon Pollock, *The Language of the Gods in the World of Men: Sanskrit, Culture, and Power in Premodern India* (Berkeley: University of California Press, 2006).

2. Pollock characterizes Sanskrit and, in the case of later north India, Persian as 'superposed' languages that not only monopolized the privileged position of being mediums of literary and intellectual exchange, but also consequently served as models for those seeking to establish literary cultures in the vernacular. See Pollock, *The Language of the Gods*, 283–98, 392–3.

3. Audrey Truschke, 'Cosmopolitan Encounters: Sanskrit and Persian at the Mughal Court', diss., Columbia University, New York, 2012, 186–90.

4. Shantanu Phukan, '"Through Throats Where Many Rivers Meet": The Ecology of Hindi in the World of Persian', *Indian Economic and Social History Review* 38, no. 33 (2001): 33–58.

5. Conspicuously absent from this list is Punjabi, and experts on this period of north India could no doubt add more languages to the list. Their absence is not at all a deliberate omission, but rather a reflection of the conference as it finally took shape in July 2012. It is the editors' hope that future meetings of the conference will find Punjabi and other languages well represented in the programme since they were an integral part of the literary and devotional landscape of early modern north India.

6. Pollock, *The Language of the Gods*, 298.

7. Pollock, *The Language of the Gods*, 435–6.

8. Yigal Bronner, Whitney Cox, and Lawrence McCrea, eds, *South Asian Texts in History: Critical Engagements with Sheldon Pollock* (Ann Arbor: Association for Asian Studies, 2011).

9. Sanjay Subrahmanyam, 'Hearing Voices: Vignettes of Early Modernity in South Asia, 1400–1750', *Daedalus* 127, no. 3 (1998): 75–104.

10. John S. Hawley, *A Storm of Songs: India and the Idea of the Bhakti Movement* (New York: Oxford University Press, 2015), 295–397.

11. For an exclusive focus on the eighteenth century, see Richard Barnett, *Rethinking Early Modern India* (New Delhi: Manohar Publishers and Distributors, 2002). For assuming the referents of early modernity, see Rosalind O'Hanlon and David Washbrook, *Religious Cultures in Early Modern India: New Perspectives* (New Delhi: Routledge, 2011). For questioning the usage of the term, see Dipesh Chakrabarty, 'The Muddle of Modernity', *American Historical Review* 116, no. 3 (2011): 663–75.

12. Subrahmanyam, 'Hearing Voices', 99.

13. Subrahmanyam, 'Hearing Voices', 99. Also see Sanjay Subrahmanyam, 'Connected Histories: Notes towards a Reconfiguration of Early Modern Eurasia', *Modern Asian Studies* 31, no. 3 (1997): 735–62.

14. C. A. Bayly, *Empire and Information: Intelligence Gathering and Social Communication in India, 1780–1870* (New York: Cambridge University Press, 1996).

15. Maya Burger, 'Encountering Translation: Translational Historiography in the Connected History of India and Europe', in *India in Translation through Hindi Literature: A Plurality of Voices*, ed. Maya Burger, Maya and Nicola Pozza (Bern: Peter Lang, 2010), 39–40.

16. O' Hanlon and Washbrook, *Religious Cultures*, 2.

17. Narayana Rao, David Shulman, and Sanjay Subrahmanyam, *Textures of Time: Writing History in South India, 1600–1800* (Bangalore: Orient Longman, 2001); Velcheru Narayana Rao and Sanjay Subrahmanyam, 'History and Politics in the Vernacular: Reflections on Medieval and Early Modern South India', in *History in the Vernacular*, ed. Raziuddin Aquil and Partha Chatterjee (Bangalore: Orient Longman, 2008), 25–64; Subrahmanyam, 'Connected Histories'.

18. Raziuddin Aquil and Partha Chatterjee, 'Introduction', in *History in the Vernacular*, 6.

19. Aquil and Chatterjee, 'Introduction', 9.

20. Pollock, The *Language of the Gods*, 26.

21. Rao, Shulman, and Subrahmanyam, *Textures of Time*.

22. Anshu Malhotra and Siobhan Lambert-Hurley, *Speaking of the Self: Gender, Performance, and Autobiography in South Asia* (Durham: Duke University Press, 2015).

23. Aquil and Chatterjee, 'Introduction', 20.

24. Romila Thapar, *The Past as Present: Forging Contemporary Identities Through History* (New Delhi: The Aleph Book Company, 2014), 7. Thapar comments that when a historical tradition claims to narrate the events of the

past, it distinguishes it from fiction; and that when a contemporary witness transmits events keeping in mind posterity as an audience, it is participating in a historical tradition.

25. Pollock, The *Language of the Gods*, 4.

26. Bayly, *Empire and Information*, 13, 40.

27. Muzzafar Alam and Sanjay Subrahmanyam, 'The Making of a Munshi', *Comparative Studies of South Asia, Africa and the Middle East* 24, no. 2 (2004): 61–72.

28. O'Hanlon and Washbrook, 'Introduction', in *Religious Cultures*.

29. Strnad gives the example of the metaphor of the mystical plantlet that grows inside the body and its semantically varying treatment by the Nathpanthis and the Kabirpanthis owing to the difference in their core beliefs (the former attuned to the psychophysical nature of the cosmos and the latter to the *nirguni*, or 'unqualified', Absolute). Interestingly, the mystical plantlet also appears in the poetry of the seventeenth-century Punjabi Sufi Sultan Bahu, and that its meaning is derived from the Islamic creedal formula. This strengthens the point about tracking 'routes' through which the padas travelled, including looking at the interaction between bhakti and Sufi devotional streams. Jamal Elias, *Death before Dying: The Sufi Poems of Sultan Bahu* (Berkeley: University of California Press, 1998), 37.

30. Barry Finbarr Flood, *Objects of Translation: Material Culture and Medieval Hindu–Muslim Encounter* (Princeton: Princeton University Press, 2009), 1–5.

31. Talal Asad, 'The Concept of Cultural Translation in British Social Anthropology', in *Writing Culture: The Poetics and Politics of Ethnography*, ed. James Clifford (Berkeley: University of California Press, 1986); James Clifford, 'Introduction: Partial Truths', in *Writing Culture*.

32. Christopher Minkowski, 'Advaita Vedanta in Early Modern History', in *Religious Cultures*.

33. Rosalind O'Hanlon, 'Speaking from Siva's Temple: Banaras Scholar Households and the Brahman "Ecumene" of Mughal India', *South Asian History and Culture* 2, no. 2 (2011): 253–77; Rosalind O'Hanlon, 'The Social Worth of Scribes Brahmins, Kāyasthas and the Social Order in Early Modern India', *Indian Economic and Social History Review* 47, no. 4 (2010): 563–95.

34. John S. Hawley, 'The Four Sampradayas: Ordering the Religious Past in Mughal North India', in *Religious Cultures*.

35. Bayly, *Empire and Information*, 180–2.

Bibliography

Alam, Muzzafar and Sanjay Subrahmanyam. 'The Making of a Munshi'. *Comparative Studies of South Asia, Africa and the Middle East* 24, no. 2 (2004): 61–72.

Aquil, Raziuddin and Partha Chatterjee, ed. *History in the Vernacular.* Bangalore: Orient Longman, 2008.

Asad, Talal. 'The Concept of Cultural Translation in British Social Anthropology'. In *Writing Culture: The Poetics and Politics of Ethnography,* edited by James Clifford. Berkeley: University of California Press, 1986.

Barnett, Richard, ed. *Rethinking Early Modern India.* New Delhi: Manohar Publishers and Distributors, 2002.

Bayly, C.A. *Empire and Information: Intelligence Gathering and Social Communication in India, 1780–1870.* New York: Cambridge University Press, 1996.

Bronner, Yigal, Whitney Cox, and Lawrence McCrea, eds. *South Asian Texts in History: Critical Engagements with Sheldon Pollock.* Ann Arbor: Association for Asian Studies, 2011.

Burger, Maya. 'Encountering Translation: Translational Historiography in the Connected History of India and Europe'. In *India in Translation through Hindi Literature: A Plurality of Voices,* edited by Maya Burger, Maya and Nicola Pozza. Bern: Peter Lang, 2010.

Burger, Maya and Nicola Pozza. *India in Translation through Hindi Literature: A Plurality of Voices.* New York: Peter Lang, 2011.

Chakrabarty, Dipesh. 'The Muddle of Modernity'. *American Historical Review* 116, no. 3 (2011): 663–75.

Clifford, James, ed. *Writing Culture: The Poetics and Politics of Ethnography.* Berkeley: University of California Press, 1986.

Elias, Jamal. *Death before Dying: The Sufi Poems of Sultan Bahu.* Berkeley: University of California Press, 1998.

Flood, Finbarr Barry. *Objects of Translation: Material Culture and Medieval Hindu-Muslim Encounter.* Princeton: Princeton University Press, 2009.

Hawley, John S. 'The Four Sampradāys: Ordering the Religious Past in Mughal North India'. In *Religious Cultures in Early Modern India: New Perspectives,* edited by Rosalind O'Hanlon and David Washbrook. South Asian History and Culture 7. New Delhi: Routledge, 2011.

———. *A Storm of Songs: India and the Idea of the Bhakti Movement.* New York: Oxford University Press, 2015.

Malhotra, Anshu and Siobhan Lambert-Hurley, eds. *Speaking of the Self: Gender, Performance, and Autobiography in South Asia.* Durham: Duke University Press, 2015.

Minkowski, Christopher. 'Advaita Vedānta in Early Modern History'. In *Religious Cultures in Early Modern India: New Perspectives,* edited by Rosalind O'Hanlon and David Washbrook. South Asian History and Culture 7. New Delhi: Routledge, 2011.

O'Hanlon, Rosalind. 'The Social Worth of Scribes Brahmins, Kāyasthas and the Social Order in Early Modern India'. *Indian Economic and Social History Review* 47, no. 4 (2010): 563–95.

———. 'Speaking from Siva's Temple: Banaras Scholar Households and the Brahman "Ecumene" of Mughal India'. *South Asian History and Culture* 2, no. 2 (2011): 253–77.

O'Hanlon, Rosalind and David Washbrook. *Religious Cultures in Early Modern India: New Perspectives.* South Asian History and Culture 7. New Delhi: Routledge, 2011.

Orsini, Francesca. 'How to Do Multilingual Literary History? Lessons from Fifteenth- and Sixteenth-Century North India'. *The Indian Economic and Social History Review* 49, no. 2 (2012): 225–46.

Phukan, Shantanu. '"Through Throats Where Many Rivers Meet": The Ecology of Hindi in the World of Persian'. *Indian Economic and Social History Review* 38, no. 33 (2001): 33–58.

Pollock, Sheldon. *Literary Cultures in History: Reconstructions from South Asia.* New Delhi: Oxford University Press, 2003.

———. *The Language of the Gods in the World of Men: Sanskrit, Culture, and Power in Premodern India.* Berkeley: University of California Press, 2006.

Rao, Velcheru Narayana and Sanjay Subrahmanyam. 'History and Politics in the Vernacular: Reflections on Medieval and Early Modern South India'. In *History in the Vernacular,* edited by Raziuddin Aquil and Partha Chatterjee. Bangalore: Orient Longman, 2008.

Rao, Velcheru Narayana, David Shulman, and Sanjay Subrahmanyam. *Textures of Time: Writing History in South India, 1600–1800.* Bangalore: Orient Longman, 2001.

Subrahmanyam, Sanjay. 'Connected Histories: Notes towards a Reconfiguration of Early Modern Eurasia'. *Modern Asian Studies* 31, no. 3 (1997): 735–62.

———. 'Hearing Voices: Vignettes of Early Modernity in South Asia, 1400–1750', *Daedalus* 127, no. 3 (1998): 75–104.

Thapar, Romila. *The Past as Present: Forging Contemporary Identities through History.* New Delhi: The Aleph Book Company, 2014.

Truschke, Audrey. 'Cosmopolitan Encounters: Sanskrit and Persian at the Mughal Court' (Dissertation). New York: Columbia University.

PART ONE

BETWEEN COSMOPOLITAN AND *BHĀṢĀ*

1

IMRE BANGHA*

The Emergence of Hindi Literature: From Transregional Maru-Gurjar to Madhyadeśī Narratives

The emergence of written literature in a particular language intrigued scholars for centuries, and recently the question has received renewed attention with regard to India.[1] This was all the more necessary since earlier, nationalist attempts to locate the origins of several particular languages lacked methodological consistency in delineating boundaries and systematic philological research.[2] A particularly mystifying aspect of such research was the lack of early manuscript evidence. This has also been the case with Hindi, which most twentieth-century literary historians claimed originated sometime between the seventh and twelfth centuries, either by forcing Apabhramsha, as well as purportedly oral or non-literary works, to be accepted as early Hindi literature or by assigning early dates to absent or much later compositions. Especially with regard to the non-Apabhramsha works, their arguments were based on much later manuscript material; however, manuscripts of purported early works are also often manipulated. For example, compositions may have been assigned to early authors, such as Gorakhnāth or Amīr Khusraw, and the text and the language of early compositions may have been updated through an initial oral transmission, as may have been the case with the Nāth songs.[3] Further, the absence of early manuscripts in the Jain collections of Gujarat and Rajasthan, where many later works are preserved, strongly suggests that the lack of early evidence is not merely a matter of the vicissitudes of the Indian climate.[4]

In this chapter I argue that the earliest vernacular literary tradition in north India preserved in manuscript is that of Old Gujarati, also called Maru-Gurjar, composed predominantly by Jains from its inception in the late twelfth century in Gujarat till its explosion in the fourteenth and fifteenth centuries into a supra-regional vernacular also cultivated in the so-called Hindi belt. Through its interaction with spoken dialects, Maru-Gurjar then began to diversify and regionalize into several new literary traditions. The earliest 'Hindi' language works in what I call the Madhyadeśī idiom grew out of the Maru-Gurjar tradition, both grammatically and poetically. Thus, Maru-Gurjar literature is where scholars may fruitfully look for an *ādikāl*, or 'initial era', of 'Hindi' literature. However, because this literature was produced by Jains, Hindi nationalist historiography has largely ignored it, relegating the scholarship on this early vernacular tradition to Gujarati and Jain scholars.

Nomenclature

A major methodological problem in addressing the emergence of a literary culture is that of the nomenclature of literary traditions. Though it is impossible to give generally acceptable definitions for all the terms used in this chapter, I will make an attempt to clarify the most important ones as I use them. First, I will consider 'literature' to be the written culture that Indians would perceive as leading to aesthetic enjoyment, that is, *rasa*.[5] For pre-colonial literary 'languages' in north India, I will use the term 'literary idioms', which avoids both the compartmentalized labelling of a modern *language*, such as Hindi or Gujarati, and identification with a spoken regional *dialect* or *patois*. Thus, the often highly stylized literary idiom of Brajbhasha is not identified with the Braj dialect of Hindi as described, for example, in *The Linguistic Survey of India*. One should also bear in mind that vernacular literary idioms often show composite regional features and that until the nineteenth century they lacked standardization. Old Hindi literary idioms shared a high number of linguistic features and most of their differences would be minor morphological ones. Many terms used for literary idioms are modern constructs projected back upon earlier times.[6] Terms often overlapped or lacked a fixed meaning not only during early modern times but also in modern scholarship. Therefore, the language of a composition may not easily be put into one or another category and, for example, the same work may be designated as Apabhramsha, Rajasthani, Hindi, or Maru-Gurjar by different scholars. Literary idioms in the first half of the second millennium CE are among the best examples of the fact that languages 'never exist as pure, self-identical, thinglike isolates but are instead processes, in fact mutually constitutive processes'.[7] Such processes are determined by literary traditions that continuously reinvent themselves in dialogue with other traditions and with the society that produces them.

The most problematic term in this chapter is 'Hindi' itself, which in early modern times often referred to what has come to be known as Urdu from the late eighteenth century. Its more archaic form, Hindavi, could initially refer to any Indian language, and later to the idiom of Sufi compositions. Hindi as an umbrella term for a range of spoken dialects and literary idioms owes its present scope of meaning to colonial and nationalist scholarship. Readers and listeners from early modern times have identified these literary idioms, namely Avadhi, Brajbhasha, Sadhukkari, and Khari Boli (used initially in Persian-mixed Rekhta compositions), in the Hindi belt (that is, Madhyadeśa) through a bunch of dialectal markers; for example, the dialectical markers of Braj *kahaiṁ* '(we/they) say' and *kahyau* '(said)' versus the Avadhi *kahahiṁ*, *kahĕu* and the Khari Boli *kahate* (*haiṁ*) and *kahā*, respectively. Moreover, tradition more often than not determined works along roughly literary dialectal lines since later compositions linguistically modelled themselves on successful earlier compositions in the same genre. Therefore, we have Sufi narratives in Avadhi, Krishna and *rīti* poetry in Brajbhasha, early Sant songs in Sadhukkari, and Rekhta compositions in Khari Boli. Early modern authors were more interested in aligning themselves with literary traditions earmarked by a literary idiom than in establishing linguistic identities in the modern sense of the term. I would, however, like to underline here that these idioms long lacked clear boundaries and are relatively late constructions with relatively late referents (see note 6). These traditions were mutually intelligible, shared their poetic forms, and were often anthologized together.[8] Many authors easily moved between one tradition and another.[9] Moreover, the idiom of certain works may have been switched during transmission.[10] All this suggests that the grouping together of works in Avadhi, Brajbhasha, Sadhukkari, and Khari Boli Rekhta is not just a modern phenomenon. These traditions intensively fed into each other and can be perceived as forming a 'super-tradition', which with a modern, heuristic term is called Old Hindi. As we are going to see, most of these idioms also form a linguistic and poetic continuum with the earlier Maru-Gurjar and Madhyadeśī works.

The language that Tessitori labelled as 'Old Western Rajasthani' may be referred to as Jain Gurjar, especially by modern Jain scholars, or as Old Gujarati, especially by Gujaratis.[11] Their Rajasthani colleagues prefer to call it Maru-Gurjar, a term that includes a reference to western Rajasthan as *maru* 'desert'.[12] While this designation seems to be appropriate for the fourteenth and fifteenth centuries, it may not be so fitting for earlier times when no literary work in it seems to have come from the regions of present-day Rajasthan. Nevertheless, I use the term 'Maru-Gurjar' here because many early works in this language did indeed circulate in Rajasthan during the period under review.

The initially Jain Madhyadeśī literature was cultivated east of Rajasthan. 'Madhyadeśī' is a modern term employed by one of the most outstanding scholars of early Hindi, Harihar Nivas Dvivedi, to refer to what he understood to be early Brajbhasha. I am using it in a slightly different sense to refer to the developing literary vernacular of the central Hindi regions between the mid-fourteenth and mid-fifteenth centuries, in which several features of the great literary dialects of the slightly later period, Braj and Avadhi, were not yet separated. Madhyadeśī was never standardized and in its initial form can be perceived as an extension of Maru-Gurjar into central north India. Over the late fourteenth and early fifteenth centuries it became regionalized, absorbing local linguistic features. By the end of this period it assumed forms that could be considered to be archaic manifestations of the major literary dialects of Hindi. In contrast with the abundance of compositions in Maru-Gurjar, there is only a limited corpus of compositions in it.

It should also be reiterated that the geographic regions discussed above do not correspond to their modern linguistic counterparts. The spoken languages of Lāṭa (southern Gujarat), Gurjara, and Maru (Marwar and the Thar) were perceived as three distinct languages out of eighteen spoken in India in the eighth century.[13] In most of the second half of the first millennium, these regions were part of one political entity under the Gurjara-Pratihāras, and they maintained their cultural continuity until the establishment of Ahmadabad as the capital of Gujarat in the fifteenth century.[14] The linguistic boundaries have, however, remained permeable for long. Gujarati was, for example, widely used in southern Rajasthan even in modern times.[15]

Theorizing the Emergence of Hindi Literature

As we are going to see, the case of Maru-Gurjar and Madhyadeśī forces us to rethink theories on the genesis of literatures and of literary languages, especially in light of the recent work of Sheldon Pollock and Francesca Orsini. The most influential modern idea about the emergence of literature was posited by German Romanticism and especially by J.G. von Herder (1744–1803), who in his *Fragments on Recent German Literature* (1767–68) and *Treatise on the Origin of Language* (1772) considered written literature as a continuation of oral 'folk' literature. While Herder held the view that 'poetry is the mother tongue of mankind'—referring of course to oral poetry—in literary historiography, the beginnings of a literature have tended to remain lost in a distant haze. Herder's view is formulated from a nationalist framework concerned with the emergence of national literature as a development from within the national language, independent of other peoples' literary achievements.

Hindi nationalist historiography, while also tracing the emergence of Hindi literature in orality, never neglected the South Asian multilingual environment in which this literature grew. The most widely accepted paradigm is that Hindi as a language is the final point of development in the Sanskrit–Shauraseni Prakrit–Shauraseni Apabhramsha lineage. The corresponding view of literary development, however, is only a modification on the Herderian concept since it presents Hindi as interacting mostly with its linguistic predecessors in this literary heritage, and assumes that much of Hindi's early corpus was composed orally and committed to writing only later.

In sharp contrast to the Herderian view of development from orality, Sheldon Pollock has maintained that in the case of South Asia literary cultures presented something qualitatively new by comparison with folk and oral traditions. In fact, excluding oral traditions from the field of the 'literary', Pollock argues that every literary culture has a two-phase beginning: at first a language is 'literized', that is, committed to writing in inscriptions and other documents; second, it is 'literarized', that is, literary works start appearing in writing modelled on earlier literary forms.[16]

Following on Pollock's arguments, Allison Busch suggests multiple Hindi literary beginnings, the first being in 1377 with Maulānā Dāūd's *Candāyan*.[17] The multilingual environment of north India received special treatment in a recent article by Francesca Orsini, who examined early Hindi within the matrix of the vernacular Hindi/Hindavi/Urdu and the cosmopolitan languages of Persian and Sanskrit.[18] Indeed, none of the aforementioned scholars viewed the emergence of Hindi in isolation either. Pollock, for example, proposes that one of the motivating forces of vernacularization was cultural emulation—an idea borrowed from archaeology in which the achievements of a culture are emulated by another, neighbouring one. Drawing on these scholars' writings, I would like to examine in some detail the emergence of literature in Madhyadeśa in the light of another, older literary idiom, Old Gujarati, which, as we have seen above, is also called Maru-Gurjar.

Jain Literature in Maru-Gurjar

Maru-Gurjar (or Mārū-Gūrjar) literature flourished between the twelfth and sixteenth centuries mostly in Gujarat and Rajasthan.[19] Today we know of a relatively large corpus of texts in Maru-Gurjar. Its most extensive survey, Mohanlal Dalichand Desai's *Jain gurjar kavio* (1925), lists (with samples) 899 compositions attributed to 437 authors, dating between the twelfth and sixteenth centuries.[20] Harivallabh Bhayani, in his historical grammar of the Gujarati language (1996), gives a not completely overlapping list of about 150 published items.[21] Independent of Gujarati scholars, Hindi literary historians also laid claim to the Maru-Gurjar tradition although they gained access to much less material. Karunapati Tripathi, in the most comprehensive history of Hindi literature, the *Hindi sāhitya kā bṛhat itihās*, lists only 31 Jain compositions from between the eleventh and fourteenth centuries, and mentions that about 500 works belong to this tradition and that they are mostly unknown and unpublished.[22]

The overwhelming majority of these works are Jain narratives and hymns composed initially by poets working in Gujarat (for instance, Vastig in Shatrunjay, Ambadevsūri in Vijapur, and so on) or in unknown locations, but that are equally popular in Rajasthan as attested by the profusion of manuscripts in Rajasthani archives. While the premodern Jain–Hindu interface must have been permeable, most Maru-Gurjar works are by Jain authors, as is clear from the texts' invocations.

They may draw on explicitly Jain themes or on any subject matter borrowed from Hindu scriptures or epics and reworked in a Jain fashion, in which the protagonist(s) become Jains at the end. Recent scholarship[23] claims that the earliest works of Maru-Gurjar literature were composed in the late twelfth century: Vajrasensūrī's undated *Bharahesur-bāhubali-ghor*,[24] Śālibhadrasūrī's *Bharateśvar-bāhubali-rās* (1185),[25] and his undated *Buddhi-rās*.[26]

From the thirteenth century onwards, many other works appear in an array of metres and genres: *sandhi, rās, carcarī, phāg, catuṣpadikā, caupāī, bārāmāsā, bhās, vivāhlā, dhaval, bolī, kalaś, janmābhiṣek, saṁvād*, and so on.[27] These works, produced mostly for singing, retain to a smaller or larger extent Apabhramsha elements; however, while some genres, such as rās, were already current in Apabhramsha, others, such as phāg, gained currency only in Maru-Gurjar works.[28] Moreover, certain genres, such as sandhi, were composed primarily on an Apabhramsha grammatical template, but contained vernacular linguistic elements, while others, such as the *vastu* or the *madanāvatār* metres, were composed primarily in the vernacular, but contained an abundance of Apabhramsha.[29] Some individual works composed mostly in the caupāī metre, such as Jinprabhsūrī's *Padmāvatī-copāi*, are primarily in Apabhramsha.[30] Others such as Vastig's *Cihuṁgati-copāī* (before 1405), the anonymously authored *Karmagati-copāī*, Devsundarsūriśiṣya's *Kākbandhi-caüppaī* (between 1363 and 1383), Sādhuhaṁsa's popular *Śālibhadra-rās* (1398) and *Gautampcchā-copāī*, and Jayaśekharsūrī's popular *Tribhuvandīpak-prabandh* (also called the *Paramahaṁsa-prabandh* or *Prabodhcintāmani-copāī*) are primarily in Maru-Gurjar.[31] According to H.C. Bhayani, the variation in register is due to the freedom of the authors to rely more heavily on either a literary or a colloquial style.[32]

Maru-Gurjar works were part of a dynamic literary world. The high number of manuscripts of Vinayprabh Upādhyāy's *Gautam-svāmī-rās* (1355)[33] and the fact that even today the work forms part of the standing repertoire of the recitation pieces of Shvetambara ascetics attests to the popularity of this literature.[34] It is recited by laypeople on the Gujarati New Year, one day after Diwali, and on the *Gotamsvāmī kā kevalgyān din*, the day on which it was composed. Since Gautamsvāmī himself is *labdhinidhāna*, or treasury of wealth, and the work is believed to be auspicious for obtaining wealth, many people sing it daily.

It was not only Jain monks who were on the move but also manuscripts and, sometimes, entire libraries.[35] Literary activities were not carried out in isolation from non-Jains. Many of the Jain *granth bhaṇḍārs* (literally, 'book warehouses', that is, libraries) collected non-Jain works, and in earlier times seem to have served as more 'public' institutions.[36] From the late thirteenth century, secular works also started to appear in Maru-Gurjar.

Much of Maru-Gurjar literature is available in fourteenth- and fifteenth-century manuscripts in Jain collections. The oldest manuscripts include one from 1296 containing Vinaycand's (fl. 1268–81) *Nemināth Catuṣpadikā*;[37] another one, found by Agarchand Nahta, is from Jaisalmer dating to 1327.[38] The *Bharahesur-bāhubali-ghor* is preserved in one single manuscript dating from 1381, more than 200 years after its purported composition.[39] Observations on these works, including those of Bhayani in his history of the Gujarati language, therefore, relate not necessarily to the language of their composition but to the still very early extant texts.[40] Due to the care paid to the written texts by their Jain keepers, one would expect less variation in the texts than in the primarily oral genres. As has been mentioned, it can be observed that in their extant forms these initial works are in some passages closer to Apabhramsha, and in others to later usages.

This Jain literary idiom first grew into a transregional tradition and then developed into regional literary languages. According to Agarchand Nahta, one of the foremost experts of literature in Rajasthan, substantial regional differences within Maru-Gurjar emerged in the fifteenth century, and from the sixteenth century onwards Marwari and Gujarati can be considered separate literary traditions.[41] H.C. Bhayani presents a slightly more complex picture, suggesting that from the fourteenth century Maru-Gurjar developed into two branches: Jaipuri and Gujarati-Marwari-Malwi, and that the latter three emerged as three separate vernaculars in the fifteenth century.[42] The appearance of literary Marwari by the fifteenth century can be corroborated by John Smith's study of the language of the reconstructed *Vīsāḷdevrās* (c.1450),[43] which is substantially different from Old Gujarati.[44]

The linguistic development of Maru-Gurjar into Middle Gujarati can be glimpsed from Table 1.1 that shows the phonetic changes between the fourteenth and the eighteenth centuries.

There is a scholarly consensus that the principal successor of the Maru-Gurjar tradition outside Gujarat was literary Marwari. I argue that one further successor was Madhyadeśī. Although literary Marwari, later called Ḍiṅgal,[45] represents a linguistic shift from Maru-Gurjar, it reflects continuity in its abundant poetic forms. In contrast to Marwari

Table 1.1 Phonetic Changes in Maru-Gurjar and Middle Gujarati Literary Works between the Fourteenth and Eighteenth Centuries

1300	1350	1400	1450	1500	1550	1600	1650	1700
-C*u*			-C*a*					
-C*i*								-C*(a)ya*/-C*a*
-*aü*				-*u* (for long ū)			-*o*	
-*aüṁ*				-*ūṁ*	> -*uṁ*			
-*aï*					-*i* (for ī)			
-*iu*			-*yaü*	>	-*yu* (for yū)	>	-*o*/-*yo*	
-*iuṁ*			*yūṁ*	>	-*yuṁ*			
-*iyā*			-*iā*/-*iyāṁ*		> -*yā* -*yāṁ*			
-*iya*	-*i*							
-*iï*		> *yaï*		> *ye*				

Source: Based on Bhayani, *Gujarātī bhāṣānuṁ aitihāsik vyākaraṇ*, 422–4.

compositions, which used a variety of metres, Madhayadeśī, as we are going to see, only produced works in caupāī (and occasionally *dohā*) metres for several centuries. This has also been observed by Narayan Singh Bhati, who stated that the literary tradition of Piṅgal, linked to Madhyadeśa and Braj, had a preference for caupāīs and dohās, as contrasted with the metrical profusion of Ḍiṅgal.[46]

Modern Hindi scholarship has incorporated Marwari and Madhyadeśī (perceived as early Braj) into the array of premodern Hindi, which directed the attention of some scholars to these idioms' predecessor, Maru-Gurjar. Several Hindi literary historians, therefore, include an appreciative survey of Maru-Gurjar literature into their histories, such as Chandradhar Sharma 'Guleri' (*Purāṇī Hindī*, 1948), Kamtaprasad Jain (*Hindī Jain sāhitya kā saṁkṣipt itihās*, 1947) Nathuram Premi (*Jain sāhitya aur itihās*, 1942–56), Ganpatichandra Gupta (*Hindī sāhitya kā vaijñānik itihās*, 1965), Shitikanth Mishra (*Hindī jain sāhitya kā bṛhat itihās*, 1989), and Agarchand Nahta in his various publications. Mainstream, that is, non-Jain, Hindi and Rajasthani histories, however, were generally ambivalent towards Maru-Gurjar.[47] Ramchandra Shukla does not appear to know about it and considers early Jain literature to be only in Apabhramsha.[48] The *Hindī sāhitya kā bṛhat itihās* treats it within the mass of later Hindi *rāsos* (heroic epic) and *muktakas* (independent verse). In his survey of Rajasthani literature,

Motilal Menariya states that 'this vast literature of Jain scholars is interesting from a linguistic and not so much from a literary point of view, although here and there one may even find literary beauty in it'.[49] In contrast with Hindi, Gujarati literary historians accept Maru-Gurjar as part of their tradition and identify it with Old Gujarati, which developed into Middle Gujarati in the sixteenth century.

A recurring observation of Hindi scholars made in the face of the substantial corpus of Maru-Gurjar is that, lacking institutional background similar to the Jain archives, Hindi's old literature has not been preserved;[50] however, the absence of any trace of handwritten books with purported early Hindi works in the Jain collections of Gujarat and Rajasthan, where later non-Jain Hindi works are found in abundance, suggests that non-Maru-Gurjar Hindi compositions became part of written circulation at a later stage. Perhaps as a consequence of this, non-Jain Hindi manuscript production can at present only be documented from the Mughal Era.

Narratives in Madhyadeśa

In all probability, the earliest known vernacular literary work in the Hindi belt is the 'Rāula-vela', a poem preserved not in manuscript but as a stone inscription from the twelfth century in Dhar, the capital of the Paramāras, including king Bhoja.[51] It contains the head-to-toe descriptions of heroines from six regions sprinkled with features of the heroines' respective dialects, that is, Mālvā, Ṭakka (south-east Panjab), Gauḍa (eastern region), Golla (the Godavari River region), Kānoḍa (Kannauj), and what is probably Maru-Gurjar.[52] This work, composed in the form of a single-actor play called *bhāṇa*, can be perceived as a variation on the favourite genre of inscriptions, the *praśasti*, inasmuch as it presents the beauty of heroines that possibly represent the Rājyalakṣmīs, or royal fortunes, of neighbouring countries as being inferior to that of Malwa.[53] Notwithstanding its connections to Sanskrit plays and to the much later Hindi rīti tradition, the 'Rāula-vela' stands out as a unique attempt with only a meagre oral or cosmopolitan link to the subsequent vernacular traditions that were upheld by manuscript culture and that operated in a single literary idiom or in some vernacular-Apabhramsha combination. Since the inscription was unmoveable and remained in a place that lost its importance after the Paramāras, the 'Rāula-vela' was excluded from the circulation of literature.

To what extent then can we stipulate the existence of pre-Mughal vernacular literary culture from the Hindi belt in the light of later manuscript evidence? Given the monsoon climate of the region, manuscripts tend to decay within a few centuries. The earliest literary manuscripts produced in the region appear only as early as the mid-sixteenth century.[54] Nevertheless, several works explicitly claim to have been created in locations in the Hindi belt, and their date of composition is either stated in the manuscript or can be inferred by the dates of a patron.[55] More and more such works were produced from the late fifteenth century onwards, attesting to a fledgling literary culture. Parallel to this, a primarily oral poetic culture was also in existence in late Sultanate times, which in its metres and aesthetics represented continuity with written literature. Poets such as Kabīr composed orally and their poetry has been in oral circulation since. Yet the majority of the early Kabīr corpus, all the *sākhīs* (distichs) and the *ramainīs* (a mixed form of distichs and quatrains) along with more than half of the *pads* (as published in *The Millennium Kabir Vāṇī*), was composed in dohās and caupāīs, the favourite poetic forms of literary Madhyadeśī. Nevertheless, the situation before 1450 needs more historical and philological investigation. Historicizing prosody or examining the earliest forms of language can be of particular help here.

Narratives in the caupāī metre and genre were produced in Madhyadeśa from the mid-fourteenth century onwards. In their surveys of early Brajbhasha works, Shiv Prasad Singh and Harihar Nivas Dvivedi made reference to several vernacular works composed between the mid-fourteenth and early fifteenth-centuries.[56] Although in the light of more recent research many of them cannot be considered to be as early as these scholars claimed, the dates of at least two narratives have not since been questioned seriously—the Jain Sadhāru's *Pradyumna-Carit* from 1354 and Jākhū Maniyār's (Jāṁkho Maṇihār) *Haricand Purāṇ* from 1396.[57] To these one can add Viddhaṇū's *Jñānpañcamī* (or *Siyapañcamī*) *Caupāī* from 1367 and Raïdhū's *Bārah Bhāvanā*.[58] H.N. Dvivedi also mentions another narrative, Lakhansenī's partially available *Haricarit* (*Virāṭparv*) written in 1424, and quotes four lines from it.[59] These works are the most outstanding products of a fledgling vernacular literary culture in the Hindi belt east of Rajasthan, and one may suspect that there were many similar works in circulation but, due to the limited scope of initial Hindi manuscript culture and to changing tastes, have been lost over time. Works such as Mualānā Dāūd's *Candāyan* (1379), Viṣṇudās's epics (*Pāṇḍav-Carit* and *Rāmāyan*) and the *Vīsāḷdev-rās* (c. 1450) have been perceived to be at the fountainheads of Avadhi, Brajbhasha, and Rajasthani literary traditions respectively; however, they may also be connected to the Maru-Gurjar idiom.

Literary works in Madhyadeśa were produced at important administrative, military, or commercial centres indicating that the emergence of new works was somehow linked to the circulation of people and, eventually, of ideas. Sadhāru wrote his *Pradyumna-Carit* in Erach on the river Betwa in Bundelkhand. Although in 2001 this small town in Jhansi district had only 9,531 inhabitants,[60] Erach, the alleged birthplace of Prahlāda, was already an urban centre with rulers and a mint during the Maurya–Gupta interlude.[61] In the fourteenth and fifteenth centuries it was the seat of local governors from Delhi, Jaunpur, and then from Malwa, and it even had its spell of independence.[62] Viddhaṇū wrote his *Jñānpañcamī Caupāī* in 'Bihār-nagar', a designation he used for Rajgir in Bihar, and Lakhansenī produced his *Haricarit* (*Virāṭparv*) in Jaunpur-Chausa, which in modern terms would belong to the Avadhi-speaking area. The Jain poet Raïdhū, better known for his Apabhramsha compositions, was active in Gwalior in the mid- and late-fifteenth century. This may also account for the fact that just like other Maru-Gurjar compositions, some of these works had a relatively widespread circulation.

The choice of a literary idiom also suited the requirements of a particular genre or metre. It is well illustrated in the case of Jākhū Maniyār's *Haricand Purān*. This narrative is composed mostly in caupāīs; however, on the pattern of Apabhramsha and Maru-Gurjar works, the caupāīs are interspersed with *vastus* (a strophic metre associated with Apabhramsha). While the caupāīs in the extant text can be perceived to be in archaic Brajbhasha, that is, Madhyadeśī, the vastus' language may be marked by Apabhramsha features:

Caupāī:
baiṣampāyana śiṣya haṁkāri, kisna dīpāyana kahai bicāri;
janmejaya bhārata sunāva, brahma hatyā ko phere pāva. (26)
bhārata suṇāyõ paraba aṭhāra, miṭī hatyā bhayo jayajayakāra. (27)

Vastu:
jāī pātika sayala asesa, hoi dharama bahu dukkhe hā̃ṇijjaï;
devapriyā rana raṁbhāvato eka līha kema thūṇijjaï.
kr̥ṣṇa dīpāyana uccarai je yahi chanda suṇantu;
manasā vācā karmaṇā ghora pāpa phīṭantu.[63]

Caupāī:
Vyasa called out to his disciple, Vaiṣampāyana
and after reflecting he said,
Janamejaya, listen to the Bhārata,
which removes even the sin of killing a Brahmin.
I am telling you the Bhārata in eighteen *parvas*—
the sin of killing is (thus) removed and celebration arises.

Vastu:
All the sins without exception disappear;
exceeding dharma arises and removes sorrow.
The beloved of the gods roars in the battle,[64]
how can he follow the same way (of his ancestors)?[65]
Whoever listens to these verses
pronounced by Vyāsa,
His sins of thought, word and action
will be erased.

Three out of the five works mentioned above are *caritkāvyas*, that is, reworkings of epic and puranic themes, and four are composed primarily in rhyming sixteen-mora caupāī couplets. Although the rhyming sixteen-mora metre called *pādākulak* (or *vadanak, aḍill,* or *maḍillā*)[66] was already popular in Apabhramsha, its use for epic purposes in Hindi indicates that in Madhyadesha, unlike in Bengal in the east or Rajasthan in the west, there existed a tradition of composing epic poetry primarily in caupāīs in literary vernaculars, that is, in the language of the place.

At present, out of the pre-1450 Hindi works, only Sadhāru's *Pradyumna-Carit*, the *Candāyan*, the *Vīsāḷdev-Rās*, and Viṣṇudās's *Pāṇḍav-Carit* have critical editions. The *Pradyumna-Carit* was edited on the basis of four manuscripts—three of which date back to the sixteenth century, a unique occurrence in Hindi editing history.[67] Despite the claim that the *Pradyumna-Carit* is in Brajbhasha,[68] with its retained Rajasthani and Apabhramsha phonology, morphology, and vocabulary, Sadhāru's language represents continuity with Maru-Gurjar, and with its preference for vowel clusters over diphthongs it foreshadows Avadhi. The language of the *Haricand Purāṇ* also retains vowel clusters and Apabhramsha elements.[69] In contrast, the idiom of the *Haricarit* (*Virāṭparv*), at least from what can be assessed in the four-line excerpt published by Dvivedi, differs from that of the other works and agrees with later Brajbhasha usage.[70] This could be the result of a serious reworking. Although Raïdhū's *Bārah Bhāvanā*, a short work in thirty-nine stanzas, dates probably from the decades after 1450, its language is very close to that of the *Pradyumna-Carit*, using both archaisms and wider regional features.

* * *

Viddhaṇū's *Jñānpañcamī* (or *Siyapañcamī*) *Caupāī* (1367) is one of the earliest dateable vernacular works in Madhyadeśa that has not been discussed by non-Jain Hindi literary historians. The little that is known about Viddhaṇū's life and the circulation of his work illustrates the link between Madhyadeśī and Maru-Gurjar, and importantly between the emergence of literary works and the movement of ideas. Viddhaṇū was the son of Ṭhakkar Mālhe and a disciple of Jinodaysūri (1318–75). Jinodaysūri, the author of works that have been labelled as Apabhramsha, Prakrit, and Rajasthani compositions,[71] lived very much in the peripatetic mode moving between Palanpur (north Gujarat), Jaisalmer, Khambat, and Patan.[72] Viddhaṇū, on the other hand, became involved with the Jains in a remote area of Bihar. An inscription in thirty-eight shlokas in the Pārśvanāth temple of Rājgṛh (Rajgir, Bihar) dating from 1355 states that it was made by the Jain *śrāvak* (layman) scholar, Vīdhā, son of Ṭhakkar Mālhe.[73]

The *Jñānpañcamī Caupāī* is a composition of 548 stanzas about the importance of the fast on the day of Jñānpañcamī or Śrutpañcamī illustrated by the adventurous story of Bhaviṣyadatta. Jñānpañcamī is the fifth day of the month of Kārtik, on which Jains worship both the knowledge contained in the books and the physical manuscripts themselves.[74] The only manuscript of Viddhaṇū's work, called *Siyapañcamī* in the text and *Ṇānapañcamī* in the colophon, is preserved in Patan.[75] While the Gujarati cataloguers and lexicographers designated its language as Apabhramsha[76] or Rajasthani,[77] Hindi scholars interested in its linguistic features found it to be closer to Hindi. Premsagar Jain took it as an early Hindi work and noted that already Nathuram Premi had drawn attention to the fact that this work is more Hindi than Gujarati when compared to the works of the Maru-Gurjar tradition.[78] The sample text below shows that the Maru-Gurjar of the poem is indeed close to Brajbhasha and Avadhi:

jiṇavara sāsaṇi āchaï sāru; jasu na lambhaï anta apāru;
paḍhahu guṇahu pūjahu ni sunehu; siya-pañcami phalu kahiyaü ehu. (1)

siya-pañcami phalu jānaü loi; jo naru karaï [so] duhiyaü na hoi;
saṁjama mana dhari jo naru karaï; so naru niścaï duttaru taraï. (2)

The teachings of the Jina are the best of all things;
they are infinite in extent; one never exhausts them.
Read them, recite them, worship them and listen to them.
The fruit of carrying out the vow of worshiping the Jain teachings is told here;
Let everyone know it.
The person who carries out these rituals will never suffer;
The one who, restrained in mind, carries out these rituals,
will surely cross over that which is difficult to cross over.
(Translated by Phyllis Granoff)[79]

ūṁva-kāraṁ jiṇahaṁ caübīsa, śārada sāmini karaüṁ jagīsa;
vāhaṇa haṁsa bahnī kara vīṇa, so jiṇa sāsaṇi achaï līṇa. (3)
aṭhadala kamala upanī nāri, jeṇi payāsiya vejaī cāri;
sasiharaviṁvu amia rasu pharaï, namaskāra tasu viddhanu karaï. (4)

The goddess Śāradā, goddess of the universe,
utters the sound *oṁ*, in which dwell the twenty-four Jinas
Her vehicle is the wild goose, she holds a *vina* in her left hand
and is immersed in the Jina's teaching.
The lady who arose from the eight-petalled lotus,
who made apprehensible the four Vedas,
and whose moon-like face sheds nectar—
Viddhaṇu salutes her.

cintā sāyara jaṁvi naru paraï, ghara dhandhali sayalaī vīsaraï;
kohu mānu māyā māya mohu, jara phajhaṁpe pariyaü sandehu. (5)[80]
dānu na dinnaü munivara jogu, nā tapu tapiü na bhogeu bhogu; (6)

When a man plummets into a sea of troubles,
he forgets all the household works,
Covered in pride, illusion, intoxication
and senselessness he falls into doubt,
Does not give appropriate donation to the excellent ascetics,
neither does he undertake asceticism nor does he enjoy delights.

sāvaya gharahiṁ liaü avatāru, anadinu mani cintahu navakāru.
tinni rayaṇa jo jhāṇahaṁ ṭhāiṁ, tisu jiu naraya ṇa kavahūṁ jāi. (7)
bhayi yaha munivara kahaü sanehu, siya-paṁcami phalu kahiyaü ehu.
caüdaha saï teīsā sāra, maṇḍala magadha nayara bīhāra. (8)

When one took human birth in the house of a Jain
one should daily meditate on the *ṇamokāra*.

The one who remains in meditation for three nights
 will never go to hell.
As the best of *munis* told it with affection
 I will explain the fruit of carrying out the vow of worshiping the Jain teachings.
It is in fourteen twenty-three
 in the country of Magadha in the town of Rajgir.[81]

* * *

Viṣṇudās has sometimes been presented as the founder of Brajbhasha.[82] In the form in which it has come to us, Viṣṇudās's language is Brajbhasha with a slight touch of archaisms.[83] The presence of these non-Braj forms puzzled some modern scholars and it must have baffled earlier scribes as well. An analysis of the linguistic layers of Viṣṇudās's works, often preserved in the variant readings of his editions, shows that his language has been subjected to a 'modernizing process'.[84] (A similar 'Brajifying drive' in the eighteenth century has been documented in the case of Svāmī Haridās's rekhta quatrain and of an Awadhi *chappay* metre of Tulsīdās's *Kavitāvalī*).[85] For example, we know that Caturbhuj Caube, the scribe of 'manuscript *ka*' of the *Pāṇḍav-Carit* copied in 1728 in Datiya, has reworked its language.[86] To quote just a few examples, in Caube's manuscript the *tadbhava* Apabhramsha *suravai* becomes the *tatsama* Braj *surapati*; similarly *dobai* becomes *draupatī* and *bairāre* is changed into *birāṭa*.[87] He also changes the words to be more in line with Brajbhasha, whereas the other manuscript of the *Pāṇḍav-Carit,* copied in 1757, keeps the language closer to Apabhramsha or Avadhi by separating the diphthongs into two syllables. In Caube's version *akāsaha* becomes *akāsaĩ*; *dīsahi* becomes *dīsaĩ*; *kahahu* becomes *kahau*.[88] Similarly, as McGregor has already noted, one of the two *Rāmāyan* manuscripts retains and the other eschews tadbhava archaisms.[89] The retained Apabhramsha elements as well as the use of tadbhava rather than *ardha-tatsama* words, such as *bhuvāra* (Sanskrit: *bhūpāla*); *pasāu* (Sanskrit: *prasāda*); *sāyara* (Sanskrit: *sāgara*); *dinayara* (Sanskrit: *dinakara*); *ruharu* (Sanskrit: *rudhira*); *paisār* (Sanskrit: *praveśamārga*); *tivaī* (Sanskrit: *strī*) still link Viṣṇudās's language diachronically to that of Sadhāru and, eventually, to Maru-Gurjar. Geographically, McGregor presents a complex picture by observing the closeness of Viṣṇudās's 'archaisms' to both early Rajasthani and Gujarati (that is, Maru-Gurjar and Marwari) on the one hand and to Bundelkhandi and Avadhi on the other.

Tables 1.2 and 1.3 show some prominent linguistic features of Maru-Gurjar and of early vernacular works of which we possess critical editions. As can be seen, none of the editions are based on manuscripts contemporaneous with the compositions themselves. If the editions are based on early manuscript material, the likelihood of the work having been reworked into later literary idioms is somewhat reduced. The two most problematic authors from this point of view are Viṣṇudās and Dāūd. (Elements that Viṣṇudās shares with Maru-Gurjar and with Sadhāru are in bold. The sign '+' indicates the presence and the sign '–' of the absence of a specific feature.)

It is the language of the two Jain works at Madhyadeśa, the *Pradyumna-Carit* as well as Raïdhū's *Bārah Bhāvanā* (a short work not listed in the table), and the earlier Maru-Gurjar works that share the most linguistic peculiarities with the archaisms of Viṣṇudās. His use of postpositions links him even more markedly to Sadhāru and to Maru-Gurjar than to later Brajbhasha (see Table 1.3).

While the poetic and linguistic features clearly indicate a diachronic continuity between early Maru-Gurjar, the language of Sadhāru, of Viṣṇudās, and Brajbhasha, what about the archaisms Sadhāru and Viṣṇudās share with Marwari and Avadhi? A few of Viṣṇudās's archaisms may also bring his language closer sometimes to the language of the *Candāyan*, written in Dalmau in the Avadhi area in 1379, and sometimes to the reconstructed language of the *Vīsāḷdev-rās*, composed in Rajasthan. It can also be observed that Dāūd's Avadhi shares more features with Viṣṇudās than it does with Marwari. The shared poetic form of the caupāī suggests continuity with Madhyadeśī, and there might even have been more linguistic overlap between Madhyadeśī works and the idiom used by Dāūd in earlier stages of transmission than is reflected in the critical editions. That is why one of the editors of the *Candāyan*, Parameshvarilal Gupta, could stress with some exaggeration that the *Cāndāyan* participated in literary circulation from its inception,

> *Cāndāyan* was neither composed in an Awadhi environment nor was it initially recited for the benefit of the Awadhi speaking public.... *Cāndāyan*, as it is clearly stated by Abdul Qadir Badayuni, was composed in honour of Jauna Shah, the prime minister of Delhi.... Obviously, *Cāndāyan* was composed in a language which could be understood by the prime minister as well as by the local population.[90]

TABLE 1.2 Comparison of Some Prominent Phonological, Morphological, and Lexical Features of Representative Works of Maru-Gurjar, Madhyadeśī, Old Marwari, Old Avadhi, and Later Braj

	Maru-Gurjar		Madhyadeśī		Old Marwari	Old Avadhi	Later Braj
	Aitihāsik vyākaraṇ[91]	*Gurjara-rāsāvalī*[92]	Sadhāru: *Pradyumna-Carit*	Viṣṇudās: *Rāmāyan*	Nālha: *Vīsāḷdev-rās*	Dāūd: *Candāyan*	
Date of the works (CE)	1150–1550	1353–1428	1354	1442	c.1450	1379	
earliest manuscripts	1273–c.1600	1493–1547	1548	1728	1576	1616	
vowel clusters	+	+	+	+ –	–	+	–
(use of the retroflex '*ṇa*')	+	+	+	–	+	–	–
Cases apart from nom., and voc.	loc/instr.; gen.		loc./instr.	obl.	loc/instr.	loc.; instr.	obl.
Apabhramsha names	+	+	+	+	n/a	n/a	–
abundance of tadbhavas	+	+	+	+	n/a	n/a	–
obl. dem. pron.	*teh*		*tihi*	tām	*tihi, tahi*	*teiṁ, tehiṁ*	*tihi*
'then'		*pachaī*	*phuni*	*phuni*	*pachai*		*puni*
'speech', 'matter'		*sār*	*sār*	*sār*	*vāta*	*bāta*	*bāta, kathā*
'woman'		–	tivaī, *tiriya*	tivaī	*tirī, trī, trīyā, astir*	*tiriyā*	*tiya*

Source: Author.

Table 1.3 Comparison of Postpositions Used in Representative Works of Maru-Gurjar, Madhyadeśī, Old Marwari, Old Avadhi, and Later Braj

	Maru-Gurjar		Madhyadeśī		Old Marwari	Avadhi	Later Braj
	Aitihāsik vyākaraṇ	*Gurjara-rāsāvalī*	Sadhāru: *Pradyumna-Carit*	Viṣṇudās: *Rāmāyan*	Nālha: *Vīsāḷdev-Rās*	Dāūd: *Candāyan*	
(instrumental postp.)	***sahū***, *saũ, siũ, syũ, śũ*	***saha***, *syaũ, siũ*	***sahu***, *siu*	***sahã***	*saũ, syaũ*	*seũ, setī, saïṁ*	*saũ*
(associative postp.)	***sarasaüṁ***, *samaüṁ*	***sarisaü***	*gohiṇa*	***sarisa***	***sarisa***	*gohana*	*saṅga, sātha*
(dative postp.)	*māṭi, bhaṇi, lagī, resi*	*naï, lagaï*	***kaha, kahũ***	***kahã***	*nũ*	***kahã***, *lāgi*	*kaũ*
(ablative postp.)	*thaü, thiu, thī, thakī*	*thuṁ*			*saũ, syaũ*	*huta, seũ, setī, saïṁ*	*saũ*
(genitive postp.)	***taṇaü***, *naü, keraü*	***taṇaü/tanaï***, *naü, keraü*	***taṇaü*** (rarely *kau*)	***tanau*** (rarely *kau*)	***taṇaü***	*kara/ka, kaï, ke*	*kau*
'on' (locative postp.)	*ūpari, māthaï*	*ūpari, pāhi* (for abl.)	***pahã***	***pahã***	*ūpari*		*pai*

Source: Author.

This question needs more investigation, but the shared linguistic features in the three above-mentioned texts, at the fountainhead of subsequent literary traditions, suggest that in the fifteenth century the dividing line that existed between later literary idioms was not yet prominent.

One can even go further and assume that there existed a literary idiom in Madhyadeśa with an array of features, the particular elements of which later became peculiar to crystallized idioms. This early, composite literary language can indeed be called Madhyadeśī bhāṣā, 'the vernacular of the central region of India'. Later, it shed its Apabhramsha/Rajasthani features and formed into the separate literary dialects of Braj and Avadhi, while its non-standardized form that mixed elements from a wide region was maintained by the Sant poets and was later given the name Sadhukkaṛī, 'the idiom of the sadhus'. At the same time, courtly works in this early Madhyadeśī, such as Vishnudas's *Rāmāyan*, were gradually dragged in the direction of Braj, and perhaps Avadhi, during the centuries of their transmission, losing many of their archaic features. The view that the geographically widespread Madhyadeśī vernacular becomes more and more regionalized over the centuries is paralleled by the better-documented development of the transregional Maru-Gurjar, within which the emergence of regional usages eventually resulted in the separate Gujarati, Rajasthani, and, now we may add, Madhyadeśī literatures.[93]

Manuscripts of our early vernacular works travelled throughout Gujarat, Rajasthan, and Madhyadeśa. Modern Hindi and Gujarati can be mutually comprehensible if one listens carefully or has some informal training; one can also conjecture that the distance between some spoken dialects of these languages may have even been smaller during the time under review. A composition in a literary idiom based originally on a form of Gujarati would be accessible to most learned speakers in Rajasthan and Madhyadeśa. Yet in order to be fully comprehensible, works committed to writing had to comply with certain linguistic and poetic conventions. Local dialects played a secondary role resulting in the regionalization of Maru-Gurjar. Originally regional features may only have been used to give a local flavour to these cosmopolitan vernacular works; however, when the cosmopolitan vernacular was no longer relevant for a readership, regionalisms eclipsed many of the transregional features, which were perceived as archaisms.

A good example of the regionalization of Madhyadeśī is Viṣṇudās's language. In its later form it has been drawn towards what has subsequently been called Brajbhasha, the language of Gwalior, as exemplified in the 1405 inscription of Birammadeva, just a few years after the establishment of the Tomar dynasty. The language of the inscription is not that of Viṣṇudās; rather, with its openness towards Persian vocabulary and its use of *ko* instead of Viṣṇudās's *tanau*, it shows the direction that Brajbhasha would take later (non-Sanskrit elements are in bold):

> om siddhiḥ| **saṁvatu** 1462 varṣe mārga **sudi** (15)
> somadina mahārājādhirāja **srībīramadeva**
> śrī aṁbikā **kau maṁḍapu karavāyau| pradhānu** paṁ
> janārdana| **phujdāru** ... sūtradhāra **haridāsu**|
> **māṭhā**pati goviṁda **candrānyavarī**|[94]

> Om. Success. In the Vikrama year of 1462 on Monday the 15th of the bright half of Mārgaśīrṣa Śrī Vīramdev, overlord of the rulers, had the mandapa of Śrī Ambikā made. The chief was pandit Janārdan, the military commander ..., the mason Haridās, the stone-carver[95] Govind Candrānyavarī.[96]

The modern locations of the two best-known fourteenth-century Hindi works, Erach and Dalmau, are small settlements with 8,000–9,000 inhabitants. Many of these inhabitants may not even know that these little towns once experienced some of the most defining events in the literary history of what is now one of the largest languages of the world. Early literary cultures were closely linked to manuscript circulation, and one of the primary aims of manuscript production was circulation. Erach on the Betwa River and Dalmau on the Ganges are found on important points in the network of Indian trade and military routes. A composition was able to participate in the literary culture when it entered into circulation, and one of the best networks of literary circulation in the early centuries of the second millennium was maintained by the Jains. In contrast, the consequences of non-participation in cultural circulation are well illustrated by the fact that the 'Rāula-vela', an inscription at a royal centre but excluded from circulation, was not able to create a subsequent literary tradition.

The period between the mid-fourteenth and mid-fifteenth centuries links Maru-Gurjar to later Braj, Avadhi, and Sadhukaṛī traditions through its dominant literary idiom, Madhyadeśī. Literature in Madhyadeśī represents continuity with Maru-Gurjar in language, themes, metres, and even in its style of relying heavily on Apabhramsha vocabulary. Over the period, it grew into a distinct intermediary tradition, more and more distanced from Maru-Gurjar, and through its regionalization came to be considered as the immediate ancestor of Brajbhasha and of other Hindi literary idioms.

Conclusion

To what extent can we address the question of the emergence of Hindi as a literary language? Can we locate a boundary between Apabhramsha and the vernacular Maru-Gurjar when the early works of the latter seem to consist of a mixture of the two? Did Hindi literature start with the non-consequential 'Rāula-vela'?[97] Or did it start with the emergence of Maru-Gurjar, that is, Old Gujarati, in the twelfth century?[98] Can one present a continuously developing literary tradition from Maru-Gurjar via Madhyadeśī and Brajbhasha through to Modern Hindi? Or shall one consider Hindi to come about only when vernacular works emerge in Madhyadeśa in the mid-fourteenth century in Maru-Gurjar?[99] Or perhaps when the first regionalized Hindi work, the *Candāyan*, appears in 1379? Or shall each Hindi tradition be allocated a different beginning? Thus, should Brajbhasha start with Viṣṇudās's *Pāṇḍav-Carit* in 1435? There are also questions of geography: shall Hindi include early works from Rajasthan or later compositions in Marwari? The obscurity of both chronological and geographical boundaries for Hindi indicates that one cannot give uncontested answers to these questions. These are, however, primarily questions of nomenclature. If one goes beyond them, one can see the continuous development of vernacular literary idioms through geographic expansion and regionalization, beginning in the twelfth century.

Scholars in the nineteenth and twentieth centuries, in a true Herderian manner, tried to root the language of a particular early work of literature in the modern dialect of the region where it was composed. Yet the role of literary patterns coming from existing traditions cannot be underestimated. It was primarily these linguistic and poetic patterns that defined a work and allowed it to participate in a transregional or, to use Sheldon Pollock's term, cosmopolitan vernacular literary world beyond the confines of a (spoken) dialect. Moreover, these linguistic and poetic patterns also informed oral poetry and facilitated its wider circulation.[100]

Although hardly known today, some of the Maru-Gurjar and Madhyadeśī narratives once enjoyed widespread popularity, as attested by a considerable number of manuscripts.[101] Their archaisms, such as the presence of a case system or the use of Sanskrit-derived, that is, tadbhava, words instead of the Sanskrit ardhatatsama loanwords dominant in later poetry, underline the continuity with the rich Apabhramsha narrative tradition. While Jain narratives preserved these archaisms, non-Jain works such as Maulānā Dāūd's Sufi *Cāndāyan* and Viṣṇudās's epics seem to have lost a considerable portion of them during transmission. In early times, features that later became peculiar to Braj or Avadhi were not marked in these works. More importantly, their language and the caupāī metre were imitated and developed by subsequent Hindi authors. In fact, the overwhelming majority of Hindi narratives produced during the pre-Mughal Era were written in caupāīs. The only development on this front is that the monotony of caupāī was broken in some works by the insertion of Sanskrit *ślokas* or of Hindi couplets, usually dohās.

As their language was felt to be more and more archaic, unless their literary idiom was updated, Madhyadeśī works became marginalized. Due to the popularity of Braj from the seventeenth century onwards, processes of transmission may have reworked early narratives into a more standardized Braj. While grammatical updating during transmission obscured the origins of a tradition, it kept the early tradition alive as it helped maintain access to archaic works in a changing world. Whether modernized or not, Madhyadeśī works receded from the view of later poets and the intermediary tradition that linked Maru-Gurjar with Braj, Avadhi, and other early modern Hindi literary idioms was lost. However obscured this tradition may be today, it contains the earliest known vernacular works in the Hindi belt that can be considered to be at the fountainhead of literature in the largest language of India.

Notes

* I am grateful to Professor John Cort, Professor Allison Busch, Professor Christopher Minkowski, Professor Phyllis Granoff, Dr Eva de Clercq, and Dr Steven Vose for their comments on various aspects of the article.

1. Dates referring to early modern India are converted from the Vikram era (VS) by subtracting fifty-seven years. Although in Gujarat the new year

starts only at Diwali and not in the spring and the subtraction of only 56 years would be more appropriate, I consistently keep the 57-year difference since I often deal with authors who travelled throughout Gujarat and Rajasthan, and we cannot always be sure whether they used the local system or not.

2. The seminal work is Sheldon Pollock, *The Language of the Gods in the World of Men: Sanskrit, Culture, and Power in Premodern India* (New Delhi: Permanent Black, 2007). For Hindi, see Allison Busch, 'Hindi Literary Beginnings', in *South Asian Texts in History*. ed. W. Cox, Y. Bronner, and L. McCrea (Ann Arbor: Association for South Asian Studies, 2011), 203–25.

3. Much of this has been pointed out already in 1965 in Ganapati Candra Gupta, *Hindī sāhitya kā vaijñānik itihās*, 5th revised edition, 2 vols (Allahabad: Lokbharati, 1999), vol. 1, 68–79, especially, 68–70 and 75–6. For an array of representative cases, see Imre Bangha, 'Rekhta, Poetry in Mixed Language: The Emergence of Khari Boli Literature in North India', in *Before the Divide: Hindi and Urdu Literary Culture*, ed. Francesca Orsini (New Delhi: Orient BlackSwan, 2010), 29–36, and for a discussion on how Hindi historiography saw this problem, see Busch, 'Hindi Literary Beginnings', especially 205–8.

4. I owe this idea to Steven Vose, personal communication, 17 July 2012.

5. A good example of what should not be considered Hindi literature is the Sanskrit manual *Ukti-vyakti-prakaraṇa*, composed by Dāmodara Paṇḍita in Benares in the early twelfth century, which is a treasury of translations of spoken Sanskrit sentences into a language that was termed 'Old Kosalī' or 'Old Avadhī'. The work is published and studied in Jinvijay Muni, *Uktivyaktiprakaraṇa* (Bombay: Singhi Jaina Shastra Sikshapitha, 1953). Its position within Sanskrit is discussed in Richard Salomon, 'The Ukti-Vyakti-Prakaraṇa as a Manual of Spoken Sanskrit', *Indo-Iranian Journal* 24, no. 1 (1982), 13–25.

6. The term 'rekhta' was first used to name a literary style in the 1650s (Bangha, 'Rekhta, Poetry in Mixed Language', 56, see also 24–6). Brajbhasha, or 'the language of Braj', dates back to the late seventeenth century; see Allison Busch, *Poetry of Kings: The Classical Hindi Literature of Mughal India* (New York and Oxford: Oxford University Press, 2011), 8. The word 'Avadhī' does not figure in two of its pre-eminent works, the *Padmāvat* and the *Rāmcaritmānas*, while the term 'Sadhukkarī' (sadhukkaṛī) is a term conceived by Ramchandra Shukla in his *History of Hindi Literature* (first published in 1929 as the introduction to the *Hindī śabd sāgar* of Shyamsundar Das, and later as *Hindī sāhitya kā itihās* [Kashi: Nagari Pracharini Sabha, 1942]).

7. Sheldon Pollock, *Literary Cultures in History: Reconstructions from South Asia* (New Delhi and London: Oxford University Press, 2003), 15.

8. The famous Fatehpur manuscript, for example, contains Sadhukkari poems of Kabīr along with the Brajbhasha poems of Sūrdās. A facsimile of this manuscript is published in Gopal Narayan Bahura and Kenneth E. Bryant, *The Padas of Sūrdās* (Jaipur: Sawai Mansingh II Museum, 1982).

9. In Ālam's *Mādhavānal-Kāmkandalā*, Braj-Avadhi caupāīs alternate with Braj dohās as published in the critical edition, which, interestingly, conceives the work to be in Avadhi. See Ramkumari Mishra, ed., *Ālam kṛt mādhavānal kāmkandalā: Avadhī premākhyānak* (Prayag: Ratnakumārī Svādhyāy Sansthān, 1982). All authors of Nāgarī Rekhtā produced texts in either Sadhukkari or Brajbhasha dialects (see Bangha, 'Rekhta, Poetry in Mixed Language', 53–61, 71–80).

10. A good example of dialect change is chappay 117 of the *Kavitāvalī* of Tulsīdās. In manuscripts dating from the seventeenth and eighteenth centuries, this poem has Avadhi verbal forms, such as *kīnheu* or *dīnheu*. Several manuscripts from the nineteenth century present the Braj forms *kīnhau*, *dīnhau* instead, and these variants make it into the *Tulsī Granthāvalī* and into the Gita Press editions. Cf. Imre Bangha, Dániel Balogh, Eszter Berki, and Eszter Somogyi, eds, *The Kavitāvalī of Tulsīdās: Critical Edition* (work in progress).

11. This name derives from the first description of the language; see Luigi Pio Tessitori, 'Notes on the Grammar of the Old Western Rajasthani with Special Reference to Apabhramça and to Gujarati and Marvari', *Indian Antiquary* 43–5. John Smith, the editor of one of the earliest texts in literary Marwari, rejects this name, stating that 'Tessitori's error seems to have been to assume that, since Old Gujarati was widely used in Rajasthan, it must be a direct relative of Rajasthani'. See John Smith, *The Vīsaḷadevarāsa: A Restoration of the Text* (Cambridge: Cambridge University Press, 1976), 47n1. Gujarati scholars do not reject the term but note that this idiom is called by various names. See Harivallabh Chunilal Bhayani, 'Prācīn gujarātī phāgu', in *Śodh ane svādhyāy: prācīn madhyakālīn sāhityaviṣayak saṃśodhanparak lekhsaṅgrah* (Mumbai: R. R. Shethni Company, [1965]), 34n1.

12. The languages of Maru and Gurjara were two of the eighteen regional languages described by Udyotana Sūri in his *Prakrit Kuvalayamālā* composed in 779 (vv. 153.3–4). See Christine Chojnacki, *Kuvalayamala: Roman Jaina de 779, composé par Uddyotanasuri* (Marburg: Indica et Tibetica Verlag, 2008), 449. According to Chojnacki, Maru referred to Marwar and Thar.

13. As described in Udyotana Sūri's Prakrit *Kuvalayamālā*, vv. 153.3–4. See Chojnacki, *Kuvalayamala*, 449.

14. Cf. Harivallabh Chunilal Bhayani, *Gujarātī bhāṣānuṃ aitihāsik vyākaraṇ: ī.sa. 1150 thī 1550 sudhī* (Amdāvād: Parśva Pablikeśan, 1996), 420.

15. Many books printed in the past century by Śvetāmbar saṅghs in 'southern Rajasthan', from places such as Jalor and Sirohi, were published in Gujarati script and language (Personal communication of John Cort, 11 January 2013).

16. Pollock, *The Language of the Gods*. Pollock's idea is not an isolated case. A recent work on the origins of Latin literature, Denis C. Feeney,

Beyond Greek: The Beginnings of Latin Literature (Cambridge, Massachusetts: Harvard University Press, 2016) argues that not every nation had literature. For example, the Puns and the Egyptians lacked it. In the case of others, such as the Latins, literature arose first in the language of another dominant culture and was then vernacularized. Feeney demonstrates that Latin literature started with the translations of Greek plays by Livius Andronicus for the Ludi Romani celebrations at the end of the Pun war in 240 BCE.

17. Allison Busch, 'Hindi Literary Beginnings', in *South Asian Texts in History: Critical Engagements with Sheldon Pollock*, ed. Whitney Cox, Yigal Bronner, and Lawrence McCrea (Ann Arbor: Association for Asian Studies, 2011).

18. Francesca Orsini, 'How to Do Multilingual Literary History? Lessons from Fifteenth- and Sixteenth-Century North India', *Indian Economic and Social History Review* 49, no. 2 (2012): 225–46.

19. The grammar of this language was first examined in detail in Tessitori, published in fifteen instalments between 1914 and 1916. Tessitori's treatment is based on a selection of relatively late texts available to the author. A more recent analysis can be found in H.C. Bhayani, *Gujarātī bhāṣānuṃ aitihāsik vyākaraṇ: ī.sa. 1150 thī 1550 sudhī* (Amadāvāda: Pārśva Pablikeśana, 1996). A brief survey of Maru-Gurjar scholarship is given in Orsini, 'How to Do Multilingual Literary History', 413–20.

20. Mohanlal Dalichand Desai and Jayant Kothari, *Jain gurjar kavio*, 2nd edition, vol. 1 (Bombay: Mahavir Jain Vidyalaya, 1986).

21. Bhayani, *Gujarātī aitihāsik vyākaraṇ*, 40–5. Forty compositions are published in Harivallabh Chunilal Bhayani and Agaracand Nahta, *Prācīn gurjar kāvyasañcay* (Amadābād: Lālabhāī Dalapatabhāī Bhāratīya Saṁskṛti Vidyāmandir, 1975). A volume with historical poetry, Agaracand Nahta and Bhamvarlal Nahta, *Aitihāsik Jain kāvyasaṅgrah* (Calcutta: Shankardas Shubhairaj Nahta, 1937), presents twenty-four compositions from between the twelfth and sixteenth centuries.

22. Karunapati Tripathi, 'Hindi sāhitya kā ādikāl', in *Hindi sāhitya kā bṛhat itihās: Hindi sāhitya kā ādikāl*, ed. Karunapati Tripathi (Benares: Nāgarīpracāriṇī Sabhā, 1983), 41–2.

23. Bhayani, *Gujarātī aitihāsik vyākaraṇ*, 40. Sitanshu Yashaschandra, 'From Hemachandra to Hind Svaraj: Region and Power in Gujarati Literary Culture', in *Literary Cultures in History*, ed. Sheldon Pollock (Berkeley: University of California Press, 2003), 574.

24. Published in Bhayani and Nahta, *Prācīn gurjar kāvyasañcay*, 15–18. See also Tripathi, 'Hindi sāhitya kā ādikāl' 317–18. This work seems to have been unknown to Desai. The *Bharahesur-bāhubali-ghor* is undated, but scholarly consensus in India puts it in the second half of the twelfth century. See Bhayani and Nahta, *Prācīn gurjar kāvyasañcay*, 15; Jayant Kothari and J. Gadit, *Gujarati sahityakoś*, vol. 1 (madhyakāl) (Ahmadabad: Gujarati Sahitya Parishad, 1989), quoted in Yashaschandra, 'From Hemachandra to Hind Svaraj', 574.

25. Desai and Kothari, *Jain gurjar kavio*, 2nd edition, vol. 1, 4. See also Tripathi, 'Hindi sāhitya kā ādikāl', 318–20.

26. Desai and Kothari, *Jain gurjar kavio*, vol. 1, 4–5. (The commentator does not exclude the possibility of it being composed by a different Śālibhadrasūri.)

27. Harivallabh Chunilal Bhayani, 'Saṅgrahit racnāoṁ kī bhāṣā', in *Prācīn gurjar kāvyasañcay*, ed. Harivallabh Chunilal Bhayani and Agaracand Nahta (Amadābād: Lālabhāī Dalapatabhāī Bhāratīya Saṁskṛti Vidyāmandir, 1975), 6. Nahta counted 117 different genres, often based on metre. See Tripathi, 'Hindi sāhitya kā ādikāl', 40.

28. Bhayani, 'Prācīn Gujarātī phāgu', 34. See also M. Avasthi, *Hindī sāhitya kā adyatan itihās*, enlarged edition (Allahabad: Sarasvatī Pres Prakāśan, 1990), 78.

29. Bhayani, 'Saṅgrahit racnāoṁ kī bhāṣā', 10.

30. Desai and Kothari, *Jain gurjar kavio*, vol. 1, 17.

31. 1405 (VS 1462) is the date of the first extant manuscript of the *Cihuṁgati-Copāī*. See Desai and Kothari, *Jain gurjar kavio*, vol. 1, 19–20. The work is published in Balavantray Kalyanray Thakore, Mohalal Dalichand Desai, and M.C. Modi, *Gurjararāsāvalī* (Baroda: Oriental Institute, 1956), 77–87. For the *Karmagati-copāī*, see Desai and Kothari, *Jain gurjar kavio*, vol. 1, 26–7. For Devsundarsūriśiṣya (that is, 'Devsundarsūri's disciple', whose name may have been Kusamaṇḍsūri), Sādhuhaṁsa, and Jayaśekharsūri, see Desai and Kothari, *Jain gurjar kavio*, vol. 1, 39–41, 42–4, and 46–50, respectively.

32. Bhayani, *Gujarātī aitihāsik vyākaraṇ*, 421.

33. Published in Bhayani and Nahta, *Prācīn gurjar kāvyasañcay*, 41–7, on the basis of a manuscript copied in 1373. On the author, see also Premsagar Jain, *Hindī Jain bhakti-kāvya aur kavi* (Benares: Bhāratīy Jñānpīṭh Prakāśan, 1964), 37–42. He is also mentioned within the 'Uttar-prārambhik Hindī: 1348–1444' section of Ganeshbihari Mishra, Shyambihari Mishra, and Shukdevbihari Mishra, *Miśrabandhu-Vinod, athavā Hindī-sāhitya kā itihāsa tathā kavi-kīrttana*, new revised edition (Lucknow: Gaṅgā Pustakmālā, 1972), vol. 1, 92, no. 71 (but missing from earlier editions). Desai and Kothari, *Jain gurjar kavio*, vol. 1, 32–4 lists eighteen manuscripts of *Gautam-svāmī-rās* and mentions that there are many more available. I found that the Jaipur branch of the Rajasthan Oriental Research Institute alone has twenty manuscripts dating from 1522 onwards. See Omkarlal Menariya and Mahopadhyay Vinaysagar, *Rājasthānī Hindī hastalikhit granth-sūcī*, ed. Rajasthan Oriental Research Institute, vol. 5 (Jodhpur: Rajasthan Oriental Research Institute, 1983), 166–9.

34. Charlotte Krause, 'Ancient Jaina Hymns', in *German Jaina Śrāvikā Dr. Charlotte Krause: Her Life and Literature*, ed. Hazarimull Banthia and Luitgard Soni (Varanasi: Pārśvanātha Vidyāpītha, 1999), 313–464, 90.

35. John E. Cort, 'The Jain Knowledge Warehouses: Traditional Libraries in India', *Journal of the American Oriental Society* 115, no. 1 (1995): 86.

36. As can be deduced from the references to the many bhaṇḍārs established in Chalukya Gujarat by Kumārapāla, Vastupāla, and Tejaḥpāla. See Cort, 'The Jain Knowledge Warehouses', 77–87. Jain literati may have taken up positions in non-Jain institutions. The heads of the Bhuj Brajbhāṣā Pāṭhśālā, for example, were initially Jains. See Françoise Mallison, 'The Teaching of Braj, Gujarati, and Bardic Poetry at the Court of Kutch: The Bhuj Brajbhāṣā Pāṭhśālā (1749–1948)', in *Forms of Knowledge in Early Modern South Asia*, ed. Sheldon Pollock (Durham: Duke University Press, 2011), 175–6.

37. Desai and Kothari, *Jain gurjar kavio*, vol. 1, 13.

38. Agaracand Nahta, 'Prastāvnā', in *Prācīn gurjar kāvyasañcay*, ed. Harivallabh Chunilal Bhayani and Agaracand Nahta (Amdābād: Lālabhāī Dalapatbhāī Bhāratīya Saṁskr̥ti Vidyāmandir, 1975), 2.

39. Bhayani, *Gujarātī aitihāsik vyākaraṇ*, 51.

40. Bhayani, *Gujarātī aitihāsik vyākaraṇ*, 11.

41. Nahta, 'Prastāvnā', 1.

42. Bhayani, *Gujarātī aitihāsik vyākaraṇ*, 34.

43. This early date of *Vīsāḷdev-rās* is established by Smith on the basis of the culture they present and because of the existence of sixteenth-century manuscripts. See Smith, *The Vīsaḷadevarāsa*, 26.

44. Smith, *The Vīsaḷadevarāsa*, 31.

45. According to Menariya, literary western Rajasthani was first called Ḍiṅgal as late as in 1814. Motilala Menariya, *Rājasthānī bhāṣā aur sāhitya*, 4th edition (Prayag: Hindi Sahitya Sammelan, 1978), 20.

46. Narayansimh Bhati, *Prācīn ḍiṅgal gīt sāhitya* (Jodhpur: Rajasthan Granthagar, 1989), i, 1–18, 24-–6 as quoted in Yashaschandra, 'From Hemachandra to Hind Swarāj', 575. Brajbhasha in Rajasthan was often called Piṅgal. This word in more recent usage came to refer to Rajasthani-mixed Brajbhasha. Menariya, *Rājasthānī bhāṣā aur sāhitya*, 101.

47. This negligence is noted in Shitikanth Mishra, *Hindī Jain sāhitya kā br̥hat itihās*, ed. Sagarmal Jain, 4 vols (Varanasi: Parshwanath Vidyashram Shodh Sansthan, 1989), vol. 1, 16. Mishra considers Ramchandra Shukla's dismissal of this literature as merely religious teachings to be the primary reason for this general neglect. However, Shukla dismisses directly only the Siddha and Nāth texts and does not mention the Jain bhāṣā works.

48. Shukla, *Hindī sāhitya kā itihās*, 17th edition, 15–18.

49. Menariya, *Rājasthānī bhāṣā aur sāhitya*, 104.

50. Nahta, 'Prastāvnā', 1; Menariya, *Rājasthānī bhāṣā aur sāhitya*, 105.

51. Harivallabh Chunilal Bhayani, *Rāula-vela of Roḍa: A Rare Poem of C. Twelfth Century in Early Indo-Aryan* (Ahmedabad: Parshva Prakashan, 1996).

52. Timothy Lenz, 'A New Interpretation of the Rāula-Vela Inscription', in *Studies in Early Modern Indo-Aryan Languages, Literature, and Culture: Research Papers, 1992–1994*, ed. Alan W. Entwistle, Michael C. Shapiro, Heidi Pauwels, and Carol Salomon (New Delhi: Manohar, 1999), 203–5. See also

Namvar Singh, *Hindī ke vikās meṁ apabhraṁśa kā yog*, 5th revised edition (Allahabad: Lokbharati, 1971; [2006]), 83–8.

53. Lenz, 'A New Interpretation', 203–6.

54. These earliest dated manuscripts include a *Pradyumna-Carit* from 1548 (VS 1605) at the Baddhicandjī kā Digambar Jain Mandir (see Kasturcand Kashlival and Chainsukhdas, eds, *Pradyumna-Carit: ādikālik mahākāvya* [Jaipur: Di. Jain A. Kshetr Shri Mahavirji, 1960], 9–10.); a *Qutubśatak* manuscript from 1576 (VS 1633) in the Anup Sanskrit Library in Bikaner (used in the critical edition Mata Prasad Gupta, *Qutubśatak aur uskī Hinduī*, Lokodaya [Varanasi: Bhatatiya Jnanpith, 1967], 1); and the famous Fatehpur manuscript from 1582 (VS 1639) at the Sawai Mansingh II Museum, Jaipur (published in facsimile in Bahura and Bryant, *Pad Sūrdāsjī kā*). The hardly accessible manuscripts known as the *Mohan* or *Goindval pothis* in the Gurmukhi script are claimed to date from 1570–2. See Winand M. Callewaert, Swapna Sharma, and Dieter Taillieu, *The Millennium Kabīr Vāṇī: A Collection of Pads* (New Delhi: Manohar, 2000), 10; Gurinder Singh Mann, *The Goindval Pothis* (Cambridge, MA: Harvard University Press, 1996), 16–25. An attempt to question this early date is Balwant Singh Dhillon, *Early Sikh Scriptural Tradition: Myth and Reality* (Amritsar: Singh Brothers, 1999), 89–182.

55. 'Sūrpūrva', that is, pre-Mughal, Bhasha works have been surveyed in S. P. Singh, *Sūr-pūrv brajbhāṣā aur uskā sāhitya* (Banaras: Hindi Pracharak Pustakalay, 1964) and in the various works of Harihar Nivas Dvivedi.

56. Singh, *Sūr-pūrv brajbhāṣā*, 143–72; Harihar Nivas Dvivedi, *Mahābhārat: Pāṇḍav-Carit: 1435 ī viracit mahākāvya: mahākavi Viṣṇudās kṛt* (Gwalior: Vidya Mandir Prakashan, 1973), 99–103.

57. In some manuscripts the date of the *Pradyumna-Carit* is read as Samvat 1311 (1254 CE) or Samvat 1511 (1454 CE), but the most reliable manuscript evidence supports Samvat 1411 (1354 CE). See Agaracand Nahta, 'Pradyumna-Carit kā racnākāl va racayitā', *Anekānt* 14, no. 6 (1957): 170–2, and Kashlival and Chainsukhdas, *Pradyumna-Carit*, 24–5. The *Haricand Purāṇ* was first described in Shyamsundar Das, *Annual Report on the Search for Hindi Manuscripts for the Year 1900* (Allahabad: United Provinces Government Press, 1903; repr., Varanasi: Nāgarīpracāriṇī Sabhā, 1998), 76–7n89. The same manuscript seems to have been acquired by Agarchand Nahta (Singh, *Sūr-pūrv brajbhāṣā*, 148.) A manuscript copy of this work can be found at the Abhay Jain Pustakalay in Bikaner. Passages from this manuscript are published in Singh, *Sūr-pūrv brajbhāṣā*, 385–7.

58. For a description of the *Jñānpañcamī Caupāī*, see Desai and Kothari, *Jain gurjar kavio*, vol. 1, 35–7, and Jain, *Hindī Jain bhakti-kāvya*, 47–9. Viddhaṇu Jain is already mentioned in G. Mishra, S. Mishra, and S. Mishra, *Miśrabandhu-Vinod*, vol. 1, 92. The *Bārah Bhāvanā* is preserved in an undated manuscript (Digambar Jain Mandir, Godhan, Jaipur, MS 241) and published in R.R. Jain, *Raydhū sāhitya kā ālocnātmak pariśīlan* (Vaishali: Research Institute

of Prakrit, Jainology and Ahimsa, Department of Education, Governmentof Bihar, 1974), 448–52.

59. Dvivedi, *Pāṇḍav-Carit*, 101–2. Harihar Nivas Dvivedi, *Madhyadeśīy bhāṣā: gvāliyarī* (Gwalior: Navaprabhat Press, 1955) and Singh, *Sūr-pūrv brajbhāṣā*, do not appear to know about it. Lakhansenī is mentioned in the in the *Khoj* Report 1944, 370 (Vidyabhushan Mishra, ed. *Khoj meṁ upalabdh hastalikhit Hindī granthoṁ kā aṭhārahvāṁ traivārṣik vivaraṇ: san 1941–43 Ī* [Kashi: Nāgarī Pračāriṇī Sabhā, 1958 [VS 2015]). According to Kishnadevprasad Gaur et al. eds, *Hastalikhit Hindī granthõ kā saṅkṣipt vivaraṇ*, 2 vols (Varanasi: Nāgarīpracāriṇī Sabhā, 1964), vol. 2, 338, he was possibly under the patronage of Rājā Baijaldās, and according to *Khoj* Report 09, 167 (Shyam Behari Mishra, *The Second Triennial Report on the Search for Hindi Manuscripts for the Year 1909, 1910, 1911* [Allahabad: Indian Press, 1914], 255), also composed a *Mahābhārat*, which, if indeed from the early fifteenth century, has been thoroughly reworked into more recent Brajbhāṣā with no archaism at all in the published samples. Interestingly, Dvivedi did not mention this work while talking about early Hindi.

60. Office of the Registrar General and Census Commissioner, India, available at http://www.censusindia.gov.in/pca/SearchDetails.aspx?Id=176108, last accessed on 19 September 2017.

61. Shailendra Bhandare, 'Numismatics and History: The Maurya–Gupta Interlude in the Gangetic Plain', in *Between the Empires: Society in India 300 BCE to 400 CE*, ed. Patrick Olivelle, South Asia Research (New York: Oxford University Press, 2006), 89–90.

62. M. Habib and Khaliq Ahmad Nizami, *The Delhi Sultanate, A Comprehensive History of India* (New Delhi: People's Publishing House, 1970), 398, 716–7, 720, 802, 917, 918. According to James Sutherland Cotton and William Stevenson Meyer, *Imperial Gazetteer of India*, vol. 14 (Oxford: Clarendon Press, 1908), 139, 'at Erach (Irich) the fragments of ancient buildings have been used in the construction of a fine mosque, which dates from 1412'.

63. Singh, *Sūr-pūrv brajbhāṣā*, 386.

64. This phrase is unclear.

65. līha thūṇijjaī—Braj: *thūr*, 'to strike' and Hindi: *lakīr pīṭnā*, 'to follow the way'.

66. Gaurishankar Mishra 'Dvijendra', *Hindī sāhitya kā chandovivecan* (Patna: Bihār Hindī Granth Akādmī, 1975), 19–20.

67. Dvivedi (*Pāṇḍav-Carit*, 101) promised an edition of the early works but it seems never to have been published. The passages he cites are very close to later Brajbhasha and are mostly devoid of the archaisms found in Viṣṇudās.

68. Singh, *Sūr-pūrv brajbhāṣā*, 143.

69. Singh, *Sūr-pūrv brajbhāṣā*, 149.

70. Dvivedi, *Pāṇḍav-Carit*, 102.

71. According to Vinaysagar in the *Khartargach sāhitya koś* (Jaipur: Prakrit Bharati, 2006), 83, 198, his *Trivikram Rās* (1368) is a rās caupaī in Apabhramsha, his *Śāśvata jina bimba stotra* is in Prakrit, and his *Yu.* [*Yugapradhāna*] *jinadattasūri chanda* is a *gīt stavan* in Rajasthani. The latter is printed in *Dādāgurubhajanāvalī* (Jaipur: Prakrit Bharati, 1993), 26–8.

72. Desai and Kothari, *Jain gurjar kavio*, 34–5.

73. 'utkīrṇāca suvarṇā ṭhakkura ṅālhāṅgajena puṇyārthaṁ; vaigyānika suśrāvakavareṇa vīdhābhidhānena'. The inscription is no. 236 in Puran Chand Nahar, *Jaina Inscriptions: Containing Index of Places, Glossary of Names of Shrāvaka Castes, and Gotras of Gachhas, and Achāryas with Dates*, vol. 1, Jaina Vividha Sahitya Shāstra Mālā (Calcutta: V. J. Joshi, 1918), 57–62.

74. On this festival, see John E. Cort, *Liberation and Wellbeing: A Study of the Śvetāmbar Mūrtipūjak Jains of North Gujarat* (Harvard University, 1989), 198–203.

75. It is called *Jñānpañcamīmāhātmya Copaībandh* and numbered as 3233 in Muni Punyavijay, *Catalogue of Manuscripts in Shri Hemachandracharya Jain Jnanamandira, Patan* (Patan: Shri Hemachandracharya Jain Jnanmandir, 1972), 151. The cataloguer conjectures that the manuscript was produced in the sixteenth century of the Vikram Era. Its first six and final five stanzas are also published in Desai and Kothari, *Jain gurjar kavio*, vol. 1, 36.

76. Punyavijay, *Catalogue of Manuscripts*, 151.

77. Vinaysagar, *Khartargach sāhitya koś*, 80.

78. Jain, *Hindī Jain Bhakti-Kāvya*, 47. (The reference that Jain gives to Premi, however, is erroneous.)

79. Personal communication (email), 23 June 2012.

80. The syllable *pha* is struck in the manuscript itself.

81. Viddhaṇū, *Siyapañcamī*, MS 3233, Shri Hemachandracharya Jain Jnanmandir. For details regarding the manuscript, see note 74.

82. Singh, *Sūr-pūrv brajbhāṣā*, 152 called him *brajbhāṣā kā saṁsthāpak* (founder of Brajbhasha). See also Pollock, *The Language of the Gods*, 394.

83. Although his language is also labelled as Madhyadeśī or Gvāliyarī (Cf. Dvivedi, *Madhyadeśīya bhāṣā*, 137–8; Dvivedi, *Pāṇḍav-Carit*, 90–123; Pollock, *The Language of the Gods*, 394), these terms are used to refer to Brajbhasha.

84. Ronald Stuart McGregor, 'An Early Hindi (Brajbhāṣā) Version of the Rāma Story', in *Devotion Divine: Bhakti Traditions from the Regions of India: Studies in Honour of Charlotte Vaudeville*, ed. Diana L. Eck and Françoise Mallison, Groningen Orientals Studies (Groningen: E. Forsten, 1991), 185.

85. For the rekhta-like verse 6 of Haridās's *Aṣṭādas Siddhānt*, see Lucy L. Rosenstein, *The Devotional Poetry of Svāmī Haridās: A Study of Early Braj Bhāṣā Verse*, Groningen Oriental Studies (Groningen: Egbert Forsten, 1997), 107. This poem is composed in Khari Boli, but some manuscripts give Braj variants, such as Braj *karī* for *kiyā* or Braj *bhaī* and *bhayā* for *huā*. In the *Kavitāvalī Uttarakāṇḍa*, 117 chappay words such as *niradaheu*, *kīnheu*, and

dīnheu have been Brajified in later transmission as *niradahyau, kīnhau,* and *dīnhau.* See Bangha et al., *The Kavitāvalī of Tulsīdās.*

86. Dvivedi, *Pāṇḍav-Carit,* 27–30.

87. The term 'tatsama' refers to words adopted from Old Indo-Aryan languages (that is, Sanskrit) without any phonetic change; 'tadbhava' refers to words derived from Old Indo-Aryan languages that have gone through phonetic changes over time.

88. Dvivedi, *Pāṇḍav-Carit,* 29.

89. Ronald Stuart McGregor, 'Viṣṇudās and His Rāmāyan-Kathā', in *Studies in Early Modern Indo-Aryan,* 245–6.

90. Parameshvarilal Gupta, *Cāndāyan* (Bombay: Hindi Granth Ratnakar, 1964), 32, translated in Nasim Hines, *Maulana Daud's Cāndāyan: A Critical Study* (New Delhi: Manohar, 2009), 54.

91. Bhayani, *Gujarātī aitihāsik vyākaraṇ.*

92. Thakore, Desai, and Modi, 'Gurjararāsāvalī'.

93. Agarchand Nahta also suggests that Hindi is a third branch of this regionalization. Nahta, 'Prastāvnā', 1. Cf. Bhayani, *Gujarātī aitihāsik vyākaraṇ,* 34.

94. Quoted in Dvivedi, *Pāṇḍav-Carit,* 51. A slightly different version is published in Gulab Khan Gauri, *Gvāliyar kā rājnaitik evaṁ sāṅskṛtik itihās: san 1392–1565 ī. tak* (New Delhi: B.R. Publishing Corporation, 1986), 55, based on the *Archeological Survey Report 1961–62,* no. 1584.

95. The meaning of this word is unclear. The most likely meaning can be derived from the Rajasthani verb *māṭhṇau* 'to shape and finish a stone' (*ghaṛāī karke patthar ko sāf kranā*); see Sitaram Lalas, *Rājasthānī sabad koś* (Chaupasni: Rajasthani Research Institute, 1962–1988).

96. The meaning of this word is unclear.

97. As suggested in Kailash Chandra Bhatiya, *Rāulavela: Prārambhik Hindī kā pahlā śilāṅkit kāvya* (New Delhi: Takṣaśilā Prakāśan, 1983).

98. This is the position of Gupta, *Hindī sāhitya kā vaijñānik itihās,* vol. 1, 89–109 and Tripathi, 'Hindi sāhitya kā ādikāl', 41–2, in regard to Rajasthani literature of Hiralal Maheshwari, *History of Rajasthani Literature* (New Delhi: Sahitya Akademi, 1980), 21, and, with some inconsistency, of Lakshmisagar Varshney, *Hindī sāhitya kā itihās,* 17th edition (Allahabad: Lokabhāratī Prakāśan, 1989), 44.

99. As seems to have been proposed by Jain, *Hindī Jain Bhakti-Kāvya,* 32–50.

100. For the argument that the primarily oral author Kabīr shared the literary forms of the written world, see Imre Bangha, 'Kabir's Prosody', in *Bhakti Beyond the Forest: Current Research on Early Modern Literatures in North India, 2003–2009* (New Delhi: Manohar, 2013).

101. Out of the five manuscripts of the *Pradyumna-Carit* inspected for the critical edition, three date from the sixteenth century. (See Kashlival and

Chainsukhdas, *Pradyumna-Carit*, 9–11.) Considering the extreme scarcity of extant manuscripts from that century, it can be judged that it was a particularly popular work at that time.

Bibliography

Bahura, Gopal Narayan, and Kenneth E. Bryant. *The Padas of Sūrdās*. Jaipur: Sawai Mansingh II. Museum, 1982.

Bangha, Imre. 'Rekhta, Poetry in Mixed Language: The Emergence of Khari Boli Literature in North India'. In *Before the Divide: Hindi and Urdu Literary Culture*, edited by Francesca Orsini, 22–83. New Delhi: Orient BlackSwan, 2010.

———. 'Kabir's Prosody'. In *Bhakti Beyond the Forest: Current Research on Early Modern Literatures in North India, 2003–2009*, edited by Imre Bangha, 284. New Delhi: Manohar, 2013.

Bangha, Imre, Dániel Balogh, Eszter Berki, and Eszter Somogyi. *The Kavitāvalī of Tulsīdās: Critical Edition*, work in progress.

Bhandare, Shailendra. 'Numismatics and History: The Maurya–Gupta Interlude in the Gangetic Plain'. In *Between the Empires: Society in India 300 Bce to 400 Ce*, edited by Patrick Olivelle. South Asia Research, 67–112. New York: Oxford University Press, 2006.

Bhati, Narayansimh. *Prācīn Ḍiṅgal gīt sāhitya*. Jodhpur: Rajasthan Granthagar, 1989.

Bhatiya, Kailash Chandra. *Rāulavela: prārambhik Hindī kā pahlā śilāṅkit kāvya*. New Delhi: Takṣaśilā Prakāśan, 1983.

Bhayani, Harivallabh Chunilal. 'Prācīn Gujarātī phāgu'. In *Śodh ane svādhyāy: prācīn madhyakālīn sāhityaviṣayak saṃśodhanparak lekhsaṅgrah*, 34–9. Mumbai: R. R. Shethni Company, [1965].

———. 'Saṅgrahit racnāoṁ kī bhāṣā'. In *Prācīn gurjar kāvyasañcay*, edited by Harivallabh Chunilal Bhayani and Agaracand Nahta, 10–12. Amadābād: Lālabhāī Dalapatabhāī Bhāratīya Saṁskṛti Vidyāmandir, 1975.

———. *Gujarātī bhāṣānuṃ aitihāsik vyākaraṇ: ī.sa. 1150 thī 1550 sudhī* [in Gujarati]. Ahmedabad: Pārśva Pablikeśan, 1996.

———. *Rāula-Vela of Roḍa: A Rare Poem of C. Twelfth Century in Early Indo-Aryan*. Ahmedabad: Parshva Prakashan, 1996.

Bhayani, Harivallabh Chunilal and Agaracand Nahta. *Prācīn gurjar kāvyasañcay*. Amadābād: Lālabhāī Dalapatabhāī Bhāratīya Saṁskṛti Vidyāmandir, 1975.

Busch, Allison. 'Hindi Literary Beginnings'. In *South Asian Texts in History: Critical Engagements with Sheldon Pollock*, edited by Whitney Cox, Yigal Bronner, and Lawrence McCrea, 203–25. Ann Arbor: Association for Asian Studies, 2011.

———. *Poetry of Kings: The Classical Hindi Literature of Mughal India*. New York: Oxford University Press, 2011. Available at http://dx.doi.org/10.1093/acprof:oso/9780199765928.001.0001.

Callewaert, Winand M., Swapna Sharma, and Dieter Taillieu. *The Millennium Kabīr Vāṇī: A Collection of Pads*. New Delhi: Manohar, 2000.

Chojnacki, Christine. *Kuvalayamala: Roman jaina de 779, composé par Uddyotanasuri*. Marburg: Indica et Tibetica Verlag, 2008.

Cort, John E. *Liberation and Wellbeing: A Study of the Śvetāmbar Mūrtipūjak Jains of North Gujarat*. Harvard University, 1989.

———. 'The Jain Knowledge Warehouses: Traditional Libraries in India'. *Journal of the American Oriental Society* 115, no. 1 (1995): 77–87.

Cotton, James Sutherland and William Stevenson Meyer. *Imperial Gazetteer of India* (vol. 14). Oxford: Clarendon Press, 1908.

Das, Shyamsundar. *Annual Report on the Search for Hindi Manuscripts for the Year 1900*. Allahabad: United Provinces Government Press, 1903. Varanasi: Nāgarīpracāriṇī Sabhā, 1998.

Desai, Mohanlal Dalichand and Jayant Kothari. *Jain gurjar kavio* (2nd ed., vol. 1). Bombay: Mahavir Jain Vidyalaya, 1986.

Dhillon, Balwant Singh. *Early Sikh Scriptural Tradition: Myth and Reality*. Amritsar: Singh Brothers, 1999.

Dvivedi, Harihar Nivas. *Madhyadeśīy bhāṣā: gvāliyarī*. Gwalior: Navaprabhat Press, 1955.

Feeney, Denis C. *Beyond Greek: The Beginnings of Latin Literature*. Cambridge, Massachusetts: Harvard University Press, 2016.

Gauri, Gulab Khan. *Gvāliyar kā rājnaitik evaṁ sāṃskṛtik itihās: san 1392–1565 ī. tak*. New Delhi: B. R. Publishing Corporation, 1986.

Gaur, Kishnadevprasad et al., eds. *Hastalikhit Hindī granthõ kā saṅkṣipt vivaraṇ* (2 vols). Varanasi: Nāgarīpracāriṇī Sabhā, 1964.

Gupta, Ganapati Candra. *Hindī sāhitya kā vaijñānik itihās* (5th revised ed., 2 vols). Allahabad: Lokbharati, 1999 [1965].

Gupta, Mata Prasad. *Qutubśatak aur uskī hinduī*. Lokodaya. Varanasi: Bharatiya Jnanpith, 1967.

Gupta, Parameshvarilal. *Cāndāyan*. Bombay: Hindi Granth Ratnakar, 1964.

Habib, M. and Khaliq Ahmad Nizami. *The Delhi Sultanate: A Comprehensive History of India*. New Delhi: People's Publishing House, 1970.

Hines, Nasim. *Maulana Daud's Cāndāyan: A Critical Study*. New Delhi: Manohar, 2009.

Jain, Premsagar. *Hindī Jain bhakti-kāvya aur kavi*. Benares: Bhāratīy Jñānpīṭh Prakāśan, 1964.

Jain, R.R. *Raydhū sāhitya kā ālocnātmak pariśīlan*. Vaishali: Research Institute of Prakrit, Jainology and Ahimsa. Department of Education, Government of Bihar, 1974.

Jinvijay Muni. *Uktivyaktiprakaraṇa*. Singhi Jaina Granthamala. Bombay: Singhi Jaina Shastra Sikshapitha, 1953.

Kashlival, Kasturcand and Chainsukhdas, eds. *Pradyumna-Carit: ādikālik mahākāvya*. Jaipur: Di. Jain A. Kshetr Shri Mahavirji, 1960.

Kothari, Jayant and J. Gadit. *Gujarati Sahityakoś* (vol. 1) (madhyakāl). Ahmadabad: Gujarati Sahitya Parishad, 1989.

Krause, Charlotte. 'Ancient Jaina Hymns'. In *German Jaina Śrāvikā Dr. Charlotte Krause: Her Life and Literature*, edited by Hazarimull Banthia and Luitgard Soni, 313–464. Varanasi: Pārśvanātha Vidyāpītha, 1999.

Lenz, Timothy. 'A New Interpretation of the Rāula-Vela Inscription'. In *Studies in Early Modern Indo-Aryan Languages, Literature, and Culture: Research Papers, 1992–1994*, edited by Alan W. Entwistle, Carol Solomon, Heidi Pauwels, and Michael C. Shapiro, 199–207. New Delhi: Manohar, 1999.

Maheshwari, Hiralal. *History of Rajasthani Literature*. New Delhi: Sahitya Akademi, 1980.

Mallison, Françoise. 'The Teaching of Braj, Gujarati, and Bardic Poetry at the Court of Kutch: The Bhuj Brajbhāṣā Pāṭhśālā (1749–1948)'. In *Forms of Knowledge in Early Modern South Asia*, edited by Sheldon Pollock, 171–82. Durham: Duke University Press, 2011.

Mann, Gurinder Singh. *The Goindval Pothis*. Cambridge, MA: Harvard University Press, 1996.

McGregor, Ronald Stuart. 'An Early Hindi (Brajbhāṣā) Version of the Rāma Story'. In *Devotion Divine: Bhakti Traditions from the Regions of India: Studies in Honour of Charlotte Vaudeville*, edited by Diana L. Eck and Françoise Mallison. Groningen Orientals Studies, 181–96. Groningen: E. Forsten, 1991.

Menariya, Motilal. *Rājasthānī bhāṣā aur sāhitya* (4th ed.). Prayag: Hindi Sahitya Sammelan, 1978.

Menariya, Omkarlal and Mahopadhyay Vinaysagar. 'Rājasthānī hindī hasta-likhit granth-sūcī'. In *Rājasthān purātan granthmālā*, edited by Rajasthan Oriental Research Institute. Jodhpur: Rajasthan Oriental Research Institute, 1983.

Mishra, Ganeshbihari, Shyambihari Mishra, and Shukdevbihari Mishra. *Miśrabandhu-Vinod, athavā Hindī-Sāhitya kā itihāsa tathā kavi-kīrttana* (new revised ed.). Lucknow: Gaṅgā Pustakmālā, 1972. VS 1970.

Mishra, Gaurishankar 'Dvijendra'. *Hindī sāhitya kā chandovivecan*. Patna: Bihār Hindī Granth Akādmī, 1975.

Mishra, Ramkumari, ed. *Ālam kṛt mādhavānal kāmkandalā: Avadhī premākhyānak*. Prayag: Ratnakumārī Svādhyāy Sansthān, 1982.

Mishra, Shitikanth. *Hindī Jain sāhitya kā bṛhat itihās*. Parshwanath Vidyashram Series, edited by Sagarmal Jain (4 vols, vol. 1) (Maru-gurjar). Varanasi: Parshwanath Vidyashram Shodh Sansthan, 1989.

Nahar, Puran Chand. *Jaina Inscriptions: Containing Index of Places, Glossary of Names of Shrāvaka Castes, and Gotras of Gachhas, and Achāryas with Dates*. Jaina Vividha Sahitya Shāstra Mālā (vol. 1). Calcutta: V. J. Joshi, 1918.

Nahta, Agaracand. 'Pradyumna-Carit kā racnākāl va racayitā'. *Anekānt* 14, no. 6 (January 1957): 170–72.

———. 'Prastāvnā'. In *Prācīn gurjar kāvyasañcay*, edited by Harivallabh Chunilal Bhayani and Agaracand Nahta, 1–10. Ahmedabad: Lālabhāī Dalapatabhāī Bhāratīya Saṁskr̥ti Vidyāmandir, 1975.

Nahta, Agaracand and Bhamvarlal Nahta. *Aitihāsik jain kāvyasaṅgrah*. Abhay Jain Granthamla. Calcutta: Shankardas Shubhairaj Nahta, 1937.

Nivas, Harihar. *Mahābhārat: Pāṇḍav-Carit: 1435 ī viracit mahākāvya: mahākavi viṣṇudās kr̥t*. Gwalior: Vidya Mandir Prakashan, 1973.

Orsini, Francesca. 'How to Do Multilingual Literary History? Lessons from Fifteenth-and Sixteenth-Century North India'. *Indian Economic and Social History Review* 49, no. 2 (April–June 2012): 225–46.

Pollock, Sheldon. *Literary Cultures in History: Reconstructions from South Asia*. New Delhi and London: Oxford University Press, 2003.

———. *The Language of the Gods in the World of Men: Sanskrit, Culture, and Power in Premodern India*. New Delhi: Permanent Black, 2007.

Punyavijay, Muni. *Catalogue of Manuscripts in Shri Hemachandracharya Jain Jnanamandira, Patan*. Patan: Shri Hemachandracharya Jain Jnanmandir, 1972.

Rosenstein, Lucy L. *The Devotional Poetry of Svāmī Haridās: A Study of Early Braj Bhāṣā Verse*. Groningen Oriental Studies. Groningen: Egbert Forsten, 1997.

Salomon, Richard. 'The Ukti-Vyakti-Prakaraṇa as a Manual of Spoken Sanskrit'. *Indo-Iranian Journal* 24, no. 1 (1982): 13–25.

Shukla, Ramchandra. *Hindī sāhitya kā itihās* (17th ed.). Kashi: Nagari Pracharini Sabha, 1972 [1942].

Singh, Namvar. *Hindī ke vikās meṁ apbhraṁśa kā yog* (5th revised ed.). Allahabad: Lokbharati, 1971 [2006, 1952].

Singh, Shiv Prasad. *Sūr-pūrv brajbhāṣā aur uskā sāhitya* (2nd ed.). Banaras: Hindi Pracharak Pustakalay, 1964 [1958].

Sitaram Lalas, *Rājasthāṃnī sabad kos*. Chaupasni: Rajasthani Research Institute, 1962–1988.

Smith, John. *The Vīsaḷadevarāsa: A Restoration of the Text*. Cambridge: Cambridge University Press, 1976.

Stuart, Ronald. 'Viṣṇudās and His Rāmāyan-Kathā'. In *Studies in Early Modern Indo-Aryan Languages, Literature, and Culture: Research Papers, 1992–1994*, Presented at the Sixth Conference on Devotional Literature in New Indo-Aryan Languages, Held at Seattle, University of Washington, 7–9 July 1994, edited by Alan W. Entwistle, Carol Solomon, Heidi Pauwels, and Michael C. Shapiro, 239–48. New Delhi: Manohar, 1999.

Tessitori, Luigi Pio. 'Notes on the Grammar of the Old Western Rajasthani with Special Reference to Apabhramça and to Gujarati and Marvari'. *Indian Antiquary* 43–5 (From February 1914 to 1916): 21–26, 55–63, 84–91, 181–86, 213–6, 45–52 (1914); 3–11, 30–36, 52–58, 74–81, 96–105, 119–126, 159–163 (1915); 6–7, 93–99 (1916).

Thakore, Balavantray Kalyanray, Mohalal Dalichand Desai, and M.C. Modi. *Gurjararāāalī*. Baroda: Oriental Institute, 1956.

Tripathi, Karunapati. 'Hindi sāhitya kā ādikāl'. In *Hindi sāhitya kā bṛhat itihās: Hindi sāhitya kā ādikāl*, edited by Karunapati Tripathi, 1–45. Benares: Nāgarīpracāriṇī Sabhā, 1983.

Varshney, Lakshmisagar. *Hindī sāhitya kā itihās* (17th ed.). Allahabad: Lokabhāratī Prakāśan, 1989.

Vinaysagar, ed. *Dādāgurubhajanāvalī*. Jaipur: Prakrit Bharati, 1993.

———. *Khartargach sāhitya koś*. Jaipur: Prakrit Bharati, 2006.

Yashaschandra, Sitanshu. 'From Hemachandra to Hind Svaraj: Region and Power in Gujarati Literary Culture'. In *Literary Cultures in History*, edited by Sheldon Pollock, 567–611. Berkeley: University of California Press, 2003.

2

ARTHUR DUDNEY

Urdu as Persian

Some Eighteenth-Century Evidence on Vernacular Poetry as Language Planning

In the mid-eighteenth century, poetry written in Urdu—although it was not yet known by that name, being generally called *rekhtah*, or 'mixed'—became a serious business in Delhi.[1] In the early eighteenth century and before, Urdu composition was a kind of novelty act. Prestigious poetry in north-central India had been written either in Persian or in another literary dialect of Hindi, such as Brajbhasha or Awadhi.[2] Between 1720 CE, when the collected works of the poet Vali arrived in Delhi from the Deccan, and 1751 CE, when the first north Indian *tażkirah* (biographical compendium) of Urdu poets was written, this had changed. An Urdu literary culture seemingly appeared fully formed in those three decades. Of course, complex literary systems do not appear out of nothing (even if that is what a cursory glance at the historical record might suggest), but rather reconfigure and amplify what exists in their environment.[3] We should use contemporary sources to explain the 'language planning', to borrow a useful concept from sociolinguistics, that went into the construction of Urdu literary language during this period.[4] Language planning is worth considering because it reminds us that people were actively thinking about how to change the vernacular language of Delhi to make it suitable for the kind of literature they wanted to create (just as European languages went through a similar evolution).[5] The difficulty is that no one wrote about Urdu analytically before the 1750s.[6] Our use of the sources must, therefore, be curiously roundabout: Before Mir Taqi Mir's *Nikāt al-shuʿarā* (1751) and Shah Hatim's preface to his revised collected Urdu poems (1756), both of which bear on this discussion, we are limited to critical writings in Persian, nominally about Persian literature, but whose conceptual framework was designed to contain Urdu as well. Sirajuddin ʿAli Khan, who died in 1756 and is known by his pen name Arzu, wrote a number of such works. We can fruitfully bring them into dialogue with the usual sources for writing about the development of Urdu. Arzu made his reputation as a Persian poet and critic, but is nonetheless recognized in most tażkirahs of Urdu literature as the first important teacher of Urdu composition in Delhi. Indeed, a generation later, he was being called the Abu Hanifah of Urdu poetry (Abu Hanifah being the great eighth-century CE jurist whose interpretations of Islamic law, the so-called Hanafite School, are dominant in Central and South Asia).[7] In brief, Arzu's theory on the commonality of Persian and what he calls *hindī* (referring to Sanskrit and various Indian vernaculars related to it) allows for Persian and Urdu to be considered in the same frame.[8] In other words, the dividing line between the two traditions is *formally* recognized as porous, and the centuries-old discourse of Perso-Arabic literary theory can be brought to bear on the nascent Urdu tradition.[9] One of Arzu's younger acquaintances (though not officially his student), Mirza Muhammad Rafiʿ Sauda, paraphrases the advice of an unnamed Persian litterateur (*fārsī-dān*), whom we are perhaps meant to understand as Arzu, in a satire (*ḥajv*) against Mirza Fakhr Makin:

> No matter what the language, excellence lies in the quality of the expression [*khūbī-ye maẓmūn*].
> Poetry does not depend on Persian alone.
> You cannot always use their language correctly,
> You should express colorful ideas in your own language.[10]

The emphasis in later scholarship has been on the supposedly nationalistic aspects of this and other similar conversations recorded for posterity; in this reading, it is a simple matter of starting to use 'our' language (Hindi–Urdu) to replace 'theirs' (Persian).[11] The view that this was necessary because Indians as non-native speakers of Persian felt they could not compose literature in it at the same level as native speakers is contradicted by Arzu's own writings. Interpreting the verse quoted above is further complicated by its circumstances: It comes from a satire referring to a specific incident, when Makin unjustly butchered some Persian verses of Sauda's that Sauda had submitted to him for correction, and its bleak conclusion that no Indian Persian poets except Khusrau, Faizi, Arzu, and Faqir were any good is clearly a satirical exaggeration. From rather poor evidence like this a 'crisis of confidence' in Indo-Persian has been taken as a self-evident cause of Urdu vernacularization (perhaps in dialogue with linguistic nationalism in nineteenth-century Europe and Iran).[12] However, more interesting for us and apparently more relevant to the writers' contemporary concerns are the parameters for a dialogue between Persian and Urdu poetry. The expression *ḳhūbī-ye maẓmūn* in Sauda's poem is in fact a term of art. 'Maẓmūn' corresponds to topos in Western rhetoric and so Sauda's unnamed interlocutor is implicitly arguing that the construction of topoi is fundamental in poetry, and that such topoi transcend individual languages. Sauda's use of the expression 'ḳhūbī-ye maẓmūn' in an Urdu poem illustrates the point since it is a completely Persian phrase. Nor is this literary influence unidirectional (moving only from the some-would-say over-determined Persian tradition to the less developed Urdu tradition). Arzu argues at length that the use of Indic words must be allowed in Persian poetry by analogy with Persian's own historical borrowing of Arabic and Turkish words and phrases.[13]

Rozmarrah, which we will define more precisely later, served as a conceptual tool for mediating between Persian and Urdu. It appears in critical writing on poetry and yet is also anchored to the world of daily experience, thereby, forming a junction between the largely formal realm of Persian and the mostly unofficial world of Hindi–Urdu in the eighteenth century. In modern Urdu usage, the meaning of rozmarrah is almost always 'colloquial' or 'everyday' language as opposed to formal language.[14] On the other hand, in modern Iranian Persian, it usually refers to a daily allowance or occurrence.[15] In Persian in the eighteenth century and before, it meant both (as illustrated by *Bahār-i ʿAjam*, an enormous Persian dictionary written by Arzu's friend Lalah Tek Chand Bahar).[16] The difference between Urdu and other north Indian literary dialects such as Brajbhasha is that Urdu grammar is based on Khari Boli, the actual spoken dialect of Delhi (which also happens to be the basis for Modern Standard Hindi). Poetry, which is what concerns us here, is obviously a linguistic domain bound by precise rules and is by definition not the prose of normal, everyday communication. And yet it has the notion of conversation built into it: *sukhan*, literally 'speech', is used throughout the Persian tradition as a metonym for poetry.[17] One does not typically 'write' poetry in classical Persian, but rather one 'speaks' it (*sh'ir guftan*). Similarly, the locus of poetic appreciation (at least in South Asia) was the literary gathering, or *mushā'irah*, an oral performance involving a great deal of audience interaction.

The later critical consensus has been that Indo-Persian writers sought complexity to the exclusion of comprehensibility—for example, Ehsan Yarshater memorably writes of interpreting such poetry that 'the game eventually becomes so complex and demands so much mental effort that it kills the pleasure of playing'[18]—however, comprehensibility as measured against the rozmarrah was in fact a contemporary concern. Let us first turn to the three prefaces of Arzu's *Dād-i sukhan* (A Poetic Gift, or Justice for Poetry, depending on the reading of *dād*), which Arzu himself claims offers an original contribution to the critical tradition. In the third preface, Arzu distinguishes between two kinds of poetic interpretation: the first is the 'common path of people [who know] the language' (*ṭarīq-i 'āmah-yi ahl-i zabān*).[19] In some contexts *ahl-i zabān* (literally, 'people of the tongue') refers to native speakers, but much of the time it simply means people who use the language competently—we can think of them as the 'community of language users'. These 'ahl-i zabān', according to Arzu, understand the meaning of words and the common interpretations that they have heard from their elders. Arzu writes that 'both common people and experts share in this interpretation',[20] but he cautions that this shallow reading is not the last word. The second kind of interpretation is that to which only true experts have access. He goes on to mock a number of so-called experts such as schoolmasters or people obsessed with metaphor to the exclusion of other kinds of interpretation. Arzu quotes a famous retort from 'one of the greats of India [addressed] to one of the contemporary poets of Iran' (which is elsewhere attributed to Abu'l Fazl with 'Urfi Shirazi as his interlocutor) that 'we have learned your language from your most eloquent [that is, written works by classic authors], and you've learned it from your old men [*pīrzāl-hā*]'.[21] Arzu's argument is simple—knowing a language is a prerequisite for interpreting and composing poetry, but the real work cannot begin until someone masters poetic interpretation. His complaint against the *mullās* (religious educators) is telling. He writes that their comprehension of poetry is 'other than that of the people of the rozmarrah'.[22] In other words, their reading of poetry is casuistry rather than a commonsense understanding of how the language is actually used. Indeed, Arzu's first preface begins with a slightly tautological invocation of the rozmarrah. He writes, 'Of that which is current [*vāqiʿ*] or not for the people of the rozmarrah, it is mostly that which is current.'[23] What does this mysterious pronouncement mean? Simply that most poetic rules follow natural speech (with the exception of metrical requirements for certain words, which Arzu admits trip people up). In the third preface, he describes interpretation 'according to the taste of the poets' (*muvāfiq-i mażāq-i shuʿarā*), and argues that it depends on comparing one's own rozmarrah with that of the poet in order to find the particularities in the poet's language.[24]

A similar concern for poetry's necessary relationship with the rozmarrah presents itself in Shah Hatim's preface to his second *dīvān* (collected works). His first dīvān had been released about a quarter century before and was both hard to find and out of date, according to the preface. Shah Hatim pared it down and gave the new edition the cheeky name *Dīvānzādah* (literally, 'born of the dīvān', or the 'dīvān's son').[25] He asserts that certain words have an inherent ugliness/inappropriateness (*qabāḥat*), and that he has tried to give them up. The words he lists are all derived from Sanskrit, such as *jag*, meaning 'world'.[26] This has usually been seen as the first salvo in the *Kulturkampf* whose armistice terms in the early twentieth century were that Hindi was to be 'the language of Hindus' (and hence the national language of India) and Urdu was to be 'the language of Muslims' (and, therefore, of Pakistan). But re-evaluating Shah Hatim's exact formulation is important; he rejects 'the Hindavī which they call "*bhākhā*"' (in other words, Brajbhasha) in favour of 'the rozmarrah of Delhi'.[27] More specifically, he states that he 'has chosen purely the rozmarrah which is understood by common people and acceptable to experts' (note the parallel to Arzu's invocation of common people and experts). Thus, he is arguing not against some kind of 'Hindu language', but rather in favour of the Delhi rozmarrah, which Braj is patently not.[28] On the other end of the cultural spectrum, he condemns poets who use Persian clumsily in Urdu. He lists *dar*, *bar*, *az*, and *ū* as examples of Persian words that should not be used in Urdu. The first three are prepositions and the last is the third person singular pronoun (in Persian grammar, they are each known as *ḥarf*, or what we would call an indeclinable particle). He approvingly cites an Urdu poem by his contemporary Shah Mubarak Abru, mocking people who use the wrong sort of Persian in their Urdu:

> vaqt jin kā reḳhte kī shā'irī meṃ ṣarf hai
> un satī kahtā hūṃ būjho ḥarf merā zharf hai
> jo kih lāve reḳhte meṃ fārsī ke fa'l-o ḥarf[29]
> laġhv haiṃ-ge fa'l us ke reḳhte meṃ ḥarf hai.[30]
>
> Those whose time is spent in *reḳhtah* poetry,
> To them I say: Consider my words deep.
> Whoever brings Persian verbs or particles into *reḳhtah*
> His deeds will be trifling; his *reḳhtah* verses will be questionable.[31]

Thus, not only are the conventions of Braj poetry to be eschewed, but also the use of Persian in a forced, artificial way. This is crucial in the self-definition of Urdu literary culture.

The importance of this shift to the colloquial in the development of Urdu poetry has been noted before, for example, by Shamsur Rahman Faruqi regarding Arzu's estranged nephew Mir, who has been regarded as a master of the colloquial.[32] Integrating everyday language into the domain of poetry was an aesthetic problem, which Mir himself addressed critically. In his taẕkirah *Nikāt al-shu'arā*, which happens to be the first north Indian taẕkirah devoted solely to Urdu poets, he notes in the conclusion (*ḳhātimah*) that

> The fourth [style of reḳhtah] is that which they adorn with Persian constructions [*tarkībāt*]; often a construction which is conformable to the reḳhtah dialect [*zabān-i reḳhtah*] appears and that is allowed, and those other than poets cannot judge it; a construction which is not familiar in reḳhtah [that is, does not seem to fit] is faulty and judging [literally, knowing] it is based on the good taste of a poet. The preference of this wretch [that is, the author, Mir] is the same: if a Persian form is acceptable to conversation [*guftagū*] in reḳhtah then there is no difficulty.[33]

In other words, if a Persian expression is already naturalized in reḳhtah—that is, it has already become part of the rozmarrah (although in this case Mir uses the similar term 'guftagū')—then it is automatically acceptable. If not, then a poet's judgement determines whether it is good reḳhtah or an inelegant intrusion of Persian. Here, the slippage of the term 'rozmarrah' is evident; it has the sense both of idiomatic natural language and acceptable poetic language, with each meaning constituting the other.

Theorizing the colloquial is not a peculiarity of Urdu literary culture, but rather was adopted from the Persian criticism of the eighteenth century. Critics of this period, including Arzu, frequently comment on whether a verse follows rozmarrah or not. For example, in *Dād-i suḳhan*, a poet's associating *ḥukm* (command) with *t̤ug̈hrā* (a royal seal) is called into question as a problem of rozmarrah since 't̤ug̈hrā' is connected with *farmān* (another kind of command) and not with 'ḥukm'.[34] Rozmarrah is mentioned frequently in *ʿAt̤īyah-i kubrá*, his treatise on *ʿilm-i bayān* (rhetoric), and *Mauhibat-i ʿuẕmá*, his treatise on *ʿilm-i mā ʿnī* (semiotics).[35] He invokes *rozmarrah-dānān* (rozmarrah-knowers) as judges of whether a metaphor has been properly used. Mocking the rozmarrah of others is fair game for Persian satirists, such as Mir Yahya Kashi (d. 1653), who apparently identified with Shiraz, despite his name (*kāshī* means 'from Kashan'), and wrote some vicious lines, quoted by Arzu, about the absurdity of the speech of Kashan.[36]

We should consider the apposition of rozmarrah and *muḥāvarah*, two terms which occupy nearly the same semantic range in this period. 'Muḥāvarah' is usually translated as 'idiom', and is used perhaps twice as frequently as rozmarrah in the critical texts considered here. Shah Hatim uses the two in a telling contrast since he mentions the 'rozmarrah of Delhi that the nobles of India and the eloquent among the flâneurs have in their *muḥāvarah*', so for him the latter is clearly a broader category than the former.[37] Since they are so similar in meaning, drawing sharp distinctions between the two words is difficult, but perhaps the difference is akin to what we would call diachronic and synchronic analysis. That is to say that rozmarrah is conceptually the usage that is current at one time, namely the present, and so a diachronic phenomenon, while muḥāvarah can refer to the set of usages over time and can, therefore, be a synchronic phenomenon. While muḥāvarah is sometimes used with a historical reference, rozmarrah is not in the texts examined here. Arzu, for example, refers to the 'rozmarrah of the Persians' (*rozmarrah-yi fārsiyān*) in order to address the differences between current usages in Indian Persian and Iranian Persian.[38] This is obviously a diachronic rather than a synchronic comparison, since it is concerned with space and not time. Crucially, rozmarrah is not an observed speech pattern as we would expect in a modern linguistic survey because for eighteenth-century literati such as Arzu, Hatim, and Mir, rozmarrah is subject to criticism.[39] (Today, in contrast, we rigorously separate the gathering of linguistic data from judgements about proper usage.[40])

It is precisely because rozmarrah is subject to criticism that language planning is a useful framework for thinking about Arzu, Shah Hatim, and Mir's interventions in the vernacular poetics that would later be called Urdu. Persian did not merely percolate into the vernacular and produce Urdu literature as we know it, but rather intellectuals provided the catalyst that modified the spoken language of Delhi into a form that was seen as appropriate for literature. We should close by mentioning one more way in which the barrier of prestige between Urdu and Persian was lowered. One aspect of a Persian or Urdu poet's self-presentation was claiming in verse to have exceeded the success of his illustrious predecessors. Far from being considered ill-tempered or presumptuous, such boasting was institutionalized in Persian and later Urdu poetry. It was called *ta'allī* (exalting one's self) or *tafaḳhḳhur* (boasting). For example, Amir Khusrau (1253–1325) wrote his own *ḳhamsah* (cycle of five poems) based upon Nizami's ḳhamsah, and declares in one of the poems that 'the star of my sovereignty has risen/And hurled an earthquake in Nizami's grave.'[41] For our purposes, the relevant boast is when an Urdu poet contrasts himself with a Persian poet. For example, Mir has a couplet referring to Naziri that goes:

> kyā qadr hai reḳhte kī go maiṃ
> is fann meṃ naẕīrī kā badal thā[42]
>
> What respect does Rekhtah receive?—even though I
> was the peer of Naziri in this art.

Ghalib, who was born when Mir was an old man, mentions Zuhuri (d. 1615):

> hūṃ ẓuhūrī ke muqābil meṃ ḳhafā'ī ġhālib
> mere da've pah yah ḥujjat hai kih mashhūr nahīṃ[43]
>
> I am, in confrontation with Zuhuri [literally, 'manifest'], secret, Ghalib
> For my claim there is this proof: that I am not famous.

Thus, Urdu poets rhetorically declare their art—generally in the final couplet (*maqṭa'*) of a ġhazal, a place where poetic self-reflection often occurs—to be a continuation of the Persian tradition, as these two examples of many demonstrate.[44] Indeed, there is an intriguing possibility that rozmarrah became established as a concept in Indo-Persian criticism because of contact with vernacular literature, in the same way that Latin literary culture was retooled during the Renaissance partially in response to vernacular literary movements for which Latin literature had itself provided the basis. Not only did Indian vernaculars absorb a great deal of vocabulary from Persian, but Persian itself had pulled in Indic words for centuries, as Arzu takes pains to elucidate in *Mus̄mir* and his three dictionaries, especially *Navādir al-alfāẓ* (Wonders of Words, 1743), a lexicon of vernacular words in Persian as used in Delhi. For Arzu, the boundary between languages was a productive zone and not a cause for anxiety as it was for some later critics.

There has never been any question that Urdu became Urdu by absorbing the literary conventions and vocabulary of Persian, but this transformation has often been a source of embarrassment for later critics. Muhammad Husain Azad, writing in the 1880s, argued from an essentially nationalist position that the adoption of Urdu liberated Indians from the foreign Persian, and that it was too much Persian that led to artificiality in Urdu. In his aesthetic programme, good Urdu was 'natural', meaning linguistically unplanned and devoid of wordplay. Though it may seem odd to frame an intellectual issue in our time around the arguments made about it over a century ago, Azad's prose is so beguiling that these preconceptions about Urdu and Persian have remained commonplace. In this chapter, I have tried to nuance the relationship of the two literary traditions, which at its crucial moment was deliberately constructed rather than accidental. The nascent Urdu tradition fit into an intellectual ecosystem centred on Delhi, which was still a focal point for north Indian culture even if the emperor's precarious political situation meant that he no longer could project his power much beyond the city. Litterateurs in Arzu's time were concerned with literary standards and identifying who had the authority to judge the newly constituted literary tradition. It is certainly no coincidence that Shah Hatim's definition of the reḳhtah community is an exact parallel with Arzu's description of how Persian came to be standardized centuries before, namely as the linguistic standard that crystallized in the imperial court, which he referred to as *zabān-i urdū-yi mu'alla*—the name which some decades later would apply to the vernacular literary language of Delhi.[45] Whether participants in other Indian literary traditions saw themselves as creating a cosmopolitan literary culture out of the idiom of a particular group of elites is an open question, but we see the focus on the spoken language of the court as the basis for vernacular poetry across early modern Europe.[46] Composition in reḳhtah was not intended as a proletarian revolt against elite culture (this is the Marxist critics' reinvention of Azad's basic argument), but rather theorized by elites with the expectation that elites would set its rules. For Arzu, a sodality of elite poets is found in every literary tradition, and thus he is able to make arguments about the Persianate literary community through the analogy of reḳhtah poets. Although Arzu draws a distinction between common and expert poets, what he means is best thought of as amateur and professional poets, rather than in socio-economic terms as plebeians and elites. Another likely contribution of Arzu's to the construction of the Urdu literary community is his focus on the origins of words. Shah Hatim flags this in his discussion of the need to spell and pronounce Arabic and Persian loanwords as in the original languages. While Perso-Arabic words were present to a greater or lesser degree in every Indian literary language, attempts were made only in this context to restructure them in a kind of language planning. The early Urdu tradition's orality gave rozmarrah a particularly important role, and also explains how Arzu's views could be so deeply engrained in vernacular poetics even though his extant writing in Urdu is represented by a few paltry lines quoted in taẕkirahs. Arzu died at the cusp of a literary and cultural revolution, whose foundation he and his literary circle had built.

Notes

1. Based on a paper given at the Association of Asian Studies Conference, Toronto, March 2012. Thanks to Alexander Jabbari, Walt Hakala, Abhishek Kaicker, and Frances Pritchett for their advice. Unless otherwise noted, all translations are my own.

2. Hindi, like Urdu, is a problematic name in the precolonial period. What the Persian sources call *zabān-i hindī* should not be conflated with Modern Standard Hindi because it could refer to any north Indian language, including Sanskrit (as '*hindī-yi kitābī*'), depending upon the context. For the sake of clarity, this chapter refers to the literary tradition in question as 'Urdu' throughout even though this name would not be applied to it until late in the eighteenth century (indeed, it was still being called 'hindī' well into the nineteenth century).

3. A famous Western example of a tradition that has no extant antecedents is medieval French troubadour poetry. We can surmise that it developed from some oral tradition rather than the moribund Latin poetry of the time, and yet no trace of this unwritten literature exists.

4. The larger cultural influence of Persian literary culture on Urdu is outside the scope of this chapter, but two major themes are worth noting: first is the tendency among critics to compare Urdu poets stylistically to Persian poets. For example, Mirza Muhammad Hasan Qatil writes in his tażkirah *Chārsharbat* that Sauda has both the same stature and style in reḳhtah that Zuhuri, a great seventeenth-century poet active in the Deccan, has in Persian, an observation which is cited by Muhammad Husain Azad in *Āb-e ḥayāt* (Lahore: Naval Kishore, 1907), 155. Second, in the same passage, Mir describes his work as creating *sanad*, or literary precedent, which is at the heart of the Persian critical enterprise but new in Urdu. To recognize that the system of literary authority would work along similar lines in Urdu is highly significant.

5. Language planning is generally considered positive or value-neutral, which stands in stark contrast to the almost universal but anachronistic idea in later Urdu criticism that such interventions made Urdu 'artificial'. On language planning generally, see Robert L. Cooper, *Language Planning and Social Change* (Cambridge: Cambridge University Press, 1989).

6. Muhammad Sadiq, *History of Urdu Literature* (London: Oxford University Press, 1964), 79. Lest we be concerned by this lacuna, it is worth noting that the great programmatic statement in favour of the vernacular in medieval Europe, Dante's *De Vulgari Eloquentia*, was itself a rather limited project: 'Dante elevates the vernacular poets to the dignity of a standard. Promoting the vernacular languages to the status of authority is one of his unique achievements.... Yet Dante never mentions more than the first line of any poem or discusses its content in detail, nor does he articulate a theoretical framework for their evaluation' (Marianne Shapiro, *De Vulgari Eloquentia* [Lincoln: University of Nebraska, 1990], 42).

7. See *Majmūʿah-yi naġhz* by Qudratallah 'Qasim' (1750–1830), dated 1806 CE (Sadiq, *History of Urdu Literature*, 42). Hadi Hasan reports that the phrase appears in an earlier tażkirah by Arzu's student Hakim Husayn Shuhrat of Shiraz, but I have been unable to trace the reference (Hadi Hasan, *History of Indo-Persian Literature* [New Delhi: Iran Culture House, 2001], 850). The first tażkirah to deal solely with Urdu poets, Mir's *Nikāt al-shuʿarā*, uses the slightly less hyperbolic formulation that all teachers of Urdu were taught by Arzu ('All teachers connected with the art of reḳhtah [that is, Urdu] are classmates [studying under] this great man [that is, Arzu]' [hamah ustādān mażbūṭ-i fann-i reḳhtah hamshāgirdān-i ān buzurgvār-and] (Quoted from Sadiq, *History of Urdu Literature*, 43).

8. This commonality is *ishtirāk* (literally, 'sharing'), and it encompasses several kinds of linguistic relationships. The most evocative of these

is *tavāfuq* (concordance), which implies a historical understanding of how languages developed from one another akin to later Western philology. Some scholars have proposed that Sir William Jones took this idea from Arzu without attribution (summarized in Rajeev Kinra, 'This Noble Science: Indo-Persian Comparative Philology, ca. 1000–1800 CE', in *South Asian Texts in History: Critical Engagements with Sheldon Pollock*, ed. Yigal Bronner, Whitney Cox, and Lawrence McCrea [Ann Arbor: Association for Asian Studies, 2011]). My own view is that although Jones certainly knew of Arzu, there is no solid evidence that he would not have come to his conclusions had he never encountered Arzu's work. On this question, see Arthur Dudney, 'A Desire for Meaning: Ḵhān-i Ārzū's Philology and the Place of India in the Eighteenth-Century Persianate World', PhD diss., Columbia University, 2013), 123–30.

9. Shah Hatim recognizes the newness of the practice, pointing out that Vali's dīvān was the first 'in this art' (that is, composing in reḵhtah) in the preface to *Dīvānzādah*, ed. Ghulam Husain Zulfiqar (Lahore: Maktabah Khiyaban-e Adab, 1975), 39. He is, of course, unaware of earlier Deccani dīvāns.

10. 'ko'ī zabān ho, lāzim hai ḵhūbī-ye maẓmūn/zabān-e fars pah kuch munḥaṣir suḵhan to nahīṃ/kahān tak un kī zabān tū durust bolegā/zabān apnī meṃ to bāndh ma'nī-ye rangīn' (Sauda, *Kulliyāt*, 403–4; quoted from Jamil Jalibi, *Tārīḵh-i adab-i urdū*, vol. 2 [Lahore: Majlis-i Taraqqi-yi Adab, 1975], 654; translated at C. M. Naim, ed, *Żikr-i mīr* [New Delhi: Oxford University Press, 1999], 177).

11. A parallel account cited in *Āb-e ḥayāt* leaves out the crucial idea that solid use of maẓmūns is what matters (Azad, *Āb-e ḥayāt*, 142). Furthermore, famous conversation along these lines between Arzu and Sauda, which has been taken as historical fact, was apparently first reported in a comparatively late tażkirah whose account we should not necessarily credit. (*Nishtar-i 'ishq* [Love's Lancet, 1233/1817] by Husayn Quli Khan Ashiqi of Azimabad [that is, Patna], 84–5, trans. Muzaffar Alam, *The Languages of Political Islam: India 1200–1800* [Chicago: University of Chicago, 2004), 180–1]).

12. See, for example, *Dād-i suḵhan*'s second preface (7–9), and *Mus̱mir*'s chapter 'dar bayān ānkih ġhalaṯ az ahl-i zabān ṣādir shavad yā na-shavad' [In the matter of whether a mistake can arise from the (usage of the) ahl-i zabān or not] (Sirajuddin 'Ali Khan Arzu, *Mus̱mir*, ed., Rehana Khatoon [Karachi: Institute of Central and West Asian Studies, University of Karachi, 1991], 34ff).

13. For example, 'Using words from Arabic, Turkish, and Armenian in Persian is allowed leaving Indic words, and even these in the school of thought of the author [Arzu] are not prohibited in this language' [āvardan-i alfāẕ-i 'arabiyah va turkiyah balkih zabān-i arāminah dar fārsī musallam ast bāqī mānad alfāẕ-i hindī va ān nīz ba-mażhab-i mū'allif dar īn zabān mamnū' nīst] (Arzu, *Mus̱mir*, 160). Sirus Shamisa emends *zamān* to *zabān* and that

makes more sense (Sirus Shamisa, ed., *Aṯīyah-i kubrá va mauhibat-i ʿuẓmá* [Tehran: Chapkhanah-i Ramin, 2002], 31).

14. The title of Shamsur Rahman Faruqi's Urdu dictionary, *Luġhāt-i roz-marrah*, is a case in point.

15. Sulayman Hayyim, *New Persian-English Dictionary: Complete and Modern* (Tehran: Librairie-imprimerie Beroukhim, 1934–6), 970.

16. Bahar writes:

> *rozmarrah*: This word is used in two situations: the first meaning idioms and words that are well known among the people, and the other meaning ration and sustenance, derived from 'day' [*roz*] and '*marrah*', which is an Arabic word in the meaning of a time/turn, that is, what one receives once a day and that which one says [*bar zabān buguẓārad*] daily. Thus, the word is established as not originally Persian.
>
> [rozmarrah: īn lafẓ rā dar do mauẓaʿ istiʿmāl kunand: yakī bah maʿnī-yi muḥāvarāt va alfāẓ-i mashhūrah bain al-nās va dīgar bah maʿnī-yi rātibah va vajh-i maʿāsh, murakkab az 'roz' va 'marrah' kih lafẓ-i ʿarabi ast bah maʿnī-yi bār, yaʿnī ānchih har roz bah yak bār barasad va ānchih har roz bah yak bār bar zabān buguẓārad. pas lafẓ mustaḥadis̤ bāshad nah fārsī aṣl] (Lalah Tek Chand Bahar, *Bahār-i 'ajam*, ed. Kazim Dizfuliyan [Tehran: Talayah, 2001], vol. 2, 1114).

Cf. *Madār al-afāẓil* (1592/3 CE /1001 AH): '*rozmarrah* (Persian): that which one uses daily and furthermore is known presently therefore they say "everyday language" [zabān-i rozmarrah]' [rozmarrah (f[ārsī]): ānchih bā-ū rozgār guẓarānand va nīz ʿurf-i ḥāl chunānkih gūyand zabān-i rozmarrah] (Allahdad Faizi Sirhindi, *Madār al-afāẓil*, ed. Muhammad Baqir [Lahore: Punjab University, 1959–70], vol. 2, 336).

17. As it is in other Indian literary traditions.

18. Ehsan Yarshater, 'The Indian or Safavid Style: Progress or Decline?', in *Persian Literature*, ed. Ehsan Yarshater (New York: Columbia University Press, 1988), 273.

19. Arzu, *Dād-i suḳhan*, 9ff.

20. 'dar īn ṯarīq ʿawāmm wa ḳhawāṣṣ sharīk-and' (Arzu, *Dād-i suḳhan*, 9ff).

21. Arzu, *Dād-i suḳhan*, 9; cf. Arzu, *Mus̤mir*, 33. For the nineteenth-century poet Ghalib, there is an addendum, namely a withering response from ʿUrfi, to the effect that of course the great poets of Iran, whose work Indians study, learned from these very same old people (Shamsur Rahman Faruqi, 'Unprivileged Power: The Strange Case of Persian (and Urdu) in Nineteenth Century India', *Annual of Urdu Studies* 13 [1998]: 27). Faruqi notes that he has not been able to trace this incident to a source earlier than Ghalib, but in fact this must be the same—a version nearly identical with Ghalib's is quoted by *Dād-i suḳhan*'s editor from a manuscript of Arzu's contemporary, Mirza

Muhammad ʿAli Tamanna, apparently quoting the critic of Shah Jahan's period Jalala-yi Tabatabaʾi. (Arzu, *Dād-i sukhan*, lxi).

22. ʻān ġhair-i fahmīd-i ahl-i rozmarrah bāshad' (Arzu, *Dād-i sukhan*, 10).

23. Arzu, *Dād-i sukhan*, 2.

24. Arzu, *Dād-i sukhan*, 12.

25. Besides *Dīvānzādah* itself, see Ghulam Hamadani Mushafi, *Tażkirah-yi hindī* (Lucknow: Uttar Pradesh Urdu Academy, 1985), 88–9.

26. He also argues for the correct spelling of words derived from Arabic and Persian.

27. ʻhindavī kih ān rā bhākhā goyand mauqūf kardah.' We can contrast this sense of linguistic boundaries with Azad's *Āb-e ḥayāt*, which discusses the poet Sauda's use of Hindi; tellingly, this passage is written with an assumption that there are two separate literary traditions, one called Hindi and one Urdu (150–2). The relationship of Hindi and Urdu in Arzu's period (and the many anachronistic assumptions about it) is outside the scope of this chapter, but it is treated at length in Dudney, 'Desire for Meaning', ch. 4.

28. The Braj tradition treats it as the everyday speech of the Braj country to the south-west of Delhi but this bucolic simplicity is undermined by its use as a transregional, cosmopolitan, literary idiom (see, for example, Busch, 'Hidden in Plain View'). This need not concern us here.

29. The phrase *ḥarf wa faʿl* is operative: when Mir enumerates the kinds of reḳhtah in the conclusion (ḳhātimah) of *Nikāt al-shuʿarā*, he notes that what he defines as the third kind of reḳhtah in which Persian verbs and particles appear is ineloquent [sīwum ānkih ḥarf va faʿl-i pārsī ba-kār mī-burdand va īn qabīh ast] (Muhammad Taqi Mir, *Nikāt al-shuʿarā* [Karachi: Anjuman-e Taraqqi-ye Urdu], 1979, 161). The first two kinds of reḳhtah are formally linguistically mixed, the first being in the style typical of works attributed to Amir Khusrau, namely with one line of the couplet in Persian and one in 'hindī', while the second has each language alternate at the middle of each line. The fourth is considered later in this chapter (see fn. 33). The fifth and sixth are *īhām* and *andāz*.

30. The wordplay on 'ḥarf' is notable: in the second line, it seems to be used along the lines of the Persian idiom '*ḥarf zadan*' (literally, 'to strike a word') meaning 'to speak'. In the third, the context tells us that it is being used in the technical grammatical sense of an indeclinable particle. The fourth line uses an idiom defined by Platts as follows: '*ḥarf honā* (*-par*), To be a stigma, stain, spot, or disgrace (upon); to be derogatory (to)' (*Dictionary of Urdu Classical Hindi, and English* [London: W. H. Allen, 1884], 476). Likewise, *faʿl* is used in its grammatical sense as a 'verb' in line three, but is made concrete in line four as 'action'.

31. Zuhur al-Din Hatim, *Dīvānzādah*, ed. Ghulam Husain Zulfiqar (Lahore: Maktabah Khiyaban-e Adab, 1975), 39–40.

32. Shamsur Rahman Faruqi, *Shi'r-e shor angez: ġhazaliyāt-i mīr kā muḥaqqiqānah intiḳhāb, mufaṣṣal muṭāli'e ke sāth* (New Delhi: Taraqqi-yi Urdu Bureau, 1990), 57ff.

33. Translation condensed from this passage:

> chahārum ānkih tarkībāt-i fārsī mī ārand, akṡar tarkīb kih munāsib-i zabān-i reḳhtah mī uftad ān jā'iz va īn rā ġhair shā'ir na-mī dānand va tarkībī kih nāmānūs–i reḳhtah mī bāshad ān ma'yūb ast va dānistan-i īn nīz mauqūf-i salīqah-yi shā'ir ast va muḳhtār faqīr ham hamīnast. agar tarkīb-i fārsī muvāfiq-i guftagū-yi reḳhtah būd maẓāyiqah na-dārad (Mir, *Nikāt al-shu'arā*, 161; cf. Naim, *Żikr-i mīr*, 179).

34. Arzu, *Dād-i suḳhan*, 52.

35. The glosses 'rhetoric' and 'semiotics' should be understood as approximate. References to 'rozmarrah' in *'Aṯīyah-i kubra* are on pages 53, 67, and 91, and in *Mauhibat-i 'uẓmá* on pages 99, 125, 135, 136, and 181.

36. Arzu, *Muṡmir*, 5–6.

37. 'rozmarrah-yi dihlī kih mīrzāyān-i hind va faṣīḥān-i rind dar muḥāvarah dārand' (Hatim, *Divānzādah*, 40). 'Flâneur' is obviously not a satisfying translation for the culturally specific 'rind'.

38. Arzu, *Muṡmir*, 38; also page 79 notes that the 'people of the *rozmarrah*' (*ahl-i rozmarrah*) criticize Sā'ib (d. 1676), who had by this time just gone out of living memory. In Arzu's commentary on Sa'dī's *Gulistān*, titled *Ḳhiyābān-i gulistān* (The Road to the Gulistān), ed. Mehr Nur Muhammad Khan (Islamabad: Markaz-e Tahqiqat-e Farsi-ye Iran va Pakistan, 1996), he contrasts the muḥāvarah of different periods (15, 16). He does refer to 'current *rozmarrah*' [*rozmarrah-yi ḥāl*] in *Mauhibat-i 'uẓmá*, in *'Aṯīyah-i kubra va mauhibat-i 'uẓmá*, ed. Sirus Shamisa (Tehran: Chapkhanah-i Ramin, 2002), 125, which could imply the possibility of a 'non-current *rozmarrah*', but since such a historical formulation never appears, it is safe to assume that 'current' is redundant in this context.

39. For example, Shah Hatim mentions 'ġhalaṯī rozmarrah' (erroneous rozmarrah). The preface of Arzu's lexicon *Chirāġh-i hidāyat* justifies its composition by noting that 'although the meaning [of a particular word] was famous and known, in the *rozmarrah* of the eloquent, confusion has often arisen as to its correctness' (ma'ānī-yi ān agarchih ma'rūf wa ma'lūm būd lekin dar ṣiḥḥat būdan-i ān az rozmarrah-yi fuṣaḥā-yi ahl-i zabān ba'ẓī rā taraddud ba-ham-rasīdah) (copied from British Library MS Or 2013, and compared with Or 264 and IO Islamic 71).

40. A typical modern linguistic approach to such issues is Rizwan Ahmad, 'Shifting Dunes: Changing Images of Urdu in India', PhD diss., University of Michigan, 2007.

41. Shamsur Rahman Faruqi, quoted and trans., 'Stranger in the City: The Poetics of *Sabk-i Hindi*', *Annual of Urdu Studies* 19 (2004): 69.

42. Ġhazal 1057, 4; see also 1056, 7 (Mir, *Kulliyāt-e mīr*, 575). There are at least twelve other references to reḳhtah in Mir's ġhazals.

43. Ġhazal 100, 9 (Pritchett, 'A Desertful of Roses'). My translation modifies Pritchett's. In his verse 36, 11, Ghalib explicitly evokes Mir making that verse a fascinating comment on the history of Urdu literature (Pritchett, 'A Desertful of Roses'). While in Calcutta, reports Hali, Ghalib wrote a *mas̱navī* called 'Bād-i muḳhālif' (A Contrary Wind), in which he references the five poets he most admires: Hazin, Asir, Talib, ʿUrfi, Naziri, and above all Zuhuri (Altaf Husain Hali, *Yādgār-e ġhālib* [Kanpur: Nami Press, 1897], 23).

44. On the other hand, we should not take boastful statements (or indeed *any* declaration in poetry) as a fact: Ghalib famously dismissed his Persian poetry when writing in Urdu and dismissed his Urdu poetry when writing in Persian. See, for example, Faruqi, 'Unprivileged Power', 30.

45. Arzu, *Mus̱mir*, 13.

46. For example, Standard French in the seventeenth century was thought of as that of 'the court and the city' (*la cour et la ville*), reflecting a courtly/urban bias just as in Arzu's formulation (Peter Burke, *Languages and Communities in Early Modern Europe* [Cambridge: Cambridge University Press, 2004], 99–100).

Bibliography

Primary Sources

Arzu, Sirajuddin ʿAli Khan. *Navādir al-alfāẕ*, edited by Sayyid Abdullah. Karachi: Anjuman-e Taraqqi-ye Urdu, 1951.

———. *Dād-i suḳhan*, edited by Sayyid Muhammad Akram. Rawalpindi: Iran Pakistan Institute of Persian Studies, 1974.

———. *Muthmir* [*Mus̱mir*], edited by Rehana Khatoon. Karachi: Institute of Central and West Asian Studies, University of Karachi, 1991.

———. *Ḳhiyābān-i gulistān*, edited by Mehr Nur Muhammad Khan. Islamabad: Markaz-e Tahqiqat-e Farsi-ye Iran va Pakistan, 1996.

———. *ʿAṯīyah-i kubrá*. In *ʿAṯīyah-i kubrá va mauhibat-i ʿuẓmá*, edited by Sirus Shamisa. Tehran: Chapkhanah-i Ramin, 2002.

———. *Mauhibat-i ʿuẓmá*. In *ʿAṯīyah-i kubrá va mauhibat-i ʿuẓmá*, edited by Sirus Shamisa. Tehran: Chapkhanah-i Ramin, 2002.

Azad, Muhammad Husain. *Āb-e Ḥayāt*. Lahore: Naval Kishore, 1907.

Bahar, Lalah Tek Chand. *Bahār-i ʿajam*, edited by Kazim Dizfuliyan. Tehran: Talayah, 2001.

Hali, Altaf Husain. *Yādgār-e ġhālib*. Kanpur: Nami Press, 1897.

Hatim, Zuhur al-Din. *Dīvānzādah*, edited by Ghulam Husain Zulfiqar. Lahore: Maktabah Khiyaban-e Adab, 1975.

Mir, Muhammad Taqi. *Nikāt al-shuʿarā*. Karachi: Anjuman-e Taraqqi-ye Urdu, 1979.

———. *Kulliyāt-e mīr*, edited by Zill-e ʿAbbas ʿAbbasi, vol. 1. New Delhi: National Council for the Promotion of the Urdu Language, 2003.

Mushafi, Ghulam Hamadani. *Taẕkirah-yi hindī*. Lucknow: Uttar Pradesh Urdu Academy, 1985.

Sauda, Mirza Muhammad Rafiʿ. *Kulliyāt-i saudā*, edited by ʿAbdul Bari Asi. Vol. 1. Lucknow: Naval Kishore, 1932.

Sirhindi, Allahdad Faizi. *Madār al-afāẕil*, edited by Muhammad Baqir. Lahore: Punjab University, 1959–70.

Secondary Sources

Abdullah, Sayyid. *Mabāḥis̤*. Lahore: Majlis-e Taraqqi-ye Urdu, 1965.

Ahmad, Rizwan. 'Shifting Dunes: Changing Images of Urdu in India', PhD diss., University of Michigan, 2007.

Alam, Muzaffar. *The Languages of Political Islam: India 1200–1800*. Chicago: University of Chicago, 2004.

Burke, Peter. *Languages and Communities in Early Modern Europe*. Cambridge: Cambridge University Press, 2004.

Busch, Allison. 'Hidden in Plain View: Brajbhasha Poets at the Mughal Court'. *Modern Asian Studies* 44, no. 2 (2010): 267–309.

Cooper, Robert L. *Language Planning and Social Change*. Cambridge: Cambridge University Press, 1989.

Dudney, Arthur. 'A Desire for Meaning: Ḳhān-i Ārzū's Philology and the Place of India in the Eighteenth-Century Persianate World', PhD diss., Columbia University, 2013.

Faruqi, Shamsur Rahman. *Shiʿr-e shor angez: ġhazaliyāt-i mīr kā muḥaqqiqānah intiḳhāb, mufaṣṣal muṯāliʿe ke sāth*. New Delhi: Taraqqi-yi Urdu Bureau, 1990.

———. 'Unprivileged Power: The Strange Case of Persian (and Urdu) in Nineteenth Century India'. *Annual of Urdu Studies* 13 (1998): 3–30.

———. 'A Stranger in the City: The Poetics of *Sabk-i Hindi*'. *Annual of Urdu Studies* 19 (2004): 1–93.

Hasan, Hadi. *History of Indo-Persian Literature*. New Delhi: Iran Culture House, 2001.

Hayyim, Sulayman. *New Persian-English Dictionary, Complete and Modern*. Tehran: Librairie-imprimerie Beroukhim, 1934–6.

Jalibi, Jamil. *Tārīḳh-i adab-i urdū*. Lahore: Majlis-i Taraqqi-yi Adab, 1975.

Kinra, Rajeev. 'This Noble Science: Indo-Persian Comparative Philology, ca. 1000–1800 CE'. In *South Asian Texts in History: Critical Engagements with Sheldon Pollock*, edited by Yigal Bronner, Whitney Cox, and Lawrence McCrea. Ann Arbor: Association for Asian Studies, 2011.

Marshall, P.J. 'Johnson, Richard (1753–1807)'. In *Oxford Dictionary of National Biography*. Oxford: Oxford University Press, 2004. Available at http://www.oxforddnb.com/view/article/63514, last accessed on 28 June 2012.

Naim, C. M., ed. *Żikr-i mīr*. New Delhi: Oxford University Press, 1999.
Platts, John T. *A Dictionary of Urdu, Classical Hindi, and English*. London: W. H. Allen, 1884.
Pritchett, Frances. 'A Desertful of Roses' (website). Available at http://www.columbia.edu/itc/mealac/pritchett/00ghalib/index.html, last accessed on 21 September 2013.
Sadiq, Muhammad. *A History of Urdu Literature*. London: Oxford University Press, 1964.
Shamisa, Sirus, ed. *'Aṭīyah-i kubrá va mauhibat-i 'uẓmá*. Tehran: Chapkhanah-i Ramin, 2002.
Shapiro, Marianne. *De Vulgari Eloquentia: Dante's Book of Exile*. Lincoln: University of Nebraska, 1990.
Yarshater, Ehsan. 'The Indian or Safavid Style: Progress or Decline?' In *Persian Literature*, edited by Ehsan Yarshater. New York: Columbia University Press, 1988.

3

LUTHER OBROCK*

Muslim *Mahākāvyas*

Sanskrit and Translation in the Sultanates

How does the mystical poetry of the great Naqshbandī Sūfī Abdur Raḥmān Jāmī become a poem of Śaiva devotion in Kashmir? How is the sultan of Gujarat like the heroes of the Rāmāyaṇa and Mahābhārata? Why would the Biblical story of Bathsheba and David become an occasion for an in-depth study of the erotics of the Kāmaśāstra? The contents of these three Sanskrit texts—the *Kathākautuka*, *Rājavinoda*, and *Sulaimaccarita*, respectively—force the modern reader to ask such questions and to confront the role of Sanskrit in Islamicate elite culture in north India. This small sample of surviving Sanskrit texts from the pre-Mughal Sultanate period shows a creative and experimental literary culture patronized in Muslim courts. Despite the evocative contents of these works, Sanskrit texts are seldom registered in histories of the regional Sultanates, and they are rarely used to nuance historical processes such as vernacularization or regional identity formation. Yet in reading these Sultanate Sanskrit texts, one is struck by the self-assured audacity of Śrīvara's retelling of a Sufi poem in the *Kathākautuka*, of Kalyaṇa Malla's reframing of a Biblical story in terms of the Sanskrit four ends of man (*puruṣārtha*) in the *Sulaimaccarita*, and the superimposition of 'Hindu' heroes on Gujarati sultans in Udayarāja's *Rājavinoda*. Such texts have the capacity to shed much light on the creation of an Indo-Persian elite culture in South Asia.

In her essay 'How to Do Multilingual History? Lessons from Fifteenth- and Sixteenth-Century North India', Francesca Orsini shows the necessity of looking outside Persian and Arabic sources to study Sultanate South Asia.[1] While her article stresses the role of vernacular sources, this chapter attempts to further her insight by introducing a small but vibrant archive of Sanskrit texts. Here I show that a dichotomy between Indic vernacular and Perso-Arabic elite literatures elides the fascinating role of Sanskrit in Sultanate courts. The *Kathākautuka, Rājavinoda,* and *Sulaimaccarita,* although from different areas of northern India (Kashmir, Gujarat, and Awadh respectively), were all produced within a fifty-year span between the late fifteenth and the early sixteenth century. Each text was patronized by and presented within the court of a local Muslim ruler. Further, from the self-confident presentation of the texts themselves it seems that each were the products of ongoing conversations about literature, religion, and representation. These three texts invite us to rethink the literary culture of medieval South Asia as well as the circulation of knowledge in the Sultanate Period in terms of Sanskrit and the Sanskritic.[2]

The *Kathākautuka, Rājavinoda,* and *Sulaimaccarita* offer Sanskrit poetry for and about Islamicate courts, and as such push the boundaries of what can be expressed in Sanskrit. Each of these texts deal with specific forms connected to Islamicate conceptions of polity or elite culture, and each must translate cultural contexts in a more or less literal way. With this in mind, it is worth highlighting that the Sultanate period—contrary to the conception of the 'death of Sanskrit' following the Turco-Muslim invasion of northern India in the thirteenth century—did witness moments when Sanskrit literature was afforded the opportunity to reassert its status as an elite language. In the process, however, the hitherto circumscribed world of the Sanskritic literary imagination had to engage Islamicate ideas, texts, and traditions.

Viewing the phenomenon of Sanskrit production in Sultanate courts from this vantage, we are left to answer several questions: how can one delineate the contours of translation into Sanskrit in pre-Mughal South Asia? What does it mean to produce Sanskrit in a Sultanate court? What genealogies are being invoked, transformed, or denied to produce such works? This short chapter does not intend to provide a thorough analysis of each of these texts, nor does provide an overarching theory of Sanskrit textual production in the

Sultanate period. Rather, it offers a brief snapshot of each of these three texts in order to hint at the richness and possibilities of the Sultanate Sanskrit and to gesture towards the benefit of Sanskrit's integration into a fuller multilingual history of pre-Mughal South Asia.

The Sanskrit texts left by authors working within and patronized by the Sultanate elite provide fascinating windows into processes of change, accommodation, appropriation, and transformation. Sanskrit as a language of political power had been utilized and refined in the courts of medieval South Asia for the previous millennium; Sanskrit was not just a language, rather it was both a way of being and a way of encoding the world. As such, Sanskrit stood as the pre-eminent vehicle of political and aesthetic orientation throughout the subcontinent.[3] The establishment of the first Muslim—and more importantly Islamicate[4]—states in north India challenged the power of the Sanskrit cosmopolis as the sole arbiter of elite culture in South Asia. After the twelfth century not only are north Indian vernaculars established as languages of political power in their own right, but also the Islamicate languages of high culture such as Arabic and particularly Persian become deeply connected with new forms of polity.

In the face of this political and cultural change, Sanskrit does not pull back from the world of public literary production. In fact, although the neat periodizations of colonial and nationalist historiography clearly demarcate the Sanskritic Hindu period from that of the Islamicate Muslim, even the fifteenth and sixteenth centuries show new and innovative articulations of Sanskrit and the Sanskritic along with an experimental attitude towards textual composition and thematic inclusiveness. Concomitantly, although often using Arabic and Persian with their different ecologies of poetic beauty and artistic representation, the Sultanate courts were not impervious or unaffected by Sanskritic high culture. Sanskrit poets sought patronage within Sultanate courts, and were sought out by members of the political elite. The works discussed in this chapter are the products of conversations in which Sanskritic and Islamicate ideas and ideals influence each other, often in surprising ways. What comes into sharp focus is the importance of translation in the cultural processes shaping the Sultanate period.

The utility of translation as a hermeneutic device has begun to be recognized by scholars, and has been used to map the dynamics of cultural change in premodern Asia. While much impressive scholarship has dealt with the Hindu–Muslim encounter (two of the most influential works being Richard Eaton's *The Rise of Islam and the Bengal Frontier* and Phillip Wagoner's '"Sultan among Hindu Kings": Dress, Titles, and the Islamicization of Hindu Culture at Vijayanagara'), too often it is theorized as unidirectional, propelled by dynamic and powerful Islamicate forms. Two recent monographs, Finbarr Flood's *Objects of Translation* and Ronit Ricci's *Islam Translated*, have traced cultural change through the lens of translation. Flood stresses that the world of contact in premodern South Asia cannot be seen in simple binaries of Hindu and Muslim, Islamic and Indic, Perso-Arabic and Sanskrit. For Flood, works of cultural translation are not the product of a singular moment of encounter; rather, they are embedded in dense networks of meaning conditioned by exchange and transference. In *Islam Translated*, Ricci argues that translation is a two-way process in which both the translator and the translated are simultaneously formed. For Ricci, the process of translation is intimately tied to religious conversion. The Sanskrit texts highlighted in this chapter hint to another sort of transformation: the rooting of new lineages, ideas, and stories in Sanskritic vocabulary, patronized and approved by the Sultanate elite.

The texts of Śrīvara, Udayarāja, and Kalyāṇa Malla are products of a dynamic culture of transmission and appropriation, in short, of circulatory translation. With Flood, I frame these three texts as moments of textual production crystallized within the larger context of exchange; however, I want to move the focus back from objects to texts. With Ricci, I stress that the process is always conditioned; however, I concentrate on elite aesthetics rather than religious communities. Sanskrit literary production in pre-Mughal north India provides an important voice in the multilingual world of Sultanate elite production.

The *Rājavinoda*

The first case study focuses on the fascinating *Rājavinoda*, a text that describes a Muslim ruler in almost completely Indic terms. The *Rājavinoda* was prepared at the court of the Muzaffarid sultan, Maḥmūd Begaḍā of Gujarat (r. 1458–1511), most probably between 1458 and 1469.[5] As such, it forces us to rethink both Persianate tellings of courtly life and Sanskrit's role in elite presentation. The text survives in a single manuscript brought by Georg Bühler to Bombay's Prince of Wales Museum in 1875, from which one printed edition was made.[6] Judging by the contents of the manuscript, its intended audience was regional-based and elite. Styling itself as a *mahākāvya* (epic poem) in the colophons, the *Rājavinoda* is a Sanskrit poem divided into seven chapters. It recounts the entertainments, pastimes, and accomplishments of Sultan Maḥmūd Begaḍā.

The first chapter frames the rest of the work. Sarasvatī, the goddess of speech and learning, engages in conversation with Indra, the king of the gods, and asks why should she return to heaven when such a ruler as Maḥmūd Begaḍa rules the earth? Sarasvatī implies that the sultan has made the earth a paradise for the goddess of (Sanskrit) language. The second chapter presents a genealogy of the sultan's dynasty, often providing fascinating Sanskritic parallels to the lives of the previous sultans, comparing their deeds to the great heroes of the epics such as Bhīma, Arjuna, and Karṇa. Over the remaining five chapters, the text offers an idealized picture of Sultan Maḥmūd's reign. He is eloquent in the *sabhā*, the meeting place for intellectuals and elites, he is a world conqueror in battle, he is a veritable god of love to women, and so forth. The tenor of this work, with its choice of topics, its metaphorical referents, its organization, its spatial imagination, and its sumptuary outlook is completely Sanskritic in orientation. If it were not for the name Maḥmūd and the other Islamic names celebrated in his genealogy, this work could be taken as a work on a 'Hindu' king in a fully Sanskritized court.

So why write such an account of a Muslim king? Before beginning to analyse Udayarāja's work, one must keep in mind the crucial, but too often ignored observation that the Persian histories of these regional Sultanates are written long—sometimes centuries—after the actual reigns of the sultans that the texts purport to describe. This insight on the limitations of Persian historiography when dealing with the Sultanate is not new; however, still history writing on the Sultanate tends to limit itself to only Persian (and Arabic) material.[7]

While the concern of the *Rājavinoda* is not 'historical', the poem places the king (and his lineage) within an imagined space of kingship, one that makes sense in terms of Sanskritic tropes, organization, and idiom. The king and his world thus become subsumed into the carefully controlled and crafted Sanskritic vocabulary of kingship and power. The very existence of a text such as the *Rājavinoda* demands a radical rereading of the Gujarati sultans. Udayarāja's poem shows the ideological translation of kingship undertaken within a completely Sanskritic vision of the world. In highlighting the courtly pleasures (*vinoda*) of the king, Udayarāja is placing the sultan and his family within a well-theorized and elaborately mapped-out typology and taxonomy of Sanskritic courtly, sumptuary, and erotic discourse.[8]

In her study of the *Rājavinoda*, 'The Last Chakravartin: The Gujarati Sultan as "Universal King" in Fifteenth Century Sanskrit Poetry' (2013), Aparna Kapadia holds that the *Rājavinoda* marks a terminal point, the last time during which a Muslim ruler could be represented as a Hindu *cakravartin*, or a world conqueror. Arguing that scholars such as Eaton have taken Islamicate practices as the baseline for elite culture in the Sultanate period, Kapadia uses the *Rājavinoda* to show 'the simultaneous existence of a reverse process' in which 'the classical Indic notion of the *cakravartin* ... could be also used to accommodate a Muslim sultan'.[9] Kapadia's intervention is important in that it shows that other factors were at play in the literary world of Sultanate courts.

However, the question remains: Leaving aside the validity of the term 'cakravartin', why is Udayarāja appealing to a universalized discourse of Sanskritic kingship? Kapadia understands the work as a last instance where Sanskrit can be used as an elite language of kingship before the rise of other languages of political power. Rather than seeing Sanskrit as something that is supplanted by vernaculars and Persian, I see it as taking active part in a fluid literary ecology. That is to say, rather than as an attempt to bring Maḥmūd Begaḍā into a 'cosmopolitan' Sanskrit discourse, the *Rājavinoda* should be read as a regional usage of a Sanskritic political idiom that attempts to contain new lineages and political ideologies. I see Sanskrit as acting as one possibility among many in the fluid intellectual world of the regional Sultanates.

The idealization of Maḥmūd in Sanskrit points towards a complex world of courtly representational practices which not only valorized a 'cosmopolitan' vision provided by Sanskrit, but also attempted to localize this power within the particular historical and geographical space of Sultanate Gujarat. The political imagination evinced in the *Rājavinoda* shows him first and foremost bound within the strictures of the Sanskritic language of power. The poetic and political vocabulary of the *Rājavinoda* is drawn entirely from the Sanskrit tradition: take, for example, a verse describing Maḥmūd's predecessor Muḥammad:

> The Sun lights up the earth only (*eva*) by day, the moon spreads its radiance [only] by night. The illustrious (*śrī*) King (*narādhipati*) Muḥammad's appearance having vigor (*pratāpa*) and fame (*yaśas*) [on the other hand] was seen on the earth perpetually.[10]

Udayarāja illustrates quite clearly here the common vocabulary of kingly might found throughout royal encomia in the subcontinent. Martial glory attributed to the king uses the same word as that used for the sun's fiery brilliance (*pratāpa*). Likewise, fame (*yaśas*) is in the Sanskritic poetic universe a white substance, luminous like moonlight. The hyperbole of the verse is obvious and the cliché well worn, yet Maḥmūd's lineage is placed within that literary imagination. This verse is followed soon after by this comparison:

> He was versed in both politics (*naya*) and acting (*abhinaya*) through the employment of both the Mahābhārata and Bharata's *Naṭyaśāstra*. Heroic in battle and especially powerful in giving, he approached [the status of] the world-famous Karṇa and Arjuna, too.[11]

In this verse, Sultan Maḥmūd Begaḍā is imagined without irony or contradiction in completely Sanskritic terms, and being completely educated in Sanskritic texts of politics and aesthetics. The verse culminates in the identification of the sultan with the epic heroes Arjuna (who was of course a skilled warrior) and Karṇa (who is remembered within the Sanskrit tradition for his generosity).

Here I want to suggest that this Sanskritic vocabulary also must be contextualized in the larger world of courtly politics in Sanskritic South Asia; the very form of the *Rājavinoda*, with the telling term 'vinoda', meaning 'entertainment' or 'leisure'. What is striking about the *Rājavinoda* is precisely this focus on vinoda, which places the king in a deep engagement with the Sanskritic sumptuary practices of rule. Udayarāja places the Gujarati sultans firmly within the carefully controlled and constructed world of courtly aesthetic norms, and in so doing is presenting a vision of Sultanate power informed by and ultimately taking part in the Sanskritic ideas of kingship. Yet I want to stress that this is not just about elevating Maḥmūd to cosmopolitan cakravartin status; the *Rājavinoda* also demonstrates the suitability of Sanskrit in articulating specifically regional elite identities.

The *Sulaimaccarita*

The *Sulaimaccarita* is a poetic work in four chapters which again brings Sanskritic and Islamicate idioms into conversation. It retells the Biblical story of David and Bathsheba and the birth of their son, Solomon (Sulaimat of the title). Produced in Awadh for a noble named

Laḍ Khān, the text traverses the Sanskritic four classical ends of man (puruṣārtha), concentrating especially on *kāma* (sensual enjoyment) and dharma (righteous behaviour) before ending in an unexpected retelling of the story of the jinn and the fisherman from *The Thousand and One Nights*. Although in some ways the *Sulaimaccarita* shows parallels with *Rājavinoda*, the experience of reading Kalyāṇa Malla's text is distinctly different—most obviously since the work imports its main characters and fundamental situations from outside of the Indic milieu. This tale does not imagine a Muslim ruler in the aesthetic space of Sanskritic rule. Rather, it superimposes the expectations of courtly vinoda (and later *dharmic* expectations of rule) on a tale from outside of the Indic sphere.

Malla himself was an expert on kāmaśāstra, or erotics, and this orientation is clearly shown in the first and second chapters, which describe David's desire for Bathsheba. David's lust becomes the occasion for a moralizing sermon on dharma put in the mouth of Nathan, which occupies the third chapter of the work. After this point, the *Sulaimaccarita* moves away from the Mosaic tradition of David into the terrain of story literature. The fourth and final chapter of the text translates and expands the story of the jinn and the fisherman from the Arabic classic of story literature, *The Thousand and One Nights*.

In translating this story, the *Sulaimaccarita* attempts, in a sophisticated way, to allow for the participation of the Islamicate in terms of the Sanskritic. While a needed study of the contents and structure of the entire work is impossible here, I will turn briefly to to *The Thousand and One Nights* in the fourth chapter and the role of story literature in Kalyaṇa's work of translation and re-imagination. In the story of the jinn and the fisherman, Malla finds a shared genre and shared sensibility that can be simultaneously incorporated and adapted. In a sense, Malla brings a story from the Islamicate world into Sanskrit and puts Sanskrit stories into the Arabic original. Yet in the *Sulaimaccarita*, this becomes truly an act of transformation as the retelling subtly positions itself within the expectations of Indic story literature.

Here I look to Malla's reworking of one of the sub-stories in the tale of the jinn and the fisherman, the story of the truth-telling parrot and the merchant. He translates:

> Long ago, there lived a righteous merchant named Dhanada, generous and intent upon the values of his own family. A certain sailor brought

a miraculous parrot, five-coloured and vivacious, from the islands and gave it to him. Taking him, the merchant deposited him into a fantastic golden cage, studded with gems, and nourished him as if he were his devoted son, possessed of all virtues, with various fruits and sugar lumps from sugarcane. Skilled in every language and proficient in every type of knowledge, the parrot grew and grew, delighting his keeper. His wife, wide-eyed, was unparalleled in beauty on the earth. Rejecting her husband (*vibhu*) constantly, she became the mistress of others. Constantly waiting outside the door for her lovers, when her husband went to the shop, she smeared a mixture of saffron and sandal as well as a paste of musk[12] on her breasts and went forth to her tryst. [...]

The parrot observed the wife living like this for days and days and became angry with her. As he (that is, the merchant) made known he was leaving the house, the [parrot] announced what he had seen earlier: 'O king, your wife is an unchaste woman, a [mere] store of flattery. Day by day she enjoys herself with other men, meeting them joyfully. Whatever excellent young man who has presented himself in front [of her] she sees, him she embraces, gives sexual pleasure joyfully, then sends on his way again.'

She plotted in her heart with her conspiring friends to kill the parrot who thus was constantly making known the daily events within the household. Once the best of merchants heard the words [of the parrot] considering them true, he beat his wife with scoldings and lashings again and again.

Thus chastised, his wife was enraged, and perceiving a means [towards revenge] she placed chick-peas on a stone near the parrot's cage and ground them with a loud sound. From above there was a sprinkling of water on the body of the parrot. In the darkness having lit a lamp she caused it to move [in front of him]. The parrot thought it was the thundering of the clouds reverberating with thunderbolts; he considered the falling of drops of water to be rain; he thought the quick flashes (*paribhramaṇa*) in the mirror near the lamp to be lightning. Then he said respectfully to the merchant when he came, 'During the night, where were you? Were you not tormented by the rain?'

As soon as he had said 'There was so much rain last night!' [the merchant] said to the bird: 'Parrot, what's this rain falling in the night? Tell me, right away! Today you have become a liar—your speech has been found out! Just so you must have spoken previously too, alas, always about my wife!'

Once he spoke thus, the merchant, the ends of his eyes reddened with anger, then, seizing a stick, struck the parrot in a rage. After he killed the parrot without reflection, he saw the behaviour of his wife,

> and afterwards, tortured, the merchant remembered the parrot with constant lamentations, and was killed by regret (*cintā*).[13]

I have chosen to translate this story at length since the story of the parrot and the merchant receives one of the longer retellings in the *Sulaimaccarita*—it seems that Malla found it especially compelling. We can see parts that Malla focuses on and others that he elides. For instance, in contrast to *The Thousand and One Nights*, Malla places greater emphasis on the fantastic nature of the parrot and the promiscuity of the wife. The Sanskrit text also does not mention the killing of the wife's paramour. Yet these small differences are not the point; rather, I think this translation shows the ease with which one can move from the Islamicate original into the Sanskritic translation. Malla's story in the last chapter of the *Sulaimaccarita* shows the possibility of equivalence. Although taken from the Islamicate tradition, the story feels completely Sanskritic in its tone and telling.

The *Sulaimaccarita* allows in a sophisticated and experimental way for the participation of the Islamicate in the Sanskritic. The final chapter of the *Sulaimaccarita* points to an intellectual milieu in which two traditions of story literature could coexist and interact in a congruent vocabulary of the story. In the case of Malla's retelling, it is clear that the Sanskrit text was cognizant of certain markers of both Sanskritic and Islamicate norms, and he worked creatively with these markers that defined and distinguished the two. In the end, the *Sulaimaccarita* presents characters, ideas, and stories made Sanskritic. While the story of David and Bathsheba is defined and shaped by ideas of dharma and kāma, Malla finds in *The Thousand and One Nights* a common idiom to expand on and explore in his Sanskrit retelling.

The *Kathākautuka*

The final text to which I turn is the startling and little-studied translation of Jāmī's Persian masnavī *Yūsuf wa Zulaykhā* into Sanskrit verse. Paṇḍit Śrīvara, who was a court historian and musician to a number of Kashmiri Shāhmīrī rulers, offered this text to Sultan Muḥammad Shāh in the spring of 1505. The *Kathākautuka* is based on Jāmī's skillful telling of the story of Yūsuf (the Biblical Joseph) and Zulaykhā (Potiphar's unnamed wife). Drawing on Yūsuf's story in the twelfth *sūra* of the Qur'ān, Jāmī transforms it into a stunning meditation on beauty and devotion to God. Jāmī's *Yūsuf wa Zulaykhā* offered a compelling poetic and religious vision and quickly moved throughout the Persianate and Islamicate world, eventually coming to the attention of Paṇḍit Śrīvara in the valley of Kashmir.[14]

Śrīvara's translation of Jāmī's poem is audacious, ignoring or explicitly excising certain Islamic elements (including the *bismillah*, the opening religious invocation) while actively turning Jāmī's Sūfī text into a poem of religious devotion to Śiva. Śrīvara's strongly stated Śaivism does not spring from an ignorance or avoidance of the religious philosophy contained in the original; his translation is not a religious polemic. He is well aware of the Persian version and its cultural context; indeed, some verses are almost exact translations of Jāmī's stanzas. To drive home Śrīvara's proficiency, the colophons after each chapter refer to Śrīvara as *yavana-bhāṣā-pāraṅga* (having gone to the far shore of the language of the Yavanas). Yet, despite—or perhaps because of—his knowledge of Jāmī's language and the expectations of Islamicate poetry and religion, he makes striking translational choices. While he states, hearkening back to Somadeva's *Kathāsaritsāgara*, that he is adhering closely to the original text, changing only the language of its expression, in actuality he moves the text from a Persianate and Islamicate context to a Sanskritic (particularly Kashmiri[15]) and Śaiva orientation. One example offers some insight into Śrīvara's translational strategies.

Joseph's beauty is his main characteristic in the Qur'ānic version of the narrative. Jāmī picks up and amplifies Joseph's beauty, creating a striking inversion of usual Sūfī (and for that matter Sanskritic) gendered roles. Joseph is the male beloved who pushes the female lover towards union with God. Throughout Jāmī's tale, the mere sight of Joseph pushes men and women (but usually women) into states of wonder and lust. Such moments are occasions for Joseph to counsel his audience to turn away from the beauties of this world, which are mere pale imitations of the beauty of the transcendent God. These sermons and the subsequent narratives of conversion utilize Sūfī ideas and tropes and are deeply intertwined with Jāmī's own Naqshbandī Sūfī ideas. In the process of translating such episodes, Śrīvara transforms not only the Persian words, but also the Persianate and Islamicate religiosity underlying his source, as is evident in the thirteenth chapter of Śrīvara's retelling.

Joseph has been captured and is to be sold as a slave. Men and women come from all over to marvel at his perfect form. A rich woman comes to spend all her wealth to attain this most handsome of men. Joseph counsels her against such attachment to beauty and goes on to preach to this woman, after which she has what one might call a conversion experience. This is how Śrīvara describes it: after Joseph's beauty is praised, he admonishes the woman to not contemplate upon earthly but divine beauty. He states:

> Know all of this that is seen endowed with many splendours to exist like a reflection in the mirror of Bhava. Beautiful browed one, just as the mind, after beholding some reflection in a mirror, instantaneously runs there alone in order to decide about it, so too after seeing the universe, fixed and moving, created from his power of illusion, do the wise meditate upon Śambhu alone. Fine-hipped lady, if [you have] a strong mental attachment to the appearance of beauty, see in your heart that the one recourse is the joyful god, charming. Beautiful-browed one, once you see my beauty as transient—[and] your happiness—therefore look towards the stable [beauty] of Śambhu, containing everything.
>
> After she heard his speech, she became freed from delusion. At that instant, she paid reverence to his lotus feet again and again. Then the thin-waisted woman gave up her fine elephants and her riches, took on a single ochre robe [of the mendicant], anointed all of her limbs with ash, gave up her affection towards family, and went to the deep forest to perform austerities like a renunciant. Her mind was cleansed through fasts and vows—each more difficult than the last. Stainless, her body became purified through bathing at all of the sacred fords.[16]

This passage demonstrates the remarkable transformation that underlies Śrīvara's translation. Here the entire cultural context is changed while the ideas and the events remain somehow similar. A tale of Sūfī devotion to God becomes a tale of Śaiva devotion to Śambhu. While Joseph's remarkable beauty remains the same, as does his power to bring women to religion, the religion and indeed the world view are changed. The Sūfī tale is fully re-imagined in a Śaiva world of austerities and sacred bathing places.

When describing his translational project, Śrīvara characterizes Jāmī's original tale (*kathā*) as 'connected to the treatises (*śāstra*) of the Muslims' (*yavanaśāstrabaddhā*).[17] In saying this, Śrīvara sees Jāmī's entire work as bound up in the textual and intellectual tradition of the Islamicate world. Tacitly underlying this observation is his retelling (once he composes it in the un-ageing language of Sanskrit, *viracitā mayā nirjarābhāṣāyām*), being bound to a different śāstra, a different world view, with different expectations. Like for Malla, the process of translation for Śrīvara is an appropriation and a transformation.

Interestingly though, Śrīvara's translational methodology is totalizing, that is to say, not just the words and ideas are translated, but also the underlying world view. Jāmī's text itself undergoes a type of religious conversion; the Islamic Sufism of the *Yūsuf wa Zulaykhā* becomes a tantric-tinged Śaivism in the *Kathākautuka*. Yet given the nature of the text and its context within the Sultanate court of Muḥammad Shāh, it seems unlikely that religion was the sole driving impetus behind the creation of the *Kathākautuka*. Rather Śrīvara, with all of his knowledge of the Persianate world, presented a vision of Jāmī's text deeply imbricated in the Sanskritic elite outlook. Instead of a religious polemic, the *Kathākautuka* reads as courtly cleverness directed towards an elite and multilingual Sultanate conversant in both Sanskritic and Persianate expectations.

Conclusion

Pre-Mughal north India saw the influx of a tremendous amount of new cultural forms. However, it is important to remember that the Sanskrit language and literature became one important site of such exchange, in which ideas were appropriated, transformed, and enriched. The three works briefly discussed here were each produced in a different regional court, for different rulers, and with different attitudes towards their sources; however, each of these three texts share in a common culture of translation and exchange, at once experimental and full of possibility. The very existence of these texts does much to break down simple and pernicious binaries of religious community, defining historiographical periodicization or clearly demarcated boundaries of literary cultures, yet they do much more. The 'encounter' shown in each of these texts suggests a modulated and complex reaction to the inclusion of new texts and ideas. But more than that, Sanskrit was finding a way to be relevant in the changing literary ecology of the regional Sultanates in the fifteenth and sixteenth centuries. As both a source of elite expression and site of exchange, Sanskrit texts are deeply embedded in the literary fabric of Sultanate South Asia and are key to creating a truly multilingual history of South Asia.

These texts show translation as much more than the simple search for word-for-word equivalence. Rather, the *Rājavinoda*, the *Sulaimaccarita*, and the *Kathākautuka* attempt to make room for the Islamicate within the structures and expectations of the Sanskritic, while actively presenting Sanskrit as a viable medium for elite

Sultanate texts. The *Rājavinoda* does this by presenting Sultanate kingship as nothing different than classically conceived Sanskritic kingship. The king is the cultured enjoyer (*bhoktṛ*) placed within the controlled universe of cultured sumptuary pleasure. The *Sulaimaccarita* takes this formula one step further, reorganizing a Biblical narrative along the lines of the Indic ends of man (puruṣārtha). Its celebration of the story in the final chapter shows the fluidity of textual translation, appropriation, addition, and transformation. The story remains fundamentally the same; however, the telling places it in conversation with Sanskritic expectations which moulds its final form. Finally, the *Kathākautuka* presents a translation that makes the Sūfī *Yūsuf wa Zulaykhā* legible in a Śaiva linguistic and literary register. Each of these texts use the Sanskrit, mediated through regional courts (each of these texts mentioned specific requests from specific rulers) for the sake of innovative acts of translation.

Śrīvara, by far the most honest and self-conscious of the authors here discussed, recognizes the distance between works bound by different cultural assumptions, and in attempting to translate, he came to the limit of what can be said in Sanskrit. He refers to his source text, the Persian *Yūsuf wa Zulaykhā*, as *yāvanaśāstrabaddhā* (tied to the Muslim [*yāvana*] sciences).[18] In recognizing the Islamicate cultural world as bound by a set of normative expectations, Śrīvara presents a world view in which the Islamicate world is bound to its own underlying theories and structures. A corollary of this is a recognition of the śāstras that underlie the Sanskritic world view, and which undergird any translational attempt. Each of these three texts in engaging with the Islamicate order encodes its own view of Sanskritic, tacitly presenting a reflexive commentary on what Sanskrit is and does.

The sources discussed here pose more questions about the role of Sanskrit in the fifteenth and sixteenth-century sultanates than they answer. By way of conclusion, I return to the idea of multilingual histories and the possible role of Sanskrit in studying the historical processes of change and continuity in second-millennium South Asia. Historical scholarship when confronted with aesthetic artefacts from the past tend to emphasize narratives of pragmatic power dynamics encoded within artistic gestures. Encounter, when seen as a purely pragmatic fact, creates a logic for cultural appropriation that papers over the far richer—and far more difficult—question of the role of aesthetics. Viewing the process of translation from the perspective of aesthetics could perhaps provide a way to capture some of the complexity and depth involved in the cultural negotiations of pre-Mughal South Asia.

Notes

* I would like to thank Hannah Lord Archambault, Munis Faruqui, and Tyler Williams for their insightful comments and criticisms on earlier drafts of this chapter.

1. Francesca Orsini, 'How to Do Multilingual History? Lessons from Fifteenth- and Sixteenth-Century North India', *IESHR* 49, no. 2 (2012): 225–46.

2. Here I use the term 'Sanskritic' to refer to elite productions and dispositions encoded in the Sanskrit language. In her recent dissertation 'Cosmopolitan Encounters', Audrey Truschke prefers the term 'Indic' as the South Asian equivalent. However, I employ the term 'Sanskritic' almost as a counterpart to 'Persianate' to emphasize the cultural-linguistic aspect of these texts. Such an identification can further nuance the investigation of multilingualism in Sultanate South Asia by seeing Sanskritic authors and works also trying to find purchase in the changing literary landscape of Sultanate South Asia. For the purposes of this chapter, the Sanskritic is set in conversation with the notion of the Islamicate (see note 5).

3. This particular way of understanding Sanskrit has been persuasively argued by Sheldon Pollock. Pollock writes: 'The work Sanskrit did do was beyond the Quotidian and the instrumental; it was directed above all toward articulating a form of political consciousness and culture, politics not as transaction of material culture ... but as celebration of aesthetic power' (Sheldon Pollock, *The Language of the Gods in the World of Men: Sanskrit, Culture, and Power in Premodern India* [Berkeley: University of California Press, 2006], 14).

4. Here and throughout I utilize Marshall Hodgson's useful term 'Islamicate' as it (following Hodgson) 'refer[s] not directly to the religion, Islam, itself, but to the social and cultural complex historically associated with Islam and the Muslims, both among Muslims themselves and when found among non-Muslims' (Marshall Hodgson, *The Venture of Islam: Conscience and History in a World Civilization* [Chicago: University of Chicago Press 1974], 59). An equivalent term to explain a similar cultural complex based on classical Indian cultural expectations is needed in order to undertake any sort of historical discussion involving the engagement of two elite cultural spheres.

5. For the date of the *Rājavinoda*, see P.K. Gode's essay 'Date of Udayarāja and Jagaddhara', *Journal of the University of Bombay* 9, no. 2 (1940): 101–15.

6. For a history of the reception of the work by modern scholarship, see Aparna Kapadia, 'The Last Chakravartin: The Gujarati Sultan as "Universal King" in Fifteenth Century Sanskrit Poetry', *The Medieval History Journal* 6, no. 1 (2013): 71–2.

7. Peter Hardy has emphasized the ideological biases underlying Persian portrayals of kingship and the disciplinary biases that color modern scholars' writings of histories of the Sultanates in his *Historians of Medieval India: Studies in Indo-Muslim Historical Writing* (London: Luzac, 1960).

8. For the representation of sumptuary culture in Sanskritic courts, see Daud Ali, *Courtly Culture and Political Life in Early Medieval India* (Cambridge: Cambridge University Press, 2006), especially chapter 6. This work has interesting parallels to the nearly contemporaneous works of Kalyāṇa Malla. The role of sumptuary and erotic discourse in the *Sulaimaccarita* will be mentioned briefly later, but it should be noted that the Sultanate elite patronized Malla's famous manual on erotics entitled the *Anaṅgaraṅga* (The Theater of Love).

9. Kapadia, 'The Last Cakravartin', 68.

10.
sūryo divaiva kurute jagati prakāśaṃ
kāntiṃ śaśī vitanute niyataṃ niśāyām
śrī manmahammadanarādhipateḥ pṛthvyāṃ
dṛṣṭaḥ pratāpayaśasor yugapat pracāraḥ //2.16// (*Rājavinoda* of Udayarāja. Here and throughout, all translations from the Sanskrit are my own).

11.
Yo bhāratasya bharatasya ca samprayogāt
Uccair ajāyata naye 'bhinaye pravīṇaḥ |
Vīro raṇe vitaraṇe ca viśiṣṭaśaktiḥ
karṇārjunāv api jigāya jagatprasiddhau //2.17//

12. The text reads 'vividhālaṃkārasaṃkumuda* paṅkam' here. Unable to make sufficient sense of this reading, I follow Raghavan's suggestion in the notes: 'vividhālaṃkārā mṛgamadapaṅkam ity atrāpekṣ itaṃpadadvayam'.

13. Here I quote the text as it appears in Raghavan's edition, noting with an asterix forms that seem grammatically or semantically suspect. Raghavan has already noted these and has sometimes provided emendations in the text or in the notes.

> Purā viśalānagare dhanado nāma dhārmikaḥ | vaiśyokaḥare badhudhanī svakulācāratatparaḥ ||4.89|| tasya* kaścic chukaṃ divyaṃ pañcavarṇaṃ mahaujasam |
>
> nāvikaḥ samupānī ya dattavān dvīpasambhavam ||4.90|| taṃ gṛhītvā vaṇig divye kāñcane ratnamaṇḍite | pañjare nyasya vividhaiḥ phalaiḥ puṇḍrekṣujair guḍaiḥ ||4.91|| pupoṣa nirataṃ putram iva sarvaguṇānvitam | sarvabhāṣāsu nipuṇaḥ sarvavidyāviśāradaḥ ||4.92|| vivardhata śukaḥ prītiṃ janayan pālakasya saḥ | tasya bhāryā viśālākṣī rūpeṇāpratimā bhuvi ||4.93|| vibhuṃ nirasya satataṃ parakīyā babhūva ha | bahir dvāre sadā sthitvā kāminaḥ saṃpratī kṣatī* ||4.94|| vipaṇiṃ gatavati nāthe vividhālaṃkārasaṃkumuda* paṅkam | kuṃkumacandanamiśraṃ liptvā

kucayoḥ prayāti saṃketam ||4.95|| madanabhūtaparājitamānasā vadar ājitamauktikacitrakā | sadanamāgatakāmukamaṇḍalī hṛdayarañjanam ācaratī* babhau ||4.96|| madhuravacanaiḥ kāṃścid yūnaḥ kaṭākṣ-avilokanaiḥ vividhamadhurāhāraiḥ kāṃścid viśeṣadhanārpaṇaiḥ | ghanakucaparī rambhaiḥ kāṃścit kaṭītaṭasevanaiḥ pratidinam iyaṃ santarpyās te manobhavavaibhave ||4.97|| evaṃ vasantīṃ gṛhiṇīṃ dine dine vilokya kīraḥ pracukopa tāṃ prati | gṛhāgatāyāśunivedayad* yathā tathā purā dṛṣṭam upetya so viśe ||4.98|| taveyaṃ gṛhiṇī deva kulaṭā caṭulāśayā | ahardivaṃ paraiḥ puṃbhī ramate militā mudā ||4.99|| yaṃ yaṃ paśyati puruṣaṃtaruṇaṃ śaraṇāgataṃ paraṃ purataḥ | taṃ taṃ parirabhya mudā datvā rataṃ punaḥ preṣayati ||4.100|| evaṃ pratyaham antargṛhavṛttaṃ bodhayantam anuvelam | hantuṃ śukam ātmani sā cintām akarot sakhībhir anvartham ||4.101|| śrutvā śukavacaḥ satyaṃ manvāno vaiśyasattamaḥ | dārān santāḍayāmāsa tarjanair marjanair muhuḥ ||4.102|| evaṃsantarjitā tasya gṛhiṇī krodhasaṃyutā | upāyaṃ kancid ālocya śukapanjarasannidhau ||4.103|| caṇakān upale kṣiptvā pipeṣa dhvanim udvaman* | upariṣṭāc chukasyāṅgeva varṣodakavipruṣaḥ ||4.104|| timire dīpam uddīpya darpaṇaṃ bhrāmayat*puraḥ | śilācakradhvaniṃ megharāvaṃ mene śukas tadā ||4.105|| ambhaḥ pṛṣatkapatanaṃ varṣodakam amanyata | dīpāntikādarś aparibhramaṇaṃ vidyud ity ayam ||4.106|| mene tataḥ samāyātaṃ vaiśyam āha sa sādaram | niśāyāṃ kva sthito 'siv ṛṣṭyā kiṃ nu na cārditaḥ ||4.107|| rātryāṃ vṛṣṭir mahaty āsīdity uktaḥ prāha* taṃ khagam | kva vṛṣṭiḥ patitā rātryāṃ śukatūṣṇīṃ* bravīṣi mām ||4.108|| mṛṣāvādī bhavān adya vijnātaṃ bhāṣitaṃ tava | evam eva purāpi tvam uktavān ayi nityaśaḥ ||4.109|| majjāyāṃ praty apīty uktvā krodharaktāntalocanaḥ | jaghāna daṇḍam ādāya śukaṃ kopād athorujaḥ ||4.110|| avicārya śukaṃ hatvā dṛṣṭvā ca gṛhiṇī gatim | paścat tāpasamāyuktaḥ śukam smṛtvā rudan sadā ||4.111|| (Kalyaṇamalla, 'Sulaimaccarita', in *Mālayamarutam: A Collection of Minor Works in Sanskrit: Poems, Plays, Hymns, and Anthologies*, ed. V. Raghavan [Tirupati: Central Sanskrit Institute, 1966]).

14. The wide and rapid diffusion of Jāmī's work is the focus of an ongoing interdisciplinary working group organized by the University of Chicago, the Neubauer Collegium, and the Franke Institute, titled 'A Worldwide Literature: Jāmī (1414–1492) in the Dār al-Islām and Beyond'. For more information on Jāmī and on the extent and magnitude of the textual tradition his work inaugurated, see the project's website: http://lucian.uchicago.edu/blogs/jamidaralislam/.

15. The regional specificity of Śrīvara and his *Kathākautuka* are discussed at greater length in my PhD thesis ('Translation and History: The Development of a Kashmiri Textual Tradition from ca.1000–1500', PhD diss, University of California Berkeley, 2015).

16. The Sanskrit quoted from the *Kathākautuka* is based on the edition of Schmidt:

> Yad idam dṛśyate sarvaṃ nānākautukasaṃyutam | tadavaihi bhavādarśe pratibimbam iva sthitam ||12.32|| yathā kiṃcit samālokya darpaṇe pratibimbitam | mano dhāvati tatraiva kartuṃ tan niścayaṃ muhuḥ ||12.33|| tathaiva sakalaṃ subhru jagat sthāvarajaṅgamam | dṛṣṭvā māyāmayaṃ śambhuṃ dhyāyanty ekaṃ manīṣiṇaḥ ||12.34|| mānasaṃ ced varārohe rūpadarśanalālasam | paśyaikaṃ śaraṇaṃ mattaṃ hṛdi devaṃ manoramam ||12.35|| dṛṣṭvaiva māmakaṃ rūpaṃ vinaśyat kiṃsukhaṃ tava | sthiraṃ sarvagataṃ tasmāt subhru śambhor vilokaya ||12.36|| iti tadvacanaṃ śrutvā gatamoheva sābhavat | tatkṣaṇāt tatpadāmbhojam praṇanāma muhur muhuḥ ||12.37|| tatas sā gajaratnāni tāni tāṃ sampadaṃ tathā | vihāyādāya kāṣāyapaṭṭam ekaṃ sumadhyamā ||12.38|| bhasmabhūṣitasarvāṅgā bandhusnehavivarjitā | vratājinī va tapase jagāma gahanaṃ vanam ||12.39|| kṛcchrātikṛcchraprāka-vratadhūtamano 'malā | sarvatīrthāvagahena śuddhadehābhavat tadā ||12.40||

17. Śrīvara, *Kathākautuka*, v. 1.2. Here I cite from my own provisional edition of the *Kathākautuka*, which is based on a close reading of the two published editions (Schmidt, 1893 and Shivadatta and Parab, 1901).

18. In the *Kathākautuka*, the half-verse containing this term reads as a statement, in brief, of Śrīvara's translational methodology. He writes:

> Viracyate yāvanaśāstrabaddhā kathā mayā nirjarabhāṣ ayeyam. ||1.2 cd||
>
> This story (*kathā*), bound to Muslim *śāstra*, is fashioned (*viracyate*) by me through the unaging language [=Sanskrit].

(Śrīvara, *Kathākautuka*).

Bibliography

Ali, Daud. *Courtly Culture and Political Life in Early Medieval India*. Cambridge: Cambridge University Press, 2006.

Eaton, Richard. *The Rise of Islam and the Bengal Frontier, 1204–1760*. Berkeley: University of California Press, 1993.

Flood, Finnbar. *Objects of Translation: Material Culture and the Medieval 'Hindu-Muslim' Encounter*. Princeton: Princeton University Press, 2009.

Gode, P.K. 'Date of Udayarāja and Jagaddhara'. *Journal of the University of Bombay* 9, no. 2(1940): 101–15.

Hardy, Peter. *Historians of Medieval India: Studies in Indo-Muslim Historical Writing*. London: Luzac, 1960.

Hodgson, Marshall. *The Venture of Islam: Conscience and History in a World Civilization*. Chicago: University of Chicago Press, 1974.

Kalyaṇamalla. *Sulaimaccarita*. In *Mālayamarutam: A Collection of Minor Works in Sanskrit: Poems, Plays, Hymns, and Anthologies*, edited by V. Raghavan. Tirupati: Central Sanskrit Institute, 1966.

Kapadia, Aparna. 'The Last Chakravartin: The Gujarati Sultan as "Universal King" in Fifteenth Century Sanskrit Poetry'. *The Medieval History Journal* 16, no. 1 (2013): 63–88.

Mahdi, Muhsined. *The Arabian Nights*, translated by Husain Haddawy. New York: Norton, 1990.

Minkowski, Christopher. 'King David in Oudh: A Bible Story in Sanskrit and the Just King at an Afghan Court'. Available at http://users.ox.ac.uk/~ball2185/Minkowski.Inaugural.pdf, last accessed on 7 March 2006.

Orsini, Francesca. 'How to Do Multilingual History? Lessons from Fifteenth- and Sixteenth-Century North India'. *IESHR* 49, no. 2 (2012): 225–46.

Pollock, Sheldon. *Language of the Gods in the World of Men: Sanskrit, Power, and Culture in Premodern India*. Berkeley: University of California Press, 2006.

Ricci, Ronit. *Islam Translated: Literature, Conversion and the Arabic Cosmopolis of South and Southeast Asia*. Chicago: University of Chicago Press, 2011.

Śrīvara. *Śrīvara's Kathākautuka: Die Geschichte von Joseph in Persisch-Indischem Gewande Sanskrit und Deutsch*, edited by Richard Schmidt. Kiel: C.F. Haeseler, 1898.

———. *The Kathâkautuka of Śrîvara*, edited by Mahamahopadyaya Pandit Shivadatta and Kashinath Pandurang Parab. Bombay: Nirnayasagar Press, 1901.

Truschke, Audrey. 'Cosmopolitan Encounters: Sanskrit and Persian at the Mughal Court', PhD diss., Columbia University, 2012.

Udayarāja. *Rājavinodamahākāvyam*, edited by G.N. Bahura. Jaipur: Rajasthan Oriental Research Institute, 1954.

Wagoner, Phillip. '"Sultan among Hindu Kings": Dress, Titles, and the Islamicization of Hindu Culture at Vijaynagara'. *Journal of Asian Studies* 55, no. 4 (November 1996): 851–80.

'A Worldwide Literature: Jāmī (1414–1492) in the *Dār al-Islām* and Beyond'. Last modified on 14 February 2014. Available at http://lucian.uchicago.edu/blogs/jamidaralislam/.

4

SAMUEL WRIGHT*

Making Sense of *Bhāṣā* in Sanskrit

Rādhāmohan Ṭhakkur's *Mahābhāvānusāriṇī-ṭīkā* and Literary Culture in Early Eighteenth-Century Bengal

In a volume that primarily addresses the literary cultures of north India, I would like to shift that centre slightly and focus upon the literary cultures of eastern India, specifically Bengal. I say slightly because, despite the fact that Bengal and north India constitute separate regions, their boundaries were indeed porous—a conterminous location being literary culture, especially Vaiṣṇava literary culture, between the fifteenth and eighteenth centuries. For example, the north Indian city of Vrindavan played a central role not only in the literary imagination of north Indian authors of Vaiṣṇava devotional lyrics such as Surdas and Hariram Vyas, but also in the imagination of their counterparts in Bengal, who included this and other locales of north India as part of the literary geography of their compositions.[1]

Yet, while it is from these lyrics that we learn about some of the categories of Vaiṣṇava literary culture in Bengal—literary geography being only one of many—it is from engaging with these lyrics that we also learn about their fascinating history of preservation. Indeed, one hallmark of Vaiṣṇava lyrics from Bengal is that they are preserved primarily in anthologies compiled from the beginning of the eighteenth century by scholars and poets from within the Gauḍīya Vaiṣṇava tradition itself. These anthologists travelled widely throughout the region in order to collect these lyrics and, in all likelihood, recorded many of them in writing for the first time. It is these anthologies (*padāvalīs*) from Bengal upon which I want to focus here.

Among those who collected lyrics or songs (*gītas*)[2] in Bengal, Visvanath Cakravartin, a well-known Sanskrit scholar, is credited with compiling the first padāvalī entitled the *Kṣaṇadāgītacintāmaṇi* (The Gem of Night Songs) in approximately 1700 CE. This was followed in approximately 1725 CE by two more padāvalīs: the *Padāmṛtasamudra* (The Ocean of Lyrical Nectar) of Radhamohan Thakkur and the slightly later *Gītacandrodaya* (The Moonrise of Song) of Narahari Cakravartin.[3] Perhaps the most well-known padāvalī, however, is the *Padakalpataru* (The Wishing Tree of Heaven in Lyrical Form), also called the *Gītakalpataru*, of Vaisnavadas compiled around 1750 CE. Of all the anthologies, this has the largest number of songs (over 3,000), and has been treated in modern secondary literature as the high-water mark for the anthology genre while other padāvalīs are mentioned in only a cursory manner.[4]

This elision of other padāvalīs occurs despite the fact that Vaisnavadas understood his work not as a superior outlier in the genre, but as modelled after and dependent upon previous anthologies and anthologists in Bengal. At the end of his *Padakalpataru*, he makes known his dependence upon Radhamohan's *Padāmṛtasamudra*:

> Within the lineage of *ācārya-prabhu* [Srinivasacarya] is Sri Radhamohan....
> He compiled a book called the *Padāmṛtasamudra*.
> I became obsessed with that book and sung songs (*kari gān*) from it.
> So, having collected *pads* by traveling widely to many places and taken all of his pads as well, I have modeled this book after that foundational work (*mūla-grantha*). It takes as many old pads and compiles them into a single work entitled the *Gītakalpataru*.[5]

If Radhamohan's anthology is considered to be a foundational work according to Vaisnavadas, then what makes it so? Two reasons are notable. First, Radhamohan's *Padāmṛtasamudra* is the first large collection of songs and seems to have eclipsed Visvanath's anthology in importance due its unprecedented breadth: 740 songs and 51 authors in the *Padāmṛtasamudra* versus 308 songs and 48 authors in Visvanath's work. In addition, Radhamohan includes a number of songs by Candidas (fifteenth century), one of the most famous and earliest authors of songs in Bengal, whereas he is absent in Visvanath's anthology.[6] Second, the *Padāmṛtasamudra* is the only anthology to contain a comprehensive scholarly apparatus—a commentary that deals with each song included in the collection. Radhamohan's commentary, entitled the *Mahābhāvānusāriṇī-ṭīkā* (A Gloss according to the Foremost Sentiment), is significant because it is written in Sanskrit—one of only three known Sanskrit commentaries on vernacular compositions from Bengal.[7]

The language difference between the vernacular of the songs, on the one hand, and Sanskrit, the language of the commentary, on the other, is not minor: aside from obvious lexical and grammatical differences, the orthography of the songs follows the phonaesthetic preferences of *Brajbuli* and grammatical rules are regularly flaunted for the purpose of achieving poetic aims.[8] This means that Radhamohan must make sense of a very informal register—what we might call a casual register—of the vernacular in Sanskrit.[9]

Focusing on Radhamohan's commentary, this chapter is divided into two large sections each with its own subsections. The first section closely examines the language of the commentary and provides a number of examples from the text. This section is divided into three parts: the first discusses the language categories used by Radhamohan, the second discusses the literary tropes of the songs identified by Radhamohan, specifically *śleṣa* (punning), and the third discusses Radhamohan's translations or renderings from the vernacular into Sanskrit. The second section steps back from the text and attempts to provide somewhat broad conclusions about the significance of Radhamohan's work for the history of literary culture in Bengal. This section is divided into two parts: the first discusses how Radhamohan engages with the vernacular and the second discusses two literary projects I consider to be part of Radhamohan's commentary.[10]

Bhāṣā and Sanskrit

Thus far, we have been using the terms 'vernacular' and 'Sanskrit' as if they are natural categories—and the full extent of categories—for Radhamohan. Before we proceed further, it is necessary to determine the language categories that Radhamohan actually uses in his commentary.

The term Radhamohan uses throughout his commentary to refer to non-Sanskrit words is 'bhāṣā'—language.[11] This usage seems to follow the practice in premodern India of using this term to contrast the vernacular with Sanskrit, although there is evidence that the vernacular could also be referred to as *subhāṣā* (high language/vernacular) in some places.[12] Bhāṣā is a major category for Radhamohan, and is used throughout his commentary primarily to refer to words in the songs that are etymologically related to Sanskrit but whose orthography has changed. For example, a line by Balaram (sixteenth century) reads:

> She is happy—but then awakes again
> In that trickery (*biẏāj*) of dreams.
>
> [Radhamohan glosses:] The bhāṣā of '*vyāja* (Sanskrit: trickery, deceit)' is 'biẏāj'.[13]

In other places, however, a word is not labelled as bhāṣā. Rather, this label is implied from the context and is used when Radhamohan wants to simply place the word in apposition to Sanskrit. For example, a couplet from a song by Vidyapati (fifteenth century) reads:

> When he'll insist on grabbing hold of my bodice (*kām̐cūẏā*),
> I will stop his hand with mine—casting side-glances
> With my eyes half open.
>
> [Radhamohan glosses:] 'kām̐cūẏā' '*kañculī* (Sanskrit: bodice)'.[14]

More complex examples are also found that illustrate the popular component required for a word to be called bhāṣā. A couplet in a song by Govindadas (sixteenth century) reads:

> The sounds of his flute are faint and far away—
> At every passing moment, the heart is consumed (*bharipūr*) with a burning fire.
>
> [Radhamohan glosses:] At every moment, it [the heart] is consumed (*paripūrṇa*) by a fire—a fire of sexual passion.
> Even today, the bhāṣā 'bharipūr' is spoken.[15]

In another example, a couplet in a song by Simha Bhupati (fifteenth to sixteenth century) reads:

> With timidity, submissiveness, and hesitation, she comes near—
> The lord of Braj, though, versed in the ways of love,
> Remains calm inside.

> Such skills in lovemaking then this business (*kājar*) of deception—
> Finally, hc appears in all his glory.
>
> [Radhamohan glosses:] The line that reads 'such skills in lovemaking then this business (kājar) of deception' means skill in relation to lovemaking and frustration related to that. In other words, the business related to that, which is a special type of trickery or deception (*kaitava*). Therefore, the bhāṣā of [the Sanskrit word] 'kārya' is 'kājar'.[16]

The issue here is the word 'kājar', which is usually read as a variation on the word 'kājal' (kohl). Radhamohan explains, however, that here this word is rather the bhāṣā of the Sanskrit word *kārya* (Sanskrit: action, affair, business).

While these types of examples are the most numerous, Radhamohan also identifies words that are more localized and employs a special category for them: *deśa-bhāṣā*. For example, Radhamohan comments on a couplet in a song by Govindadas that reads:

> He is the shining color of an emerald mirror—
> Kamdev is a guard (*anaṅga āgor*) of his body for viewing pleasure.
>
> [Radhamohan glosses:] With regard to the phrase 'anaṅga āgor'—here *āgor* means *āgol* since a change in the letters *ra* and *la* gives the same meaning; the meaning [of the word] is 'guard (*rakṣaka*)'. Even today, the word 'āgol' in the language of a particular region (deśa-bhāṣā) is meant in the sense of a guard of houses, and so on, or of granaries, and so on.[17]

The category of deśa-bhāṣā or similar localizing terminology is used frequently throughout Radhamohan's commentary. A song by Campati (sixteenth century?) contains the word *paiṛ*, which is glossed by Radhamohan as bhāṣā belonging to Utkal (*utkala-deśīya*), meaning 'raw coconut' (*apakva-nārikela*).[18] A song by Vidyapati contains the word *oj*, which Radhamohan glosses as bhāṣā from another region (*deśântarīya*) that means 'lotus' (*abja*).[19] Commenting on another song by Govindadas, Radhamohan tells us that it contains the regional bhāṣā word (*daiśika-bhāṣā*) *lunik*, which means 'fresh butter' (*nava-nīta*).[20] In yet another song by Govindadas containing the reduplicated word *ḍaha ḍaha*, Radhamohan glosses the word as the bhāṣā of a particular region (deśa-bhāṣā) that 'is indicative of the meaning of "burning" (*dāhârtha-vācaka*)'.[21]

All of these examples show Radhamohan employing a certain language category (bhāṣā or deśa-bhāṣā) and glossing words within those categories with their Sanskrit equivalents. Yet what of Radhamohan's use of Sanskrit as a category? Surprisingly, he seems to only use the word 'Sanskrit' once in his commentary in relation to one of his own compositions. The relevant line from his song and commentary reads:

> Beautiful songs made up of lyrics of accolades showered (*girata*) Gaurī (Rādhikā).
>
> [Radhamohan glosses:] Special compositions—songs composed with lyrics that have rustic melodies containing many accolades—*girata*, that is, 'describe (*kathayati*)' [Rādhikā] in such a way through bhāṣās beginning with Sanskrit, and so on.[22]

In the context of our above discussion, this apparent inclusion of Sanskrit within the category of bhāṣā is definitely confusing. To be sure, the *Padāmṛtasamudra* does contain Sanskrit lyrics by Jayadeva and Radhamohan. This could mean that bhāṣā, as used here, ought to be taken in a very general sense of 'language', rather than as a spoken or regional language. Or, it could mean spoken Sanskrit literature (*kāvya*) as opposed to Vedic verse (*chandas*). However, this remains a source of confusion for me in Radhamohan's conception of language categories that is not easily resolved.[23]

To sum up, Radhamohan's language categories move from Sanskrit to a more localized language he calls bhāṣā and then finally to a very localized language he calls deśa-bhāṣā. This appears to fall in line with much older categories of language, namely the categories of *tatsama, tadbhava,* and *deśī*. Leaving aside the category of tatsama, Radhamohan's glosses of bhāṣā words we examined earlier (and throughout the commentary) do seem to be glosses of tadbhava words, that is, words that come from Sanskrit but which have gone through some type of orthographic or semantic change; and his glosses of deśa-bhāṣā words seem to be 'deśī' words, that is, words not etymologically related to Sanskrit. But Radhamohan is clearly not concerned with the etymological relationship (or lack thereof) between these words and Sanskrit. Rather, he is concerned with the semantic relationship between these words and Sanskrit.

Literary Tropes of *Bhāṣā*

Radhamohan's commentary also highlights specific literary tropes of the vernacular. While this includes the trope of *vyañjanā* or *dhvani* (suggestion), his commentary highlights a more sophisticated literary trope: śleṣa.[24] The reading of śleṣa in the songs is significant and will be addressed conceptually later in the chapter in relation to other vernaculars and Sanskrit. Here, due to space constraints, I examine only two examples in order to gauge how it has been used according to Radhamohan. In both examples below, I provide the song followed by Radhamohan's commentary that highlights the śleṣa; then I provide my own śleṣa reading of the song.

Perhaps the most complex use of śleṣa highlighted by Radhamohan occurs in an erotic song composed by Govindadas. Govindadas's song begins:

> Blowing on his flute, he stokes the
> Desire of the group [of cow-herding girls]. A fire-like exhilaration in the heart.
> Beholding (*daraśan*) and imbibing (*pān-i*),
> Then amorously touching and caressing (*paraś sohāgan*).
> Sweat of the brow is added to the mix.
> Her friend says 'he is a master goldsmith (*chaila sonār*)'.

> [Radhamohan glosses:] 'Chaila sonār' means a skillful/master goldsmith. In other words, having taken that my jewel, my love, through sheer power and then having soldered it with his jewel, his own love, and making a necklace, he placed it around my neck. Through the trope of exceeding expectations (vyatireka)[25], namely 'that he won me over because of his own jewel, which is exceedingly more valuable or important [than mine]', an expertise in that, that is, his skill in goldwork, is made known. The meaning of the 'śleṣa' is that 'kul' means 'wood', that is, wood of the jujube tree.

Radhamohan identifies 'kul' as the śleṣa in the song, which enables not just a rereading of that word but also this entire portion of the song. This is a result of the vast difference in meaning: kul means not simply a group or assemblage (namely, of cow-herding girls), but, as Radhamohan tells us, this word in the song is part of a śleṣa that refers to the wood of the jujube tree used by goldsmiths in their kilns. As a result, the line beginning with the word 'beholding/examination' can be read as describing the work of a goldsmith as well as the act of seduction.

> Blowing on his blowpipe, he stokes the
> Fuel—the jujube wood. A powerful breath in the chest.[26]
> Examination and water, then borax and striking,[27]
> Sweat of the brow is added to the mix.
> Her friend says 'he is a master goldsmith'.[28]

Another important aspect of Radhamohan's commentary here is the identification of the trope of vyatireka (exceeding expectations). If I read this correctly, this is the result of Krishna placing his jewel (identified here as his love) around the neck of the devotee. This implies an inversion of the normal direction of devotion from devotee to Krishna: Krishna is joining his love with the heart of the devotee instead of the devotee joining his/her love with Krishna's.

The second example, a song by Vidyapati, illustrates that śleṣa can be found in poems composed by authors who are quite early. The opening lines read:

> Her friend says—today I experienced such wondrous confusion in the temple-like flower grove!
> It was as if the clouds were covered over by lightening
> And the moon was a blue lotus.
> Seeing that the most excellent jewel—a single unornamented braid (*pheṇī*)[29]—was exhibited, the other peahens went elsewhere.
> On the peak of Mt Meru the river of the gods (*sura-taraṅgiṇī*)
> Rose up in waves.
>
> [Radhamohan glosses the last line:] Then, the *sura-taraṅgiṇī*, that is, the Gaṅgā—compared to the movement of a pearl necklace—became rough (*taral bhela*), in other words [that is, in Sanskrit], rose up in waves (*ūrmi-taralā babhuva*) on the twin peaks of Mt Meru [or, upon the breasts]. And so on that view, the meaning of that [that is, sura-taraṅgiṇī], which includes the meaning of 'a necklace' (*hāra*), is made known through a segmentation (*śabda-śleṣa*), that is, that which is swaying or moving in lovemaking (*surate raṅgiṇī*).[30]
>
> [The last line might then read:]
> Over her voluptuous breasts, the pearl necklace swung about.[31]

Through a clever use of segmentation, Radhamohan is providing an alternative reading for the song: the Gaṅgā is equated with Rādhā's pearl necklace and the waves of the river equated with the swaying of the necklace. This śleṣa is a śabda śleṣa, that is, it segments the word in a different way to create a different meaning.[32] Here *suratataraṅgiṇī* can be either *sura-taraṅgiṇī* (the river of the gods, that is, the Gaṅgā) or *surata-raṅgiṇī* (that which is swaying or moving in lovemaking); and Mt Meru is often used to refer to the breasts.

Radhamohan's identification of śleṣa in the songs—both *artha śleṣa* and śabda śleṣa—means that these poems in the vernacular can do what Sanskrit does. To be sure, the mentioned examples are not as complex as we see in Sanskrit works. Nor, as discussed in more detail later, is this usage as complex as the use of śleṣa in other vernaculars. Yet, it is significant. Even if Radhamohan is simply making explicit a standard but non-formalized reading practice of these songs that already existed, his analysis is the first attempt to formally employ Sanskrit literary tropes into the analysis and reading of Vaiṣṇava songs from Bengal (and perhaps even the vernacular in general in Bengal).

Bhāṣā into Sanskrit

In our discussion so far, we have examined Radhamohan's commentary in terms of its language categories and the literary trope of śleṣa identified by him. Here we briefly examine how Radhamohan makes sense of the imagery in the songs as well as his translations and/or renderings of the songs into Sanskrit.

A line by Govindadas, which contains a reduplicated word, reads:

> Her beautiful, voluptuous (*ḍal ḍal*) body—
> A shimmering rain cloud.
> Enchantingly dressed.
>
> [Radhamohan glosses:] The phrase 'ḍal ḍal' refers to an almost lascivious beauty (*tāralyam iva lāvaṇyam*).[33]

Notice that Radhamohan does not suggest a Sanskrit equivalent for this reduplicated word, but rather glosses the imagery: a sexually charged beauty.

Radhamohan also translates descriptive terms in the vernacular whose meaning is important for conveying the poetic imagery of a song. A line from one of his songs reads:

> Praise the one whose shimmering body (*jalada-śarīr*) resembles
> The water of the Yamunā.
>
> [Radhamohan self-glosses:] The phrase 'shimmering body (jalada-śarīr)' in the line where it is compared to the water of the Yamunā means a body that is 'resplendent or shining extremely brightly (*dedīpyamāna*)'.[34]

In other places, Radhamohan explains the conventional tropes used in a song. A line from a song by Govindadas reads:

> Having powdered her nose and dressed-up (*nās beś kari aṇge*),
> She goes along the main road.
> Radha is a decent girl.
>
> [Radhamohan glosses:] The line beginning with 'she goes along the main road' means that she has skill in arranging a rendezvous. 'Nose (*nās*)' means a placement of a jewel [on the nose]. 'Garb or clothing (*beś*)' means with those things such as *sindur* in the hair and perfume.[35]

Radhamohan's commentary here presents a full picture of the scene only implied in the song. His commentary highlights the tongue-in-check statement that Radha 'is a decent girl'. On the contrary, she is arranging a secret tryst with Krishna and has dressed up for this purpose with perfume and jewellery—only going on the main road to make people think she has nothing to hide.

While limitations of space preclude us from examining additional areas of interest, other examples would highlight Radhamohan's references to Sanskrit texts such as the *Ujjvalanīlamaṇi*, the *Haribhaktirasāmṛtasindhu*, the *Lalitamādhavanāṭaka*, and the *Haṃsadūta*, all composed by Rupa Goswami (1490–1563 CE), in order to explicate the songs. The choice of these texts is significant because Rupa is one of the founding scholastic figures of Gauḍīya Vaiṣṇavism and by connecting his commentarial analysis with Rupa's textual authority Radhamohan enables the songs to conform doctrinally to this scholastic tradition.[36]

Situating *Bhāṣā*

We have examined with some specificity the ways in which Radhamohan glosses and makes sense of the songs in his commentary. Given the above, what conclusions can we draw with respect to the vernacular in early eighteenth-century Bengal? I now turn to examine three areas of importance: (*a*) language and meaning, (*b*) śleṣa, and (*c*) lexicography.

One of the most striking aspects of Radhamohan's commentary is the largely unproblematic movement between languages and meanings: Sanskrit and bhāṣā as well as Sanskrit and deśa-bhāṣā can stand in apposition. While this may not be so surprising in the case of tatsama words since a lexical relation was already established, this relation with deśa-bhāṣā words is more problematic since there is no formal or historically instantiated lexical relation between a deśa-bhāṣā word and Sanskrit. Despite these issues, Radhamohan appears to completely ignore the debate in Sanskrit linguistic theory about whether the vernacular contains an expressive power (*śakti*) just like Sanskrit or whether it conveys meaning by referencing the Sanskrit word from which it deviates.[37] As this goes unaddressed by him, we must assume that for Radhamohan, bhāṣā, including deśa-bhāṣā, not only has a Sanskrit equivalent and vice versa, but that the type of lexical relationship between bhāṣā or deśa-bhāṣā words and Sanskrit no longer needs to be theorized or the debate is not relevant to his work.

To be sure, Radhamohan is engaging with the vernacular in a unique manner for Bengal. Consider the fact that his commentary quotes from the *Amarakośa* in order to explain words in the vernacular. For example, a line from Govindadas in which Krishna entices Radha reads:

> In a dark-blue pond (*kāsar*) are quivering blue lotuses
> Where no one takes any notice.
>
> [Radhamohan glosses:] That place where blue lotuses quiver in a pool of dark-blue water goes unnoticed by everyone and anyone. The *Amara* [*kośa*] gives these words for 'pool' or 'lake': *kāsāra, sarasi,* and *sara*. The reading of kāsar is in the bhāṣā [from the Sanskrit '*kāsāra*]' (*bhāṣāyāṃ kāsar iti pāṭhaḥ*).[38]

This passage demonstrates that, for Radhamohan, Sanskrit lexical materials are useful for making sense of vernacular texts as well. Whether this is indicative of the broader consensus among scholars at this time requires further research.

The second important aspect of Radhamohan's commentary is his identification of śleṣa as a literary device in the songs. While we have nothing close to the type of engagement with śleṣa as found in Sanskrit works, it is significant that Radhamohan identifies śleṣa in the vernacular. As Yigal Bronner discusses, bi-textual works in the vernacular occurred first in Telugu from the late 1500s. These examples in Telugu are sustained experiments that show an intense interaction with this technique that resulted in works of 'simultaneous narration'.[39] The examples of śleṣa in the songs referenced here only concern one word or small phrases, which means that the experiment with śleṣa in Radhamohan's reading is far more limited and forms a very small area of poetic concern. At the same time, the fact that

Radhamohan highlights the use of śleṣa by poets as old as Vidyāpati as well as in his own songs may indicate that our poets knew about and were experimenting tentatively with śleṣa, but that it never became a popular technique. A less significant alternative is that the use of śleṣa could simply be Radhamohan's own interpretation, rather than a device purposefully used by the poets themselves. Yet, even if this were so, it would still indicate that Radhamohan is expanding the type of literary analysis possible vis-à-vis vernacular poetry.

The third important aspect of Radhamohan's commentary is its significance for the history of lexicography in Bengal. Radhamohan's commentary stands as the first (and likely the only) in-depth attempt in Bengal at glossing the vernacular with Sanskrit—neither of Visvanath's Sanskrit commentaries on vernacular works noted in our introduction come near to the type of analysis undertaken by Radhamohan. While this aspect needs further research, it is clear that we have to consider these works in any account of the history of lexicography in Bengal rather than simply focus on missionary or colonial works from the eighteenth century.[40]

Readership and Prestige

There are arguably two major projects at work in Radhamohan's commentary, both of which raise more questions than answers. First, the commentary provides the Sanskrit reader the necessary tools to make sense of the songs. In each aforementioned case—glossing bhāṣā and deśa-bhāṣā words, indicating examples of śleṣa and dhvani, expounding on the cultural context of a song, rendering or translating parts of a song into Sanskrit, and referencing Sanskrit works of literary theory—the Sanskrit reader is able to turn towards the vernacular with an improved skill set for understanding the songs. Radhamohan does not tell us if this was his intention, though he does tell us that older songs were being increasingly sung, suggesting a rise in their popularity and a literary possibility for a work such as his.[41] This rise in popularity may have meant that Sanskrit readers unacquainted with these songs—both linguistically and aesthetically—constituted a primary audience for Radhamohan. While we cannot confirm this, Radhamohan's commentary, as it is in Sanskrit, would have theoretically been intelligible to Sanskrit scholars outside of Bengal. At the same time, my initial research shows that the distribution of manuscripts is confined to Bengal (where the work continued to be transcribed) despite the work's relevance to scholars in neighbouring regions and Radhamohan's sensitivity to the category of region[42] in his analysis.[43] A possibility may be that Radhamohan had an extra-regional audience in mind when writing, but that his work was never distributed outside of Bengal.

Let us turn now to a second possible project of the commentary. From a purely external perspective, an argument can be made that a purpose of Radhamohan's commentary is to establish the literariness of the songs, in other words, to move these lyrics from the oral (as song) to the literary (as text). This possible shift from orality to textuality as it relates to the vernacularity of Gauḍīya Vaiṣṇava songs has never been theorized, but must form a part of any serious analysis of the anthology genre.

As we are dealing with the category of song, we need to know how song was theorized in Sanskrit literary theory since this is the dominant perspective from which song has been analysed prior to and during our period. As Sheldon Pollock has discussed in detail, premodern Sanskrit scholars theorized song as a place of vernacularity that was 'subliterary', that is, it was a form in which the qualities that constituted the literary were absent.[44] In order to argue, then, that Radhamohan is establishing the literariness of the songs, we would have to demonstrate how his commentary challenges this notion of a 'subliterary' category for song argued for by premodern Sanskrit scholars.

As such, any treatment of this complex issue would need to address a number of aspects and an initial list would include at least five components: first, we would need to show that Radhamohan understands the songs as becoming written works, that is, that they have some form of textual existence when included in his anthology; second, that there is a full range of figures of speech in the songs parallel to Sanskrit; third, that they are connected to literary theory; fourth, that they can be separated as a distinct genre; and fifth, that they contain knowable or learnable lexical, and possibly orthographic, features. While a full treatment of this cannot be undertaken here, a general sketch can be offered.[45]

Reference to a textualizing project as part of the anthology genre—as we saw earlier—is made by Vaisnvadas in his anthology, the *Padakalpataru*. When he speaks of collecting pads (*saṃgraha karā*), he is likely to be speaking of collecting and textualizing these compositions, although a few may have been preserved in writing. More significantly, however, Radhamohan often says that a song included in his anthology is now 'written down'. For example, in introducing the seventh song of the anthology by Govindadas, he says: 'Next, he [Radhamohan] writes down (*likhati*) a song composed by Srimad Govindadas Kaviraj that begins with the words "marigolds and yellow..."; the song destroys all things inauspicious and is in the mode of *śrīmad gauracandra*.'[46] This demonstrates that Radhamohan was aware that he was textualizing oral compositions simply by recording them in his anthology. Radhamohan also performs the function of an editor by (*a*) noting when songs have alternative 'readings (*pāṭha*)'[47] and (*b*) telling us that he has taken it upon himself to finish composing (*racanaṃ kr̥*) songs by Candidas and Vidyapati in which entire stanzas are missing.[48] These editorial activities impose a textual stability on a song as the lacunas and/or alternative readings that may have been part of a song's oral form becomes subsumed into a more editorially authoritative textual form, where these variations can be appreciated, discussed, and marked as non-standard.

We have already discussed the literary tropes of the songs. While metaphor and simile (including categories such as vyatireka) are commonly used, the inclusion of śleṣa and dhvani as figures of speech demonstrates that we are far from a 'subliterary' domain for Gauḍīya Vaiṣṇava song.[49] In fact, Radhamohan demonstrates here, perhaps for the first time, that the vernacular in Bengal is afforded a full range of figures of speech parallel to the Sanskrit literary tradition. This is a large claim and requires more investigation; nevertheless, it cannot be denied that the vernacular now warrants a close reading both aesthetically and semantically precisely because of the literary possibilities of the vernacular made explicit by Radhamohan.

Radhamohan's commentary also connects the songs to a larger body of theoretical writings on *rasa* and typologies of poetic characters: he quotes from Rupa Goswami's works, for example, in order to provide definitional and analytical support. This affords the songs an aesthetic and theoretical authority precisely because they conform to this body of literary-devotional theory, which in turns refers further to standard works of Sanskrit literary theory.[50]

Radhamohan also specifies that the songs in his collection conform to the genre of *kīrtan* not through some popular definition, but through formal definitions found in systematic manuals of song (*gīta-śāstra*).[51] He does not tell us which works he has read, but his intent is clear: to codify the kīrtan as a formal genre in vernacular literary culture.

Finally, Radhamohan's commentary, through the use of the *Amarakośa*, displays how the vernacular lexicon can be learned or at least derived in part from Sanskrit lexical materials in the absence of similar types of texts for the vernacular. In addition, the apposition noted by Radhamohan between Sanskrit and bhāṣā as well as Sanskrit and deśa-bhāṣā theoretically helps to standardize the vernacular in its semantic variations—again, in the absence of lexical materials for the vernacular. Whether this also translates into orthographic standardization remains uncertain.[52]

Again, this is only a very broad sketch; yet it raises serious questions about the work that Radhamohan's *Mahābhāvānusāriṇī-ṭīkā* did for increasing the prestige or literary status of the songs. Indeed, this function of the genre of anthology in general is little discussed in the historiography of literary culture in Bengal,[53] and it occurred as a result of the efforts undertaken not by the poets themselves but by scholars and poets in the eighteenth century who, looking back onto their oral tradition, decided to act as anthologists of that tradition. This demonstrates that the songs, at least from 1700 CE, were a literary success and increased in prestige in part because scholars took them seriously as a literary form and preserved them; and, in the case of Radhamohan, took it upon themselves to explain their literariness.

Notes

* I would like to thank all the participants of the conference for a lively engagement with the ideas in this chapter as well as Thibaut d'Hubert and Tyler Williams for a critical reading of an earlier draft of this chapter. I would also like to thank Shweta Banerjee for musing with me on the ways to describe the lotuses in the *pukur* near our house in Bhowanipore.

1. For north Indian authors, see Allison Busch, *Poetry of Kings: The Classical Hindi Literature of Mughal India* (Oxford: Oxford University Press, 2011), 26. For Gauḍīya Vaiṣṇava authors and Vrindavan, see Radhamohan's *Padāmr̥tasamudra*, ed. Uma Ray (Kalikata: University of Calcutta, 1391 BS [c. 1984]), §63 and §736; for Mathura, see §63 and §736, §459; for Yamunā River, see Cakrvartin (Ghanasyam) Narahari, comp., *Gītacandrodaya* (Navadvip: Haridas Das, 463 Gaurabda, 1948), §3, 185, and Radhamohan, *Padāmr̥tasamudra* §486.

2. Our authors refer to these lyrics as both gītas (songs) and *padas*. I follow Radhamohan Thakkur's preference in the chapter: 'padâmr̥tasamudrâkhyaḥ sad-bhakta-gīta-saṃgrahaḥ' (*Padāmr̥tasamudra, maṅgala* v. 21, 3, [Ray]).

3. Narahari also authored an anthology consisting solely of his own compositions entitled the *Gauracaritracintāmaṇi* (Tony K. Stewart, *The Final*

Word: The Caitanya Caritamrta and the Grammar of Religious Tradition [Oxford: Oxford University Press, 2010], 162–3).

4. J. C. Ghosh, *Bengali Literature* (London: Oxford University Press, 1948), 64; D. Dineshchandra Sen, *History of Bengali Language and Literature* (Calcutta: University of Calcutta, 1954), 562–3. The earliest padāvalī would be the now lost (or perhaps never-existing) *Padasamudra* by Manoharadas (sixteenth century) (Sen, *Bengali Language and Literature,* 479–80). Govindadas is said to have collected his own songs (Dineshchandra Sen, *Vaiṣṇava Literature of Mediaeval Bengal* [Calcutta: University of Calcutta, 1917], 202); while we have no record of the text, it is likely that Radhamohan used it (see Radhamohan, *Padāmr̥tasamudra,* commentary on §7, 501 [Ray]). Rupa Goswami compiled a collection of songs, but these are in Sanskrit (see Lutjeharms in this volume for a treatment of this work). For additional anthologies, see Vaisnavadas, comp., *Padakalpataru: An Anthology of Vaiṣṇava Lyric,* ed. Satishcandra Ray (Calcutta: Bangiya Sahitya Parishat, 1322–30 BS, 1915–23), vol. 5, 1–16.

5. Vaisnavadas, *Padakalpataru,* fourth *śākhā,* 2224. All translations are my own unless otherwise noted. Transliteration is provided except in (*a*) the names of the authors of the songs (as well as Krishna and Radha) and honorific prefixes to names such as Sri (that is, Śrī) and (*b*) place–names. For Sanskrit, standard transliteration is used; for Bangla, the Library of Congress (2012) rules are followed except in the case of the final inherent vowel. This is not transliterated unless a word is the first member of a compound (for example, 'jalada-śarīr'), when a word ends in a conjunct (for example, 'grantha'), when a word is a past passive participle (for example, 'girata'), and when a word ends in/*h*/(for example, 'ḍaha'). This method concerning the final inherent vowel is also followed in the names of the authors of the songs.

6. Radhamohan, *Padāmr̥tasamudra,* 26 (Ray's introduction). It is possible that Visvanath did not finish compiling his anthology.

7. The two others are the *Payāraṭīkā* on the *Caitanyacaritāmr̥ta* and the *Ṭippanī* on the *Premabhakticandrikā*, both by Visvanath Cakravartin. There is some disagreement about the authenticity of Visvanath's *Payāraṭīkā* (personal communication with Tony K. Stewart). I would like to thank the Bhaktivedanta Research Centre (Kolkata) for providing me access to the *Payāraṭīkā*. Also important to note is Bharatcandra Ray's bilingual octet, *Nāgāṣṭaka* (An Octet for [Ramdev] Nag), written prior to 1749, composed in Sanskrit with accompanying Bangla translation (see Sukumar Sen, *Bāṅgālā sāhityer itihās, dvitīya khaṇḍa, saptadaś—aṣṭadaś śatābdī* [Kolkata: Ananda Publishers, 1975], 429).

8. See Edward Dimock and Roushan Jahan, ed., *Bengali Vaiṣṇava Lyrics: A Reader for Advanced Students* (Chicago: South Asian Languages Research Program, 2006), 13–15, for more discussion.

9. Radhamohan seems at home in Sanskrit and the vernacular, composing songs in both for inclusion into his anthology. Despite the importance of Radhamohan's *ṭīkā*, I can find no treatment of the work outside Ray's lengthy introduction to her edition.

10. Radhamohan tells us in his commentary that he is the great-grandson of Srinivasacarya (Radhamohan, *Padāmṛtasamudra*, 684), and that (via a pun in his verse) Jagadananda is his guru (Radhamohan, *Padāmṛtasamudra*, 488). From two well-known letters, we know he flourished between 1719 and 1731 CE (Yajnesvar Chauduri, ed., *Nabadvīp Mahimā of Kānticandra Rāṛhī* [Nabadvip: Nabadvip Puratattva Parishad, 2004], 342–46). It is said that he was from Malihati (Bardhaman) and was the teacher of Maharaja Nandakumar, Rabindranarayan, and Krsnaprasad Thakur (Radhamohan, *Padāmṛtasamudra*, 26 [Ray's introduction]).

11. This is the standard English gloss of the term. Radhamohan does not give any definition or explanation of this term, although he does suggest that one aspect of bhāṣā is that it is spoken and/or part of popular usage. See notes 15 and 18.

12. See Busch, *Poetry of Kings*, 8, for Braj, and Rich Freeman, 'Genre and Society: The Literary Culture of Premodern Kerala', in *Literary Culture in History: Reconstructions from South Asia*, ed. Sheldon Pollock (Berkeley: University of California Press, 2003), 437–43, for Malayalam. Examples of *subhāṣā* are known in Tripura (Sen, *History of Bengali Language and Literature*, 14).

13. §579 and commentary: 'vyājasya bhāṣā biẏāj iti' (662). All references are to Uma Ray's edition unless otherwise noted. I provide the text here (as well as for song §127 and §235 later) to demonstrate how Radhamohan relates the bhāṣā term with Sanskrit.

14. §539 and commentary. I thank Thibaut d'Hubert for correcting my earlier reading of this song.

15. §127 and commentary: 'anukṣaṇaṃ madana-dahanena tad agninā paripūrṇaḥ | adyâpi loke bharipūr iti bhāṣā ucyate' (561).

16. §541 and commentary.

17. §34 and commentary.

18. §235 and commentary: 'raw coconut' is spoken using the bhāṣā word *paiṛ* by those belonging to the place of Utkal (*apakva-nārikelam utkala-deśīyaiḥ paiṛ iti bhāṣayôcyate*).

19. §293 and commentary.

20. §421 and commentary.

21. §440 and commentary.

22. §366 and commentary. Radhamohan glosses 'Gaurī' with 'Rādhikā' here.

23. For the orality and social performance of Sanskrit kāvya, see Sheldon Pollock, *Language of the Gods in the World of Men: Sanskrit,*

Culture and Power in Premodern India (Berkeley: University of California Press, 2006), 84–6.

24. For *vyañjanā* or dhvani, see these songs and corresponding commentaries: §40, §113, §127, §136, §142, §158, §474, and §571. For śleṣa, see these songs and corresponding commentaries: maṅgala v. 4 (Radhamohan), §176 (Govindadas), §215 (Govindadas), §296 (Radhamohan), §302 (Vidyapati), §335 (Anantadas), §336 (Govindadas), §404 (Vidyapati), §488 (Govindadas), and §599 (Govindadas). I have tried to be comprehensive in both these lists.

25. For this trope, see Busch, *Poetry of Kings*, 76.

26. §599:

beṇuk phuk buk madanânal
kul-indhan māhā jāri |

The word *buk* reads *buke* in the *Padakalpataru* (§101). Incorporating this śleṣa into these two *caraṇ*s is not easy. I have read 'buk' as 'kiln', 'anala' as 'breath' (an extension of one of its Sanskrit meanings, 'wind'), and *madana* in a somewhat strained manner as 'powerful'.

27. I read 'pānī' as 'water' and *sohāgan* as *sohāgā* or borax (as per Ray in Radhamohan, *Padāmr̥tasamudra*, 409).

28. §599 and commentary.

29. Radhamohan glosses *pheṇī* as *veṇī*—an unornamented braid of the hair worn by a woman signifying that her husband is away.

30. The reading 'surateraṅgiṇī' is taken from Vidyaratna's edition—a variation from 'surata-raṅgiṇī' in Ray's edition.

31. §302 and commentary. The Gaṅgā, especially its physicality, is often compared to a pearl necklace. See commentary on §307 (613): 'sur-dhunī gaṅgā dhārā muktâhāra iti jñeyam |'.

32. See Abhinavagupta, *Dhvanyāloka of Abhinavagupta with the Locana and Bālapriyā Commentaries*, ed. Pattabhiram Sastri (Benaras: Kashi Sanskrti Series, 1940), 218–19, for a discussion on śabda-śleṣa (or *śabda-bhaṅga-śleṣa*) in Sanskrit literary theory.

33. §35 and commentary. Another song by Govindadas (§150) contains the reduplicated word *diśi diśi*, glossed by Radhamohan as 'in every direction (*sarvāsu dikṣu*)'.

34. §486 and commentary.

35. §330 and commentary.

36. For an example referencing the *Ujjvalanīlamaṇi*, see §177 and commentary.

37. Sheldon Pollock, 'Languages of Science in Early Modern India', in *Forms of Knowledge in Early Modern Asia: Explorations in the Intellectual History of India and Tibet, 1500–1800*, ed. Sheldon Pollock (Durham: Duke University Press, 2011), 30–2.

38. §153 and commentary. I have used Vidyaratna's edition for the commentary (137, §14) as Ray's edition contains a misprint (*kasār* instead of *kāsar*). The reference here is to Amara, *Amarakośa with Sudhā Commentary*, ed. Visvanath Jha (Varanasi: Motilal Banarsidas, 2011), 1, vārivarga, 28.

39. Yigal Bronner, *Extreme Poetry: The South Asian Movement of Simultaneous Narration* (New York: Columbia University Press, 2010), 133–9.

40. Tarapada Mukherji, 'Bengali Lexicography up to 1800', in *S.K. De Memorial Volume*, ed. R.C. Hazra and S.C. Banerji (Calcutta: Firma KL Mukhopadhyay, 1972).

41. Commentary on maṅgala v. 17, 491.

42. For yet another example of this sensitivity, see his identification of the word *abahan* as 'western *bhāṣā* (*pāścāttya-bhāṣā*)' (commentary on §548). Interestingly, this is defined via another bhāṣā word, *aichan* (Sanskrit: *īdṛśa*).

43. The *Catalogus Catalogurum of Bengali Manuscripts* lists twenty extant manuscripts (Jatindramohan Bhattacharya, comp. and ed., *Catalogus Catalogurum of Bengali Manuscripts* [Kolkata: Asiatic Society, 1978], vol. 1, 134–5). The geographic distribution is: Kolkata, Birbhum, Rajshahi, Tripura, and Dhaka. I have not examined all these manuscripts to determine their provenance and scripts. Volume 12 of the *New Catalogus Catalogurum* (NCC) only lists the Rajshahi holding under *Padāmṛtasamudra*. Volume 19 of the NCC lists the *Mahābhāvānusāriṇī-ṭīkā*, but only as a printed work (Vidyaratna's edition). Most importantly, Uma Ray in the introduction to her edition of the text provides detailed notes on the many manuscripts she uses (Radhamohan, *Padāmṛtasamudra*, 98–104). I have not determined if the anthology and commentary were always transcribed and/or travelled together.

44. Pollock, *Language of the Gods*, 299–300. Pollock employs arguments from the *Bhāvaprakāśaṇa* (twelfth century) and the *Mānasollāsa* (1131, Kerala) in his account.

45. This list is informed by Pollock, *Language of the Gods*, 298–318. I select this treatment by Pollock since his account is based upon a fine historical reading of what makes Sanskrit literature literary according to various Sanskrit authors from the premodern period vis-à-vis song. Of course, these criteria may not be applicable at all times and places (the criteria may prove to be more heterogeneous in north India, for example [I thank Tyler Williams for this observation]), but my aim is to provide a list of possible areas of investigation. Needless to say, these issues need to be addressed more fully in a larger treatment.

46. Radhamohan, *Padāmṛtasamudra*, commentary on §7, 501.

47. See §153, §177, and §335.

48. See maṅgala vv. 18–19 (3) and auto-commentary, 491.

49. Pollock, *Language of the Gods*, 299–300. For metaphor and simile, see Dimock, *Bengali Vaiṣṇava Lyrics*, 93, 31 respectively.

50. Compare the passage from *Ujjvalanīlamaṇi* in the commentary on §177, 577 with *Sāhityadarpaṇa* §3, 121. Rupa's texts make a sustained argument for the application of Sanskrit literary-aesthetic categories (rasa theory) onto the emotional states of devotees in Gauḍīya Vaiṣṇavism. In his view, the principal emotion of the devotees, *rati* or love, is a *sthāyibhāva* of the rasa called erotic love or *śr̥ṅgāra*. This adoption of Sanskrit literary theory enables Rupa to develop his theory of love (also a theory of praxis) of Krishna as *rāgānugā bhakti* in which the relationship between Krishna and the devotee is likened to one between lovers. This type of relationship between Krishna and the devotee formed the inspiration for much, if not all, of Gauḍīya Vaiṣṇava songs. This position of the Gauḍīya Vaiṣṇava authors was also recognized by scholars of the period: for a précis of this theory by a *nyāya* author, see Gadadhara Bhattacarya 'Viṣṇuprītivāda', in *Vādavāridhi by Śrī Śrī Gadādhara Bhaṭṭācārya and others*, ed. Balakrishna Misra and Dhundiraj Shastri, Chowkhamba Sanskrit Series no. 446 (Chowkhamba Sanskrit Series Office: Benares City, 1936), 140 (fl. 1661, Bengal).

51. Maṅgala v. 17, 3: But having studied manuals of song composed by true devotees, beautiful songs conforming to the genre of kīrtana are collected here ('ālokyagīta-śāstrāṇi sad-bhaktānāṃ kr̥tāni tu | saṃgr̥hyantesu-gītāni kīrtanasyânusārataḥ ||').

52. I have not examined all extant manuscripts to determine the scripts used, although my initial research shows a uniformity of Bangla script.

53. Sudipta Kaviraj, 'Two Histories of Literary Culture', in *Literary Culture in History: Reconstructions from South Asia*, ed. Sheldon Pollock (Berkeley: University of California Press, 2003), 525–8.

Bibliography

Primary Sources

Abhinavagupta. *Dhvanyāloka of Abhinavagupta with the Locana and Bālapriyā Commentaries*, edited by Pattabhiram Sastri. Benaras: Kashi Sanskrti Series, 1940.

Amara. *Amarakośa with Sudhā Commentary*, edited by Visvanath Jha. Varanasi: Motilal Banarsidas, 2011.

Bhattacarya, Gadadhara. 'Viṣṇuprītivāda'. In *Vādavāridhi by Śrī Śrī Gadādhara Bhaṭṭācārya and Others*, edited by Balakrishna Misra and Dhundiraj Shastri. Chowkhamba Sanskrit Series no. 446. Chowkhamba Sanskrit Series Office: Benares City, 1936.

Dimock, Edward and Roushan Jahan, eds. *Bengali Vaiṣṇava Lyrics: A Reader for Advanced Students*. Chicago: South Asian Languages Research Program, 2006.

Krsnadas Kaviraj. *Caitanyacaritāmṛta of Kṛṣṇadāsa Kavirāja with the Payāraṭīkā of Viśvanāth Cakravartī and the Editor's Commentary Sudhāsañcāriṇī-vyākhyā*, edited by Makhanalala Dasa Bhagavatabhusana. Kalikata: Candra and Co. Oriental Printing Works, 1315 BS [c. 1908].

Narahari (Ghanasyam) Cakrvartin, comp. *Gītacandrodaya*. Navadvip: Haridas Das, 463 Gaurabda [c. 1948].

Thakkur, Narottamadas. *Premabhakticandrikā with the Ṭippanī of Viśvanatha Cakravartin and Sudhākaṇikā by AnantadasBabaji Maharaj*. Mathura: Sri Krishna Caitanya Sastra Mandir, 2010.

Thakkur, Radhamohan, *Padāmṛtasamudra*, edited by Uma Ray. Kalikata: University of Calcutta, 1391 BS [c. 1984].

———. comp., *Padāmṛtasamudra* (second edition), edited by Ramnarayan Vidyaratna. Murshidabad, 1315 BS [c. 1908].

Vaisnavadas, comp. *Padakalpataru: An Anthology of Vaiṣṇava Lyrics*, edited by Satishcandra Ray. Calcutta: Bangiya Sahitya Parishat, 1322–30 BS [c. 1915–23].

Visvanatha. *Sāhityadarpaṇa*, edited by Durgaprasad. Bombay: Nirnaya Sagar Press, 1922.

Secondary Sources

Bhattacharya, Jatindramohan, comp. and ed. *Catalogus Catalogurum of Bengali Manuscripts*, vol. 1. Kolkata: Asiatic Society, 1978.

Bronner, Yigal. *Extreme Poetry: The South Asian Movement of Simultaneous Narration*. New York: Columbia University Press, 2010.

Busch, Allison. *Poetry of Kings: The Classical Hindi Literature of Mughal India*. Oxford: Oxford University Press, 2011.

Chaudhuri, Yajnesvar, ed. *Nabadvīp Mahimā of Kānticandra Rāṛhī*. Nabadvip: Nabadvip Puratattva Parishad, 2004.

Freeman, Rich. 'Genre and Society: The Literary Culture of Premodern Kerala'. In *Literary Culture in History: Reconstructions from South Asia*, edited by Sheldon Pollock. Berkeley: University of California Press, 2003.

Ghosh, J.C. *Bengali Literature*. London: Oxford University Press, 1948.

Kaviraj, Sudipta. 'The Two Histories of Literary Culture in Bengal'. In *Literary Culture in History: Reconstructions from South Asia*, edited by Sheldon Pollock. Berkeley: University of California Press, 2003.

Mukherji, Tarapada. 'Bengali Lexicography up to 1800'. In *S. K. De Memorial Volume*, edited by R.C. Hazra and S.C. Banerji. Calcutta: Firma KL Mukhopadhyay, 1972.

Pollock, Sheldon. *The Language of the Gods in the World of Men: Sanskrit, Culture and Power in Premodern India*. Berkeley: University of California Press, 2006.

———. 'The Languages of Science in Early Modern India'. In *Forms of Knowledge in Early Modern Asia: Explorations in the Intellectual History of India and Tibet, 1500–1800*, edited by Sheldon Pollock. Durham: Duke University Press, 2011.

Raghavan, V.K. Kunjunni Raja, C.S. Sundaram, N. Veezhinathan, and N. Gangadharan. *New Catalogus Catalogorum: An Alphabetical Register of Sanskrit and Allied Works and Authors*. Madras: University of Madras, 1949.

Sen, Dineshchandra. *Vaiṣṇava Literature of Mediaeval Bengal*. Calcutta: University of Calcutta, 1917.

———. *History of Bengali Language and Literature*. Calcutta: University of Calcutta, 1954.

Sen, Sukumar. *Bāṅgālā sāhityer itihās. Dvitīya khaṇḍa, saptadaś—aṣṭadaś śatābdī*. Kolkata: Ananda Publishers, 1975.

Stewart, Tony K. *The Final Word: The Caitanya Caritamrta and the Grammar of Religious Tradition*. Oxford: Oxford University Press, 2010.

5

TYLER WILLIAMS

Commentary as Translation

The *Vairāgya Vṛnd* of Bhagvandas Niranjani

The *Vairāgya Vṛnd* (Collection of [Verses on] Non-Attachment, 1673 CE), a commentary in Brajbhasha on the Sanskrit *Vairāgya Śataka* of Bhartrihari, provides insight into not only the devotional but also the intellectual world of early modern north India, particularly the region now known as Rajasthan. In the *Vairāgya Vṛnd*, the Niranjani monk and poet Bhagvandas (fl. 1671–1713 CE) uses the then recently established genre of the vernacular commentary in a novel manner, translating and explicating the original text of Bhartrihari (itself a collection of independent epigrams), and also transforming that poetic anthology in such a way that it could be used as a religious treatise as well as a literary anthology. This manipulation of genre prompts us to reconsider the contours of the distinction between religious and literary writing in this period—for such a distinction did indeed exist, but it was continuously contested, arbitrated, and revised. This also means reconsidering the distinction, often made in modern scholarship, between 'popular' *bhakti* poetry and more elite, 'scholastic' writings. Both the structure of the *Vairāgya Vṛnd* and the history of its circulation and reception—gleaned through a study of available manuscripts—complicates two major assumptions prevalent in Hindi literary historiography: the implicit binary between the monastery (or devotional community) and the royal court as two separate literary cultures, and the characterization of poets of a *nirguṇ* persuasion (who worship a formless Divine) as being generally anti-scholastic and even anti-literary in outlook and style.[1] Finally, the *Vairāgya Vṛnd*, because it mediates between a Sanskrit source text and an audience more conversant in the vernacular of Brajbhasha, draws our attention to the need for what Francesca Orsini has called 'multilingual literary history', an approach that attempts to link the literary traditions of multiple languages in a geographical region rather than study each in isolation.[2]

The *Vairāgya Vṛnd* belongs to a whole class of texts that have been largely forgotten in modern literary histories, but that in the seventeenth and eighteenth centuries fulfilled the important function of giving various audiences access to the literary, religious, and intellectual material locked away in Sanskrit, while simultaneously creating a body of such material in the vernacular. Although neither the *Vairāgya Vṛnd* nor Bhagvandas is found in any modern history of Hindi literature or Indian religion, manuscript copies of the *Vairāgya Vṛnd* are found across Rajasthan and beyond its borders, in the libraries of powerful Rajput dynasties as well as in the manuscript collections of other religious communities such as the Dadu Panth, thus revealing that it was a work of some importance and influence. The *Vairāgya Vṛnd* and similar works from the period have suffered neglect from scholars for supposedly being derivative or unoriginal, for being mere translations of (implicitly superior) Sanskrit originals.[3] Yet the translation aspect of these highly innovative works is one of the things that make them such a fascinating and important part of Hindi literary culture.

In this chapter, I attempt to understand the intellectual and aesthetic work performed by the *Vairāgya Vṛnd* and its location in the broader picture of vernacularization and literary innovation taking place at the time in north India. The concept of translation can be helpful in this regard since much of what the text does is translation in one sense or another. At perhaps the most obvious level, the *Vairāgya Vṛnd* is a work of 'iconic translation', a rendering of a text taken from one language into another, with a more or less one-to-one correspondence (in this case, Sanskrit to Brajbhasha).[4] In this respect, it was part of a vibrant scene of interlingual and intralingual exchanges between cosmopolitan languages (Sanskrit and Persian) and the vernaculars, between the cosmopolitan languages themselves, and between the various vernaculars in the early modern period before colonialism.[5]

At a second, more conceptual level, Bhagvandas's 'commentary' is a site of translation between different traditions, ideologies, or symbolic orders, including the courtly tradition of the Sanskrit poetic anthology and the devotional tradition of which Bhagvandas was a part, the Niranjani Sampraday.[6] Finally, the *Vairāgya Vṛnd* was an event of translation in the sense employed by Bruno Latour and Michel Callon: its savvy author, Bhagvandas, deployed it as a node in a network of people, texts, and ideas, a node through which the other things in this network—for example, the Sanskrit *Vairāgya Śataka*, the figure of Bhartrihari, notions of the prestige of Sanskrit, notions of asceticism, and ideological elements of his own Niranjani tradition such as yogic practice and bhakti, and so on—were reinterpreted.[7]

The Niranjani Sampraday: From Local Roots to Trans-regional Literary Activity

To appreciate the work that the *Vairāgya Vṛnd* performs, we must first situate it within its immediate tradition, that of the Niranjani Sampraday of Rajasthan. This religious community of saint-poets, monks, and householders was numerically small but wielded a disproportionately large amount of influence through the literary and theological compositions of its poets. These works (all composed in the vernacular) were not only sophisticated but often travelled great distances in written form, demonstrating the importance of literacy and learning to the ability of a devotional group to broadcast its thought and influence.

Tradition recognizes the saint-poet Haridas (d. c. 1644 CE) of Didwana as the founder of the sampraday, and his compositions constitute the innermost textual core of the Niranjanis' thought and literature.[8] In these works—mostly *pads*, *sākhīs*, and *candrāyaṇ*, verse forms suited to singing and oral recitation, and composed in a Brajbhasha inflected by local Marwari phonology and usage—he cites Kabir and Gorakhnath as his gurus, and preaches devotion to a nirguṇ, formless Absolute, combining yogic practice with *prem-bhakti*.[9] His oeuvre thus closely resembles those of preceding and contemporary nirguṇ saints such as Kabir, Ravidas, and Dadu Dayal, and sets the mould for the hymns and diptychs of the Niranjani poets who would come after him, such as Khemdas, Dhyandas, Manohardas, Bhagvandas, Sevadas, Tursidas, and Hariramdas. This then is one textual tradition within the Niranjani Sampraday: nirguṇ and yogic in orientation, renouncing worldly ties, but with a Vaishnava influence as well, connecting it to popular genres of song and verse in the period.

As the community grew during the seventeenth century and developed a monastic structure, spreading to nearby cities such as Nagaur, Ajmer, Jodhpur, Fatehpur, and Pokhran (Pokaran), it drew a substantial number of lay followers (and thus patronage) from the Bihani community, an affluent division of the Maheshwari merchant caste that was scattered across these urban trading centres.[10] This partnership appears to have generated two important and related developments in the Sampraday: relatively high levels of literacy and education among Niranjani monks and prodigious scribal activity within the community, meaning the copying of large numbers of texts authored by both Niranjanis as well as by poets hailing from other traditions. Works by Niranjani monks evince literacy in Sanskrit as well as in literary Brajbhasha, and hagiographic texts record that some initiates were sent to Banaras for study.[11] Manuscript colophons reveal that these initiates copied a large numbers of works from other traditions *into* the Sampraday, including such diverse works as Dadu Dayal's devotional pads, Tulsidas's epic *Rāmcaritmānas*, and Biharilal's *Satsaī* literary anthology, even as they broadcast their own thought *outwards*, copying Niranjani works for householder patrons and even occasionally for members of royal courts in the region.

This chapter reveals the Niranjanis' social connections with other religious communities (such as the Dadu Panth) and courts (particularly the Rajput Rathores of Jodhpur and Nagaur), and the connection of their thoughts and writings to various contemporary discourses, including Vaishnava bhakti, Advaita Vedanta, and even literary theory (*alaṁkāraśāstra*, or the science of poetic figures, and *chandaśāstra*, the science of metrics). After Haridas, Niranjani poets continued to compose hymns and diptychs in a popular style of nirguṇ bhakti, but they also (quite literally) penned erudite works of a more scholastic nature, elaborating their nirguṇ theology and metaphysics through the genres and sciences mentioned above. Bhagvandas is a perfect example of these later Niranjani poets, as he composed not only evocative hymns in an accessible style, but also sophisticated didactic and poetic texts: these include works of Advaita Vedanta—the *Amṛt Dhārā* (Stream of Nectar, 1671), *Bhakt Virudāvalī* (Panegyric of the Devotee, n.d.), and *Pañcīkaraṇ manorath mañjharī* (Bouquet of Desire to Comprehend the Five Elements, n.d.); commentaries—the *Vairāgya Vṛnd* (Collection of Verses on Non-attachment, 1673), *Bhāgavat daśamskandh bhāṣā*

(Commentary on the Tenth Chapter of the *Bhāgavata Purāṇa*, 1703), *Bhāgavat Gīt bhāṣā ṭīkā* (Commentary on the *Bhagavad Gītā*, 1704); and vernacular renderings of Sanskrit *itihās* and purāṇa texts—the *Adhyātma Rāmāyaṇa* (Spiritual *Ramāyaṇa*, 1684), *Kārtik māhātmya bhāṣā* (Commentary on the Greatness of Kārtika, 1686), and *Jaimanī Aśvamedh* (The Horse Sacrifice of Jaimini, 1698).[12]

This is the second textual tradition within the sampraday, a tradition that quite often involved translation in one form or another. Niranjani poets never use any term equivalent to the English word 'translation' when describing their activities; certainly the equivalents in modern Hindi-Urdu (*anuvād, tarjamah*) do not appear.[13] Yet these poets are clearly aware of the 'trans' nature of their enterprise, in the sense that something is being shifted 'across', 'beyond', or 'through' two or more languages, discourses, or systems of thought. They are aware of the novel and, perhaps, transgressive nature of this act, and the attendant anxiety is evident in their introductory apologetics (something we will investigate in detail later in the context of the *Vairāgya Vṛnd*).[14] Most often they refer to their activity as *bhākhā kar-*, making (a text or an utterance) into the vernacular or spoken speech; the ostensible simplicity of this phrase conceals a much more sophisticated understanding of the language ecology of their time.[15] Indeed, the very absence of 'translation' as a literary or epistemic concept tells us something important about how these authors imagined the relationships between the many languages in their multilingual world. So let us now see how Bhagvandas's *Vairāgya Vṛnd* 'translates' its source material in different ways and at different levels, beginning with a brief description of the source text itself.

The *Vairāgya Śataka* of Bhartrihari

The *Vairāgya Śataka* (One Hundred Verses on Non-attachment) is one of the three *śataka*s (poetic anthologies) attributed to the poet-intellectual Bhartrihari (fl. fifth to seventh century CE), the other two being the *Nīti Śataka* (One Hundred Verses of Worldly Wisdom) and the *Śṛṅgāra Śataka* (One Hundred Erotic Verses). The attribution of all these verses to one historic individual is not without problems, and it is clear that the collation of the verses into these three collections probably took place over centuries.[16] Even the contents of the *Śatakatraya* (the collective name for the three śatakas) are not totally fixed: different recensions include or exclude particular verses, or include the same verse in different divisions of the corpus.[17] This diversity need not concern us too greatly here; what is important is that by the period in which Bhagvandas was writing, there existed an idea of the *Vairāgya Śataka* (and its two sister collections) as textually stable anthologies authored by a single enlightened poet. The figure of that enlightened poet is important as well: tradition relates that Bhartrihari was a king who, after enjoying the many sensual pleasures of the court, became disgusted with worldly life and renounced it completely, taking up an ascetic life in the forest.[18] Though the historical veracity of this biography may be questioned, this is, nevertheless, how Bhartrihari was *remembered* by Bhagvandas and his contemporaries in the Niranjani Sampraday, as well as in the nearby Dadu Panth and Ramanandi Sampraday: as an exemplary renunciate.[19]

The *Vairāgya Śataka* participates in the genre of *subhāṣita*, or 'well-spoken' verse, collections of unordered, independent epigrams that served a dual, didactic purpose: to educate elites in proper conduct through their content and acculturate those same elites into the appreciation of good literature through their form.[20] The verses contained in the *Vairāgya Śataka* (the majority of which are composed in the metres of *śārdūlavikrīḍitā, śikharinī, vasantatilaka*, or *anuṣṭubh*) are all obviously related, to some degree, to the theme of non-attachment. Bhartrihari is particularly critical of the pursuit of worldly aims such as wealth and power, of sexual desire and worldly love, and of the practice of physical asceticism without an accompanying practice of mental discipline. In this regard, his poetry was ideally suited for translation and consumption within the Niranjani monastic community: Bhagvandas and his fellow Niranjani poets advocated 'being in the world but not of it', fiercely criticizing worldly desires and pursuits and preaching mental detachment from them, but stopping short of advocating an ascetic life over that of a householder.[21]

The *Vairāgya Vṛnd*: Commentary and Translation

Although ostensibly a commentary on the *Vairāgya Śataka*, the *Vairāgya Vṛnd* of Bhagvandas does much more than simply explicate or elaborate upon its source text—it transforms it into a different type of composition that can do the literary and intellectual work of both a subhāṣita and a religious treatise. The *Vairāgya Vṛnd* contains 120 Sanskrit verses attributed to Bhartrihari, which Bhagvandas explicates and elaborates upon in 293 Brajbhasha verses composed in the form of *dohās, sorathās, kavitts, arills, chappays, caupaīs, kuṇḍaliyās, savaiyās,* and *samān savaiyās.*[22] He calls his text a *ṭīkā*, simultaneously referencing the prestigious commentarial tradition of Sanskrit and making an argument for the authority of his own text by claiming fidelity to Bhartrihari's original. As he writes in the final section (*prakāś*) of the *Vairāgya Vṛnd*:

bhāṣā kṛta ṭīkā yaha/sata tīnyūṁ parakāśa
dohā savaiyā caupaī/kuṇḍala kavita bigāsa
chappaya chanda aru soraṭhā/chanda rūp yaha jāṃna
ati nirmala vairāgya tara/sāra sāra paramāna[23]

This is a commentary (ṭīkā) made in the vernacular,
One hundred [verses] in three chapters,
Developed [in] dohās, savaiyās, caupaīs,
Kuṇḍaliyās, and kavitts,
Chappay, chand and soraṭhā—
Know these to be the forms of metre [used].
Exceedingly pure and overflowing with non-attachment,
The essence of its essence is made evident [here].

Bhagvandas also prefaces his commentary by stating that he has faithfully represented Bhartrihari's original text to the best of his intellectual ability:

grantha nāma paramāna/vairāga vṛnda so jāniye
bhāsauṁ budhi unamāna/mūla bhṛtihari bhāsa taiṁ[24]

The authoritative name of the *granth*—
Know it to be the *Vairāg Vṛnd.*
I speak according to my intellect
From the original utterances of Bhartrihari.

At the end of the text he again insists that he has neither added nor subtracted from the original work, recreating it 'just as it was' (*jathā tathā*):

jathā tathā yā graṃtha kū bhākhā sūṁmana baṃdha[25]

I have tied together this book (*granth*) in the vernacular
And according to my intellect, just as it was [in the original]

Claiming fidelity to the source text was clearly an attempt to tap into the authority and prestige of Bhartrihari's original, and to establish Bhagvandas's commentary as an authoritative rendering or interpretation. The verse also recalls the ubiquitous phrase *apnī mati anusār* (according to my understanding), which, as Allison Busch has demonstrated, was used by prominent Brajbhasha poets such as Keshavdas and Bhikharidas to signal their original interventions and innovations.[26]

Accordingly, this claim to a transparent rendering was not meant to diminish the importance or prestige of Bhagvandas's own intellectual contribution to the work; indeed, composing a commentary was understood to be a great feat of scholarship. The preceding commentarial tradition within Sanskrit had involved far more than the straightforward explication of meaning, and Bhagvandas appropriated some of its techniques and prestige when he chose to write the *Vairāgya Vṛnd*. A vast array of texts on different subjects was composed in the commentarial style, making it the largest body of expository works in Sanskrit.[27] As commentaries, these works (including ṭīkā and *bhāṣya*) acknowledged a pre-existing discourse on their subject and positioned themselves in relation to it without being *bound* by it—indeed, many 'commentaries' are magisterial treatises in their own right, sometimes departing markedly from the texts upon which they purport to comment (usually referred to as *mūl*, literally 'root'). Consequently, commentaries and their authors received as much prestige as the so-called mūl texts. By styling his work as a commentary, Bhagvandas presented himself as participating in this scholarly tradition, and partook of its prestige.

He was certainly not the first vernacular writer to do so: around seventy years earlier, at the turn of the seventeenth century, the Bundela Rajput Prince Indrajit of Orccha had composed a prose commentary in Brajbhasha on all three of Bhartrihari's śatakas.[28] Indrajit, in turn, was building upon an existing commentarial literature on the śatakas in Sanskrit, and may have even drawn from commentaries in Rajasthani vernaculars.[29] Meanwhile, at Indrajit's court, the poet Keshavdas had inaugurated the tradition of śāstra-like compositions in the vernacular on the science of poetry, and these in turn inspired their own commentarial tradition by the end of the seventeenth century, around the same time that Bhagvandas was writing.[30] Just preceding Indrajit and Keshavdas, the poet Nandadas had composed the *Rāsapancādhyayī*, which was both a translation of and a commentary on the portions of the tenth book of the *Bhāgavata Purāṇa* that describe the *rās-līlā* dance of Krishna and the *gopīs* (cowherd girls).[31] So Bhagvandas's *Vairāgya Śataka* should not be understood as an anomaly, but rather as a text that participated in the emerging tradition of vernacular commentaries on both Sanskrit and vernacular works.[32]

This tradition, though already several decades old, was still in the process of being consolidated when Bhagvandas composed the *Vairāgya Vṛnd*, and so his work reflects an awareness of the freedom to experiment and even a certain confidence, but also a lingering anxiety that attended vernacular composition in the shadow of the Sanskrit tradition.[33] Therefore, Bhagvandas's apologetics at the beginning and end of his work should be understood as attempts to establish the literary and intellectual merit of his enterprise. After the initial *maṅgalācaraṇ*, or invocation to god, he makes the formulaic dismissal of his own poetic skill and the appeal to the learned to correct and to forgive his errors that begin many works of *kāvya* (poetry or literature):

piṅgula amara lakhyau nahī nahi kavita kī rīti
grantha artha parakāśa kūṁ antari upajī prīti

chanda bhaṅga akṣara kaṭita aratha vipara jai hoi
dūkhana taiṁ bhuṣana karaiṁ kauvida kahiye soi[34]

I have not seen the *Piṅgala Śāstra* or the *Amara Kośa*,
Nor the rules of poetry composition.
[Yet] a passion arose within
To illuminate the meaning of the granth.

If the metre be broken, or syllables omitted,
Or a contradictory meaning is produced,
Those who change these flaws into adornments
Are called the learned.

Though he appears to be excusing himself as a literary neophyte, Bhagvandas's verses are meant to establish just the opposite: that the text he is about to present is a serious work of literature. Such apologetics are absent from contemporary hymns and works of strictly religious interest; it was only when literary merit was at stake that composers felt the need to address the topic, and so the works in which we find such apologetics include Tulsidas's *Rāmcaritmānas* (c. 1600 CE) and Manohardas's *Vedānt mahāvākya bhāṣā* (1660 CE), works that could make a plausible claim to the status of vernacular kāvya (even if the poets themselves were not ready to make such a claim expressly). It is also noteworthy that Bhagvandas attributes the power and success of his creation not to his own poetic skill, but to spiritual inspiration—the 'passion' that 'arose within' him. We first see this idea articulated in Tulsidas's *Rāmcaritmānas*, and then repeatedly in works by bhakti poets in the seventeenth century: the assertion by a poet that his creation derives its affective power not from its formal literariness, but from its devotional *feeling*.[35] This logic is particularly noticeable in the compositions of Niranjani poets, who refer to themselves both as *kavi* (poets) and as *bhakt* (devotees).

Just as he felt the need to establish his literary credentials, Bhagvandas was apparently aware that a case still needed to be made for the vernacular as a medium of intellectual discourse (including religious scholarship). In the final section of the *Vairāgya Vṛnd*, he makes an interesting assertion regarding the suitability of the vernacular to his intellectual purpose:

> śāstra aratha su kūṃpa jala bhāṣā silatā siṃdha
> jathā tathā yā graṃtha kū bhāṣā sūṁ mana baṃdha[36]
>
> In regard to artha (meaning/purpose of action),
> The śāstras are well water,
> And the vernacular a cool river.
> I have tied together this book (granth) in the vernacular,
> And according to my intellect, just as it was [in the original].
>
> mūla hāṃni kīnhi nahī karyau suvāka vilāsa
> bāla budhi bhākhā lakhain piṃḍata mūla prakāsa[37]
>
> I have not done harm to the original
> I have created pleasurable, fine speech
> In the vernacular speech of my child-like mind
> Wise ones will perceive the light (meaning) of the original.

The former verse recalls the famous *sākhī* attributed to Kabir—'saṃsakarita hai kupa-jala, bhākhā bahatā nīra' (Sanskrit is well water, the vernacular flowing water)—so often quoted by modern scholars to demonstrate the iconoclastic bhakti poets' attitude towards Sanskrit and its privileged knowledge systems. Kabir's sākhī characterizes Sanskrit as a 'dead' language, and celebrates the dynamism and 'life' of the vernacular, establishing it as the superior medium of religious and literary content. Bhagvandas's critique, however, is quite different as he juxtaposes the śāstras, not Sanskrit, with *bhākhā*. Sanskrit maintains a place of prestige in his text: he emphasizes his fidelity to the Sanskrit mūl text as the basis of authority of his work, and most available manuscripts of the *Vairāgya Vṛnd* include the original Sanskrit verses in addition to the commentary. Bhagvandas instead appears to be arguing that śāstra as a textual genre is a poor source for teaching or learning about the primary artha (purpose or goal) with which his text is concerned, that is, non-attachment (*vairāgya*). For this purpose, the more poetic *Vairāgya Śataka* and even his vernacular renderings of its epigrams are more effective. As we shall see in specific examples of his exegesis, Bhagvandas no doubt believed that it was his vernacular rendering that made clear the didactic import of Bhartrihari's verses, which otherwise might have been lost in the swirl of multiple emotions conveyed in the original text.

How does Bhagvandas maintain the literary quality of the mūl text while also foregrounding Niranjani religious ideology in his interpretation of it? Bhagvandas adopted certain elements of the Sanskrit commentary such as the dialectic style, paraphrasing, and references to texts and composers while abandoning others such as word glosses and the analysis of compounds. It was through this selective application of commentarial elements that Bhagvandas was able to turn the *Vairāgya Śataka* from simply a work of subhāṣita into a work that could be used for both religious and, more generally, moral and even literary instruction (not to mention aesthetic pleasure).

Bhagvandas first frames the text by prefacing it with a brief discussion of the three types of vairāgya: *manda*, *tīvra*, and *taratīvra*, defining each and associating them with Shuka, Shukhadeva, and Bhartrihari respectively.[38] Interestingly, he associates taratīvra, the highest state of non-attachment, with Bhartrihari himself, placing him above the puranic figures of Shuka/Shukhadeva. Bhagvandas then turns to his explication of Bhartrihari's text.

Bhagvandas arranges the unordered verses of the original *Śataka* thematically into five prakāś, or chapters, titled 'nām-kām' (desire for fame), 'dhan-mad' (the intoxication of wealth), 'tṛṣṇā' (thirst), 'śānti-sukh-nived' (peace, happiness, and indifference), and 'atitar vairāg' (complete non-attachment). Although a number of Bhartrihari's verses do not lend themselves to this type of categorization and thus sit somewhat awkwardly in their various chapters, the division itself reflects a certain logic, beginning with a diagnosis and description of different states of attachment (nām-kām, dhan-mad, and tṛṣṇā), and ending with verses that describe the different levels of non-attachment (śānti-sukh-nived and atitar vairāg). Bhagvandas further stitches several of the verses together by using the structure of a dialogue (*saṁvād* or *goṣṭhī*), sometimes between guru and disciple, sometimes between mental states such as 'greed' and 'contentment', sometimes between God and a generic devotee.[39] This results in a text that reads as a sort of treatise, rather than as a collection of independent epigrams.

Bhagvandas is not completely consistent in the number of verses or in the types of metres that he uses to translate or to comment on each Sanskrit verse; nevertheless, a general pattern is easily discernible. He begins by giving the original Sanskrit verse, and then an exegetical verse in Brajbhasha that explains the meaning of the original in detail. For this purpose he most often employs kavitts, although he also uses chappay, caupaī, arill, savaiyā, and samān savaiyā in places. These longer metres provide plenty of space for exegesis, and rather than simply translating the content of the original, Bhagvandas typically adds details or comments to explicate metaphors and references and to emphasize the spiritual lesson to be learned. He then presents a dohā or soraṭhā that neatly encapsulates the meaning of the original verse. Within this shorter form, though he tries to recreate at least some of the literal content of the Sanskrit, Bhagvandas's primary concern is clearly to compose an aesthetically powerful epigram that conveys the didactic message or emotional content of the original. Having thus established the theme or lesson, he then expands upon it, adding one or more verses in dohā, soraṭhā, arill, chappay, or caupaī metres. The use of so many different metres in a single text, while relatively rare for a devotional poet (especially a poet within the *nirguṇ sant* tradition), was common among those poets associated with royal courts who composed *prabandha kāvya* (epic or long narrative poetry).[40] By employing so many different (and some relatively more complex) metres, Bhagvandas was demonstrating his own virtuosity and taking the Niranjani tradition's poetry into an area that overlapped with more 'literary' genres.[41]

To see in detail how he did so, let us take an example that also reveals some choices regarding the content. Though the *Vairāgya Śataka* itself is a collection of verses that reject worldly pursuits and extol the virtues of asceticism, it is clear that Bhagvandas was also quite deliberate in his selection of verses to translate, including not only verses from the *Vairāgya Śataka*, but also those that he found appropriate from the *Nīti* and *Śṛṅgāra* śatakas.[42] Among the verses that appear to be imported from the 'other' śatakas is the following well-known śloka, which is recorded as part of the *Śṛṅgāra Śataka* in most recensions:

yaṁ cintayāmi satataṁ mayi sā viraktā
sāpyanyamicchati janaṁ sa janonyāsaktaḥ

asmatkṛte ca pariśuṣyati kācidanyā
dhiktāṁ ca taṁ ca madanaṁ ca imāṁ ca māṁ ca

She of whom I think ceaselessly is indifferent to me,
She yearns for another man, and he is attached to a third person,
While some other woman pines away for me.
Fie on that woman, on him, and on Kāmadeva,
as well as on this woman and on me.[43]

The original verse is satirical, and while it lampoons worldly love, it does not reject it as inherently corrupt. In his exegesis, however, Bhagvandas employs the verse to make a critique of worldly love, desire, and sexual relations as obstacles to spiritual progress and the attainment of liberation:

jāsūṁ merā mana lagyau sau tau mau virakta hvai kai
rata mānī aurahūṁ sūṁ sau tau anya rata hai
mai tau jānī merī triyā triyā hū na merī mo kūṁ
taji ma so puruṣa puruṣa āsa cita hai
tarunī triyā kūṁ tyāgi aisau mahā mandana rava
syau jai vesyā ghari andhitā ucita hai
dhṛga kaṃma dhṛga vāṃma dhṛga nara narī nāṃma
bhagavāna vināṁ gyāṃna mokūṁ dhṛga niti hai[44]

The one for whom my heart pines feels no attachment for me;
she desires another, and he's desirous of another.
The woman I understood to be mine is not mine and renounced me,
and is desirous of a man like me.
The blindness of quietly going to a house of prostitutes
is more appropriate than leaving an attractive young woman like this.
Fie on desire, fie on Kāmadeva, fie on man and woman;
to me, knowledge without the name of god is a contemptible way of living!

Most of Bhagvandas's kavitt follows Bhartrihari's originally closely, but the third and fourth lines introduce important new elements. In the third line, Bhagvandas critiques infidelity—that is, desire run amok, desire for multiple objects—by comparing it unfavourably with the patronage of prostitutes. The only relationship that is implied to be beyond critique is the monogamous relationship of marriage, which is both the reality of the householder and the archetype of pure love in the bhakti poetry of traditions like that of the Niranjanis. In spite of finding one's self bound in a web of worldly relations, one can transcend them through knowledge of and devotion to god. Bhagvandas establishes this through opposition when he states that any knowledge 'without the name of God is a contemptible way of living'.

Bhagvandas then adds an additional verse in the arill metre that expands upon the theme of the futility of sexual desire while also relating a popular narrative about the origins of Bhartrihari's own detachment from worldly life:

amṛta phala nṛpa pāi diyau jāi vāma kauṁ
vāṃmma ratī pratihāra diyau jāi kāṃmma kau
sau vesyāṁ rata bhayau diyau phala tāsa hai
parihāṁ vesyāṁ phala lai hāthi gaī nṛpa pāsi hai[45]

The king obtained the fruit of immortality
and having gone to his wife gave it [to her].
[His] wife went and gave it to the door-guard out of lust.
He became infatuated with a prostitute and gave the fruit to her,
And yes! The prostitute took the fruit in her hand and brought it to the king.

In the case of several other verses as well, Bhagvandas uses what was originally a satirical verse or a maxim intended to instruct the listener in the ways of the world to reject worldly affairs in their entirety, or to characterize them as obstacles to spiritual progress and liberation. Several modern critics have commented on the range of emotions expressed by Bhartrihari in all three of his śatakas; even in his epigrams on non-attachment, Bhartrihari reveals a lingering ambivalence towards women and worldly pleasures, finding it difficult to completely give up such desires.[46] In his commentary, however, Bhagvandas says unequivocally that attachment to women, children, home, and wealth can only lead to further and disastrous entanglement in the web (*jāl*) of maya or illusion.

Yet Bhagvandas regularly punctuates this sober sermon with verses that, if taken independently, could pass for the high literary and romantic style of *rīti* poetry. For example, in the middle of a discussion of the danger posed by women, we find the following verse:

caupaī
kāma vāṇa asaṭ adhā jākai, ramaiṁ naraka prāpati hoi tākai
naiṃna pheri soī vāṃṇa calāvai, citavata sava kau cita curāvai[47]

The one who is squarely hit with the arrow of erotic love (*kāma*)

Wanders and obtains Hell.
She lets loose the arrows by turning her eyes,
And steals the mind of all those who have one.

These well-crafted verses, along the introductory formulae and apologetics discussed above, give one the distinct impression that Bhagvandas was attempting to compose a work that would be appreciated as much for its literary qualities as for its devotional and didactic content.

Circulation, Performance, and the Devotional, Literary, and Intellectual World of Early Modern Rajasthan

The manuscript record of the *Vairāgya Vṛnd* would appear to confirm Bhagvandas's success in crafting a text that had both literary as well as devotional appeal, since it circulated far beyond the boundaries of the Niranjani devotional community. Most available copies of the *Vairāgya Vṛnd* are found in *pothīs* (wide-format folios, usually unbound) and in copies of the Niranjani *Vāṇī*, a large anthology of works by Niranjani and non-Niranjani sant poets that served as a vade mecum for high-ranking monks of the community and as an object of worship at Niranjani shrines. The colophons of most of these manuscripts reveal that they were copied by monks for their gurus. This evidence, along with the structure of the text itself, suggest that Niranjani gurus taught from it in the context of *pravacan* (sermonizing): with the *Vairāgya Vṛnd* the guru had on hand not only the original Sanskrit verses—which carried religious and social prestige—but also the tools with which to explain and elaborate upon their meaning in the vernacular.[48] The shorter verses—the dohās and soraṭhās—were pithy encapsulations of each lesson and ideally suited to memorization. Prefaced with a discussion of the different levels of renunciation, and loaded with moral and spiritual advice, the *Vairāgya Vṛnd* was an ideal textbook for Niranjani initiates.

Yet the colophons of some manuscripts tell us that the *Vairāgya Vṛnd* was also copied for householder patrons and even Rajput courts. That it was read by non-renunciate members of the Niranjani community appears consistent with the householder-friendly orientation of the text and the Sampraday noted earlier, and the existence of manuscripts of similarly scholastic works copied for Niranjani householders suggest that there may have been a culture of collective study (perhaps reading groups?) among Bihani devotees, similar to that described by the contemporary merchant Banarasidas in the context of the Jains.[49] A manuscript of the *Vairāgya Vṛnd* was copied for the Kacchwaha court of Jai Singh II at Jaipur in 1737 (copies of some other Niranjani works also made their way into that collection, but it is more difficult in their cases to determine when or how).[50] Some of Bhagvandas's other compositions, such as the *Jaimanī Aśvamedh*, made it into the collections of the Rathore courts at Jodhpur and Nagaur.[51] This is where the potential of Bhagvandas's text to be meaningful beyond a sectarian and even beyond a religious context becomes clear: more than just a treatise on renunciation, it was also a guidebook to a famous work of Sanskrit literature and thus the key to an important piece of cultural capital. As mentioned above, since at least the tenth century CE, Sanskrit subhāṣita anthologies had been compiled for the purpose of educating elites about literature, religion, politics, and comportment. By familiarizing oneself with the contents of such anthologies (often including memorization), an individual sought to cultivate connoisseurship and a worldly persona.[52] The satakas of Bhartrihari—covering worldly ethics, erotic love, and detachment from worldly concerns—were well-known collections of this type, praised not only for the wisdom of their verses but also for Bhartrihari's literary craft. By providing explanations of Bhartrihari's verses and, moreover, condensed equivalents in Brajbhasha, Bhagvandas was rendering the valuable service of providing knowledge of the prestigious Sanskrit tradition to kings, princes, and courtiers who were more comfortable in the vernacular. This was a major driver of vernacularization as the market for vernacular intellectuals continued to expand in north India in the seventeenth century.[53] Seen in this context, Bhagvandas appears not as a simple nirguṇ sant-poet concerned only with world denial, but rather as a participant in the broader intellectual network of the region, which was comprised of both religious and more 'secular' scholar-poets.

Bhagvandas's *Vairāgya Vṛnd* is a delightful read full of verbal artistry, sober reflection, and occasional flashes of wit. It is also an important document of the literary, religious, and intellectual world in which it was composed and enjoyed. We should not let the poet's own modest description of his work as a commentary, nor our own prejudice against translation as a 'second order' activity in comparison to 'original' composition, blind us to the inventiveness, ingenuity, and popularity of the *Vairāgya Vṛnd* and works like it. Though perhaps not one of the most popular works of the period, this anthology-cum-treatise did enjoy circulation across a wide geographical and social expanse, and was one of the 'everyday' texts through which peoples of the seventeenth and eighteenth centuries educated themselves on religion, worldly ethics, and literature. Commentary then, or rather commentary as a practice of translating not only language but also systems of thought and value, was one of the more important aspects of vernacularization, and one of the principle practices through which 'Hindi literature' was created in the early modern period.

Notes

1. The most influential scholar to draw a line between the devotional poetry of bhakti and the more 'secular' or scholastic literature (generally referred to as rīti) of royal courts is Ramchandra Shukla in his *Hindī sāhitya kā itihās* (1929), who goes so far as to posit bhakti and rīti as two separate periods or literary epistemes. Shukla was also one of the earliest critics to characterize nirguṇ saints as being more religious reformers than poets. See Ramchandra Shukla, *Hindī sāhitya kā itihās,* second edition (Allahabad: Lok Bharatiya Prakashan, 2003 [1940]), 39–48. The prevailing view of such nirguṇ saints is succinctly articulated by another influential critic, Nagendra: 'The poet-saints of the nirguṇ stream of poetry ... arose in an environment without resources and were deprived of the knowledge of literature, language, grammar, etc. For this reason, in the language of their poetry there is no embellishment, refinement, standardization or literariness' (Nagendra, *Hindī sāhitya kā itihās* [New Delhi: National Publishing House, 1973], 109). The distinction in scholarship between bhakti and rīti has been thoroughly critiqued in recent years; see Allison Busch, 'Questioning the Tropes of "Bhakti" and "Riti" in Hindi Literary Historiography', in *Bhakti in Current Research, 2001–2003: Proceedings of the Ninth International Conference on Early Devotional Literature in New Indo-Aryan Languages, Heidelberg, 23–26 July 2003,* ed. Monika Horstmann (New Delhi: Munshiram Manoharlal, 2006), 33–46, and Rupert Snell, 'Bhakti versus Riti? The Satsai of Biharilal', *Journal of Vaishnava Studies* 3, no. 1 (1994): 153–69.

2. Francesca Orsini, 'How to Do Multilingual Literary History? Lessons from Fifteenth- and Sixteenth-Century North India', *The Indian Economic and Social History Review* 49, no. 2 (2012): 225–46.

3. In this regard, translations and transcreations of Sanskrit texts of a devotional bent have suffered largely the same fate as more 'secular' works of the rīti register; a critique of the treatment of such texts by colonial and nationalist critics can be found in Allison Busch, *Poetry of Kings: The Classical*

Hindi Literature of Mughal India (New York: Oxford University Press, 2011), 202–39. However, there are also important exceptions to this treatment of translations and transcreations: prominent among them are the regard with which modern scholars have treated the *Rāmcaritmānas* of Tulsidas and the *Bhāgavata Purāṇa* based compositions of Nandadas.

4. The concept of iconic translation is outlined by Charles Sanders Peirce in his essay 'Logic as Semiotic: The Theory of Signs', in *Philosophical Writings of Peirce*, ed. Justus Buchler (New York: Dover, 1955 [1897]), 98–119. The first scholar to put Peirce's ideas in conversation with South Asian material was A. K. Ramanujan; see 'Three Hundred *Rāmāyaṇas*: Five Examples and Three Thoughts on Translation', in *Many Rāmāyaṇas: The Diversity of a Narrative Tradition in South Asia*, ed. Paula Richman (Berkeley: University of California Press, 1991), 44. I thank John Cort for bringing this to my attention and for sharing his excellent article on translation within the Jain tradition that makes productive use of this and other characterizations of translation ('Making It Vernacular in Agra: The Practice of Translation by Seventeenth-Century Digambar Jains', in *Tellings Not Texts: Music, Literature and Performance in North India*, ed. Francesca Orsini and Katherine Butler Schofield [Cambridge: Open Press Books, 2015], 61–106). My use of the term is slightly different in that Ramanujan uses 'translation' to refer to a one-to-one correspondence between elements in a narrative, whereas I use it to refer to an even closer correspondence between linguistic elements in the source text and in its translation. This is because the source text under consideration here, the *Vairāgya Śataka*, is not a narrative but rather a collection of short utterances.

5. Recently there has been an increase in interest in precolonial acts of translation in South Asia; for a representative selection of the rich variety of approaches relating to north Indian languages in particular, see Aditya Behl, 'Presence and Absence in *Bhakti*: An Afterword', *International Journal of Hindu Studies* 11, no. 3 (2007): 319–24; Cort, 'Making It Vernacular in Agra'; Thomas de Bruijn, 'Many Roads Lead to Lanka: The Intercultural Semantics of Rama's Quest', *Contemporary South Asia* 14, no. 1 (2005): 39–53; Deven Patel, 'Source, Exegesis, and Translation: Sanskrit Commentary and Regional Language Translation in South Asia', *Journal of the American Oriental Society* 131 no. 2 (2011): 245–66; Sheldon Pollock, *The Language of the Gods in the World of Men: Sanskrit, Culture, and Power in Premodern India* (Berkeley: University of California Press, 2006); Tony K. Stewart, 'In Search of Equivalence: Conceiving Muslim-Hindu Encounter Through Translation Theory', *History of Religions* 40, no. 3 (2001): 260–87; and Audrey Truschke, 'Cosmopolitan Encounters: Sanskrit and Persian at the Mughal Court', PhD diss., Columbia University, 2012. See also Samuel Wright's and Luther Obrock's chapter in this volume.

6. In thinking through texts and objects as sites of translation between different social and ideological worlds, I have taken significant help from

the following studies: Finbarr B. Flood, 'Pillars, Palimpsests, and Princely Practices: Translating the Past in Sultanate Delhi', *RES: Anthropology and Aesthetics*, no. 43 (April 2003): 95–116, as well as his monograph *Objects of Translation: Material Culture and Medieval Hindu-Muslim Encounter* (Princeton: Princeton University Press, 2009); Stewart, 'In Search of Equivalence'; and Phillip Wagoner, 'Sultan among Hindu Kings: Dress, Titles, and the Islamicization of Hindu Culture at Vijayanagara', *Journal of Asian Studies* 55, no. 4 (1996): 851–80.

7. 'To designate this thing which is neither one actor among many nor a force behind all the actors transported through some of them but a connection that transports, so to speak, transformations, we use the word translation—the tricky word 'network' being defined ... as what is traced by those translations in the scholars' accounts. So, the word "translation" now takes on a somewhat specialized meaning: a relation that does not transport causality but induces two mediators into coexisting' (Bruno Latour, *Reassembling the Social* [New York: Oxford University Press, 2005], 108).

8. Although Haridas is universally accepted to be the founder of the community by Niranjanis today and no compelling evidence to the contrary is currently known to exist, it is difficult to establish his preeminence in Niranjani texts earlier than the eighteenth century, when the Niranjani poet Hariramdas composed his hagiography of Haridas, the *Haridās kī pañc paricai* (n.d.). In fact, the earliest text to mention Niranjani saints, the *Bhaktamāl* (1660 CE) of Raghavadas, a member of the nearby Dadupanth, appears to refer to one 'Jagan' as the figurehead of the Niranjani *panth* (path), though it gives no details upon which we can ascertain who this Jagan was. Raghavadas also praises twelve saints of the Niranjani sect, including Haridas, but gives no information as to their chronological order or spiritual preeminence. See Tyler Williams, 'Sacred Sounds and Sacred Books: A History of Writing in Hindi', PhD diss., Columbia University, New York, 2014, 140–56. C.f. Ratanlal Mishra, *Nirañjanī sampradāy: sādhanā evaṁ sāhitya* (Navalagarh: Mahamaya Mandira, 1998), 61–77, 92–3.

9. The only published collection of Haridas's poetry is the *Śrī Mahārāj Haridāsjī kī vāṇī* edited by Swami Mangaldas. Although Swami Mangaldas (a monk and scholar of the Dadu Panth) clearly had access to a large number of manuscripts of Haridas's works belonging to both the Niranjani Sampraday and the Dadu Panth, the collection lacks a critical apparatus, making it of marginal utility to textual scholars (my research on seventeenth-century manuscripts has already uncovered some important variants not addressed in his edition). Nevertheless, this impressive work of research and collation is indispensable to anyone who wishes to know about the Niranjanis and their poetry.

10. Though dating from a later period in the development of the Sampraday, the earliest hagiographic texts of the Niranjani tradition, including

the *Dayāl jī kī pañc paracaī* (c. 1760–70 CE), of Hariramdas and the *Paracaī* (c. 1800) of Raghunathdas make a clear connection between the Niranjanis and the Bihani community, reporting that Haridas's first two disciples were Pada Devi, the clan goddess of the Bihanis, and Dwarkadas, a prominent Bihani merchant of Didwana. Ragunathdas in particular stresses the reverence that these merchants demonstrated towards Haridas as he travelled, in a manner strikingly similar to that used by Jangopal of the Dadu Panth when narrating the story of his own guru, Dadu Dayal, in the *Dādū janm-līlā* (c. 1620). That the Bihanis also numbered among the more prominent devotees and saints of the Dadu Panth raises the interesting question of whether these two groups were competing for the patronage of these wealthy traders (Williams, 'Sacred Sounds and Sacred Books', 196–210). The Bihanis are one of the many divisions of the Maheshwari caste that trace their lineage to the Rajputs of Khandela; see Lawrence A. Babb, *Alchemies of Violence: Myths of Identity and the Life of Trade in Western* (New Delhi: SAGE Publications, 2004), 98–116.

11. For example, it is often mentioned that Tursidas Niranjani, one of the more prominent poets of the Sampraday whose verses explain aspects of Advaita Vedanta in a relatively accessible style, was sent to Banaras, which was at the time a major centre of learning and a particularly important centre for Advaita Vedanta. On the early modern scholastic scene of Banaras, see Rosalind O'Hanlon, 'Speaking from Siva's Temple: Banaras Scholar Households and the Brahman "Ecumene" of Mughal India', *South Asian History and Culture* 2, no. 2 (2011): 253–77, and in the same issue, Christopher Minkowski, 'Advaita Vedānta in Early Modern History', 205–31.

12. Unfortunately, none of these works has been published. I am currently working on a critical edition of the *Vairāgya Vṛnd*; the rest of Bhagvandas's oeuvre continues to await scholarly attention.

13. The term *anuvād*, at least, can be shown to have a rather modern origin. See Brian Hatcher, 'Writing Sanskrit in the Vernacular: The Semantics and Practice of Translation in Early Colonial Bengal' (unpublished paper) and 'Sastric Modernity: Mediating Sanskrit Knowledge in Colonial Bengal', in *Modernities in Asian Perspective*, ed. Kausik Bandyopadhyay (Kolkata: Setu Prakashani, 2010), 117–49; see also Cort, 'Making it Vernacular in Agra'.

14. This anxiety is similar to that described by Allison Busch as 'the anxiety of innovation' felt by rīti scholar-poets such as Keshavdas. See Allison Busch, 'The Anxiety of Innovation: The Practice of Literary Science in the Hindi Riti Tradition', *Comparative Studies of South Asia, Africa and the Middle East* 24, no. 2 (2004): 46–53; see also the first chapter of Busch, *Poetry of Kings*, especially 23–6.

15. On the idea of an ecology of languages in a multilingual society, see Shantanu Phukan, '"Through Throats Where Many Rivers Meet": The

Ecology of Hindi in the World of Persian', *Indian Economic and Social History Review* 38, no. 33 (2001): 33–58. See also Orsini, 'How to Do Multilingual Literary History?'.

16. Bhartrihari, *Poems*, ed. Barbara Stoler Miller (New York: Columbia University Press, 1967), 'Introduction', xvi; Ludwik Sternbach, *Subhasita, Gnomic and Didactic Literature* (Wiesbaden: Otto Harrassowitz, 1974), 4.

17. Bhartrihari, *The Epigrams Attributed to Bhatṛhari (Bhartṛhari-viracitaḥ śatakatrayādi-subhāṣitasaṅgrahaḥ)*, ed. D. D. Kosambi (New Delhi: Munshiram Manoharlal Publishers, 2000 [1948]), 56–78.

18. Miller, 'Introduction', in Bhartrihari, *Bhartrihari*, ixvi–xvii. The most famous story about Bhartrihari relates how he was given a fruit of immortality by a brahmin; this he gave to his wife, who gave it to her lover, who gave it to another, and so on, until it reached the king again, at which point he became disillusioned with worldly love. This tradition is related, for example, in the *Vikramacarita*. See Judit Törzsök, ed. and trans., *Friendly Advice by Nārāyaṇa and King Vikrama's Adventures* (New York: New York University Press, 2007), 566–77.

19. *Vairāgya Vṛnd*, 1st prakāś, *arill* 16. The verse does not name Bhartrihari, but refers to an anonymous king while recounting the story. There is little ambiguity as to the king's identity, however, as the verse is a part of the commentary on Bhartrihari's famous śloka lampooning worldly love and infidelity. For more on that verse (beginning 'amṛta phala nṛpa pāi…'), see below. Bhartrihari is eulogized as a saint and devotee in the *Bhaktamāl* (c. 1600 CE) of the Ramanandi poet Nabhadas; Raghavadas of the nearby Dadupanth, another *sant* community with which the Niranjanis maintained close ties, describes Bhartrihari in a similar manner in his *Bhaktamāl* (1660 CE). Verses in Brajbhasha attributed to Bhartrihari are also to be found in the *Sarvāṅgī* anthology (1627 CE) of the Dadu Panthi monk Gopaldas. See Winand Callewaert, ed., *The Sarvāṅgī of Gopaldas: A 17th Century Anthology of Bhakti Literature* (New Delhi: Manohar, 1993).

20. Ludwik Sternbach, *Subhasita*, 4.

21. The large role played by Bihani merchants in the development of the Niranjani Sampraday probably has something to do with this orientation. In his *Paracaī* (1800 CE), Raghunathdas Niranjani lays heavy emphasis on Haridas's instructions for merchant householders, which (according to Raghunathdas) include the fulfilment of worldly obligations while being unattached to the objects of those obligations.

22. The *Vairāgya Vṛnd* has never been published, and I have yet to complete a critical edition of the text. For the purpose of this chapter, I have relied primarily on MS 37973 of the Rajasthan Oriental Research Institute, Jodhpur, which, judging by the evidence contained in other sections of the *guṭakā*, dates from the mid-eighteenth century CE. There is remarkable consistency in the available manuscripts; however, I cite this manuscript having compared

it with other copies, and believe it to be sufficiently representative of the contents of the manuscript tradition. Any exceptions are noted below in the notes for individual verses.

23. 5th prakāś, dohās 77, 78. All translations are mine unless otherwise noted.

24. 1st prakāś, soraṭhā 3.

25. 5th prakāś, v. 68.

26. Busch, 'The Anxiety of Innovation', 45–59; Busch, *Poetry of Kings*, 109–20.

27. Gary Tubb and Emery Boose, *Scholastic Sanskrit: A Manual for Students* (New York: American Institute of Buddhist Studies, 2007), 1.

28. Ronald Stuart McGregor, *The Language of Indrajit of Orchā: A Study of Early Braj Bhāṣā Prose* (London: Cambridge University Press, 1968), 11. Unfortunately, there is no known manuscript available of Indrajit's commentary on the *Vairāgya Śataka*; if one were to become available, a comparison with the *Vairāgya Vṛnd* might reveal whether Bhagvandas was familiar with Indrajit's work.

29. Ronald Stuart McGregor, 'The Progress of Hindi, Part 1: The Development of a Transregional Idiom', in *Literary Cultures in History: Reconstructions from South Asia*, ed. Sheldon Pollock (New Delhi: Oxford University Press, 2003), 928.

30. Busch, *Poetry of Kings*, 37. Vishvanathprasad Mishra, 'Tīkāeṁ aur ṭīkākār', in *Keśavdās*, ed. Vijaypal Singh (New Delhi: Radhakrishna Prakashan, 1970), 230–4. The earliest commentary Mishra mentions is a commentary (in Sanskrit no less!) on the *Rasikapriyā*, dated VS 1755/ 1698–9 CE.

31. Ronald Stuart McGregor, *The Round Dance of Krishna, and Uddhav's Message* (London: Luzac, 1973); Nandadas, *Rāsapañcadhyayī*, in *Nandadās Granthāvalī*, ed. Babu Vrajaratnadas (Varanasi: Nagari Pracharini Sabha, 1958).

32. That tradition continued well into the colonial period, and Brajbhasha poets continued to compose commentaries on Bhartrihari's śatakas long after Bhagvandas. We find, for example, a Brajbhasha commentary on the *Nīti Śataka* composed by one Nainsiha in 1729 at Ahmedabad at the bequest of Anand Singh, prince and son of Anup Singh, the Rathore king of Bikaner (MS 160.14, Abhay Jain Granthalaya, Bikaner).

33. Busch, 'The Anxiety of Innovation', 46–50. Pollock, *Language of the Gods*, 439.

34. Bhagvandas, *Vairāgya Vṛnd*, 1st prakāś, vv. 4–5.

35. Tulsidas introduces his vernacular adaptation of the Ram narrative by saying: 'Kabita bibeka eka nahiṁ moreṁ/satya kahauṁ likhi kāgada koreṁ. Bhaniti mori saba guna rahita bisva bidita guna eka/so bicāri sunihahiṁ sumati jivha keṁ bimala bibeka' (Tulsidas, *Rāmcaritmānas*' [Gorakhpur: Gita Press, 2003], 'Bālkāṇḍ', v. 1.9).

36. Bhagvandas, *Vairāgya Vṛnd*, 5th prakāś, v. 68. For this particular verse, I take the reading from MS 2165; MS 37973 gives 'syaṃdh' for 'sindh', which maintains the rhyme but obscures the meaning of the verse.

37. Bhagvandas, *Vairāgya Vṛnd*, 5th prakāś, v. 68, 5th prakāś, v. 71. For this verse as well, I take the reading from MS 2165; in MS 37973, the scribe has written 'vās' for 'bāl', which does not render any satisfactory meanings.

38. Bhagvandas, *Vairāgya Vṛnd*, 5th prakāś, v. 68. , 1st prakaś, vv. 6–9. It is not clear if these two names, Shuka and Shukhadeva, refer to the same individual, that is, the son of Vyasa, or to two separate individuals. In Bhagvandas's hierarchical scheme of the levels of non-attachment, they are certainly treated as if they were two distinct persons.

39. Some copies of the *Vairāgya Vṛnd* contain additional clarifications or 'rubric' in prose that introduce and frame Bhartrihari's verses in the manner of a commentary; for example, we find phrases such as 'now Bhartrihari discusses the *bhāgavat* ... ' (MS 2165, 832). Other examples can be found on pages 829 and 831 of the same manuscript.

40. Busch, *Poetry of Kings*; Dalpat Rajpurohit, 'Language and Metres in the *Himmatbahādurvirudāvalī*' in this volume.

41. The use of multiple metres in courtly poetry was often intended as a demonstration of the poet's virtuosity; Keshavdas's *Rāmcandrikā* and Padmakar's *Himmatbahādurvirudāvalī* are prime examples of such metrical performance.

42. As mentioned earlier, the contents of the individual śatakas were not consistent across manuscript traditions; nevertheless, the number of verses included in Bhagvandas's text that are generally included in the *Nīti* and *Śṛngār* śatakas in other recensions, and the content of these same verses suggest that Bhagvandas was familiar with all the three śatakas and intentionally drew his content from all three (as opposed to the possibility that he was working from a single recension of the *Vairāgya Śataka* that included all the 118 ślokas that he translates).

43. Translation by M.R. Kale, *The Nīti and Vairāgya Śatakas of Bhartrhari* (Bombay: Motilal Banarsidass, 2013 [1902]), 113. In Kale's edition, this verse is included within the *Nīti Śataka*.

44. 1st prakāś, kavitt 15.

45. Bhagvandas, *Vairāgya Vṛnd*, 1st prakāś, arill 16.

46. Bhartrihari, *Epigrams Attributed to Bhartṛhari*, 80–1; Bhartrihari, *Bhartrihari: Poems*, 17–24.

47. 1st prakāś, caupaī 7.

48. Monika Horstmann has made an excellent study of the different types of manuscripts to be found in the neighbouring Dadu Panth and their various uses, including *pravacan*. It seems likely that Dadupanthi manuscripts provided a model for the Niranjanis, particularly the *Vāṇī*. See Monika Horstmann, 'Dādūpanthi Anthologies of the Eighteenth and Nineteenth

Centuries', in *Bhakti in Current Research: Proceedings of the Ninth International Conference on Early Devotional Literature in New Indo-Aryan Languages, Heidelberg, 23–26 July 2003*, ed. Monika Horstmann (New Delhi: Manohar, 2006), 164–71.

49. Banarasidas, *Half a Tale: A Study in the Interrelationship between Autobiography and History: The Ardhakathanaka of Banarasidasa*, ed. and trans. Mukund Lath (Jaipur: Rajasthan Prakrit Bharati Sansthan, 1981).

50. MS 2440.28, Maharaja Sawai Singh II Museum, Jaipur.

51. MS 5.1 and 6.2, Maharaja Man Singh Pustak Prakash, Jodhpur.

52. Sternbach, *Subhāṣita*, 2–4.

53. See Pollock, *Language of the Gods*, 405–36.

Bibliography

Manuscripts

Bhagvandas. *Vairāgya Vṛnd*. Accession Number 37973, Rajasthan Oriental Research Institute, Jodhpur.

Hariramdas. *Dayāl jī kī pañc paracaī*. Accession Number 24778, Rajasthan Oriental Research Institute, Jodhpur.

Miscellaneous authors. *Santdās jī kī vāṇī*. Accession Number 2165, Rajasthan Oriental Research Institute, Jaipur.

Primary Sources

Banarasidas. *Half a Tale: A Study in the Interrelationship between Autobiography and History: The Ardhakathanaka of Banarasidasa*, edited and translated by Mukund Lath. Jaipur: Rajasthan Prakrit Bharati Sansthan, 1981.

Bhartrihari. *Bhartrihari: Poems*, edited by Barbara Stoler Miller. New York: Columbia University Press, 1967.

———. *The Epigrams Attributed to Bhatṛhari (Bhartṛhari-viracitaḥŚatakatrayādi-subhāṣitasaṅgrahaḥ)*, edited by D.D. Kosambi. New Delhi: Munshiram Manoharlal Publishers, 2000 [1948].

———. *The Nīti and Vairāgya Śatakas of Bhartrhari*, edited and translated by M.R. Kale. Bombay: Motilal Banarsidass, 2013 [1902].

Gopaldas. *The Hindi Biography of Dadu Dayal (Dādū Janm-Līlā)*, edited and translated by Winand Callewaert. Delhi: Motilal Banarsidass, 1988.

———. *The Sarvāṅgī of Gopaldas: A 17th Century Anthology of Bhakti Literature*, edited by Winand Callewaert. New Delhi: Manohar, 1993.

Haridas. *Śrī Mahārāj Haridāsjī kī vāṇī*, edited by Swami Mangaldas. Jaipur: Nikhil Bharatiya Niranjani Mahasabha, 1962.

Nabhadas. *Bhaktamal, With the Commentary of Priyadas*, edited by Rupkala. Lucknow: Tejkumar Press, 1914.

———. *Nandadās Granthāvalī*, edited by Babu Vrajaratnadas. Varanasi: Nagari Pracharini Sabha, 1958.

Narayana. *Friendly Advice by Nārāyaṇa and King Vikrama's Adventures*, translated by Judit Törzsök. New York: New York University Press, 2007.

Raghavdas. *Bhaktamāl*, edited by Agarchand Nathata. Jodhpur: Rajasthan Oriental Research Institute, 1965.

Goswami, Rupa. *The Bhaktirasāmṛtasindhu of Rūpa Gosvāmin*, translated by David Haberman. New Delhi: Indira Gandhi National Centre for the Arts and Motilal Banarsidass Publishers, 2003.

Sundardas. *Sundardās Grantāvalī*, edited by Pandit Harinarayan Sharma. Calcutta: Sri Dadu Dayalu Mahasabha, 1936.

Tulsidas. *Rāmcaritmānas*. Gorakhpur: Gita Press, 2003.

Secondary Sources

Babb, Lawrence A. *Alchemies of Violence: Myths of Identity and the Life of Trade in Western India*. New Delhi: SAGE Publications, 2004.

Behl, Aditya. 'Presence and Absence in *Bhakti*: An Afterword'. *International Journal of Hindu Studies* 11, no. 3 (2007): 319–24.

Busch, Allison. 'The Anxiety of Innovation: The Practice of Literary Science in the Hindi Riti Tradition'. *Comparative Studies of South Asia, Africa and the Middle East* 24, no. 2 (2004): 45–59.

———. 'Questioning the Tropes of "Bhakti" and "Riti" in Hindi Literary Historiography'. In *Bhakti in Current Research, 2001–2003: Proceedings of the Ninth International Conference on Early Devotional Literature in New Indo-Aryan Languages, Heidelberg, 23–26 July 2003*, edited by Monika Horstmann. New Delhi: Munshiram Manoharlal, 2006, 33–46.

———. *Poetry of Kings: The Classical Hindi Literature of Mughal India*. New York: Oxford University Press, 2011.

Cort, John E. 'Making It Vernacular in Agra: The Practice of Translation by Seventeenth-Century Digambar Jains'. In *Tellings and Texts: Music, Literature and Performance in North India*, edited by Francesca Orsini and Katherine Butler Schofield. Cambridge: Open Press Books, 61–105.

De Bruijn, Thomas. 'Many Roads Lead to Lanka: The Intercultural Semantics of Rama's Quest'. *Contemporary South Asia* 14, no. 1 (2005): 39–53.

Dwivedi, Hazariprasad. *Hindī sāhitya kī bhūmikā*. Bombay: Radhakrishnan, 1963.

Eaton, Richard Maxwell. *The Rise of Islam and the Bengal Frontier, 1204–1760*. Berkeley: University of California Press, 1993.

Flood, Finbarr Barry. 'Pillars, Palimpsests, and Princely Practices: Translating the Past in Sultanate Delhi'. *RES: Anthropology and Aesthetics*, no. 43 (April 2003): 95–116.

———. *Objects of Translation: Material Culture and Medieval Hindu-Muslim Encounter*. Princeton: Princeton University Press, 2009.

Hatcher, Brian. 'Writing Sanskrit in the Vernacular: The Semantics and Practice of Translation in Early Colonial Bengal' (unpublished manuscript).

———. 'Sastric Modernity: Mediating Sanskrit Knowledge in Colonial Bengal'. In *Modernities in Asian Perspective*, edited by Kausik Bandyopadhyay. Kolkata: Setu Prakashani, 2010, 117–49.

Horstmann, Monika. 'Dādūpanthi Anthologies of the Eighteenth and Nineteenth Centuries'. In *Bhakti in Current Research: Proceedings of the Ninth International Conference on Early Devotional Literature in New Indo-Aryan Languages, Heidelberg, 23–26 July 2003*, edited by Monika Horstmann. New Delhi: Manohar, 2006, 164–71.

Latour, Bruno. *Reassembling the Social*. New York: Oxford University Press, 2005.

McGregor, Ronald Stuart. *The Language of Indrajit of Orchā: A Study of Early Braj Bhāṣā Prose*. London: Cambridge University Press, 1968.

———. *The Round Dance of Krishna, and Uddhav's Message*. London: Luzac, 1973.

McGregor, Ronald Stuart. 'The Progress of Hindi, Part 1: The Development of a Transregional Idiom'. In *Literary Cultures in History: Reconstructions from South Asia*, edited by Sheldon Pollock. New Delhi: Oxford University Press, 2003, 912–57.

Minkowski, Christopher. 'Advaita Vedānta in Early Modern History'. *South Asian History and Culture* 2, no. 2 (2011): 205–31.

Mishra, Ratanlal. *Nirañjanī sampradāy: sādhanā evaṁ sāhitya*. Navalagarh: Mahamaya Mandira, 1998.

Mishra, Vishvanathprasad. 'Ṭīkāeṃ aur ṭīkākār'. In *Keśavdās*, edited by Vijaypal Singh. New Delhi: Radhakrishna Prakashan, 1970, 230–4.

Nagendra. *Hindī sāhitya kā itihās*. New Delhi: National Publishing House, 1973.

O'Hanlon, Rosalind. 'Speaking from Siva's Temple: Banaras Scholar Households and the Brahman "Ecumene" of Mughal India'. *South Asian History and Culture* 2, no. 2 (2011): 253–77.

Orsini, Francesca. 'How to Do Multlingual Literary History? Lessons from Fifteenth- and Sixteenth-Century North India'. *The Indian Economic and Social History Review* 49, no. 2 (2012): 21.

Patel, Deven. 'Source, Exegesis, and Translation: Sanskrit Commentary and Regional Language Translation in South Asia'. *Journal of the American Oriental Society* 131, no. 2 (2011): 245–66.

Peirce, Charles Sanders. 'Logic as Semiotic: The Theory of Signs'. In *Philosophical Writings of Peirce*, edited by Justus Buchler. New York: Dover, 1955 [1897], 98–119.

Phukan, Shantanu. '"Through Throats Where Many Rivers Meet": The Ecology of Hindi in the World of Persian'. *Indian Economic and Social History Review* 38, no. 33 (2001): 33–58.

Pollock, Sheldon. *The Language of the Gods in the World of Men: Sanskrit, Culture, and Power in Premodern India*. Berkeley: University of California Press, 2006.

Ramanujan, A. K. 'Three Hundred *Rāmāyaṇas*: Five Examples and Three Thoughts on Translation'. In *Many Rāmāyaṇas: The Diversity of a Narrative Tradition in South Asia*, edited by Paula Richman. Berkeley: University of California Press, 1991.

Shukla, Ramchandra. *Hindī sāhitya kā itihās* (second edition). Allahabad: Lok Bharatiya Prakashan, 2003 [1940].

Singh, Bachan. *Hindī sāhitya kā dūsrā itihās* (third edition). New Delhi: Radhakrishna Prakashan, 2004.

Snell, Rupert. 'Bhakti versus Riti? The Satsai of Biharilal'. *Journal of Vaishnava Studies* 3, no. 1 (1994): 8.

Sternbach, Ludwik. *Subhasita, Gnomic and Didactic literature.* Wiesbaden: Otto Harrassowitz, 1974.

Stewart, Tony K. 'In Search of Equivalence: Conceiving Muslim-Hindu Encounter through Translation Theory'. *History of Religions* 40, no. 3 (2001): 260–87.

———. *The Final Word: The Caitanya Caritamrta and the Grammar of Religious Tradition.* New York: Oxford University Press, 2010.

Truschke, Audrey. 'Cosmopolitan Encounters: Sanskrit and Persian at the Mughal Court', PhD diss., Columbia University, 2012.

Tubb, Gary and Emery Boose. *Scholastic Sanskrit: A Manual for Students.* New York: American Institute of Buddhist Studies, 2007.

Wagoner, Phillip B. 'Sultan among Hindu Kings: Dress, Titles, and the Islamicization of Hindu Culture at Vijayanagara'. *Journal of Asian Studies* 55, no. 4 (1996): 30.

Williams, Tyler. 'Sacred Sounds and Sacred Books: A History of Writing in Hindi', PhD diss., Columbia University, 2014.

PART TWO

POETIC GENRES AND PERSONALITIES

6

RAMAN P. SINHA

Poetry in *Ragas* or *Ragas* in Poetry?

Studies in the Concept of Poetic Communication

Some poetry communicates like literature; some like music or painting. The poetry which communicates like literature uses literary devices, whereas poetry communicating like music or painting uses the non-referential devices of these media. But sometimes the boundary blurs and the relative importance of the component parts defines a new sort of category altogether. Hence, Bharatmuni (second century) defines *gāndharva* as a composition involving *svara* (notes), *tāla* (rhythm), and *pada* (words), and differentiates it from *gāna* (song) on the ground that gāndharva gives more importance to svara and tāla, whereas gāna is comprised primarily of pada-centred compositions.[1] Svara and tāla are musical devices, whereas pada is a literary one. Abhinavagupta (950–1030 CE) further elaborates this distinction in his *Abhinavabhāratī*, stating that the importance of pada in gāna is of one type whereas in gāndharva it is of a different type. Svara and tāla are important in gāndharva and since it is impossible to present them without any vehicle, pada as a vehicle becomes useful. That is why Abhinava says pada is a felicitator (*anubhavaka*) of svara and tāla.[2]

Another category that had been developed in Sanskrit in this context is *raga* poetry, or *rāgakāvya*. It can be traced at least to the time of Kohal (third century), who defined and classified it as a subcategory of *uparūpaka* (minor play). This was later quoted by Abhinavagupta in *Abhinavabhāratī*.[3] Abhinavagupta cites two examples of this subcategory—*rāghava-vijaya* and *marīcavadham*—and informs us that the former work was based on raga *thakkā*, while the latter work was composed in raga *kukubh*. Basically, rāgakāvya was meant to be enacted with dance, but it can also be sung as a song. It is composed in a single raga or multiple ragas, and *dhruvak* or a combination of *sthāī* (primary movement) and *antarā* (secondary movement) is also used in it. Jayadev's *Gītagovinda* is a pioneering work in the tradition of rāgakāvya,[4] but before the *Gītagovinda*, the *Caryāpada* of *siddha* poetry (eighth to twelfth century) also provided an indication of the ragas appropriate to it. The *Caryāgītikośa*, which is considered to be the earliest specimen of New Indo-Aryan vernacular literature, was composed in various metres; it also indicates the raga that is appropriate to each composition.[5] It is interesting to note that the famous thirteenth-century treatise on Indian music, *Sangītaratnākara*, categorizes *Caryāgīti* in the group it calls *prakīrṇakaprabandhagīti*, in which songs are composed in metre with end rhyme.[6] The question arises as to whether it was *suras* (tunes) or rather words that comprised the more central element in this kind of composition, or is it possible to take both into account simultaneously? Studying early eastern New Indo-Aryan versification, Nilratan Sen opines that 'from the context of the songs it [becomes clear] that the text of the song was no less important … than the tune. So, obviously, the composers were inclined to maintain a recital verse-meter, side by side with the raga-tune. Versification and musical notes therefore often overlapped'.[7]

Subsequently this style came down to Hindi poetry, as Ganapatichandra Gupta proclaims, but only after bifurcating into two streams. In one stream, Sanskrit poets such as Kshemendra and Jayadeva adopted and developed it after being influenced by Apabhramsha poets. This tradition was adopted from Jayadeva by Maithili poets such as Vidyapati, and that in turn was later popularized by Krishnaite poets. In the other stream the lyric style of siddhas was developed by the Nāthpanthī yogis and the Maharashtrian *sants*, creating a tradition that later came down to the Hindi sant poets.[8] Thus, a tradition was established in north India where metre or music became a part of an overall communication strategy; and in this regard there was no difference between *saguṇa* and *nirguṇa*, between *krishnabhakta* and *rāmabhakta*, or between *prem-margī* and *gyān-mārgī*.

We can see the importance of musical systems of classification in the case of the *Ādi Granth*.[9] This great book classifies its contents on the basis of various ragas. After the initial three sub-sections (Japji, Rahirasa, and Kirtan), the remaining poems, comprising the great bulk of the collection, are arranged in thirty-one ragas. The same is the case with Sindhi poetry, where, in the words of Ali S. Asani,

> the thematic relationship between musical mode and Sindhi mystical poetry is demonstrated explicitly in early manuscripts in which poems were arranged in chapters according to the *sur* in which they were intended to be sung. The first collection to be so arranged was that of Miyān Shāh 'Ināt ('Ināyatullāh Rizwī), whose poems were grouped under nineteen *surs*. The great classical compendium of Sindhi mystical poetry, Shāh 'Abdul Latīf's *Risālo*, is arranged into thirty chapters, each devoted to a *sur*, and most of these are associated with either a specific folktale or a certain theme.[10]

As evident in the case of *Caryāgītikośa*, there were two ways of presenting poetry in the north Indian tradition—one way was reciting and the other was singing. Both these traditions were developed, it seems, in the process of acquiring better skills in communication. Recitation requires familiarity with metre (*chand*), whereas knowledge of raga is a must for singing. It is no coincidence that before elaborating various ways of poetry recitation in his *Kāvyamīmāṃsā*, Rajashekhara (tenth century) establishes the importance of recitation itself in no uncertain terms: 'Experts in poetry writing may somehow compose poems, but only the accomplished can recite poetry.'[11] *Prabandhas* (larger works) were meant for recitation, so a prabandha such as the *Rāmcaritmānas* mentions the name of its chands, whereas smaller works (*muktakas*) were for singing. No wonder most of the padas of Kabir, Mira, or Surdas, or of Tulsī's *Vinaya Patrikā* and *Gītāvalī*, indicate the names of the ragas to which they were to be sung.[12] But both the traditions were one in aiming at *rasa* as the fruition of the performance process overall.

Kshemendra (990–1065 CE) instructs poets that they should select the metres (chand) they use according to the subject being described and the rasa that is inherent in the poetry.[13] Bhanukavi also provides a table of favourable and unfavourable metres according to rasas and the subject matters being described. But he emphasizes that the system works better for Sanskrit than for bhasha. Vernacular metres such *dohā, chaupaī, soraṭh, savaiyā*, and so on, are suitable for all kinds of rasas and subjects.

The question of the relation between raga and rasa has been addressed since the time when the *Nāṭyaśāstra* was written. When Bharatamuni discusses 'the occasions and *rasas* of the *dhruvās*', he says:

> There are two kinds of occasions: one which relates to others, and one which relates to oneself.
>
> The Apakṛṣṭa Dhruvā should be sung in the Karuṇa Rasa on the following occasions: when captured, when obstacles are encountered, and during a fall, illness, fainting or death.
>
> A Sthita Dhruvā (a Dhruvā with the Vilambita Laya) should be sung on these occasions: when in a desperate hurry, when dissimulating, when worried, when tired, when extremely depressed, when in despair.
>
> When these emotions are being expressed in the Karuṇa Rasa, the Karuṇa emotions should be expressed in the Druta Laya.
>
> Grief on personally seeing someone dead or wounded should be acted in the Sthita (Vilambita) Dhruvā and the Karuṇa Rasa.
>
> The Dhruvā should be sung in the Druta Laya on these occasions: on seeing unexpected calamities, when intensely happy, on seeing something astounding, or when depressed, when pleased, in anger, on seeing heroic acts, or when personally reporting the heroic, the furious and the terrible. The Dhruvā should be sung in the Druta Laya on occasions of excitement.
>
> The Prāsādikī Dhruvā should be sung in the Madhya Laya on these occasions: when pacifying another, when making a request, when remembering (various things), when making an exaggerated speech, in a first meeting, on seeing the unusual in love.
>
> The Antarā Dhruvā should be sung continuously when there is physical distress, in anger, and when wielding weapons.
>
> The Dhruvā should not be sung when the character enters weeping or singing, or when there is a hasty action, or when giving a message, or if a mishap (falling, stumbling, etc.) or something surprising occurs when entering.
>
> The Dhruvā-s should thus be used after taking into consideration the theme, the region, time, season, the characters, and emotions.[14]

The relation of a raga to a mental state is a complex albeit intriguing subject. Acharya Brhaspati, in his pioneering work *Bhārat kā sangīt siddhānt*, proposes a clear-cut relationship between *sthāyī-svara* (major notes), rasa, and *sthāyī-bhāva* (major emotions):[15]

Table 6.1 Interrelationship between *Sthāyī-svara*, *Rasa*, and *Sthāyī-bhāva*

Major notes (sthāyī-svara)	Rasa	Major emotions (sthāyī-bhāva)
ṣadaja (*sā*)	valour (*vīra*), amazement (*adbhuta*), terror (*raudra*)	enthusiasm (*utsāha*), wonder (*vismaya*), anger (*krodha*)
ṛṣabha (*re*)	valour (vīra), amazement (adbhuta), terror (raudra)	enthusiasm (utsaha), wonder (vismaya), anger (krodha)
gāndhāra (*ga*)	pathos (*karuṇa*)	sorrow (*śoka*)
madhyama (*ma*)	erotic (*śṛṅgāra*), humour (*hāsya*)	love (*rati*), laughter (*hāsa*)
pañcama (*pa*)	erotic (śṛṅgāra), humour (hāsya)	love (rati), laughter (hāsa)
dhaivata (*dha*)	disgust (*vibhatsa*), dread (*bhayānaka*)	fear (*bhaya*), repulsion (*jugupsa*)
niṣāda (*ni*)	pathos (karuṇa)	sorrow (śoka)

Source: Author.

Picking up the same subject, Omkarnath Thakur, the great musician of twentieth-century India, once remarked that it is not merely the notes which produce a mood but also various other factors such as grace notes, tempo, octave levels, and so on. According to him, those ragas that move in the upper octaves are never sombre and dignified; they express faster-paced emotions such as anger, excitement, and enthusiasm. Those with an emphasis on the *sā–ma* relation, by contrast, are peaceful and mature. Ragas of the *khamaj* group are erotic and lighter in vein. Those with *ri*, *dha*, and *ma* as the major notes have pathos as their predominant tendency. Ragas with *ri*, *dha*, and *ma* show tiredness, lack of enthusiasm, and so on.[16] Thus, classical aesthetic criticism offers us an array of matters to be considered when we assess the relationship between poetry and music.

To test such notions in relation to the devotional poetry of early modern north India, let us consider the poems and associated ragas of four major poets of the *bhakti* period—Kabir, Surdas, Mira, and Tulsidas. The 403 padas of Kabir as they appear in the Shyamsundar Das's edition of his work net us a total of sixteen ragas. For the 201 padas of Mira in Parshuram Chaturvedi's edition, an aggregate of 70 ragas are indicated. Tulsidas's *Gītāvalī* in the Gita Press edition consists of 330 padas, in which 22 ragas are mentioned, while the

Gita Press edition of his *Vinaya Patrikā* offers 279 padas, for which 23 ragas are listed. As for Surdas, if you accept the *skandha* method of arranging poems in the *Sūrsāgar* and restrict your attention to only the first canto (*prathama skandha*), you come up with 343 padas, for which 28 ragas are indicated. These distributions can be seen in Tables 6.2 and 6.3.

If we take as our guide the editions mentioned in Table 6.2, then we see in Table 6.3 that in comparison to the other three poets Mira used the greatest variety of ragas, even though she composed the smallest number of padas. If we agree with the critics' general evaluation of Mira's limited life experience and the relative monotony that it produced in her poetry,[17] then it is quite understandable that she would have wanted to introduce variety into her oeuvre by means of the numerous ragas she employed. Contrary to this, Kabir is considered to be well-informed about the world[18] and, like Narsimha Mehta, a witness to varied and sometimes almost impossible situations,[19] so it is no wonder that, in comparison to the other three poets, he has the least need to introduce variety into his poetry by means of a plethora of ragas. Can we draw a conclusion from this contrast, proposing that the choice of ragas that would be appropriate to their verse had different meanings for different poets?

Table 6.2 Number of *Pada*s and Indicated *Raga*s in *Bhakti* Poetry

Poet	Edition	Total number of padas	Total number of padas for which raga is indicated	Number of indicated ragas
Kabir	*Kabīr Granthāvalī* (ed. Shyamsundar Das)	403	403	16
Surdas	*Sūrsāgar Saṭīk* (ed. Hardev Bahari)	343	324	28
Mira	*Mīrāṅbāī kī padāvalī* (ed. Parshuram Chaturvedi)	201	115	70
Tulsidas	*Gītāvalī* (14th edition, Gita Press)	330	143	22
	Vinay Patrikā (52nd edition, Gita Press)	279	46	23

Source: Author.

Table 6.3 Preferred *Ragas* of Individual Poets

Poets	Five most common rāgas in individual poet's oeuvre (arranged according to numerical prevalence)					Ragas specific to individual poet	Ragas common to all poets
Kabir	Gauḍī 152	Āsāvarī 60	Rāmakalī 49	Soraṭhī 38	Bhairav 37	3	9
Surdas	Dhanāśrī 83	Sāraṅg 55	Bilāval 35	Kedār 26	Kānharā 19	6	
Mira	Pīlū 6	Sāraṅg 5	Bihāg 4	Soraṭh 4	Bilāval 3	50	
Tulsidas	Kedār 29	Bilāval 16	Kānharā 13	Gauḍī 13	Jaitaśrī 11	3	

Source: Author.

I think we can. For someone like Mira, raga was a device; it seems to compensate for her limited experience and exposure. Since every raga has a distinct form that interprets or colours the sensibilities of a text in a distinct way, the varieties expressed in ragas turn out to indicate varieties in sensibilities. Poets such as Kabir, Tulsi, or Surdas, however, draw no extra weight from or attention to a given raga in relation to their poetic compositions. They feel little need to expand their sensibilities. This argument can be substantiated by the number of ragas that we can discover to be specific to individual poets. In the case of Mira, we have fifty such ragas, whereas Surdas has six, and Kabir and Tulsi three each, as documented in Tables 6.3 and 6.4.

These tables present information that further amplifies our sense of the landscape of word and song in bhakti poetry. In Table 6.4 we have a representation of the ragas most commonly used by our four major poets, taken in the aggregate. Then in Table 6.3 we see the ragas individually preferred by the poets concerned. The ragas that they hold in common are *dhanāśrī, āsāvarī, sārang, rāmkelī, bilāval, malār, māru*, and *todī*.

Surveying the data presented in Tables 6.3 and 6.4, we have two options. Either we see the structure of a particular raga—what it 'expresses' by its constituent notes—and then see how this accords with the contents of a particular poem, imagining each to be invariant in time; or we try to perceive a particular raga and its corresponding poem in a diachronic setting, judging that neither the raga's structure

Table 6.4 Most Common *Ragas* in *Bhakti* Poetry

	Kabir	Surdas	Mira	Tulsidas
Dhanāśrī	6	83	1	8
Āsavarī	60	9	1	10
Sāraṅg	2	55	5	9
Soraṭh	38	12	5	14
Rāmkelī	49	11	1	7
Bilāval	12	35	3	16
Malār	2	10	1	6
Mārū	3	7	1	6
Ṭoḍī	2	3	1	9

Source: Author.

nor the poem's meaning is static. To acquire the additional data that would make this latter approach feasible is very difficult. It is almost impossible to ascertain the structure of a given raga as it would have been performed in the bhakti period. It is equally difficult to know how our four bhakti poets might have perceived such a raga at that point of time, a bit of information that would seem to be required to determine a given poem's communicability with the raga in question.[20] From the early twentieth century onwards, when gramophone companies started recording in India, we have enough data to show that singers hardly make a habit of following the ragas indicated on the page as they prepare to render the compositions of bhakti poets. How is this to be understood? Maybe the sensibilities expressed in the meaning of the poems have changed in the course of time or, alternatively, there have been changes in the interpretation of the ragas involved. Or perhaps both.

The situation is complex. We can see what is involved by considering the example of raga bilāval. Bilāval is a morning raga, intended to be sung between 6 a.m. and 9 a.m., preferably in the rainy season, and with a feeling of deep devotion and repose. Bilāval was a popular raga in the early modern period. No wonder, then, that over 170 hymns were composed to this raga by Guru Nanak, Guru Amar Das, Guru Ram Das, Guru Arjan, and Guru Tegh Bahadur, as recorded in the *Ādi Granth*. It later became a basic *ṭhāṭh* (musical mode) in Hindustani classical music. Bilāval is considered by most authorities to be of the *sampūrṇa-sampūrṇa jāti* (all seven notes in ascending and descending). Others, however, are of the opinion that it should be considered *śadav-sampūrṇa* (six notes in ascending and seven notes in descending) due to the weakness of its *ga* in the ascent (*ārohana*) of the raga. In ascending, the following svaras appear: *sā re ga ma pa dha ni sā*. In descending, the following: *sā ni dha pa ma ga re sā*. Its *vādi* (evocative note) is *dha* and its *saṃvādi* (co-note) is *ga*. The *calan* or *pakaḍ* (characteristic gait) is: *ga re, ga ma dha pa, ma ga, ma re sā*. So there are some uncertainties in evaluating bilāval as we presently know it, but there are well-accepted generalizations as well.

Now what can we see if we consider four actual uses of bilāval on the part of our exemplary bhakti poets? Tulsidas's *Vinaya Patrikā* begins with a hymn to Lord Ganesha in this raga:

gāïe ganapati jagabandana, saṁkara-suvana bhavānī-nandana
siddhi-sadana gajabadana bināyaka, kṛpā-sindhu sundara saba lāyaka

modaka-priya mudra-maṅgala-dātā, vidyā varidhi buddhi-vidhātā
māṁgata tulasidāsa kara jore, basahiṁ rāmasiya manasa more[21]

Surdas also begins his *mangalācaraṇ* (invocation) in raga bilāval:

carana kamala bandau harirāī,
jākī kṛpā paṁgu giri laṁghai andhe kau saba kaghu darasāī[22]

On one occasion, Mira employs bilāval for a poem that starts thus:

āvo manamohanājī mīṭhī thāro bol (ṭek)
balapanāṁ kī prīta ramaiyā jī, kade nāhi āyo tharo tola
darasaṇa vaṇi mohi jakaṇa parata hai, catti mero ḍāvāṁḍola
mīra kahai maiṁbhaī bāvarī, kahī bajāüṁḍola[23]

Finally, Kabir gives us a pada in raga bilāval that begins as follows:

bāra bāra hari kā guṇa gāvai, gura gami bheda sahara kā pāvai (tek)[24]

If we analyse these poems, we find a certain similarity in their contents as well as in their forms, and each of these seems well-suited to the patterns of raga bilāval as they have been set out earlier. So far, then, we seem to be on solid footing. But in our contemporary times, if we take, for example, Tulsidas's first Ganesha hymn, so very popular across the musical genres, we find that hardly anybody sings it in raga bilāval. Three symptomatic examples can be cited: Ashwini Bhide's rendering of this poem in raga *bihāg*,[25] Pandit Rajan and Sajan Mishra's rendering in raga *kiravāṇī*,[26] and Ahmed Hussain and Muhammad Husain's rendering in raga *mārvā*.[27] If we compare the characteristics of these ragas with those appropriate to raga bilāval, we get the following spread (Table 6.5).

As the table shows, these four ragas are so different in nature that their suitability for the above-mentioned poem can only be interpreted as an act of individual perception on the part of the performer. Ragas

Table 6.5 One Poem in Four *Ragas*

Raga	Nature	Jati	Performance time
Bilāval	Devotional	sampūrṇa-sampūrṇa	morning
Bihāg	Serious	audav-sampūrṇa	late night
Kiravāṇī	Melancholic	sampūrṇa-sampūrṇa	midnight
Mārvā	Contemplative	śadav-śadav	sunset

Source: Author.

have different possible meanings just as poems do; there are multiple possibilities in each case. Ragas not only differ from one another as a class, they also vary according to individual usage. When it comes to an act of poetic communication between words and music, then, it is not just a question of which raga will best suit a given poem, but which is best suited to communicate its meaning in a given moment. Or, to work backwards, which poem is best suited to give 'voice' to a given raga?

In the end, then, we can only return to the conundrum with which we began: Is it poetry in ragas or ragas in poetry? It seems it must indeed be both.

Notes

1. 'gāndharva trividhaṁ vidhyāt svaratālahadātmakam' (R.S. Nagar, ed., *Naṭyaśāstra of Bharatmuni with the Abhinav Bharati Commentary* 4: 28/11 [New Delhi: Parimal, 1998]).

2. 'kintvanyathā tasya (padasya) prādhāvyaṁ gane'nyathā cagandharve. tatra hi svaratālau pradhānam. tau canādharau va śakyau prayoktumitthādhārayā tadupayogi tadāha svartālānubhāvakamiti. Abhinava Bhāratī' (Nagar, *Naṭyaśāstra of Bharatmuni*, 302).

3. 'eka eva tu prakāraḥ kalāvidhinā nibadhyamāno rāghavavijayamārī cavadhādikaṁ rāgakāvyabhedamudbhāvayatīti. yathokta (kohalena)—"layāntaraprayogena rāgaiścāpi vivecitam. nānārasaṁ sunirvāhma kathaṁ kāvyamiti smṛtam". layataścāsya gī tyādhāratvevāprādhāvye gītereva prādhānamiti va kāvyārthaviparyāsavaśena rāgabhāṣādiviparyāso nāṭya iva. tathā hi rāghavavijayasya hi ṭhakkarāgeṇaiva vicitravarnīyatve'pi nirvāḥ. mārīcavadhasya kakubhagrāmarāgeṇaiva. ateva rāgakāvyānītyucyaṁt etāni. rāgogītyātmakatvāstava (kaḥ sva) rasya tadādhārabhūtaṁ kāvyamitī' (Nagar, *Naṭyaśāstra of Bharatmuni*, 184).

4. Rādhavallabha Tripāṭhī, *Saṁskṛta shitya kā abhinav itihās* (Varanasi: Viśvavidhyālay Prakāśan, 2001), 205.

5. Out of the forty-seven songs in *Caryāgītikoṣa*, thirty-six are composed in Padakulaka, eleven in doha, chaupai, and other chands, and the following ragas are indicated in the text: *patamanjari, gabadi, malasi, malasi gabuda, aru, gujari, kahnugunjari, debakri desakh, bharabi, kamoda, dhanasi, ramakri, gauda badadi, sibari, baladdi, mallari,* and *bangala*. See Nilratan Sen, ed., *Caryāgitikoṣa* (Shimla: Indian Institute of Advanced Study, 1977).

6. Sarangadeva, *Saṅgītaratnākara*, ed. and trans. R.K. Shringy and Premlata Sharma (New Delhi: Munshiram Manoharlal, 1991), 292–4.

7. Nilratan Sen, *Early Eastern NIA Versification* (Shimla: Indian Institute of Advanced Study, 1973), 4.

8. Ganpati Candra Gupta, *Sāhityak Nibandh* (Allahabad: Lokabhārati Prakāśan, 1987), 364.

9. The *Ādi Granth* was compiled over a course of five centuries (twelfth to seventeenth centuries). Its final editing was completed in 1604, but earlier manuscripts also indicate ragas.

10. Ali S. Asani, 'At the Crossroads of Indic and Iranian Civilizations: Sindhi Literary Cultures', in *Literary Cultures in History: Reconstructions from South Asia*, ed. Pollock (Berkeley: University of California Press, 2003), 633.

11. 'karoti kāvyaṁ prayeṇa saṁskṛtātmā yathā tathā. paṭhituṁ vethi sa paraṁ yasya siddhā sarasvatī' (Rajaśekhara, *Kāvyamimāṁsā* [Patna: Bihār Rāṣtrabhāṣā Pariṣad, 2000], 82).

12. It is also worth mentioning that that poetry of the so-called *rīti* period (a period of 'conventions', seventeenth–eighteenth century) does not mention either the raga's name or that of the chand (metre), Bhartendu Harishchandra (1850–1885) tries it again in the nineteenth century. He not only indicates both, but sometimes also in the same text. In the Chayavad Movement, both Sumitranandan Pant and Suryakant Tripathy 'Nirala' thought it was necessary to delve into the relationship between chand and rasa in their poetry, albeit from different angles.

13. 'kāvye rasānusareṇa varṇanānuguṇena ca. kurvīta sarvavṛttānāṁ viniyogaṁ (7)' (Kṣemendra, *Suvṛttatilakam* [Varanasi: Chaukamba Sanskrit Series, 1968], 109).

14. Adya Rangacharya, ed., *Nāṭyaśāstra* (New Delhi: Munshiram Manoharlal, 2003), 287–8; in the original 1986 edition, 190–1.

15. Kailāś Candradev Bṛhaspati, *Bharat kā saṅgīt siddhānt* (Lucknow: Uttar Pradesh Hindi Sansthan, 1991), 271.

16. Quoted in B. Chaitanya Deva, *The Music of India: A Scientific Study* (New Delhi: Munshiram Manoharlal, 1995), 142.

17. Parshuram Chaturvedi, ed., *Mīrāṅbāī kī padāvalī* (Prayag: Hindi Sahitya Sammelan, 1993), 31–2.

18. Śyāmsundar Dās, *Kabīr Granthāvalī* (Allahabad: Lokbharti, 2011), 37.

19. Hazārīprasād Dvivedī, *Kabīr* (New Delhi: Rajkamal, 1994), 144.

20. Here we also take note of Winand M. Callewaert who, looking for the original version of Kabir, found 'musical' variants very important. He says:

> It would appear that first the singers sang a particular song in a particular *rāg*, then they grouped together the songs which were to be sung in the same *rāg*. Consequently, a *rāg* is like an identity card for the earliest period of oral transmission. The same song, however, could be sung to different *rāga*-s. As a result we find songs classified under different *raga*-s in different manuscripts. This variation in classification is obviously not due to a scribe's intervention, but stems from the oral period itself when the songs were transmitted in the hands of the singers. Subsequently, the songs were under different *rāga*-s and appeared as such

in the manuscripts (Winand Callewaert, *The Millennium Kabīr Vāṇī* [New Delhi: Manohar, 2000], 103).

21. Tulsidas, *Vinay Patrikā* (Gorakhpur: Gita Press, 2000), 13.

22. Hardev Bāharī and Rājendra Kumār, eds, *Sūrsāgar Saṭīk*, vol. 1 (Allahabad: Lokbhārati Prakāśan, 1991), 1.

23. Chaturvedi, *Mīrāṅbāī kī padāvalī*, 129.

24. Dās, *Kabīr Granthāvalī*, 205.

25. Available at http://www.youtube.com/watch?v=D01xA03C8yE, last accessed on 10 September 2016.

26. *Bhaktimala: Ganesh*, vol. 1. Music Today, 1991.

27. *Shradha*, T-series, 1995.

Bibliography

Bahiri, Hardeo and Rajendra Kumar, eds. *Sūr Sāgar*. Allahabad: Lokbharti, 1991.

Banukavi, Jagannath Prasad. *Chandaprabhākar*. Bombay: Shrivenkateshvar, 1931.

Brihaspati, Acharya. Kailashchandradev. *Bhārat kā saṅgīt siddhānt*. Lucknow: Uttar Pradesh Hindi Sansthan, 1991.

Callewaert, Winand. *The Millennium Kabīr Vāṇī*. New Delhi: Manohar, 2000.

Chaturvedi, Parshuram, ed. *Mīrāṅbāī kī padāvalī*. Prayag: Hindi Sahitya Sammelan, 1993.

Coomaraswamy, Anand K. *Essays on Music*. New Delhi: Manohar, 2010.

Das, Shyamsundar. *Kabīr Granthāvalī*. Allahabad: Lokbharti, 2011.

Deva, B. Chaitanya. *The Music of India: A Scientific Study*. New Delhi: Munshiram Manoharlal, 1995.

Dvivedi, Hazariprasad. *Kabīr*. New Delhi: Rajkamal, 1994.

Gupta, Ganpatichandra. *Sāhityak Nibhandh*. Allahabad: Lokbharti, 1987.

Kshemendra. *Suvrittatilakam*. Varanasi: Chaukhamba, 1968.

Mitra, Rajyeshwar. *Mughal bhārat kā saṅgīt cintan*. New Delhi: National Publishing House, 1993.

Nagar, R. S., ed. *Naṭyaśāstra of Bharatmuni with the Abinava Bharati Commentary*. New Delhi: Parimal, 1998.

Pant, Sumitranandan. *Pallav*. New Delhi: Rajkamal, 1977.

Pollock, Sheldon, ed. *Literary Cultures in History: Reconstructions from South Asia*. Berkeley: University of California Press, 2003.

Rajshekhar. *Kāvyamīmāṁsa*. Patna: Bihar Rashtra Bhasha Parishad, 2000.

Rangacharya, Adya, ed. *Nāṭyaśāstra*. New Delhi: Munshiram Manoharlal, 2003.

Sarangadeva. *Saṅgītaratnākara*, edited and translated by R.K. Shringy and Premlata Sharma. New Delhi: Munshiram Manoharlal, 1991.

Sen, Nilratan, ed., *Caryāgītikoṣa*. Shimla: Indian Institute of Advanced Study, 1977.

Singh, Mahip. *Ādi Granth*. New Delhi: Rajpal, 2009.

Tripathy, Radhavallabh. *Saṁskṛt sāhitya kā abhinav itihās*. Varanasi: Vishvavidyalaya Prakashan, 2001.

Tripathy, Suryakant 'Nirala'. *Parimal*. New Delhi: Rajkamal, 1988.

Tulsidas. *Vinay Patrikā*. Gorakhpur: Gita Press, 2000.

7

JAROSLAV STRNAD

Searching for the Source or Mapping the Stream?

Some Text-Critical Issues in the Study of Medieval *Bhakti*

The study of medieval manuscripts that contain verses of north Indian devotional poetry, particularly those attributed to thinkers of the so-called *sant dhārā*, can be profitably pursued by methods that require the skills of a pure philologist, but in this there is more to be considered than classical models of philology suggest. The language of many texts available in manuscript collections datable to the sixteenth–eighteenth centuries is a peculiar mix of north Indian dialectal forms that shows the language to be a process rather than a polished product of learned poets informed by the tradition of classical Sanskrit literature and grammar. To the philologist, the unpolished language of *pad*s and *sākhī*s (couplet) contained in the manuscript collections represents an invaluable source for the study of an important phase in the history of New Indo-Aryan languages. We can follow the gradual phonological erosion of endings and suffixes and observe a concomitant emergence of postpositional phrases and analytical verbal forms. Collections with different but identifiable dates and places of origin show these processes in different stages of progress and leading in different directions.

Scholars pursuing this line of research will find the original manuscript material to be of greater interest and better use than printed collections with a lot of editing and sometimes even phonological and grammatical 'normalization' of non-standard forms. A critical apparatus given in footnotes below a reconstructed text may be helpful, but inevitably it makes the reconstitution of original sources rather difficult. A welcome attempt at a solution to this problem is represented by the latest edition of Kabir's pads prepared by Winand Callewaert and Swapna Sharma—*The Millennium Kabīr Vāṇī* published in the year 2000. Here the pads (sākhīs and *ramainī*s [a longer poem with esoteric meaning] have been omitted) transcribed from nine manuscript collections—to which the *Ādigranth* versions, if available, were added—have been ordered synoptically *in extenso* on the same page or adjoining pages. This is probably the first time that scholars have received the opportunity to see the variant forms and phrases in their original contexts. If there is a drawback, at least for a pedant philologist, it is merely a feature inherent in all editions: by necessity the transfer of the handwritten text to the printed page includes a lot of interpretation (segmentation of the original *scriptura continua* into meaningful words, handling of nasalizations, and so on) and sometimes brings unwelcome printing errors. These notwithstanding, the *Millennium Kabīr Vāṇī* represents a very helpful aid to further research and also an incentive for the inquisitive scholar to go back to the original manuscripts. This brings us to the urgent desideratum of New Indo-Aryan philology—the necessity of digitizing at least that part of the manuscript material which had been already photographed and is now available on microfilm reels, and, as the next step, the exact transliteration (as far as possible) that would prepare the text for processing in concordancers and related linguistic software. To chart the main currents in language change, the quantitative aspect is of great importance, particularly if a scholar tries to distinguish short-term variations and scribes' idiosyncrasies from long-term trends.

This quantitative approach to texts can yield interesting results in other ways too—when the main attention turns to a comparative study of the content and meaning of the extant creations. Study of a greater number of manuscripts containing utterances attributed to a particular author may reveal significant variations in their form and not infrequently also in content. It can be argued that this kind of variation is closely related to the predominantly performative character of many poems—either authored by the *sant*s themselves or inspired by them and composed by others. It may be futile to search for the 'authentic' or original version of a particular poem that has come down to us embedded in the broad current of a living tradition borne for centuries by predominantly oral and performative presentations that involve a significant degree of improvisation. Rather than looking for 'Ur-texts', philological and comparativist methods might be used to map the dynamic flows—the cross-currents and undercurrents—that constitute, in the long term, a particular tradition.

From this perspective, studies of north Indian bhakti literature and vernacular poetry may profit from the recent methodological advances made in the study of oral poetry, particularly by Finnish scholars, some of whom have devoted considerable attention to Indian oral traditions as well.[1]

Considering the fact that Kabir and other medieval poets of the so-called sant tradition presented their ideas and poetry in oral form (several sākhīs attributed to Kabir advocate this in an unambiguous way), the organic variation concept introduced by Lauri Honko and his colleagues can offer us a useful methodological tool in our search for possible 'original' versions of bhakti poems. In Honko's understanding, the term 'organic' refers to a textual variation that arises in a specific situation and context, in which a particular text (song, poem) is presented or performed before a public. In an oral tradition there may be more than one authorial version and, of course, more than one variant of each of these several authorial versions in consequence of their having been presented by still other performers before their different audiences. The extant Kabirian texts incorporated into different collections (be it *pañcvāṇīs* [an anthology of works attributed to five major authors canonized by the Dādūpanth: Dādū, Kabīr, Nāmdev, Hardās, and Raidās], *sarvāṅgīs* [Dādūpanthī anthology of texts by different authors in different poetic forms on a broad range of topics], or other types of anthologies) reflect this orality-based diversity. Yet the texts that have come down to us in the manuscripts appear to be products not only of oral traditions but of written ones as well—two traditions, sometimes parallel and sometimes intersecting.

Under such circumstances, any attempt by authors of 'critical editions' to arrive at the original version of a poem (an Ur-text) amounts to little more than the addition of another variant to the already existing ones. Actually, the structure of the pad, with its relatively free ordering of, more or less, self-contained distichs, is an ideal form for variation through interpolations and/or elisions, as the need may be, of lines, distichs, and even larger blocks of text. These can emphasize, dilute, or subtly modify the basic idea of the pad without destroying its internal coherence.

Comparisons of texts found in the Kabirian collections with works attributed to other medieval poets (particularly other sants and *nāths* [sādhus belonging to an order founded by Gorakhnāth]) may bring to light surprising parallels with word-for-word correspondences not only of particular phrases, but whole distichs, and in several cases even complete pads attributed in their colophons (*bhaṇitās*) variously to different authors. In the case of Kabirian literature from Rajasthan, we can see striking parallels with phrases and verses found in the works of Dadu, Gorakhnath, and to a lesser extent those attributed to Namdev. Modern literary theories working with the (variously articulated) concept of intertextuality may help in providing useful guidelines and frameworks for a systematic mapping of this so far little studied aspect of medieval Indian literature.

Probably the most obvious candidates for a mutual comparison are the texts of sākhīs and pads found in the same scribal collection (manuscript) and attributed to the same author. In the case of Kabir's Rajasthani corpus it is possible to identify several instances of sākhīs, or parts of them, which can be found to form an integral part of a larger composition, a pad—a group of ideas or images that serve as an axis around which a singer could build such a poem. Seen in this context, sākhīs may be identified as one possible source of inspiration to singers whose task was to compose larger poetic structures. As an example, we can take the first three sākhīs from Jaipur MS 3190,[2] chapter 'citāvanī kau āga' (MS 3190 fol. 263a), and set them alongside the pad published in the *Millennium Kabīr Vāṇī* under the number 367 (corresponding to MS 3190 fol. 227a):

kabīra naubati āpaṇī // dina dasa lehu bajāi //
ai pura pāṭaṇa ai galī // bahuṛi na deṣisi āi //1//
Kabir [says]—your festive music
 you may play for a few days;
[then] this quarter, town, this lane—
 you will not come back and see [them] again.

Kabīra jyãha kai naubati bājatī // maĩgala bãdhate bāri //
aikai hari kai nãva bina // gaye janma saba hāri //2//

Kabir [says]—they whose festive music is heard all the time,
who chain the musth elephants as a matter of course:
without [remembering] the name of the One Hari
[their] whole birth is lost.

Kabīra ḍholā damā̃mā̃ duṛabaṛī // sahināī sā̃gi bheri //
ausara cale bajāi kari // hai ko lyāvai pheri //3//
Kabir [says]—drum, kettledrum, timpani,
cymbals together with pipe:
once played, [these] shows are gone;
is there anybody who can call them back?[3]

prā̃ṇī lāla ausara cale re bajāi //
mūṭhī aika kaṭhiyā̃ mū̃ṭhī aika mā̃ṭiyā / **hā̃sā̃gi kāhū kai na jāi** //ṭeka//
deharī laga terī sagī re maherī // phalisā lagī samī i i [read: sagīmāī] //
marahaṭa laga saba loka sagau re // hā̃sa akelau jāi //
kahā̃ vai loga kahā̃ pura paṭā̃ṇa / bahuri na deṣisi āi //
kahai kabīra rā̃ma nā̃ma bhajana bina // janama avirathā jāi //12//

People, dear ones, played out, [your] shows are gone;
a single fistful of bones, a single fistful of flesh—
no one takes with him when he dies.
Your wife is your [closest] relative within the door-step [of your house],
your mother within the border of [your] village;
all the world is [your] relative up to the cremation ground;
[then] the swan (soul) flies away alone.
Where are those people, where is the quarter, the town [you have lived in]?
You will not come back and see [them] again.
Kabir says—without worshipping the name of Ram/God
life will pass in vain.[4]

A comparison of passages printed in bold letters in the sākhīs and in the pad shows close correspondences not only in meaning but also in form, as shown by the phrases 'ausara cale bajāī', 'pura paṭā̃ṇa', and 'bahuri na deṣisi āī'. The author of the pad probably knew many sākhīs by heart and was able to join them, with the help of additional material, into a larger meaningful whole. In this work, he was helped by the structure of many sākhī collections: typical for them was a grouping of topics into thematic chapters and within each chapter an ordering process structured by dominant or significant phrases or words that they contained. Thus, for example, the first two sākhīs contain the phrase 'naubati baj-/bāj-', which means literally 'to beat the drum', thus, 'to play one's own music' or 'to have a good time'. The metaphor of musical instruments is carried over to the third and fourth sākhīs that also use the verbs 'baj-' (to sound) and 'bāj-' (to play). Similarly, a little bit further down in the same chapter, sākhīs 9 to 12 contain the phrase *kahā grabiyau* (Why do you pride yourself?) followed by the admonition to realize the futility of self-aggrandizement and attachment to worldly pursuits. This kind of ordering appears to be followed more or less consistently throughout the sākhī section of the *Kabir Vāṇī*, at least in the older collections.

Related to this predilection for thematic ordering is the habit followed by the scribes to leave an empty space at the end of each thematic sākhī and pad chapter, obviously with the intention to fill it later with new, thematically related material. This peculiar feature of the scribal collections can be detected only by a study of the original manuscript—the existence of inserted portions and the fact that they are often written by a different hand, probably at a later time, is typically not reflected in printed editions. The study of manuscripts, therefore, helps us understand some of the ways the material circulating in oral form was gradually collected, written down, and sorted in such a way as to help the singers in mobilizing the appropriate words, phrases, and ideas suitable for a particular performance context. The same purpose was served by ordering the pads according to different rāgas sung on different occasions and in different parts of a day.

These observations make a strong case for looking at the texts not—or not only—as independent units but as a series, each characterized by a peculiar inner ordering of its constituent parts. In the case of sākhīs, the features worth recording are the names and the sequence of chapters, and, at a lower level, the number and ordering of sākhīs within each chapter. The collation of different manuscripts of known date and place of provenance, laborious as it may be, may help us build a chronological and spatial map showing the gradual accretion of new material added to an older core. An analysis of sākhī collections may be a good starting point for such an endeavour, since they are easier to study than pads with their greater internal variability.

As far as pads are concerned, comparative analysis may focus on the variability of their internal structure in so far as it shows the limits of singers' freedom to improvise—a freedom which may be relatively narrow within a certain school or tradition (Dadupanthi, Vaishnava, and so on), or significantly broader, as in the case of Kabir vāṇīs with borrowing and adaptation that become evident if we compare the Rajasthani (Dadupanthi and Vaishnava), Panjabi (Sikh), and Eastern

(Kabirpanth, *Bījak*) traditions. The number of pads (or what can still be counted as one and the same pad) common to all these three main traditions is quite small—not more than a dozen—but their comparison can still be instructive.

As an example of this internal variability, we can look at a famous pad attributed by all three traditions to Kabir. In the oldest Rajasthani version, it begins with the words *lokā re mati bhorā re*. Apart from the substantial reordering of individual verses within the pad as it occurs in the three traditions and the omission of certain verses in the Rajasthani and Panjabi versions, we can also detect more subtle shifts in the meaning. Thus, Kabir's introductory exclamation is interpreted in two different ways: the *Ādigranth* version states unambiguously *hari ke logā mai ta:u mati kā bhorā* (O people of Hari, I am such a fool!), an ironical exclamation through which Kabir ('maĩ', that is, 'I') distances himself from the 'wiser' people for whom devotion to a holy city is more important than devotion to the one God within. The *Bījak* takes the more direct way of saying the same thing: *logā tumahī̃ mati ke bhorā* (People, you are fools!), addressing them directly (*tumahī̃*, 'you'). The oldest Rajasthani version of Jaipur MS 3190 *lokā re mati bhorā re* ('O people, foolish in mind!') is less explicit: it can be understood either as '[I am] foolish in (my) mind' or '[You are] foolish in mind'. Parallel readings extant in later Dadupanthi and Vaishnava Rajasthani manuscripts have the unambiguous *lokā mati ke bhorā re*, where the plural form *ke* of the postposition, missing in the oldest variant where both the singular form *kā* and plural *ke* can be supplied, points to people as fools. The difference between the direct scolding found in the *Bījak* and the irony of the *Ādigranth* version and possibly the second oldest Rajasthani manuscript with Kabir's poems may be a subtle one; but such subtleties can be looked upon as constituent parts of a peculiar style.

An example showing a different aspect of textual variation is presented in pad no. 416 of the *Millennium Kabīr Vāṇī* edition.[5] Despite the fact that it is missing in the oldest Jaipur Dadupanthi manuscript (MS 3190), it still can be counted as belonging to the older layer of Kabir's (or Kabirian) poetry: a Panjabi version of it is found in the *Mohan Pothī* manuscript (dated to ca. 1570 CE), a predecessor of the *Ādigranth*. Winand Callewaert has selected as the main Rajasthani version the text included in a pañcvāṇī manuscript of 1675 CE:

raĩni gaī jaisaĩ dina bhī jāi / bhavara uḍe vaga vaiṭhe āi //ṭeka//
tharahari kā̃pyau vārā jīva / ko jā̃naī kā karihai pīva //1//

kācai bhā̃ḍai rahai na pā̃nī̃ / hā̃sa calyau kāyā kumilā̃nī̃ //2//
kahi kavīra yahu kathā sirā̃nī̃ / kāga uḍāvata vā̃ha pirā̃nī̃ //3//

As the night has passed, the day will pass too;
Black bees have flown, the herons have come and settled down. // refrain//
Shaking and shivering, the bride's soul trembled:
Who knows what the bridegroom will do. //1//
The water will not stay in the unbaked pot;
The swan has flown, the body has withered away. //2//
Kabir says: this is the end of the story;
Chasing away the crows the arm has begun to ache. //3//

Several features make this short poem interesting, one of them being the fact that it is entirely composed of metaphors. Black bees stand for black hair, herons for white hair; the refrain reminds us of the inexorable process of ageing. The first verse likens the relationship of the soul and God to the young bride expecting with trembling anxiety the way her bridegroom will treat her. The second verse represents the impermanent body as an unbaked pot that cannot hold the water (life) for long. The second part of the verse uses different images to express the same idea: since the time of early Upanishads the swan (*haṃsa*) has been understood as a symbol of the soul. Idiomatically, chasing away the crows means to indulge in useless work. Interpreted in a somewhat different way, the phrase may refer to the habit of unmarried girls who chase away crows and try to guess from their patterns of flight whether their beloved will come or not—or from what direction the bridegroom will come. The latter idiomatic meaning may not carry as strong a connotation of uselessness as the former: it can be interpreted as a sign of longing, perhaps even laudable, but in itself not sufficient to bring the desired result. This might be the reason for a change of the last line in the oldest Dadupanthi version of the poem that is included in the *Sarvāṅgī* of Gopaldas (compiled in 1627 CE). Here the poem ends with a stronger and more direct warning:

kahai kabīra kachu kīyā na hoi / tau daragaha pālāna pakarai koi //3//

Kabir says: if nothing is done,
somebody [else] will capture the throne of royalty.[6]

This change makes the meaning of the message quite straightforward—by 'somebody else' is here meant *kāl* (Death)—but the new phrase blends in neither with the general, perhaps, somewhat melancholic tone of the poem, nor with the metaphor of the bride and bridegroom (which in Gopaldas's *Sarvāṅgī* directly precedes the last verse). Here we see how the locally or regionally specific interpretation of certain phrases or idioms may figure as one of the reasons for selective rephrasings of received texts.

Equally interesting as rephrasings and shifts of emphasis in texts of the Kabirian tradition is the evidence of mutual influencing and mingling of different strands within the broad current of sant religiosity. As the general outlook of the *nirguṇī* poets was very similar, the occurrence of similar ideas in their pads and sākhīs should not be a matter of surprise. What is certainly worthy of note, however, particularly when studying the internal structure of a number of pads, is the incorporation of phrases and clauses that appear in identical or nearly identical form in works attributed to other authors. Some of these may have been drawn from a common pool of public wisdom accumulated in the course of the long history of religious thinking, teaching, debating, and disputing. Many sākhīs attributed to different authors may be of this origin. But others are more specific, and their co-occurrence in the textual corpora of two or more authors may point to closer contacts between communities of singers and scribes that handed down the words of their spiritual masters.

What is particularly striking in the case of the old Rajasthani Kabirian corpus is the great number of ideas and phrases (or rephrasings) borrowed from the *bānī* of the Nathpanthi guru Gorakhnath. Probably the most notable example is pad no. 186 of the *Millennium Kabīr Vāṇī* edition (corresponding to pad no. 9 of the *rāga rāmagrī* section of Jaipur MS 3190), which is nearly identical with pad no. 17 of *Gorakhbānī* in the Barthwal's edition.[7] In the symbolical language of Nathpanthi religious philosophy, the pad describes the mystical plantlet that grows inside the body—its paradoxical nature and behaviour. The version extant in the Kabir corpus appears to be corrupted at several places, which the scribe may not have understood correctly; but, more significant is the change at the very beginning of the pad. The version in the *Gorakhbānī* as extant in the Jaipur MS 3190 begins with the words:

tatva belī lo tatva belī lo // avadhū gorașanātha jā̃nī //

Gorakhnath has known the plant of the true substance, o *avadhūta*![8]

In the pad of the Kabir corpus in the same manuscript, this sentence is changed to:

rā̃ma gū̃na belaṛī re avadhū gorașanāthi jā̃ṇī //

Gorakhnath has known the plantlet of the praise of the Lord, o *avadhūta*!

The change of the character of the subject of the pad from the mystical essence attained by a process of psycho-physical exercises developed, practised, and described in the Nathpanthi communities into the activity of praising the name of God as recommended by nirguṇī sants can be seen as an example of subtle reinterpretation of tenets held by a closely related, but independent and distinct traditions.

Similar shifts of emphasis can be detected in two other pads, one in the *Gorakhbānī* corpus and the other in the Rajasthani collection of Kabirian poetry.[9] Both pads describe the human body as an alembic and the production of the true substance as a result of mystical distillation. They are similar in content and in the elated tone that suggests a state of joyful intoxication; still, they should not be understood as two versions of one and the same poem. Apart from other differences of more or less formal character, there is one of special interest. Namely, in contrast to Gorakhnath, Kabir does not forget to mention the destruction of the baser human qualities that occurs during the process of distillation and the resultant detachment from the worldly pursuits:

kā̃ma krodha dou kīyā balītā // chū̃ṭi gaī sā̃sārī //

Of both, lust and anger, [I have] made the wick/igniter.
Attachment to the world (or worldliness) has disappeared.[10]

Similar observations can be made about several other pads attributed to Gorakhnath and Kabir: the general idea, the dominant image, and the structure may be (nearly) identical, but the description differs in details. Gorakhnath's pad no. 18 and the pad found in the *Millennium Kabīr Vāṇī* at number 182[11]—both describe the paradoxical character of the ultimate reality that is called brahma and *paramāratha* in Gorakhnath's pad and *gobinda* and *hari* in Kabir's. The opening line in both is similar:

pūchau paṇḍita brahma giyā̃nā

Ask, o pundit, about the knowledge of Brahma (Gorakhnath).

jāi pūchau gobinda paḍhiyā paṇḍita
Go to inquire about Gobinda, o learned pundit (Kabir).

In both pads some of the concrete examples by means of which the paradoxical nature of the Ultimate is demonstrated are different, while some are identical but expressed in different terms. Thus, the first verse of both pads contains these words:

bā̃jha kerā balūṛā pyā̃gula taravari caṛhiyā (Gorakhnath)

Son of a barren woman, [although] lame, has climbed a tree.

bā̃jha kā pūta bāpa bina jāyā / bina pā̃u taravari caḍhiyā (Kabir)

Son of a barren woman, born without a father,
[although] without legs, has climbed a tree.

Comparing these and several other pads attributed to these two authors, one wonders whether what one is reading are two different works, or just two variants of one and the same pad handed down by two different lines of tradents in two different dialectal environments. In Gorakhnath's language we can see a stronger western or Marwari influence (*kerā, caṛhiyā*) than in Kabir. In this context, it should be noted that grammatical forms typically occurring in Nathpanthi texts, for example, the past participles with the inserted *-i-* that are common in western dialects, appear mainly in those Kabirian pads that show close parallels with verses of the *Gorakhbānī*. This seems to indicate that at least some singers may have been versed in both traditions, capable of improvising and accommodating their performances to the expected disposition of the public. The more popular or successful presentations might have been written down in songbooks as handy reminders for similar future occasions.

This brings us to the important question of what should count as the legitimate unit of analysis in the study of the historical development of a tradition of the sant dhārā type. If we attempt the task of reconstructing the single, original, and authentic version of a poem or aphorism, the so-called critical editions that result will be of limited use. When we look at the history of the formation of the Rajasthani Kabirian corpus, as we have seen, we are faced with a number of influences and cross-currents coming from several directions, whose existence can be demonstrated by occurrences of specific terms, phrases, and images. In the Rajasthani pads attributed to Kabir, we can see clear Nathpanthi influences; the whole corpus was passed on and written down by members of the Dadupanthi community; and the geographical closeness to the Braj area was probably responsible for a noticeable imprint of Vaishnava images. How best to register all this? I would argue that the firmest ground for a study of such traces and identifications is the available manuscript material itself. Many manuscripts housed in the public and private libraries of north India can be best described as extensive collections of religious literature of the age—storehouses of texts considered relevant to the spiritual needs of broad strata of the population, compendia whose content is not restricted to just one religious authority or tradition. We should take this as the great resource that it is, and, therefore, use such manuscripts as we have been given them, yet without insisting that any such text be seen as definitive for the genre as a whole.

To give just one example of what I mean, let me point to the manuscript I have all along been using as a source of Kabir's pads. It was discovered and brought to the attention of scholarly public by Winand Callewaert in the *Millennium Kabīr Vāṇī*. In the introduction of that work, Callewaert gives only a very short description of the manuscript (just eight lines) and characterizes it as a *pañcvāṇī*—a term used for Dadupanthi collections of sākhīs and poems attributed to five sants who enjoyed exceptional popularity and authority in the Dadupanth: namely Dadu, Kabir, Namdev, Raidas (Ravidas), and Hardas.[12] But an inspection of the contents of the manuscript presents quite a different picture: the original is a huge *pothī* (book, codex) of 692 folios; as first items, it lists a *vānī-saṃgrah* (collection of vānīs or anthologies) of Dadu, *vāṇī-saṃgrah* of Kabir, and next a *vividh vāṇī-saṃgrah* (collection of different vānīs) that contains, apart from the texts of the remaining three *pañcvāṇī sants* (authors represented in pañcvāṇī type of anthology) mentioned above, other works of more than seventy different authors. These vāṇī sections are followed by works of other medieval bhakti authors (pads of Surdas are also included) and also by Nathpanthi texts. The text of the *Gorakhbānī* included in this manuscript is, to my knowledge, the earliest extant version of this important work.

All authors included in this collection and in many other sarvāṅgīs and anthologies of a similar kind were considered relevant first of all as authoritative carriers of important spiritual truths—truths that could be presented in different forms, eliciting different but always desirable and salvific emotional and intellectual responses from those who listened to them. An important requirement for the singer was to be faithful to this primary meaning of the message. The exhortative, inspirative, and practically oriented character of a large part of this literature is summed up tersely by Kabir in the last verse of one of his pads:

yahu terau ausara yā terī bāra // ghaṭahi̐ bhītari soci bicāri //
kahai kabīra jīti bhāvai hāri // bahu bidhi kahyau pukāri pukāri //

This is your opportunity, this is your time:
 think, contemplate within [your] heart!
Kabir says: you may either win or lose.
 In many ways I have explained and entreated.[13]

Obviously, the purpose of this literature was to reveal the truth about life and its ultimate meaning—truth or truths of cosmic rather than worldly character. Those who preached them and stood behind them had to be men of great spiritual authority and moral integrity. Their authorship was considered to be of different kind from that of, say, classical kāvya or rīti poets.[14] Preaching and spreading the messages of sants was a collective effort on the part of many generations of tradents. The memories and social contexts of different actors active in that process brought more or less subtle changes in the form and, to some extent, the content of the message. The Jaipur 3190 manuscript that Callewaert has brought to light can also be seen as an important link in this long chain.

The field of possible comparisons that emerges within and in relation to that manuscript is vast. So is the range of subtle textual manipulations and reinterpretations that it displays. These have been so far little explored. The research that is needed should include, inter alia, a thorough study of Indian traditions of memorization. When compared to the very specific tradition of Vedic recitation, the study of other ways and methods has received, to my knowledge, considerably less attention.[15] Closely related to this problem is the fact that in the period under study, at least, the oral tradition already existed side by side with the written one; it is highly probable that each influenced the other. Errors that typically occur in the process of handing down a longer utterance or a poem known by heart are of a different kind from the typical run of scribal errors. Extant manuscripts contain numerous instances of both these types; recording and analysing them not as individual examples, but in a systematic way in the framework of a broadly based quantitative study may be helpful in charting out various currents of a tradition across space and time.

As far as the study of the historical development of a specific religious 'current' is concerned, an important advantage the Rajasthani Kabirian textual tradition has over that of the *Ādigranth* and the *Bījak* is its relatively large amount of written texts. These are available in the form of manuscripts, covering the long span of the seventeenth and eighteenth centuries. One of the more pressing requirements for future research is to make available as many manuscripts as possible to the scholarly community, preferably in the form of digitized images. Scholars engaged in this type of research should be expected either to have the memory comparable to that of the medieval singers themselves or to own a computer with a sophisticated concordancer and a lot of transcribed texts. In the advancing decadence of the *kaliyuga*, we must probably settle for the second option. Transferring the digitized images into computer-readable text formats will, therefore, be our next important task.

Notes

1. See, for example, the collection of articles edited by Lauri Honko, *Thick Corpus, Organic Variation and Textuality in Oral Tradition* (Helsinki: Finnish Literature Society, 2000). From the methodological point of view, of particular interest is the editor's introductory chapter, 'Thick Corpus and Organic Variation: An Introduction', 3–28. The Indian material there analysed was published by Lauri Honko and Anneli Honko, *The Siri Epic as Performed by Gopala Naika*, 2 vols (Helsinki: Suomalainen Tiedeakatemia, 1998). A shorter report of this project, in the form of an article, 'Variation and Textuality in Oral Epics: A South Indian Case', can be found in Honko, *Thick Corpus*, 351–72.

2. The manuscript which has served as the source of all verse quotations in this chapter is part of a large private manuscript collection housed in the Sanjay Sharma Museum and Research Institute, Jaipur, registered there as MS 3190. The date of its origin is given as 1614–19 CE, the scribe as Ram Das Dadupanthi, and the place Kadela, Rajasthan. I have been working with a digitized copy of a microfilm of the Kabir portion of the MS made by Winand Callewaert back in the 1980s. The microfilm reel is deposited in the library of the Südasien Institute, Heidelberg.

3. MS 3190 fol. 263a, sākhī, citāvanī kau ãga.

4. MS 3190 fol. 227a, rāga kedārau, pad 12 (Winand M. Callewaert with Swapna Sharma, *The Millennium Kabīr Vāṇī* [New Delhi: Manohar, 2000], pad no. 367).

5. Callewaert with Sharma, *The Millennium Kabīr Vāṇī*, 527, pad 416.

6. Callewaert with Sharma, *The Millennium Kabīr Vāṇī*, 527, *pad* 416—Gop109; 39.3.

7. Pitambardas Barthwal, *Gorakha-bānī* (Prayāg: Hindī Sāhitya Sammelan, 1960), 108–9.

8. Jaipur MS 3190, fol. 563b, pad 9.1.

9. Barthwal, *Gorakha-bānī*, 122–23, pad 28; Callewaert, *The Millennium Kabīr Vāṇī*, 137–8, pad 19; Jaipur MS 3190, fol. 191b, pad 15 of the *rāga gauṛī* section.

10. Jaipur MS 3190, fol. 191b, pad 15.2 of the *rāga gauṛī* section.

11. Barthwal, *Gorakha-bānī*, 108–9, pad 18; Callewaert with Sharma, *The Millennium Kabīr Vāṇī*, 291–2, pad 182; Jaipur MS 3190, fol. 205b–206a, pad 6 of the *rāga rāmagrī* section.

12. Callewaert with Sharma, *The Millennium Kabīr Vāṇī*, 21.

13. Jaipur MS 3190, fol. 231a, pad 16 in the section of *rāga bhairu*; Callewaert with Sharma, *The Millennium Kabīr Vāṇī*, 517–20, pad 408.

14. Excellent treatment of this aspect of medieval bhakti poetry can be found in the article of J. S. Hawley, 'Author and Authority in the Bhakti Poetry of North India', *Journal of Asian Studies* 47, no. 2 (1988): 269–90, reprinted in Hawley, *Three Bhakti Voices: Mirabai, Surdas, and Kabir in Their Times and Ours* (New Delhi: Oxford University Press, 2005), 21–47.

15. An inspiration for more detailed studies in this direction may be found in the current research done in the field of literary traditions of medieval Europe; cf., for example, Murray McGillivray, *Memorization in the Transmission of the Middle English Romances* (New York, London: Garland Publishing, 1990).

Bibliography

Barthwal, Pitambardas (Pītāṃbaradāsa Baḍathvāla). *Gorakha-bānī*. Prayāg: Hindī Sāhitya Sammelan, 1960.

Callewaert, Winand M. with Swapna Sharma. *The Millennium Kabīr Vāṇī: A Collection of Pads*. New Delhi: Manohar, 2000.

Hawley, J. S. 'Author and Authority in the Bhakti Poetry of North India'. *Journal of Asian Studies* 47, no. 2 (1988): 269–90.

———. *Three Bhakti Voices: Mirabai, Surdas, and Kabir in Their Times and Ours*. New Delhi: Oxford University Press, 2005.

Honko, Lauri, ed. *Thick Corpus, Organic Variation and Textuality in Oral Tradition*. Helsinki: Finnish Literature Society, 2000.

———. 'Thick Corpus and Organic Variation: An Introduction'. In *Thick Corpus, Organic Variation and Textuality in Oral Tradition*, edited by Lauri Honko. Helsinki: Finnish Literature Society, 2000.

Honko, Lauri and Anneli Honko. *The Siri Epic as Performed by Gopala Naika*, 2 vols. Helsinki: Suomalainen Tiedeakatemia, 1998.

———. 'Variation and Textuality in Oral Epics: A South Indian Case'. In *Thick Corpus, Organic Variation and Textuality in Oral Tradition*, edited by Lauri Honko. Helsinki: Finnish Literature Society, 2000.

McGillivray, Murray. *Memorization in the Transmission of the Middle English Romances*. New York, London: Garland Publishing, 1990.

8

HIROKO NAGASAKI

Duality in the Language and Literary Style of Raskhan's Poetry

Fragments of Information about Raskhan's Life

The Krishnaite poet Raskhan (Raskhān) is familiarly regarded as a convert from Islam to Hindu *bhakti*, but little is known about who Raskhan really was because he does not tell much about himself in his work. Only at the end of his *Prem-Vāṭikā* (*dohās*, 48–50)[1] do we come across couplets mentioning that Raskhan, who was a Pathan of Delhi, left his noble family background, broke a beautiful woman's heart, ran for safety from the upheaval in Delhi, and took refuge in Vrindavan. However, as Rupert Snell says, it is difficult to identify which war it was that he fled,[2] and scholars such as Baṭekr̥ṣṇa even claim that the *Prem-Vāṭikā* is not Raskhan's authentic work.[3]

Faced with such problems, we may turn to outside sources such as hagiographical texts in hopes of uncovering clues as to his life. Probably the oldest and most famous reference to Raskhan is found in the *Do sau bāvan vaiṣṇavan kī vārtā*, which portrays his conversion to the worship of Krishna as a disciple of Viṭṭhalnāth (1516–1586) after suffering from the agony of unfulfilled love directed to a boy.[4] Veṇīmādhavdās, a biographer of Tulsīdās who was supposedly his contemporary, also refers to him in his *Mūl gosāīṃ carit* (VS 1687).[5]

The information provided and date of composition given at the end of this work, however, have provoked much controversy and some scholars have concluded that this work has no credibility as a historical resource.[6] The *Mūl gosāīṃ carit* tells us that Raskhan listened to Tulsīdās's *Rāmcaritmānas* on the banks of the Yamuna for a period of three years, but it is hard to know whether this should be believed. Nābhādās and Priyādās, authors of the *Bhaktamāl* and its principal commentary, do not mention Raskhan, even though both wrote about Tulsīdās. It was not until the eighteenth century that Vaiṣṇavdās, a grandson of Priyādās, referred to Raskhan in his *Bhaktamāl Prasaṅg* (VS 1844). In line with these hagiographical sources, the editors of Raskhan's works report a few additional rumours, but they do not seem to connect to each other; so it is not easy to put the pieces of information together and create an integral image of Raskhan.

It is considered that the real name of Raskhan was Sayyad Ibrahim. However, according to Hazarī Prasād Dvivedī, there were two poets called Sujān Raskhān, the first being Sayyad Ibrahim of Pihani and the second being a disciple of Viṭṭhalnāth.[7] Sujān Raskhān is also the title given to a work of Raskhan's that editors created, leading to a further element of confusion about the name Raskhan on the part of Dvivedī and others. Dvivedī claimed that the Raskhan who was a disciple of Viṭṭhalnāth is different from the Raskhan who was the author of the *Sujān Raskhān*. Raskhan himself did not mention Viṭṭhalnāth as his guru. Still, if we may portray a single Raskhan based on the above-mentioned facts, it is possible to assume that there was a poet called Raskhan who was a Muslim by birth and devoted himself to Krishna in the bhakti period. If he was a disciple of Viṭṭhalnāth, as is usually believed, then his lifetime would have fallen sometime in the seventeenth century, as confirmed by the date VS 1671 mentioned by Raskhan at the end of his work *Prem-Vāṭikā*.[8]

The Works of Raskhan and Their Editions

The works attributed to Raskhan are the *Sujān Raskhān*, the *Prem-Vāṭikā*, and some other small pieces (*Dān Līlā* and *Sphuṭ Pad*). However, Heidi Pauwels argues that not all the works attributed to Raskhan may actually have been written by him.[9] This accords with the fact that the numbers of the verses included in editions of his work differ considerably from each other. For example, the first published edition of the *Sujān Raskhān* by Kiśorīlāl Gosvāmī in 1892 contained

128 stanzas, but after half a century Viśvanāthprasād Miśra's edition expanded to 214 stanzas. Kiśorīlāl Gosvāmī collected Raskhan's poems with the help of his friends, and he does not mention which manuscript(s) his edition is based on. Viśvanāthprasād Miśra, by contrast, edited his *Raskhāni Granthāvalī* mainly on the basis of manuscripts which were found in the course of the *khoj* project of the Nāgarī Pracāriṇī Sabhā. The *Raskhān Granthāvalī* prepared by Deśrāj Siṃh Bhāṭī and published in 1972 contains even more poems, these coming from unidentified sources. In a still more recent edition by Vidyānivās Miśra, Miśra[10] says he found new verses in a manuscript housed in the K.M. Institute, Agra.

One obvious question arises: Why have Raskhan's poems continuously increased in number with the passage of time? The verses of the *Sujān Raskhān* lack unity or continuity and often look abrupt. According to scholars such as Nirmalā Nārāyaṇ, Raskhan did not compose the *Sujān Raskhān* as an integral, connected work. Rather, he composed separate verses and editors subsequently put together his verses under the title *Sujān Raskhān*. According to Nirmalā Nārāyaṇ, the *savaiyā*s of Raskhan are found in the *Rāg Ratnākar*, the *Bṛhad rāg ratnākar*, the *Rāg Kalpadrum*, and so on, which are anthologies of savaiyās and *kavitt*s that were prepared in Raskhan's own time.[11] Because of variations between these, she says, the order of the verses of the *Sujān Raskhān* has come to be different in each edition. Viśvanāthprasād Miśra reordered them according to fifty-one subtitles. Some scholars believe that there might be more verses of Raskhan which have not been found yet. The general picture is that when editors found the word Raskhan used as the *chāp* (pen name) in otherwise unknown poems, they seem to have simply added them to their new editions, even though a chāp does not automatically confirm a poem's authenticity. The manuscript on which Viśvanāthprasād Miśra's edition is based is in the collection of Nāgarī Pracāriṇī Sabhā now, but it contains only 93 verses, while the edition Miśra prepared contains 214. Miśra himself admits that he included verses traditionally attributed to Raskhan but bearing no further authentification.

Clearly, therefore, we still need to determine the authenticity of Raskhan's works. As a contribution to this effort, in this chapter I hope to provide a minimum standard for assessing the literary style that can be identified as pertaining especially to Raskhan. This I will do by analysing the metrical characteristics that undergird it.

Characteristics of Each Metrical Form Used by Raskhan

The *Sujān Raskhān* is composed in savaiyā, kavitt, dohā, and *soraṭhā* metres. The greater part of this work is composed in savaiyā, while the *Prem-Vāṭikā* consists solely of dohās.[12] Table 8.1 shows metrical forms used in the *Sujān Raskhān*. I have arrived at this by scanning the metre of Kiśorīlāl Gosvāmī's edition, which is the smallest version. Except for six stanzas, its entire contents are included in all other editions as well.

Savaiyā, which made Raskhan famous, is a class of metre consisting of eight occurrences of the same foot and allowing variation in the last of these. In the savaiyā of Raskhan, the feet '-⏑⏑' and '⏑⏑-' are found.[13] The following is the example of a savaiyā of the '-⏑⏑' type:

Example 1
kānani dai aṁgurī rahibo jabahīṁ muralī dhuni manda bajaihai/
\- ⏑⏑ - ⏑ ⏑ - ⏑⏑ - ⏑ ⏑ - ⏑ ⏑ - ⏑ ⏑ - ⏑ ⏑ - -
mohanī tānani soṁ rasakhāni aṭā caṛhi godhana gai*hai* tau gai*hai*/
ṭeri kahauṁ sigare braja logani kālhi *k*oū su kitau samujhaihai/
māi *rī* vā mukha kī musakāni samhā*rī* na jai*hai* na jai*hai* na jaihe//

—*Sujān Raskhān*, 56[14]

When the melody of Krishna's flute sounds sweet, even if someone covers my ears with fingers or even if Krishna climbs to the attic and sings the fascinating melody of a cowherd's song, I will call out to people of Braj that however hard someone persuades me, I cannot manage to look [straight] at his smiles.

As already mentioned, a savaiyā consists of eight occurrences of the same foot, and this metre has a variation in the last foot. Thus, the verse consists of seven instances of '-⏑⏑' plus a single '--', making it *mattagayand* savaiyā. The foot of savaiyā metre is originally found in the Sanskrit *vārṇikchand*. Similar long metrical forms are listed in Sanskrit poetics, though not much used.

Table 8.1 Metrical Forms Used in the *Sujān Raskhān*

Savaiyā	Kavitt	Dohā	Soraṭhā
105	12	8	3

Source: Author.

The savaiyā metre, although being a vārṇikchand in Hindi prosody, allows irregular mora scansion, such as the scansion of the diphthongs *-e-* and *-o-* as short. Keśavdās and Tulsīdās usually follow the rules of moras strictly, but in their savaiyās as well some irregular scansions are found. The above-mentioned example of Raskhan, however, shows more uncommon scansions than this: *ā*, *ī*, *e*, *ai*, and *o* are occasionally scanned as one mora for the sake of metre (light *ā*, *ī*, *e*, *ai*, and *o* are in italics in the previous citation). An extreme case of inconsistent scansion is the syllable *-hai-*. In the last *gaṇa* of each line, *-hai-* is scanned as having two moras, that is, a heavy syllable, but in the last line the *-hai-* of *-jaihai-* is light even though the preceding syllable *-jai-* is heavy.

The next characteristic of Raskhan's savaiyā is the frequent use of *durmil* savaiyā. Durmil savaiyā is composed of eight times of '⏑⏑-'. The following is an example of his durmil savaiyā:

> kala kānani kuṇḍala morapakhā ura pai banamāla birājati hai/
> ⏑⏑ - ⏑⏑ - ⏑⏑ - ⏑⏑ - ⏑⏑ - ⏑⏑ - ⏑⏑ - ⏑⏑ -
> muralī kara maiṁ adharā musakāni-taraṁga mahāchabi chājati hai/
> rasakhāṅi lakheṁ tana pīta paṭā sata dāmini kī duti lājati hai/
> vaha bāṁsurī kī dhuni kāna pareṁ kula kāni hiyo taji bhājati hai//
>
> —*Sujān Raskhān*, 25

> Adorned with earrings on gentle ears, a peacock feather, a forest garland on the chest,
> A flute in hand, a wave of smile on the lips—such great beauty befits him.
> Having seen the yellow sash on Krishna's body, the brightness of a hundred lightning bolts feels ashamed.
> Their ears having heard the melody, [the *gopi*s find that] the shame of family [that is, modesty] that rests in their hearts gives up the cause and flees.

Tulsīdās and Keśavdās composed verses in the form of savaiyā metre, but durmil savaiyā is not used as often as mattagayand savaiyā by poets of the bhakti period other than Raskhan. Why did Raskhan use durmil savaiyā so much then? For one reason: in durmil savaiyā, Raskhan could easily place his chāp Raskhan at the beginning of the line. Its syllabic weight is *ra-sa-khā-na* ⏑⏑-⏑.[15] At the end of each line, the copula verb *hai* has only the role of a refrain and does not carry any grammatical value. It is just there to fill out the moras. Therefore, the *hai* which is needed only for the refrain can be replaced by any other two-mora syllable. Indeed, for this function Raskhan prefers the copula verb or *rī*, while the preceding *-ājati* carries out the end rhyme in this example.

Kavitt/*kabitt* is also defined under the rubric of vārṇikchand. It is not a foot metre like savaiyā, but a syllabic one (vārṇikchand). Like savaiyā, kavitt is a generic term for the poetic forms that have thirty to thirty-two syllables in each line, so there is no rigid rule. The following is an example of a kavitt attributed to Raskhan:

> kāhā rasakhāni sukha saṃpati sumāra kahā, kahā tana jogī hvai lagāye aṅga chāra ko/
> kahā sādhe pañcāvala kahā soye bīca nala kahā jīta lāye rājasindhu āra pāra ko/
> japavāra bāra tapa saṃjama bayāra vrata tīratha hajāra are būjhata lavāra ko/
> kīnhoṃ nahīṃ pyāra nahīṃ seyo darabāra cita cāhyo nihāra jo pai nanda ke kumāra ko//
>
> —*Sujān Raskhān*, 101

> Raskhan says: Happiness? Counting of wealth? Putting ashes on the body to become an ascetic? To be heated in the five suns? Meditation in water? Triumphing over the region over the ocean? Repeating a name many times? Meditation with self-control? Restraining the breath? Doing pilgrimage a thousand times? He who considers doing any of these is stupid if he does not love Nanda's son, does not resort to him for refuge, does not want to see him with his heart.

Kavitt/kabitt is preferred by many poets, and Raskhan is one of them. Verses in vārṇikchand as described in treatises on Hindi metre were required to follow rigid patterns of syllabic weight, but Raskhan chose metrical forms of vārṇikchand which have few such restrictions and hence are easier to follow.

Hazārī Prasād Dvivedī says that the savaiyā–kavitt metrical complex first appeared in Braj literature.[16] Unlike kavitt, which is a native Indian metre, savaiyā is a mixture of indigenous north Indian traditions and Persian ones. Persian metres brought into India by poets of the Muslim dynasties could easily assimilate to the Sanskrit vārṇikchand because both Persian metres and vārṇikchand are syllabic metres defined by foot. Accordingly, Persian prosodists gave the name 'Hindi metre' to savaiyā and defined it in terms of feet. For example, they regard the foot of mattagayand savaiyā as '-ᵕᵕ' (*fe'lun* foot) and that of durmil savaiyā as 'ᵕᵕ-' (*faʿilun* foot).[17] Another characteristic of savaiyā is its end rhyme, which is not an inheritance of Sanskrit metre but was probably borrowed from Persian metre.[18] During the bhakti period, the Braj area was home to a literary circle in which Muslim and Hindu poets influenced each other. It is not difficult to imagine how the savaiyā might have emerged as a new metrical trend under such circumstances.

Along with vārṇikchand, Raskhan used two forms of *mātrikchand*, dohā and soraṭhā, which are mora metres of Prākrit-Apabhraṃśa taken over into Hindi. In a sharp contrast to the metrical license in his vārṇikchand, Raskhan rigidly follows the mora rules when it comes to mātrikchand. The following is an example of a dohā of the *Prem-Vāṭikā* attributed to Raskhan:

> kāma krodha mada moha bhaya lobha droha mātsarya/
> ina saba hī teṁ prema hai pare kahata munivarya//
>
> —*Prem-Vāṭikā*, 14

> Passion, anger, intoxication, fascination, fear, greed, hostility, and jealousy—all of these are far away from love. So says a sage of real excellence.

A dohā, a couplet which consists of lines of 13 + 11 moras, ends in *guru-laghu* (heavy-light) and rhymes at the end of the lines. In this example, there is no fault in metrical construction. This dohā looks just like Vaishnava bhakti poems by other contemporary bhakti poets with respect to the metre as well as the subject, and we see little sign of the Persian environment to which Raskhan is considered to have belonged.

Summing up this section, three characteristics are observed in Raskhan's metrical style. The first is that he preferred savaiyā, kavitt, and dohā, while other poets of the bhakti period who wrote about Krishna in the Braj region preferred other metrical forms, especially pads. Raskhan's use of savaiyā and kavitt is not unique, however. *Aṣṭchāp* poets of the Vallabhan sect such as Paramānanddās, court poets of Akbar such as Gaṅg (b. [?] 1538), Caturbhuj, and Pr̥thvīrāj, and early Rādhāvallabhite *bhaktas* such as Harivaṃś ([?]1502–52) and Kalyāṇ 'Pujārī' (sixteenth century) all used them.[19] But savaiyā metre was not as popular in those early days as it became in the following periods. While dohā had been a popular form of mora metre (mātrikchand) from the Prakrit period onwards, savaiyā and kavitt, which adopt syllabic metre (vārṇikchand), are probably a more recent fashion. Kavitts were popularized by influential poets such as Raskhan and Tulsīdās. The mixed form of kavitt, savaiyā, and *chappay* reaches its height in the *Kavitāvalī* composed by Tulsīdās, but we see little metrical variation of this sort in Raskhan's works.[20] For example, the metre used in the *Sujān Raskhān* is mostly savaiyā, and in the *Prem-Vāṭikā* it is mostly dohā.

The contrast of the irregular scansion of mora counting in savaiyās and the rigid observance of the rules of mora metre in dohās are a second characteristic of Raskhan's poetry. Compared with the dohās of Muslim poets, in which irregularities are often found, the dohās of Raskhan are exceptionally rigid, like those of Abdurrahīm Khānkhānā. Thus, it is hard to imagine that Muslim poet Raskhan did not know the rules of mātrikchand and that he made many mistakes in his savaiyās. It is much easier to suppose that Raskhan composed savaiyās not by the rules of Sanskrit *varṇa* metre, but by those of Persian prosody. Then the problem as to why there are many instances of irregular scansion in his savaiyās is solved. Consider, for example, the syllable *-ai-* of the *jaihai* mentioned earlier. In Sanskrit, the syllable rhyme '-ai-' is phonologically or morphologically (if not phonetically) heavier than '-e-', and scansion of the former is always heavy. In contrast, in the Persian prosody which is adopted later by Urdu, both '-e-' and '-ai-' can be scanned as light depending on the need of metre.

A third characteristic of Raskhan's metrical style can be observed in his use of the imperfect participle plus copula verb, as found in his savaiyās. This too reminds us of later Urdu verses composed in adapted Perso-Arabic metrical conventions. As already mentioned, savaiyā can be defined in terms of Persian metre. Raskhan's savaiyās generally look like Urdu ghazals, which rhyme at the end of each line by means of an imperfect participle plus a copula verb. With respect to the metrical style of Raskhan's savaiyā, the other characteristic to be noted is that in spite of many irregular scansions of syllabic weight, he was very cautious about syllabic structure. For example, his chāp 'Raskhan' is scanned *ra-sa-khā-na* CV-CV-CVV-CV (C standing for consonant; V for vowel) according to the mora metre. While in terms of Persian metre it is disyllabic *ras-khān* CVC-CVVC and is not distinguished from the CVV-CVVC pattern we meet in words such as *rājīva*, Raskhan always chooses words with the structure CVC-CVVC to rhyme with it.

Multifaceted Poems: Bhakti versus Sufism

Metrically speaking, then, there is an admixture of Indic- and Persian-based conventions in Raskhan's poetry. When it comes to content, too, it can be observed that Krishna bhakti and Sufism merge indistinguishably in Raskhan's passionate tone of devotion. It is this dual spirituality that has captivated generations of hearers and readers.

The dohās of the *Prem-Vāṭikā* describe a love that is not always limited to the love of Krishna, while those of the *Sujān Raskhān* explicitly praise the beauty of Krishna. In the *Sujān Raskhān*, Raskhan describes the enchanting beauty of Krishna by means of a conversation between two gopis, which is a traditional style of literature dedicated to Krishna. The description of the beauty of the divine couple in this way is hardly peculiar to Raskhan: many other bhakti poets of his time share it. And there are occasions on which whole phrases are shared by Raskhan and his bhakti kin.[21] Yet the works of Raskhan, especially the *Prem-Vāṭikā*, also reflect the strong influence of Sufism in their substratum:

> akatha kahānī prema kī, jānata lailī khūba/
> Do tanahūṁ jahaṁ eka bhe, mana milāi mahabūba//
>
> —*Prem-Vāṭikā*, 33
>
> The story of love cannot be told. Laila knows it well.
> In love two bodies become one; it integrates two lovers' hearts.

In the first line of this dohā, Raskhan refers to Lailā, the heroine of the famous Perso-Arabic love story bearing her name, but the second line can be interpreted as expressing the union of human beings and God according to the idea of bhakti. Such a union, for example, appears in Rādhāvallabhī doctrine, but it is the ultimate goal in Sufism, too.[22] At the same time, however, this line might lead us to imagine the personal love of *mahabūbs* (lovers). This term has a distinctively Persian resonance, but the thought—that love can be simultaneously human and divine—is one that Sufis and bhaktas share.

Another dohā in the *Prem-Vāṭikā* (24) says that 'love is the shape of Hari and Hari is the shape of love', as if to make a Hindu readership feel relieved. In the next line of the same dohā, however, Raskhan uses a metaphor popular among the Sufi poets—God as sun and man as light—saying 'eka hoi dvai yoṃ lasaiṃ jyauṃ sūraja aru dhūpa' (Being one, they shine forth like two, like sunlight and the sun). Thus, the word 'Hari' in the first line of this dohā might not necessarily refer to Krishna. It is true that in the *Prem-Vāṭikā*, Raskhan uses only eleven Perso-Arabic words—*ajūbo, khūba, gadara, jāṃbājī, bājī, dila, nejā, bādasā, maulavī, mahabūba, lailī*, and *tūl*.[23] While he clearly prefers *tatsam* vocabulary, such as *prem* instead of *ishk*, the short verse we have just quoted nonetheless includes three Perso-Arabic words: 'lailī', 'khūb', and especially 'mahabūb'. So in the end, it seems his words can be interpreted simultaneously from the two sides. In this light, consider also the following verse:

> syāma saghana ghana gheri kai rasa barasyau rasakhāni/
> bhaī dimānī pāna kari, prema madya mana māni//
>
> —*Sujān Raskhān*, 50

> Raskhan says that Krishna, a thick cloud, veiled me and rained love on me.
> Having drunk the wine [of love] to my heart's content, I became mad.

Here Raskhan uses the common metaphor of Krishna as a cloud and the standard tatsam term *madya* for alcohol. The fact that appeal is made here to Krishna suggests what we today would call a Hindu ambience, yet we know that drinking wine is a favourite poetic expression by Sufi or Muslim poets. The most impressive phrase of this dohā is *bhaī dimānī* (I became mad), and for this sentiment Raskhan chose the Persian word *dimānī/dīvānī*, not the term *bāvalī* used so characteristically in connection with Mīrābāī ('darasaṇa kāraṇa bhaī bāvalī', I went mad at the sight [of Krishna]]).[24] In this way, a superb mixture of Hindu bhakti and Persian Islamic canons of devotion makes Raskhan's poetry both novel and attractive.

Verses dedicated to God described by means of worldly love are not surprising in either a bhakti or a Sufi context, but the verses of Raskhan are particularly suffused with an unabashedly sensual tone. Why did Raskhan use such expressions and why were his verses widely accepted by the people of Braj? The ardent devotion expressed in plain words and simple phrases gained him considerable popularity, even though he is regarded as 'non-canonical' by both Hindus and Muslims. Indeed, it might be well to say that this non-canonical status made it possible for Raskhan to establish the harmony for which he is noted. If Raskhan was a Muslim who converted to devotion to Krishna, as the hagiography says, then his literary style, which is rather different from that of Hindus, would have been acceptable for those same Hindus even if—and perhaps because—it stretches the boundaries of the canon. For Muslims as well, he is naturally non-canonical, given his Vaishnava sensibility. But for them too Raskhan's freedom clearly had its appeal, enabling him to blend the two literary traditions as many other poets of his time could not.

Duality and the Historical Raskhan

Raskhan's taste in language, metrical usage, and literary style makes it clear that his works are formed through a meeting of two literary traditions: Sanskrit-inflected bhakti on the one hand and Persian-infused Sufism on the other. But another possible duality also needs to be taken into account, and it brings us back to the issue of authenticity in Raskhan's works. The *Prem-Vāṭikā* is about love as such, while the *Sujān Raskhān* presents an image that belongs specifically to Krishna. This contrast is remarkable with respect to the dohās of both works. Dohās in the *Sujān Raskhān* are limited in number—eight dohās and three soraṭhās in the edition of Kiśorīlāl Gosvāmī (see Table 8.1)—yet all those verses are explicitly dedicated to Krishna, while love in the *Prem-Vāṭikā* seems to have a wider meaning. Metrically speaking, we have seen that the savaiyās of Raskhan are unique or irregular from the viewpoint of Hindi prosody, which leads us to believe that there must have been a long chronological gap between the *Prem-Vāṭikā* and the *Sujān Raskhān*. And there is a material difference to match. So far we know of no institution which possesses a manuscript of the *Prem-Vāṭikā*, while this can hardly be said of the *Sujān Raskhān*. Again we need to consider the possibility that the authors of the two compositions were different.[25]

As already mentioned, Hazārī Prasād Dvivedī pointed out the possibility of two Raskhans, and this contention cannot be ignored. Rāmcandra Śukla says that when poets gathered, they used to talk to each other saying 'Someone please recite a verse of Raskhan', meaning not a poet so named but 'a verse full of *ras*'.[26] We need more evidence to support the hypothesis that the term *raskhān* can have this generic meaning, but several features of the style we associate with the name of Raskhan do lend it credibility: the simple phrases, the easy metre which can be taken up by everyone, the language that bears the more modern traits we associate with Khari Boli, the frequent alliteration which is a characteristic of Urdu ghazals, the rhyme and refrain with an imperfect participle and the copula verb at the end of each line, and so on. All these suggest the possibility that someone in a period later than the seventeenth century composed verses containing the chāp Raskhan. These, then, found their way into the *Sujān Raskhān* and are now attributed to Raskhan. They really say more about the style we associate with his name than they do about Raskhan the man, if indeed there was such a person.

And yet, we still have to deal with the question of whether there was such a poet or not. Personally, I find it hard to believe there was not. The very existence of the unique style of Raskhan seems to presuppose the existence of a poet with unique talent who wrote those impressive verses. Of the two works attributed to Raskhan, the *Prem-Vāṭikā* has a uniform style and theme, and there is little reason to suggest that it was written by more than one poet. On the contrary, the *Sujān Raskhān* contains verses so diverse that they can readily be ascribed to interpolation by later poets. If we take the position that one poet wrote (at least parts of) both works, we need to assume that the original *Sujān Raskhān* was extended by later interpolation. Otherwise, if those compositions were written by different poets, the *Sujān Raskhān* consists of poems of multiple poets. Since it is possible that one poet's style and thought might well change in the course of his life, it seems to me methodologically more sound to start from the hypothesis that one poet wrote both the *Prem-Vāṭikā* and the archetype of the *Sujān Raskhān*. Or, at least, that is how things seem at present—until we find more solid evidence compelling us to ask whether in fact the two compositions may stem from different sources.

Notes

1. The edition by Viśvanāthprasād Miśra has been used for all references to *Prem-Vāṭikā* (Viśvanāthprasād Miśra, ed. *Rasakhāni* [Granthāvalī] [Varanasi: Vani-Vitana Prakashan, 1953]).

2. Rupert Snell, 'Raskhān the Neophyte: Hindu Perspectives on a Muslim Vaishnava', in *Urdu and Muslim South Asia: Studies in Honour of Ralph Russell*, ed. Christopher Shackle (London: SOAS, 1989), 29–30.

3. Baṭekr̥ṣṇa, 'Raskhān kā samay', *Nāgarī pracāriṇī patrikā* 60, no. 1 (VS 2012): 54.

4. Śrībrajbhūṣaṇ Śarmā, *Do sau bāvan vaiṣṇavan kī vārtā*, vol. 3 (Kankrauli: Shuddhadvait Academy, 1953).

5. Veṇīmādhavdās, *Mūl gosāīṃ carit* (Gorakhpur: Gita Press, n.d.).

6. Philip A. Lutgendorf, 'The Quest for the Legendary Tulsīdās', in *According to Tradition: Hagiographical Writing in India*, ed. Winand M. Callewaert and R. Snell (Wiesbaden: Otto Harrassowitz, 1994), 65–85.

7. Hazārīprasād Dvivedī, *Hindī sāhitya: uskā udbhav aur vikās* (New Delhi: Attarcand Kapur and Sons, 1964), 133. Among early works referring to the name Sayyad Ibrahim of Raskhan is the anthology *Śivsiṃh-Saroj* (Śivsiṃh Seṅgar, *Śivsiṃh-Saroj* [Prayag: Hindi Sahitya Sammelan, 1970], 784).

8. As for the date of composition mentioned by Raskhan, Viśvanāthprasād Miśra added the numbers comprising the date given in his edition as follows—*bidhu* (1), *sāgara* (7), *rasa* (6), and *indu* (1). Hence, the *subhabarasa*

that appears in the text is to be interpreted as SV 1671. Many scholars have accepted this date, but Baṭekr̥ṣṇa offers another interpretation of the date, taking rasa as 9, so that according to him the date comes out to be SV 1971.

9. Heidi Pauwels, 'Two "Gardens of Love": Raskhān's *Prem-Vaṭikā* and Nāgarīdās's *Iśk-Caman*', in *Patronage and Popularisation, Pligrimage and Procession: Channels of Transcultural Translation and Transmission in Early Modern South Asia, Papers in Honour of Monika Horstmann*, ed. Heidi Pauwels (Wiesbaden: Harrassowitz Verlag, 2009), 23fn1.

10. Vidyānivās Miśra, *Raskhān Racanāvalī* (New Delhi: Vani Prakashan, 1985), 5–6.

11. Nirmalā Nārāyaṇ, *Raskhān: vivecanātmak adhyayan* (Hyderabad: Milind Prakashan, 2008), 29.

12. It is Raskhan's characteristic metrical usage that soraṭhā, a variation of dohā, cannot be found in the *Prem-Vāṭikā*. However, Viśvanāthprasād Miśra, in his edition (1953), puts a comma after the eleventh mora in the following two dohās:

> hari ke saba ādhīna, pai harī prema ādhīna. 36.1.
> veda mūla saba dharma, yaha kahaiṁ sabai srutisāra. 37.1

While *pai* of 36.1 and *yaha* of 37.1 semantically belong to the second pādas, it is possible to put caesuras after the thirteenth mora. In addition to this, the second lines of these verses are normal dohās. Thus, these two lines can be regarded as dohās.

13. Amphibrach is not found probably because it is incompatible with the bimoraic rhythm of Hindi metre.

14. The numbering of verses is different between the edition of Kiśorīlāl Gosvāmī and Viśvanāthprasād Miśra. In this chapter, the edition of Kiśorīlāl Gosvāmī is used for the *Sujān Raskhān* (Śrī Kiśorīlāl Gosvāmī, ed., *Sujāna-Rasakhāna*, Kashi: Bhāratjīvan Press, 1892).

15. The *chāp* 'rasakhāna' ᵕᵕ-ᵕ can be applied to the savaiyā of -ᵕᵕ type as well, for example, -ᵕᵕ|- *rasa* | *khāna* ᵕ|-ᵕᵕ...; however, in this metre, this word cannot be put at the beginning of a line.

16. Hazārīprasād Dvivedī, *Hindī sāhitya kā ādikāl* (New Delhi: Vani Prakashan, 1994), 150.

17. There are eight types of feet (*fa-'ū-lun* (˘ ¯ ¯), *fā-'i-lun* (¯ ˘ ¯), *ma-fā-'ī-lun* (˘ ¯ ¯ ¯), *fā-'i-lā-tun* (¯ ˘ ¯ ¯), *mus-taf-'i-lun* (¯ ¯ ˘ ¯), *maf-'ū-lā-tu* (¯ ¯ ¯ ˘), *mu-fā-'i-la-tun* (˘ ¯ ˘ ˘ ¯), and *mu-ta-fā-'i-lun* (˘ ˘ ¯ ˘ ¯), which derive from the feet of Arabic metre and their variations such as *fe'lun* and *fa'ilun*.

18. Hiroko Nagasaki, 'Hindi Metre: Origins and Development', in *Indian and Persian Prosody and Recitation*, ed. Hiroko Nagasaki (New Delhi: Saujanya Publications, 2012), 120–4.

19. R. S. McGregor, *Hindi Literature from Its Beginnings to the Nineteenth Century* (Wiesbaden: Otto Harrassowitz, 1984), 89, 91, 120; Maheshwari

Mahesh Sinha, *The Historical Development of Mediaeval Hindi Prosody (Rāmānanda-Keśava, 1400–1600 A.D.)* (Bhagalpur: Bhagalpur University Publication, 1964), 91.

20. Imre Bangha, 'Dynamics of Textual Transmission in Premodern India: The Kavitavali of Tulsidas', *Comparative Studies of South Asia, Africa and the Middle East* 24, no. 2 (2004): 34.

21. The following dohā of Tulsīdās starts with the same phrase as the verse cited above:

> kāma krodha lobhādi mada prabala moha kai dhāri.
> tinha mahaṁ ati dāruna dukhada māyārūpī nāri.
>
> —*Dohavali*, 266.
>
> Pride passions, greed and anger are of Yearning's armies powerful wings.
> Midst these Maya's woman's body, deep passions' lasting sorrow brings (S. P. Bahadur, trans., *Dohavali: An Anthology of Verses on Dharma and Morality* [New Delhi: Munshiram Manoharlal Publishers, 1978]).

It is remarkable that both poets start verses with the same phrase 'kāma krodha mada moha lobha'. We could find that there are many other bhakti poets who shared such close similarity to Raskhan, namely Kabīr, Sūrdās, Nāgrīdās, and so on.

22. Md. Sirajul Islam, *Sufism and Bhakti* (Washington, DC: Council for Research in Values and Philosophy, 2004), 165

23. Among the eleven Perso-Arabic words used in the *Prem-Vātikā, tūla* (*Prem-vātikā*, 41) can be interpreted as Arabic word *t̤ūl* ('extent') or Sanskrit *tulya* ('comparable'). Double meaning is possible here, so I included this word in the list of Perso-Arabic vocabulary.

24. *Mīrāṃbāī kī padāvalī*, edited by Paraśurām Caturvedī (Prayag: Hindi Sahitya Sammelan, 1970), 128, v. 94.

25. The possibility that two compositions are different might be supported by the following fact: There are many verses which have the word Raskhān or Raskhāni. While in the *Prem-Vātikā*, this word always implies the author himself as the chāp, in the *Sujān Raskhān* this term refers to the author as well as Krishna.

26. Rāmcandra Śukla, *Hindī sāhitya kā itihās*, 13th edition (Varanasi: Nagaripracharini Sabha [originally 1929]), 105.

Bibliography

Bahadur, S. P., trans. *Dohavali: An Anthology of Verses on Dharma and Morality*. New Delhi: Munshiram Manoharlal Publishers, 1978.

Bangha, Imre. 'Dynamics of Textual Transmission in Premodern India: The Kavitavali of Tulsidas'. *Comparative Studies of South Asia, Africa and the Middle East* 24, no. 2 (2004): 33–44.

Baṭekṛṣṇa. 'Raskhān kā samay'. *Nāgarī pracāriṇī patrikā* 60, no. 1 (VS 2012): 47–55.

Bhati, Deshraj Singh. *Raskhāna granthāvalī saṭīkā*. New Delhi: Ashok Prakashan, 1972.

Caturvedī, Paraśurām, ed. *Mīrāṃbāī kī padāvalī*. 14th edition. Prayag: Hindi Sahitya Sammelan, 1970.

Dvivedī, Hazārī Prasād. *Hindī sāhitya: uskā udbhav aur vikās*. New Delhi: Attarcand Kapur and Sons, 1964.

________. *Hindī sāhitya kā ādikāl*. New Delhi: Vani Prakashan, 1994 [1952].

Gosvami, Shrikishorilal, ed. *Sujāna-Rasakhāna*. Kashi: Bhāratjīvan Press, 1892.

Islam, Md. Sirajul. *Sufism and Bhakti*. Washington, DC: Council for Research in Values and Philosophy, 2004.

Lutgendorf, Philip A. 'The Quest for the Legendary Tulsīdās'. In *According to Tradition: Hagiographical Writing in India*, edited by Winand M. Callewaert and R. Snell. Wiesbaden: Otto Harrassowitz. 1994, 65–85.

Mahesh, Maheshwari Sinha. *The Historical Development of Mediaeval Hindi Prosody (Rāmānanda-Keśava, 1400–1600 A.D.)*. Bhagalpur: Bhagalpur University Publication, 1964.

McGregor, R.S. *Hindi Literature from Its Beginnings to the Nineteenth Century*. Wiesbaden: Otto Harrassowitz, 1984.

Mishra, Vidyanivas, ed. *Rasakhān Racanāvalī*. New Delhi: Vani Prakashan, 1985.

Mishra, Vishvanathprasad, ed. *Rasakhāni (Granthāvalī)*. Varanasi: Vani-Vitana Prakashan, 1953.

Nagasaki, Hiroko. 'Hindi Metre: Origins and Development'. In *Indian and Persian Prosody and Recitation*, edited by Hiroko Nagasaki. New Delhi: Saujanya Publications, 2012, 107–29.

Nārāyaṇ, Nirmalā. *Raskhān: vivecanātmak adhyayan*. Hyderabad: Milind Prakashan, 2008.

Pauwels, Heidi. 'Two "Gardens of Love": Raskhān's *Prem-Vaṭikā* and Nāgarīdās's *Iśk-Caman*'. In *Patronage and Popularisation, Pligrimage and Procession: Channels of Transcultural Translation and Transmission in Early Modern South Asia, Papers in Honour of Monika Horstmann*, edited by Heidi Pauwels. Wiesbaden: Harrassowitz Verlag, 2009, 23–38.

Śarmā, Śrībrajbhūṣaṇ. *Do sau bāvan Vaiṣṇavan kī vārtā*, vol. 3. Kankrauli: Shuddhadvait Academy, 1953.

Seṅgar, Śivsiṃh. *Śivsiṃh-Saroj*. Prayag: Hindi Sahitya Sammelan, 1970 [1878].

Snell, Rupert. '*Raskhān* the Neophyte: Hindu Perspectives on a Muslim Vaishnava'. In *Urdu and Muslim South Asia: Studies in Honour of Ralph Russell*, edited by Christopher Shackle. London: SOAS, 1989, 29–37.

Shukla, Ramchandra, Bhagvandin, and Brajratnadas, eds. *Tulasī Granthāvalī*, vol. 2. Varanasi: Nagaripracharini Sabha, 1974 [1923].

Śukla, Rāmcandra. *Hindī sāhitya kā itihās*, 23rd edition. Varanasi: Nagaripracharini Sabha, 1990 [1929].

Venimadhavdas. *Mūl gosāīṃ carit*. Gorakhpur: Gita Press, n.d.

9

STEFANIA CAVALIERE*

Religious Syncretism and Literary Innovation

New Perspectives on *Bhakti* and *Rasa*s in the *Vijñānagītā* by Keshavdas

The *Vijñānagītā* (henceforth VG) is one of the many Hindi adaptations of the *Prabodhacandrodaya* by Kṛṣṇamiśra (eleventh century CE).[1] It was composed by Keshavdas (1555–1617 CE) in 1610 CE and represents a sort of farewell to his courtly and literary duties. Being a work which he wrote at an advanced age, it departs from the *rīti* (mannerist) and secular themes that had occupied Keshavdas earlier, reflecting a spiritual quest that seems new. In fact, at the very end of the text the poet expresses the wish to go and spend the last days of his life as an ascetic on the banks of the Ganges as the biggest reward for his works.[2] The VG presents a new aspect of the poetics of Keshavdas—a desire to explore philosophical matters without neglecting his literary skills.

The theme is the allegorical war between Discrimination (*viveka*) and Delusion (*mahāmoha*), both generated by the Mind (*manas*). This psychological battle arises in the process of mental awakening, with Passion (*kāma*), Rage (*krodha*), Greed (*lobha*), and so on, being obstacles to attaining liberation. Since Keshav draws on many other literary and theoretical sources to compose his work, the VG can be interpreted as an independent text rather than as a simple adaptation of a Sanskrit drama.[3] The allegory follows the same basic guidelines that we find in the *Prabodhacandrodaya*: the battle between Discrimination (viveka) and Delusion (mahāmoha) leads to the final Resignation to a life of Renunciation (*vairāgya*), which is the only way to achieve peace of mind and serves as a prelude to the dawn of Enlightenment (*prabodhodaya*) and Knowledge (*vidyā*). Yet, the VG enriches the theme by opening the discussion to embrace many other spiritual and moral issues, as found in disparate works such as the *Yogavāsiṣṭha*, the *Purāṇas*, the *Dharmaśāstras*, the *Bhagavadgītā*, and many others. The psychological battle is almost finished by the twelfth chapter, and the following nine chapters are intended to explore other topics which contribute to the portrayal of the complex religious vision offered by the VG.

The focus of my chapter will be chapter 19, entitled *Balicaritravijñānaprāptivarṇanaṃ* (Description of the Acts of Bali and His Attainment of Knowledge), which comprises a miscellany of quotations in addition to the tale of the meritorious acts of Bali. As we read at the outset:

> unaīs meṃ barniyo bali ko atibijñān
> brahmabhakta haribhakta ko kahibo sabai bidhāna.
> jyauṃ sādhyau Bali āpuhī tyauṃ sādhau bijñāna. (vv. 1–2a)

> In the nineteenth chapter Bali's exceptional knowledge is described.
> He is celebrated as a wholehearted devotee of *brahman* and the Lord.
> May you achieve knowledge in the same way as Bali achieved his.

Keshav takes his subject from the fifth book of *Yogavāsiṣṭha* (*upaśama khaṇḍa*, 'On Quietism'), chapters 22–9.[4] There we read that Bali, the son of Virocana, reigned in the infernal regions as the king of demons, and his forefathers were all destroyed by Vishnu in the form of his first four incarnations. Bali had been instructed by Śukra[5] about the long course of the soul's advancement in spiritual knowledge; by gaining control of his mind, he overcame the three worlds. When he understood that 'there is nothing to be thought besides the intellect, and nothing to be obtained anywhere except from the spacious womb of the intellect, which comprehends all the three worlds',[6] he became a *jīvanmukta* ('liberated' from worldly existence, that is, self-realized). In this way Bali exercised full authority over the three worlds by means of self-control and self-resignation, thinking of himself as the immortal and everlasting soul in a state of oneness with the Supreme. According to the dynamics of *Yogavāsiṣṭha*, being a philosophical adaptation of the *Rāmāyaṇa*,[7] the story of Bali is intended as an example for Rāma to imitate.[8] Analogously, the VG was composed to instruct King Vīrsiṃh (r. 1605–27 CE), Keshav's patron, about the supreme knowledge.[9] In this context, *bhakti* is introduced as an indispensable aspect of the king's moral elevation.

The benefits of religious commitment are presented throughout the chapter by means of many extracts from traditional texts. For instance, VG 19.13 quotes *Bhagavadgītā* 15.6[10] and VG 19.36 harks back to *Bhāgavatapurāṇa* 7.9.10.[11] Keshavdas starts with the ritual practices of religious observance—in VG 19.44 we find a passage from *Parāśarasmṛti* 8.25,[12] while VG 19.30 cites *Padmapurāṇa Pātālakhaṇḍa* 84.72[13]—then moves towards the supreme stage of meditation by offering two definitions of *navadhā bhakti*. One of these is taken from the *Bhāgavatapurāṇa* and is based on formal practices (VG 19.59), while the other aligns the inner feelings of the devotee (VG 19.66) with the nine *rasas* (VG 19.61–4). In effect he proposes a new definition of navadhā bhakti, combining literary notions such as the theory of rasas with the new metaphysics of devotion proposed by Vaishnava reformers such as Vopadeva and Rupa Gosvami. In a manner different from Madhusūdana Sarasvatī, as we shall see, Keshav fills the gap between *dvaita* and *advaita* through the aesthetics of rasas as applied to bhakti.

From Ninefold *Bhakti* to Ninefold *Rasa*

Keshavdas already mentions navadhā bhakti in *Kavipriyā* 11.20, listing it among things generally known to be ninefold (*nava-varṇana*):

> aṅgadvāra bhūkhaṇḍa rasa bāghini kuca nidhi jāni
> sudhākuṇḍa graha nāḍikā navadhā bhakti bakhāni.[14]

> The limbs of the body, the divisions of earth, the aesthetic emotions, the nipples of a tiger [?], the mythological treasures, the receptacles of ambrosia, the planets, the channels of the body, and bhakti[15] are described as being ninefold.

As usual in this 'Manual for Poets' (1601 CE), Keshavdas thus uses a *dohā* to offer some common standards for the topic he is expounding, in this case the numeral descriptions. Among the items which are commonly considered to be ninefold by tradition, he includes both the rasas and bhakti.

In the VG, Keshavdas takes things much further. In a passage that begins in verse 19.55, he explains that the bhakti path starts with the most rigorous ritualism, epitomized through the practices of sacrifice. He apparently starts by quoting the *Padmapurāṇa*, though the verse he gives actually combines two independent segments—the first *pāda* of *Padmapurāṇa, uttarakhaṇḍa* 23.2, and the third pāda of *Kriyākhaṇḍa* 24.26.[16]

> patraṃ puṣpaṃ phalaṃ toyaṃ dravyam annaṃ maṭhasya ca
> yo 'śnāti sa pacet ghore narake caikaviṃśatiḥ. (v. 55)

> He who consumes leaves, flowers, fruits, water, substances, and the earth beneath a temple will burn in a terrible hell—this is the ritual of the twenty-one offerings.[17]

The list of offerings here presented as appropriate for an act of sacrifice—which must not be dispersed or desecrated—represents a leitmotif we also encounter in Bhagavadgītā 9.26,[18] where the items being offered are meant to point to the importance of the attitude of the devotee making any such sacrifice. Whatever the devotee does, it must be done as an offering unto the Lord, since only by this attitude of complete renunciation will he or she be released from the bondage of karma.

> ina koṃ tau nṛpa chāṃḍijai kījai dvija-āsakti
> tribidha pāpa miṭi jāhiṃ ura upaji parai haribhakti. (v. 56)

> May the king abandon them [that is., the sacrifices so far mentioned], and pay respect to *brāhmaṇas*. Sin in all its three parts is extinguished wherever devotion to the Lord is generated in the heart.

> akala abidyā-rahita hai sraddhājuta haribhakti
> sādhau navadhā aṅga soṃ taji saba soṃ āsakti (v. 57)

> Devotion to the Lord, enhanced by faith, lacks any ignorance. A sage, once released from the nine limbs [of his body],[19] feels affection for everyone.

The implication is that the king whom the poet advises must abandon any formal ritualism and focus on ultimate reality with an attitude of complete renunciation, as Bali did. Bali obtained supreme understanding by realizing, as specified in *Yogavāsiṣṭha* 2.1119, that 'feelings of love and enmity are properties of the intellect (soul), and are not separated from it by the intellect's separation from the body. Hence passions and feelings are inseparable from the intellect or soul'.[20] Further (2.1120), 'Once a person becomes conscious that there is no category of existence besides himself, that person is no longer subject to states of pain and pleasure'.[21]

Keshavdas takes this general framework regarding intellect and adapts it to aesthetic experience. The passions recognized by Bali as nothing but attributes (not properties) of the intellect are thus projected into the realm of rasas. The quietness of mind attained by realizing this ultimate truth becomes *śānta* (quiet) rasa. Once the sage has no more worldly desires, he achieves quietness beyond his passions. In the same way, as we will see hereafter in some details, beyond the other rasas one obtains the supreme rasa that is śānta. This feeling must be rediscovered for enlightenment and release to be accomplished. The supreme knowledge Bali achieved through devotion is thus described as mixed with the nine rasas:

> navarasamiśrita sādhi nṛpa navadhā bhakti pramānu
> dānava[22] mānava devagana bhakti-kamala hari-bhānu. (v. 58)

> Bhakti, achieved by the king as mixed with the nine rasas, is proved to be ninefold.
> For demons, humans, and gods bhakti is the flower while the lord is the sun.

The verses explaining this passage proceed to introduce the relation between bhakti and the rasas, which are conceived as the emotional states by means of which people approach divinity. First, Keshavdas quotes the *Bhāgavatapurāṇa* (7.5.23) on the customary nine practices of devotion:

> Hearing and chanting about the Lord Viṣṇu, remembering Him, serving His lotus feet, offering Him respectful worship, offering Him prayers, becoming His servant, considering the Lord one's best friend, and surrendering everything unto Him. [These nine processes are accepted as pure devotional service.][23]

Then he turns from bhakti to rasa, bringing to bear a popular quotation from *Nāṭyaśāstra* 6.15, which he personally emends as regards the domain of rasas:

śṛṅgārahāsyakaruṇaraudravīrabhayānakāḥ
bībhatsādbhutaśāntāś ca nava kāvyarasāḥ smṛtāḥ. (VG 19.60)[24]

The nine aesthetic emotions acknowledged in poetry are the erotic, the comic, the furious, the pathetic, the abhorrent, the terrific, the heroic, the marvellous, and the quiet.

Clearly, Keshavdas understands there to be nine rasas, not eight, with 'the quiet' (śānta) as the ninth in the series.[25] As V. Raghavan points out, 'the texts on Śānta in certain recensions of Bharata's *Nāṭya-śāstra* must have been interpolated by the advocates of Śānta'.[26] Probably two parallel versions of the *Nāṭyaśāstra* circulated, one of which listed nine rasas, and it is obvious which of these Keshavdas preferred.

The dynamics of the production of the rasas has long been debated by scholars, and particular attention has been paid to the insertion of the ninth emotion. Abhinavagupta, commenting on the eight-rasa version of the *Nāṭyaśāstra*, nonetheless introduces the matter of śānta in his commentary, presenting a kind of causal relation between the rasas. First we find the erotic since it affects everyone, followed by the comic, which is qualified as 'careless'. It arises opposite to the pathetic. The comic causes also the furious, which basically consists of indignation. The heroic concerns observance of duty (dharma), while the fearful is its opponent, being based on the fear of someone heroic. Having the same determinant, the disgusting is also produced from the heroic. Coming to the culmination of the heroic, but with a separate cause, the marvellous is obtained. Therefore, it is said [in the *Nāṭyaśāstra* 18.43]: 'At the conclusion of all the plays which contain various states and sentiments, experts should always introduce the marvellous sentiment.'[27] And here comes the interesting addition by Abhinavagupta, describing śānta as the most important of all the rasas, since it is grounded on the highest goal of man: 'From that [that is, the marvellous], the quietistic [comes], having liberation as its result. It consists of the norm of resignation (*nivṛttidharma*), contrary to the norm of activity (*pravṛttidharma*) pertaining to the threefold purpose of mankind. In this case the gustation of *rasa* arises by means of an absorption into one's own self. So it has been said.'[28]

The Connection between *Bhakti* and *Rasa*

The *śloka* from the *Nāṭyaśāstra* that Keshavdas quotes receives quite a different sort of comment from his own hand. In the first two verses of his explanation, we finally see how Keshav reconciles the two nine-fold fields of bhakti and rasa. He combines each type of bhakti with a specific rasa, making the latter representative of it in every case. For example, *śravaṇa* (hearing) is linked to *adbhuta* (the fantastic) rasa, since amazement is caused by hearing something amazing. Similarly, *karuṇā* (the tragic) is prompted by an act of remembering—remembering someone who was abandoned—while *pāda sevana* (foot reverence, that is, submission) is induced by fear. *Arcana* (adoration) is stimulated by love, or possibly love is proved through adoration. Fury displays itself in chanting (!), while the act of offering oneself brings quietness.

> jītahu adbhuta sravana soṃ sumirana karunā jāni
> sahita jugupsā dāsatā pādabhajana bhaya māni. (v. 61)
>
> The marvellous is attained by hearing a [tale of] triumph, the pathetic by remembrance. Slavery is considered to be associated with the abhorrent, while foot-reverence is associated with the terrifying.
>
> bandana bīra siṅgāra syoṃ arcana sakhya sahāsa raudra
> kīratana sama sahita ātmanibeda prakāsa. (v. 62)
>
> Offering prayers is bound to the heroic, adoration to the erotic, amity to the comic, and chanting to the furious, while offering oneself displays itself with quietness.

In the last *caraṇa* (line of poetry), by the way, we notice that instead of mentioning the rasa, as in the other eight cases, Keshav gives us the *bhāva* of *śama* (quietude). Actually, the *sthāyī bhāva* (stable emotion) of śānta rasa is a matter of debate. In the case of śama (as for *nirveda* [despair] or *vairāgya* [detachment]) the external basis of the sentiment (*ālambanavi bhāva*) appears to be the phenomenal world, with reference to which one develops 'non-attachment or the state of being not disturbed by it, i.e., quietude'.[29]

As is well known, the connection between bhakti and rasa has been extensively discussed in post-Chaitanya Vaishnava circles. There the theory of aesthetic emotions is adapted to the new context of devotionalism, as classically expounded in the *Bhaktirasāmṛtasindhu* of Rupa Gosvami. In analysing the background of this work, David Haberman draws attention to Mammaṭa, who in his *Kāvyaprakāśa* insists that love for a god is only a bhāva, not a rasa, and Abhinavagupta, who inserts bhakti in his consideration of śānta rasa not as a separate rasa but as 'an emotion conducive to the tranquil state'. Haberman goes on to say that '[t]he real pioneer in presenting bhakti as a distinctive rasa seems to have been Vopadeva'.[30] In the eleventh chapter of *Muktāphala*, Vopadeva expounds the aesthetics of bhakti rasa while classifying bhaktas into nine types, corresponding to the nine rasas of Abhinavagupta.[31] In his commentary on *Muktāphala* 11.1, Hemādri defines a devotee as one who experiences bhakti rasa.[32] He establishes bhakti as a legitimate rasa having all the required constituents of sthāyi-bhāva, and so on. As Raghavan observes, 'the rhetoricians of Bengal who followed the school of Caitanya [served] as a continuation of what Bopadeva did as a pioneer'.[33]

Keshavdas, similarly, assumes a causal relationship between bhakti rasa and the other nine rasas, since bhakti is the supreme rasa and takes the form of the other nine, depending on the rasa a devotee might experience.[34] All the rasas are subservient to bhakti, even those belonging to the characters who, according to the stories, come into conflict with the Lord. Here is what Keshav says:

dīna hvai smara dīnabatsala nāma nāma nidāna
karma adbhuta bhāva soṃ suni nitya beda purāna
chāṃḍi māna amāna syauṃ upahāsa hvai jo dāsa
pādasevahu brahma ko taji sarbabhāvani trāsa. (v. 63)

Religious observance entails remembering his name as 'the compassionate with the poor' and taking refuge in his name, as well as daily listening to his acts in wonder from the Vedas and Purāṇas. Fury is set free by one who has been betrayed [by him]; while laughter those who act as his servants.[35] All creatures who abstain from the service of Brahma's feet feel terrified.

It seems to me that along with the particular rasa inspiring the various practices of bhakti, each line of this stanza depicts a different approach to devotion. The mood connected with *smaraṇa*—compassion towards the poor—suggests the parental affection (*vātsalya*) so emphasized in post-Chaitanya Vaishnavism, that is, the tenderness of parents towards their offspring, as in the case of Krishna's parents.[36] Parental fondness then becomes one of the possible ways for devotees in general to approach Krishna. The second line proposes another way to come close to the Lord—listening to his wondrous acts—as happened to the great sages who knew him. The third line, by the same token, would refer to the moods of the *gopīs* (cow herding girls), either offended by Krishna's betrayals or jeered at by his mockeries. As we have seen in the formulation of Abhinavagupta, fury can be caused by laughter. In this case the rage of the offended gopī is provoked either by the cheeky words of Krishna or by his acts of deception like, for instance, his theft of butter. The last line, finally, refers to Krishna's enemies, who are assailed by terror.

I would propose the following table as a general summary of the relations between bhakti and rasa to which Keshavdas thus alludes in his VG:

Table 9.1 Relationships between *Bhakti* and *Rasa* in the *Vijñānagītā*

Aesthetic Emotion	Practice of Bhakti	Person by Whom the Aesthetic Emotion Is Experienced
śṛṅgāra, the erotic	*arcanaṃ*	
hāsya, the comic	*sakhyam*	the gopīs/Yaśodā
karuṇā, the furious	*smaraṇaṃ*	the gopīs
raudra, the pathetic	*kīrtanaṃ*	the gopīs
vīra, the heroic	*dāsyaṃ*	
bhayānaka, the terrific*	*pādasevanam*	those who abstain from his service and his enemies
bībhatsa, the abhorrent*	*vandanaṃ*	
adbhuta, the marvellous	*śravaṇaṃ*	those who knew Lord Kṛishṇa or listened to his acts from the texts
śānta, the quiet*	*ātmanivedanam*	

Source: Author.
*The corresponding bhāva, not the rasa, is mentioned.

No allusion to the final terms, śānta rasa and *ātmanivedana*, has yet been made in portions of the text that have so far been considered. That, however, follows immediately. The last step towards liberation requires going beyond the rasas narrated in the stories concerning Krishna. These are ultimately illusions, since beyond multiplicity there is nothing but the unity of Paramabrahma. At this stage the dualistic attitude is transcended by a monistic unity, wherein one reaches the Absolute by sublimating one's own soul through the experience of the rasas. At the end of life, everyone must give up everything and retire into solitude to meditate on the Ultimate Truth beyond its forms. Thus, as Keshavdas says:

> kīrati paṛhi nīrasaka hvai rudra rūpa mana jīti
> mana jīte ura upajihai parabrahma soṃ prīti. (v. 64)

> By chanting and reading become dispassionate and overcome your mind in its furious form. When the mind is overcome, the supreme pleasure of *paramabrahma* originates in the heart.

This passage recalls some considerations by Abhinavagupta on the relation between the aesthetic experience and spiritual deliverance. For example, even though the aesthetic and the mystical states of consciousness are characterized by a particular bliss, which is full and perfect, a fundamental difference exists between śānta rasa and *brahmasvāda*. Gnoli describes Abhinava's position as follows: religious experience 'marks the complete disappearance of all polarity, the lysis of all dialexis in the dissolving fire of God', while 'in the aesthetic experience ... the feelings and the facts of everyday life, even if they are transfigured, are always present.... Art is not absence of life ... but it is life itself, pacified and detached from all passions.'[37] The nine rasas are nothing but the mental movements that constitute the bliss tasted during aesthetic experience, which cannot become a permanent feature of life.[38] This is one of the characteristics that distinguish the aesthetic experience from the ultimate experience of *mokṣa* (liberation). In contrast, the Vaishnava devotionalism theorized by Rupa Gosvami 'sought a way to maintain the experience of *rasa* outside the walls of any theatre'[39] and extended aesthetic experience into all of life. As Haberman has said, 'The aim of *bhakti* is the transformation of identity, not the Vedānt in identification with the non-differentiated One.... Rupa claims that one is ultimately a character in the Vraja-līlā—a servant, a friend, an elder, or more important, a lover of Kṛṣṇa's—but never Kṛṣṇa himself. The experience of love requires an object and a subject.'[40] Hence, the goal of bhakti is to relish Ultimate Reality aesthetically and not merely become one with it.[41]

Keshav's approach seems to sit somewhere between these two positions. He takes the religious sentiments seriously, as being cumulatively effective. Yet in the end he moves on to a more Vedāntic position, recognizing that the external world is just an illusion—along with the subjectivity that perceives it as different from itself—and assuming that this acknowledgement is the key to blissful liberation.

> kāma krodhahi jītikai mada lobha moha nivāru
> mitra jyauṃ haṃsi magna ānanda arci sāji siṅgāru
> rūpasaṃvara raudra syauṃ bapu arpiyau anayāsa
> pāya pūrana rūpa koṃ samabhūmi kesavadāsa. (v. 65)

> Once one defeats lust and rage, intoxication, greed, and delusion are destroyed,[42] just as a friend smiles, immersed in joy, when praised for being adorned with all the ornaments. Refusing the external world of shapes, the body is effortlessly delivered from the sentiment of fury and obtains all forms on the same level. So says Keshavdas.

This theoretical progress from dvaita to advaita is nothing new in the syncretic philosophical framework of sixteenth- and seventeenth-century north India. On the whole, it recalls Madhusūdana Sarasvatī's approach, as we see in the notion of bhakti being mixed with the nine rasas (*navarasamilitaḥ: Bhagavadbhaktirasāyaṇam* 1.1).[43] Still, the peculiarity of VG seems to be the idea of a navadhā bhakti based on the nine rasas that lead to liberation (*mokṣadātrī*), as we see in the verse that follows, which is attributed to the *Matsyapurāṇa*:

> mokṣadātrī ca saṃpūrṇalobhadambhādivarjitā
> jagadīśasya navadhā bhaktir navarasātmikā. (v. 66)

> It bestows liberation and lacks any avarice or hypocrisy and so forth—this ninefold devotion to the Lord of the world, composed of the nine aesthetic moods.

Drawing on this Sanskrit quotation, the author searched for an authoritative utterance to support his position, somehow departing from the *Bhagavadbhaktirasāyaṇam*. In fact, Madhusūdana Sarasvatī considers bhakti, which is a proper rasa, as the supreme aim beyond the fourth *puruṣārtha*, that is, mokṣa.[44] He explains bhakti as the *citta* (mind) taking the form of the Lord; it thus becomes the very object with which it comes into contact. For Madhusūdana, bhakti and śānta are essentially different.[45]

Madhusūdana Sarasvatī and Keshavdas converge in their attention to *vairāgya* (asceticism) as a way to *prabodha* (enlightment), but their intuitions about the nature of unity with the Absolute remain somewhat different. Here is the summary Keshavdas offers as he concludes the passage we have been analysing. Having explained the connection of bhakti with the rasas by means of an extension of aesthetics into the field of religion, he thus propounds a sort of 'yoga of emotions':

> sukrācāraja ke kahe bali sādhī saba rīti
> suddha bhayau mana sarbathā baṛhī brahma soṃ prīti. (v. 67)
>
> Bali practised in all ways what the sage Śukra had told him, so his mind became completely purified and the supreme pleasure of brahma arose in him.
>
> taiseṃ tum hūṃ chāṃṛi bhrama hou brahma soṃ līna
> pābahu paramānanda jyoṃ santata nitya navīna. (v. 68)
>
> Having thus abandoned the [duality of] you and me, absorbed in brahma, [with the firm belief that] 'I am brahma', he reached supreme bliss, ever and eternally young.

The theories of rasa bhakti analysed in this chapter try to overcome the subtle—though substantial—gap that is claimed to exist between aesthetic experience and religious bliss. The view of navadhā bhakti articulated in the VG explores a field in which many philosophical influences converge—from the Vedāntan approach of the *Prabhodacandrodaya* and of Madhusūdana Sarasvatī to the aesthetics of Abhinavagupta and the bhakti approaches theorized in Vaishnava circles. Whether, in the midst of this considerable spectrum, Keshavdas's position is distinct is a question that readers themselves are now prepared to address.

Notes

* I would like to express my deep gratitude to John Stratton Hawley for his extensive remarks and inspiring suggestions on earlier versions of this chapter. All translations, aside from those specifically marked otherwise, are my own.

1. Cf. Saroj Agravāl, *Prabodhacandrodaya aur uskī Hindī paramparā* (Prayāg: Hindi Sāhitya Sammelan, 1962). For the Sanskrit text of the *Prabodhacandrodaya* along with translations into French and English, see Armelle Pédraglio, *Le Prabodhacandrodaya de Krsnamisra* (Paris: Institut de Civilisation Indienne, 1974); *Prabodhacandrodaya of Kṛṣṇa Miśra; Sanskrit Text with English Translation, a Critical Introduction, and Index*, ed. Sita Krishna Nambiar (New Delhi: Motilal Banarsidass, 1971); Matthew Kapstein, *The Rise of Wisdom Moon by Krishnamishra* (New York: New York University Press and JJC Foundation, 2009).

2. VG 21.71:

brtti daī padabī daī dūri karauṃ dukhatrāsa
jāya karau sakalatra Śrī Gaṅgātaṭa basabāsa.

Once abandoned wealth and prestige, may I remove fear and sorrow and spend the end of my life taking shelter on the bank of the Gaṅgā.

(Keshavdas, *Vijnānagītā*, in *Keśava-Granthāvalī*, vol. 3, ed. Viśvanātha Prasāda Miśra [Allahabad: Hindustani Academy, 1959], 680.)

3. Saroj Agravāl lists the VG among the readaptations (*rūpāntar*) of the *Prabodhacandrodaya*, being those works basically inspired by the theme of the Moha–Viveka *yuddha* (war). Refer to *Prabodhacandrodaya aur uskī Hindī paramparā*, 203–4; 266–85. She also records almost twenty translations (*anuvād*, 202–3 and 206–65), and twenty independent compositions (*svatantr rūpaknāṭak*, 204 and 287–345), being those texts keeping some similarities with the *Prabodhacandrodaya* but having a different purpose, such as *Bhārat Durdāśā* by Bhartendu and *Kāmnā* by Jayshankar Prasad.

4. V. L. Mitra, *Yoga Vasishtha Maharamayana of Valmiki*, vol. 2 (Calcutta: Bonnerjee and Co., 1891), 1096–131.

5. Sukra, the planet Venus, is represented as the preceptor of demons. The admonition of Sukra to Bali is described, for example, in Mitra, *Yoga Vasishtha*, vol. 2, 1116, v. 26.13: 'Taking the intellect as something thinkable or object of thought, is the snare of the mind; but the belief of its freeness or incomprehensibility, is what confers liberation to the soul. The incomprehensible intellect is verily the universal soul, which is the sum of all doctrines.'

6. Mitra, *Yoga Vasishtha*, vol. 2, 1120, 1127. According to the myth, Viṣṇu deceived Bali by his cunning and dispossessed him of the three worlds, shutting him in the netherworld. Nevertheless, Bali, having forsaken any desire for earthly fruition, enjoyed the fullness of his mind in the privation of his wants.

7. The *Yoga Vāsiṣṭha Mahārāmāyaṇa* is a large compendium of Indian philosophy, illustrated by myths, stories, and similes. The complex theme of the construction of the text of *Yoga Vāsiṣṭha* has been deeply explored by the Mokṣopāya Project Research Group at the University of Halle (Germany), supervised by Walter Slaje (available at http://adwm.indologie.uni-halle.de/moksopaya.htm, last accessed on 24 June 2014) and Peter Thomi at the Institut für Indologie Wichtrach (available at http://indologiewichtrach.ch/werkstatt/, last accessed on 24 June 2014). Keshav's quotations certainly come from Thomi's version (only two stanzas have also been identified in Mokṣopāya), nevertheless, many discrepancies have been found with the edition we referred to. Cf. Mitra, *The Yoga Vāsiṣṭha*.

8. The path traced by the soul in elevating itself towards Brahma-hood is known as the *sapta bhūmikā* (the seven stages of the practice of yoga), described in the next chapters of *Yogavāśiṣṭa* as well as in the following chapter of VG. In the twentieth chapter of VG, the sapta bhūmikā through which the *yogin* advances are named along the phases of a growing sprout: *aṅkurai* (bud), *prakāsa* (manifestation of blossoms), *abināsa* (sprouts like a wonderful flower, stanza 49), the fourth *bhūmikā* is called *svapnavat* (where the world is seen as a dream, stanza 50), the fifth is known as *suṣupta* (hypnotism, stanza 51), liberation in life (*jīvanmukta*, stanza 52) appears as the sixth land, while the seventh bhūmikā is the pleasure of an immovable mind (*cittavilāsa*, stanza 50).

9. In the first chapter of VG, Keshavdas explains that he composed this work to awaken the curiosity about the supreme knowledge (*adhyātma jñāna*) in the heart of Vīrsiṃhadeva, and to show him how to save his soul, since *jñāna*, Hari bhakti, and ritualism are ineffective for a mind that does not abandon misbehaviour and cannot prevent from decadence.

> Once the noble king [Vīra Siṃha], sitting in an assembly of learned people, asked Keśavarāya, the king of poets, [to tell] the finest tale. (1.28): [King Vīra Siṃha said] Having achieved the holiest place that is the Gaṅgā and the greatest gift that is the gift of a cow, we heard from the Vedas and the Purāṇas about the glory of Shiva and the other gods. The glory of the *Vedas* and the Purāṇas has been described in many ways; a man practicing faith to his own possibility is praised for his merit, while a mind (*mana*) practicing devotion to his own possibility is saved from the body. [But this does not happen for] a mind (*citta*) not abandoning misbehavior, even cleansing on the bank of the Gaṅgā. (1.29) (Keshavdas, *Vijñānagītā*, vv. 28–9).

10.

na tad bhāsayate sūryo na śaśāṅko na pāvakaḥ/yad gatvā na nivartante tad dhāma paramaṃ mama (Bhagavadgītā 15.6).

The sun does not illumine there, nor the moon, nor the fire. That is My supreme abode. Having reached there they do not come back (Ramanand Prasad, trans., *The Bhagavad Gita* [Fremont USA: American Gita Society, 1988]).

11.

viprāddviṣaḍguṇayutādaravindanābha/pādāravindavimukhāt śvapacaṃ variṣṭham/
manye tadarpitamanovacanehitārtha/prāṇaṃ punāti sa kulaṃ na tu bhūrimānaḥ//
(*Bhāgavatapurāṇa* 7.9.10).

If a brāhmaṇa has all twelve of the brahminical qualifications [as they are stated in the book called *Sanat-sujāta*] but is not a devotee and is averse to the lotus feet of the Lord, he is certainly lower than a devotee who is a dog-eater but who has dedicated everything—mind, words, activities, wealth and life—to the Supreme Lord. Such a devotee is better than such a brāhmaṇa because the devotee can purify his whole family, whereas the so-called brāhmaṇa in a position of false prestige cannot purify even himself.

Cf. *Śrīmad Bhāgavatam*, at Bhaktivedanta Veda Base, available at http://vedabase.net/sb/en/, last accessed on 14 July 2012.

12. VG 19.44: 'patito 'pi varo vipro na ca śūdro jitendriyaḥ/kaḥ parityajya gāṃ duṣṭāṃ kharī ṃśīlavatīṃ duhet', corresponding to *Paraśāra* 8.25, with some interpolations in the first pāda ('duḥśīlo 'pi dvijaḥpūjyo'): 'Even a Brahman of a bad character deserves respect; but not so a Shoodra, even though his passions may have been subdued by him. Who would quit a wicked cow, and try to milk a docile female ass?' See *Parasaradharmasamhita*: Kandas 1 and 2 Input by Muneo Tokunaga, completely revised GRETIL version (2002), based on the edition with Madhava's Tika by Pandit Vaman Sastri Islampurkar (and R. G. Bhandarkar) (Bombay: Government Central Book Depot 1893–1919, Bombay Sanskrit Series), available at, http://gretil.sub.uni-goettingen.de/gret_utf.htm#Parassmr, last accessed on accessed 14 July 2012; http://ia700200.us.archive.org/6/items/ParasharaSmriti/SriParasharaSmrithiPdf.pdf.

13. VG 19.30: 'na yajñayogena tapobhir ugrair na mantratīrthair na ca mārjanena/tathā haris tuṣyati devadevo yathā mahī devasutoṣ aṇena.' See N.A. Deshpande, *The Padma-Purāṇa*, part VI (New Delhi: Motilal Banarsidass, 1990), 2033–4: 'The lord, the god of gods, is not that pleased with sacrifices, austerities and meditation or worship as he is with the bhāhmaṇas being pleased.'

14. Keshavdas, *Kavipriyā*, in *Keśava-Granthāvalī*, vol. 1, ed. Viśvanātha Prasāda Miśra (Allahabad: Hindustani Academy, 1954), 162; Lālā Bhagavān Dīn, *Priyā Prakāśa: Keśava Kṛta Kavipriyā Kī Prāmāṇika Ṭīkā*, 3rd ed. (Vārāṇasī: Kalyāna Dāsa, 1964), 235–6.

15. In his commentary to the *Kavipriyā*, Lālā Bhagavān Dīn gives details of the navadhā bhakti referring to the forms of ritual actions prescribed by the *Bhāgavata Purāṇa* that we will see hereafter. Refer to Bhagavān Dīn, *Priyā Prakāśa*, 235–6. Despite being also mentioned in VG 19.59, this seems not to be the point of Keshavdas, since he proposes a new kind of navadhā bhakti based on the nine rasas and not on the practices of devotion.

16. Cf. *Śrī Padmamahāpurāṇam*, uttarakhaṇḍa 23.2 (the parts that also occur in VG 19.55 are underlined):

patraṃpuṣpaṃphalaṃ mūlaṃśākhātvakskhandhasaṃjnitam/tulasīsaṃbha vaṃsarvaṃpāvanaṃmṛttikādikam//

Everything of Tulasī including leaves, flowers fruits, roots, branches, skin, and stem is purifying, so also the clay (where) the Tulasī-plant grows.

Kriyākhaṇḍa 24.26:

yo 'śnātitulasīpatraṃsarvapāpaharaṃśubham/taccharīrāntarasthāyipāpaṃ naśyatitatkṣaṇāt //

The sin in the body of him who eats the auspicious tulasī leaf, removing all sins, perishes at that moment (only).

Cf. Deshpande, *The Padma-Purana*, 2404, 3535.

17. The word *ekaviṃśati*, meaning twenty-one, is associated since Vedic times to sacrifice, referring to the usage of that specific number of sacred leaves, roots, stems, and so on, while performing a ritual. Refer to Uma Marina Vesci, *Heat and Sacrifice in the Vedas* (New Delhi: Motilal Banarsidass, 1985), 89.

18.

Na kevalaṃ mad-bhaktānām anāvṛtti-lakṣaṇam ananta-phalam, sukhārādhanaś cāham/katham? patraṃ puṣpaṃ phalaṃ toyaṃ yo me bhaktyā prayacchati/tad ahaṃ bhakty-upahṛtam aśnāmi prayatātmanaḥ // 9.25 // patraṃ puṣpaṃ phalaṃ toyam udakaṃ yaḥ me mahyaṃ bhaktyā prayacchati, tat ahaṃ patrādi bhaktyā upahṛtaṃ bhakti-pūrvakaṃ prāpitaṃ bhakty-upahṛtam aśnāmi gṛhṇāmi prayatātmanaḥ śuddha-buddheḥ// 9.26 //.

Worshippers of the demigods go to the demigods, the worshippers of the ancestors go to the ancestors, and the worshippers of the ghosts go to the ghosts, but My devotees come to Me (and are not born again) (9.25). Whosoever offers Me a leaf, a flower, a fruit, or water with devotion; I accept and eat the offering of devotion by the pure-hearted (9.26).

Trans. Ramanand Prasad, *The Bhagavad Gita.*

19. The nine limbs of the body are two eyes, two ears, two hands, two legs, and the nose. Cf. Syamasundara Dasa, *Hindī Śabdasāgar* (Kasi: Nagari Pracarini Sabha, 1965–75).

20. Mitra, *Yoga Vasishtha*, vol. 2, 1119. See also *Yoga Vāsiṣṭha of Vālmīki*, 607: 'citā saṃcetito dveṣo dveṣo bhavati nānyathā/tasmāddveṣādayaḥ sarve bhāvābhāvāścidātmakāḥ//(25).'

21. Mitra, *Yoga Vasishtha*, vol. 2, 1120. See also *The Yogavāsiṣṭha of Vālmīki*, 607: 'na dveṣo 'sti na rāgo 'sti na mano nāsya vṛttayaḥ/cinmātrasyātiśuddhasya vikalpakalanākṛtā //(17).'

22. Class of demons often identified with the *daityas* or asuras and held to be implacable enemies of the gods or *devas*.

23. 'śravaṇaṃ kīrtanaṃ viṣṇoḥ smaraṇaṃ pādasevanam/arcanaṃ vandanaṃ dāsyaṃ sakhyam ātmanivedanam //' (The translation has been taken with some slight modifications from *Śrīmad Bhāgavatam* 7.5, 23–4).

24. The original verse from *Nātyaśāstra* 6.15 is: 'śṛṅgārahāsyakaruṇā raudravīrabhayānakāḥ/bībhatsādbhutasaṃjñau cetyaṣṭau **nāṭye** rasā ḥsmṛtāḥ' (Cf. *Nāṭyaśāstra of Bharatamuni with the Commentary Abhinavabhāratī by Abhinavaguptācārya*, vol. 1, ed. R. S. Nagar [New Delhi: Parimal Publications, 1988], 266; Manomohan Ghosh, *The Natyasastra: A Treatise on Hindu Dramaturgy and Histrionics Ascribed to Bharata-Muni* [Calcutta: The Royal Asiatic Society of Bengal, 1950], 102). Keshava's own interpolation has been highlighted in bold, while the 'traditional' interpolation concerning the number of rasas (on which see hereafter, note 26) has been underlined.

25. In *Nāṭyaśāstra* 6.17 and 7.1–28, eight rasas are described. As Raghavan asserts, the number of rasas remains eight till the time of Daṇḍin (660–680 CE) and there is the possibility that Bhāmaha (700–750 CE) was aware of the eight rasas. Udbhaṭa (750–850 CE) in his *Kāvyalaṃkārasārasaṅgraha* accepts nine rasas with śānta included. Dhanañjaya (974–996 CE) in his *Daśarūpaka* vehemently opposed śānta as the ninth rasa, and this tells us that śānta had already been introduced by then. Ānandavardhana mentions about śānta rasa in the third *uddyota* of *Dhvānyaloka*, and from his assumptions Abhinavagupta starts his own theorization of the ninth rasa. Probably, there existed at that time two different versions of *Nāṭyaśāstra*, one of which listed nine rasas, but, as Abhinavagupta himself admits, the classification into eight rasas was more ancient. See V. Raghavan, *The Number of Rasa-s* (Madras: The Adyar Library and Research Centre, 1967), 15–16; J.L. Masson and M.V. Patwardhan, *Śāntarasa and Abhinavagupta's Philosophy of Aesthetics* (Pune: Bhandarkar Oriental Research Institute, 1969), 34–8.

26. Raghavan, *The Number of Rasa-s*, 15.

27. 'sarveṣāṃ kāvyānāṃ nānārasabhāvayuktiyuktānām/nirvahaṇe kartavyo nityaṃ hi raso 'dbhutastajñaiḥ' (*Nāṭyaśāstra of Bharatamuni*, vol. 2, 316). In Ghosh's translation, the verse is numbered as 20.46. See Ghosh, *The Natyasastra*, 362.

28. *Nāṭyaśāstra of Bharatamuni*, vol. 1, 267: tatas trivargātmakapravṛtt<i>{a} dharmaviparītanivṛtt<i>{a}dharmātmako mokṣaphalaḥ śāntaḥ/tatra svātmāveśena rasacarvaṇetyuktam.

I am indebted to Daniele Cuneo for his help with the translation and his clarifications on this point in Abhinavagupta's philosophy. The mention of pravṛtti and nivṛtti dharma seems to be highly significant for our discussion, since these two concepts are allegorically represented in the *Prabodhacandrodaya* as the two views of the mind (*manas*). Resignation (nivṛtti) generated discrimination (viveka), while activity (pravṛtti) generated delusion (mahamoha) and perished in the war together with her son. After that, the mind had to be persuaded to continue his life with resignation to achieve relief. Referring to the pre-eminence of śānta rasa in the hierarchy of rasas, see Masson and Patwardhan, *Śāntarasa and Abhinavagupta's Philosophy of Aesthetics*, 102–3.

29. Quite different is the case of Abhinavagupta, holding that *tattvajñāna* (knowledge of truth) or *ātmasvarūpa* (the true form or nature of the Self) itself is the *sthāyin* (permanent state) of śānta, being the knowledge of the very nature of the Self bringing *jñāna* (knowledge) and *ānanda* (bliss) and leading to *mokṣa* (liberation). If *ātman* (the Self) is taken as the sthāyin of śānta rasa, 'we have a unique case of a Rasa in which the Ālambana and Sthāyin are identical'. Refer to Raghavan, *The Number of Rasa-s*, chap. IV, particularly 97–101; Masson and Patwardhan, *Śāntarasa and Abhinavagupta's Philosophy of Aesthetics*, 123–88.

30. David Haberman, *Acting as a Way of Salvation* (New Delhi: Motilal Banarsidass, 2001 [1988]), xlviii.

31. V. Kameswari, 'Bopadeva and His Contribution to Bhakti Cult', in N.B. Patil, Mrinal Kaul 'Martand', *The Variegated Plumage: Encounters with Indian Philosophy* (A Commemoration Volume in Honour of Pandit Jankinath Kaul 'Kamal') (New Delhi: Sant Samagam Research Institute, Motilal Banarsidass, 2003), 289–93. Already in *Bhāgavata Purāṇa*, few kinds of devotees are mentioned: those desiring material profits from their master, being not pure devotees (7.10.5), those never desiring any kind of material opulence, either in this life or in the next, being pure devotees (7.10.11 and 21). 'By devotional service, pure devotees who incessantly think of the Supreme Personality of Godhead receive bodies similar to His' (7.10.40). Then, Prahlāda is defined as the best among exalted devotees (7.10.47). Refer to *Śrīmad Bhāgavatam*, canto 7: The Science of God, chapter 10: 'Prahlāda, the Best Among Exalted Devotees', at Bhaktivedanta Veda Base.

32. See Kameswari, 'Bopadeva and His Contribution to Bhakti Cult', 292–3:

> According to Bopadeva, the 'delectation' produced through *śravaṇa*, *manana* etc. of the story of the Bhaktas which embody the nine *rasas* in Bhakti-rasa: He then illustrates devotion through each of these nine *rasas* by bringing the relevant verses of *Bhāgavata* under each one of them: *Hāsya*: Gopīs and boy Kṛṣṇa's pranks with them. *Śṛṅgāra: Samboga*—Love of the Gopīs towards Kṛṣṇa. *Vipralambha*—Gopīs in separation. *Karuṇa*: Arjuna's lamentation before Kṛṣṇa, Sunītī's words, verses uttered by Prahlāda, Aditi, Nārada, etc. *Raudra*: Episodes of Hiraṇyakaśipu and Śiśupāla—their violent personalities subserve the purpose of the constant thought of the Lord. *Bhaya*: Similar obsession of the thoughts of Kṛṣṇa through fear—Kamsa, Durvāśas, and the expression of fear by devotees. *Bībhatsa*: Expressed through disgust towards the body and mundane pre-occupations. *Śānta*: This is intimately connected with Bhakti. The commentary answers at length the objections of *ālaṃkārikas* against *Śānta*

rasa—e.g. Kapila, Akrūra, Mucukunda. *Adbhuta*: Sudāma episode. Also the wonderful spiritual experiences of Śuka, Uddhava, Prahlāda, Akrūra. *Vīra*: Of Bali, Pṛthu, Parīkṣit, Rudra and others. Both dānavīra and dharmavīra varieties are illustrated.

33. Raghavan, *The Number of Rasa-s*, 143–4. Cf. Kameswari, 'Bopadeva and His Contribution to Bhakti Cult', 292–3.

34. 'Sa navadhā bhaktaḥ nava-vidhatve hetum āha—bhaktīti/bhaktir vihitāvihitā ca/bhakti-rasasyaiva hāsya-śṛṅgāra-karuṇa-raudra-bhayānaka-bībhatsa-śāntādbhuta-vīra-rūpeṇānubhavāt [...] vyāsādibhir varṇitasya viṣṇu-bhaktānāṃ vā caritrasya nava-rasātmakasya śravaṇādinā janitaś camatkāro bhakti-rasaḥ/tatra hāsya-rase gopyaḥ/sa ca tredhā' (*Mukta-phalam [Muktāphalam]* by Vopadeva with the commentary of Hemadri, ed. Pandit Isvar Chandra Sastri and Pandit Haridasa Vidyabagisa, Calcutta Oriental Series 5 [Calcutta: New Arya Mission Press, 1920], 125, 131). See also Raghavan, *The Number of Rasa-s*, 153.

35. Hemadri's commentary on *Muktāphalam* 11.*ad* 1–6 associates the rage to the shepherds' resentment for the butter stealing, and the laughter to the *gopīs*' amusement for Kṛṣṇa's tricks. See Vopadeva, *Mukta-phalam*, 131–2. The comic rasa in the dynamics of *nāyakanāyikābheda* (typology of heroes and heroines) has been dealt with also in *Rasikapriyā* 14.1–17, where Keshav describes four kinds of *hāsya rasa: bhaṃdhās* (feeble laughter), *kalhās* (sweet laughter), *atihās* (violent laughter), and *parihās* (loud laughter). See K. P. Bahadur, *Rasikapriya of Keshavadasa* (New Delhi: Motilal Banarsidass, 1990), pp. 120–44. The choice of different word (*upahās*) in the VG possibly aims at excluding any secular setting of the rasa.

36. Sushil Kumar De, *The Early History of the Vaishnava Faith and Movement in Bengal* (Calcutta: Firma K.L Mukhopadhyayi, 1961), 196.

37. Raniero Gnoli, *The Aesthetic Experience According to Abhinavagupta* (Varanasi: Chowkhambha Sanskrit Series, 1985[1968]), xl. Some main similarities and differences between *rasasvāda* and *brahmāsvāda* according to Abhinavagupta are listed in Masson and Patwardhan, *Śāntarasa and Abhinavagupt's Philosophy of Aesthetics*, 161–4.

38. Gnoli, *The Aesthetic Experience According to Abhinavagupta*, xliv.

39. Haberman, *Acting as a Way of Salvation*, 37.

40. Haberman, *Acting as a Way of Salvation*, 38.

41. Haberman, *Acting as a Way of Salvation*, 53.

42. Refer to *Padmapurāṇa*, Krīyā Yogasāra 2/83:

kāmakrodhavihīnā ye hiṃsādambhavivarjitāḥ/lobhamohavihīnāś ca jñeyās te vaiṣṇavājanāḥ

Those who are free from lust, anger, violence, arrogance, greed, illusion, they are said to be Vaishnavas.

43. 'nava-rasa-militaḥ vā kevalaḥ vā pum-arthaḥ paramam iha mukunde bhakti-yogaḥ vadanti [1.1ab].... etena bhaktir na puruṣārtho dharmārtha-kāma-mokṣeṣv anantarbhāvād ity ādikaḥ sarvam apāstam [1.ad1].' Cf. *Bhagavad-bhakti-rasayanam*, ed. Janardan Shastri Pandeya, Vidyabhavanprācya-vidyā-grantha-mālā 91 (Varanasi: ChowkhambaVidyabhavan, 1998 [3rd edition]).

44. 'Those who did not accept Bhakti as a separate Rasa considered it as a Bhāva, a variety of Rati, the object of which is God: *devādiviṣayāratiḥ*. To these writers, Madhusūdana Sarasvatī replies that this Bhāva-Rati described as *devādiviṣayā* refers to Rati for the lesser gods. Rati for the Supreme Being is a Rasa' (Raghavan, *The Number of Rasa-s*, 153–4).

45. Giving *nirveda/vairāgya* as a condition that precedes the *uddīpanavibhāva* (stimulant factor) of bhakti as the Lord himself, according to Madhusūdana, the sthāyin for bhakti is *bhagavadākāra-cittavṛtti* (focusing of the mind on the form of god). This is not very different from *bhagavad-rati* (enjoyment of [the apprehension of] god), since the result of this cittavṛtti, its *phala*, is intense love for God. See Raghavan, *The Number of Rasa-s*, 150.

Bibliography

Primary Sources

Bhagavad-bhakti-rasāyaṇam of Madhusūdana Sarasvatī, edited by Janardan Shastri Pandeya. Vidyabhavan prācya-vidyā-grantha-mālā 91. Varanasi: Chowkhamba Vidyabhavan, 1998 (3rd edition). Available at http://www.granthamandira.com/index.php?show=entry&e_no=521, last accessed on 15 March 2013.

Bhāgavatapurāṇa. Available at http://gretil.sub.uni-goettingen.de/gretil/1_sanskr/3_purana/bhagp/bhp_01u.htm, last accessed on 14 July 2012.

Kavipriyā of Keshavdas. In *Keśava-Granthāvalī*, vol. 1, edited by Viśvanātha Prasāda Miśra. Allahabad: Hindustani Academy, 1954, 94–228.

Rasikapriyā of Keshavdas. In *Keśava-Granthāvalī*, vol. 1, edited by Viśvanātha Prasāda Miśra. Allahabad: Hindustani Academy, 1954, 1–93.

Vijñānagītā of Keshavdas. In *Keśava-Granthāvalī*, vol. 3, edited by Viśvanātha Prasāda Miśra. Allahabad: Hindustani Academy, 1959, 643–780.

Mukta-phalam (*Muktāphalam*) of Vopadeva, with the commentary of Hemadri, edited by Pandit Isvar Chandra Sastri and Pandit Haridasa Vidyabagisa, Calcutta Oriental Series 5. Calcutta: New Arya Mission Press, 1920. (Text only available in the Grantha Mandir edition, available at http://www.granthamandira.com/index.php?show=entry&e_no=794, last accessed on 15 March 2013.)

Nāṭyaśāstra with the Commentary Abhinavabhāratī by Abhinavagupta, edited by K. L. Joshi. New Delhi: Parimal Publications, 1984.

Nāṭyaśāstra of Bharatamuni with the Commentary Abhinavabhāratī by Abhinavaguptācārya, edited by R. S. Nagar. New Delhi: Parimal Publications, 1988.

Parasaradharmasamhita (=Parasarasmrti), Kandas 1 and 2 Input by Muneo Tokunaga, completely revised GRETIL version (2002). Based on the edition with Madhava's Tika by Pandit Vaman Sastri Islampurkar (and R. G. Bhandarkar). Bombay: Government Central Book Depot 1893–1919, Bombay Sanskrit Series. Available at http://gretil.sub.uni-goettingen.de/gret_utf.htm#Parassmr; http://ia700200.us.archive.org/6/items/ParasharaSmriti/SriParasharaSmrithiPdf.pdf, last accessed on 14 July 2014.

Prabodhacandrodaya of Kṛṣṇa Miśra; Sanskrit Text with English Translation, a Critical Introduction, and Index, edited by Sita Krishna Nambiar. New Delhi: Motilal Banarsidass, 1971.

Śrī Padmamahāpurāṇam (4 vols), edited by Charudev Shastri and Shloka, index by Nag Sharan Singh. New Delhi: Nag Publishers, 1984.

The Yogavāsiṣṭha of Vālmīki, with the Commentary Vāsiṣṭhamahārāmāyaṇatātparyaprakāśa, edited by Wāsudev Laxmaṇ Śāstrī Paṇśīkar (3rd ed.). Bombay: Pāṇḍurang Jāwajī, 1937.

Secondary Sources

Agravāl, Saroj. *Prabodhacandrodaya aur uskī Hindī paramparā*. Prayāg: Hindi Sāhitya Sammelan, 1962.

Bahadur, K. P. *Rasikapriya of Keshavadasa*. New Delhi: Motilal Banarsidass, 1990.

Bhagavān Dīn, Lālā. *Priyā prakāśa: keśava kṛta kavipriyā kī prāmāṇika ṭīkā* (3rd ed.). Vārāṇasī: Kalyāna Dāsa, 1964.

Dasa, Syamasundara. *Hindī Śabdasāgar*. Kasi: Nagari Pracarini Sabha, 1965–75. Available at http://dsal.uchicago.edu/dictionaries/dasa-hindi/, last accessed on 14 July 2015.

De, Sushil Kumar. *The Early History of the Vaishnava Faith and Movement in Bengal*. Calcutta: Firma K. L. Mukhopadhyayi, 1961.

Deshpande, N. A. *The Padma-Purāṇa*, part VI, translated and annotated by N. A. Deshpande. New Delhi: Motilal Banarsidass, 1990.

Ghosh, Manomohan. *The Nāṭyaśāstra. A Treatise on Hindu Dramaturgy and Histrionics Ascribed to Bharata Muni* (cap. 1–27). Calcutta: The Royal Asiatic Society of Bengal, 1950.

Gnoli, Raniero. *The Aesthetic Experience According to Abhinavagupta*. Varanasi: Chowkhambha Sanskrit Series, 1985 [1968].

Haberman, David. *Acting as a Way of Salvation: A Study of Rāgānugā Bhakti Sādhana*. New Delhi: Motilal Banarsidass, 2001 [1988].

———. *The Bhaktirasāmṛtasindhu of Rūpagosvāmin*. New Delhi: Indira Gandhi National Centre for the Arts, 2003.

Kameswari, V. 'Bopadeva and His Contribution to Bhakti Cult'. In N.B. Patil and Mrinal Kaul 'Martand', eds, *The Variegated Plumage: Encounters with Indian Philosophy* (A Commemoration Volume in Honour of Pandit Jankinath Kaul 'Kamal'). New Delhi: Sant Samagam Research Institute and Motilal Banarsidass, 2003, 289–93.

Kapstein, Matthew. *The Rise of Wisdom Moon by Krishna-Mishra*. New York: New York University Press and JJC Foundation, 2009.

Larson, Gerald James. 'The Aesthetic (*rasāsvāda*) and the Religious (*brahmāsvāda*) in Abhinavagupta's Kashmir Śaivism'. *Journal of Indian Philosophy* 26, no. 4 (1976): 371–87.

Masson, J. L. and Patwardhan M. V. *Śāntarasa and Abhinavagupta's Philosophy of Aesthetics*. Pune: Bhandarkar Oriental Research Institute, 1969.

Mitra, V. L. *Yoga Vasishtha Maharamayana of Valmiki*. Calcutta: Bonnerjee and Co., 1891. Accessed via Project Gutenberg/Distributed Proofreaders at www.pgdp.net.

Pédraglio, Armelle. *Le Prabodhacandrodaya de Krsnamisra*. Paris: Institut de Civilisation Indienne, 1974.

Prasad, Ramanand, trans. *The Bhagavad Gita*. Fremont, CA: American Gita Society, 1988. Available at http://eawc.evansville.edu/anthology/gita.htm, last accessed on 14 July 2012.

Raghavan, V. *The Number of Rasa-s*. Madras: The Adyar Library and Research Centre, 1967.

Śrīmad Bhāgavatam at Bhaktivedanta Veda Base. Available at http://vedabase.net/sb/en/, last accessed on 14 July 2012.

Vesci, Uma Marina. *Heat and Sacrifice in the Vedas*. New Delhi: Motilal Banarsidass, 1985.

10

JOHN E. CORT*

'This Is How We Play Holī'

Allegory in North Indian Digambar Jain Holī Songs

The springtime festival of Holī has long posed a problem for Jains. Jain ideologues have criticized the celebration of Holī as contravening several key Jain ethical virtues. In response, Digambar Jain poets developed a genre of Holī songs that transformed the elements of Holī into a complex spiritual allegory, and thereby 'tamed' the transgressive festival. These songs were part of a culture of songs (*pad, bhajan*) and other vernacular compositions by Digambar laymen in the cosmopolitan centres of north India in the seventeenth through nineteenth centuries. I argue in this chapter that an investigation into this Digambar genre of Holī songs encourages us to see that the many 'Hindu' Holī songs from this same time period were also engaged in a process of reframing and taming Holī. Both Hindu and Jain songs translate its antinomian and transgressive elements into softer, less threatening sets of metaphors specific to their various spiritual traditions.

On the first night of the festival everyone gathers for the burning of a bonfire, in memory of the burning of an evil woman or demoness.[1] In many theological interpretations, this is the demoness Holikā. The bonfire clearly violates the central Jain ethical principle of *ahiṃsā*, or non-harm. Igniting a fire at night, when inevitably many insects and other small living creatures will be incinerated, is seen by Jains as an act of fearsome violence. The next morning is Dhuleṇḍī; this is a riotous time, as neighbours throw dry, coloured powders and coloured liquids on each other. Many people accentuate the festivities by consuming *bhāṅg* (cannabis) and becoming intoxicated. Holī is also a time when many people sing songs 'publicly characterized as obscene', as they focus on 'the joking [and potentially sexual] relationship between a woman and her younger brother-in-law'.[2] In many villages, women employ long phallic staffs and thick, wet-knotted ropes to beat the men.[3] All of this clearly goes against the Jain emphasis on decorum, mindfulness, and equanimity (*samatā*, *saṃyam*, and *sañjam*). Scholarship has shown the many ways that the observance of Holī involves extensive subaltern expressions of subjugated social and economic status, something in which many Jains from middle- and upper-class families, as paradigmatic 'alterns',[4] might understandably be reluctant to participate.

For these reasons Holī was included on a list of 'harmful customs' (*hānīkārik rivāz*) that Śvetāmbar Mūrtipūjak Jain reformers in the early twentieth century urged their fellow Jains to avoid.[5] In a 1940 essay published in the Hindi journal *Anekānt*, of which he was the founder and editor, the Digambar intellectual and social reformer Jugalkiśor Mukhtār (1877–1968) decried the way that Holī was commonly observed, and argued that its true essence was equanimity (samatā) and independence (*svatantratā*).[6] He argued that it was of vital interest to the cause of the nation for the Congress to take the lead in restoring the observance of Holī to its original spirit. This would help instill a true spirit of independence (*svarājya*) in the people. If Congress was unwilling or unable to take the lead in this effort, he suggested that another national religious organization such as the Hindu Mahasabha should. He concluded his essay with a ten-point plan for the reform (*sudhār*) of Holī. This included using liquid substances in the play of colours that were not harmful, eliminating the consumption of alcohol and other intoxicating substances, not trading insults, and not singing obscene songs. He accompanied his article by a poem he wrote in Hindi entitled 'Holī Holī hai', in which he played upon the oral coincidence between the Hindi 'Holī' and the English 'holy'to ask in the refrain, 'How is Holī holy?' (*kaise holī holī hai?*) The refrain was a rebuttal to the popular phrase 'Holī hai!'

This is the standard response to any criticism of the excesses of Holī, and implies, 'it is Holī, so anything goes!' He reprinted the poem in a 1948 issue of *Anekānt*, proudly noting that he had been told that the poem had been painted on the wall of the Bīspanth Koṭhī temple at the important pilgrimage shrine of Sammet Shikhar in eastern India.[7]

This is not just a modernist response to Holī. The fifteenth-century Digambar poet Brahm Jindās criticized the popular performance of Holī in his *Holī Rās*. As summarized by Premcand Rāṅvkā, Jindās described how Holī had been observed in the fourth spoke of time in Jain cosmology, a Jain version of the golden age of truth (*satyayug*): '[S]pring (*basant*) was played on the full moon of Phālgun. *Rās, bhās, kavitt, phāg* and *gīt* [all genres of songs] were sung. Virtuous people worshiped in the Jina temples. There were performances of religious stories. This was the correct Holī. The way Holī is observed nowadays is not correct.'[8] A little more than a century later, the Digambar poet Chītar Ṭholiyā in his *Holī kī kathā*, which he composed in Mozamabad in 1603, said that the play with colours and the Holī bonfire are both examples of *mithyātva* (wrong faith). According to him, not only does participating in the play of Holī result in a person being reborn in an infernal existence (*jo ṣelai holī mithyāta/so pāvai narakā kau pāta*), but just watching the bonfire will have the same result (*holī jalatī deṣai soya/naraka taṇauṃ jīva soya*).[9]

On the other hand, Holī is a neighbourhood event in which everyone in a community is expected to participate. Most Jains have done so willingly and even eagerly. It is a joyous springtime festival, the celebration of which traditionally has not been tied to any one religious community. Much of what goes on during Holī, such as visiting with friends and neighbours to express loving comradeship and eating sweets, dried fruits, and other special seasonal foods, is not opposed to Jain ethics or etiquette. Not to participate in these activities can even be seen as rude and antisocial. Despite the ideological stance that a strictly orthodox Jain should not participate in various aspects of Holī (and some indeed do not), in actual fact the vast majority of Jains in north India have done so.

Singing Spring: *Phaguā, Phāgu*

Holī in north India is more than a two-day religious and social event. It is a high point of a much larger set of cultural events that mark the season of spring. People gather in Hindu temples and other public places to sing Holī songs in a seasonal style known as *phaguā*, after the spring month of Phāgun. In traditional north India, wintertime often saw the men of a family go elsewhere, to work, trade, or soldier. In Phāgun, women expected their men to return. Many phaguā songs express *viraha* (love in absence), and are filled with emotional longing and sexual anticipation. Others express *saṃyog*, as the man has returned and the lovers are again united.

Phāg is also one of the names for the red powder that people throw on each other while playing Holī. While the various myths behind the festival indicate that most of the activities predate the Krishna-oriented Vaishnavization of north India, in large parts of north India, Holī for several centuries has been inextricably linked with imitating the ways that Krishna and his companions played it. The play of colours in particular is closely associated with the spiritualized erotic play of Krishna and the *gopī*s (cowherding girls) in the countryside of Braj.

Modern phaguā songs derive from the older genre of phāg or *phāgu*. As described by Charlotte Vaudeville, 'the main and almost sole theme of the *phāgu* is the erotic theme in its various aspects and phases: *viyoga* and *saṁyoga*, union and separation of lovers'.[10] Kantilal B. Vyas has summarized the features of a phāgu.[11] It begins with a sensuous description of spring, as all of nature exhibits new life. The poem then turns to the heroine. The fertile exuberance of spring accentuates her longing for her absent lover. The detailed descriptions of the lovesick heroine are essential to the mood of the poem, creating a sympathetic sense of longing in the audience. At length, the hero returns, the lovers are reunited, and rather than being in conflict with the surrounding natural setting, their fertile erotic play is consonant with it. The poem ends with a sense of profound fulfilment.

This genre was adopted by more theologically oriented poets in the Vaishnava and Jain traditions to express the separation of the person from his or her spiritual essence. In a Vaishnava phāgu, the poet allegorized the separation of the lovers to the separation of the soul from God as Krishna. In a Jain phāgu, the poet allegorized the separation of the person as defined externally by the transitory and deluded body and senses from the person's true being, the internal, eternal, and wise soul.

The Jain genre of *phāgu* and another genre that Vaudeville has demonstrated had extensive overlap with it, the genre of *bārahmāsā* (a cycle of songs depicting the twelve months of the year), had a significant influence on the later Digambar genre of Holī songs.[12] A third genre that overlapped extensively with phāgu was *dhamāl* (also spelled *dhamār*; in older Digambar texts, it is often spelled as *ḍhamāl*). The overlap between phāgu and dhamāl was so great that Agarcand Nāhṭā said of the two: 'There must be differences between *phāgu* and *dhamāl* in terms of meter, *rāginī* and style, but in the seventeenth century, from when most of the compositions in the genre of *dhamāl* date, both names are applied to the same compositions.'[13] We see this clearly in a text by the seventeenth-century Banārsīdās, which was entitled both *Adhyātam Phāg* and *Adhyātam Dhamār* in the same manuscripts.

Among Jains, phāgu and bārahmāsā appear to have begun in Śvetāmbar literary circles, but they did not remain exclusively Śvetāmbar genres. There was also a Digambar expression of this genre, as seen in the *Ādīśvar Phāg* by Bhaṭṭārak Jñānbhūṣaṇ, composed sometime around 1500 CE.[14] It narrated the biography of the first Jina, Ādināth or Ādīśvar. After dwelling at great length on the hero's childhood and accession to the throne as king, Jñānbhūṣan achieved a denouement in which the divine dancer Nīlañjanā was sent by the gods to remind Ādīśvar of the need to renounce the world. She danced so energetically that she fell dead. This shocked Ādīśvar into realizing the fragility of life, and caused him to renounce his throne and become a homeless mendicant. We see here a skilful redeployment of the common phāgu emphasis on viraha or bereavement at separation from one's beloved to underscore the Jain valorization of renunciation of the emotions.

A Digambar Jain Counter-tradition of Holī

Digambar Jain poets in north India developed a counter-tradition of short Holī songs (pad) in response to the popular transgressive observances. We do not know when this counter-tradition started, but it has been in existence since at least the time of Banārsīdās (1586–1643), who composed several Braj-bhāṣā poems on the subject. Included in his *Banārsī Vilās*, the collection of his poetic works compiled shortly after his death by his friend and fellow poet Jagjīvanrām, is an eighteen-verse poem entitled *Adhyātam Phāg* or *Adhyātam Dhamār*. Banārsīdās engaged in an extensive allegorization of the observance of Holī, in which he stressed the need to turn away from externalities and focus on one's inner spiritual essence. This is the basic message of the style of Digambar spirituality known as Adhyātma; Banārsīdās was a leader in one of the most important Adhyātma circles, in Agra, in the mid-seventeenth century.[15] Adhyātma involved a radical form of soteriological dualism, and in the song, Banārsīdās recommended that while deluded people play the external, physical Holī, the spiritual seeker should instead 'play in the virtues of the power of the spontaneous soul' (*sahaja śakti guṇa kheliye ho*) and thereby destroy delusion. Among the many virtues in which the seeker should revel is *sumati*, right or good thought or belief. Hiralal Jain felicitously translated sumati as 'good intention'.[16] In his poem, Banārsīdās said that sumati is like a festive black cuckoo, whose singing aids the soul (*ghaṭ*) that is wandering in a fog that is as thick as a cloud of cotton (*bharama kuhara bādaraphaṭe ho*).

Another poem that is possibly by Banārsīdās involved a more fully developed allegory, similar to what we find in the many Holī songs of subsequent centuries.[17] In it we read of the heroine Sumati. She and her friends expelled the evil woman Kumati (Bad or Wrong Thought, Belief or Intention) from their midst. In place of the passionate colours of Holī, they sprinkled the colours of samatā. Instead of a physical fire to burn the wood of the bonfire (and the small living beings who make it their home), they developed the interior fire of *dhyān* (meditation) in which they burnt up the eight forms of karma. Banārsīdās also allegorized the foods shared by people on Holī: the sweets became *dayā* (compassion), the expensive dried fruits became *tap* (renunciatory asceticism), and the betel leaf became *sat* (truth). Finally, the congregational musical performance of Holī was allegorized, as the drums and tambourines instead of music played the guru's *vacan* (speech), as well as *jñān* (knowledge) and *kṣamā* (forgiveness).

Possibly because Banārsīdās is regarded as a foundational poet for the subsequent tradition of lay Digambar poets in north India, he is also credited with the composition of an allegorical drama called *Moh vivek yuddh* (The Battle between Delusion and Discrimination). Most scholars, however, have rejected his authorship of this text.[18] In verses two and three, the author of *Moh vivek yuddh* explicitly said that he related in a more concise version what was found in three longer texts by the earlier poets Malh, Lāldās, and [Jan] Gopāl. According to Nāthūrām Premī, on the basis of information provided to him by Agarcand Nāhṭā, Malh (or Mall), also known as Mathurādās, was an Advaitin. Malh's *Moh vivek yuddh*, composed in VS 1603 (1546 CE), was a vernacular version of Kṛṣṇamiśra's *Prabodhacandrodaya*. The presence in the Digambar libraries of Jaipur of five manuscripts of *Moh vivek yuddh* attributed to Banārsīdās, however, indicates that it was copied and read by later Digambar authors, for whom the attribution to Banārsīdās would have given the text an authoritative status.[19]

In 118 verses, the text described a lengthy battle between two opposing armies. On the one side was the army of Vivek (Discrimination), who was assisted by such allies as Niṣkām (Dispassion), Dayā (Compassion), Saraltā (Straightforwardness) and Udārtā (Generosity). On the other was the army of Moha (Delusion), who was assisted by Kāma (Passion), Krodh (Anger), Māyā (Illusion), Mamtā (Egotism), and others. In the end, Vivek was victorious.

Moh vivek yuddh indicates another line of historical influence upon the Holī songs of the later Digambar poets. This is the long tradition of allegory in South Asian religious writing. The Śvetāmbar scriptures, for example, contain many symbolic and metaphorical stories, as well as several instances of formal allegory.[20] The most famous allegory in Indian literature, and one that had a significant influence on Jain literature, was the *Prabodhacandrodaya* (Moonrise of Spiritual Awakening) of Kṛṣṇamiśra. The author was an Advaita ascetic who lived in the court of the Candela king Kīrtivarman, where the play was first performed sometime soon after 1060 CE.[21] In the play, Kṛṣṇamiśra lampooned representatives of the various non-Advaita schools, such as Buddhism, Jainism, and Cārvāka, and described (with adequate accuracy) and rejected their doctrines. The hero of the play was Puruṣa (Soul), who had forgotten his identity with Parameśvara, the Supreme Being. He had been led astray by his wife, Māyā (Illusion). His son Manas (Mind), along with a companion named Ahaṃkāra (Egoism), contributed to his ignorance. Manas in turn had two wives, the bad wife Pravṛtti (Activity, that is, active engagement with the external sensory world) and the good wife Nivṛtti (Quiescence, that is, ceasing such active engagement). Pravṛtti's son was the equally bad Moha (Delusion), while Nivṛtti's son was the good Viveka (Discrimination). Moha and Viveka waged a war over their grandfather, each of them accompanied by an appropriately negative and positive army of external and internal values and practices. Manas saw that Pravṛtti had been the source of much suffering, and he became attached to Nivṛtti. He was aided by his good sons and associates, and became quiet, that is, he turned away from external stimuli and focused upon his interior spiritual essence. Viveka was then able to awaken Puruṣa to his true nature.

This play was widely read in the subsequent centuries, by intellectuals and artists in all traditions. It was also the source of extensive imitation, adaptation, and translation. Arguably the most important Digambar Jain response to the *Prabodhacandrodaya* was the Sanskrit *Jñānasūryodaya Nāṭaka* (Drama of the Sunrise of Knowledge) by the domesticated monk Vādicandra, which he wrote in VS 1649 (CE 1593) in Mahuva, in present-day Surat district in southern Gujarat. The title was a direct nod to Kṛṣṇamiśra's earlier allegorical drama, for whereas the earlier play detailed the Moonrise of (Salvific) Awakening, Vādicandra's concerned the Sunrise of (Salvific) Knowledge.

The *Jñānasūryodaya Nāṭaka* was the story of the hero Ātman (Soul). He had a number of children by his two wives Sumati (Good Intention) and Kumati (Bad Intention). Sumati's four sons were all virtues: Prabodha (Awakening), Viveka (Discrimination), Santoṣa (Contentment), and Śīla (Virtue). Kumati's five sons were all vices: Moha (Delusion), Kāma (Passion), Krodha (Enmity), Māna (Pride), and Lobha (Greed). Several of these characters reappeared in the works attributed to Banārsīdās a generation later, and still others were included in the subsequent genre of Digambar Holī poems.

While the Digambar allegories of Sumati, Kumati, and Cetan are based on the basic elements of Jain epistemology and karma theory, they do not relay the technical details. Rather, the allegories work on a simpler and more straightforward understanding that Cetan is the pure, eternal soul within the person, characterized in particular as 'consciousness'. In Sanskrit the feminine noun *cetanā* was the preferred form, but in the vernacular literature the masculine noun *cetan* was used. This allowed the poets to allegorize Cetan as a male hero. Sumati and Kumati are the positive and negative sensory mentalities—mind is considered one of the senses in Jain ontology—by which a person, as a transitory embodied being, interacts with the world. These two aid or hinder the person in realizing his or her pure, eternal essence. Sumati and Kumati comprise all the thoughts, beliefs, and intentions through which a person interacts with the external world. Since *mati* is a feminine noun, Jain poets allegorized Sumati and Kumati as feminine characters.

We do not have any definitive proof that Banārsīdās himself read or otherwise knew of Vādicandra's drama, composed a generation earlier in a different province of the Mughal Empire. It is clear that subsequent Jain poets did read it, and it had a significant influence on later vernacular Digambar literature. There are at least eight manuscripts of the drama in the Digambar temple libraries in Jaipur, and at least another half-dozen manuscripts in other Digambar temple libraries elsewhere in Rajasthan.[22] More important as evidence of its influence is that it was translated at least five times into the vernacular, making it among the most frequently translated of all Digambar Sanskrit texts.

Dyānatrāy

In the two centuries following Banārsīdās, seemingly every one of the dozens of prolific poets who made up the thriving lay Digambar vernacular literary scene in north India included several Holī songs in his repertoire. To provide continuity with my presentation at the Tenth International Bhakti Conference, held in 2009 in Miercurea Ciuc, Romania, in this chapter, I present and analyse six of the eight Holī songs by Dyānatrāy, who was also the focus of my paper on that occasion.[23] Dyānatrāy lived from 1676 to 1726 CE in Agra and Delhi. He composed more than 300 short pads, in addition to many longer liturgies (*pūjā*) to be sung during the performance of temple rituals by individuals or congregations. He remains today among the most popular of the earlier poets.

Dyānatrāy's poems do not show a single, simple allegorization of Holī. Rather, in each composition he gave different symbolic interpretations of various elements in the observance of Holī. Presumably part of the enjoyment of hearing the songs sung in performance would be the pleasure of seeing how the poet had structured equivalences in any one particular song, and then comparing them to the next song that followed in the series.

Two short songs introduce us to the larger Holī allegory within which Dyānatrāy framed most of his Holī songs. The heroine Sumati anxiously waits for her beloved spouse Cetan (also known as Ātamrām, 'bliss of the soul') to return after spending the winter months out in the world pursuing mundane concerns. Holī is the time for her separation (viraha) to come to an end. But the time of Holī has come, everyone else is celebrating in the city, and her lover has not yet arrived. Sumati says that Cetan has decided instead to live with her evil co-wife Kumati, implying that through ignorance and delusion we choose to engage in the external world of the senses and pleasures instead of mindfully 'returning home' and turning inwards to pursue the soul. She remembers playing Holī with Cetan in the past, when she mixed the saffron (*kesar*) of tranquility (*upaśam*) into the water that they sprayed upon each other, thereby calming the mind and removing the influences of the external sensory world. In her grief, Sumati turns to the Jina, and with folded hands prays to the Jina for guidance.

Horī is happening
    in the city. (refrain)[24]
My beloved Cetan
    is not at home
        so listen to my sad story. (1)
He wants to live
    with my co-wife Kumati—
        how can I bring him back? (2)
Dyānat says
    Sumati says
'Lord Jina,
    tell me what to do?' (3)

nagaramemṃ horī ho rahī ho (ṭek)
mero piya cetana ghara anāhīṃ yaha dukkha suna hai ko (1)
soti kumatike rāca hai kihi vidha lāūṃ so (2)
dyānata sumati kahai jina svāmī tuma kachu sicchā do (3)

Without my beloved
    how will I play Horī? (refrain)[25]
My beloved Bliss of the Soul
    has not come,
        my Horī is unfulfilled. (1)
Once I played
    with my dear one,
        I mixed the saffron of tranquility. (2)
Dyānat says
    when will that time come?
        Sumati folds her hands and prays. (3)

piyā bina kaise khelauṃ horī (ṭek)
ātamarāma piyā nahiṃ āye mokoṃ horī korī (1)
eka bāra prītama hama khelaiṃ upaśama kesara ghorī (2)
dyānata vaha samayo kaba pāūṃ sumati kahai kara jorī (3)

The emotion of separation, however, is not the dominant one in Holī; the poets prefer to celebrate love in union (saṃyog), as in the next four songs by Dyānatrāy. Sumati's lord and master King Consciousness (Cetan Rāy) has indeed returned home, and she can play Holī with him. In separation from him, she was distracted, but now her mind is settled. Instead of passion (*rāg*), she is adorned with dispassion (*virāg*), a term similar to one of the principal epithets of the liberated and dispassionate Jina, *vītrāg*. In one song her right faith (*samyak*), which she maintains through the twelve vows (*barat*, *vrat*) of a pious Jain layperson, is the red powder (*raṅg gulāl*). In another song right faith or world view (darshan) is her dress, which she has moistened with the colour of right knowledge (*jñān raṅg*), so that the red powder, which is the third jewel of right conduct (*caran*), can stick to her. She sprays the perfume of bliss (*ānand atar*) from the *pickārī*, and on a *bīn* (veena) she plays the unstruck sound (*anahad*). In another song, she uses the pickārī to spray the yellow colour (*gulāl pīl*) of knowledge (jñān), and the saffron (kesar) in this case is compassion (*karunā*).

O how happy,
  Horī has come,
    my King Cetan has returned. (refrain)[26]
A long time has passed
  without my dear.
    Now I can play.
      I have gathered my mind. (1)
The red color
  of right faith
    through the vows—
I adorn myself
  with dispassion
    from passion. (2)
Dyānat says
  Sumati is so happy
    I'm at a loss
      to describe her. (3)

bhalī bhaī yaha horī āī āye cetanarāya (ṭek)
kāla bahuta prītama bina bīte aba khelauṃ mana lāya (1)
samyaka raṅga gulāla baratameṃ rāga virāga suhāya (2)
dyānata sumati mahā sukha pāyo so varanyo nahiṃ jāya (3)

I will play Horī,
  King Consciousness has come. (refrain)[27]

I have moistened my dress of faith
    with the color of knowledge,
        I have applied the red powder of conduct. (1)
The pickārī sounds
    with the perfume of bliss,
        I play the unstruck on the bīn. (2)
He delights himself
    and delights his beloved.
I sing the virtues
    for my dear one. (3)
Dyānat says
    Sumati appears happy and contented
        her dear friends all approve. (4)

khelauṅgī horī āye cetanarāya (ṭek)
darsana vasana jñāna raṅga bhīne carana gulāla lagāya (1)
ānanda atara sunaya picakārī anahada bīna bajāya (2)
rījhauṃ āpa rijhāvauṃ piyako prītama lauṃ guna gāya (3)
dyānata sumati sukhī lakhi sukhiyā sakhī bhaī bahu bhāya (4)

Horī has come
    today is full of colors.
Full of color
    full of flavor
        today is full of the juices. (refrain)[28]
My beloved Cetan has come
    my mind is content
        mixed in the saffron
            of compassion. (1)
The yellow powder of knowledge
    in the *pickārī*—
the cosmic thrum
    stands alert
        in meditation. (2)
Dyānat says
    Sumati says
        to her companions in equanimity
    Now my Lord
        has granted me his grace. (3)

horī āī āja raṅga bharī hai raṅga bharī rasa bharī rasauṃ bharī hai (ṭek)
cetana piya āye mana bhāye karunā kesara ghora dharī hai (1)
jñāna gulāla pīla picakārī dhyāna mahādhuni hota kharī hai (2)
dyānata sumati kahai samatāsoṃ aba mopai prabhu dayā karī hai (3)

Finally we come upon a poem (*Cetan plays Horī*) in which Dyānatrāy engages in his most extensive allegorization. Whereas for the rest of the year the world is dominated by social hierarchies and resultant grudges and bitterness, in this season the land is ruled by forgiveness (*chimā*, kṣamā), and, so, equanimity comes to predominate. The jar in which the coloured powders are mixed with water is the mind (*man*). The saffron (kesar) is again compassion (karunā), while the water is love (*prem*). The pickārīs are filled with the rhyming pair of knowledge (jñān) and meditation (dhyān). Here the tambourines (*ḍaph*) that keep the rhythm (*tāl*) are the two aspects of logic (*naya*) at the centre of Digambar Jain Adhyātma spirituality: the relative logic (*vyavahāra naya*) of the material and intellectual world, in which differences of self and other, and good and bad are dominant; and the absolute logic (*niścaya naya*) in which one sees that the only thing that is really real is the soul.[29] One learns this twofold logic through the words of the guru (*guru ke vacan*), which are what the drum (*mṛdaṅg*) of Holī intones. After the riotous play of colours in the morning, all the participants bathe and adorn themselves with new clothes. They also make themselves attractive with perfume (*atar*), which the poet equates with equanimity (sañjam), and scented water (*covā*), which he equates with the stainless vows (*vimal vrat*). The dry red powder (gulāl) that people rub on each other's foreheads in the afternoon is devotion (*bhāv*). 'Devotion' is an inadequate translation of this central term in Jain religious practice. As Whitney Kelting has described its usage among the Śvetāmbar Jain laywomen she has studied in Pune, 'Bhāv was usually used by laywomen to mean one's emotions, attitude, or intention in performing worship. Often the word bhāv alone was used to denote bhakti bhāv—a devotional disposition toward the Jina; one either has bhāv or not'.[30] In the afternoon one also shares special seasonal treats with friends; the sweets (*miṭhāī*) are righteousness (dharma), the dried fruits (*mevā*) are the various forms of Jain asceticism (*tap*), and the bowl for food (*kaṭorī*) is now filled with the stainless bliss of harmony (*samaras ānand amal*). A union of lover and beloved, of Consciousness and Good Intention, that is based upon such a strong spiritual foundation is a union that will persist in age after age (*jug-jug*).

Cetan plays Horī. (refrain)[31]
In springtime
    forgiveness rules the land,
        equanimity is the woman

beloved by all creatures.
Saffron of compassion
is mixed into water of love
in the jar
of the mind.
Pickārīs are filled
with knowledge and meditation.
Boys compete with each other
At Horī. (1)
The drum beats the words of the guru.
The two logics are the tambourines
lightly keeping the rhythm.
Equanimity is perfume,
stainless vows are scented water.
The bag is filled
with red powder of devotion. (2)
Dharam is sweets,
asceticism the many dried fruits.
The stainless bliss of harmony
fills the bowl.
Dyānat says
Sumati says to her friends
This union will live long
in age after age. (3)

cetana khelai horī (ṭek)
sattā bhūmi chimā vasantameṃ samatā prānapriyā saṅga gorī
manako māṭa premako pānī tāmeṃ karunā kesara ghorī
jñāna dhyāna picakārī bharibhari āpameṃ chorai horā horī (1)
guruke vacana mṛdaṅga bajata haiṃ naya donoṃ ḍapha tāla ṭakorī
sañjama atara vimala vrata covā bhāva gulāla bhaira bhara jhorī (2)
dharama miṭhāī tapa bahu mevā samarasa ānanda amala kaṭorī
dyānata sumati kahai sakhiyanasoṃ cirajīvo yaha jugajuga jorī (3)

The Allegorical Songs of Holī and Jain Spirituality

We do not see in these poems a single, rigidly imposed allegorization. There are a few allegorical elements that are common to most of them: the male hero is Cetan, Consciousness (in one place Ātamrām, Bliss of the Soul); the female heroine is Sumati, Good Intention; and the wicked anti-heroine is Kumati, Bad Intention. The basic allegorical message is that of Digambar Adhyātma: the need to turn away from the external world of sensory input and karmic bondage, and focus instead on the inner spiritual path to the purity of the soul. The many ways that a person can be distracted by external sensory experience are symbolized by aspects of Holī, as are the religious virtues and practices that allow one to turn away from the externals and return to one's self, one's soul.

Right faith (darshan, samyak) in one case is Sumati's dress, in another, the red-coloured powder (raṅg gulāl). Knowledge (jñān) appears in many songs: as music, colour, water (in one case of unspecified colour, in another as yellow water) squirted from the pickārī, and as red powder. In two songs, the *Holikā* fire burns the eight logs of the eight forms of karma according to Jain philosophy. The material fire of Holikā that is criticized by Jain ideologues as a harmful practice that can only accumulate karma is transformed here into a positive spiritual practice, as the internal fire of asceticism.

The music of Holī appropriately appears in many songs. The drum in one case is the words of the guru (guru vacan), in another love (prem). The rhythm appears as three conjoined pairs, indicating its back-and-forth nature. These are the supporting pair of knowledge and meditation (jñān and dhyān), the hierarchical pair of the twofold logic (*naya*) of relative and absolute, and the opposed pair of the internal spiritual soul and the external material world, or self and other (*sva-par*).

The play of waters squirted from the pickārīs also appears in more than one poem. The saffron used to dye the water is compassion (karunā) in two poems, and the water is knowledge in one poem, and knowledge and meditation in another. Finally, other elements of the physical Holī make their appearance in metaphorical garb. The sweets people share after the play of colour are righteousness (dharma) and equanimity (sañjam), the dried fruits people also share are asceticism (tap) and meditative absorption in the soul (*magan subhāv*), and the red powder is devotional experience (bhāv) and knowledge.

Taming Holī

The Digambar Jains have not been the only ones in north India to compose and sing allegorical Holī songs. Many 'Hindu' poets have also composed Holī songs, in both the *nirguṇ* and *saguṇ* styles,[32] although it does not appear to have been as extensive a genre as among Digambar poets. Paying attention to the Jain allegorization of Holī allows us to see how non-Jain authors also strove to recast Holī as a spiritually transformative occasion rather than a socially transgressive one.

Let me give a few examples. In their critical edition of the large anthologies of songs in the Dādū Panth known as *Pañc Vāṇī*, Callewaert and de Beeck include a single Holī song each by four poets. These four nirguṇ songs also show an allegorization of Holī, although not the same as the Jain allegory with Cetan, Sumati, and Kumati. Kabīr sings:

> Play Horī with the true teacher.
> Drive away disease and death,
> bring wandering to an end[33]

He continues to sing of spraying forgiveness (*ṣimā*, kṣamā) with the pickārī, of playing Horī in the alley of knowledge (*gyāṅn galī*), and of the dramatic display of the true teacher playing phāg (*tamāsā satagura ṣelai phāga*). The songs by Hardās and Sundardās both refer to the 'red powder of knowledge' (*gyān gulāl*). In their songs, these three poets and Nāmdev all play on the image of the inner self soaked in the colour of true spiritual experience.[34]

Saguṇ poets have produced Holī songs that are in many ways quite similar to those of the nirguṇ poets, reminding us that the saguṇ–nirguṇ distinction, while heuristically useful at times, can also obscure as much as it reveals. The saguṇ Holī songs focus on the loving play with colours and liquids, in which the participants dye each other and erase visual social differences, and simultaneously dye their souls and erase the ignorant perceptions of difference between God and soul. Whitney Sanford has translated a song by the sixteenth-century Vaishnava poet Paramānand, in which the play of colours in Holī symbolizes the Vaishnava emphasis on communion: of congregants with each other, and of congregants with Krishna.[35] Paramānand emphasizes that the seeming separation of one from another, of soul from God, is in fact all part of God's creative play, his *līlā*. God experiences life as a unity, but also creates our human experience of difference. In that experience of difference, the soul feels the absence of God. For a Vaishnava, the absence of the beloved reveler at Holī symbolizes the separation of the feminized Soul from the masculine Krishna; for a Jain, it symbolizes the separation of Good Intention (feminine) from the Conscious Soul (masculine).

It is striking that all of these poets—Jain, nirguṇ, and saguṇ—present a softened, cleaned up version of Holī. It is a celebration of loving companionship, in which people gently throw coloured powder and sprinkle coloured liquid over each other and share with each other sweets and drinks. These depictions of Holī in the songs of all traditions, to symbolize the theological positions on suffering and liberation, are quite different from the descriptions we get from other sources.

Ethnographic analyses of Holī as performed today in Braj and Banaras, as well as historical accounts of how it has been performed for at least several centuries, show that it is a deeply transgressive affair.[36] Seemingly every hierarchy—of caste, class, religion, gender, age, and sexuality—is turned upside down. It is a time of freedom. But this freedom is not the calm, controlled freedom of orthodox religious ideology; rather, it is an antinomian social freedom from the forms of oppressive domination.

Some religious reformers may decry the excesses and subversions of Holī, and urge their co-religionists to avoid it as a 'harmful custom' that runs counter to religious orthodoxy. But Holī is unavoidable in north Indian life, and has been for centuries. We see, then, how religious poets from many traditions have tried to soften the subversions of Holī. Dyānatrāy and the other Jain poets employed their educated literary tools of metaphor, symbolism, and allegory to transform Holī's social transgressiveness. Instead of criticisms and reversals of the hierarchies of society, we find in Dyānatrāy's poems a gentler, more irenic religious transgressiveness, in which the listener is urged to put aside all the external constraints and ignorance of worldly existence and turn instead to an inner spiritual pursuit of that which is ultimately real.

Notes

* A version of this chapter was also delivered at the conference, 'The Intersections of Religion, Society, Polity, and Economy in Rajasthan: A Conference on the Occasion of Alan Babb's Retirement', Amherst College, USA, 13–15 July 2012. A longer version of this chapter, focusing on the Holī pads of the nineteenth-century poet Budhjan, is John E. Cort, 'Today I Play Holī in My City'. See also John E. Cort, 'Daulatrām Plays Holī'. Funding for the research in north India in 2007–8 that underlies this chapter came from a Senior Short Term Fellowship from the American Institute of Indian

Studies, Funding for further research in Jaipur and Delhi in 2011 and 2012 came from a Franklin Research Grant of the American Philosophical Association and the Denison University Research Foundation. I thank K. C. Sogani, Priti Jain, Imre Bangha, Surendra Bothara, Manish Modi, Gangaram Garg, Monika Thiel-Horstmann, T. N. Madan, Shrivats Goswami, Alan Babb, and Jack Hawley for helpful suggestions and leads, and Sombabu Sharma for his invaluable help in accessing manuscripts in Digambar libraries in Jaipur.

1. McKim Marriott's 'The Feast of Love', in *Krishna: Myths, Rites, and Attitudes*, ed. Milton Singer (Chicago: University of Chicago Press, 1966), 200–12, remains the most accessible introduction to the observance of Holī in a north Indian village, although the articles by D. B. Miller, 'Holi-Dulhendi: Licensed Rebellion in a North Indian Village', *South Asia* 3 (1973): 15–22, and Lawrence Cohen, 'Holi in Banaras and the *Mahaland* of Modernity', *Gay and Lesbian Quarterly* 2 (1994): 399–424, reprinted in *Sexualities*, ed. Nivedita Menon (London: Zed Books, 2007), 197–223, are important extensions and corrections of his analysis.

2. Smita Tewari Jassal, *Unearthing Gender: Folksongs of North India* (Durham: Duke University Press, 2012), 219.

3. Miller, 'Holi-Dulhendi', 18–19.

4. I have coined this neologism as a back-formation from 'subaltern'. Whereas the latter designates people and communities who are in subordinate social positions, the term 'altern' indicates that most Jains have occupied a more powerful position in north Indian society.

5. John E. Cort, 'Defining Jainism: Reform in the Jain Tradition', in *Jain Doctrine and Practice: Academic Perspectives*, ed. Joseph T. O'Connell (Toronto: University of Toronto Centre for South Asian Studies, 2000), 175–6.

6. Jugalkiśor Mukhtār, 'Holī kā tyauhār', *Anekānt* 3, no. 5 (1940): 350–1, reprinted as 'Holī kā tyauhār aur us kā sudhār', in *Yugvīr Nibandhāvalī*, vol. 1 (New Delhi: Vīr Sevā Mandir Ṭrasṭ Prakāśan, 1963), 342–6.

7. Jugalkiśor Mukhtār, 'Holī Holī hai', *Anekānt* 3, no. 5 (1940): 351, reprinted in *Anekānt* 9, no. 3 (1948): 89.

8. Premcand Rāṅvkā, *Mahākavi brahm jindās: vyaktitva evaṃ kṛtitva* (Jaipur: Mahāvīr Granth Akādamī, 1980), 70–1.

9. Chītar Ṭholiyā, *Holī kī kathā*, MS 1356, veṣṭan 1356 (Jaipur Amerbhaṇḍār: Jain Vidyā Saṅsthān). These passages are found in verses 95 and 96 in MS 1356, and verses 94 and 95 in MS 1357. See also Anūpcand Nyāytīrth, 'Ḍhūṇḍhārī bhāṣā kī ek prācīn kṛti—Holī kī kathā', *Anekānt* 57, no. 3–4 (2004): 86–92.

10. Charlotte Vaudeville, *Bārahmāsā in Indian Literatures* (New Delhi: Motilal Banarsidass, 1986), 21.

11. Kantilal B. Vyas, *Vasanta Vilāsa: An Old Gujaratī Phāgu* (Bombay: N. M. Tripathi Booksellers, 1942), xxxviii–xxxix.

12. On this literature, see also Agarcand Nāhṭā, *Prācīn kāvyoṃ kī rūp-paramparā* (Bikaner: Bhāratīya Vidyā Mandir Śodh Pratiṣṭhān, 1962), 36–45.

13. Nāhṭā, *Prācīn kāvyoṃ kī rūp-paramparā*, 39.

14. Bhaṭṭārak Jñānbhūṣaṇ, *Ādīśvar Phāg*, MS copied VS 1597, in collection of Digambar Jain Mandir Bhanpura, through Anekānt Jñān Mandir, Bina, available at www.idjo.org/Manuscript.asp?id=361.

15. John E. Cort, 'A Tale of Two Cities: On the Origins of Digambar Sectarianism in North India', in *Multiple Histories: Culture and Society in the Study of Rajasthan*, ed. Lawrence A. Babb, Varsha Joshi, and Michael W. Meister (Jaipur: Rawat, 2002), 39–83.

16. Hiralal Jain, 'Introduction' to his edition of Hariṣeṇa, *Mayaṇa-parājayacariu* (Varanasi: Bhāratīya Jñānpīṭh, 1962), 14.

17. 'raṅga bhayo jina dvāra calo sakhi khelana horī' (*Adhyātma-Pad-Pārijāt*, ed. Kanchedī Lāl Jain [Varanasi: Śrī Gaṇeś Varṇī Digambar Jain Saṅsthān, 1996], 192). I have translated this poem: John E. Cort, 'Foreword' to Imre Bangha and Richard Fynes', *It's a City Showman's Show! Transcendental Songs of Ānandghan* (New Delhi: Penguin, 2013), 9–10.

18. Nāthūrām Premī, 'Introduction' to his edition of Banārsīdās, *Ardha Kathānak* (Bombay: Hindī Granth Ratnākar, 1957), 83–7; Saroj Agravāl, *Prabodhacandrodaya aur uskī Hindī paramparā* (Allahabad: Hindī Sāhitya Sammelan, 1962), 265–78; Ravīndar Kumār Jain, *Kavivar Banārsīdās* (Calcutta: Bhāratīya Jñānpīṭh Prakāśan, 1966), 207–15.

19. I have consulted two of these manuscripts: MS 1622, veṣṭan 1427, Digambar Jain Mandir Baṛā Terāpanth, Jaipur, and MS 22, veṣṭan 2417, Digambar Jain Mandir Baṛā Terāpanth, Jaipur. These are numbers 665 and 2322 in the published catalogue. Kastūrcand Kāslīvāl, ed., *Rājasthān ke jain śāstra bhaṇḍāroṃ kī granth sucī*, vol. 2 (Jaipur: Digambar Jain Atiśay Kṣetra Śrīmahāvīrjī, 1945–72), 184, 330. The text was also edited by Kastūrcand Kāslīvāl and published in *Vīr Vāṇī* as Kastūrcand Kāslīvāl, 'Kyā "moh vivek yuddh" Mahākavi Banārsīdāsjī kī racnā hai?' See Nāhṭā, '"Moh vivek yuddh" ke chūṭe hue 8 padya', *Vīr Vāṇī* 14, no. 7 (1962): 95–7, for eight verses omitted by Kāslīvāl.

20. The best introductions to this literature are Jain, 'Introduction', 9–36; Rājkumār Jain, *Prastāvnā* to her edition of Nāgadeva, *Madanaparājaya* (Varanasi: Bhāratīya Jñānpīṭh Prakāśan, 1966 [1964]), 1–58.

21. Kṛṣṇamiśra, *Prabodhacandrodaya*, trans. Matthew Kapstein, *The Rise of Wisdom Moon* (New York: New York University Press and J. J. C. Foundation, 2009), xxviii.

22. Kāslīvāl, *Rājasthān ke jain śāstra bhaṇḍāroṃ*, 1945–72.

23. John E. Cort, 'God Outside and God Inside: North Indian Digambar Jain Performance of Bhakti', in *Bhakti Beyond the Forest Proceedings of the Tenth International Bhakti Conference*, ed. Imre Bangh (New Delhi: Manohar, 2013), 255–86. See also John E. Cort, 'Dyānatrāy: An Eighteenth Century Digambara Mystical Poet', in *Essays in Jaina Philosophy and Religion*, ed. Piotr Balcerowicz (New Delhi: Motilal Banarsidass, 2003) 279–95.

24. Dyānatrāy, *Dyānat bhajan saurabh*, with modern standard Hindi paraphrase by Tārācand Jain (Mahavirji: Jainvidyā Saṅsthān, Digambar Jain Atiśay Kṣetra Śrīmahāvīrjī, 2003), no. 309, 358. In the translations, I use the Braj-bhāṣā form Horī.

25. Dyānatrāy, *Dyānat bhajan saurabh*, no. 311, 361.

26. Dyānatrāy, *Dyānat bhajan saurabh*, no. 312, 362.

27. Dyānatrāy, *Dyānat bhajan saurabh*, no. 307, 355.

28. Dyānatrāy, *Dyānat bhajan saurabh*, no. 313, 363.

29. Paul Dundas, *The Jains* (London: Routledge, 2002), 107–10.

30. M. Whitney Kelting, *Singing to the Jinas: Jain Laywomen, Maṇḍaḷ Singing, and the Negotiations of Jain Devotion* (New York: Oxford University Press, 2001), 109. See also Caroline Humphrey and James Laidlaw, *The Archetypal Actions of Ritual: A Theory of Ritual Illustrated by the Jain Rite of Worship* (Oxford: Clarendon Press, 1994), 161–2, 218–23, for another discussion of this key concept.

31. Dyānatrāy, *Dyānat bhajan saurabh*, no. 308, 356.

32. The nirguṇ–saguṇ distinction has been thoroughly historicized and problematized in recent years; see John Stratton Hawley, 'The Nirguṇ/Saguṇ Distinction', in *Three Bhakti Voices: Mirabai, Surdas, and Kabir in Their Times and Ours* (New Delhi: Oxford University Press, 2005), 70–86. I use it here as a simple shorthand to distinguish between two broad and overlapping styles of religiosity in north India—on the one hand, with an emphasis on turning inwards to discover one's spiritual essence, and, on the other, with an emphasis on the need to establish a firm relationship with God (in various forms) as one's refuge and saviour.

33. 'sataguru saṅga horī ṣelie jātaṃ jarā marana bhrama jāī' (Winand M. Callewaert and Bart Op de Beeck, eds, *Nirguṇ-Bhakti-Sāgar: Devotional Hindī Literature*, 2 vols [New Delhi: Manohar, 1991, South Asia Institute, New Delhi Branch, Heidelberg University, South Asian Studies 25], vol. 1, no. 144, 327).

34. Callewaert and de Beeck, *Nirguṇ bhakti sāgar*, vol. 1, no. 70, 465 (Hardās); vol. 1, no. 200, 582 (Sundardās).

35. A. Whitney Sanford, *Singing Krishna: Sound Becomes Sight in Paramānand's Poetry* (Albany: State University of New York Press, 2008), 170–1.

36. See the sources in note 1.

Bibliography

Primary Texts

Adhyātma-pad-pārijāt, edited by Kanchedī Lāl Jain. Varanasi: Śrī Gaṇeś Varṇī Digambar Jain Saṅsthān, 1996.

Ādīśvar Phāg of Bhaṭṭāraka Jñānbhūṣaṇ. MS copied VS 1597, in collection of Digambar Jain Mandir Bhanpura, through Anekānt Jñān Mandir, Bina. Available at www.idjo.org/Manuscript.asp?id=361.

Banārsī Vilās of Banārsīdās, edited by Nāthūrām Premī. Bombay: editor, 1905.

———, edited by Kastūrcand Kāslīvāl and Bhaṅvarlāl Nyāytīrth. Jaipur: Akhil Bhāratīya Jain Yuvā Pheḍareśan, 1987 (second printing). First printing Jaipur: Nānūlāl Smārak Granthmālā, 1954.

Dyānat bhajan saurabh of Dyānatrāy. With Modern Standard Hindi paraphrase by Tārācand Jain. Mahavirji: Jainvidyā Saṅsthān, Digambar Jain Atiśay Kṣetra Śrīmahāvīrjī, 2003.

Holī kī kathā of Chītar Ṭholiyā. MS 1356, veṣṭan 1356, Amer bhaṇḍār, at Jain Vidyā Saṅsthān, Jaipur. Copied in Jaipur in VS 1811 (CE 1754) by Pt Hemcandra.

———. MS 1357, veṣṭan 1357, Amer bhaṇḍār, at Jain Vidyā Saṅsthān, Jaipur. Copied in Malpura by Pt Dayārām, n.d.

Jñānasūryodaya Nāṭaka of Vādicandra. MS in collection of Syādvād Mahāvidyālay, Banaras. Available at www.idjo.org/Manuscript.asp?id=130.

———. Modern Standard Hindi, translated by Nāthūrām Premī. Bombay: Hindī Granth Ratnākar, 1909.

Moh vivek yuddh attributed to Banārsīdās. MS 22, veṣṭan 2417, Digambar Jain Mandir Baṛā Terāpanth, Jaipur.

———. MS 1622, veṣṭan 1427, Digambar Jain Mandir Baṛā Terāpanth, Jaipur.

———, edited by Kastūrcand Kāslīvāl. 'Kyā "Moh Vivek Yuddh" Mahākavi Banārsīdās jī kī Racnā Hai?', *Vīr Vāṇī* 7, no. 1 (1954): 15–18; 7, no. 2 (1954): 31–2; 7, nos 3–4 (1954): 47–8; 7, no. 5 (1954): 66–8.

Nirguṇ-Bhakti-Sāgar: Devotional Hindī Literature. Edited Winand M. Callewaert and Bart Op de Beeck. 2 vols. New Delhi: Manohar, 1991, South Asia Institute, New Delhi Branch, Heidelberg University, South Asian Studies 25.

Prabodhacandrodaya of Kṛṣṇamiśra, translated by Matthew Kapstein as *The Rise of Wisdom Moon*. New York: New York University Press and JJC Foundation, 2009.

Secondary Texts

Agravāl, Saroj. *Prabodhacandrodaya aur uskī Hindī paramparā*. Allahabad: Hindī Sāhitya Sammelan, 1962.

Anūpcand Nyāytīrth. 'Ḍhūṇḍhārī bhāṣā kī ek prācīn kṛti—Holī kī kathā'. *Anekānt* 57, nos 3–4 (2004): 86–92.

Cohen, Lawrence. 'Holi in Banaras and the *Mahaland* of Modernity'. *Gay and Lesbian Quarterly* 2 (1994): 399–424. Reprinted in *Sexualities*, edited by Nivedita Menon. London: Zed Books, 2007, 197–223.

Cort, John E. 'Defining Jainism: Reform in the Jain Tradition'. In *Jain Doctrine and Practice: Academic Perspectives*, edited by Joseph T. O'Connell. Toronto: University of Toronto Centre for South Asian Studies, 2000, 65–91.

———. 'A Tale of Two Cities: On the Origins of Digambar Sectarianism in North India'. In *Multiple Histories: Culture and Society in the Study of Rajasthan*, edited by Lawrence A. Babb, Varsha Joshi, and Michael W. Meister. Jaipur: Rawat, 2002, 39–83.

———. 'Dyānatrāy: An Eighteenth-Century Digambara Mystical Poet'. In *Essays in Jaina Philosophy and Religion*, edited by Piotr Balcerowicz. New Delhi: Motilal Banarsidass, 2003, 279–95.

———. 'Daulatrām Plays Holī: Digambar Bhakti Songs of Springtime'. *Jaina Studies: Newsletter of the Centre of Jaina Studies* 8 (2013): 28–30.

———. Foreword to Imre Bangha and Richard Fynes, trans., *It's a City Showman's Show! Transcendental Songs of Ānandghan*. New Delhi: Penguin, 2013, 4–11.

———. 'God Outside and God Inside: North Indian Digambar Jain Performance of Bhakti'. In *Bhakti beyond the Forest: Proceedings of the Tenth International Bhakti Conference*, edited by Imre Bangha. New Delhi: Manohar, 2013, 255–86.

———. '"Today I Play Holī in My City": Digambar Jain Holī Songs from Jaipur'. *International Journal of Jaina Studies* 9, no. 7 (2013): 1–50. Available at https://www.soas.ac.uk/research/publications/journals/ijjs/archive/2013.html.

Dundas, Paul. *The Jains*. London: Routledge, 2002, second revised edition.

Hawley, John Stratton. 'The Nirguṇ/Saguṇ Distinction'. In *Three Bhakti Voices: Mirabai, Surdas, and Kabir in Their Times and Ours*. New Delhi: Oxford University Press, 2005, 70–86.

Humphrey, Caroline and James Laidlaw. *The Archetypal Actions of Ritual: A Theory of Ritual Illustrated by the Jain Rite of Worship*. Oxford: Clarendon Press, 1994.

Jain, Hiralal. 'Introduction' to his edition of Hariṣeṇa. *Mayaṇaparājayacariu*. Varanasi: Bhāratīya Jñānpīṭh, 1962, 9–36.

Jain, Rājkumār. *Prastāvnā* to her edition of Nāgadeva. *Madanaparājaya*. Varanasi: Bhāratīya Jñānpīṭh Prakāśan, 1966 [1964], 1–58.

Jain, Ravīndar Kumār. *Kavivar Banārsīdās*. Calcutta: Bhāratīya Jñānpīṭh Prakāśan, 1966.

Jassal, Smita Tewari. *Unearthing Gender: Folksongs of North India*. Durham: Duke University Press, 2012.

Kāslīvāl, Kastūrcand. *Rājasthān ke Jain śāstra bhaṇḍāroṃ kī granth sucī*, 5 vols. Jaipur: Digambar Jain Atiśay Kṣetra Śrīmahāvīrjī, 1945–72.

Kelting, M. Whitney. *Singing to the Jinas: Jain Laywomen, Maṇḍaḷ Singing, and the Negotiations of Jain Devotion*. New York: Oxford University Press, 2001.

Marriott, McKim. 'The Feast of Love'. In *Krishna: Myths, Rites, and Attitudes*, edited by Milton Singer. Chicago: University of Chicago Press, 1966, 200–12.

Miller, D. B. 'Holi-Dulhendi: Licensed Rebellion in a North Indian Village'. *South Asia* 3 (1973): 15–22.

Mukhtār, Jugalkiśor. 'Holī kā tyauhār'. *Anekānt* 3, no. 5 (1940): 350–1. Reprinted as 'Holī kā tyauhār aur us kā sudhār'. In *Yugvīr Nibandhāvalī*, vol. 1 (New Delhi: Vīr Sevā Mandir Ṭrasṭ Prakāśan, 1963), 342–6.

———. 'Holī Holī hai'. *Anekānt* 3, no. 5 (1940): 351. Reprinted in *Anekānt* 9, no. 3 (1948): 89.

Nāhṭā, Agarcand. *Prācīn kāvyoṃ kī rūp-paramparā*. Bikaner: Bhāratīya Vidyā Mandir Śodh Pratiṣṭhān, 1962.

———.'"Moh vivek yuddh" ke chūṭe hue 8 padya'. *Vīr Vāṇī* 14, no. 7 (1962): 95–7.

Premī, Nāthūrām. 'Introduction' to his edition of Banārsīdās, *Ardha Kathānak*. Bombay: Hindī Granth Ratnākar, 1957.

Rāṅvkā, Premcand. *Mahākavi brahm jindās: vyaktitva evaṃ kṛtitva*. Jaipur: Mahāvīr Granth Akādamī, 1980.

Sanford, A. Whitney. *Singing Krishna: Sound Becomes Sight in Paramānand's Poetry*. Albany: State University of New York Press, 2008.

Vaudeville, Charlotte. *Bārahmāsā in Indian Literatures*. New Delhi: Motilal Banarsidass, 1986.

Vyas, Kantilal B. *Vasanta Vilāsa: An Old Gujaratī Phāgu*. Bombay: N.M. Tripathi Booksellers, 1942.

11

TEIJI SAKATA

Hindi *Bārahmāsā* Tradition

From Narpati Nālha to Present-Day Folk Songs and Popular Publications

In Hindi, *bārahmāsā* is a genre of lyrical songs usually describing the sorrow and pain of a woman who is separated from her beloved. These songs take as their background the changing climate patterns that occur during the twelve months (*bārahmāsā*) of a given year. I will consider three kinds of sources for Hindi bārahmāsās: first, selected literary works; second, folk songs published in collections of folk literature and studies of dialects; and third, an interesting set of popular booklets that were published beginning in late nineteenth century and on into the early twentieth.

*Bārahmāsā*s Contained in Hindi Literary Works

Lālcand 'Maṅgal' Gupt, in his book *Hindī bārahmāsā sāhitya*, offers us a comprehensive list of Hindi bārahmāsās from the beginning to the present day.[1] Charlotte Vaudeville also gives us minute information on the topic in her elaborate work titled *Bārahmāsā in Indian Literatures*, where she provides us with the texts and translations of a number of important bārahmāsās.[2] These help us locate the following four bārahmāsās, which are worthy of study as representatives of different sorts of bārahmāsās that make their way into larger literary corpuses and compositions. They are:

1. A bārahmāsā describing the anguish of separation experienced and brought into song by Rājmatī, which is contained in *Bīsal dev rās* (c. 1343) by Narpati Nālha.
2. A bārahmāsā describing the anguish of separation sung by Nāgmatī and contained in the *Padmāvat* (c. 1540) of Jāyasī.
3. A bārahmāsā *Padāvalī* (mid-sixteenth century[?]) describing the anguish of separation sung by Mīrābāī, the well-known devotee of Krishna.
4. A bārahmāsā describing a wife entreating her husband not to leave home, which is found in the *Kavipriyā* (1602) of Keśabdās (Keshavdas).

I will present a brief portrait of each of these, confirming the month in which the bārahmāsā in question starts and noting whether the union of the lover with the beloved is realized in the month in which it concludes. For each, an English translation of at least one month mentioned in the bārahmāsā will also be given.

1. 'Rājmatī Bārahmāsā' Contained in Narpati Nālha's *Bīsal dev rās*

The whole of *Bīsal dev rās* consists of 128 stanzas, and the portion devoted to the 'Rājmatī Bārahmāsā' occupies stanzas 67–78. It starts in the month of Kārttik and concludes in the month of Āśvin. The union of the two lovers in the last of these months is not confirmed, but there a confident tone is established by Rājmatī's concluding remark, which is: 'Now he, my husband, will come back soon!' With very slight alterations, I offer a translation made by Charlotte Vaudeville for the month of Kārttik only, which is typical in its expression of the anguish of separation (*viraha*) experienced by Rājmatī, who has been left behind by her husband:

> He went away, the knight-errant, in the month of Kārttik.
> He left his palace, beautiful as Kailās,
>   he left his splendid terrace,
> And I, standing on the road, have lost my eyes weeping,
>   hunger and thirst have left me.
> Tell me, my friends, how can I sleep again? (§67)[3]

2. 'Nāgmatī Bārahmāsā' Contained in Jāyasī's *Padmāvat*

The whole of the *Padmāvat* consists of 653 stanzas, and the 'Nāgmatī Bārahmāsā' occupies stanzas 344–55. This bārahmāsā starts from the month of Āṣāḍh and runs to the month of Jeṭh. The union of the two lovers is not realized in the concluding month. Vaudeville's translation for the month of Āṣāḍh is as follows:

> Āṣāḍh has come, clouds rumble in the sky,
> Virah gathers his troops and beats the war-drum:
> Gray, blue-black or white, armies of clouds rush up
> and the flocks of white cranes look like floating banners.
> On all sides, flashes of lightning glisten like naked swords,
> and menacing clouds shower rain-drops hard as arrows,
> When the constellation Ārdrā appears, the earth receives the seed—
> but to me, a wife away from her husband, who will pay honor?
> Bending, the clouds come down and surround me:
> O my lord! Run to my help, I am in the power of Madan!
> Frogs, peacocks, the koil and the papīhā birds,
> all pierce me with their cries—and life ebbs out of my body.
> Now the constellation Puṣya has come over my head
> and I remain without a protector: who will repair our roof?
> Blessed are those women those husbands are at home,
> to them belong honor and pride—
> But for myself, away from my beloved spouse,
> there is no joy of any kind! (§344)[4]

3. Bārahmāsā by Mīrābāī, Contained in the *Mīrābāī kī padāvalī* of Paraśurām Caturvedī

The whole of this *Padāvalī* consists of 202 *pads*, with the bārahmāsā listed as pad 115. It starts with the month of Jeṭh and concludes in Baisākh. The union of the two is not realized in the concluding month. Again, I turn to Vaudeville's translation—this time of the entire poem:

> O my beloved,
> Grant me the vision of Yourself:
> Again and again I call on You,
> have pity on me—Ho! [Refrain]
> In the month of Jeṭh, for want of water
> the bird is in pain—Ho!
> In Āṣāḍh, the peacock throws its cry
> the Cātak-bird too calls the cloud—Ho!

In Śrāvan, the rain falls hard
  and my friends play the *Tīj*—Ho!
In Āśvin, the shell enjoys in its heart
  the drain-drop of Svāti—Ho!
In Kārttik comes the *pūjā* to the God
  and You are my God—Ho!
In Agahan, it is getting cold:
  Quick, come to my help—Ho!
In Pauṣ, there is plenty of white frost:
  hasten to my help—Ho!
In Māgh, comes the feast of Basant Pancamī
  and they all sing *Phāg* songs—Ho!
In the month of Phālgun, they all play the *Phāg*
  and the great trees shed their leaves—Ho!
In the month of Caitra, Desire spouts in the heart:
  grant me a vision of Yourself—Ho!
In the month of Baisākh, the great trees burst into flower,
  the koil throws its melodious call—Ho!
Putting crows to flight my days have passed in vain,
  in vain did I ask Paṇḍits and astrologers—Ho!
Mīrā, the lonely one, is in deep anguish:
  when will You grant me Your vision ?—Ho! (§115)[5]

4. Bārahmāsā in the *Kavipriyā* of Keśabdās, Describing the Wife Who Entreats Her Husband Not to Leave Home

The *Kavipriyā* consists of sixteen sections and the bārahmāsā is included in the tenth of these. The tenth section has thirty-five stanzas, of which the bārahmāsā takes up stanzas 24–35, starting in Caitra and concluding in Phālguṇ. Given below is a translation made by V.P. Dvivedi, which describes the month of Caitra. In it a wife beseeches her husband not to abandon her in this season when it seems the whole world is coming into bloom.

The charming creepers have blossomed and so have young trees.
  Rivers and ponds are full.
The ladies, aglow with passion, are worshipping their husbands.
  Parrots, *sārikas* and nightingales are chirping sweet sounds.
The poet Keśab says that in such a flowery season
  no one should embrace thorns (of separation),
    leaving the flowers (of union).

What to say of going out?
One should not allow one's mind to waver in the month of Caitra. (§24).[6]

All of the four examples given above express viraha, but as we have seen, the months vary markedly. The significance of variations such as these is a matter ripe for study.

*Bārahmāsā*s Sung as Hindi Folk Songs

The lyrical songs of bārahmāsā, though offering material to many literary works, have also been enjoyed by the 'folk' in various dialects of Hindi. We have abundant records of folk song versions of bārahmāsās, these having been published in collections of folk literature or in linguistically oriented studies of Hindi's many dialects. I have studied the following collections for present purposes, and will once again present four translations to give some sense of the whole:

1. Mohanlāl Bābulkar, *Gaḍhvālī lok-sāhiyakā vivecnātmak adhyayan*, Prayāg, 1964.
2. Bhaṭṭ 'Śaileś', *Gaḍhvālī bhāṣā aur sāhitya*, Lakhnaū, 1976.
3. Sarojnī Rohatgī, *Avadhī kā lok sāhitya*, Dillī, 1971.
4. Śrīvāstav 'Snehī', *Bundelī lok sāhitya*, Āgrā, 1976.
5. Laxmi Ganesh Tewari, *Folk Songs from Uttar Pradesh*, New Delhi, 2006.
6. Kṛṣṇdev Upādhyāy, ed., *Avadhī Lokgīt*, Illāhābād, 1978.
7. Kṛṣṇdev Upādhyāy, coll. and ed., *Bhojpurī Lokgīt*, vol. 1, Prayāg, 1990.

5. 'Viraha Bārahmāsā' Sung in Avadhī

This bārahmāsā covers the twelve months of a year in four portions, with each portion comprising three months. Beginning with the month of Aṣāḍh, this bārahmāsā concludes in the month of Jeṭh. I translate the first stanza only, which concludes with a poignant dream of reunion—poignant because it is not reality:

In the month of Aṣāḍh the dense clouds thunder.
In the month of Sāvan the rains pitter-patter.
In the month of Bhādau lightning flashes often.
I had a happy dream—that my beloved came back.[7]

6. 'Milan Bārahmāsā' Sung in Avadhī

In this bārahmāsā, Rādhā is expecting Krishna to come back home. It starts with the month of Jeṭh and concludes in Baisākh and shows us the rare case of an instance in which the lovers are reunited.

He did not come, my beloved Krishna,
He did not come in Jeṭh, he did not come in Asāḍhau—clouds overcast me.
He did not come in Sāvan, he did not come in Bhādau—rivers full of water....
[Four lines skipped.]
The poet Sūr expects Krishna to come. He suddenly came back to see Rādhā.[8]

7. Bārahmāsā on the Rām Story Sung in Avadhī

In the following bārahmāsā the entire life story of Rām is compressed into a month-by-month progression that starts from Caitra (Cait) and concludes in Phāgun, the former marking Rām's birth and the latter his coronation. Thus, his life is made to span exactly a year, though the return of Rām to Ayodhyā, heralding his coronation, is usually thought of as occurring in autumn, at Divali time. I translate only a portion of the tale:

Rām was born on the ninth day of the first half of the month of Cait,
There was happiness all over Avadh. Girlfriends sang auspicious songs....
[Three lines skipped.]
In the early month of Baiśāk Kaikeyī staged an uproar:
A curse on her life, Bharat's mother!...
[Nine months skipped.]
In the month of Phāgun, Rāvan abducted Sītā. Later, though, he was killed.
Śiva, Brahmā and other gods came to see.
Install Rām on the throne! (§162)[9]

8. Bārahmāsā on the Hardship of a Peasant's Life, Sung in Bundelī

Many peasants have difficulty when they suffer bad weather, and most of them are under the control of landlords and moneylenders in any case. This bārahmāsā, though not completely given in Śrīvāstav's work, seems to starts from Agahan and to be concluded in Kārttik. The extract given below shows how peasants are beset by landlords and moneylenders:

In the month of Agahan the moneylender comes to the door
  holding a ledger book in his hand.
He shamelessly collects interest, down to the last anna.
  He takes the grain we have as interest.
The lines that fate has written on my brow
  will never be erased....
    [Eight lines skipped.]
In the month of Baisākh the moneylender comes
  to collect his capital with interest.
The landlord also comes to collect his rent on the land,
  standing at the door and saying 'You come out!'...
    [Three lines omitted.][10]

Looking back over these four extracts, we can see how various are the themes that can be taken in by the bārahmāsā genre: separation, meeting, the Rām story, and the painful rhythms of peasant life. Viraha bārahmāsās predominate, but one can appreciate how the viraha theme lends itself to other closely associated moods, whether to a joyful meeting—much to be wished—or, alternatively, to an exploration of life's sadnesses, felt over long stretches of time. As the reader will have noticed, the actual months that appear in these bārahmāsās vary as to the months with which they begin or end, but the bārahmāsā rhythm rings through them all.

Bārahmāsās Appearing in Popular Publications of the Nineteenth and Twentieth Centuries

The third set of bārahmāsās I would like to present comes from booklets published in the late nineteenth and early twentieth centuries. These small books hold a particular interest because, as Francesca Orsini has observed, 'bārahmāsās were perhaps the first substantial genre in the boom in commercial publishing in north India of the 1860s.... The cheapness of lithography allowed the printers to produce books at low cost, without having to purchase a full set of type fonts'.[11] I have studied six of these pamphlets, each containing bārahmāsā songs or songs of a very similar nature. These are:

1. Sohanlāl Gosvāmī (printer), *Prempramod kī bārahmāsī*, Mathurā: Munśī Rāmnāyaṇ, 1885. Eight pages, printed by lithography, 9 paise, 500 copies printed.
2. Jagdambālāl Harīkaraṇ (printer), *Pūrāmās ko kyāl*, 1904. Thirty pages printed by lithography, 8 paise.
3. Kisān Pustak Bhaṇḍār, Mathurā (publisher), *Bārahmāsī saṃgrah: Bharat jī, Rāmcandra jī, Kṛṣṇa jī, Benī mādhav jī kī*. The portion containing date of publication and price are broken. Sixteen pages printed typographically.
4. Raghunāthsiṃh, *Bhaundū kī bārahmāsī*, Mathurā: Kisān Pustak Bhaṇḍār. The portion containing date of publication and price are broken. Eight pages printed typographically.
5. Śarmā 'Vicitra', Prayāgdatt, *Ablā kī bārahmāsī*, Mathurā, 1917. Eight pages printed typographically, 30 paise.
6. Raghunāthsiṃh 'Akelā, *Dhruv jī kī bārahmāsī*, Mathurā: Kisān Pustak Bhaṇḍār, n.d. Eight pages printed typographically, 30 paise.

Again, I will restrict my translations to a representative four songs culled from the group as a whole.

9. *Prempramod kī bārahmāsī* by Gosvāmī, Published in 1885

This is a typical viraha bārahmāsā starting with Āṣāḍh and concluding in Jeṭh. I translate the first two months in the set:

> In the month of Āṣāḍh, clouds spread all around,
> Women here are happy and sing songs of the season,
> But you, my love, are not with me now. (1)
>
> In the month of Sāman (*śrāvaṇ*), women swing and sing festival songs,
> I wish my beloved one were here to embrace me tightly,
> But alas, you are not with me now. (2)[12]

10. 'Rām kī Bārahmāsī' from the *Bārahmāsī Saṃgrah*, Published by Kisān Pustak Bhaṇḍār

Unlike the example presented above, we begin in Caitra and conclude in Phāgun. Again, I translate only excerpts:

Rām is born in the month of Caitra in Ayodhyā.
  The beautiful city is purified with sandalwood paste.
In the temples and houses people celebrate Rām's birth.
  The beautiful boy is born in our Ayodhyā city. (1)

It is getting hot in the month of Baisākh.
  It seems like fire is raining down.
Living without water, the fish writhe.
  The wicked queen Kaikeyī gives us this trouble—fire! (2)[13]

11. *Bhaundū kī bārahmāsī* by Raghunāthsiṃh, Whose Date of Publication Is Unknown

In this bārahmāsā, Bhaundū, that is, a foolish farmer, tries hard to make his wife happy, but fails every time. The bārahmāsā once again starts with the month of Caitra (Cait) and ends in Phālgun, but the familiarity of the formula seems to stop there. Any tone of serious viraha is gone.

The month of Cait has come and the silly man is happy.
He's told his wife, 'Now I'll cultivate the field each day'.
  The wife was happy to hear it
And the silly man, carrying lunch, got down to work.
  He grasped a sickle in his hand,
He went to the field, but he fumbled the sickle
  and injured his fingers.
    He was sad.
His wife lamented, too. Here's what she said:
  'This destiny—it's written on the forehead—
    the forehead of my silly man'.[14]

12. 'Ablā kī Bārahmāsī'—A Woman's Bārahmāsā from the Collection by Śarmā 'Vicitra', 1917

Here no month is mentioned, but the story is sung in bārahmāsā style. The story is of a woman making a pilgrimage around sacred places related to Lord Krishna. She was left behind by her friends and captured by villains, but thanks to the Lord this 'weak woman' (*abalā*) was not lost:

Policemen came to the place and noticed a lady was in difficulty,
They fired guns and arrested the villains. Thus she was saved.
She was in the protection of Govardhannāth, the Lord Krishna himself.[15]

Here too, as earlier, we see that various themes are accepted as bārahmāsās—from the frequently attested viraha bārahmāsās and bārahmāsās on Rām's story to a far less typical pilgrimage bārahmāsā and one that pertains to a foolish farmer. Again, the starting and ending months in the twelve-month sequence may vary, and it is not always necessary for the author to describe the climatic changes that attend them. All this seems to suggest that the genre of bārahmāsā or bārahmāsī had become so popular in the late nineteenth and early twentieth century that it could expand to include quite a number of subjects that were expected to be attractive to various hearers or readers. We might summarize by proposing three classes of songs that appeared under the label bārahmāsā by the beginning of the twentieth century:

1. Songs that mention twelve months and depict concomitantly the emotions of a woman separated from her beloved, as seen in most of the selections examined in this chapter (samples 1–6, 9);
2. Songs mentioning twelve months but without depicting the emotions of a woman separated from her beloved, as seen in the bārahmāsās of Rām's story and bārahmāsās of farmers (samples 7–8, 10–11 from our set);
3. Songs that do not depict the twelve months of a year at all, such as the 'Abalākī Bārahmāsī' that appears as sample 12 in our set.

This scheme of classification relates in interesting ways to the one proposed by Dušan Zbavitel after he had examined nearly two hundred Bengali *bāromāsī*s (that is, bārahmāsīs).[16] Zbavitel put forward five groups of songs, which I have related to our Hindi group by means of the '→' sign:

1. The religious baromāsī, giving a catalogue of the main festivals celebrated in Bengali villages throughout the year → describing the life of gods or heroes to whom a certain group of people is devoted.
2. The farmer's baromāsī, listing the main agricultural labours over the twelve months of the year → describing the everyday life of farmers and noting the difficulties they suffer.
3. The narrative baromāsī included in an epic poem. This category can be used as is to describe our Hindi bārahmāsās.
4. The baromāsī of separation, which is concerned with the suffering of a wife separated from her husband during the twelve months of the year. This too can be used as is to describe our Hindi bārahmāsās.

5. The baromāsī of a test imposed on a young wife who has been separated from her husband → no example of this sort is found in our material.

Looking back at our own classification, we find that Zbavitel's religious and farmers' bārahmāsās fall mainly within the realm of our category 2. His narrative and separation bārahmāsās correspond well with our category 1. Yet that leaves two areas where there is no overlap at all. On the one hand, Zbavitel's bārahmāsā of a wife's test does not appear in the group I have studied. On the other, the *Abalā kī bārahmāsī* (example 12, category 3) which I have uncovered, with its complete freedom from the rubric of the twelve months or the trials of being separated from one's husband, finds no way to appear on Zbavitel's list.

In some ways this abalā outlier is the most interesting case of all, since it illustrates so clearly the plasticity of the bārahmāsā genre as a whole, and it invites the mention of one last example of a bārahmāsā that also seems to break all the rules. The bārahmāsā I have in mind concerns a person whom no one would have described as a poor helpless woman (abalā nārī) after the fashion of the *Abalā kī bārahmāsī*. This is a short text called *Indirājī kī bārahmāsī: kāyar ke fāyar*, written by one Prabhudās and published by Vandna Book Depot in Mathurā in November 1984. It consists of a minute description of the assassination of Indira Gandhi, with the title indicating clearly the author's perspective on that event: *Indiraji's Bārahmāsī: Shots Fired by Cowards*.

What makes this a bārahmāsā or bāraḥmāsī? At the level of subject matter it is apparently the loneliness of Indira Gandhi's suffering that makes it so, and at the level of form it is the fact that the author felt he could depict her travail in twelve stanzas. In some obvious way this poem takes us far indeed from the classical bārahmāsā genre, and yet, when we consider the broad history of the bārahmāsā as indicated by the examples we have studied, it turns out we are really not so far away at all. From the point of view of our anonymous Mathurā author, this moment of dour crisis in 1984 that had a definite bārahmāsā feel, and the plasticity of the bārahmāsā genre enabled him to actualize this feeling in song.

Notes

1. Lālcand Gupt, *Hindī bārahmāsā sāhitya* (Dillī: Sañjīv Prakāśan, 1987), 18–27.

2. Charlotte Vaudeville, *Bārahmāsā in Indian Literatures* (New Delhi: Motilal Banarsidass, 1986).

3. English translation by Vaudeville (slightly altered), *Bārahmāsā in Indian Literatures,* 56; Hindi text: Mātāprasād Gupt and Agarcand Nāhṭā, eds, *Bīsal dev rās* (Prayāg: 1960, 2nd edition), 149.

4. English translation by Vaudeville (slightly altered), *Bārahmāsā in Indian Literatures,* 64; Hindi text: Mātāprasād Gupt, ed., *Padmāvat* (Illāhābād: Bhārtī Bhaṇḍār, 1963), 293.

5. English translation by Vaudeville (slightly altered), *Bārahmāsā in Indian Literatures,* 53–4. Hindi text: Paraśurām Caturvedī, ed., *Mīrāṅbāī kī padāvalī* (Prayāg: Hindī Sāhitya Sammelan, 1970, 14th edition), 133–4.

6. English translation by V. P. Dvivedi (slightly altered), *Bārahmāsā—The Song of Seasons in Literature and Art* (New Delhi: Agam Kala Prakashan, 1980), 129. Hindi text: Viśvnāth Prasād Miśr, ed., *Keśab Granthāvalī,* vol. 1 (Illāhābād: Hindustānī Ekeḍemī, 1977, 2nd edition), 157.

7. Kṛṣṇdev Upādhyāy, ed., *Avadhī Lokgīt* (Illāhābād: Sāhitya Bhavan, 1978), stanza 156 [my translation].

8. Sarojnī Rohatgī, *Avadhī kā lok sāhitya* (Dillī: Neśnal Pabliśiṅg House, 1971), 207 [my translation].

9. Laxmi Ganesh Tewari, *Folk Songs from Uttar Pradesh* (New Delhi: D.K. Printworld, 2006), 186–91 [English translation by Tewari].

10. Śrīvāstav 'Snehī', Rāmsvarūp, *Bundelī lok sāhitya* (Āgrā: Rañjan Prakāśan, 1976), 134 [my translation].

11. Francesca Orsini, 'Bārahmāsās in Hindi and Urdu', in *Before the Divide,* ed. Francesca Orsini (Hyderabad: Orient BlackSwan, 2010), 169.

12. Sohanlal Gosvāmī, *Prempramod kī bārahmāsī* (Mathurā: Munśī Rāmnāyaṇ, 1885), 2 [my translation].

13. Anonymous, ed., *Bārahmāsī Sangrah* (Mathurā: Vandnā Book Depot, ca. 1984), 5–6 [my translation].

14. 'Akelā' Raghunāthsiṃh, *Bhaundūkī Bārahmāsī* (Mathurā: Kisān Pustak Bhaṇḍār, n.d.), 2 [my translation].

15. Śarmā 'Vicitra', 'Prayāgdatt', in *Ablā kī bārahmāsī* (Mathurā, 1974), 2–7 [my translation].

16. Dušan Zvabitel, 'The Development of Bāromāsī in Bengali Literature', *New Orient,* no. 3 (April–June 1962): 109–12.

Bibliography

Anonymous, ed. *Bārahmāsī Saṅgrah.* Mathurā: Vandnā Book Depot, ca. 1984.

Caturvedī, Paraśurām, ed. *Mīrāṅbāī kī padāvalī* (14th edition). Prayāg: Hindī Sāhitya Sammelan, 1970.

Dvivedi, V.P. *Barahamasa—The Song of Seasons in Literature and Art*. New Delhi: Agam Kala Prakashan, 1980.
Goswāmī, Sohanlāl (printer). *Prempramod kī bārahmāsī*. Mathurā: Munśī Rāmnāyaṇ, 1885.
Gupt 'Maṅgal' Lālcand. *Hindī bārahmāsā sāhitya*. Dillī: Saṅjīv Prakāśan, 1989.
Gupt, Mātāprasād, ed. *Padmāvat*. Illāhābād: Bhārtī Bhaṇḍār, 1963.
Gupt, Mātāprasād and Agarcand Nāhṭā, eds. *Bīsal dev rās* (2nd edition). Prayāg, 1960.
Miśr, Viśvnāth Prasād, ed. *Keśab Granthāvalī*, vol. 1 (2nd edition). Illāhābād: Hindustānī Ekeḍemī, 1977.
Orsini, Francesca. 'Barahmasas in Hindi and Urdu'. In *Before the Divide*, edited by Francesca Orsini. Hyderabad: Orient BlackSwan, 2010.
Prabhudās. *Indirājī kī bārahmāsī: kāyar ke fāyar*. Mathurā: Vandnā Book Depot, 1984.
Raghunāthsiṃh 'Akelā'. *Bhaundūkī Bārahmāsī*. Mathurā: Kisān Pustak Bhaṇḍār, n.d.
Rohatgī, Sarojinī. *Avadhī kā lok sāhitya*. Dillī: Neśnal Pabliśiṅg House, 1971.
Śarmā 'Vicitra', Prayāgdatt. *Ablā kī bārahmāsī*. Mathurā, 1974.
Śrīvāstav 'Snehī', Rāmsvarūp. *Bundelī lok sāhitya*. Āgrā: Rañjan Prakāśan, 1976.
Tewari, Laxmi Ganesh. *Folk Songs from Uttar Pradesh*. New Delhi: D.K. Printworld, 2006.
Upādhyāy, Kṛṣṇdev, ed. *Avadhī Lokgīt*. Illāhābād: Sāhitya Bhavan, 1978.
Varmā, Dhīrendra et al., eds. *Hindī sāhitya koś*, vol. 1. Vārāṇasī: Gyān Maṇḍal, 1958.
Vaudeville, Charlotte. *Bārahmāsā in Indian Literatures*. New Delhi: Motilal Banarsidass, 1986.
Zbavitel, Dušan. 'The Development of Bāromāsī in Bengali Literature'. *New Orient*, no. 3 (April–June 1962): 109–12.

PART THREE

HISTORY IN HINDI

12

WILLIAM R. PINCH

War and Succession

Padmakar, Man Kavi, and the Gosains in Bundelkhand

In this chapter, I explore the careers of Anupgir (also known as 'Himmat Bahadur')[1] and Umraogir Gosain of Bundelkhand by making recourse to two eulogistic Hindi poems of the late eighteenth century—Man Kavi's *Anūp-Prakāś* and Padmakar's *Himmatbahādurvirudāvalī*.[2] Part one ('Succession') of the chapter is focused on a knotty question of ascetic politics and guru–chela primacy; part two ('War') examines how the phenomenon of the warrior ascetic was understood—at least, from the point of view of those who had considerable first-hand experience with 'fighting *gosains*',[3] namely the poets themselves. I conclude with some brief reflections on the significance of early modern Hindi poetry for history.

Anupgir and Umraogir were, as I have argued elsewhere,[4] among the most successful 'warlords' or military entrepreneurs of the late eighteenth century. Born to destitute parents in eastern Bundelkhand, they were acquired in their infancy by a warlord named Rajendragir—also a gosain. After the death of Rajendragir, the gosain brothers worked for or alongside nearly every major paymaster-prince of northern India in the latter half of the eighteenth century, including the English East India Company. They were, therefore, intimately involved in, and witness to, late-Mughal decline as well as the defeat of Maratha power, and the concurrent rise of the British. Anupgir eventually emerged as the ruler of Bundelkhand at a key turning point in South Asian history, on the eve of the Second Anglo-Maratha War. If historians are to properly assess the forces that governed the political and military dynamics of the transition from late Mughal to early British rule, and (equally important) how all this was understood and experienced by observers on the ground, figures such as Anupgir and Umraogir and those close to them need to be understood. Hindi poetry is, arguably, the best source we have for doing precisely that.

Though Anupgir is today better known than Umraogir, the 'gosain brothers' have long been understood as extensions of each other, working seamlessly in concert to advance their united interests.[5] Not surprisingly, however, the turbulence of sibling rivalry seems to have occasionally produced ripples on the placid waters of the extended gosain 'family'. Happily, the poems under review here offer some clues on this score. The following section begins with a rare airing of differences among the gosains in 1804 at the death of Anupgir. We then turn to the poets, Man Kavi in particular, for hints as to how Umraogir may have been perceived in the context of Anupgir's growing fame and success in the 1790s.

Succession

Anupgir died on 4 June 1804 in eastern Bundelkhand. The scene of his death was the gosain camp near Bhuragarh, west of Banda, by the Ken River. Umraogir, who at the time was residing at Shivrajpur, near Kanpur, rushed to Banda to take charge of the situation. When he arrived, however, he was confronted with the spectacle of John Baillie, the Company agent, placing a young boy on Anupgir's throne. Umraogir recalled the circumstances two years later, in a petition to the acting governor general, George Barlow:[6]

> It is now two years since [my brother] sent for me in haste in his last illness; and committing into my hands his ring and his chelah Kunchun Geer [or Kanchangir], resigned his soul to his creator.... While I was engaged in mourning for the death of my late brother, the above mentioned chelah [Kanchangir], in concert with the other officers of the Government, availing himself of my absence, by various pretexts carried Captain Baillie[7] to his House and persuaded him to place on the

> Musnud a child of five years of age born of a Musselman woman in my brother's family.

From Umraogir's point of view, Kanchangir had orchestrated an internal coup, placing a young boy of uncertain origins on the gosain throne. This was especially galling, and not simply because Kanchangir had, allegedly, been entrusted to Umraogir by his dying brother. Rather, in Umraogir's mind, Umraogir himself had long been senior to Anupgir. In fact, he began his petition to Barlow (quoted above) with this very point:

> The late Muha Rajah Anoop Geer Himmut Buhadur and myself were full brothers. On the death [in 1753] of Muha Rajah Rajinder Geer, my spiritual preceptor, I received from the late Nawab Sufdur Jung a Khellaut [robe of honour] investing me with the government and in concert with my Brother and the adherents and dependents of my family, I proceeded to arrange and regulate the affairs of the Province. My brother, in the spirit of our mutual harmony and friendship, adopted my eldest son [probably Rajgir—see note 21], and for a period of twenty years, continued to conduct the administration of public affairs, allowing me a jaidad of two lacks of rupees for the maintenance of myself and attendants while, I being relieved from the weight of all worldly concerns, passed my time on the banks of the Ganges in the full and undisturbed exercise of my religious duties.... With these facts all the chiefs and Rajahs of Bundlecund are acquainted but it is probable that Captain Baillie, who had the charge of the affairs of that Province, was not fully apprised of them.

Umraogir then went on to detail the conspiracy that led to the installation of the child Narindragir in 1804 and the wider political and military circumstances at the time that ultimately compelled him to acquiesce in the face of Kanchangir's bid for power.[8]

Umraogir's decline vis-à-vis his brother (and the latter's *chela*, Kanchangir) was, in fact, more gradual than is suggested by the said turn of events. To grasp this, it is helpful to backtrack to the late 1780s. In 1789, Anupgir was released from Mahadji Scindia's 'house arrest' by order of the *peshwa*. Together with the Maratha warlord Ali Bahadur, who helped release Anupgir from confinement, the two began the slow conquest of Bundelkhand. Meanwhile, Umraogir began moving between forts in Farrukhabad, in the western reaches of Awadh, only to be expelled from that region by the order of Asaf-ud Daula acting under the prodding of the Company Resident. By 1791

Umraogir was reported to have gone to Almora in Kumaon, to begin plotting with regional chiefs against the Gorkhas of Nepal, but this too seemed to produce little in the way of results.[9] A key turning point occurred in 1792. In mid-April of that year Anupgir defeated Arjun Singh, the pride of the Bundela Pamar Rajputs, at the fortress-citadel of Ajaigarh in eastern Bundelkhand. Anupgir's victory represented a significant rupture in the region's political history, as it brought to an end roughly three centuries of Bundela Rajput rule. It also seems to have drawn Umraogir southward to the Ganga, whence he divided his time between fortified mansions in Banaras and a quieter, if no less comfortable, riverine retreat in the village of Shivrajpur (Sheorajpur), west of Kanpur and near Bithur.[10] Despite what looked like a kind of retirement, however, Umraogir kept dabbling in political intrigue. This resulted in his 1799 arrest for a hazy involvement in the 'Vizier Ali conspiracy', in which the recently deposed nawab of Awadh, Vazir Ali, murdered the governor general's agent in Benares (and former Lucknow Resident), George Cherry. Umraogir was consequently held in confinement, first at Chunar and later at Lucknow, only to be released as a condition of the strategic alliance forged between Anupgir and the British in 1803, according to which Bundelkhand was ceded to Company control.[11]

Anupgir's victory over Arjun Singh at Ajaigarh in 1792 was a key event in shifting gosain fortunes, particularly in the aftermath of the heady days of service to Shuja in Awadh and Najaf in Delhi. The British noted the event with characteristic brevity. The intelligence communiqué relating the news, from the Resident at Lucknow, Edward Ives, to the governor general at Calcutta, Lord Cornwallis, consisted of one sentence:

> Intelligence was received last night of a complete victory gained on the 25th of Shaubaun [April 18th] by Rajah Himmut Behauder on the part of the Nawaub Ally Behauder over Lohny Urjun Sing, the only chief in the Bundilcund District who held out against his authority, in which Urjun Sing is reported though it is not yet absolutely certain to have lost his life and Bucktauwar Sing the Minor Rajah in whose name Urjun Sing managed the Zemindary was taken prisoner.[12]

Among gosains, by contrast, the response to Anupgir's victory consisted of an outpouring of panegyric verse—in the form of two Hindi poems of considerable length. The *Himmatbahādurvirudāvalī*, 211 verses long and composed by the young (and soon to be celebrated)

Padmakar, describes the siege of Ajaigarh and culminates with a narration of the spectacular slaying of Arjun Singh by Anupgir himself.[13] The *Anūp-Prakāś*, over 700 verses long and composed by the more obscure Man Kavi, recounts the entire career of Anupgir—beginning with the politically transformative discipleship of his and Umraogir's guru, Rajendragir, and ending with the delivery of Arjun Singh's head to Anupgir's Maratha sponsor and ally, 'Nawab' Ali Bahadur.

Given the circumstances surrounding the composition of the poems, it is not surprising that they celebrate the life and career of Anupgir. What is surprising, however, is how they each handle the figure of Umraogir. The poem by Man Kavi is particularly remarkable on this score. Recall Umraogir's petition in 1806, in which he states that he was the senior chela to Rajendragir and was invested with the command of the gosain army upon his guru's death in battle in 1753. In contrast, Man Kavi had this to say:

> Enduring continuous attacks and filled with wounds,
> King Rajendragir sacrificed his life while destroying his enemy in battle.
>
> He gave his heart, he gave his soul, to serve his overlord in the heat of battle.
> He brought glory to Sabdarjang [*sic*], he gave his head for Siva's garland.
>
> The emperor, hearing from his vazir, the service [of Rajendragir] to his overlord,
> Elevated both Rajendragir's sons to kingship, and gave them their hearts' desire.
>
> Umraogir and Anupgir, both brothers, are well known in the world.
> He increased their jagir ten-fold and divided a mansab of 7,000 between them.
>
> Seeing kingly qualities, aptitude, moral rectitude, valor, and steadfastness in battle,
> He immediately gave the title 'Himmat Bahadur' to the brave [one].
> They had a mansab of 7,000, they uprooted their enemies.
> They were both excellent swordsmen, they were protectors of the earth.
>
> They both became the protector of the earth, it was written in their fates to be king.
> The emperor invested that mighty one with kingship and gave him many gifts of cloth.[14]

In light of Umraogir's petition to Governor General Barlow in 1806, the most controversial elements of this section would have been lines 101 and 103, where it is suggested that the Mughal emperor in concert with Safdarjang, the nawab-wazir, bestowed the title of 'Himmat Bahadur' on Anupgir and recognized him as the superior of the two gosains.[15] Man Kavi goes on to elaborate both points in successive verses, repeatedly employing the title 'Himmat Bahadur' (in verses 124, 125, and 126, having only used it twice before, in the introduction).[16] Meanwhile, in verses 104–20, Man Kavi implies very strongly that it was Anupgir and not Umraogir who received top honours and command of the army under Safdarjang. He begins thus:

> The king [*bhūp*] was invested with the title solemnly, (then) went to worship Siva.
> Accompanied by all thirty-six of the Rajput clans—it was impossible to describe.[17]

The fifteen verses that follow describe the thirty-six Rajput clans and the poets and brahmans that joined in the puja of royal investiture. Finally, in verse 120, Man Kavi points to 'King Anupgir' (*nṛpanūpagir*) as the object of all these royal rituals:

> On the day of his coronation, [the vazir][18] gave him all the imperial accoutrements.
> He appointed him vanguard of his personal army, to King Anupgir's great delight.[19]

Perhaps to add insult to injury, in verse 135 Man Kavi uses the term *umrāū* to refer to the groups of nobles and braves that are arrayed like leaves around the water lily king. But what must have seemed like the final straw to Umraogir is Man Kavi's description of Safdarjang's death and the accession of Shuja-ud Daula:

> Having abandoned the painful existence of his body, he [Safdarjang] went to heaven.
> His son Shujandaula became the nawabvazir.
> He loved him ten times more than the first one.
> He gave him the vanguard in the army, and their brotherly love was praised by all.[20]

In this verse, Man Kavi does not explicitly identify which of the gosain brothers was the recipient of Shuja's affections, but given the context of the previous verses and the wider poem, the implication is clear. We have rendered the third line in the above verse as, 'he loved him ten times more than the first one [*prathamteṃ*]'. If this is correct, then the referent here is Safdarjang, that is, 'he [Shuja] loved him [Anupgir] ten times more than the first one [Safdarjang]'. However, it is possible that the line should be translated as, 'he loved him ten times more *than before*', in which case the referent would be Shuja's love for Anupgir having grown exponentially. This latter interpretation seems less likely from a stylistic point of view. Either way, the following line, referring to the brotherly love between Anupgir and Shuja, and the reiteration of Anupgir's appointment in the vanguard, could only have rubbed Anupgir's 'full brother' the wrong way.

We have no evidence that Umraogir heard Man Kavi's poem or possessed a copy. But given the frequent communication between the two gosains and the fact that at least one of Umraogir's children served under Anupgir,[21] it is difficult to imagine that he was unaware of the work. What matters more, perhaps, is that other gosains would have heard it being recited, and it would have propagated the notion that Umraogir had long been inferior to Anupgir in the military and political hierarchy of the gosain army.

That Umraogir was sensitive on the question of his relative status vis-à-vis Anupgir is clear from the 1806 petition, cited at the outset. However, there are indications that Umraogir was prickly about this matter some years earlier, in the mid or late 1790s. At some point in that decade, Umraogir began referring to himself with a new and evocative title, that is, with the name of his guru, 'Raja Rajendragir Gosain'. This fact emerges during the frantic mopping-up operations after the failed 'Vizier Ali conspiracy' of 1799, in which Umraogir was entangled.[22] James Lumsden, the Resident at Lucknow, referred to 'Rajah Rajinder Gheer Ghossein better known by the name of Rajah Omrao Gheer'; and Major General J. H. Craig, commanding the troops in Kanpur that eventually captured Umraogir, referred to 'Raja Rajinder Gheer Ghossein, more usually known by the name of Rajah Omrau Gheer'. Indeed, G. H. Barlow, secretary to the governor general in Calcutta, made reference to 'Maharajah Rujunder Gheer *Bahadre*' (italics added), suggesting either that Anupgir's reputation had rubbed off on the elder gosain, that Umraogir sought to cash in on his brother's reputation, or even that Umraogir possessed some claim to the title of 'Bahadur' as well.[23] All prior Company letters from the early 1790s and earlier (that I am aware of at any rate) refer to Rajah Omrao Gheer, or Omrow Geer, or permutations thereof, with no reference to Rajendragir in his title. Umraogir's exact reason for adopting Rajendragir's name as his own is not known, but, if nothing else, it would have served to remind anyone who needed reminding that he had a prior claim to the mantle of his guru. Indeed, given the close reading of Man Kavi's verses that we have provided earlier, there is a strong possibility that Umraogir was responding to a poetic slight with some discursive strategies of his own.

There is, as it happens, good evidence to back up Umraogir's claim to precedence. Umraogir seemed to suggest as much with his claim, as he put it in his petition to Barlow in 1806 (quoted earlier, see note 6), that 'with these facts [about his investiture as commander of the gosain army at the death of Rajendragir in 1753] all the chiefs and Rajahs of Bundlecund are acquainted'. The evidence in question was in the form of another poem, written in the early 1750s and not long after the death of Rajendragir, by Sudan Kavi at the court of Bharatpur, entitled *Sujāncaritra*. The key verses are as follows:[24]

> There, amidst the battlefield, in the hail of bullets,
> There was a massive explosion [and] a discharge of a barrage of artillery.
> Still the steadfast warrior did not retreat, [but] urged [his] horse forward.
> Then Harsukh Brahman swiftly rushed up unafraid.
> At that moment a bullet suddenly lodged in Rajendra Giri's body.
> That hero, amid the battlefield, for the sake of his overlord, set off for the supreme place.
>
> When he heard of the death of Rajendragiri, the vazir's heart was filled with sadness.
> He called all his good warriors to camp from the battleground.
> In a deep frenzy of sorrow, he realized darkly [that] Rajendra had fallen in battle.
> So the nawab summoned Umrao Girai [and] having given him many fine elephants and clothing of investiture (*sirpāv*), had him adorn the throne (*gaddī*).
>
> The *gaddī* of Rajendra was established by Giri Umrao and Anup.
> They were then returned to the battle, in two forms from one.

The first and most obvious point to be underlined here is that Sudan Kavi basically corroborates Umraogir's version of events from 1753.[25] Safdarjang had indeed placed Umraogir upon Rajendragir's gaddi, decorated him with a *khilat* (described as a 'sirpāv' by Sudan Kavi),[26] and put him in charge of the gosain army. Anupgir is mentioned in verse 10, but he appears almost as an afterthought—as though he was important and had to be mentioned, but that the main figure was Umraogir. In light of Sudan Kavi's poem, it is clear that Man Kavi, writing forty years later, had indeed inverted the order of seniority of Rajendragir's two chelas. Indeed, one might even regard his gradual progression from the use of plural to singular markers in verses 99 to 103, along with his delay in explicitly naming Anupgir in verse 120 as a kind of recognition on his part that he was tampering with the facts.[27] Why he was willing to do this is unclear. No doubt his ability to upend the historical narrative had everything to do with the fact that the younger Anupgir was the object of his panegyristic exertions. But the actors who had the most to gain, as Umraogir's 1806 petition makes clear, were Anupgir's chelas, Kanchangir being senior-most among them. It would appear, then, that Man Kavi was anxious to please the younger generation of gosain leadership.

If it is clear that Umraogir had grounds for complaint in 1806, and that he was in fact Rajendragir's senior chela and, therefore, deserving of the gosain command, it seems equally clear that bardic poetry had assisted in undermining Umraogir's position in the years following Anupgir's victory at Ajaigarh. As Baillie put it in his report immediately after the coronation, there was little cause for worry over Umraogir's public displeasure at the turn of events, as he possessed 'limited influence ... over the troops of his deceased brother'.[28] We may, I think, conclude that Man Kavi's poem is one reason why this was so. Baillie may have been 'not fully apprised' of Umraogir's former glory in the 1750s, but he seemed well aware of Umraogir's diminished stature by the early 1800s. That said, Umraogir was not left entirely empty-handed: the result of his petition was a Company pension of 1,000 rupees per month on which he could live out his days in relative comfort.[29] The elder gosain would remain at his estate at Shivrajpur till 1808, when he would shift to Banaras. He would die in that city soon thereafter, on 12 January 1809. Kanchangir had died the previous year; so perhaps Umraogir took some small pleasure in the fact that he had outlived his nemesis—or one of several, anyway.[30]

War

All this talk of combat and kingship alongside gurus and chelas raises another set of questions, questions that circle around how Anupgir and Umraogir reconciled their putatively ascetic background with their military and political ambitions—or, indeed, whether they felt any such need. Was being a 'fighting gosain'[31] simply an anachronism (at best), an abomination (at worst), or does the very question reveal more about the pervasive power of modern, Western social–scientific analytical categories and the Enlightenment assumptions that underpin them than it does about the cultural categories that conveyed meaning in eighteenth-century north India? There is not space here for a full theoretical and historiographical unpacking of this question,[32] but we can and should probe the poems for clues as to how the 'fighting gosain' was understood—whether in gosain circles or by knowledgeable observers generally. In short, can these poems help us see the political and religious meanings that animated the 'precolonial' north Indian world?

The answer, happily, is yes. Man Kavi hints at a tension between asceticism and kingship, but he also makes clear that this tension was readily resolved and productive of enormous dividends. Padmakar's take on this is more complex, focusing on the difference between the yoga of war (the Kshatriya model) versus the war-craft of the yogi (what may be termed the Yogi model)—and this is possibly a reflection of his earlier ritual connections to the entourage of Arjun Singh, Anupgir's foe, who falls in battle: he needed to please his new gosain master, and he managed to do so in a way that would not have offended his old master and the still-influential (if vanquished) Rajput sensibilities that Arjun embodied. The most obvious set of clues emerge early in Man Kavi's poem, when Rajendragir is introduced as both an obedient chela–slave and a bold yogi–raja:[33]

> His diadem disciple is the most expert in the society of sants.
> Rajendra Gir, [who is] like Raja Indra when it comes to kingly quality of rajas.
> He lovingly looked after all the arrangements at [his guru's] womb-like cave.
> He served with pleasure like a slave and daily gave his heart to his guru.

While guarding his guru's cave, the young Rajendragir blocked entrance to a strange figure, who turned out to be his guru Dhyan Nath's own guru, Nayan Nath. Nayan Nath was so pleased with Rajendragir's *guru-sevā* that he granted the young chela a wish. Rajendragir indicated that he hoped to realize the 'inner passion [*rajo*] of king Indra', to 'become a king among kings, so that other kings will obey my rule'. Nayan Nath 'clasped him to his breast' and happily granted the boon: 'Each generation will reign, equipped with horses, elephants, and cash. You will go forth with your four-part army in a royal retinue.' Then the sage entered the cave to see Dhyan Nath and 'taught him the quality of [being] a nath'.[34] It was not long before Rajendragir experienced an inner transformation: 'Indra's kingly qualities entered his heart. The effect of the blessing became manifest, a great love of kingly ways was fashioned in him.' Soon he was enjoying martial success. 'He went to Siraunj and his dominion spread', and 'wealth, elephants, and horses all attached to him'. Meanwhile, his guru Dhyan Nath, now 'the crown jewel of the nath gurus', had set off for Prayag; en route, at the fervent request of a royal devotee in Kulpahar, one 'Jagatesh', Dhyan Nath agreed to stop for some time. After some time, Rajendragir too arrived at Kulpahar.[35] Here things become interesting:

> Then there arrived Rajendra Gir, and his elephants, horses, and treasure grew.
> He received the blessings of the sage, [when] he clasped the feet of [his] guru.
>
> When the great sage saw his disciple, radiating majesty like a king,
> Appearing with his fourfold army, whose power was indescribable [,]
> Nathji offered forth his sagely wisdom, 'Oh king, what will become of you?
> The bliss of a king is worthless, the joy of the jogi-lord[36] is most excellent'.
>
> Hearing this, he renounced all power and abandoned all worldly pleasures.
> The clever King Indra Gir, became immersed in *jap* [meditative repetition].
>
> The boon that the sage gave can never be described.
> Once you have undertaken such yoga, the passion for jap cannot be erased.
>
> For some time [as he] acquired [mental] power, his martial cunning [also] grew.
> Seeing him return to the good old ways, he was pleased with Rajendra Gir.[37]

Dhyan Nath, content in the knowledge that his chela had his priorities straight, resumed his journey to Prayag. Upon reaching the spot where 'the dark and light waters look lovely [and] the three rivers meet', he 'relinquished his spirit through his skull' and 'merged with the divine essence'. As for his chela, 'King Rajendragir focused on rāja yoga'.[38]

For Man Kavi, at the heart of Rajendragir's transformation is a productive paradox: while the lifestyle of the king is incompatible with that of the ascetic, the mental cunning of the ascetic makes one a more effective warrior—a sine qua non for a king.[39] Man Kavi does not dwell on the point: part one ends after verse 46, and the action of part two takes up Rajendragir's defeat of the Maratha Naru Shankar of Jhansi, the acquisition of the citadel of Moth, and the gosain's entry into the service of Safdarjang of Awadh—which, as it happens, occurs during a pilgrimage visit to Prayag. Fortunately, by contrast, Padmakar does offer some commentary on the internal paradox that animated this new Yogi model of being—though he does so not through reference to Rajendragir, but rather by contrasting his old patron Arjun Singh with his new patron Anupgir Gosain at a key moment in the battle of Ajaigarh. Well into the siege, Padmakar launches into an extended meditation on what it means to be a Kshatriya, told in the form of a heated conversation among Arjun Singh's men who are debating whether to stay and fight from a position of safety in the fort or sally forth and engage directly with the enemy.[40] After some initial quavering on the part of one soldier, the question was revealed to be purely rhetorical: a true Kshatriya could not even imagine cowering behind the walls of a fort, thereby squandering not only the opportunity to die an honourable death in battle but sullying his name for eternity. 'The dharma of the Kshatriyas, according to the eternal proof of the Vedas and Puranas, [is] protecting brahmans and cows, removing enemies, and enduring bodily sword blows.'[41] Or, as another proclaimed: 'Honor—this is the wealth of the Rajputs—always protect your honor. If you lose your honor, not even your wife will respect you, to say nothing of others.'[42] For our purposes, the key passage occurs amidst this debate among Arjun's men, spoken by an anonymous Pamar warrior:

> There are two types of men in this world who go on to pierce the beautiful disc of the sun.
> He who has been following the path of yoga from birth and fights with calm indifference.

> And he whose passion is roused by the battle and fights to the death then and there.
> Those who hear the ballad of these two types (of men) understand the highest truth.[43]

Arjun listened to all this and 'was fully pleased'. He rewarded his Brahmins, who 'gave him an amulet containing the Bhagavad Gita to wear around his neck [and] pure Ganga water [to drink], and he resolved to wage a fierce battle'.[44] For his part, Anupgir, seeing Arjun's forces streaming out of the fort, was visibly thrilled: 'There could be seen so much redness surging and spreading in his eyes. As though he were up to his eyeballs with the frothing, juicy essence of valor.' Around his neck was also an amulet, but unlike Arjun's, Anupgir's was filled with 'Durga and Bhagavad Gita-based magical incantations', or *jantra-mantra*;[45] and though he had many brave warriors ready to die at his command, their distinctive battle cry signalled that many of them were anything but paragons of Rajput honour and virtue:

> There, (with) many Durga and Bhagavad Gita-based magical incantations,
> Around (his) neck, an amulet shines that brings victory in battle.
> Two three-hand-long *khagā* swords are bound gleaming to his waist.
> The sight of his foreign *jamadhar* sword frightens even the God of Death.
>
> A quiver full of arrows and a great bow were strapped on to a horse.
> The (clamor of their) glorious approach spread and awakened all the direction points.
> There the sound of 'harakhi har har harakhi har har harkhi har har' rippled in the wind.
> The sound of the 'har har' chant weakened the liver of the enemy.[46]

Thereupon follows descriptions of set-piece combat, as various components of Anupgir's army challenge Arjun's forces and Arjun himself,[47] followed by a dozen or so verses devoted to descriptions of the array of weapons used in the battle.[48] The dénouement occurs with Anupgir himself finally delivering the death blow to Arjun, and offering the Rajput's head to Parvati, consort of the primal yogi, Shiva:[49]

> There was a great tumult, fierce clashing, then suddenly Arjun was getting tuckered out.
> Then King Anupgir crossed over the great ocean army and challenged Arjun, sword in hand.

> Urging his horse Kanhaiya, he remembered God,[50] and attacked at the elephant's shoulder.
> Waving his sword, taking aim and striking, he grabbed the forearm of the mighty Pamar.
>
> He knocked him off the elephant, rushed forward, grabbed the enemy's head and cut it off.
> He offered his foe's body to the Earth, and took its head and offered it to Shakti.[51]
> Taking Arjun's head, Parvati[52] strung it,[53] and began to dance indescribably.
> She's beating the *damru* drum, singing the praises, she sets the spirits a'dancing gloriously.
>
> Chandi screeched, she took her piece, she swelled and radiated with pleasure.
> She brought her demon-girl-gang, they clapped to the beat, cracked-chewed the bone marrow.
> The gathering of *yoginis*, [full of] grim delight, gorged themselves on the meat.
> Filling the skull bowls with blood, they reveled and danced about.

The logic of Padmakar's 'argument', as it were, is signalled in verse 105. Padmakar relies, in this verse, on Arjun Singh's Pamar Rajputs to provide the commentary that explains the decisive difference between Anupgir Gosain and Arjun Singh: whereas Arjun is one 'whose passion is roused by the battle and fights to the death then and there', Anupgir 'has been following the path of yoga from birth and fights with calm indifference'. In the end, calm indifference won the day—even if it was a calm indifference that sometimes appears ferocious and uncontrollable, causing even the eyeballs to overflow with the 'frothing, juicy essence of valor'.[54] Though Padmakar does not make the point explicitly, Anupgir's frothy, calm indifference allowed him the luxury of choosing when and how to fight. There was no compulsion for the gosain to meet the enemy in an even contest, man to man—or Kshatriya to Kshatriya. He waited while his subordinates and followers gradually wore Arjun down, and then he rode in—when Arjun was 'tuckered out'—and delivered what otherwise might be interpreted as the coup de grâce. Parvati got to add another skull to her necklace, and the cavorting yoginis got to enjoy their feast. Not pretty, but effective.

Aftermath

Anupgir's mental cunning, as Man Kavi would put it, has earned him the opprobrium of later commentators, including none other than Bhagvandin, the editor of the first published edition of Padmakar's *Himmatbahādurvirudāvalī*. Bhagvandin could not fathom why Padmakar would choose to eulogize Anupgir rather than Arjun Singh, and offered a host of reasons for why the Rajput was by far the more attractive hero:

> 1– Arjun Singh was a *kshatriya*, and a true *kshatriya*. Himmat Bahadur was the son of a *Sanadhya* brahman beggar and the disciple of a thieving *gosain*. 2– Arjun was a *kshatriya* who was completely devoted to *kshatriya* patriotism. Himmat Bahadur was a brave brahman and a *gosain* devotee of Siva who served the foreigner and the irreligious *yavana* [foreigner, Muslim]. 3– Arjun Singh never begged the assistance of anyone, he always fought with his own personal strength and helped others. Himmat Bahadur always sought the aid of others. 4– Himmat Bahadur fought with his own self interest in mind, he wanted to establish his own state come what may. The villages and territories that Arjun Singh won in battle he always offered to his ward [Bhakta Singh], and if he had wanted he could have established a state at any time. 5– Even on his deathbed Himmat Bahadur was engaged in trickery and deceit, which for a man of courage and honor is a great sin. One hears nothing of this sort concerning Arjun Singh. 6– Himmat Bahadur was a kind of traitor to his country. Arjun Singh was innocent of this treachery. Indeed, because he fought against a traitor we can speak of him as a lover of his country. As a result of all these points, the name of Arjun Singh is accorded such great respect that Himmat Bahadur's name pales in comparison.[55]

Thomas Brooke, a judge of Banaras who dabbled in intelligence, put it more succinctly on 4 June 1804, unaware that Anupgir had died the previous day:

> Himmut Behadhur is not to be trusted, by the inhabitants of every class he is detested, and whilst he stays in Bundelcund we can never prosper. A native speaking of him, said he was like a man who in crossing a river kept a foot in two boats, ready to abandon the one that was sinking.[56]

Blinded by the high moral dudgeon of their emergent political formations (British imperialism and Indian nationalism, respectively),

Brooke and Bhagvandin could not understand that reputation and honour matter little when the world around you is sinking into a pit of corruption. The only logical course of action is to seek a higher morality. Padmakar certainly saw this, and it suggests that he also understood that the old order was giving way—and its moral codes along with it. He thus made necessity a virtue. Anupgir, he wrote, 'is a sacred ship (sailing) on the ocean of *Kali Yuga*, his work is to fulfill the wishes of all'.[57]

What might this brief foray into the gosain past reveal about the use of early modern Brajbhasha poetry for our own historical writing, in a post-nationalist, post-imperial mode? Certainly the fine-grain details that emerge in the late eighteenth-century poems enable a sharper narrative and a thicker description. In labouring to understand the poets' words, we begin to see the world through their eyes; we move closer to an experience of the past, which is increasingly necessary if we are to properly apprehend temporally distant meanings in a blindingly all-consuming present.[58]

Should we worry about the fact that both poets were occasionally willing to subordinate questions of historical fact to concerns of genre and politics? Hardly. As Allison Busch points out in her chapter on Padmakar in this volume, such behaviour was entirely in keeping with the expectations of *praśasti* stylistics and should not negate the many ways in which *rīti* poetry met the needs of history. And in any case, as Hayden White has reminded us, modern historians are hardly guiltless when it comes to moulding substance to style. Rather than look askance at such politico-aesthetic moves, we would do well to read them for the meta-historical messages they seek to convey. Thus, Padmakar's invention of a final encounter between Anupgir and Arjun Singh (and, no doubt, the speechifying that preceded it) did not simply serve to bring the battle narrative to a fitting climax. It also allowed Padmakar to engage in a different kind of truth-telling—more akin, perhaps, to political theory and sociology than to history. Freed of the constraints of chronology by the compressed temporal frame of his poem, and no doubt mindful of his recent connections to Arjun Singh, his narrative offered both a celebration and comparison of the Kshatriya and Yogi's ways of war. Padmakar's thoughtful attention to this juxtaposition suggests that it was a matter of some local import that observers were conscious of the fact that Anupgir's gosain victory marked the termination of Rajput dominance in Bundelkhand. And that Padmakar was able to make this point while employing the *alaṃkāra-śāstra* ornamentation typical of Rajput court poetry is no mean hermeneutic feat; it speaks not only to the breadth of his imagination, but also to the capaciousness of the literary genre in which he operated.

The larger sociopolitical point that Padmakar was making would, arguably, have rendered his narrative inventions seamlessly acceptable to his audience. It is hard to imagine anyone objecting that some violence was being done to the historical record by the depiction of Anupgir personally delivering the death blow to Arjun Singh. After all, it was Anupgir's army that had vanquished the pride of the Bundelas. By contrast, it is easy to imagine Padmakar's listeners nodding with an inkling awareness that indeed the era of Kshatriya valour was coming to an end; they may have even wondered, casting a nervous eye towards Calcutta, what other political-cultural changes were in the offing.

What of Man Kavi's inventions? These seem to be of a different order altogether. Man Kavi seems to have crossed a line, and he seems to have been aware of the fact. In suggesting that it was Anupgir and not Umraogir whom Safdar Jang placed in command of the gosain army in 1753, Man Kavi was not simply inventing the recent present: he was subverting the well-known past. And it was a subversion that seemed calculated to benefit Anupgir's chelas—Kanchangir especially—more than Anupgir himself. I would hazard the suggestion that Man Kavi's language here is purposefully ambiguous not so that the reader might choose an interpretation that favoured either Umraogir or Anupgir, but to hint at a cautious admission on his part that he was treading on extremely thin ice when it came to issues of historical fact. And I would suggest, as well, that we should interpret his rather-too-obvious discursive sleights of hand as an expression of narrative anxiety and as yet more evidence—negative evidence—that early modern Hindi poets did indeed possess well-developed historical sensibilities. Political realities and aesthetic codes notwithstanding, they wanted to tell the truth. The hard part is figuring out how they managed to do so.

Notes

1. 'Himmat Bahadur' is a hybrid Indo-Persianate title bestowed on Anupgir by the Awadh nawab Shuja-ud Daula, though, as I have noted later, this may well have been a point of dispute. *Himmat* is from Hindi and means courage, resolve, spirit, and boldness; *bahādur* comes from Persian

and means brave (adjective) or hero (noun) and it was often used as an honorific title. A figurative translation of the combination of the two terms might be 'the bravest of the brave'. I use the spelling *Anupgir* in this chapter rather than *Anupgiri* (which I have used elsewhere), though both spellings (and various permutations thereof) were used in Hindi and English records, often in the same documents. For some contemporary observers, the suffix 'gir' will have hinted at—perhaps not inappropriately—Maratha as well as Mughal connections. The term *bargir*, for example, was generally associated with the Maratha armies and signified a mounted soldier who rode a horse owned by his leader. Similarly, 'bargir-*girī*' referred to a 'style of warfare based on light cavalry which emphasized mobility rather than frontal attack in a plains battle'. See Stewart Gordon, *The Marathas: 1600–1818* (Cambridge: Cambridge University Press, 1993), xii (for the quote) and 41–5. As we shall see, a preference for mobility rather than frontal attack is appropriate in the context of Anupgir. Another use of the term 'gir' is as a Persian suffix, often employed in formal titles, connoting 'grasping', 'taking', or 'grabbing hold of'—thus, the imperial title adopted by Akbar's son Salim, 'Jahangir', 'world conqueror'. The Hindi term *girī*, by contrast, means mountain, and in a modern Hindu context connotes inclusion in a *Dasnami sanyasi* lineage, usually connected to a military *akhārā* (order). Meanwhile, as the term 'bargir-girī' suggests, the suffix 'girī' can also refer to 'style', 'doings', or 'behaviour', as in *gundāgirī* (mischief, hooliganism) or *Gandhigirī* (the kind of principled do-goodism that the latter-day Gandhians might promote, as in the 2006 film *Lage Raho Munna Bhai*).

2. All translations of the poems in this chapter, including the verse by Sudan Kavi, are from a book in progress, provisionally entitled *Poems for a Warlord*, by Allison Busch, Dalpat Rajpurohit, and William Pinch. I hereby record my gratitude to my colleagues for their generosity and patience in the face of my halting and, at times, painful attempts at deciphering early modern Hindi. The bibliographic details of each poem are given in the relevant notes.

3. The term 'gosain', properly transliterated as *gosāiṃ*, is functionally synonymous with *sanyāsī* in that it refers to an ascetic; however, whereas the latter derives from *sanyās*, or renunciation, the former derives from *go* or *gau*—which can have a multitude of meanings including cattle, arrows, the world, the senses, and the four compass points—and *saiṃ*, often thought to be a corruption of '*swāmī*' or lord, master, husband, the Supreme Being. Thus, 'gosain'/'gosāiṃ' can be taken to mean 'lord of the world' or 'master of the senses', or even 'lord of cows' (it is often used in this latter sense in the Krishna-bhakti context). In some senses, then, 'gosain'/'gosāiṃ' carries the opposite meaning of renunciation.

4. William R. Pinch, *Warrior Ascetics and Indian Empires* (Cambridge: Cambridge University Press, 2006).

5. See, for example, P. N. Bhalla, 'The Gosain Brothers', *Journal of Indian History* 23, no. 2 (August 1944): 128–36; Jadunath Sarkar and Nirod Bhusan Roy, *History of the Dasnami Naga Sanyasis* (Allahabad: Mahanirvani Panchayati Akhbara, n.d. [1952?]).

6. 'Translation of an Arzee from Omrao Geer', no. 83 of 2 April 1807 (received 1 November 1806), BPP (see the list of records from the India Office Records, British Library, for abbreviations). The purpose of the petition was to request pensionary support.

7. Baillie claimed that Anupgir's dying wish was that the British protect his son, but this evolved over the course of two days into a request that the boy be made the full heir and successor. He acknowledged in his official report that Umraogir did not accept the boy's authority and 'departed from the [coronation] tent with some appearance of displeasure' (Baillie to Mercer, no. 232 of 21 June 1804, d/4 June 1804, BSPP). For more on Baillie, see note 30.

8. Interestingly, Umraogir absolved Baillie of complicity and placed responsibility for the plot at the feet of the senior chela Kanchangir who acted 'in concert with the other officers of the Government'. This does not mean that Umraogir actually believed Baillie to be blameless in the affair. Rather, it is more likely that he did not wish to accuse that increasingly influential officer of malfeasance as doing so could have compromised the success of his petition. Baillie would soon become the Resident at Lucknow, perhaps the most desirable post in the Company's political service.

9. For Anupgir's doings, see the sources cited in Pinch, *Warrior Ascetics*, Chapter 3. Umraogir's movements are more difficult to track but are suggested in reports by Edward Ives, Resident in Lucknow, to the governor general, no. 12 of 3 December 1790, dated 24 November 1790, BPP; and Ives to the governor general, (no number given) of 12 October 1791, dated 3 October 1799, BPP. If nothing else, Umraogir's reported movements belie his claim, in the 1806 petition cited earlier, that 'for a period of twenty years ... I passed my time on the banks of the Ganges in the full and undisturbed exercise of my religious duties'.

10. See S. Davis, Magistrate Benares, to G. H. Barlow, Secretary to the Governor General, no. 2 of 3 September 1799, dated 25 August 1799, BSPP. One of the Banaras mansions was known in the early nineteenth century as 'Oomraogir Pooshta'; see William R. Pinch, 'Hiding in Plain Sight: Gosains in Banaras, 1809', in *Benares Urban History, Architecture, Identity*, ed. Michael Dodson (New Delhi: Routledge India, 2012), 77–109. The other was a 'garden house' in 'the western suburb of Benares'; on this latter structure, Davis remarked that it 'has been possessed by [Umraogir] and his fraternity since the time that Benares appertained to the Dominion of Oude' (that is, prior to 1781). Thus, it was probably acquired when the gosains were in the service of Shuja, between 1753 and 1775.

11. See Pinch, *Warrior Ascetics*, 132. On Umraogir's involvement in the 'Vizier Ali Conspiracy,' see below.

12. Ives to the Governor General (Cornwallis), no. 8 of 2 May 1792, BPP. Edward Ives was the British Resident to the court of Asafud-Daulah, the nawab of Awadh.

13. The two published versions are almost identical, though they use slightly different spellings for the title of the poem. They are Padmakar, *Padmākar kṛt himmatbahādur birdāvalī*, ed. Lala Bhagvandin (Varanasi: Kashi Nagarani Pracharani Sabha, n.d. 1930[?], 2nd edition) and Padmakar, '*Himmatbahādurvirudāvalī*', in *Padmākar (Granthāvalī)*, ed. Vishwanathprasad Mishra (Varanasi: Nagaripracarini Sabha, 1959), 3–30. In his introduction to *Padmākar kṛt himmatbahādur birdāvalī* (xxiv and xxxi–xxxv), Bhagvandin relates the Bundela legend that Arjun died at the hands of one of his own men, thus fulfilling a prophecy of a sadhu whom he served in his youth.

14. Man Kavi, '*Anūp-Prakāś*', MSS Hin. D9a, Asia, Pacific, and Africa Collections, BL, vv. 97–103.

15. While the nom de guerre 'Himmat Bahadur' was widely known to refer to Anupgir, all accounts (save Man Kavi) agree (or assume) that it was bestowed upon him by Shuja-ud Daula, Safdarjang's son and heir, several years later in the late 1750s or early 1760s. See, for example, Bhagvandin's introduction to *Padmākar kṛt himmatbahādur birdāvalī*, xxi.

16. Man Kavi's only prior references to the title 'Himmat Bahadur', before verse 101, occur in verses 5 and 12, amid the *maṅgalācaraṇ* section in the introduction: 'On the strength of the wisdom granted by Kesavdev, I will sing the praises of Himmat Bahadur' (v. 5.b) and 'One gains the treasure of the strength and intelligence granted by Shri Lord Kesavdev by describing the courageous deeds of Himmat Bahadur, Protector of the Earth' (v. 12.b). (The wording of the latter is related to the refrain verse in Padmakar's poem, indicating that one poet knew about the other's work.) After verse 126, most uses of the title 'Himmat Bahadur' occur in Man Kavi's own refrain verse, 'Sing the glorious praises, of Himmat Bahadur the king' (for example, vv. 129, 144, 197).

17. Man Kavi, *Anūp-Prakāś*, v. 104.

18. The previous verse makes clear that 'Safdarjangvazir' was bestowing these gifts 'with the emperor', that is, Ahmad Shah Bahadur.

19. Man Kavi, *Anūp-Prakāś*, v. 120.

20. Man Kavi, *Anūp-Prakāś*, v. 139. I am grateful to Tyler Williams for his suggestions on and corrections to the translation with respect to verse 139.c.

21. Padmakar's sole reference to Umraogir in his poem occurs in verse 143, where Rajgir is described as 'the son of Umraogir'.

22. Soon after Vazir Ali, the deposed claimant to the *nawābī* (rulership) of Awadh killed George Frederick Cherry, agent to the governor general in Banaras, in a bid to mount a rebellion and reclaim the throne, a cash of letters and allied documents were discovered that directly implicated Umraogir in the plot. See, for example, no. 11 of 3 June 1799, Barlow to Davis, d/28 May 1799; and no. 8 of 20 August 1799, Davis to Barlow, d/6 August 1799—all in BSSP. In his letter of 28 May, Barlow noted that 'Maharajah Rujunder Gheer Bahadre was concerned in Vizier Alli's conspiracy and that he had taken measures for assembling a body of Nagah's [*sic*] to assist Vizier Alli in the execution of his designs'. Along these lines, D. Vanderheyden, agent to the governor general in Cawnpore, noted in a letter to Barlow that 'Omrao Gheer is a more likely person, than any yet apprehended, to find desperate adherents, being brother to Himmut Behadur in Ally Bahadur's service, and chief of a numerous class of fighting gosains' (no. 6 of 20 August 1799, Vanderheyden to Barlow, d/6 August 1799, BSSP).

23. No. 7 of 9 July 1799, J. Lumsden to J. H. Craig, dated 25 June 1799, BPP; no. 7 of 20 August 1799, J. H. Craig to D. Vanderheyden, undated, BSSP; and no. 3 of 13 May 1799, G. H. Barlow to Samuel Davis, Magistrate of Benares, undated but probably 13 May 1799, BSSP.

24. Sudan Kavi, *Sudan kavikṛt sujān caritra*, comp., Shri Radhakrshndas (Allahabad: Kashi Nagari Pracharini Sabha, 1902), 172–3. These lines occur in section four of part five of the poem, vv. 7–10; the verse numbers restart in each section. Sudan wrote the *Sujān Caritra* for the Jat ruler Sujan Singh (also known as Surajmal) of Bharatpur. It praises that ruler 'against the background of Jat alliances and hostilities with the Mughals, Afghans and Marathas during the years 1745–53' (R.S. McGregor, *Hindi Literature from Its Beginnings to the Nineteenth Century* [Wiesbaden: Otto Harrassowitz, 1984], 197). According to A. L. Srivastava:

> Although a great admirer of his hero, Sudan has given the virtues of his patron's enemies side by side with the virtues of Surajmal. The work describes the battles that Surajmal fought either on his own account or on behalf of his friends. It is written in a difficult and highly figurative style and the whole work is a panegyric; yet most of the occurrences described by the author are quite true (as I found them by subjecting them to a comparison with the contemporary Persian and Marathi works). He has given month and year for each battle, which too are correct. It seems that Sudan was an eye witness of most of these battles and described each one of them soon after its conclusion. (Srivastava, *The First Two Nawabs of Oudh* [Lucknow: Upper India Publishing House, 1933], 294).

25. Srivastava (*The First Two Nawabs of Oudh*, 236) cites Sudan's verse (though the page number given appears to be incorrect), but notes as well

that Umraogir's account is supported by the anonomously authored *Tarikh-i Ahmad Shahi*, f. 59b.

26. The gifting of robes was central to courtly ritual in early modern South Asia. See Stewart Gordon, ed., *Robes of Honour: Khil'at in Pre-Colonial and Colonial India* (New York: Oxford University Press, 2003).

27. With this in mind, several features of this passage invite closer examination. In verse 99 Man Kavi acknowledges that the emperor elevated *both* of Rajendragir's chelas, using the phrase *Rājendragir ke suvan jug* (Rajendragir's handsome pair). Then, in verse 100, he identifies them each by name. In verse 101, however, Man Kavi shifts to the singular, indicating that the emperor bestowed the title 'Himmat Bahadur' on the *vīr*, or 'brave'. In the following verse, 102, Man Kavi reverts to the plural, namely, *bhaye jugul taravāriyā*, which we have translated as 'they were both excellent swordsmen'. In verse 103, by contrast, Man Kavi moves from the plural in the first line, indicated by the term *donoṃ*, 'both', to the singular in the second line, referring to *bali*, 'that mighty one'. After this point, all of Man Kavi's references are to the singular and not to both *gosains*, usually employing the prefix *bhūp*, 'earth-lord', or *nṛp*, 'king'—sometimes explicitly but often implicitly in reference to Anupgir, the hero of the poem. I return to this matter in the concluding section of this essay.

28. Baillie to Mercer, no. 232 of 21 June 1804, d/4 June 1804, BSPP.

29. J. Richardson, Agent in Bundelkhand, to N. B. Edmonstone, Secretary to the Governor General, no. 5 of 25 August, d/10 August 1807, BPP. Richardson took over from Baillie in April of 1807, but Baillie was consulted on, and concurred with, the amount awarded. Significantly, however, the amount was only half of what Kanchangir had been granted.

30. As the sun set on the gosains, it rose on Baillie. Based on his success in Bundelkhand, in 1807 he was made Resident at Lucknow, one of the plum postings in the Company's political service. He returned to Britain in 1816, won a parliamentary seat in 1820, and was elected to a Company directorship in 1823. By the early 1830s, during his third term in parliament, he had begun building a castle near Inverness, his ancestral home. He died suddenly in London in 1833, aged 61, struck down by an outbreak of influenza. His life awaits a full biographical treatment. Key among his qualities was a gift for 'Oriental languages'. On the strength of these talents he was appointed, in 1801 and at the rank of lieutenant in the Bengal Army, a professor of Arabic and Persian and of Mahommedan Law at Fort William College. He amassed a huge collection of Persian and Arabic manuscripts, which were donated to Edinburgh University Library by his grandson in 1876. This also includes a small collection of 'Hindustani Manuscripts'. For glimpses of his career, see Casey, 'Baillie, John (1772–1833)', available at http://www.historyofparliamentonline.org/volume/1820–1832/member/baillie-john-1772–1833, last accessed on 21 April 2013; Edinburgh University's 'Gallery of Benefactors',

available at http://www.docs.is.ed.ac.uk/docs/lib-archive/bgallery/Gallery/records/eighteen/baillie.html, last accessed on 22 April 2013.

31. This term is employed in no. 6 of 20 August 1799, D. Vanderheyden to G. H. Barlow, d/ 6 August 1799, BSSC. Vanderheyden was the agent to the Governor General at Cawnpore (Kanpur).

32. See the introduction to Pinch, *Warrior Ascetics*, for a beginning on this head.

33. Man Kavi, *Anūp-Prakāś*, v. 16.

34. Man Kavi, *Anūp-Prakāś*, vv. 17–22.

35. Man Kavi, *Anūp-Prakāś*, vv. 23–9. Though Man Kavi does not mention the fact in his poem, Rajendragir acquires Umraogir and Anupgir in Kulpahar.

36. The term is *jogiś*.

37. Man Kavi, *Anūp-Prakāś*, vv. 30–5.

38. Man Kavi, *Anūp-Prakāś*, vv. 44–6.

39. Cf. J. C. Heesterman, *The Inner Conflict of Tradition: Essays in Indian Ritual, Kingship, and Society* (Chicago: University of Chicago Press, 1985), and his more recent 'Warrior, Peasant and Brahmin', *Modern Asian Studies* 29, no. 3 (1995): 637–54. There would appear to be much convergence between what Rajendragir experiences and the inner conflict (resolvable only by sacrifice) that Heesterman describes. A key difference is that whereas for Heesterman the role of the warrior and of the brahman alternate temporally according to season, here (as embodied in Rajendragir and his descendants), they necessarily coexist in time—and rather than seeing the tension as a conflict in need of brahmanical sacrificial resolution, the ascetic, through *rāja* yoga, is able to contain the powerful forces within his own being.

40. Padmakar, *Himmatbahādurvirudāvalī*, vv. 91–110.

41. Padmakar, *Himmatbahādurvirudāvalī*, v. 101.

42. Padmakar, *Himmatbahādurvirudāvalī*, v. 110.

43. Padmakar, *Himmatbahādurvirudāvalī*, v. 105.

44. Padmakar, *Himmatbahādurvirudāvalī*, v. 111.

45. Padmakar, *Himmatbahādurvirudāvalī*, vv. 118–19.

46. Padmakar, *Himmatbahādurvirudāvalī*, vv. 119–20.

47. Padmakar, *Himmatbahādurvirudāvalī*, vv. 121–90.

48. Padmakar, *Himmatbahādurvirudāvalī*, vv. 191–202.

49. Padmakar, *Himmatbahādurvirudāvalī*, vv. 206–8.

50. Note that this is based on the text in Mishra's edition, *Himmatbahādurvirudāvalī*, as 'Kanhaiya' is used thrice in this line; in the earlier Bhagvandin edition, *Padmākar kṛt himmatbahādur birdāvalī*, the second and third terms are 'Kandhaiya', which can either mean shoulder or is the name of Arjun's elephant.

51. *Hara hi hara ko.*

52. *Girijā*, or 'the Goddess of the Mountain', a name of Parvati.

53. Presumably, through its nostrils or eye sockets or ear holes, onto her garland of skulls.

54. Padmakar, *Himmatbahādurvirudāvalī*, v. 118.

55. Bhagvandin, 'Introduction', *Padmākarkṛt himmatbahādur birdāvalī*, xxxvi. Of course, Bhagvandin conveniently ignores the fact that it was Anupgir who was Padmakar's main patron in the region after Arjun's demise.

56. 'Correspondence of Thomas Brooke at Benares with Major M. Shawe, Secretary to Lord Wellesley, 1803–1805', Wellesley Papers, series II, volume VIII, Add. MS 37, 281 (MSS Reading Room, BL, London), ff. 228b–229a.

57. Padmakar, *Himmatbahādurvirudāvalī*, v. 10.a.

58. Frank Ankersmit, *Sublime Historical Experience* (Stanford: Stanford University Press, 2005), Introduction.

Bibliography

Primary Sources

Anon. *Tarikh-i Ahmad Shahi*, Ms. Or. 2005, British Library, London.

BPP: Bengal Political Proceedings. India Office Records, British Library, London.

BSPP: Bengal Secret and Political Proceedings. India Office Records, British Library, London.

BSSP: Bengal Secret and Separate Proceedings. India Office Records, British Library, London.

'Correspondence of Thomas Brooke at Benares with Major M. Shawe, Secretary to Lord Wellesley, 1803–1805', Wellesley Papers, series II, volume VIII, Add. MS 37, 281 (MSS Reading Room, BL, London).

Man Kavi. *Anūp-Prakāś*. MSS Hin. D9a, Asia, Pacific, and Africa Collections, BL.

Padmakar. *Himmatbahādurvirudāvalī*. In *Padmākar (Granthāvalī)*, edited by Vishwanathprasad Mishra. Varanasi: Nagaripracarini Sabha, 1959.

Padmakar. *Padmākar kṛt himmatbahādur birdāvalī*, edited by Lala Bhagvandin, (2nd edition). Varanasi: Kashi Nagarani Pracharani Sabha, n.d. (1930[?]).

Sudan Kavi. *Sudan kavi kṛt sujān caritra*, compiled by Shri Radhakrshndas. Allahabad: Kashi Nagari Pracharini Sabha, 1902.

Secondary Sources

Ankersmit, Frank. *Sublime Historical Experience*. Stanford: Stanford University Press, 2005.

Bhalla, P. N. 'The Gosain Brothers'. *Journal of Indian History* 23, no. 2 (Aug 1944): 128–36.

Casey, Martin. 'Baillie, John (1772–1833), of Leys Castle, Inverness and Devonshire Place, Mdx'. In *The History of Parliament: The House of Commons 1820–1832*, edited by D. R. Fisher. Cambridge: Cambridge University Press, 2009.

Gordon, Stewart. *The Marathas, 1600–1818*. Cambridge: Cambridge University Press, 1993.

Gordon, Stewart, ed. *Robes of Honour: Khil'at in Pre-Colonial and Colonial India*. New York: Oxford University Press, 2003.

Heesterman, J. C. *The Inner Conflict of Tradition: Essays in Indian Ritual, Kingship, and Society*. Chicago: University of Chicago Press, 1985.

———. 'Warrior, Peasant and Brahmin'. *Modern Asian Studies* 29, no. 3 (1995): 637–54.

McGregor, R. S. *Hindi Literature from Its Beginnings to the Nineteenth Century*. Wiesbaden: Otto Harrassowitz, 1984.

Pinch, William R. *Warrior Ascetics and Indian Empires*. Cambridge: Cambridge University Press, 2006.

———. 'Hiding in Plain Sight: Gosains in Banaras, 1809'. In *Benares: Urban History, Architecture, Identity*, edited by Michael Dodson, 77–109. New Delhi: Routledge India, 2012.

Sarkar, Jadunath and Nirod Bhusan Roy. *History of the Dasnami Naga Sanyasis*. Allahabad: Mahanirvani Panchayati Akhbara, n.d. (1952[?]).

Srivastava, A. L. *The First Two Nawabs of Oudh*. Lucknow: Upper India Publishing House, 1933.

13

ALLISON BUSCH*

The Poetics of History in Padmakar's *Himmatbahādurvirudāvalī*

Padmakar and the Corpus of Hindi Historical Poetry

Padmakar (1753–1833), one of the most influential Brajbhasha writers at the turn of the nineteenth century, is often considered the last of a dying breed of Indian court poets, a representative of an old literary order that was destined for obsolescence as the new expressive regimes of Khari Boli Hindi became entrenched during the colonial period. The nationalist turn in Hindi literary criticism that took hold by the 1920s and has yet to be fully superseded did much to propagate the view that there is little worthwhile in *rīti* literature, the modern name generally accorded to the Brajbhasha courtly texts that had flourished for centuries. Supposed to be suffused through and through with *vilāsitā* (decadence) and *sāmantvād* (feudalism), the Hindi courtly past is often thought to be best forgotten.

As I have argued elsewhere, literary scholars are ill-advised to do so.[1] The same holds true for historians. To some extent, the subfield of *aitihāsik kāvya* (historical poetry) has in fact been allowed to escape the usual 'rīti taint' because unlike the more erotic styles of court poetry it can at least be said to embody a spirit of martial vigour, a trait that colonial discourse held to be in short supply among 'effeminate' Hindus and a purported failing that nationalist-period writers were keen to redress.[2] Although several valuable studies of historical poetry exist in Hindi,[3] this corpus has yet to be widely appreciated for its enormous historiographical significance. The Rajput rulers of early modern India (c. 1500–1800) were the main patrons of rīti literature and there are dozens if not hundreds of Braj and Rajasthani works that shed light on the dynamics of Rajput–Mughal political interactions; many also give voice to something we can call local history. Padmakar's *Himmatbahādurvirudālī* falls into the latter category.

This martial ode pays tribute to Anupgir Gosain, a Brahman warrior-ascetic who rose to the status of a king after decisively defeating Arjun Singh Pamar, his main political rival in Bundelkhand and scion of the Bundela Rajputs, a clan that had controlled the region for centuries.[4] It makes good sense that when Anupgir was burnishing his kingly credentials he would have found the literary skills of Padmakar, who hailed from a well-known local family of court poets, a useful tool in public relations. Kings needed their court poets; an aspiring young court poet would also have needed a king. This mutual dependency has a long history in India and is aptly expressed in a Sanskrit adage:

> jñāyate jātu nāmāpi na rājñaḥ kavitāṃ vinā
> kaves tadvyatirekeṇa na kīrtiḥ sphurati kṣitau.
>
> Even the name of a king would not be known if it were not for poetry.
> And without kings the glory of poets would not emanate throughout the world.[5]

Poets were kingmakers, then, and kings were poet-makers, a pattern that can be readily attested throughout Indian cultural history. It is certainly relevant to Padmakar and his patrons: after writing *Himmatbahādurvirudāvalī* he went on to have a distinguished career, serving various other rulers, including the prestigious Kachhwaha house of Jaipur under Pratap Singh (r. 1778–1803) and Jagat Singh (r. 1803–18).[6]

There is something poignant about the figure of Padmakar in Indian literary history. He comes at the tail end of a two-millennia tradition of *kāvya*, or formal (often specifically courtly) literary production. A tendency—even teleology—propagated by literary historians has been to view late poets such as Padmakar as doomed to decadence and failure, as though the lake of poetic creativity had already dried up by the time these ill-timed poets came upon the scene.[7] Seventeen years after Padmakar's death, Bharatendu Harischandra (1850–1885), the so-called founder of modern Hindi literature, was born, and soon the very purpose of poetry and other literary arts would be dramatically re-conceptualized. New genres and registers, many imported from the West under colonial conditions, would displace the old. Padmakar did not see any of this coming. He was confidently rooted in his traditions.

The use of the plural 'traditions' is deliberate, for Padmakar—and this is true of rīti poets generally—was heir to several cultural streams. As a professional poet writing at Anupgir Gosain's court, his most obvious literary antecedents would have been the rīti traditions that had been born in his very own Bundelkhand two centuries earlier during the long reign of Akbar (1556–1605). Here I refer to the pioneering work of Keshavdas, who served the Bundela kings of Orccha, writing innovative treatises on literary theory and works of historical kāvya in a style that came to be widely adopted in Rajput courtly settings. Rīti authors—especially the earliest ones—drew considerable inspiration from Sanskrit literary topoi and yet they were also of necessity very much engaged with their present political contexts. During Akbar's reign, most of the Rajput houses of India came under Mughal dominion. Engaging with the present meant a cognizance of the Mughal political order, and a whole lexicon pertinent to Persianized military and courtly culture. A new influx of Perso-Arabic vocabulary into Hindi is one reason why the kāvya of 1600 looks nothing like the earlier Sanskrit kāvya of 600.[8] Additionally, because of the importance of Rajputs from western India in the Mughal imperial system, the literary trends of that region were bound to have an impact. Historical poetry in Hindi, much of it rich in martial imagery, is thus an interesting distillation of older Sanskritic kāvya modes that aspired to invoke *vīra rasa* (the martial sentiment, according to classical aesthetics), blended with the more contemporary styles such as Ḍiṅgal that were popular in Rajasthan.[9] Literary elements skilfully meshed with more documentary concerns drawn from contemporary political life. All of this is deeply pertinent to the historical poetry of Padmakar.

Though a compact work of just 211 verses, the *Himmatbahādurvirudāvalī* executes a variety of functions. As the title suggests, it is a *virudāvalī* (chain of epithets), a subgenre of praise poetry that will be briefly introduced. This genre, when performed, would have been a mechanism for publicly asserting a patron's martial or kingly disposition. Another concern for Padmakar was history—in particular, a battle that took place between his patron Anupgir Gosain and Arjun Singh Pamar, which he dates and, to some extent, records for posterity. The work's historical mission ultimately proves inseparable from its poetic features, which evince connections to earlier martial poetry produced by Sanskrit literati as well as the vibrant oral traditions of Rajasthan.

The *Virudāvalī* Genre and the Poetry of Praise

Different inflections of the virudāvalī (also *birudāvalī*) genre can be found throughout Indian cultural history. *Viruda* is originally a Tamil word and lists of titles, often inscribed, had a significant function in Pallava and other south Indian political cultures.[10] Cynthia Talbot has remarked on the importance of the genre for the Kakatiya dynasty of medieval Andhra, where *biruda*s were hard-won material and symbolic accolades:

> *Birudas* were not just bardic pleasantries meant to flatter a patron but were often physical objects in the form of an anklet or insignia—what we consider a medal of honor—as well as titles announced in public appearances and enumerated in inscriptions. *Birudas* could not be adopted freely but had to be inherited from a predecessor, bestowed by an overlord, seized from an enemy, or justified by some deed. A list of *birudas* was a synopsis of a lineage's achievements, in effect, a summary of a person's claim to fame.[11]

Sanskrit rhetoricians, for their part, took up the subject as a genre of poetry. Vishvanatha in his *Sāhityadarpaṇa* (Mirror on Literature, c. 1250) defined the *virudam* as 'a praise poem for a king, composed in verse and prose'.[12] Vishveshvara proposed a more prescriptive or educative function in *Camatkāracandrikā* (Moonlight of Poetic Wonder, c. 1385): 'The *birudāvalī* is marked by multiple titles. Its purpose is to indicate what [a king] is supposed to do on any given occasion.'[13]

During the early modern period in north India, the virudāvalī could likewise function as a synopsis of achievements or an incitement to good works, but both documentary and didactic features were overlain with panegyric, often in a martial vein.[14] One also sees variations with a more devotional cast, such as the bhakta virudāvalī ('chain of devotees'), or Rupa Goswamin's Krishna-centred *Govinda virudāvalī*.[15]

Padmakar, for his part, made the virudāvalī the basis for two entire narrative poems in Brajbhasha, interweaving martial and historical elements with royal panegyric.[16] One can well imagine the power that a recitation of a text like the *Himmatbahādurvirudāvalī* would have had in a courtly assembly. The repetition of the verb *hai* (is) in these lines from the opening verses imparts a stately, percussive regularity:

> himmata bahādura bhūpa hai, subha saṃbhu rūpa anūpa hai
> dila-dāna-bīra dayāla hai, ari-bara-nikara ko kāla hai
> sukha sāhibī amaresa hai, bhuva bhāra dhara abhujaṃgesa hai
> manu mauja deta mahesa hai, guna-jñānavāna ganesa hai...
>
> duti dipati deha manoja hai, manu mauja detani bhoja hai
> subha-ḍīla sīla-samudra hai, ghamasāna meṃ janu rudra hai
> cauṃsaṭhi kalāni prabīna hai, duja-devatāni adhīna hai
> mukha-bola kahata aḍola hai, gaja-bāji deta amola hai...
>
> jaga autaryau ju anūpa hai, mahipāla navarasa-rūpa hai
> nija nāikana ju siṃgāra hai, ari lakhata bīra apāra hai
> lakhi dīna karunā-batsa hai, khala-katala meṃ bībhatsa hai
> nija khilavatina meṃ hāsa hai, bhaya-rūpa durajana-pāsa hai
> haya caṛhata adbhuta hota hai, sara leta rudra-udota hai
> siva-bhajana sānta sujāna hai, jihi kī samāna na āna hai
> himmata bahādura nṛpa balī, jihiṃ sena satruna kī dalī.
>
> Himmat Bahadur is King, he is the unparalleled form of Siva.
> His heart is generous and compassionate,
>   to his host of enemies he is death.
> Refined as Amaresh (Indra),
>   he supports the weight of the world like Sheshnag.
> Like Mahesh (Shiva) he delights the heart,
>   like Ganesh his essence is wisdom....
>
> His form is lustrous like Manoja.
>   Like Bhoja he lavishes worldly pleasures.
> He is of solid build, his character strong. In battle he becomes Rudra.
> He is expert in the 64 arts,
>   he is subordinate (only) to Brahmans and the gods.

His spoken word is unbreakable,
the horses and elephants he gives are priceless....

He has taken unprecedented form in the world;
as a king he embodies the nine *rasas*.
His women find him irresistible (*sṛṅgāra*), his enemies indomitable (*vīra*).
Seeing the helpless he is compassionate (*karuṇa*);
in slaughtering the vile he is disgusting (*bībhatsa*).
With close friends he is comic (*hāsya*);
for opponents he is terror incarnate (*bhaya*).
On horseback, he inspires wonder (*adbhuta*);
lopping off heads he is fierce (*rudra*).
Adept at chanting Siva-bhajans, he is quiescent (*śānta*);
there is no one else like him.
Himmat Bahadur is a powerful king, who destroys enemy armies.[17]

This section is by far the most classical and *kāvya-esque* of the work. Brajbhasha, like modern standard Hindi, can be used in a variety of registers, such as *tatsama* (pure Sanskrit), *ardhatatsama* (modified Sanskrit), or *tadbhava* (words more radically vernacularized); it may also be inflected with Persian or more local Indic dialects, often Rajasthani. Note the dense compounding, which feels like a nod to classical style. To speak of his king as being radiant like Manoja (the god of love, v. 6) and adept in the sixty-four arts (v. 7) is to conjure up ideals of royal comportment that date back at least to the Gupta period.[18] Padmakar here also invokes a significant concept from another courtly art—Indian literary theory—in an elaborate sequence that depicts his patron as an embodiment of the nine rasas.[19] When vernacular poets needed gravitas, they turned to a Sanskrit register. Still, the ready assimilation of Persian and Arabic words (such as *dil* [heart], in v. 3; *sāhibī* [grandeur], in v. 4; and *qatl* [slaughter], in v. 12) at the same time forcefully reminds us that this is an early modern kāvya in Brajbhasha.

The elegant language serves to reinforce the passage's emphasis on kingliness, and this can hardly be accidental. The political dispensation that Anupgir ushered in was something profoundly new and unsettling. After a period of political turmoil, a Shaivite[20] *gosain* had just defeated the ruling Kshatriya dynasty.[21] Padmakar here stresses the moral components and responsibilities of kingship, as though these were special concerns. Court poets are too often considered shameless sycophants who merely prop up the egos of their patrons in exchange for recompense but, as Julie Scott Meisami has noted in the case of Persian poetry, panegyric is often a powerful instrument of ethical suasion.[22] Here the poet reminds his patron (and perhaps reassures others who are listening) that kingly duty means not just the vanquishing of foes but also requires good character and the protection of one's subjects from harm.

Padmakar, Historian and *Kavi*

If Padmakar mobilizes elements of cosmopolitan Sanskritic poetics to invoke its moral imaginary of kingship, some features of the *Himmatbahādurvirudāvalī* fall more squarely in the realm of local politics. Here we meet Padmakar the historian. Immediately following the encomiastic opening lines, Padmakar briskly telescopes the historical backdrop of his tale into a few terse verses, and the world of early modern Bundelkhand comes into view. We are introduced to local notables such as Chatrasal, the famous seventeenth-century anti-Mughal rebel, and the poet zooms in on the redoubt of Ajaigarh near the Ken River, home of Arjun Singh Pamar, Anupgir Gosain's contemporary and rival.[23]

In a move that would have been virtually unthinkable for a Sanskrit *kavi* (poet) but is relatively commonplace for early modern Hindi writers, Padmakar dates the events of which he speaks. This grounding of narratives in the here and now rather than in a timeless framework marks a changed sensibility during the early modern period and can be considered a significant development in the Hindi historiographical tradition. Still, non-prosaic concerns about temporality persist: Padmakar records how Anupgir summons an astrologer to determine a suitable time to engage in warfare, and it is for this reason that we come to know the exact date of the battle:

He called the favored astrologer,
  respectfully asking him to name an auspicious date.
Now speak, when shall we fight?
  Name a suitable day, then we will wage war.

Hearing this order by the maharaja,
  the royal astrologer's heart was gladdened.
The well-named Sarup Sinha spoke words to ensure victory.

He perused all the astral treatises,
  settled upon an auspicious date, and announced it.
Listen, (take) Samvat 1800, and count forty-nine more.

The twelfth day of the dark half of Baisakh, make a note of Wednesday—
an auspicious day for fighting, for young men,
    warriors, and the best of kings.[24]

This is a poetic way of proclaiming that the storied battle between Anupgir Gosain and Arjun Singh took place in Vikram Samvat 1849, or CE 1792.

A typical example of the interplay between history and poetry is a moving catalogue of the many warriors who lost their life fighting for Anupgir. Mandhata Kayasth, the son of one Sabsukhray, is singled out for his pivotal role in the vanguard of Anupgir's army. He delivers a long speech recognizing the generosity of Anupgir to his family before bravely entering the fray.[25] His inevitable death in the service of his overlord (*svāmikāraja*) is described in a lively passage:

In this way the brave Mandhata put himself
    in mortal danger to fight out in front.
Wielding spear, sword, and dagger,
    he cut and sliced through the enemy army.
Then, separated from his horse, he joined the ranks of foot soldiers.
How many blows did he fend off with his shield,
    repulsing the enemy assault?

There he leaped and pounced, slapping away blows.
Sacrificing his body for his overlord, he was first in line to enter heaven.
Laughing and shouting, he faced Arjun Pamar
    and endured the assault of his weapons.
Even as he breathed his last on the battlefield, he continued the fight.

This is how the good Mandhata died, rushing forth into battle.
Ascending the celestial chariot, he paid obeisance
    to his king and became immortal.[26]

A full twenty other names are singled out (even if their contributions are not explained with the same level of detail), and Padmakar describes in each case these brave men's heroic but ultimately unsuccessful engagements with the forces of Arjun Singh Pamar.[27] Many of these figures would not have lived on in history at all, were it not for Padmakar. At the same time, this is powerful poetry.

In narrative terms, all of this is a fitting lead-up to the climax of the work: Anupgir's own fateful encounter with Arjun Singh. The poet chooses not to render this event with verisimilitude. Padmakar the historian cannot be seen as distinct from Padmakar the kavi. Padmakar sought a consummately dramatic tone for his finale. His technique can be glimpsed in these lines (and to perceive the full effects of Padmakar's poetry, it helps to read the Braj out loud):

nikasīṃ tahaṃ khaggaiṃ, umaṛi umaggaiṃ,
    jagamaga jaggaiṃ duhuṃ dala maiṃ
bhāṃtina-bhāṃtina kī, bahu jātina kī, ari-pāṃtina kī kari kalamaiṃ
tahaṃ kaṛhīṃ magarabī, arī-gana carabī, cāpaṭa karabī sī kāṭaiṃ
jagi jora junabbai, phaharata phabbaiṃ, suṇḍani gabbaiṃ phara pāṭaiṃ

bijjula-sī camakaiṃ, ghāina ghamakaiṃ, tīkhana tamakaiṃ bandara kī
bandarī su khaggaiṃ jagamaga jaggaiṃ lapakata laggaiṃ nahiṃ barakī
sohaiṃ subha suratī, ghalata na muratī, rana meṃ phuratī birana koṃ
līlama taravāraiṃ, jhuki-jhuki jhāraiṃ, taki-taki māraiṃ dhīrana koṃ

Then the swords came out, raised with zeal. Both sides were as if ablaze.
So many men, comprising many different communities—
    the enemy lines were cut down.
The unsheathed sword sliced the flesh of the enemy host,
    as though it were a stalk of millet.
The mighty lance awoke, wielded masterfully—
    the ground teemed with elephant trunks.

Like lightning they shone, they wounded deeply,
    the fierce sting of the *bandar* blades.
The fine blades dazzled the world, never wavering upon attack.
The fine *surati* swords of the spirited braves,
    once implanted are never extracted.
The *lilam* swords swooped and swayed, aimed and maimed,
    and killed the steadfast braves.[28]

The *tribhaṅgī* metre with its 'triple folds' of internal rhyme are the perfect way to convey martial intensity. The long sequence catalogues how a host of exotic weaponry was unfurled and heightens the pace to a spectacular crescendo. Poetic flourishes—note the power of the alliteration—are far more important in this scene than documentary precision. *Yamaka* (repeating the same word in more than one sense) is another aural technique used to interesting effect:

Taba nṛpa anūpa giri subhaṭa sindhu tiri arjuna soṃ bhiri khaṛaga gahī
Haya dābi kanhaiyā, sumiri kanhaiyā, su gaja kanhaiyā para pahuṃcau

Then King Anupgir crossed over the great ocean-army
    and challenged Arjun, sword in hand.

Urging on his horse Kanhaiya, he remembered God,
and attacked at the elephant's shoulder.[29]

The second line excerpted here cleverly uses the word *kanhaiyā* in three different senses, meaning the name of the hero's horse; Lord Krishna; and shoulder (cf. modern standard Hindi *kandhā*). In the final verses where Anupgir is portrayed decapitating Arjun Singh with his sword, the advent of supernatural beings such as Shiva and the corpse-loving *yoginīs* elevates the scene to a more transcendent register of the wondrous (known as adbhuta rasa). There is also not a little bloodthirstiness and gore in the spirit of the bībhatsa rasa (disgust) from classical poetics.[30]

Rajasthani Inflections and the Performance of History

Here we find ourselves squarely in the realm of what can be termed the 'poetics of history'. In fact, in many places Padmakar shies away from realistic description and instead adopts dazzling literary strategies to add depth and zest to his account.

In an early scene where Anupgir's soldiers first set out for Ajaigarh, Padmakar describes the troops not in terms of who Anupgir's allies actually were but instead uses a more formulaic conception of the thirty-six canonical Rajput clans. The motif can be traced at least as far back as Kalhana's *Rājataraṅgiṇī*, an important twelfth-century Sanskrit chronicle,[31] and it also occurs in the *Pṛthivīrājrāso* attributed to Chand Bardai, a text that in its current form dates to the sixteenth century (even if it purports to describe twelfth century events).[32] In the hands of the Mughal-period Hindi poets, the Rajput clans became a common literary 'set piece' that was perfect for waxing poetic about Rajput valour. Thirty-six was merely a convenient rubric since each author evidently felt free to elaborate upon the concept in his own way.[33]

For Padmakar, who devotes one line to each of the Rajput groups, the point is to set the scene for the impending battle. The sounds *ka*, *jha*, and retroflex *ṭa* in the second half of each line of this verse, for instance, perfectly conjure up the swishing of swords and the cutting down of enemy soldiers:

bara baisa bīra jujhāra je, jhuki jhamaki jhārata sāra je
gautama tamaki je rana karaiṃ, ari kāṭi kaṭi-kaṭi kai laraiṃ

The fine brave soldiers of Baiswara handled their swords with finesse.

The Gautams were fierce in battle: even when cut by the enemy
they kept on slaughtering.

The passage's focus on the exemplary martial excellence of specific clans also contributes an element of Rajput pride, strengthened by clever homonyms such as *paṛihāra hāra na mānahīṃ* (Pariharas never surrender):

paṛihāra hāra na mānahīṃ, jina koṃ haraṣa ghamasānahīṃ
uddhata sulaṃkī sāhasī, je karata rana meṃ rāha-sī

rajapūta rānā haiṃ saje, jinake khaṛaga rana meṃ jage
haraṣe su hāṛā himmatī, jinakī jagata rana kimmatī

The Pariharas never surrender, taking delight in warfare.
Valorous are the Sulanki braves,
who cut a swathe through the battlefield.

All the Rajput kings have marshaled their forces, swords ready for battle.
The courageous Haras are riled up, whose worldly worth is in battle. [34]

This brings us to another important feature of the work: much of its expressive punch stems from its performative features—the rhythm of its cantering metres, the heavy reliance on alliteration. A virudāvalī was intended for oral recitation, not just for silent reading.

In this excerpt from an extended passage in the *ḍillā* metre we are whisked up into the bustle of activity as the army advances, the thud of elephants and horses creating a deafening ruckus:

ghanaghanāta gajaghaṇṭa umaṅgani
sanasanāta sura-śruti subha aṅgani
ghumaṛi calata ghummata ghana ghorata
suṇḍana nakhata-jhuṇḍa jhakajhorata

calata mataṅgani takki tamaṅkiya
pakhkharaita haya huṛaka humaṅkiya
sira jhārata na sahata mṛga-sobhani
kahuṃ-kahuṃ calata chuvata chiti chobhani

The thrilling clanging of the elephant bells,
the whooshing sounds of their stately limbs!
Rolling and massing like dense thunder clouds,
their upraised trunks rocked the heavens.

The intense, enraged elephants were on the move,
and the armoured horses were chomping at the bit.

Spry forest creatures were no match for their swaying and bucking.
Wherever they went, the earth groaned under their weight.[35]

The harsh velars, retroflexes, and geminate (doubled) consonants effectively convey the jostling of war animals and soldiers. The strategic deployment of alliteration and onomatopoeia was a long-standing practice of Indian poets, particularly for works that were intended to convey the *vīra* (heroic sentiment).[36]

As a rīti poet, Padmakar may have been taking his cues from traditions of *yuddha-varṇanam* (descriptions of war) in Sanskrit poetry. This excerpt from a verse by the acclaimed Sanskrit playwright Bhavabhuti (c. 700) is brimming with sound effects intended precisely to animate the audience with an intensely martial experience. A *vidyādhara* (wise supernatural being) reports vividly to his wife on the fierce combat he witnessed between the heroes Chandraketu and Lava:

jhaṇajjhaṇitakaṅkaṇa
kvaṇitakiṅkiṇīkaṃ dhanur
dhvanadguruguṇāṭanī
kṛtakarālakolāhalam
vitatya kiratoḥ śarān
aviratasphuraccūḍayor
vicitram abhivardhate
bhuvanabhīmam āyodhanam

They bend the bows that sound with ringing
golden bells and raise an awful
ruckus from their heavy strings
twanging at their tips, all the while
showering down arrows as their topknots
swing constantly and the battle
rages with dramatic intensity,
bringing terror to all the world.

And for the welfare of both the war drums
of heaven boom as deeply as stormclouds.[37]

Bhavabhuti's carefully chosen language is extremely effective at conjuring up the twanging of bow strings and the booming of war drums.

There were also, of course, more proximate poetic models. It seems likely that Padmakar's exposure to the Ḍiṅgal traditions of western India would also have conditioned his poetic choices.[38] This excerpt from a set piece in the *bhujaṅg-prayāt* metre renders vivid the armamentarium and terror of war through the Ḍiṅgal technique of *vaiṇa-sagāī* (also *vayan-sagāī*), or structured assonance:

tupakkaiṃ tapakkaiṃ dharakaiṃ mahā haiṃ
pralai-cillikā-sī jhaṛakkaiṃ jahāṃ haiṃ
khaṛakkaiṃ kharī bairi-chātī bhaṛakkaiṃ
saṛakkaiṃ gae sindhu majjai gaṛakkaiṃ

calai gola-golī atolī sanaṅkaiṃ
manau bhauṃra-bhīraiṃ uṛātīṃ bhanaṅkaiṃ
caṛhī āsamānai chaīṃ bepramānaiṃ
mano meghamālā gilai bhāsamānaiṃ

The crack and throb of the guns is great,
like the crashing intensity of the apocalypse.
The harsh clashing pounds the hearts of the enemy,
who escape into the churning ocean.

Countless shots whizz by—
like a swarm of bees buzzing,
they rise up and suddenly shadow the sky,
as though a mass of clouds has swallowed up the light.[39]

Here and elsewhere, the poet uses Ḍiṅgal styles, charged with cacophony, to mimic the sounds of guns and powerful weaponry. We can just about hear the explosions and see the dust clouds rising and may even feel like running for cover.

A rīti poet par excellence, Padmakar is adept at aestheticized description but he also skillfully conveys the human dimensions of war in a brief scene that captures the mood in the enemy's camp. Arjun Singh delivers an inspiring discourse on Kshatriya dharma to his troops, a few brief highlights of which are excerpted here:

These are attestations of kshatriya dharma,
  according to the Vedas and Puranas:
Protecting brahmans and cows, routing enemies,
  and enduring wounds inflicted by weapons.
In this world, a soldier never says 'no' to war, not even in a dream.
When these prime Rajputs fall in battle,
  they have their pick of heavenly brides....
There are two types of men in this world
  who go on to pierce the beautiful disc of the sun:

He who has been following the path of yoga from birth never feels grief,
and he whose passion is roused by the battle
  and fights to the death then and there.
He who speaks or hears of their virtues understands the highest truth....

Over time all wells and tanks get filled in.
  Dense forests and gardens get cut down.
Palaces and splendid homes all collapse—nothing escapes decay.
One day your body and wealth will evaporate.
  Cities and towns will also burn to the ground.
In this world, only two things remain: fame and ignominy.[40]

The passage consists of an interesting combination of lofty maxims and everyday speech. As observed by Dalpat Rajpurohit (this volume), the tone becomes somewhat colloquial, which lends verisimilitude to a scene that Padmakar—a court poet to the opposing side—could never himself have witnessed.

The episode also brings a complex emotional tenor to the text. It sets Arjun Singh up as a worthy opponent of Anupgir and renders poignant the plight of his warriors, who are apprehensive about their imminent fate. Arjun consoles his troops, and rouses them to action using a combination of rhetorical strategies. He reminds them that they are Kshatriyas, a social role that carries responsibilities prescribed by hallowed Sanskrit texts. He speaks of the world's impermanence, while also playing to the soldiers' sense of honour. He tempts them with the rewards that await victorious heroes upon death: celestial damsels and everlasting fame. Arjun Singh's noble attempt to inspire his troops seems absolutely of a piece with the Rajput values that we read about in many a tale from the early modern period and there are also notable parallels from classical India, such as Krishna's famous exhortation to Arjuna to fight, in chapter two of the Bhagavad Gītā.[41] Narrative strategy also surely underlies this interlude: giving voice to the concerns of the opponent builds tension. It may also be that in real life Padmakar felt a certain affection for Anupgir's rival, at whose court he is said to have had a brief sojourn as guru and court poet.[42]

Padmakar's work is, in short, conditioned by both timeless and time-bound features. He had multiple resources for kāvya at his disposal and he used them judiciously to craft his captivating poetics of history.

Conclusion

The *Himmatbahādurvirudāvalī* is an outstanding example of Hindi historical poetry, and one concern here has been to signal some of Padmakar's techniques while situating the work in a larger literary context by drawing attention to various textual layers and their possible sources. A close reading of the work also prompts us to think more about both *Hindi in history* and *history in Hindi*. Kāvya was one of the predominant genres in which premodern Indian history was composed, and the specifically Hindi incarnations of kāvya are as rich as they are underexplored.

Padmakar's *Himmatbahādurvirudāvalī* is both more and less than history in the mainstream sense of the term. We see a combination of historical specificity with more generic motifs drawn from a poet's toolbox—Padmakar was both a historian and kavi, and the two roles were not in the least incommensurable. He describes a historical episode of great import in the local politics of Bundelkhand at the end of the eighteenth century, but he only sometimes recounts the events historically. Often, he was more interested in poetic effectiveness. It is possible to track the shifting textures of the work and to analyse them with some clarity.[43] The opening, we noted, was in a more classical register—both lexically and thematically—which was an excellent choice for highlighting Anupgir's status as a king. Martial themes are also an important element of Padmakar's narrative, as when he invokes the motif of the thirty-six Rajput clans or in Arjun Singh's sermon on Kshatriya dharma delivered to his troops at a pivotal moment. The poem with its vivid battle scenes evinces both its earlier kāvya heritage and a more contemporary Ḍiṅgal poetics, sourced from western India during the early modern period.

We can speak of the work's *style* or *themes*, as is typical of literary analysis, but we can also consider its profile as a historical document, especially with respect to the attention it gives to commemorating the main heroes who took part in the signal battle between Anupgir and his Bundelkhandi rival. Often, this account of local history takes on an aura of epic grandeur that renders it larger than life.

We also see glimpses of yet other genres besides the central dyad of poetry and history stressed here. The *Himmatbahādurvirudāvalī* functions as a *praśasti* (praise address) and has certain noteworthy didactic features; poets have always reminded kings and warriors of their duties. As a virudāvalī with aural features designed to mimic the atmospherics of a battlefield, the poem further functions as a heroic ode that in its recitation may have instilled courage in warriors who were headed to an uncertain fate. The *Himmatbahādurvirudāvalī* is a rich and multilayered text that requires a complex engagement, but this should only inspire us all the more to continue to probe the marvellous poetics of history evident throughout the early modern period in Hindi historical kāvya.

Notes

* I owe many insights about Padmakar's *Himmatbahādurvirudāvalī* to my colleagues William (Vijay) Pinch and Dalpat Rajpurohit, with whom I have been collaborating on a translation. I thank Ronnie Dreyer, my assistant at Columbia University, for her help in transcribing passages from the text and following up with references. I am also grateful to the American Council of Learned Societies, New York, for a grant that partially supported this work.

1. Allison Busch, *Poetry of Kings: The Classical Hindi Literature of Mughal India* (New York: Oxford University Press, 2011), 240–8.

2. Constructions of masculinity and virility loom large in colonial and nationalist appraisals of Indian literature. For a discussion of this problem in relation to Nirala, see Heidi Pauwels, 'Diptych in Verse: Gender Hybridity, Language Consciousness, and National Identity in Nirālā's "Jāgo phir ek Bār"', *Journal of the American Oriental Society* 121, no. 3 (2001): 455–9; cf. Christopher King, *One Language, Two Scripts: The Hindi Movement in Nineteenth Century North India* (New Delhi: Oxford University Press, 1999 [1994]), 33–7.

3. An interested reader might turn to Bhagavandas Gupta, *Mughaloṃ ke antargat bundelkhaṇd ke itihās-saṃskṛti ke Hindī sāhityik srotoṃ kā mūlyāṅkan* (Jhansi: Bhavan Printers and Publishers, 2001); D. B. Kshirsagar and Omprakash Sharma, eds, *Rājasthān kā aitihāsik gadya sāhitya* (Jodhpur: Rajasthan Pracyavidya Pratishthan, 2000); Omprakash Sharma, ed., *Rājasthān ke aitihāsik bhāṣā kāvya* (Jodhpur: Rajasthan Oriental Research Institute, 1999).

4. See William R. Pinch, this volume, and *Warrior Ascetics and Indian Empires* (Cambridge: Cambridge University Press, 2006), 108–47.

5. *Bhojaprabandha* of Ballaladeva, ed. Jagdishlal Shastri (Bankipur [Patna]: Motilal Banarsidass, 1900), v. 120.

6. Basic details about Padmakar's career and larger oeuvre are available in R. S. McGregor, *Hindi Literature from Its Beginnings to the Nineteenth Century* (Wiesbaden: Harrassowitz, 1984), 183; Vishvanathprasad Mishra, 'Sampādakīya', in *Padmākargranthāvalī* (Varanasi: Nagari Pracarini Sabha, 1959), 41–7.

7. I have critiqued this formulation in my paper for the 9th ICEMLNI conference. See Allison Busch, 'Questioning the Tropes about "*Bhakti*" and "*Rīti*" in Hindi Literary Historiography', in *Bhakti in Current Research, 2001–2003*, ed. Monika Horstmann (New Delhi: Manohar, 2006), 33–47.

8. Some of the radical new Hindi adaptations of the kāvya form are discussed in Allison Busch, 'The Classical Past in the Mughal Present: the Brajbhasha Rīti Tradition', in *Innovations and Turning Points: Toward a History of Kāvya Literature*, ed. Gary Tubb, Yigal Bronner, and David Shulman (New Delhi: Oxford University Press, 2014).

9. Ḍiṅgal is a literary dialect-cum-genre of Marwari. A useful recent study is Janet Kamphorst, 'In Praise of Death', PhD diss, Leiden University, 2008, 31–6.

10. See T. Burrow and M. B. Emeneau, *A Dravidian Etymological Dictionary* (Oxford: Clarendon Press, 1984): entry 5414 on Tamil *virutu*, 491; Sheldon Pollock, '*Praśasti*: A Small Note on a Big Topic', in *Rajamahima: C. Rajendran Congratulatory Volume*, ed. N. K. Sundareswaran (Calicut: University of Calicut Press), 30–1.

11. Cynthia Talbot, *Precolonial India in Practice: Society, Region, and Identity in Medieval Andhra* (Oxford: Oxford University Press, 2001), 144.

12. *Sāhityadarpaṇa* of Vishvanatha, ed. Krsnamohan Sastri (Banaras: The Chowkhamba Sanskrit Series Office, 1947–8), v. 6.337.

13. *Camatkāracandrikā* of Vishveshvara, ed. Pandiri Sarasvati Mohan (New Delhi: Meharchand Lachhmandas, 1972), v. 3.60.

14. See, for instance, the striking virudāvalī of Man Singh Kachhwaha composed by Amrit Rai, *Māncarit*, in *Māncaritāvalī: amber ke suprasiddh rājā mānsiṃh ke carit se sambandhit pāṃc rājasthānī racnāoṃ kā saṅkalan*, ed. Gopalnarayan Bahura (Jaipur: Maharaja Savai Man Singh II Sangrahalay, 1990), 2.

15. On the former, see G. N. Bahura, *Literary Heritage of the Rulers of Amber and Jaipur with an Index to the Register of Manuscripts in the Pothikhana of Jaipur (I. Khasmohor collection)* (Jaipur: Maharaja Sawai Man Singh II Museum, 1976), 292, 320; on the latter, see David Buchta, 'Pedagogical Poetry: Didactics and Devotion in Rūpa Gosvāmin's 'Stavamālā'', PhD diss., Department of South Asia Regional Studies, University of Pennsylvania, 2014, 292–312.

16. The other poem (not discussed here) was for Raja Pratap Singh of Jaipur. See *Pratāpsiṃhvirudāvalī* of Padmakar, in *Padmākargranthāvalī*, ed. Vishvanathprasad Mishra (Varanasi: Nagari Pracarini Sabha, 1959).

17. *Himmatbahādurvirudāvalī* of Padmakar, in *Padmākargranthāvalī*, ed. Vishvanathprasad Mishra (Varanasi: Nagari Pracarini Sabha, 1959), vv. 3–4, 6–8, 11–14. Unless otherwise specified, all citations of the *Himmatbahādurvirudāvalī* refer to the Mishra edition. Here and elsewhere, I draw (occasionally with minor modifications) from the draft of a forthcoming translation of *Himmatbahādurvirudāvalī* by Busch, Pinch, and Rajpurohit.

18. Daud Ali, *Courtly Culture and Political Life in Early Medieval India* (Cambridge: Cambridge University Press, 2004), 74–7.

19. Here Padmakar may be taking a page from the book of Keshavdas, who opened his landmark *Rasikpriyā* with just such a verse about Krishna. See the *Rasikpriyā* of Keshavdas, in vol. 1 of *Keśavgranthāval*, ed. Vishvanathprasad Mishra (Allahabad: Hindustani Academy, 1954), v. 1.2; Keshavdas himself had drawn on the Sanskrit rhetorician Rudrabhatta, cf. *Śṛṅgāratilaka* of Rudrabhatta, ed. R. Pischel and trans. Kapildev Pandey (Varanasi: Prachya Prakashan, 1968), v. 1.1.

20. Note how Anupgir is repeatedly compared to Shiva in the passage just cited.

21. For further on this point, see William Pinch, this volume.

22. Julie Scott Meisami, *Medieval Persian Court Poetry* (Princeton: Princeton University Press, 1987), 11–14. The same holds true for Brajbhasha court poets. Keshavdas is a case in point. See Busch, *Poetry of Kings*, 43–55.

23. Padmakar, *Himmatbahādurvirudāvalī*, vv. 15–19.

24. Padmakar, *Himmatbahādurvirudāvalī*, vv. 20–3.

25. Padmakar, *Himmatbahādurvirudāvalī*, vv. 122–6.

26. Padmakar, *Himmatbahādurvirudāvalī*, vv. 132–4. The last line references one commonly held belief that brave fighters attained immortality at the moment of death since divine beauties awaited them with a chariot. Another was the idea that warriors pierced the sun and were absorbed into its light.

27. These are, in order, Gangagiri Dilavarjang, vv. 135–9; Jagat Bahadur, vv. 139–41; Rajgiri, vv. 141–5; Uttamgiri, vv. 146–51; Zulfikar Nawab, vv. 151–3; Umrao Singh, vv. 153–6; Naval Singh Pamar, v. 157; Narind Singh Pamar and Jagat Singh Pamar, v. 158; Buddh Singh Sengar, v. 159; Sarupgiri Kumvar, v. 160; Nidhan Singh Parihar, v. 161; Khuman Singh, v. 162; Hiralal, v. 163; Hindupati Pamar, v. 164–68; Bahadur Singh, vv. 168–70; Dilip Singh Gaur, vv. 170, 172; Niwaj Singh Gaur and Durjan Singh Gaur, v. 171; and Uttam Singh Gaur, v. 172.

28. Padmakar, *Himmatbahādurvirudāvalī*, vv. 192–3.

29. Padmakar, *Himmatbahādurvirudāvalī*, v. 206.

30. See, for instance, verses 207–8. For further analysis of this passage, see the papers by Dalpat Rajpurohit and William Pinch, this volume.

31. This reference occurs in a section about King Harsha (r. 1089–1101) from *Kalhaṇa's Rājataraṅgiṇī: A Chronicle of the Kings of Kaśmīr*, vol. I, Introduction, Books I–VII, translated, with an introduction, commentary, and appendices, by M. A. Stein (New Delhi: Motilal Banarsidass, 1900), vv. 1617–18, p. 393.

32. For a thorough discussion and contextualization of the *Pṛthivīrājrāso*, see Cynthia Talbot, *The Last Hindu Emperor: Prithviraj Chauhan and the Indian Past, 1200–2000* (Cambridge: Cambridge University Press, 2016).

33. Select examples of the literary motif include *Anūp-Prakāś* of Man Kavi (London: OIOC. British Library, Hin.D.9 [a]), vv. 105–16; *Kānhaṛade Prabandh* of Padmanabha, ed. Kantilal Baldevram Vyas (Jodhpur: Rajasthan Oriental Research Institute, 1997), vv. 3.37–3.39; *Vīrsiṃhdevcarit* of Keshavdas, vol. 3 of *Keśavgranthāvalī*, ed. Vishvanathprasad Mishra (Allahabad: Hindustani Academy, 1959), vv. 8.15–8.20. Related examples are Amrit Rai, *Māncarit*, v. 136; *Binhairāsau* of Maheshdas Rao, ed. Saubhagyasingh Shekhavat (Jodhpur: Rajasthan Oriental Research Institute, 1966), v. 61. For further on the thirty-six clans, see Norman P. Ziegler, 'Action, Power, and Service in Rajasthani Culture: A Social History of the Rajputs of Middle Period Rajasthan', PhD diss, Department of History, University of Chicago, 1973, 36–9. Also note the early mention of the thirty-six clans by Colonel James Tod (he called them *rajkula*, or 'royal linages'), who compiled various iterations of the concept from Rajput sources. See James Tod, *Annals and Antiquities of Rajasthan*, vol. 1 (London: Humphrey Milford; Oxford University Press, 1920), 97–145. I am grateful to Cynthia Talbot for the reference.

34. Padmakar, *Himmatbahādurvirudāvalī*, vv. 30–2.

35. Padmakar, *Himmatbahādurvirudāvalī*, vv. 51–2.

36. The poetics of martial description—for instance, a desire to convey *ojas* or 'spirit'—was in fact a topic taken up by several leading Sanskrit rhetoricians, including Anandavardhana, Abhinavagupta, and Mammata, who tied the notion to specific rasas, especially vīra (the heroic), raudra (the terrible), and bībhatsa (the disgusting). See V. Raghavan, *Bhoja's Śṛṅgāraprakāśa* (Madras: Punarvasu, 1963), 348.

37. *Rama's Last Act* of Bhavabhuti, trans. Sheldon Pollock (New York: New York University Press, 2007), 316–17.

38. On Ḍiṅgal poetry, see also Rajpurohit, this volume.

39. Padmakar, *Himmatbahādurvirudāvalī*, vv. 63–4.

40. Padmakar, *Himmatbahādurvirudāvalī*, vv. 101, 105, 109 (drawing on the Lala Bhagvandin edition for v. 109, which includes his reconstruction of line 2).

41. A fruitful comparison can be made with Keshavdas's *Ratanbāvanī* (c. 1583), a poignant martial ode about the Mughal takeover of Orccha. Prince Ratnasena displays exemplary Rajput conduct and delivers a sermon on Kshatriya dharma that has some resonances with Arjun Singh's. This lesser known work of Keshavdas is discussed in Busch, *Poetry of Kings*: pp. 29–32; also see Heidi Pauwels, 'The Saint, the Warlord, and the Emperor: Discourses of Braj Bhakti and Bundelā Loyalty', *Journal of the Economic and Social History of the Orient* 52, no.2 (2009): 196–207.

42. See Mishra, 'Sampādakīya', 42, and Pinch, this volume.

43. Rao, Shulman, and Subrahmanyam have proposed that south Indian historiography of approximately the same period exhibits varying textures, weaving together both literary and more factual elements that were parsed as

such by contemporary audiences. Velcheru Narayana Rao, David Shulman, and Sanjay Subrahmanyam, *Textures of Time: Writing History in South India* (New York: Other Press, 2003).

Bibliography

Primary Sources

Annals and Antiquities of Rajasthan of James Tod, edited by William Crooke. Vol. 1. London: Humphrey Milford; Oxford University Press, 1920.

Anūp-Prakāś of Man Kavi (c. 1800), OIOC. British Library, no. Hin.D.9(a), London.

Bhojaprabandha of Ballaladeva, edited by Jagdishlal Shastri. Bankipur (Patna): Motilal Banarsidass, 1900.

Binhairāsau of Maheshdas Rao, edited by Saubhagyasingh Shekhavat. Jodhpur: Rajasthan Oriental Research Institute, 1966.

Camatkāracandrikā of Vishveshvara, edited by Pandiri Sarasvati Mohan. New Delhi: Meharchand Lachhmandas, 1972.

Himmatbahādurvirudāvalī of Padmakar. In *Padmākargranthāvalī*, edited by Vishvanathprasad Mishra. Varanasi: Nagari Pracarini Sabha, 1959.

Himmatbahādurvirudāvalī of Padmakar. In *Padmākar kṛt himmatbahādur birdāvalī*, edited by Lala Bhagvandin. Varanasi: Nagari Pracarini Sabha, 1930 [?].

Kalhaṇa's Rājataraṅgiṇī: A Chronicle of the Kings of Kaśmīr, translated by M.A. Stein. Vol. 1. New Delhi: Motilal Banarsidass, 1900.

Kānhaṛade Prabandh of Padmanabha, edited by Kantilal Baldevram Vyas. Jodhpur: Rajasthan Oriental Research Institute, 1997.

Māncarit of Amrit Rai. In *Māncaritāvalī: amber ke suprasiddh rājā mānsiṃhke carit se sambandhit pāṃc rājasthānī racnāoṃ kā saṅkalan*, edited by Gopalnarayan Bahura. Jaipur: Maharaja Savai Man Singh II Sangrahalay, 1990.

Pratāpsiṃhvirudāvalī of Padmakar. In *Padmākargranthāvalī*, edited by Vishvanathprasad Mishra. Varanasi: Nagari Pracarini Sabha, 1959.

Rama's Last Act of Bhavabhuti, translated by Sheldon Pollock. New York: New York University Press, 2007.

Rasikpriyā of Keshavdas. In vol. 1 of *Keśavgranthāvalī*, edited by Vishvanathprasad Mishra. Allahabad: Hindustani Academy, 1954.

Sāhityadarpaṇa of Vishvanatha (with the Lakṣmī Commentary), edited by Krsnamohan Sastri. Banaras: The Chowkhamba Sanskrit Series Office, 1947-48.

Śṛṅgāratilaka of Rudrabhatta, edited by R. Pischel, translated by Kapildev Pandey. Varanasi: Prachya Prakashan, 1968.

Vīrsiṃhdevcarit of Keshavdas. In vol. 3 of *Keśavgranthāvalī*, edited by Vishvanathprasad Mishra. Allahabad: Hindustani Academy, 1959.

Secondary Sources

Ali, Daud. Courtly *Culture and Political Life in Early Medieval India*. Cambridge: Cambridge University Press, 2004.

Bahura, Gopalnarayan. *Literary Heritage of the Rulers of Amber and Jaipur with an Index to the Register of Manuscripts in the Pothikhana of Jaipur (I. Khasmohor Collection)*. Jaipur: Maharaja Sawai Man Singh II Museum, 1976.

Buchta, David. 'Pedagogical Poetry: Didactics and Devotion in Rūpa Gosvāmin's *Stavamālā*', PhD diss., Department of South Asia Regional Studies, University of Pennsylvania, 2014.

Burrow, T. and M. B. Emeneau. *A Dravidian Etymological Dictionary*. Oxford: Clarendon Press, 1984.

Busch, Allison. 'Questioning the Tropes about "*Bhakti*" and "*Rīti*" in Hindi Literary Historiography'. In *Bhakti in Current Research, 2001–2003*, edited by Monika Horstmann. New Delhi: Manohar, 2006.

———. *Poetry of Kings: The Classical Hindi Literature of Mughal India*. New York: Oxford University Press, 2011.

———.'The Classical Past in the Mughal Present: The Brajbhasha Rīti Tradition'. In *Innovations and Turning Points: Toward a History of Kāvya Literature*, edited by Yigal Bronner, David Shulman, and Gary Tubb. New Delhi: Oxford University Press, 2014.

Gupta, Bhagavandas. *Mughaloṃ ke antargat bundelkhaṇḍ ke itihās-saṃskṛti ke hindī sāhityik srotoṃ kā mūlyāṅkan*. Jhansi: Bhavan Printers and Publishers, 2001.

Kamphorst, Janet. 'In Praise of Death', PhD diss., Leiden University, Leiden, 2008.

King, Christopher. *One Language, Two Scripts: The Hindi Movement in Nineteenth Century North India*. Delhi: Oxford University Press, 1999 [1994].

Kshirsagar, D. B. and Omprakash Sharma, eds. *Rājasthān kāa itihāsik gadya sāhitya*. Jodhpur: Rajasthan Pracyavidya Pratishthan, 2000.

McGregor, R. S. *Hindi Literature from Its Beginnings to the Nineteenth Century*. Wiesbaden: Harrassowitz, 1984.

Meisami, Julie Scott. *Medieval Persian Court Poetry*. Princeton: Princeton University Press, 1987.

Mishra, Vishvanathprasad. 'Sampādakīya'. In *Padmākargranthāvalī*. Varanasi: Nagari Pracarini Sabha, 1959.

Pauwels, Heidi. 'Diptych in Verse: Gender Hybridity, Language Consciousness, and National Identity in Nirālā's "Jāgo phir ek Bār"'. *Journal of the American Oriental Society* 121, no. 3 (2001): 449–81.

———. 'The Saint, the Warlord, and the Emperor: Discourses of Braj Bhakti and Bundelā Loyalty'. *Journal of the Economic and Social History of the Orient* 52, no. 2 (2009): 187–228.

Pinch, William R. *Warrior Ascetics and Indian Empires*. Cambridge: Cambridge University Press, 2006.

Pollock, Sheldon. '*Praśasti*: A Small Note on a Big Topic'. In *Rajamahima: C. Rajendran Congratulatory Volume*, edited by N. K. Sundareswaran. Calicut: University of Calicut Press, 2013, 21–39.

Raghavan, V. *Bhoja's Śṛṅgāraprakāśa*. Madras: Punarvasu, 1963.

Rao, Velcheru Narayana, David Shulman, and Sanjay Subrahmanyam. *Textures of Time: Writing History in South India*. New York: Other Press, 2003.

Sharma, Omprakash, ed. *Rājasthān ke aitihāsik bhāṣā kāvya*. Jodhpur: Rajasthan Oriental Research Institute, 1999.

Talbot, Cynthia. *Precolonial India in Practice: Society, Region, and Identity in Medieval Andhra*. Oxford: Oxford University Press, 2001.

———. *The Last Hindu Emperor: Prithviraj Chauhan and the Indian Past, 1200–2000*. Cambridge: Cambridge University Press, 2016.

Ziegler, Norman P. *Action, Power, and Service in Rajasthani Culture: A Social History of the Rajputs of Middle Period Rajasthan*, PhD diss., Department of History, University of Chicago, 1973.

14

DALPAT RAJPUROHIT*

Making the War Come Alive

Ḍiṅgal Poetry and Padmakar's *Himmatbahādurvirudāvalī*

The *Himmatbahādurvirudāvalī*[1] of Padmakar Bhatt (1753–1833) is a poetic tale of a war fought in 1792 in Bundelkhand between the armies of Anupgir Gosain and Arjun Singh Pamar.[2] Chronologically the *Himmatbahādurvirudāvalī* is the first of the eleven texts written by Padmakar. The poem sings the glories of Anupgir (d. 1804), also known as Himmat Bahadur, a major warlord and ascetic in the second half of the eighteenth century.[3] Also depicted in this poem are the disciples and nephews of Anupgir and other warriors whom he patronized. Padmakar takes great interest in describing bards, war drums, weapons, cannons, swords, armours, elephants, and horses. He includes, in addition to these worldly elements, some supernatural characters who appear on the battlefield when the war ends, including the goddess Caṇḍī as well as *yoginīs*, *baitālinī* (female vampires), and *bhūt* (ghouls) who dance, eat human flesh, drink the blood of the dead, and collect skulls to make a garland for Lord Shiva.

The *Himmatbahādurvirudāvalī* contains five distinct sections, which are each devoted to the description of a particular subject. The first section consists of the traditional *maṅgalācaraṇ* (benediction), as well as panegyric verses about Anupgir which evoke the concept of *navrasa* (the nine sentiments of poetry) and the glories of the thirty-six clans of the Kshatriyas. The second section describes the armies of Anupgir advancing towards war, with kettledrums sounding and bards singing the praises of the warriors. The third portion of the text catalogues the strength of various kinds of cannons and guns. The fourth and largest piece of the text chronicles the major events of the war. It describes the warriors and their tactics, presents discourses on Rajput honour—*swāmī-dharma*, the traditional conception of martial service to an overlord—and the inevitability of death. The fifth and last section details various kinds of swords and the final battle between Anupgir and Arjun Singh. The poem concludes by describing Arjun's death and Anupgir's victory.

Padmakar thus structures the *Himmatbahādurvirudāvalī* as a *prabandh kāvya*, or long-form poem, much like other Brajbhasha *carit kāvyas* (description of great deeds) of the early modern period. Padmakar not only creatively uses generic features for literary and performative purposes but also fashions his Gosain patron Anupgir as a Kshatriya king. *Virudāvalī/birdāvalī* literally means 'string of titles'. It is a praise-poem of a king which situates that king in a glorious genealogy. In most cases they are the glories of the Kshatriya clans or lineages. However, as the poem's title suggests, Padmakar sings the glories of a warrior ascetic who is not a Kshatriya but a Gosain Brahmin. Padmakar goes on to depict him as a king like Indra, an incarnation of Shiva, a generous patron of poets, and a protector of Hindu dignity. In order to fashion his patron as a Rajput king, Padmakar gives the *Himmatbahādurvirudāvalī* a carit-kāvya-like structure and incorporates most of the elements present in the tradition of historical poetry in Hindi as well as in Sanskrit.[4]

Padmakar and his *Himmatbahādurvirudāvalī* stand at a significant historical, literary, and linguistic juncture. The standard modern literary histories mention that, on the one hand, classical Brajbhasha literature was coming to its apex with the writings of Padmakar and, on the other, the very same period saw the rise of Khari Boli literature.[5] In this traditional understanding, Brajbhasha literature was beginning to be considered archaic or medieval in contrast to the self-consciously modern literature of Khari Boli Hindi. In contrast to this narrative, this chapter shows that Brajbhasha literary culture was as strong and as pluralistic in its linguistic registers at the turn of the nineteenth century as it was in its earlier history by exploring some linguistic, literary, and performative aspects of the *Himmatbahādurvirudāvalī*.

This chapter studies the literary history of war descriptions in north Indian vernacular literatures. It explores the interaction and influence of the Ḍiṅgal, or Marwari, poetic tradition—well regarded for its alliterative, onomatopoeic and pictorial descriptions of wars—with other vernacular literary traditions such as Brajbhasha and Awadhi. Taking linguistic and literary elements of war descriptions from Sanskrit and Apabharamsha, the Ḍiṅgal poetic tradition modified them according to its own performative need and local song genres. When Brajbhasha carit kāvya tradition was developing under the Mughal and Rajput domain, it had Ḍiṅgal poetic tradition to look for certain genres. Taking the kāvya elements from the long-established Sanskrit tradition, Brajbhasha kāvya tradition inherited the style of war descriptions from Ḍiṅgal. Exploring the intertextual topos of Ḍiṅgal into Brajbhasha and Awadhi literary traditions, this chapter shows the interaction of these poetic traditions among themselves. By doing this, I question the notion in the modern historiography of Hindi and Rajasthani literatures where these traditions are often described as mutually disconnected.[6] Including this, I argue that the performance of virudāvalīs by communities such as Charans and Bhats of Rajasthan—bards or record keepers of consanguinities and singer of encomiums—as seen from the sixteenth-century influential Brajbhasha (or Pingal) poem the *Prithvirāj Rāso* to the eighteenth-century poem the *Himmatbahādurvirudāvalī* of Padmakar are the result of taking the Ḍiṅgal poetic features into Brajbhasha carit kāvya tradition. The following section discusses how the virudāvalīs were performed in two early bhāṣā texts—the *Prithvirāj Rāso* attributed to Chand Bardai and the sixteenth-century Awadhi *bhakti* poem the *Rāmcaritmānas* of Tulsidas.

Performing the *Virudāvalīs*: Two Early Examples from Hindi Literature

In the early vernacular court poetry such as the influential *Prithvirāj Rāso*,[7] the poet Chand Bardai appears as a court poet of this magnificent Brajbhasha kāvya and also a Bhat of Prithviraj Chauhan's consanguinities. On one hand, the *rāso* genre contains courtly kāvya features from Sanskrit literature and, on the other, it contains the metrical and linguistic features of Apabhramsha as well as some performative aspects related with the Bhat tradition. In the following example, the virudāvalī is performed in a warlike situation at an enemy's (Muhammad Ghauri) court to inspire the poet's patron-king Prithviraj Chauhan, who has been captured and blinded, for the final round of combat:

ghat siṃci vīr pāvakka jhar, rīs ravat tan prajjaryau
kahi bhaṭṭ birdāvālī, dūt rāj raj sambharyau[8]

The deceit watered the fire of the brave (Prithviraj),
Anger burst through the king's body.
The bard (Chand) recited the birdāvalī,
And the king remembered the envoy from his own soil and kingdom.

The popularity of Chand Bardai and the rāso genre needs to be better understood. Chand Bardai was celebrated greatly among the emerging community of court poets at Mughal and Rajput courts.[9] The legacy of the poet Chand inspired the creation of further rāso kāvya such as the influential *Hammīr Rāso* (seventeenth century[?]).[10] The Bhat community of Rajasthan considers Chand Bardai to be their ancestor and as a community has produced a large amount of historical poetry in Hindi.[11]

Another early Hindi source for the performance of the virudāvalīs is the *Rāmcaritmānas* (1574 CE), in which Tulsidas depicts the *rāj sabhā* (royal court) of Janak. He describes the Bhats or *bandījan* (bards) as a part of this rāj sabhā. The bandījan here recite the virudāvalī of King Janak on the auspicious occasion of Sita's *svayaṃvar* (selection of a husband):

tab bandī jan janak bolāye, birdāvalī kahat cali āye
kaha nripu jāi kahahu pan morā, cale bhāṭ hiyaṃ harṣu na thorā[12]

Then Janak called the bards,
They came while reciting the birdāvalī.
'Go and tell my pledge to the kings!'
The bards left with no little joy in their hearts.

When Padmakar describes Anupgir as an ideal Kshatriya king and his army as a typical Kshatriya army, he employs virudāvalī-like features.[13] He also describes the Bhat or bandījan who sing the virudāvālī at the time of war:

bandī jana virāvalī bullahi, sunat subhaṭṭ drigkamal praphullahi[14]

The bards sang the virudāvalī,
[And] hearing it the lotus-eyes of the great warriors bloomed.

Given that many Hindi court poets proudly relate themselves to Chand Bardai and his poetic legacy, which exerts great influence on Hindi historical kāvya, raises a noteworthy question: How did the circulation of vernacular poetry inspire creation and lead to interaction between the vernacular literary cultures such as Brajbhasha and Awadhi? In the following pages, I discuss the Ḍiṅgal literary tradition of western Rajasthan, which was established in the early modern period. It had a clear historical orientation and influenced the courtly kāvya idiom of later Hindi poetry, including Padmakar's *Himmatbahādurvirudāvalī*.

War Description in Ḍiṅgal Style: An Intertextual Topos in Hindi Historical Poetry

Padmakar describes the historical events in the *Himmatbahādurvirudāvalī* when Anupgir sets off on his *muhim* (military campaigns) to Bundelkhand in the 1790s.[15] Anupgir's conquest of this area, especially his attacks against Arjun Singh, the pride of Bundelas, makes him a maharaja-like figure. Padmakar writes that after his powerful campaign around Delhi, Anupgir reaches Bundelkhand. Historically, penetrating the fort of Ajaigarh and defeating Arjun Singh was the main challenge for Anupgir in this area. He first captures the state of Datia and then goes for combat with Arjun Singh, who rules (*amal karai*) at Ajaygarh. He sets up his camp on the River Ken and after consulting his *jyotiṣi* (astrologer) sets a date for the initial siege. Once Padmakar finishes this episode, he painstakingly describes the advancing of the armies armed with cannons, guns, and hundreds of warriors. Finally, he describes the war itself. We see some distinctive linguistic features in these descriptions, namely single consonantal gemination and frequent use of retroflex sounds—both of these features are the prime characteristics of Hindi war poetry. The gemination relates to the intervocalic stops on a single consonant:

> ān phirat cahuṃ ca**kk**a dhāk tha**kk**an gaṛh dhu**kk**ahiṃ
> lu**kk**ahiṃduvan digant jāi jahṅ tahṃ tan mu**kk**ahiṇ[16]
>
> [His] fame spreads in all directions [and] so many forts are terrified of his notoriety.
> The enemy hide themselves going far away; here and there they place their bodies.
>
> kari kha**gga** ja**ggi** uda**ggi** ati ari va**gga** āe umṛi kai
> gaj ghaṭ ni māhiṅ mahābalī ghālat ha**tth**ārani ghumṛi kai

prithu **ritti nitta** suvi**tta** dai jag ji**tti** ki**tti** Anūp kī
var varniye virudāvalī himmat bahādur bhūp kī

Having propitiated his blade, [he] rushed forward to face the advancing enemy.
The powerful one swirled [into the fray] and stabbed the elephants to the quick.
Like Prithu, [who] always bestowed much wealth and won the world, his fame spread.
The virudāvalī of King Himmat Bahādur is described (herein).

The consonantal gemination[17](ca**kka**, kha**gga**, and ri**tti**, and so on) increases when Padmakar summarizes a chapter, often with a conscious use of *chappay* and *harigītikā* metres. The last two lines of the aforementioned verse are used as a refrain throughout the text. By employing this technique of keeping two long metres at the end of each section in the poem, Padmakar gives the *Himmatbahādurvirudāvalī* a performative character through which the reader can summarize the previous episode and prepare for the next one. The harigītikā metre is used in the same fashion—to summarize what has already been said—in the *Rāmcaritmānas*.[18]

Padmakar frequently uses retroflex letters along with the consonantal gemination. In his description of the war fought in 1792, Padmakar focused on describing the sounds made by cannons and guns. This description of cannons and guns is unique because traditionally in war poems bows, arrows, swords, and lances were described. The increasing use of cannons and guns in wars could be the reason that Padmakar greatly emphasized their sounds. Proving his firm grasp on *bhāṣā* (vernaculars), Padmakar uses multiple onomatopoeic verbs—rarely repeated in the poem—to represent various sounds. By rhyming internally with alliterative retroflex sounds, Padmakar creates an aural effect in which the reader can hear the sounds of the battleground:

tupakkai taṛakkai dhaṛakkai mahā haiṅ,
    pralai cillikā sī jhaṛakkai jahāṅ haiṅ
khaṛakkaiṅ kharīṅ vairī chātī bhaṛakkai,
    saṛakkaiṅ gaye sindhu majjai gaṛakkaiṅ[19]

The crack and throb of the guns is great
Like the lightning flashes of the apocalypse.
The harsh clashing pounded the hearts of the enemy,
[Who] escape into the churning ocean.

These linguistic features in the war descriptions are not particular to the *Himmatbahādurvirudāvalī* and can be seen throughout Hindi historical poetry. Interestingly, single consonantal gemination and frequent use of retroflex sounds can also be seen in the 'Laṅkā-Kāṇḍ' (the chapter of Lanka) of the *Rāmcaritmānas* where Tulsidas depicts the war between Ram and Ravan:

> jambuka nikar kaṭakkaṭa kaṭṭhiṃ, khāhi huahim aghaim dapattahim
> koṭinha ruṇḍ muṇḍ binu dollahiṃ, sīs pare mahi jay jay bollahiṃ[20]
>
> There were jackals eating the dead,
> Making noises, attacking each other.
> Billions of trunks were rolling without heads,
> While others lay on the battlefield intoning their chants of victory.

Among the linguistic features that we have seen in the war descriptions of the *Himmatbahādurvirudāvalī* (Brajbhasha) and *Rāmcaritmānas (*Awadhi), the consonantal gemination was historically an Apabhramsha feature. Consonantal gemination, in the process of prosodic alteration, is one of the main linguistic features of Apabhramsha literature.[21] However, the question arises as to why it became typical of Hindi martial poetry? Did Brajbhasha and Awadhi adopt it from Apabhramsha or were they transmitted through another vernacular tradition? Here the Ḍiṅgal poetic tradition, which arises at the same time as Brajbhasha and Awadhi, and its acceptance in the martial poetry genres in Hindi, is to be noted since scholars have noticed the linguistic features discussed earlier prominently in Ḍiṅgal.

While working on the Apabhramsha poem *Sandeśrāsak* (thirteenth century) of Abdul Rahaman, the renowned Apabhramsha scholar Harivallabh Bhayani writes about the gemination of consonants for the reason of prosodic alteration in Apabhramsha and its influence on Ḍiṅgal poetry:

> It may be remarked en passant that later on the tendency of consonantal gemination for metrical reasons noted above [in case of *Sandeśrāsak*] becomes stronger and stronger so much that it comes to form a striking characteristic of the language of *Diṅgala* (old Mārvaṛī poetic) literature cultivated by the bards of Rājputānā.[22]

One of the reasons that consonantal gemination became a characteristic of Ḍiṅgal poetry is that the Apabhramsha metres, mostly *dūhā* (*dohā*), chappay, and *paddharī*, were very popular among Ḍiṅgal poets. Composing in chappay, paddharī, and dūhā belongs to the same tradition of Apabhramsha poetry as these phonetic pyrotechnics. The two enter in Ḍiṅgal poetry together. However, Ḍiṅgal poets regionalized them by modifying these metres according to their local song genre called *vayaṇsagāī*.[23] Vayaṇsagāī[24] is a distinctive kind of alliteration—not found in Sanskrit, Prakrit, or in Apabhramsha literature—and the Charans and Bhats of Rajasthan, who were the leading purveyors of Ḍiṅgal poetry, were an authority on it. From the sixteenth century onwards, Ḍiṅgal poetry starts to cross the trajectories of Brajbhasha, Sanskrit, and some dialects of eastern Rajasthan such as Dhundhari, since Ḍiṅgal was a poetic tradition of the Marwar region of western Rajasthan. The circulation of Ḍiṅgal poetry within and outside Rajasthan had a huge impact on the historical poetry of Hindi. Particularly important to mention here is the popular sixteenth-century Ḍiṅgal poem on love and war called *Krisan Rukmaṇī rī velī* (The Vine of Krishna and Rukmani) by Prithviraj (Prithiraj) Rathore (d. 1600) of Bikaner.[25] Prithviraj was famous as a poet of the period, being praised and eulogized in multiple religious anthologies, hagiographies, and Mughal chronicles.[26] The Ḍiṅgal poem *Krisan Rukmaṇī rī velī* by Prithviraj gained great fame among Brajbhasha, Dhundhari (a dialect of Rajasthan), and Sanskrit poets, as is evident from the circulation of its manuscripts and the number of Brajbhasha, Dhundhari, and Sanskrit commentaries on the text. Prithviraj depicts a war among Krishna, Shishupal, and Rukman in Ḍiṅgal vayaṇsagāī style. He suggests that one needs to consult with Charans and Bhats and other language experts (*bhākhā-catur*) in addition to well-versed poets (*sukavi*) in order to understand his poem.[27] Here, Prithviraj is not only indicating the authority of the Charans and Bhats[28] in describing wars, but is also bringing the localized Ḍiṅgal poetic tradition of Marwar to the notice of the Brajbhasha poets who were being patronized by the Rajput states under Mughal domain.[29] These Rajput states were becoming centres of a widely circulating historical poetry in Brajbhasha.

From the late sixteenth century, we see instances of Brajbhasha poets adopting the Ḍiṅgal vayaṇsagāī style to describe wars. In his biography of Mansingh Kachvaha of Amer (*Māncarit* c.1600), Narottam Kavi's description of the war of Haldighati is informed by this style.[30] The Braj poet Vrind (1643–1723)—patronized by the Mughal emperor Aurangzeb, his successor Muazzam (Bahadurshah), and Raj Singh of Kishangarh—wrote two historical poems in Brajbhasha called the *Vacanikā* (1707[?]) and the *Satya sarūp pūpak* (1707), which describe the wars of succession among Shahjahan's and Aurangzeb's sons respectively. Both of the poems describe wars entirely in the Ḍiṅgal style of vayaṇsagāī; observe this example from the *Satya sarūp pūpak*, in which the repeated syllables have been emphasized:

> **sa**bai sūr sāvanta rāvanta **sa**tyaṅ
> **la**rai loha sauṅ choha sauṅ **la**tpattha
> **du**taṅg autaṅga turaṅga **da**baṭṭai
> **bi**kaṭṭa gaṭaṅ gajja ghaṭṭaṅ **bi**ghaṭṭai[31]
>
> All brave warriors and kings
> Fight passionately with their weapons and body smeared in blood.
> Horses from both sides attacked forcefully,
> Elephants broke each other's tusks.

The Ḍiṅgal method of describing wars was appropriated in Brajbhasha because the tradition concentrated mainly on martial value, a subject that lent itself to alliterative, onomatopoetic, and pictorial description or poetics.

While the tradition of Brajbhasha historical poetry (including rāso literature) hardly neglected war, it also contained other typical kāvya elements such as the *nagar-varṇan* (city description), *nava-rasa* (the nine poetic sentiments), and descriptions of the *ṣaḍ-ritu* (six seasons). The language of the rāso is often described as Brajbhasha (or Pingal); however, these rāsos have some Ḍiṅgal influence as many of them were written in Rajasthan. From the seventeenth century, we find rāsos written in Ḍiṅgal as well. There was a magnificent rāso—*Sagat Rāso*—written by a seventeenth-century Charan poet, Girdhar Ashiya.[32] This rāso contains none of the elements found in the Brajbhasha rāso tradition such as the nagar-varṇaṇ, nava-rasa, or ṣaḍ-ritu and only describes the wars fought by the Shakti Singh, the younger brother of Rana Pratap Singh. It proves how the Ḍiṅgal tradition invested much into the war description and modified the established Brajbhasha genres such as rāsos according to their need. Some Brajbhasha rāsos, such as the *Khummāṇ Rāso*, follow the Ḍiṅgal vayaṇsagāī style in their descriptions of war.[33] These examples suggest that the descriptions of war in the Ḍiṅgal style were considered a topos in Brajbhasha historical poetry. It can, therefore, be argued that distinctive linguistic features such as consonantal gemination and frequent use of retroflex sounds found in Brajbhasha historical poetry—especially in descriptions of combat and in metres such as the chappay, *padhharī*, and *dūhā*—were an effect of mixing Ḍiṅgal features into other martial poetry traditions of Hindi. These definitely influenced the eighteenth-century Brajbhasha poet Padmakar, who was also patronized by kings in Rajasthan. The following section describes the poetic techniques and creative use of bhāṣā by Padmakar in crafting the *Himmatbahādurvirudāvalī*. It brings his *bhāv-mūrti-vidhān* (creating the images of emotions) into discussion for which he is well known in the history of Hindi literature.

The *Bhāv-Mūrti-Vidhān* of Padmakar

While appropriating these generic features to give his poem a performative aspect and create aural effects, Padmakar also presents a didactic account of war for a Brajbhasha-knowing audience. For Padmakar, literary purposes and the need to tailor his poetic style to individual contexts were the main factors behind word choice and adaptation of certain styles. Whether he is describing a war in progress or the sentiments of warriors, Padmakar not only captures the specific context but also creates moving images of the situation through the creative use of language:

> sar bhare tarkas aru kamān mahān ghoṛe saum̥ lagī
> tihim̥ samaya kī vah ān disā disān viṣai jagī
> tahm̥ harakhi har har harakhi har har harakhi har har kari pillyau
> vah kahani har hark kī sudhuni suni jigar satrun kau hillyau[34]

> A quiver full of arrows and a great bow were strapped on to a horse.
> The (clamor of their) glorious approach spread and awakened all the direction points.
> There the sound of 'harkhi har har harkhi har har harkhi har har' rippled through the air.
> The sound of the 'harhar' chant weakened the liver of the enemy.

Padmakar draws attention to the fact that his hero and patron Anupgir is a Shaivite warrior and so are many of his disciples and relatives. In the verse given above, he captures the enthusiasm of these warriors in chanting the slogan *har-har* while attacking the enemy. This slogan gives Anupgir's army a unique identity among eighteenth-century warrior clans. The other warrior ascetics I am thinking of are the Rāmānandīs and the Dādūpanthīs, which, of course, would not enchant this Shavaite slogan. In order to express both of these—the aural effect of chanting 'har-har' and the enthusiasm of the Shaivite ascetics—Padmakar creatively uses the verb *harakhanā*. This verb contains both *har* (Shiva) and *harakh* (from the Sanskrit *harṣa*—meaning joy, enthusiasm) and is skillfully integrated into the slogan to create a powerful effect.

In the following verse, Chandi (skillfully rhymed with *khaṇḍī*, 'tax' in the Budelkhandi dialect) comes to the battlefield with yoginīs, baitālinīs, and bhūts. This marks the triumphant end of the war, and each line gives a moving image of the goddess' actions:

> Kil kilkata caṇḍī lahi nij khaṇḍi umaṛi umaṇḍi harakhati hai
> saṅga lai baitālini dai dai tālani majjā jālani karakhati hai
> jugganani jamātī hiya harkhatīṅ khad khad khatim masan kau
> rudhiran sauṃ bhari bhari khappar dhari dhari nacatī kari kari hāsan kau[35]

> Chandi screeched, she took her piece,
>   she swelled and radiated with pleasure.
> She brought her demon-girl-gang, they clapped to the beat,
>   cracked-chewed the bone marrow.
> The gathering of yoginīs, [full of] grim delight,
>   gorged themselves on the meat.
> Filling the skull bowls with blood, they reveled and danced about.

Summoning Chandi on the battlefield is common in Hindi historical poetry but the way Padmakar presents it—the noise, the screams, the clapping, the cracking of bones, the chewing, the onomatopoeic alliteration *khad-khad* (the sound of eating warm flesh), the laughing and dancing—is a significant innovation on the trope. In a long description where Arjun Singh is telling his warriors about the inevitability of death and the need to adhere to Rajput codes of honour, whatever the cost, the language is idiomatic and gives a feeling of colloquial speech:

> ab ran tajai jo hūjiye it ajar amar jahān maiṅ
> tau choṛi hathiyārin dharahi kaha kaṛhat hai ghamsān maiṃ
> jab ek din marnau mukarrar janam pāi sunījiye
> tātaiṃ galin dar galin hūṃ jas vrithā malin na kījiye[36]

> When you depart the battlefield [in death], [then] you become immortal here in the world.
> So if you renounce your weapon, what will you wield in battle?
> Listen, once you gain birth into this world, it is a given that you will die.
> So do not pointlessly sully your name across all the highways and byways.

Conclusion

The rise of historical kāvya tradition in Brajbhasha took many elements from its vernacular predecessor such as the Ḍiṅgal poetry, written and performed mostly by Charans and Bhats. The Ḍiṅgal tradition presents the metrical and linguistic discourse prominent in the Apabhramsha literature and also takes elements from the Sanskrit kāvya tradition; however, it modifies them according to its performative need and local song genres. Within the Sanskrit prabandha-kāvya-like structure for his Brajbhasha poem, Padmakar employs elements that are closely associated with vernacular literature which emerged in the early modern period and, in particular, within the Ḍiṅgal tradition of Rajasthan. Ḍiṅgal poetry had a strong martial ethos, a clear historical orientation, and a special repertoire of poetic techniques. For many vernacular poets, writing on a historical or martial theme entailed using the techniques of Ḍiṅgal poetry. For Padmakar in particular, these themes presented him with opportunities for innovation within the framework of a traditional generic topos—not just another exercise in the old *vīra-rasa* style. The very linguistically fluid nature of Brajbhasha gave Padmakar an opportunity to craft his poem according to the need of various descriptions and performative purposes, which reminds us of the vibrant Brajbhasha literary culture at the dawn of colonialism in India. Besides its descriptions of weapons and its accounts of historical personalities, the *Himmatbahādurvirudāvalī* narrates a major recent war.

Notes

* I am grateful to Allison Busch, Vijay Pinch, Andrew Ollett, and Yogi Trivedi for their comments and criticism on an earlier draft of this chapter.

1. Padmakar, *Padmākar kṛt himmatbahādur birdāvalī*, ed. Lala Bhagvandin (Varanasi: Nagari Pracharini Sabha, 1930 [?]). All dates are in Common Era unless otherwise noted.

2. Padmakar, *Himmatbahādur birdāvalī*, vv. 22–3.

3. Historians Jadunath Sarkar (1950) and William Pinch (2006) have written extensively on the warrior ascetics, including Anupgir Gosain.

4. Allison Busch writes about this in great detail; see her chapter in this volume.

5. Ramchandra Shukla, *Hindi sāhitya kā itihās* (Ghaziabad: K.L. Pachauri Publishing, 2002). Shukla considers the beginning of *ādhunik kāl* (modern period) with the emergence of Khari Boli Hindi prose. Although the date he

sets for the modern period is 1843, he writes that the era of Khari Boli Hindi prose started around 1800 with texts produced at the Fort William College in Calcutta and a few texts written before that time.

6. Motilal Menariya writes two separate literary histories of Ḍiṅgal (Marwari) as *Rājasthānī bhāshā aur sāhitya* and Brajbhasha (Pingal) as *Rājasthān kā pingal sāhitya.* Ramchandra Shukla does not give Ḍiṅgal literature any place in his influential history of Hindi literature. He states that 'the literary form of the pure Rajasthani language mixed with Apabhramsha was called *ḍiṅgal.* Therefore we can only discuss the texts written in Pingal (Brajbhasha) in the history of Hindi literature' (Shukla, *Hīndī sāhitya kā itihās,* 21). We assume from Shukla's statement that Ḍiṅgal literature has no relation with Hindi literature.

7. The date of creation of the *Prithvirāj Rāso* is highly debated; however, written records show the existence of some poetry about Prithvirāj Chauhān in Hindi attributed to Chand Baliddiya or Chand Bardai as early as the fifteenth century. Both the editors of *Prithvirāj Rāso,* Hazari Prasad Dvivedi and Namwar Singh, establish the existence of some poetry about Prithviraj written by poet Chand Baliddiya (Chand Bardai) on the basis of a fifteenth-century text *Purātan prabandh saṅgrah,* which contains two verses of Chand Baliddiya about Prithviraj. They also reject the existence of the poem *Prithvirāj Rāso* in the form in which it is found today before the period of the Mughal emperor Akbar. See *Prithvirāj Rāso,* ed. H. P. Dwivedi and Namwar Singh (Allahabad: Sahitya Bhawan, 1998), 178.

8. Dvivedi and Singh, *Prithvirāj Rāso,* 164

9. In 1585 CE while writing the biography of Mansingh Kachwaha, the *Māncarit,* Amrit Rai invokes the blessings of Chand Baliddiya. Refer to *Māncharitāvalī,* ed. G.N. Bahura (Jaipur: Sawai Mansingh II Museum Trust, City Palace, 1990), 2. Also, see *Cand chand barnan kī mahimā* (A Praise of Chand's Poetry) attributed to Kavi Gang (Bhat), who is believed to have lived at the courts of the Mughal emperors Akbar and Jahangir. This poem—whose authenticity is questioned along with other poetry attributed to Gang—places Chand Bardai and his *Prithvirāj Rāso* at a place of very high prestige in Mughal court culture. See *Kavi gaṅg racnāvalī,* ed. Bate Krishna (Jodhpur: Rajasthani Granthagar, 2009). Whether this poem was written by Gang or not, it shows the prominence of Chand Bardai and the *Prithvirāj Rāso* within the Bhat community of Rajasthan.

10. Mahesh Kavi, *Hammīr Rāso,* ed. Agarcand Nahta (Jodhpur: Rajasthan Oriental Research Institute, 1982). See dohā 19 where Mahesh Kavi invokes Chand Bardai.

11. Bhati Narayan Singh, *Prācīn ḍiṅgal gīt sāhitya* (Jodhpur: Rajasthani Granthagar, 1989), 235.

12. Tulsidas, *Srī Rāmacaritmānas* (Gorakhpur: Gita Press, 2002), 213.

13. Padmakar, *Himmatbahādur birdāvalī, hakal cand* 2–3.

14. Padmākar, *Himmatbahādur birdāvalī*, 10. All translations from the *Himmatbahādur birdāvalī* in this chapter are from a book in progress, provisionally entitled *Poems for a Warlord*, by Allison Busch, William Pinch, and Dalpat Rajpurohit.

15. For Anupgir's military career during this period, see William R. Pinch, *Warrior Ascetics and Indian Empires* (Cambridge: Cambridge University Press, 2006), Chapter 3.

16. Padmakar, *Himmatbahādur birdāvalī*, 7.

17. Harivallabh Bhayani defines consonantal gemination as: 'It relates to the intervocalic stops which otherwise are elided in middle Indo-Aryan, *paṇḍit= paṇḍitta, manmath= maṇmattha*' (Abdul Rahaman, *Sandeśrāsaka*, ed. Harivallabh Bhayani [Ahmadabad: Prakrit Text Society, 1999], 6).

18. Philip Lutgendorf writes about the similar use of harigītikā in the *Rāmcaritmānas*. Refer to Lutgendorf, *The Life of a Text: Performing the Rāmcaritmānas of Tulsīdās* (California: University Press California, 1991), 16.

19. Padmakar, *Himmatbahādur birdāvalī*, 11.

20. Tulsidas, *Sri Rāmcaritmānas*, 788.

21. Rahaman, *Sandeśrāsaka*, 3. Bhayani notes that the gemination of simple consonants is done in two ways in Apabhramsha: either in the seam of compounds *maṇmattha* and/or in the body of the word (confined mostly to continuants such as nasal, sibilants, and liquids *tammāl*). I thank Andrew Ollett for leading the Apabhramsha and Prakrit reading groups at Columbia University where I got a chance to read a few Apabhramsha texts.

22. Rahaman, *Sandeśrāsaka*, 3.

23. In Ḍiṅgal, three types of dohā (*baṛau* [big], *tuṃverī*, and *khodo dūho* [half broken]) are used in a modified *mātrā* structure of the traditional dohā metre (used in Braj, Awadhi), which follows a particular way of recitation. Even *soraṭhā* is called a dūhā in Ḍiṅgal. The chappay has also been modified in three ways, namely kavitt/chappay, *śudhh kavitt* (pure kavitt used in Braj), and *dauṛo kavitt* (one and a half kavitt). See the introduction to the Mansaram Sevag, *Raghunāth Rūpak*, ed. Mahtab Chandra Khared (New Delhi: Sahitya Academy, 1999); Motilal Menariya, *Rājasthān kā pingal sāhitya* (Jodhpur: Rajasthani Granthagar, 2006); Kamphorst, *In Praise of Death: History and Poetry in Medieval Marwar* (Leiden: University Press, 2008).

24. *Vayaṇsagāī* means engagement or relation between similar sounds or letters. It is a Marwari song genre, which can be vaguely characterized as a type of *anuprās* (alliteration). There are three kinds of vayaṇ sagāī used in Ḍiṅgal. According to the most common vayaṇ sagāī (called *adhik/uttam*, increased/best), the first letter of the first word in a *caraṇ* (metrical foot) should be identical with the first letter of the last word in the same caraṇ. See Khared, *Raghunāth Rūpak*.

25. *Krisan Rukamaṇī rī velī, Prithvirāj rī kahi*, ed. Swami Narottamdas (Jodhpur: Rajasthani Granthagar, 1998), 34. According to Swami, a

manuscript dated 1607 is the earliest of all manuscripts of the *Velī* found in the seventeenth century.

26. Prithviraj Rathore was the younger brother of Akbar's ally Rai Singh. Abul Fazl (*The Akbarnāmah*, vol. 3, trans. H. Beveridge [New Delhi: Ess Ess Publication, 1977], 518) and the court historian of Marwar, Muhtan Nainsi, (fl. seventeenth century) (*Mumhatā Nainsi rī khyāt*, part 1, ed. Sākariya BadarīPrasād, 256 [Jodhpur: Rajasthan Oriental Research Institute, 1960]), mention Prithviraj serving at Akbar's court. Akbar awarded him a *jagir* in Gagaron. Prithviraj is mentioned in sixteenth- and seventeenth-century Braj hagiographies. Nabhadas, who was a contemporary of Prithviraj, calls him a king of poets (*kavirāj*) in his *Bhaktmāl*, c. 1600 (*Bhaktmāl-Paṭhanuśilan evam vivecan*, ed. Narendra Jha [Patna: Anupam Prakashan 1978], 48, chappay 133). Later on, the Dadupanthi Raghavdas extols Prithviraj as *the* poet on the earth: 'prithī par prithīrāj kabī' (Prithvirāj is *the* poet on earth) in his *Bhaktmāl*, ed. Agarcand Nahta (Jodhpur: RORI, 1964), 209, chappay 452. There is an entire chapter (*vārtā*) on Prithviraj in the *Do sau bāvan vaiṣṇvan kī vārtā* (Story of Two Hundred and Fifty-Two Vaiṣṇavas) ascribed to the Vallabhaite Gokulnath (Niranjandev Sharma, ed., *Dau sau bāvan vaiṣṇavan kī vārtā* [Mathura: Shri Govardhan Granthmala Samiti, Dauji Ghat, 1965], 341–2).

27. Swami, *Krisan Rukamaṇī rī velī*, 62, v. 296.

28. The Rathores of Bikaner and Charans have a very strong bond with the Rathores rising as rulers in Bikaner who patronized Charans. The figure which relates both of these is the goddess of Marwar Karni Mata, who is a Charan by birth and historically related with the foundation of the Bikaner kingdom. Her temple is in town Deshnok, which is very close to the Bikaner city and is famous as the 'Rat temple' (G. H. Ojha, Bīkāner rājya kā itihās [Jodhpur: Rajasthani Granthagar, 2007]; Rajvi Amar Singh, *Medieval History of Rājasthān* [Jaipur: Premier Press, 1992]; and Menariya, *Rājasthān kā pingal sāhitya*).

29. Allison Busch, 'Poetry of Kings', *The Classical Hindi Literature of Mughal India* (New York: Oxford University Press, 2011), Chapter 5.

30. Busch, 'Poetry of Kings', 89–90.

31. Vrind, *Vṛnd Granthāvalī*, ed. Janardan Rao Cheler (Agra: Vinod Pustak Mandir, 1971). *Satya sarūp pūpak* (262–303). In this poem, the *vayaṇsagāī* can be seen primarily in verses 153–5, 227–33, 236–99, 305–12. In *Vacanikā* (115–261) the *vayaṇsagāī* can be seen in verses 49–51, 53–83, 86–9, 234–41, 268–80, 289–313, 316–20, 255–60, 409–16, 457–66, 479–508, 526–50.

32. Girdhar Asiya, *Sagat Rāso*, ed. Hukam Singh Bhati (Udaipur: Pratap Shodh Sansthan, 1987). This magnificent rāso describes the wars of Maharana Pratap's younger brother Shakti Singh of Mewar and his successors.

33. Brajmohan Javaliya, ed., *Dalpativijay krit khummāṇ rāso*, vol. 2 (Udaipur: Maharana Pratap Smarak Samiti, 2001), 461. The long war description is entirely in *vayaṇsagāī*.

34. Padmakar, *Himmatbahādur birdāvalī*, 24.
35. Padmakar, *Himmatbahādur birdāvalī*, 43.
36. Padmakar, *Himmatbahādur birdāvalī*, 20.

Bibliography

Primary Sources

Abul Fazl, *The Akbarnāmah*, translated by H. Beveridg. New Delhi: Ess Ess Publication, 1977.

Asiya, Girdhar. *Sagat Rāso*, edited by Hukam Singh Bhati. Udaipur: Pratap Shodh Sansthan 1987.

Chand Bardai. *Prithvirāj Rāso*, edited by H.P. Dwivedi and Namwar Singh. Allahabad: Sahitya Bhawan, 1998.

Gang. *Kavi gaṅg racnāvalī*, edited by Bate Krishna. Jodhpur: Rajasthani Granthagar, 2009.

Dalpativijay krit khummāṇ rāso, edited by Brajmohan Javaliya Udaipur: Maharana Pratap Smarak Samiti, 2001.

Dau sau bāvan vaiṣṇavan kī vārtā, edited by Niranjandev Sharma. Mathura: Shri Govardhan Granthmala Samiti, Dauji Ghat, 1965.

Mahesh Kavi. *Hammīr Rāso*, edited by Agarcand Nahta. Jodhpur: RORI, 1982.

Māncharitāvalī, edited by G.N. Bahura. Jaipur: Sawai Mansingh II Museum Trust, 1990.

Nabhadas. *Bhaktmāl*, edited by Narendra Jha. Patna: Anupam Prakashan, 1978.

Padmakar. *Padmākar kṛt himmatbahādur birdāvalī*, edited by Lala Bhagvandin. Varanasi: Nagari Pracharini Sabha, 1930 (?).

———. *Padmākar Granthāvalī*, edited by Vishwanathprasad Mishra. Varanasi: Nagari Pracharini Sabha, 1959.

Prācīn ḍiṅgal gīt sāhitya, edited by Narayan Singh Bhati. 235, Jodhpur: Rajasthani Granthagar, 1989.

Prithviraj. *Krisan Rukamaṇī rī velī, Prithvirāj rī kahī*, edited by Narottamdas Swami. Jodhpur: Rajasthani Granthagar, 1998.

Raghavdas. *Bhaktmāl*, edited by Agarcand Nahta. Jodhpur: RORI, 1964.

Rahaman, Abdul. *Sandeśrāsaka*, edited by Harivallabh Bhayani. Ahmadabad: Prakrit Text Society, 1999.

Sevag, Mansaram. *Raghunāth Rūpak*, edited by Mahtab Chandra Khared. New Delhi: Sahitya Academy, 1999.

Tulsidas. *Śrī Rāmcaritmānas*. Gorakhpur: Gitapress, 2002.

Vrind. *Vṛnd Granthāvalī*, edited by Janardan Rao Cheler. Agra: Vinod Pustak Mandir, 1971.

Secondary Sources

Busch, Allison. 'Rīti and Register: Lexical Variation in Courtly Brajbhāṣā Texts'. In *Hindi-Urdu before the Divide*, edited by Francesca Orsini. New Delhi: Orient Blackswan, 2010.

———. *Poetry of Kings: The Classical Hindi Literature of Mughal India*. New York: Oxford University Press, 2011.

Kamphorst, Janet. *In Praise of Death: History and Poetry in Medieval Marwar*. Leiden: University Press, 2008.

Lutgendorf, Philip. *The Life of a Text: Performing the* Rāmcaritmānas *of Tulsīdās*. California: University Press California, 1991.

Menariya, Motilal. *Rājsthanī bhāṣā aur sāhitya*. Jodhpur: Rajasthani Granthagar, 2006.

———. *Rājasthān kā pingal sāhitya*. Jodhpur: Rajasthani Granthagar, 2006.

Ojha, G. H. *Bīkāner rājya kā itihās*. Jodhpur: Rajasthani Granthagar 2007.

Pinch, William R. *Warrior Ascetics and Indian Empires*. Cambridge: Cambridge University Press, 2006.

Shukla, Ramchandra. *Hindi sāhitya kā itihās*. Ghaziabad: K.L. Pachauri Publishing, 2002.

Singh, Namwar. *Hindī ke vikās meṁ apabhraṁś kā yug*. Allahabad: Lokbharati, 2002.

Singh, Rajvi Amar. *Medieval History of Rājasthān*. Jaipur: Premier Press, 1992.

Sarkar, Jadunath. *Daś nām nāge saṅyāsiyoṅ kā itihās*, 2 vols. Prayag: Shri Panchayati Akhara Mahanirvani, 1950.

15

SHREEKANT KUMAR CHANDAN

Alam

A Poet of Many Worlds

Alam is well known to scholars of Hindi literature as a Bhasha or vernacular poet in the precolonial past, but remains an unknown figure to the world of historians primarily because of the neglect of Bhasha[1] texts as a credible sources for writing history. Although the Hindi literary world has immortalized Alam's verses in its literary historiography, literary scholars seldom explore other facets of the polyglot poet named Alam and confine him to a stereotyped image of 'a poet in love' in their literature. This stereotyped image fails to fully appreciate Alam's versatility and his dynamic career which this chapter seeks to explore. Alam was well versed in Sanskrit as well as in Persian, the languages of power and high culture, and was an active participant in the Bhasha literary movement. He was a poet, critic, and an expert in *ilm-i-tib* (medicine). This chapter is divided in two sections; the first section problematizes the question of the poet's agency and his historical consciousness in courtly society while the second section explores Dakhani influence on Alam's religious thought and literary production stemming from his sojourn in the Deccan during the closing decades of the seventeenth century.

Historicizing Alam

Alam's dedicatory verses to Muazzam Shah in the *Śyāmsnehī* inform us of his presence in the Deccan in the late seventeenth century. It was a common practice for princes and military generals—Mughals as well as Rajputs—to carry their entire retinue comprising entertainers, poets, musicians, and others along with them as they journeyed to the military camps where they would be staying. A contemporary source which gives us an eyewitness account of various Mughal military campaigns against the Marathas in the Deccan from 1689 to 1707 also tells us about the protracted nature of the warfare and how military generals of warring camps exchanged musical parties at night to entertain themselves.[2] Our poet was part of such a milieu where he interacted with a number of types of individuals including poets, scholars, and Sufis during his stay in the Deccan.

Alam's retelling in Dakhani Urdu of *Sudāmā Carit*, a work on the theme of Sudama and Krishna's friendship in Dakhani Urdu, should be seen as a product of the Dakhani influence that he came to experience during his sojourn as part of the Mughal prince's retinue in this frontier region. Alam's retelling of the Sudama–Krishna tale represents his interaction with the Dakhani literary trends being practised by Chishti Sufis of the Deccan as well as his negotiation with Sufi *taṣawwuf* (philosophy). Maulana Daud's *Candāyan* (1379) and Qutban's *Mṛgāwatī* (c. 1503) can be seen as providing representative texts for this Sufi corpus. The former uses the folk tale of Lorik and Chanda (popular among the Ahir pastoral community) and the latter the theme romance of prince Qutban and the celestial nymph Mrigawati to construct an allegorical narrative of the Sufi quest for *ishq-i ḥaqīqī* (divine love).[3] Closer to Alam's period, we know of Akbar's penchant for getting works from Sanskrit translated into Persian for the Persianate world through a bureau of translation especially devoted to facilitating intercommunity dialogue in the late sixteenth century.[4] Faizi's Persian translation of the narrative of Nala and Damyanti, a very popular love tale in the Indic tradition, is another attempt to facilitate intercultural dialogue and to explore the Indic literary heritage.[5]

The Historical Consciousness of a Poet

For a long time the independent agency of poets has been underestimated owing to the assumption that court poets were mere sycophants patronized for the purpose of praising the monarch or the ruling class. Such a jaundiced understanding of the *kavikul* (poet fraternity) denies any subjectivity to the poet concerned and also clouds his larger role in the early modern world. This stereotypical view has been questioned in recent scholarship.[6] In this context, Alam's poetry provides a useful entry point for revisiting the role of poets in the early modern world and unsettling the easy characterization of poets as mere sycophants—persons devoid of a critical awareness of their surroundings and contemporary political and cultural developments. Alam's dedicatory verses in his first epic-based poem, the *Śyāmsnehī*, contain layers of meaning. They illuminate the poet's critical understanding of complex political developments in the Deccan and the changing relationship between the emperor and Prince Muazzam on the one hand, and the rivalry between Prince Muazzam and Prince Azam on the other, as evident from the following verses:

Janata auliya kitabāna ko je nisāfa ke māne kahe hai to cinhe
Palata ho ita alama uta nike rahima ke nāma linhe
Mojama śāhi tumhe karatā karibe ko dilīpati haiṃ bara dinheṃ
Qābil haiṃ te rahe kithahuṃ kahūṃ qābila hota haiṃ qābila kinheṃ[7]

Well versed in the holy book(s) and the true knower of justice,
The keeper of this world and devoted to the one true God,
Muazzam Shah blessed by the Lord of Delhi himself
The so-called worthy should pay heed
No one becomes worthy by self proclamation.

To fully appreciate Alam's poetic ecumene, one needs to situate him in the midst of the fast-changing world of the Deccan in the 1680s and the rivalry among Aurangzeb's sons accentuated by their claim to be the *qābil* (worthy) successor to the imperial throne. The Mughal prince Muazzam was sent to the Deccan as viceroy to keep an eye on the growing menace of the Deccani sultanates and the Marathas, and to force both to accept Mughal suzerainty. During his military expedition in October 1685, Prince Muazzam captured Hyderabad from the Qutbshahi ruler Abul Hasan and forced him to sign a treaty acknowledging Mughal suzerainty. This, however, assured continued Qutabshahi rule of Golkonda.[8]

Aurangzeb could not abide by the terms of this treaty, however, and launched a surprise attack on the Qutbshahi kingdom and conquered Golkonda in open violation of the imperial treaty signed under the leadership of Prince Muazzam. The conquest of Golkonda served the cause of Mughal hegemony but damaged Muazzam's personal integrity, as the 1685 treaty had guaranteed that there would be no Mughal annexation of Golkonda. Muazzam looked at the imperial conquest of Golkonda as unjust and as a breach of faith, since it was signed under the witness of the holy Quran. As a result, Muazzam developed a soft spot in his heart for the deposed ruler of Golkonda, Abul Hasan, and indulged in clandestine correspondence with him. On 20 February 1687, a letter from the prince to Abul Hasan was intercepted by the imperial officers and was brought to the notice of Aurangzeb.[9] As a result, Muazzam and his entire family were imprisoned and suffered the worst days of their lives as prisoners in the shifting imperial camp in the Deccan, deprived of all comforts. One year later, in April 1688, Aurangzeb showed kindness to Prince Muazzam and offered to release him, but Prince Muazzam considered his freedom from imperial incarceration to be futile unless it was accompanied by the freedom of the Qutbshahi ruler Abul Hasan. Only this would restore his personal prestige. As this was not acceptable to the emperor and the request was denied, Muazzam continued to live on in a state of incarceration.

Alam's stress on Muazzam being well-versed in *auliya kitābān* (texts such as the Quran and Hadith) and knowing the true meaning of *nisāf* (justice) alludes to the above-mentioned incident. In his correspondence with the emperor during his incarceration, the Mughal prince highlighted the sanctity of a treaty signed under the witness of a holy text and hence the illegitimacy of imperial aggression, as well as his own deep sense of having lost personal prestige. In contrast, Aurangzeb wanted the prince to repent of his illegal, clandestine correspondence with the enemy. Clearly, the difference in understandings of *insāf* (justice) between the emperor and the prince was well understood by our poet, who alluded to Prince Muazzam's commitment to the notion of justice even if it demanded a huge sacrifice—in this case a diminished chance of succeeding his father on the throne. In all this we see that Alam was acutely aware of the contemporary political developments in the Deccan as well as of the importance attached to the concept of 'justice', a critical part of the discourse of kingship under *akhlāqī* traditions.[10]

Alam as a Dakhani Literary Figure

Alam's sojourn in the Deccan during the closing decades of the seventeenth century had a profound impact on his religious thought as well as on his literary production. Alam's verse compositions in Bhasha, prior to coming to Deccan, reveal his deep engagement with popular devotion woven around the cult of Krishna, geographically located in the region of Braj (Mathura and Vrindavan). However, during his stay in the Deccan, Alam was influenced by the Sufi milieu and by the Dakhani vernacular literary trends produced by the Chishti Sufis of Bijapur, among others. The most easily discernible influence was the shift of language, from Bhasha to Dakhani Urdu, reflected primarily in his recasting of the popular tale of Krishna–Sudama in Dakhani Urdu and in some miscellaneous verses.

There were other subtle mutations besides the temporary shift from Bhasha to Dakhani for versifying a popular tale. Our poet was also going through an intense churning of ideas on various questions pertaining to the domain of religion and spirituality during this period. Issues such as the notion of god, the nature of a devotee's relationship with god, and the role of a *pīr* (spiritual leader) in one's spiritual journey engaged his attention. These were the questions which Alam seriously pondered over when he roamed around in a Deccani landscape dotted by the *khānqāhs* (hospice) and *dargāhs* (shrine) of various Sufi *silsilāhs* (orders) as he travelled with the imperial camp. We see them represented handsomely in Alam's *Sudāmā Carit*, which evinces two reciprocal processes: the growing indigenization or localization of Sufi thought and the Sufi-ization of a popular Indic tale having its root in Puranic literature.[11] Earlier, Sufism was accessible to the masses through the architectures of its khānqāhs and dargāhs and by means of the ceremonies linked to these structures, but Alam's Deccani rendering of the *Sudāmā Carit* shows how basic ideas of Sufism such as monotheism and the powerful agency of the pīr in the spiritual pursuit of a *murīd* (disciple) could further penetrate popular perceptions of religious truth by means of the oral recitation of popular lyrical poetry.

Let us see how Sufi influences on Alam's thought are refracted in his *Sudāmā Carit*, in his short work *Rāmlīlā*, and in his *rekhtā* compositions.[12] Alam seems to be intensely influenced by the Sufi ideal of *fanā* (annihilation of the Self into the Divine Reality) and the agony of suffering that is experienced during the soul's separation from the beloved (that is, god). Majzubs such as Shah Amin went into insensate raptures (*bekhudī*) during their practice of *samā* (spiritual music). Hagiographical literature interpreted this as union with the Divine, but such a meeting was not a permanent: once these adepts recovered from their raptures, they found themselves in the mortal world once again and intensely longed for a return to the state of union. This they expressed in their poetry, and we see traces of such poetry in Alam's compositions.[13] Consider the following verses by Alam in the rekhtā style:

> Dauri dauri dwāre āvai aise dila bhi na pāwai,
> Kiyā hai pakheru taiṃ daryāva ke navāre kā,
> Parā terī sūrati ke nūra giradāba bīc,
> Phūla sā faqīra phirai sāñjha lauṃ saba re kā,
>
> . . . .
>
> Sārā dina phirā karai tereī hī firaqa bīc,
> Jau na cāhe citamauṃ tau cārā kyā bicāre ka.
>
> I keep running to the door, no one should have such a heart.
> I have turned into a sea-bird who only hovers over the ship.
> The lines of the light of your visage among the bees,
> As if they were a flower-like mendicant wandering from dusk to dawn.
>
> . . . .
>
> All day long I wander in separation from you,
> Even if I were not to want [you] in my heart, what relief would there be for this wretch?[14]

In another of Alam's compositions the narrative of the *Rāmlīlā* is moulded to represent a Sufi's quest for divine love. Sita is separated from 'Pīr' Raghubir (that is, Ram) and her craving for union becomes the ideal model for a Sufi who has to go through the agony of separation from the beloved. It is also possible to argue that the same verses represent Alam's personal voice of carnal love and separation given the fluidity of meaning in such poetry, reflected in the verses given below:

> Nainā nīra dhoi hāryo lohū saba rāi tāteṃ,
>   Jhūro hvai kai jhūro aba lohū na lahatu hai.
> Ālama na āve bāt pire mukha sīre gāta,
>   Tāto hiyo rāto kari sūlahi sahatu hai.

Bhītara kī bhīt kahuṃ lagyo hai pachīt thaki,
  Rīti yahai nehi kī bidehī nibahatu hai.
Eka ṭak herata hiraï rahuo citta binu,
  Mitra ko biyogī māno citra hvai rahatu hai.

Her eyes were exhausted from crying,
And suffused with redness.
They dried up till they were parched
And now could not become redder.
Alam cannot even describe how
Her mouth pained,
Her limbs went numb,
And her heart endured spears
That bloodied it.
Were I to venture to say,
This is the custom of love
By which Bidehi (Sita) abided.
With unwavering glance,
Lost and senseless,
She was like a painting
Of a woman separated from her lover.[15]

Similarly, Alam's *Sudāmā Carit* begins with eight lines of invocation which not only attest to Alam's familiarity with Sufi vocabulary, but also reveal his negotiation between the two irreconcilable positions of monotheism and polytheism. Influenced by the idea of one supreme god, the cornerstone of Islam and Sufism, Alam appropriated the doctrines of Sufi philosophy and rendered his invocation ambiguous in order to navigate between the two worlds of popular Hinduism and the monotheistic Sufi milieu without clearly taking a side.

Rāma ramāpati viṣṇu su keśava kṛṣṇa gupāla gubardhanadhārī,
Nādara saba ke sira para sāhaba sundara tana ghanaśyāma murārī.
Sūrata khūba ajāyaba mūrata ālama kā mahabūba bihārī,
Jagamaga jagai jamālaṃ jagata meṃ hilamila dila kīje balihārī.
Sada salāma aru bahuta bandagī tisakūṃ jo apane dila āne,
Jyoṃ jyoṃ yāda kare vaha bandā tyoṃ tyoṃ vaha nīkā kari jāne.
Dekho karama kiyo bāmana para diyo ju kachu usake mana manai,
Aisa kauna binā giradhārī jo garība ke dukha ko bhānai.

Ram, Lord of Ram, Vishnu, Keshav,
  Krishna, Gopal, the Lifter of Govardhan,
The master revered by all the indigent,
  the dark and handsome-bodied Murari.

With beautiful face and amazing form, Alam's beloved, Bihari!
May I offer up my heart to be mingled with His brilliant beauty (jamāl)
that shines throughout the universe?
A hundred salutations and many obeisances to him who loves [Krishna],
The more his servant thinks of Him, the more beneficence He shows.
See how he showed mercy on the Brahmin (Sudama)
and gave whatever his heart desired.
Who other than the Mountain Lifter
understands the pain of the wretched?[16]

As we can see, epithets such as *mahbūb* (beloved) and *sāhab*, used by Sufis to refer to the Ultimate Reality, were fully appropriated by Alam. Yet although he was intensely influenced by the notion of one god, he retained his faith in a personal, visible, and loving god as borne out in the first and third lines of the above-mentioned invocation. The influence of Sufism on Alam becomes further visible when he refers to Sudama's destination, that is, Krishna's palace in Dwarka—as 'dargāh baḍe sāhab ke', a Persianate idiom for 'the great master's court' that suggests the court of god, rather than simply referring it to as a king's palace:

Jo tū kahatī rahatī hai to jānā mujhe jarūra bhayā hai,
Para daragāha baḍe sāhab ke binā bheṭa kahu kauna gayā hai.
Kyā tuhafā lijai usa ghara ko jahāṃ tahāṃ jagadīsa dayā hai,
Khālī hātha nātha soṃ milanā yahī sukana kā soca bhayā hai.

I definitely know what you are talking about,
But who has ever gone to the great master's court without an offering?
What gift should one bring to that home upon which the Lord of the
World shows his mercy?
To go to the Lord empty-handed—this is the idea that you've come up with?[17]

Indeed, Alam's *Sudāmā Carit* can be read as an allegorical account of a Sufi's spiritual journey. On that understanding the 'dargāh baḍe sāhib ke' would represent the soul's *manzil*, its final destination. The possibility of such a reading shows Alam to have become an active participant in the Dakhani Sufi milieu of the late seventeenth century. We see this also in passages where he seems to side with the dervishes as he charts out what might be considered a legitimate *tarīqā* (spiritual path). While recounting the indigent Sudama's discussion with his wife over whether or not to meet his rich friend Krishna, the poet ridicules any attachment to material wealth, echoing the Majzub's denunciation of worldly Sufis who take on the roles of *pīrzādā* and *ināmdār*:

> Jar khātira hajāra fikaro meṃ dila kūṃ fikaramanda nahiṃ karanā,
> Jar khātara yoṃ bhārī apanā haluvā kari āge lai dharanā.
> Jar khātira yoṃ mitra soṃ milanā tina soṃ bahuta bhalā hai maranā,
> Aisai hāla musākat rahanā jo dukha hoya to sukha kara bharnā.
>
> Out of the thousands of worries, don't trouble your heart with thinking about gold.
> Take this burden of thinking about gold, turn it into halva, and take it with you.
> It's better to die than to meet a friend for the sake of gold.
> In this situation, keep smiling and transform this pain into joy.[18]

Looking back we see that Alam's poetry opens a window onto the complex cultural processes that transpired in the late seventeenth-century Deccan—a window to which vernacular usage gives us especially direct access. Other facets of his work, directly reflecting his thoughtful presence at the Deccan court of Aurangzeb, help to fill out the picture, giving a sense of the poet's historical consciousness and his fully engaged poetic agency. Alam was a poet of many worlds, and yet of one.

Notes

1. I prefer to use the term 'Bhasha' over 'Hindi' or 'Braj' because the poets of the concerned period refer to their language as *bhāṣā* or *bhākhā*, as opposed to 'Hindi' or 'Brajbhasha' (which is of later coinage). Additionally, the term 'Braj' tends to restrict Bhasha literary culture to the Braj geography and also comes with the baggage of suggesting predominantly devotional poetry. In contrast, Bhasha poetry is incredibly diverse, encompassing courtly poetry, love tales, war narratives, epic compositions, ethical discourse, and so on.

2. Bhimsen Burhanpuri, *Nuskha-i-Dilkasha*, trans. Jadunath Sarkar (Bombay: The Department of Archives, 1972), 207–10.

3. Aditya Behl, 'The Magic Doe: Desire and Narrative in a HIndavi Romance', circa 1503, in *Cultural History of Medieval India*, ed. Meenakshi Khanna (New Delhi: Social Science Press, 2007), 175–7.

4. Athar Ali, *Mughal India* (New Delhi: Oxford University Press, 2010, fifth impression), 173–80.

5. Muzaffar Alam and Sanjay Subrahmanyam, *Writing the Mughal World* (New Delhi: Permanent Black, 2011), 205–48.

6. Allison Busch, 'Hidden in Plain View: Brjbhasha Poets at the Mughal Court', *Modern Asian Studies* 44, no.2 (2010): 267–309.

7. Shivsingh Sengar, *Śivasiṁh Saroj*, ed. Trilok Narayan Diksit (Lucknow: Tejkumar Book Depot, 1966 [1878]), 70.

8. Jadunath Sarkar, *Studies in Aurangzeb's Reign* (Calcutta: Orient Longman, 1989), 32–4.

9. Sarkar, *Studies in Aurangzeb's Reign*, 35.

10. Muzaffar Alam, *The Languages of Political Islam in India c.1200–1800* (New Delhi: Permanent Black, 2004), 50–5.

11. For Puranic lineage of Krishna devotional poetry in medieval period, see Manager Pandey, *Bhakti āndolan aur Sūrdās kā kāvya* (New Delhi: Vani Prakashan, 2003, fourth edition), 68–75.

12. It is important to bear in mind that the captions given to miscellaneous poetry are not by the poet himself but it has been done by Vidyaniwas Mishra, the editor of *Ālam Granthāvalī*. These captions bind Alam's poetry in a fixed framework, while multiple readings of the same verses are possible. Hence, such labelling fails to do justice to the fluid meaning of Alam's poetry.

13. Richard M. Eaton, *Sufis of Bijapur: 1300–1700* (New Delhi: Munshiram Manoharlal Publishers, 1996), 43–4.

14. Vidyaniwas Mishra, ed., *Ālam Granthāvalī* (New Delhi: Vani Publication, 1991), 96.

15. Mishra, *Ālam Granthāvalī*, 96.

16. Mishra, *Ālam Granthāvalī*, 263.

17. Mishra, *Ālam Granthāvalī*, 266.

18. Mishra, *Ālam Granthāvalī*, 265.

Bibliography

Primary Sources

Alam. *Ālam Granthāvalī*, edited by Vidyaniwas Mishra. New Delhi: Vani Prakshan, 1991.

Bhuranpuri, Bhimsen. *Nuskha-i-Dilkasha*, translated by Jadunath Sarkar. Bombay: The Department of Archives, 1972.

Secondary Sources

Athar Ali, M. *Mughal India*. New Delhi: Oxford University Press, 2010.

Alam, Muzaffar. *The Languages of Political Islam in India c.1200–1800*. New Delhi: Permanent Black, 2004.

Alam, Muzaffar and Sanjay Subrahmanyam. *Writing the Mughal World.* New Delhi: Permanent Black, 2011.

Bangha, Imre. *The First Published Anthology of Hindi Poets.* New Delhi: Rainbow Publishers Limited, 2000.

Behl, Aditya. 'The Magic Doe: Desire and Narrative in a Hindavi Romance, circa 1503'. In *Cultural History of Medieval India,* edited by Meenakshi Khanna. New Delhi: Social Science Press, 2007.

Busch, Allison. 'Hidden in Plain View: Brabhasha Poets at the Mughal Court'. *Modern Asian Studies* 44, no. 2 (2010): 267–309.

Eaton, Richard M. *Sufis of Bijapur, 1300–1700.* New Delhi: Munshiram Manoharlal Publishers, 1996.

Pandey, Manager. *Bhakti āndolan aur Sūrdās kā kāvya.* New Delhi: Vani Prakashan, 2003, fourth edition.

Sarkar, Jadunath. *Studies in Awrangzeb's Reign.* Calcutta: Orient Longman, 1989.

Schimmel, Annemarie. 'The Influence of Sufism on Indo-Muslim Poetry'. In *Anagogic Qualities of Literature,* edited by Joseph P. Strelka. University Park, Pennsylvania State University Press, 1971.

Sengar, Shivsingh. *Śivasiṁh Saroj,* edited by Trilok Narayan Diksit. Lucknow: Tejkumar Book Depot, 1966 (1878).

16

HEIDI R. M. PAUWELS*

The Pursuit of Pilgrimage, Pleasure, and Military Alliances

Nāgarīdās's *Tīrthānanda*

When we think of centres of pilgrimage, we rarely think of their role in military campaigns. Scholars of religion sometimes tend to conceive of pilgrimage centres as above place and time, removed from the political and military vicissitudes surrounding them. Yet the famous and well-studied pilgrimage centre of Braj was also eminently located on the road between Delhi and Agra built by Sher Shāh Sūr in the eventful sixteenth century. This new road may have been built primarily to allow for military movements, but it also allowed mercantile travel and, at the same time, provided easy access for pilgrims, a major condition for the flourishing of a place of pilgrimage.[1] Its location near the centre of Mughal power made it a natural stop for delegations on the way to and from the capital. This is often mentioned in chronicles or other historical accounts. In Akbar's time, his Rajput general Mān Singh took a vow to build the fabulous Govindadeva temple in Vrindāban, just before leaving on his campaign to Gujarat in Mughal service.[2] In Shāh Jahān's time, a court chronicle for the Kishangarh ruler Rūp Singh describes him as receiving felicitations from the emperor in Delhi after his successful participation in a 1646 Mughal campaign in Balkh and Qandahār. Before returning home he stopped in Braj, where he received a divine image to install in his newly founded capital, Rūpnagar.[3] Likewise, at the beginning of Muhammad Shāh's reign, Kotah's king, Bhīm Singh I (1707–20), went to Delhi to congratulate the new emperor and on his way back home stopped in Braj, where he also obtained the tutelary image of Śrī Brajanātha jī.[4] Even during Aurangzeb's rule, in 1678 (1735 VS), a delegation sent by Rāj Singh of Mewar under his son (and later successor) Jai Singh stopped in Mathura and Vrindāban on its way back from Delhi so that the entourage could perform acts of pilgrimage.[5] These are only a few examples with regard to Braj, but they could be multiplied and broadened to other pilgrimage sites. In short, travel for military purposes and for alliance-building with the Mughals could naturally be combined with pilgrimage to a site that lay along on the way, so that religious symbols could be acquired to legitimate Hindu rule back home and even, perhaps, in the course of the journey itself. No contradiction was felt in earning such double mileage from a business trip.

This chapter focuses on a remarkable account of such a case of a double-mileage pilgrimage travel. It is an autobiographical pilgrimage account, *Tīrthānand* (The Joy of Pilgrimage), written in 1753 (Māgh 1810 VS) by Nāgarīdās, alias Sāvant Singh of Kishangarh (1699–1764). Superficially this appears to be a purely religious text, celebrating the joys of religious travel, but as we discover from studying the historical circumstances, there is quite a bit more to it than meets the eye.

Sāvant Singh's Crisis

Sāvant Singh is celebrated as the main sponsor of the distinctive Kishangarhi style of Rādhā–Krishna miniatures. Secondary sources often mention that he abdicated his throne and retired to Vrindāban. This may give the impression that he was somewhat other-worldly. While he certainly was a great devotee, that was by no means the whole story. Surely, he had a firm footing in Krishna's world: Sāvant Singh produced an enormous corpus of poetry in praise of Rādhā and Krishna. It is clear he was attracted to *bhakti* early on in his life, as his earliest dated work, *Manoratha Mañjari*, or 'Blossoming Wish' (1723 or VS 1780), already expresses his desire to spend time in Vrindāban. As the crown prince of Kishangarh, he had the luxury of having his own poetry illustrated with miniatures, such as famously his *Bihār Candrikā* and the matching miniature 'Boat of Love', now to be found in the National Museum, New Delhi.[6]

In 1748, however, everything changed, and when it did, it must have seemed to Nāgarīdās like the end of the world as he knew it. Since the Kishangarhi house was a vassal of the Mughals, he had been called to Delhi by the emperor Muhammad Shāh in a crisis situation. All nobles were to respond to an 'external' threat: Ahmad Shāh Abdālī 'Durrānī', the newly chosen leader of the Afghan tribes, had invaded India in 1748. The Afghans confronted the Mughals at the Battle of Sirhind, where they were temporarily defeated, though they would soon return with a vengeance. Sāvant Singh did indeed travel to Delhi where, although he himself did not actually partake in the battle, he suffered severe personal setbacks. First, he learned the news of his father's passing away in his absence. And second, as if that was not enough, his younger brother Bahādur Singh usurped the throne before he could come home to be crowned.[7]

Yet Nāgarīdās's personal hardship was dwarfed by the disastrous and complex political developments in the empire. Wherever he turned for help, he found people preoccupied with bigger worries. Nāgarīdās's first reflex must have been to seek the emperor's help, but Muhammad Shāh had his hands full warding off Abdālī. Though the Afghan was defeated, the cost of this first temporary victory was high Mughal casualties; the most influential nobles lost their lives. Shortly thereafter, the emperor himself died.[8] Thus, Sāvant Singh was practically orphaned in two ways: first, his own father passed away, then the father figure of the emperor also vanished. Delhi was now rife with strife. The major senior noblemen had died and the young new emperor, Ahmad Shāh (1748–54), who had only barely won the victory against Durrānī, was insecure himself. Several court intrigues led to an all-out civil war in 1753, in which the Marathas played a decisive role.[9] Amidst all this chaos, it must not have been easy to see whom to turn to. Little wonder Sāvant Singh retreated temporarily—this is exactly the time he went on his pilgrimage to Braj—but that did not mean he gave up his political designs.

Bahādur Singh could not have chosen a better moment to advance his ambitions in Kishangarh. It seems there was chaos and transition everywhere during this period. Sāvant Singh could expect no substantial support from any of the friendly Rajput kingdoms, because nearly all of them were embroiled in conflicts surrounding their own thrones. Indeed, the middle of the eighteenth century was dominated by Rajput succession struggles. All parties were appealing for help to the power brokers of the time, the Marathas.[10] Several Maratha players had established control over vast areas and were only too happy to mediate in local conflicts—for a price. They were at times at odds among themselves about which party to support in the local conflicts. This made it easy for them to take a less-than-forthright approach. Whenever they did not receive the payment they expected, they would turn against the protégé in question and recuperate the prize by force. Their favourite solution was to weaken the Rajput kingdoms by encouraging a process through which they could become divided into quarrelling parties. At the same time, the Marathas would extract several concessions for themselves. Sāvant Singh was merely following the trend when he ended up seeking Maratha help against his brother, and it led him into exactly such a morass.

We first find mention of the enmity between Bahādur Singh and Sāvant Singh in Maratha sources—in a letter dated 20 September 1750 to the Peshwa 'Nānāsāhib' Bālājī Bājirāo by Rāgho Nīlkaṇṭh, where he also talks about his upcoming campaign against the Afghan Rohillas of the Doāb area.[11] Eventually it was Raghunāth Rao, the peshwa's brother, whom Sāvant Singh approached for help. His troops under Jaya Appā Sindhia and Mahar Rao Holkar were fighting the Rohillas in the north in 1751, driving them to the Terai region and Kumaon.[12] Sāvant Singh followed them to negotiate a contract, as he mentions obliquely in his pilgrimage report. Eventually, he succeeded in enlisting the help of the Marathas and got Kishangarh on their agenda as a stop on the way in their more extensive Rajput campaign of 1753–5. By this time, however, Sāvant Singh seems to have settled in Braj, and it was his son, Sardār Singh, who actually fought with the Marathas. The peshwa's diaries give us the full itinerary of encampments established in the course of Raghnāth Rāo's campaign in the north from 1753 to 1755. There we learn that he was encamped in Rūpnagar during March 1755, but is unclear what the results were.[13] It seems that a solution came only after the Marwar treaty was signed, at which point Dattaji Sindhia moved towards Rūpnagar to wage war.[14] Peace came to Kishangarh in June 1756, but at a price.[15] The kingdom was divided in two—Kishangarh for Bahādur Singh and Rūpnagar (with Salemabad) for Sāvant Singh's son, Sardār Singh.

The signing of the peace treaty prompted Sāvant Singh to return home from Braj.[16] The timing was excellent, for he narrowly escaped the massacres of the Braj area by Abdālī in February–March 1757.[17] A memorandum of understanding between Sāvant Singh and Bahādur Singh was signed in Salemabad in the presence of the Nimbārkan abbot Govinddev Ācārya in October 1757.[18] Thereby, Sāvant Singh recognized his brother's son, Birad Singh, as the legitimate heir of Kishangarh. The brothers also made provisions for their stepmother and her son, their half-brother.

Thus, the upshot was that Sāvant Singh managed to recover only part of his kingdom, the area around Rūpnagar, and only in 1756.[19] Instead of ruling himself, he placed his son, Sardār Singh, on the throne and retired, apparently to Vrindāban, where he died in 1764 (1821 VS), as attested by the inscription on his samādhi in Vrindāban. The amazing thing is that he himself represents all this upheaval in his life—his effective exile from his kingdom and his wanderings to find military help—in a text that focuses on none of the events we have just described but celebrates instead the joys of religious travel. It is an autobiographical pilgrimage account, which he calls *Tīrthānanda* (The Joy of Pilgrimage).

Tīrthānanda for Healing the Soul

Tīrthānanda is fascinating in several respects. First, it provides a wealth of information on eighteenth-century networks and itineraries of pilgrimage. In addition, it documents local rituals and festivals as celebrated in Braj at the time. Since Sāvant Singh undertook his extensive pilgrimage for the better part of two years, his narrative roughly follows the seasonal calendar. Thus, it documents not just sacred locale but sacred time—*tīrtha* as well as *utsava*. We get a lively glimpse of Braj culture as it was in 1753, including a description of the Holī festivities, just five years before the horrible massacres by Ahmad Shāh Abdālī in 1757, which turned that year's Holī into an orgy of blood rather than red powder.[20] Moreover, we get vivid vignettes of gatherings of devotees in which religious songs were composed and transmitted. And most remarkable of all, we get a rare record of one man's personal experience of the meaning of pilgrimage. If 'the real meaning of these journeys lies in people's individual experiences, in the depth of meaning with which they invest them', as James Lochtefeld says at the conclusion of his study of Haridvar, then

Sāvant Singh's *Tīrthānand* is a wonderful source text.[21] If people 'categorize their experience by using culturally mediated categories', as Lochtefeld goes on to say, then we see here how the framework of the pilgrimage account is used to justify a trip undertaken to rally support for a political cause, with the religious narrative apparently overtaking any political motivations. And, in the bargain, the *Tīrthānand* gives us a good sense of the problems involved in reconstructing such an elusive thing as 'individual experience' in the first place—particularly if the experience in question requires the investigative tools of an historian.

Although this is Nāgarīdās's only autobiographical work, it does not seem out of place in his oeuvre. It fits seamlessly with other poems of Nāgarīdās that celebrate the Braj area and its seasonal festivals. It seems a natural outgrowth of his lifelong production of such poetry, which here he ties together in the course of reporting an actual journey in historical time. Rather than the somewhat 'impersonal' style of that other type of poetry, this pilgrimage account is obviously shot through with personal experience. There is a strong autobiographical factor, with repeated references, even if downplayed, to the military objective of the trip, which was to muster support for his cause from the Marathas in Kumaon and the Mughal court in Delhi. As simultaneously Sāvant Singh and Nāgarīdās—the ruler and the devotee—the author of the *Tīrthānand* helps us appreciate the extent to which, as Lochtefeld says, pilgrimage is 'a polysemous way of acting' that 'contains multiple meanings and cannot be rendered intelligible by any single explanation'.[22]

Pleasure and Pilgrimage

One of the most striking characteristics of this work is what its title promises: 'The Joy of Pilgrimage'. What is foregrounded is indeed *ānand*—here, the spiritual bliss that results from participating in ceremonies at a holy place. Theorists of the phenomenon of pilgrimage may be disappointed to learn that there is hardly any reference to the hardships of the journey in this work—only a single remark about mountainous territory (*TĀ*, 55). In fact, hardly any practical details are mentioned. We get no sense of the cost of the journey, the minutiae of money transfers, or purchases made along the road. We do not even know how big Nāgarīdās's party was—just the odd reference to his 'camp' (*śivira*: *TĀ*, 18, 44, 60). He totally neglects matters such as official meetings, economic transactions, and ethnographic musings—features that become prominent in more modern pilgrimage reports, which come closer to travel accounts and reserve a great deal of space for the curiosities of the strange places visited. These tend to be bazaar-centred, whereas Nāgarīdās's text is more temple-oriented—or rather, celebration-oriented, as many of the religious celebrations he attends are held in the open air.

Nāgarīdās's silence about hardships is all the more remarkable given the existential situation of the author: his exile as a consequence of his throne being usurped. In fact, a more apt title would be 'The Joy of Pilgrimage in a Time of Distress'. In the *Tīrthānand*, however, Sāvant Singh's efforts to secure political help become at best a sideshow—the main objective being pilgrimage. He mentions en passant some political affairs he had to take care of but dismisses them as unpleasant distractions (*TĀ*, 69 and 73 respectively). By contrast, his eagerness to visit Vrindāban is deep. When on his way to Delhi he sees the land of Braj across the Yamuna and finds no boats to get there, he simply swims across the river (*TĀ*, 61–8). One cannot miss his joy in doing so. And if there is a note of sorrow in the work, it is the sorrow of parting, of leaving the hallowed ground of Braj (*TĀ*, 18, 39).

Yet as his title makes clear, it is the pleasures of pilgrimage that Nāgarīdās foregrounds. If we thought the combination of pilgrimage and tourism is a modern phenomenon, we should reconsider. There are moments where Nāgarīdās gives us a sense of how pilgrimage is combined with leisure activities. As a prince in Kishangarh, Nāgarīdās had always loved excursions on Lake Gundalao, and no sooner did he reach Mathura that he went boating. He speaks of enjoying a boat ride (*naukā vihāra*) opposite Viśrām ghāṭ at dusk (*TĀ*, 19). The pleasures of travel are described in a very tactile way: one can feel the refreshment of the beautiful bucolic setting of Devyānī (*TĀ*, 5), cool Galta (*TĀ*, 6–7), and tree-shaded Braj upon arrival (*TĀ*, 10). Especially attractive are the evocations of the view of Barsānā from a distance (*TĀ*, 71–3), and his descriptions of how the deities appear (*darśan*) in Vrindāban (*TĀ*, 33) and Barsānā (*TĀ*, 74). In good calendrical fashion, he describes the joys of the seasons of the monsoon (*TĀ*, 76ff.), autumn (*TĀ*, 120ff.), the cold season (*TĀ*, 160ff.), and spring, especially Holī (*TĀ*, 164ff.). There is the beautiful and lush description of the offering of lights (*āratī*) that is made to the Yamuna at dusk in Mathura, and we feel his voyeuristic pleasure in seeing the women participate in the rites (*TĀ*, 21–4). In similar fashion, he lovingly describes the women who sell flowers at Jñān Gudarī in Vrindāban (*TĀ*, 35). He also expresses the aesthetic delight of witnessing his well-dressed concubine Rasik Bihārī as she sings before the image of Bihārī in Vrindāban (*TĀ*, 33–4). The joy and beauty of musical gatherings and the pleasures of satsaṅg are repeatedly described throughout the work (*TĀ*, 12–13, 16–17, 35–7, 67–8). This sense of joy is not trivial or unmarked. At one point in the text, he explicitly elevates enjoyment above *mukti* (*TĀ*, 37).

In its single-minded focus on ānand, Nāgarīdās's work differs appreciably from other accounts of royal pilgrimage, these being usually written in the third person by a courtier in order to commemorate the journey as an auspicious occasion for the accumulation of merit (*puṇya*) and to record for posterity the king's religious gift-giving and acts of charity along the way. One example of this kind of narrative from south India is the *Śarabhendra Tīrthāvalī*, which describes the Tanjore Maratha ruler Serfoji Bhosle II's 1801–2 pilgrimage in the south. Similarly, the *Trishtaḷ yātrecyā lāvanyā* records his journey to the north in 1820–2.[23] As a rule, such works foreground the king's donations and acts of largess and the Sanskritic rites performed by Brahmins. Interestingly, however, Serfoji II's pilgrimages also served to legitimize the Maratha ruler's tenuous position, as he had been adopted by the previous king only on his deathbed and his coronation with British support had been much contested.[24] One might argue that Nāgarīdās was in a comparable situation, with a need to justify his case of succession, yet the *Tīrthānand* bypasses practically all Brahmins, ritual details, and gift-giving. Possibly, Nāgarīdās did not have much charity to offer as a king in exile, but the omission of this sort of activity seems rather to express a different conception of what pilgrimage is about. There is no obvious trace of the pilgrimage goal of gaining worldly prestige through lavish displays of wealth. Nāgarīdās seems interested not in royal self-aggrandizement but personal experience and that act of partaking in mythological events.

One could look upon this foregrounding of joy in pilgrimage as escapism. Indeed, such a postulation would seem to be supported by the beginning of the work. Nāgarīdās's first *kavitt* contrasts dry Rajasthan, with its prickly cactus vegetation, to what we could term 'the green, green grass of Braj' (*TĀ*, 1). His dismissal of majestic Vaikuṇṭha in his first *savaiyā* (*TĀ*, 2) as being no match for bucolic

Braj has likewise an autobiographical ring in light of his having to give up his majestic throne. Yet we should keep in mind, however his extensive work on this theme, the *Braj-vaikuṇṭh tulanā*, was composed in 1744 (1801 VS), well before the tragic events of 1748. And, in any case, escapism may not have been his motive.

It is more fruitful, I think, to look upon such exclamations about the glories of Braj in a positive way—as a quest for psychological relief and healing. I would venture to propose this as a motivation for pilgrimage that complements the practical goals about which we otherwise frequently hear—the accomplishment of life cycle rituals, the 'transactional' realm of vow-fulfilment, the allaying of concerns about fertility, the general acquisition of merit, and the overarching but rarely expressed desire for release from this world (*mokṣa*).[25] Here instead we have as a practical goal the desire for relief and the hope of healing—benefits that pilgrimage could bring in a situation of crisis.[26] Obviously, the process of going on pilgrimage represents a change of scenery, and the travails of the journey certainly distract the mind from whatever hardships one was working through at home.[27] But these are at best only part of the picture.

Pilgrimage Patterns in the Eighteenth Century

Nāgarīdās's itinerary begins with shrines along the road from Rajasthan to Braj. He seems to have started out from Rūpnagar in 1748 and headed towards Sambar Lake, the mineral-rich area that was a bone of contention between different parties at the time. Then he must have retraced his steps slightly, taking the route to Delhi that passes over Sursurā and skirts the south-east corner of the lake.[28] Facing Sāmbhar Lake at that point is a pond dedicated to Devyānī.[29] The legend associated with the place is that Shukrācārya, the guru of the demons, lived there, whose daughter married Yayāti. The pilgrimage site, built around a pond, has many buildings from the eighteenth and nineteenth century, though nearly all are in ruins now.[30]

Nāgarīdās's itinerary does not include a stop in the city of Jaipur, though on the way out of Devyānī, Sāvant Singh speaks of making obeisance to 'Govind, the Lord of Gokul'. It naturally comes to mind that this might be the famous Govindadev image that by this time was installed in Jaipur in the Jaynivās.[31] If he indeed paid a visit to Jaipur, however, most likely Sāvant Singh did so not in the course of his trip to Delhi but around September 1750, when he successfully sought the help of Ishvari Singh, then the Jaipur king. We know from Maratha sources that Ishvari Singh marched with him to Rūpnagar, helping him lay siege to the city occupied by Sāvant Singh's brother, but then left for lack of funds, leaving only a small contingent under Kṛpārām with Sāvant Singh to continue the siege, which was ineffectual.[32] In any case, it would be odd if Nāgarīdās entered the city of Jaipur on the occasion of his pilgrimage without mentioning it at all. Hence, it seems likely that he instead bypassed Jaipur, possibly because of the dynastic struggles going on at the time.[33] If Sāvant Singh, for whatever reason, did not enter Jaipur, he may have meant not the 'real' Govindadeva image in Jaipur, but one of the shrines where the deity had been installed on his way to Jaipur about half a century earlier, and where after the transfer a 'replacement image' had been installed.[34] If so, that too might have found mention in the *Tīrthānand*, but it does not. It is remarkable how all the political strife of the times is simply bypassed in the *Tīrthānand*'s pilgrimage narrative.

Sāvant Singh's next stop is the Rāmānandī monastery of Galtā, right outside Jaipur.[35] Given the importance of this monastery and its political and military clout in Jaipur at the time,[36] one wonders whether possibly Nāgarīdās had also the intention of enlisting the help of the powerful Rāmānandī Nāgās for his cause. If he did, he did not succeed: he simply describes the site. He also remembers happily his meeting with the *mahant* at the time, Hariācārya, who was the first householder-abbot at Galta (*TĀ*, 6–8). The two men had much in common. They were both poets interested in the divine love play and they were both active as sponsors for this type of religious event.[37] Hariācārya started a tradition of organizing *rāslīlās* in Galtā on the festival of Rām's wedding.[38] Nāgarīdās too had a special interest in rāslīlā, which he reports attending shortly afterwards in the Braj area. Thus, their conversations likely dwelled not just on military plans but on religious matters as well.

The first stop in Braj for the party travelling from Rajasthan was Govardhan, which was circumambulated (*TĀ*, 10, 12), with ensuing stops at nearby Rādhā- and Krishna-*kuṇḍas* (*TĀ*, 14). This involved *kīrtan* with musical accompaniment and drew a lot of attention to the party performing the rite as other enthusiasts joined the group. Persons named Bansīdās and Murlīdās are singled out for mention as members of a local all-night singing party (*TĀ*, 14–17).[39] Murlīdās also had visited Rūpnagar when Nāgarīdās was still the crown prince, as we know from another of his works.[40]

Mathura, referred to by its Sanskritic name Madhupurī, is next on the itinerary (*TĀ*, 18). Here the only specific site mentioned is Viśrānt Ghāṭ, where, as we have mentioned, Nāgarīdās witnesses the āratī of the Yamuna at dusk (*TĀ*, 19). Next en route is Vrindāban, where we know the family possessed a residence now called Nāgarī Kunj.[41] In Vrindāban, Sāvant Singh mentions his reception by the local community. He says sādhus come running to meet not Prince Sāvant Singh but Nāgarīdās, the author of wonderful songs. It seems that, like modern-day pilgrims, Nāgarīdās had darśan in the Bihārī temple, although the reference is slightly ambiguous (*TĀ*, 33).[42] The only other site described in Vrindāban is Jñān Gudarī, where an all-night devotional singing party ensues (*TĀ*, 35–7).

But Sāvant Singh did not stay in Braj. As he travelled onwards, his first stop was at Soron, an ancient pilgrimage centre on the west bank of the Ganges, east of Aligarh. This makes sense in terms of Rajput pilgrimage patterns. For instance, in 1648, the Mewar royal family made an extended pilgrimage trip from Mathura and Gokul to Prayāg, Kāśī, and Ayodhyā with a stop in Soron (Śukra) on the way. The party included the young prince and future ruler Rāj Singh (r. 1652–80),[43] who later commissioned an illustrated manuscript (finished in 1655) of the Sanskrit *Sukara kṣetra mahāpurāṇa*, a text celebrating the miraculous power of the Soron Tīrtha.[44] In 1724, Savāī Jai Singh II too, while he was the governor of Agra and engaged in a campaign against the Jats, extended his pilgrimage to Braj with a jaunt to Soron.[45] It is also a site where people immerse the ashes of their deceased family members, but Sāvant Singh does not mention doing that.

It is possible that he had intended to set out for Prayāg, like some of the other parties mentioned, but instead he turned north to meet the Marathas. The latter, under Jaya Appā Sindhia and Mahar Rao Holkar, were fighting the Rohillas in the north in 1751, driving them up into the Terai region and Kumaon.[46] En route, Sāvant Singh once again finds opportunities for pilgrimage: he mentions Rāmeśvaram and the ashram of Kapila.[47] He also mentions approaching Dhavalāgiri[48] 'where not even birds fly' (*TĀ*, 55) and bathing in the Kauśikī river, supposedly the modern Kosi river, though its course may have been different. Yet he gives very little description of these Himalayan sites. Instead he describes rushing back down the mountains, keen on returning to Braj.

Delhi too is in his sights: he is pursuing the second of his two bids of alliance-building with the Mughals. But as he travels up the left bank of the Yamuna towards Delhi, he sees the land of Braj at the other side of the river and cannot contain himself:

> I saw the woods of Vrindā at the other side,
> but in between flowed a deep river.
> No boat, no other means,
> O God, how to get across? (*TĀ*, 61)
> Staying on this side brings shame to my zeal;
> Going across would fulfill all my designs....(*TĀ*, 62)
> Even as I was considering this
> I jumped into the water, gaining the middle of the stream.
> As my feet moved, running frantically,
> My zeal became my rescue.... (*TĀ*, 64)
> Then a wave of politics swept me away.
> To Indraprastha I went, separation burning my heart.
> Where are Delhi's walls? Where begins the Holy Land?
> Then again Shyām brought me back.
> I left that place and with it all worldly cares.
> With mounting excitement, I turned back towards Braj. (*TĀ*, 69)

From this fragment, we can see the tension between the political goals that prompted the journey—covert from the point of view of the narrative—and the stated goal of visiting holy places. Sāvant Singh consciously foregrounds the pilgrimage experience over the building of political alliances. Unable to resist the call of Krishna's flute when no boats are available, he makes his way across the river—half running, half swimming. He poignantly puts it as a choice between 'this side' and 'the other side'. For the homeless king, the question of his true residence takes on poignant dimensions. He sees himself compelled to go to Delhi and involve himself in military alliance-building, but where is his heart? In Braj.

Soon, indeed, Nāgarīdās returns to Braj. This time, approaching from Delhi, he first reaches Barsānā. He vividly describes the road to Barsānā, with the white palace temple in the distance (*TĀ*, 71). It is here that Sāvant Singh seems to have been based for the rest of the time he describes in his pilgrimage account. Bucolic as it may seem, however—certainly in legend—Barsānā at this time was far from being provincial and isolated, lost in a devotional world. This is exactly the period when Barsānā was being built up under the influence of Rūp Rām, a Brahmin who served as priest and negotiator of the Jat rulers Sūraj Mal and Javāhar Singh.[49] Rūp Rām built the Lārilījī temple on the hill, which superseded the earlier one attributed to Vīr Singh of Orcchā, and this is probably the one Nāgarīdās describes seeing from a distance. Other wealthy families also chose to reside there, including a Thākur who is said to have made his fortune in Lucknow.[50]

Actually, in the mid-eighteenth century, there was a big real estate boom in this area. One suspects that Sāvant Singh actively chose to be in this 'happening place', since for this second lengthy stay it served as the centre of his activities, rather than Vrindāban, which was equally accessible from Delhi. The rites he describes may well reflect Barsānā's new-found prominence. They represent not so much the time-honoured traditions as what was 'in' for the new elites that were involved in the Barsānā boom. All festivals described are in locations within striking distance of Barsānā: Nandagāṃv, Uṃchāgāṃv, Karaharā, Kadam Khaṇḍī, and so on. All these places were trendy at the time and were being built up by those associated with the Jats and others. Karaharā, for instance, the place where everyone gathered for the birth festival of Lalitā, one of Rādhā's friends (*sakhīs*), is described at length (*TĀ*, 98–100). A monarch no less than Savāī Jai Singh of Jaipur had built a mansion there for the leader of a rāslīlā group called Vikram.[51]

Breakthrough to Krishna's Mythical Realm

The pilgrimage described by Nāgarīdās involves many opportunities for participatory rites. One way this is facilitated is by joining in communal singing, but he partakes in processions and enactments of the divine līlā as well, and in merrymaking and riotous revelry generally. The Braj rāslīlās are choreographed in such a way that they elicit intense audience participation; their audiences are indeed transported to Krishna's mythical world.[52] We see this repeatedly in Nāgarīdās's accounts of festivals, but it also conditions his personal experiences. About the moment when he swam across the Yamuna, for instance, he says that 'Taranijā allowed me to cross; the Lord of the forest grabbed my hand' (*TĀ*, 65).[53] Later, he ascribes his ability to stay in Barsānā to an invitation issued from Rādhā's father Vrishabhānu and delivered by Rādhā herself (*TĀ*, 70–5). This ability to be transported into the world of the gods via participation in their rites comes out most strongly at the climax of the work, when Nāgarīdās describes the reenactment of the Holī rites undertaken by the villagers of Nandagāṃv and Barsānā.

These Holī festivities involve processional movements, in which the actors impersonating Nanda, Yaśodā, Krishna, and Balrām on one side, and Vrishabhānu, his wife, and Rādhā on the other accompany the people in song, merrymaking, and colour-throwing. In his description, Nāgarīdās stresses not the role played by the actors themselves, but rather that of the audience. This is where Nāgarīdās himself joins the fun and gets caught by the ladies of Barsānā. He is literally swept off his feet, drenched in coloured paint, and has his clothes tied to theirs while they sing mock (and mocking) wedding songs. He declares that now he truly feels he has 'arrived' in Braj (*TĀ*, 201–2). He proclaims the festival of Phāg as the essence of Braj, and Barsānā and Nandagāṃv as the essence of its special joy (*TĀ*, 208–11). He begs Rādhā and Krishna to keep him in Braj forever, and with that he ends the work. This climax of audience participation in the festivals leads for Nāgarīdās to a breakthrough into the divine world.

Conclusion

In his *Tīrthānand*, Sāvant Singh's search for political and military support becomes transformed into an account of a pilgrim's progress. Remarkably, he casts his peregrinations in exile as an account of joy, mainly the joy of visiting Braj. 'Business' does intrude upon the eternal bliss of Vrindāban, but only minimally. God's play—Krishna's līlā as enacted in Braj—becomes the real world for him, whereas his efforts to gather troops and build alliances become mere shadow play. Thus, the *Tīrthānand* is an extended effort on the part of Nāgarīdās to write himself into Krishna's world. In the miniatures he sponsored in happier days, Krishna was depicted enjoying naukā vihāra on Lake Gundalao, as Prince Savant Singh himself also did. Now, similarly, we see Nāgarīdās go boating on the Yamuna. Whereas earlier he tried to draw Braj into his courtly world, now he and his courtiers are drawn quite literally into Braj. The *bhakta*s who used to visit his court in Rūpnagar now invite him into their huts in Rādhākuṇd, asking him to partake in all-night kīrtan sessions.

This entrance into Braj is not exactly a retirement from the world, however. Sāvant Singh settled in the trendy places that were part of the contemporary Jat-inspired real estate boom. The area of Barsānā and Nandagāṃv was where things were happening, and where noblemen, successful businessmen, and shrewd political agents had settled. Like so many others at his time, Sāvant Singh was drawn into Krishna's world, while at the same time bringing his own world to Braj. Sāvant Singh inscribed his own life into myth by participating into the rites enacting Krishna and Rādhā's adventures. The participatory rites of Braj, especially the seasonal ones, were well designed to facilitate just this transformation. Nāgarīdās describes the riotous climax of the process in the Holī celebrations of Barsānā and Nandagāṃv. When the women of Braj molest him as part of those rites, he feels completely accepted, absorbed in the world of myth. By describing a moment when the boundaries between spectator and participant begin to blur, Nāgarīdās allowed the carnival that is Braj to unleash its creative powers[54] and his pilgrimage to fulfil its healing goal. Did this happen in the moment or in retrospect, in the experience lived or the experience relived in memory? Rightly, perhaps, the *Tīrthānand* does not provide us the means to decide.

Notes

* A longer version of this chapter was circulated under the title 'The Joy of Pilgrimage' or 'Seeking Maratha Help?' for the Shimla Conference. It is the basis of a chapter in my forthcoming book *On the Move from Court to Temple*, which includes a full translation of the text. In interlinear references in the text, I shorten the title *Tīrthānanda to TĀ*.

1. Alan W. Entwistle, *Braj: Centre of Krishna Pilgrimage*, Groningen Oriental Studies, 3 (Groningen: Egbert Forsten, 1987), 159.

2. Gopal Narayan Bahura, 'Śrī Govinda Gāthā: Service Rendered to Govinda by the Rulers of Āmera and Jayapura', in *Govindadeva: A Dialogue in Stone*, ed. Margaret H. Case (New Delhi: Indira Gandhi National Centre for the Arts, 1996), 199–200.

3. Janardan Rāo Celer, *Vṛnd Granthāvalī* (Agra: Vinod Pustak Mandir, 1971), 135–7, 143–7.

4. Norbert Peabody, 'In Whose Turban Does the Lord Reside: The Objectification of Charisma and the Fetishism of Objects in the Hindu Kingdom of Kota', *Comparative Studies in Society and History* 33, no. 4 (1991): 735–7.

5. *Rājapraśasti sarga* 22.8–9; Motilal Menaria, *Mahākavi Ranchoḍ Bhaṭṭ praṇītaṃ rājpraśasti˙ mahākāvya* (Udaipur: Sāhitya Sansthān, 1973), 233.

6. Vijay Kumar Mathur, *Marvels of Kishangarh Paintings from the Collection of the National Museum, New Delhi* (New Delhi: Bharatiya Kala Prakashan, 2000), plate 4.

7. Mathur, *Marvels of Kishangarh Paintings*, 11.

8. This was on 15 April 1748 (Vaisākh *badi* 14). For the exact date, see Raghubir Sinh, *The Julusi Saneh's of the Mughal Emperors of India (1556–1857 A.D.)* (Sitamau: Shri Natnagar Shodh Samsthan, 1984), 22; for the background, see Zahir Uddin Malik, *The Reign of Muhammad Shah (1719–1748)* (New York: Asia Publishing House, 1977), 176–84, who gives a different date, but does not provide a source.

9. Jagannath Sarkar, *A History of Jaipur* (Hyderabad: Orient Longman, 1984 [1964], revised edition), 290–315.

10. They did so at their own peril. Jai Singh had foreseen the threat of the Marathas and tried to unite against them with the Hurda agreement of 1734. Kishangarh had been party to this, as well as Marwar, Mewar, Bikaner, Kota, and Karauli (G. R. Parihar, *Marwar and the Marathas (1724–1843 A.D.)* [Jodhpur: Hindi Sahitya Mandir, 1968], 50–1).

11. G. I. Sardesai, ed., *Selections from the Peshwa Daftar*, 46 vols (Bombay: Government Central Press, 1930–4), 21: 29, no. 31.

12. Sarkar, *A History of Jaipur*, 1.253–8.

13. Sardesai, *Selections from the Peshwa Daftar*, 27: 76, no 79.

14. Sardesai, *Selections from the Peshwa Daftar*, 27: 76, no 79; a letter by him dated 9 May 1756; Parihar, *Marwar and the Marathas*, p. 90.

15. VS 1813, *āṣāḍh baḍī* 5; Vrajvallabh Śaraṇ, *Śrī Nāgarīdāsjī kī vāṇī: Nāgarīdāśjī ke jīvanvṛtta evaṃ vāṇiyoṃ kā sanśodhit sanskaraṇ* (Vrindaban: Śrī Sarveśvar Press, 1966 [1972]), 246. It is not clear what Śaraṇ's sources are. He also quotes an epic on Sardār Singh, called *Sardār Sujas*, authored by Hīrālāl Sanāṛya of Karaulī in VS 1816 (*Śrī Nāgarīdāsjī kī vāṇī*, 246).

16. He is said to have set out in 1756 (1813 VS; Bābū Rādhākṛṣṇadās, 'Śrīnāgrīdāsjī kā jīvan caritra', in Śrīdharātmaja Kisanlāl Gauḍ, ed. *Nāgarasamuccaya* (Mumbai: Jnānsāgar, 1898), 5.

17. This is described in gruesome detail twenty-five years later by the eyewitness Samīn, as translated in William Irvine, 'Ahmad Shāh Abdālī and the Indian Wazzīr, Imād-ul-Mulk (1756–7)', *Indian Antiquary* 36 (1907): 60, 62. Another eyewitness report is by the devotee Cācā Vrindābandās who describes two different attacks, the second in 1760–1, see Imre Bangha, 'Courtly and Religious Communities as Centres of Literary Activity in Eighteenth-Century India', in *Indian Languages and Texts through the Ages*, ed. Csaba Dezsö (New Delhi: Manohar, 2007 [1997]), 232.

18. Āśvin sudi 9, Thursday, in VS 1814; Bangha, 'Courtly and Religious Communities', 247.

19. See K. A. Acharya, *Maratha-Rajput Relations from 1720 to 1795 A.D.* (Akola: Sitabai Arts College, 1978), 216–18.

20. Entwistle, *Braj*, 197–8; Irvine, 'Ahmad Shāh Abdālī and the Indian Wazzīr', 70.

21. James Lochtefeld, *God's Gateway: Identity and Meaning in a Hindu Pilgrimage Place* (New York: Oxford University Press, 2010), 228.

22. Lochtefeld, *God's Gateway*, 173.

23. Irina Glushkova, 'Moving God(s)ward: The Idea of Tīrtha-yātrā', *Bulletin of the Deccan College. Professor Ashok R. Kelkar Felicitation* 62–3 (2004): 265–83.

24. Glushkova, 'Moving God(s)ward', 269.

25. Ann Grodzins Gold, *Fruitful Journeys: The Ways of Rajasthani Pilgrims* (Berkeley: University of California Press, 1988), 149. For an overview of these goals, see, for example, Surinder M. Bhardwaj and James G. Lochtefeld, 'Tīrtha', in *The Hindu World*, ed. Sushil Mittal and Gene Thursby (New York: Routledge, 2004).

26. This is somewhat related to what Ann Gold describes under her section 'Troubles Relieved, Wellbeing Procured: What Happens at Shrines', in *Fruitful Journeys*, 146–54, though she talks more about concerns of physical health and desire for offspring, all within a *do ut des* mentality. What I intend to stress here comes closer perhaps to Bhardwaj and Lochtefeld's 'peace' and relieving 'mental tension' (Surinder M. Bhardwaj and James G. Lochtefeld, 'Tīrtha', 493–4).

27. For a similar example, see the case for the pilgrimage of Raghunath Rao of Vincur (Maharashtra) in the mid-nineteenth century, who embarked on his first pilgrimage after the loss of his wife and daughter (Glushkova, 'Moving God(s)ward', 218).

28. Irfan Habib, *An Atlas of the Mughal Empire: Political and Economic Maps with Detailed Notes, Bibliography, and Index* (Aligarh: Centre of Advanced Study in History, Aligarh Muslim University; Delhi and New York: Oxford University Press, 1982[1978]), plate 6B; 26–7° by 75°.

29. Faiyāz Alī Khan, *Nāgarīdās Granthāvalī* (New Delhi: Kendrīya Hindī Nideśālay, 1974), 364.

30. The pond was dry when I visited on 27 July 2011, and the site seems now quite far from an active pilgrimage centre. Apparently, though, it was very popular in the eighteenth and nineteenth centuries, judging from the architecture.

31. Nath R. Śrī Govindadeva's 'Itinerary from Vṛndāvana to Jayapura, c. 1534–1727', in *Govindadeva: A Dialogue in Stone*, ed. Margareth H. Case (New Delhi: Indira Gandhi National Centre for the Arts, 1996), 180–1.

32. Nath, 'Itinerary from Vṛndāvana to Jayapura', 239; Sardesai, *Selections from the Peshwa Daftar* 2: 17 and 23.

33. Ishvari Singh was Savāī Jay Singh's oldest son and heir, but his throne was contested by his half-brother. If Sāvant Singh's pilgrimage took place immediately after the death of his father, around August 1748, it was right at the time of the battle of Bagru between the contender Madho Singh (who had the Peshwa Balaji Rao on his side) and Ishvari Singh (who had the Jat leader Suraj Mal on his side). Throughout August, the battle was raging and the Marathas were plundering the area around Sambhar Lake

(Sarkar, *A History of Jaipur*, 236–8). That seems an unlikely time for Sāvant Singh to be travelling. Alternatively, Sāvant Singh may have travelled in the course of the next year or so, but again by April 1750 another major battle was going on. This time, Ishvari Singh was involved in the succession battle of Marwar on the side of the beleaguered Rām Singh against Bakht Singh and his supporter, Mīr Bakhśī Salabat Khān. This battle took place in Raona (south of Merta), so he would have been absent from Jaipur. Alternatively, Sāvant Singh's trip may have taken place after 1750, perhaps after the abortive seige of Rūpnagar. By that time, Ishvari Singh had committed suicide and Mādho Singh would have been on the throne. Since the latter was an ally of Sāvant Singh's brother Bahādur Singh, one might think Sāvant Singh would have detoured around the city. Moreover, in January 1751, there had been the massacre of Marathas in Jaipur, which caused significant upheaval (Sarkar, *A History of Jaipur*, 243–4).

34. This would most likely have been Rūpāheḍā (also known as Govindapurā), situated southwest of Galtā (Nath, 'Itinerary from Vṛndāvana to Jayapura', 174). Alternatively, it could have been Kanaka Vrindāvana near Āmer (Nath, 'Itinerary from Vṛndāvana to Jayapura', 174–8).

35. Mentioned here by its Sanskritic name Gālavāśrama, after the ashram of another Vedic sage, whose shrine is in the complex.

36. In 1730, the then abbot, Vrijānand, signed a document promising to conform with his Nāgās to Jai Singh II's stipulations of orthodoxy. After Jai Singh's death in 1743, Vrijānand fought on the side of Ishvari Singh, and took part in the Bundī succession wars at the latter's side. Fascinatingly, Vrijānand had strong connections with the Braj area, where he died (his samādhi is still at Govardhan) (Monika Horstmann, 'Power and Status: Ramanandi Warrior Ascetics in 18th-Century Rajasthan', in *Asceticism and Power in South and Southeast Asia*, ed. Peter Flügel and Gustaaf Houtman [London: Routledge, forthcoming], available online at https://uniheidelberg.academia.edu/MonikaBoehmTettelbach).

37. Hariācārya composed poetry with the *chāpa* 'Hari-sahacarī', which shows his *Rām-rasik* inclinations (Bhagavatī Prasād Siṃha, *Rāmbhakti meṃ rasik sampradāy*, Rasik Granthmālā 1 [Balrāmpur: Avadh Sāhitya Mandir, 1957], 408–9). He was heavily influenced by Krishnaite models: he wrote a Hindī *Aṣṭayām* and a Sanskrit *Jānakīgīta*, modelled after *Gītagovinda*.

38. Monika Horstmann, 'The Rāmānandīs of Galtā (Jaipur, Rajasthan)', in *Multiple Histories: Culture and Society in the Study of Rajasthan*, ed. L. Babb, V. Joshi, and M. Meister (Jaipur: Rawat Publications, 2002), 170; Siṃha, *Rāmbhakti meṃ rasik sampradāy*, 408–9.

39. Nāgarīdās mentions staying again with Bansīdās later, during the all-night singing for the Kārtik-bathing festival at Rādhākuṇd (*TĀ*, 133). Nāgarīdās is very positive about his gatherings in Rādhākuṇd with Bansīdās and Murlīdās. It is possible that the former was a follower of the

unorthodox party of Rūpa Kavirāja, the so-called *sauramya–mat*, who lived at Surmā Kunj. They had been socially excluded for their defiance of Savāī Jai Singh's measures (Horstmann, *Der Zusammenhalt der Welt*, 75–86). Bansīdās maybe the Vaṃśīdāsa, mentioned in one of the VRI documents regarding the theologocial debates about Radha's nature as *svakīyā* or *parakīyā* (wife as against paramour), as a second-generation follower of Rūpa Kavirāja (Horstmann, *Der Zusammenhalt der Welt*, 121). This would interestingly place Nāgarīdās in the middle of a group that opposed Savāī Jai Singh's religious reforms to ensure orthodoxy, be it after the Jaipur king's death.

40. Kiśorīlāl Gupta. *Nāgarīdās*, 2 vols (Banaras: Nāgarī Pracāriṇī Sabhā, 1965).

41. Vrajvallabh Śaraṇ, *Śrī Nāgarīdāsjī kī vāṇī: nāgarīdāśjī ke jīvanvṛtta evaṃ vāṇiyoṃ kā sanśodhit sanskaraṇ* (Vrindaban: Śrī Sarveśvar Press, 1966), 15.

42. There are several other deities named 'Bihārī', the one near Nāgarī Kuñj and the old residence of Śrījī Mahārāj on Bihār Ghāṭ that was originally worshiped by Aṭalbihārī, the Nimbārkī Nāgā mentioned in *Bhakt-māl*. This deity seems to have been prominent for the Bharatpur Jats in this period (Entwistle, *Braj*, 140).

43. The party also included the young prince's grandmother Jambāvatī, Jagat Singh's mother, who seems to have been fond of pilgrimage, as she also went to Dvārkā in 1641 (Sri Ram Sharma, *Maharana Raj Singh and His Times* [New Delhi: Motilal Banarsidass, 1971], 16–17).

44. Andrew Topsfield, 'Saving Power of Soron: Sahibdin of Udaipur and the Sukarakshetra Mahatmya', in *Court Painting in Rajasthan*, ed. Andrew Topsfield (Mumbai: Marg Publications, 2000), 29.

45. Entwistle, *Braj*, 190.

46. Sarkar, *A History of Jaipur*, 1.253–8.

47. It is unclear where this shrine is located. It seems very unlikely it would be the shrine near Banaras, or near the sources of the Narmada River (Surinder Mohan Bhardwaj, *Hindu Places of Pilgrimage in India (A Study in Cultural Geography)* [Berkeley: University of California Press, 1973], 49). The one at Gaṅgāsāgar at the mouth of the Ganges seems even further afield.

48. Probably not Daulagiri, now in Nepal, more likely one of the bright white peaks in the neighbourhood of Badrinath, such as Gauriparbat (6, 727 m) or Dunagiri (7,066 m).

49. Entwistle, *Braj*, 370–1.

50. Entwistle, *Braj*, 271.

51. Entwistle, *Braj*, 383.

52. John Stratton Hawley and Shrivatsa Goswami, *At Play with Krishna: Pilgrimage Dramas from Brindavan* (Princeton, NJ: Princeton University Press, 1981), 104.

53. A related feature of the text could be characterized as the interpretation of events as miraculous. Thus, a flood of the Ganges at Soron is interpreted

by Nāgarīdās as a manifestation of the river's anger about the slaughter of a goat by someone in his company (*TĀ*, 42–4). It is unclear what happened. Apparently, there was a sudden flash flood and his party had to flee the riverbanks. Nāgarīdās also directs on two occasions a prayer to the Ganges that he may be able to return to Braj (*TĀ*, 47–9, 59). His wish, of course, is granted.

54. Cf. Bakhtin's analysis of medieval carnival and its creative forces as compared to modern-day Mardi Gras that has degenerated into a mere spectacle (Michael Bakhtin, *Rabelais and His World*, trans. Hélène Iswolsky [Bloomington: Indiana University Press, 1984 [1965]], 7).

Bibliography

Acharya, K. A. *Maratha-Rajput Relations from 1720 to 1795 A.D.* Akola: Sitabai Arts College, 1978.

Bahura, Gopal Narayan. 'Śrī Govinda Gāthā: Service Rendered to Govinda by the Rulers of Āmera and Jayapura'. In *Govindadeva: A Dialogue in Stone*, edited by Margaret H. Case. New Delhi: Indira Gandhi National Centre for the Arts, 1996.

Bakhtin, Michael. *Rabelais and His World*, translated by Hélène Iswolsky. Bloomington: Indiana University Press, 1984 (1965).

Bangha, Imre. 'Courtly and Religious Communities as Centres of Literary Activity in Eighteenth-Century India'. In *Indian Languages and Texts through the Ages*, edited by Csaba Dezsö. Delhi: Manohar, 2007.

Bhardwaj, Surinder M. and James G. Lochtefeld. 'Tīrtha'. In *The Hindu World*, edited by Sushil Mittal and Gene Thursby. New York: Routledge, 2004.

Bhardwaj, Surinder Mohan. *Hindu Places of Pilgrimage in India (A Study in Cultural Geography)*. Berkeley: University of California Press, 1973.

Celer, Janardan Rao. *Vṛnd Granthāvalī*. Agra: Vinod Pustak Mandir, 1971.

Entwistle, Alan W. *Braj: Centre of Krishna pilgrimage*. Groningen Oriental Studies, 3. Groningen: Egbert Forsten, 1987.

Glushkova, Irina. 'Moving God(s)ward: The Idea of Tīrtha-yātrā'. *Bulletin of the Deccan College. Professor Ashok R. Kelkar Felicitation Volume* 62–3 (2004): 265–83.

Gold, Ann Grodzins. *Fruitful Journeys: The Ways of Rajasthani Pilgrims*. Berkeley: University of California Press, 1988.

Gupta, Kiśorīlāl. *Nāgarīdās* (2 vols). Banaras: Nāgarī Pracāriṇī Sabhā, 1965.

Habib, Irfan. *An Atlas of the Mughal Empire: Political and Economic Maps with Detailed Notes, Bibliography, and Index*. Aligarh: Centre of Advanced Study in History, Aligarh Muslim University; Delhiand New York: Oxford University Press, 1982.

Hawley, John Stratton and Shrivatsa Goswami. *At Play with Krishna: Pilgrimage Dramas from Brindavan*. Princeton, NJ: Princeton University Press, 1981.

Horstmann, Monika. 'The Rāmānandīs of Galtā (Jaipur, Rajasthan)'. In *Multiple Histories: Culture and Society in the Study of Rajasthan*, edited by L. Babb, V. Joshi, M. Meister. Jaipur: Rawat Publications, 2002, 141–97.

———. *Der Zusammenhalt der Welt: Religiöse Herrschaftslegitimation und Religionspolitik Mahārājā Savāī Jaisinghs (1700–1743)*. Wiesbaden: Otto Harrassowitz, 2009.

———. 'Power and Status: Ramanandi Warrior Ascetics in 18th-Century Rajasthan'. In *Asceticism and Power in South and Southeast Asia*, edited by Peter Flügel and Gustaaf Houtman. London: Routledge, forthcoming. Available online at https://uni-heidelberg.academia.edu/MonikaBoehmTettelbach.

Irvine, William. 'Ahmad Shāh Abdālī and the Indian Wazzīr, Imād-ul-Mulk (1756–7)'. *Indian Antiquary* 36 (1907): 10–18, 43–51, 55–70.

Khān, Faiyāz Alī. *Nāgarīdās Granthāvalī*. New Delhi: Kendrīya Hindī Nideśālay, 1974.

Lochtefeld, James. *God's Gateway: Identity and Meaning in a Hindu Pilgrimage Place*. New York: Oxford University Press, 2010.

———. 'Pilgrimage'. In *Oxford Bibliography Online: Hinduism*, edited by Alf Hiltebeitel. New York: Oxford University Press. DOI: 10.1093/OBO/9780195399318-0096, last accessed on 4 October 2017.

Malik, Zahir Uddin. *The Reign of Muhammad Shah (1719–1748)*. New York: Asia Publishing House, 1977.

Mathur, Vijay Kumar. *Marvels of Kishangarh Paintings from the Collection of the National Museum, New Delhi*. Delhi: Bharatiya Kala Prakashan, 2000.

Menaria, Motilal. *Mahākavi Ranchoḍ Bhaṭṭ Praṇītaṃ Rājpraśasti˙ Mahākāvya*. Udaipur: Sāhitya Sansthān, 1973.

Nath, R. 'Śrī Govindadeva's Itinerary from Vṛndāvana to Jayapura, c. 1534–1727'. In *Govindadeva: A Dialogue in Stone*, edited by Margareth H. Case. New Delhi: Indira Gandhi National Centre for the Arts, 1996.

Parihar, G.R. *Marwar and the Marathas (1724–1843 A.D.)*. Jodhpur: Hindi Sahitya Mandir, 1968.

Peabody, Norbert. 'In Whose Turban Does the Lord Reside: The Objectification of Charisma and the Fetishism of Objects in the Hindu Kingdom of Kota'. *Comparative Studies in Soceity and History* 33, no. 4 (1991): 726–54.

Rādhākṛṣṇadās, Bābū. 'Śrīnāgarīdāsjī kā jīvan caritra'. In *Nāgarasamuccaya*, edited by Śrīdharātmaja Kisanlāl Gaud. Mumbai: Jnānsāgar, 1898, 1–25.

Śaraṇ, Vrajvallabh. *Śrī Nāgarīdāsjī kī vāṇī: Nāgarīdāśjī ke jīvanvṛtta evaṃ vāṇiyoṃ kā sanśodhit sanskaraṇ*. Vrindaban: Śrī Sarveśvar Press, 1966.

Sarkar, Jagannath. *A History of Jaipur*. Hyderabad: Orient Longman, 1984, revised edition.

Siṃha, Bhagavatī Prasād. *Rāmbhakti meṃ rasik sampradāy*. Rasik Granthmālā 1. Balrampur: Avadh Sāhitya Mandir, 1957.

Sinh, Raghubir. *The Julusi Saneh's of the Mughal Emperors of India (1556–1857 A.D.)*. Sitamau: Shri Natnagar Shodh Samsthan. 1984.

Sharma, Sri Ram. *Maharana Raj Singh and His Times*. New Delhi: Motilal Banarsidass, 1971.

Topsfield, Andrew. 'Saving Power of Soron: Sahibdin of Udaipur and the Sukarakshetra Mahatmya'. In *Court Painting in Rajasthan*, edited by Andrew Topsfield. Mumbai: Marg Publications, 2000, 26–40.

PART FOUR

SAMPRADĀY AND BEYOND

17

SHRIVATSA GOSWAMI

Gopal Bhatt

Carrier of *Bhakti* to the North

He who has mastered all the steps and gestures (in dance),
Who loves drama and music,
Who enhances the bliss in people's minds,
Who dwells in the divine pastimes,
Whose speech is ingenious and full of variety,
Who is best amongst the wise—
May this godlike man, Gopal Bhatt, protect a fallen soul like me.

—Kavikarnapura[1]

In this chapter I shall explore how Gopal Bhatt, in interaction with Chaitanya Mahaprabhu, transformed and transcreated the Chaitanyites' philosophy and rituals for the new *sampradāy* (community sharing common beliefs and practices) that was under formation at Vrindavan in the first half of the sixteenth century.[2] I will do so by introducing Gopal Bhatt's two major works—the *Ṣaṭ-Sandarbha* (Six Treatises), which is his pre-eminent philosophical formulation, and the *Haribhaktivilāsa* (The Pleasure of Worshiping Hari), where he provides what today might be called a lifestyle code for the new Vaishnava community of which he was a part. As we survey these works, we will begin to see how Gopal Bhatt, an immigrant from the south, became a prominent catalyst for important conceptual and aesthetic canons that took hold in the Braj region in the first half of the sixteenth century. We will also see, however, that there is an element of mystery in the matter of how his philosophical statements relate to his pronouncements on devotional practice.

Bhakti—the Link between South and North

Streams and rivers have a universal nature, which is to flow, and *bhakti* too is such a flowing mass (*dhārā*), albeit a current of Indian culture and history. Yet bhakti is different from other streams and rivers. They normally flow from east to west or north to south, while bhakti is believed to have flowed upwards from south to north as it played its formative role in Indian history. The connecting point between the Brajs of southern and northern India is bhakti, which moves effortlessly from place to place. As we read in the *Bhāgavata Māhātmya*, where bhakti is personified as a beautiful woman, bhakti was born in the Tamil land, grew up in Karnataka, and came of age in Maharashtra and Gujarat.[3] For bhakti, it was an existential requirement to reach Vrindavan because it was only there that she could repair herself from the damages she had suffered from hypocrites and heretics. Indeed, as the *Māhātmya* tells us, when bhakti reached Vrindavan, she was rejuvenated; she danced for joy.

The *Bhāgavata Māhātmya* describes this movement from south to north as if it were a single event, but a closer look enables us to flesh out the details and see how it was actually not a one-time affair. Some of this information comes from the *Bhaktamāl* of Nabhadas—his portrait of saints such as Ramanand—but we meet it in more recent scholarship as well. Friedhelm Hardy,[4] for instance, has emphasized the role that was played by Madhavendra Puri in this broad process. As vehicles by means of which bhakti could travel to the north in the fifteenth and sixteenth centuries, Ramanand and Madhavendra Puri were not alone. Gopal Bhatt Gosvami's life story follows just the sort of trajectory that the *Bhāgavata Māhātmya* summarizes so beautifully. He belonged to the famous 'six *gosvāmīs*' who played leadership roles in the community dedicated to Sri Chaitanya Mahaprabhu as it developed in Vrindavan in the course of the sixteenth century. Gopal Bhatt is somewhat less well known than gosvāmīs such as Rup, Sanatan, and Jiv, but, as we shall see, his role in their common enterprise was no less crucial than theirs.

Finding and Grooming Gopal Bhatt

The story of Gopal Bhatt begins with that archetypal non-resident Bengali, Sri Chaitanya Mahaprabhu (1486–1533), who, after taking *sannyāsa* (renunciation—classically, the fourth stage in an individual's life) in 1509, wanted to live at Vrindavan. At the request of his mother, Sachi Devi, however, he settled in Jagannath Puri instead, where she would be able to visit him on a periodic basis. Not much later, in 1510–11, Chaitanya travelled to the south of India, the land of bhakti and the *Bhāgavata Purāṇa*. There, on the banks of the Godavari, he met Ray Ramanand, a governor serving under the Gajapati king Pratap Rudra of Orissa (Odisha). As he conversed with Ray, Chaitanya was successful in envisioning a grand framework that would make possible a proper systemic discourse about bhakti, including a number of subsidiary classifications.[5] The picture we get from the *Caitanya Caritāmṛta* is that Chaitanya Mahaprabhu, like an ocean, had all these doctrines and ideas assembled in his own mind, but in the service of humanity he wanted them to be distilled and then showered to earth by a gifted structural thinker such as Ray Ramanand, who would thereby act like a cloud on his behalf. In connecting with Ray Ramanand, the first stage of Chaitanya's mission was accomplished.

Yet further resources also needed to be brought to bear. Chaitanya proceeded farther south to Srirangam, the great centre of Vaishnava experience and expression that was heir to the glorious tradition of bhakti elaborated by Ramanujacharya. What Chaitanya required at this point was very clear in his mind. He was looking for a functioning doctrinal system supported by codes of conduct that set out a comprehensive and coherent Vaishnava lifestyle. To gain access to these codes, Chaitanya lodged himself as the guest of Vainkata Bhatt, the chief priest of the great Srirangam temple, for a considerable period of time. During this time, Gopal Bhatt, Vainkata's son,[6] who was some ten years old at the time, was put in the service of the illustrious visiting *sannyāsī* from Bengal.[7]

In the course of his four-month stay at Srirangam, traditional for an ascetic in the monsoon season, Sri Chaitanya trained the prodigy Gopal Bhatt in the Bhāgavata tradition as he understood it. Using the framework elaborately worked out on the banks of Godavari with Ray Ramanand, he initiated and indoctrinated Gopal Bhatt into the philosophy and spiritual discipline of *premā bhakti* (devotion out of love). At the end of his *cāturmāsya* stay, the time when wandering sannyāsīs camp at one place and remain there for the four-month duration of the rainy season. Chaitanya received the child as a gift from his family. Instead of carrying him along on his travels, however, Chaitanya ordered Gopal Bhatt to stay at home, become fully educated in the systematic, text-oriented *śāstric* tradition, and wait for further orders. That moment came in about 1521, when Gopal Bhatt was asked by Chaitanya to go and settle at the recently discovered Vrindavan in north India along with Sanatan, Rup, and other gosvāmīs. They became its first settlers. Chaitanya had already communicated to each of the others different aspects of the framework he was intent on developing in this new and pioneering bhakti site.

Gopal Bhatt's First Act of Service: The *Bhāgavata Sandarbha*

Exactly what was Chaitanya Mahaprabhu up to? Among other things, he was ringing in a silent Vedantic revolution. Any school of Vedanta philosophy and religion would take off by commenting upon the *prasthāna trayī* (three authoritative texts)—the Upanisads, the Gita, and the Brahma Sutras. Paying due respect to all three, Chaitanya took the further step of proposing that the *Bhāgavata Purāṇa* be acknowledged as the real fifth Veda,[8] the essence of all the Upanisads,[9] and a natural commentary upon the Brahma Sutras.[10] The *Bhāgavata Purāṇa* thus became the *śāstra* par excellence, especially in our present age.[11] As Srinath Cakravarti has said:

> In the Caitanyite formulation, which declared that because the object of worship is Krishna of Braj, whose eternal abode is Vrindavan on earth, the best path of religious realization is bhakti as practiced by the gopis of Braj. The means of valid knowledge is therefore the *Bhāgavata Purāṇa* [where their deeds are described], and loving service [in the spirit of the gopis' path] is the *summum bonum* for humanity.[12]

The Vaishnava *acharyas* before Chaitanya Mahaprabhu had also been moving in this direction, but half-heartedly. Ramanuja, Madhva, and others had accepted the Mahabharata and *Bhāgavata Purāṇa* as valid śāstras, but had fallen short of according the *Bhāgavata Purāṇa* the sui generis status that Chaitanya thought it deserved—an independent authority in matters spiritual and religious. To bring the *Bhāgavata Purāṇa* into the mainline philosophical discourse of the Vedanta tradition, a proper philosophical treatise on the *Bhāgavata Purāṇa* was required. It was Gopal Bhatt who delivered these goods. He did so by writing the *Bhāgavata Sandarbha*, a treatise on the *Bhāgavata Purāṇa* in six parts; for this reason it is also called the *Ṣat-Sandarbha*, as we have mentioned earlier. The first four parts or treatises are the *Tattva*, *Bhāgavata*, *Paramātma*, and *Śrīkṛṣṇa Sandarbhas*, which explain that reality is essentially a set of relationships. The fifth volume, the *Bhakti Sandarbha*, talks about the means of realizing this relationality. Finally, the sixth volume, the *Prīti Sandarbha*, concerns the goal to which each of the spiritual disciplines described in the first five treatises leads.[13–14]

Here we must stop for a moment to look at the question of the authorship of the *Bhāgavata Sandarbha*, since it is generally ascribed to Jiv Gosvami, the youngest of the six gosvāmīs, rather than to Gopal Bhatt. This is just a half-truth, as we can judge by hearing what Jiv Gosvami himself has to say on this issue, a point that has generally been glossed over in prior scholarship. He refers to himself in the third person:

> All glories to Sri Rup and Sanatan, the residents of the land of Mathura (*vrajamaṇḍala*), who got this treatise written so as to make the truth (*tattva*) known. A certain friend of theirs, a Bhatt born in a south Indian Brahman family, properly wrote this text, having critically examined the writings of earlier Vaishnavas [Ramanuja, Madhva, Sridhara Svami, and others]. Some parts of that original work [by Gopal Bhatt] were in order, others were not, and some were damaged. Now, with his permission,[15] after careful study, Jiv is rewriting [that text].[16]

These crucial two verses (4 and 5) from the beginning of the *Tattva Sandarbha*, the first treatise of the six, represent an honest declaration on the part of Jiv about his role in the publication of the six sandarbhas. And lest there be any confusion about authorship of Gopal Bhatt, Jiv repeats both these verses at the beginning of all six sandarbhas. Jiv Gosvami is very clear about the fact that his role is a purely editorial one: he is preparing for the final publication of Gopal Bhatt's *Ṣaṭ-Sandarbha*. Whenever he had something to add to these already existing sandarbhas, he did so by writing an independent commentary named *Sarvasaṃvādinī*, which is extant so far as it concerns the first four sandarbhas but not the final two.[17]

To elaborate his viewpoint on the *Bhāgavata Purāṇa*, Jiv also wrote a comprehensive commentary called *Krama Sandarbha*.[18] At its outset, Jiv says:

> Having seen the *Bhāgavata Sandarbha* and the *Vaiṣṇava Toṣaṇī*, I am here writing a commentary upon the *Bhāgavata* as per my understanding (*mati*). If I have failed in my understanding or comprehension, it is not due to the authors of these works, but is to be known as a fault that results only from my gathering together (*samāhāra*) [of what they have already written].[19]

Once again it is very evident that Jiv is consciously distinguishing himself from the author of *Bhāgavata Sandarbha*, whom he clearly identifies as Gopal Bhatt. The same attribution of authorship was later made by Baladev Vidyābhūṣaṇ when he wrote a commentary on the *Tattva Sandarbha*.[20]

We may then safely conclude that Gopal Bhatt wrote the *Bhāgavata Sandarbha*, and that it was later comprehensively edited and published by Jiv. In this regard, we should also take note of a so-far unremarked list of manuscripts prepared by Jiv Gosvami himself in the year 1597 (VS 1654).[21] This list is classified into packets or bundles (*kothalī*), which are arranged subject-wise. The kothalī labelled *Sandarbha Granthāḥ* mentions a *Purātana Sandarbha* in addition to the *Bhāgavata Sandarbha*, probably indicating that an older version of the text was in existence before Jiv began his editorial project, which he then dubbed the *Bhāgavata Sandarbha*. Later, Baladev Vidyābhūṣaṇ also makes mention of this earlier version, and he follows suit in calling it *purātana* (older, earlier).[22] Unfortunately, we no longer have access to this older version of the *Ṣaṭ-Sandarbha*, the pre-edited text, but it seems clear that it did exist and that Jiv regarded his changes to it as being merely editorial in nature.

As is well known, Jiv also edited the works of his mentor and uncle, the famous Rup Gosvami. The eighteenth-century *Bhaktiratnākara*[23] gives us some sense of what the process must have been like. It reports an interesting exchange between Rup and Sanatan Gosvami in which the matter of Jiv's editorial assistance arises. It says:

> Sanatan Gosvami asked Rup for news: 'When is *Bhaktirasāmṛtasindhu* expected?' Rup said, 'The writing almost done. Had Jiv been around, it would have been edited (*śodhana*) quickly.'

Clearly, Jiv was responsible for editing and finishing Rup Gosvami's writing. This applies not only to the philosophical *Bhaktirasāmṛtasindhu* but also to Rup's poetic works, which were collected and published by Jiv as the *Stavamālā*.[24] Yet in none of these instances are Rup's works actually ascribed to Jiv in popular memory. Why then should we continue to believe the situation was any different in the case of Gopal Bhatt's *Bhāgavata Sandarbha*?

Let us then return to the subject matter of the sandarbhas. Gopal Bhatt, concurring with a *mahāvākya* (central proposition) of the *Bhāgavata Purāṇa*,[25] declares ultimate reality to be 'non-dual knowledge', which the Vedantic tradition, with due humility, tries to define as having the three essential characteristics *sat, cit,* and *ānanda* (being, consciousness, and bliss).[26] Yet to parse absolute reality as being *saccidānanda* in this way opens a floodgate of questions: Why does ultimate reality have three characteristics, not less or not more? If the ultimate reality is non-dual, then must these three characteristics be regarded as synonyms? Finally, if these three are in some sense sui generis, then does absolute reality have internal or external differences in its being?

Gopal Bhatt attempts to respond to such queries by making a distinction between the absolute that is *advayatva* (non-dual, indivisible, transcending all discursive knowledge) and the absolute as it appears when regarded from the standpoint of any viewer. In the latter case, it is cast in the mould of a particular human make-up. Generally, this happens in relation to three psychological characteristics—knowledge (pertaining to sat), will (pertaining to cit), and feeling (pertaining to ānanda)—where any of them may be predominant. According to Gopal Bhatt, the absolute can be approached through each of these three ways.[27]

These three approaches may be understood as the three functions of consciousness and may be conceived as modes of relating attention to content. The absolute in the *jñāna* (knowledge) approach is pure being (brahma). It is pure will (*paramātma, parama ahantā*) from the standpoint of karma (will). But with regard to these two, objectivity and subjectivity are false respectively, and the confusion of the two is also false. This is because the absolute is essentially non-relational. In the third alternative—the path of bhakti (feeling)—the nature of the absolute as relational emerges distinctively, since relation is always between two terms. In this mode of approach, we see that the absolute is dipolar. Abstraction in this case emerges as being intrinsically false. In love, separation is suffering and there is always an attempt to overcome that separation through union, where the sense of mutual exclusiveness is transcended. Religion establishes man's relation to the *parama tattva*, the supreme reality, in this way.[28]

For many centuries before the time of Gopal Bhatt, the historical development of Vedantic logic had been oscillating dialectically between familiar pairs of opposites: I and you, subject and object, phenomenon and noumenon, *vyavahāra* and *paramārtha*. This ongoing polemics of binary opposition sometimes grew to amusing limits. On the one hand, the objective absolute from the standpoint of knowledge was celebrated in its own right by Sankara. On the other hand, the subjective absolute from the point of view of will or karma was celebrated by the Vijñānavādīs, Kashmir Shaivites, and others. In all this, bhakti was waiting for its due.

Gopal Bhatt entered the scene with the following consolidated perspective. He held that if the paramatattva, the absolute reality as per Vedic spiritual experience, is *raso vai saḥ* (*Taittirīya Upaniṣad*, 2.7.1), then the taster and the object of tasting are both required. Only if that is acknowledged can the act of tasting be regarded as having been completed. *Rasāsvāda* has its own logic, where neither the subject nor the object of experience is negated, but both are bound together in alliance. Their dialogue in the presence of one another leads to a dalliance, *rāsa*. Rasa as ultimate reality is thus an inclusive transcendence. Ramanuja and other Vaishnavas, through their systems of *Viśiṣṭādvaita-vāda*, *Bhedābheda-vāda*, and so on, had prepared the ground for Gopal Bhatt's *acintya-bheda-abheda-vāda* (the path of inconceivable difference and non-difference), which resolves the dilemma of the logic of binary opposites. In pursuing this formulation, Gopal Bhatt was aware of and indebted to the broad philosophical traditions to which he was heir.[29]

For Gopal Bhatt, the *Bhāgavata Purāṇa* is not just another text. It is a definitive dialogue in which jñāna, karma, and bhakti—in other words, sat, cit, and ānanda—are all talking to each other, as we see especially in the section having to do with the sage Kapil (3.28) and in the *Uddhav Gītā* (11.19–29). To be a successful text of dialogue, the *Bhāgavata* has to be a text in which an alliance is forged between speaker and listener, humanity and divinity, humanity and nature, and so on. Since the *Bhāgavata* focuses on dialogue and alliance both, it naturally becomes the text of dalliance, that is, dialogue plus alliance. The five chapters on the *rāsalīlā* (10.29–33) are the essential five vital breaths of this text.

In this rāsa, opposite viewpoints are included and transcended. Bhagavān includes and transcends Brahma and Paramātma without excluding them. Loving service becomes the mother both of jñāna and of karma/*vairāgya*. In the course of all this, it is emphasized by Gopal Bhatt that one can subscribe to the *Bhāgavata Purāṇa* only when one resolves not to denounce or disrespect any other śāstra.[30] This logic of inclusive transcendence as adopted by Sri Chaitanya Mahaprabhu and Gopal Bhatt did in fact become instrumental in shaping the interfaith history of India. Such a perspective made it possible and indeed natural for the gosvāmīs of Vrindavan to enter into dialogue with the Grand Mughal Akbar, who in 1598 decreed that their Vrindavan be regarded not only as a genuine, secure settlement reality but as a revenue entity. Here in the interaction between the Mughal throne and the Gauḍīya theologian-administrators we see an amazing instance of ideology being translated into action.

Returning to the text of the *Ṣaṭ-Sandarbha*, we can see how Gopal Bhatt characteristically takes ideas and motifs to which he was heir and carries them to their logical conclusions. His philosophy of 'acintyabhedābheda' had major implications for the way in which the Braj-based Chaitanyite community developed in the course of the sixteenth century. In the spirit of sixness that we observe in the organization of the sandarbha itself, let me mention six of these.

First, Gopal Bhatt took the *parakīyā bhāva* of Radha, which is generally interpreted as an extramarital relationship, and broadened its interpretation so that it shone forth as a form of love that includes and transcends all social vested interests. Radha's parakīyā bhāva is then a relationship for the sake of relation itself—relation without any ulterior motive.[31] As a consequence, Gopal Bhatt prepared the ground for an image of Radha to be installed by the Chaitanyite Gosvamis alongside Govind Dev in Vrindavan in the third decade of the sixteenth century.[32] Also as a consequence, *mādhurya* (amorous attraction) came to be regarded as the king of the emotions, all of which realized in absolute love.[33] Fourth, one saw in the theology and praxis of the new community being established in Vrindavan a total humanization of the divine.[34] The lordly or *aiśvarya* image of how divinity and humanity are interrelated came to be widely shunned.

Fifth, *gopībhāva*, the sentiment of the *gopīs*—what one might call the ultimate feminism and modeled on the parakīyā mode—came to be regarded as the supreme form of spiritual discipline.[35] This was an explicit emphasis of Chaitanya Mahabrabhu himself. After his stay in Srirangam, he travelled in the southwestern part of the country, where he discovered a partial manuscript of the *Brahma Saṃhitā* in which it was taught that Krishna alone is male; all other actors, right up to Brahmā himself, the creator, are female.[36] We see the legacy of this perspective in the regular worship that is performed in the Gopīśvara Mahādev temple in Vrindavan. There Shiva's lingam, the absolute icon of masculinity, is daily decorated as a beautiful woman.

Finally, let me mention the fact that on the same trip Chaitanya also discovered the manuscript of the *Kṛṣṇa Karṇāmṛta* by Līlāśuka Bilvamaṅgala. This work is a remarkable anthology of poetry celebrating the mādhurya *līlā*s of Radha and Krishna. It is important to note that Gopal Bhatt devoted an elaborate commentary to this text.[37]

Gopal Bhatt's Second Act of Service: The *Haribhaktivilāsa*

The second major work of scholarship by which Gopal Bhatt is typically known, however, is of quite a different nature from either the *Bhāgavata Sandarbha* or the *Kṛṣṇa Karṇāmṛta*. This is Gopal Bhatt's *Haribhaktivilāsa* (enjoyment of the worship of Hari) or, as it is also called, the *Bhagavadbhaktivilāsa*.[38] This voluminous text, which may be classified as a *smṛti nibandha* (code book of conduct), is a veritable encyclopedia of what one might call the Vaishnava lifestyle—how a Vaishnava should behave on a daily, fortnightly, monthly, and annual basis, and with respect to a huge range of textual, ritual, and initiatory realms of practice. In the course composing the *Haribhaktivilāsa*, Gopal Bhatt quotes copiously from 230 prior texts. One may well wonder how he accomplished this feat in Vrindavan, where his reference resources were apparently quite few. All one can think is that he carried the bulk of his reference library in his head, having transported it from south to north India as he played his major role in transplanting bhakti from the southern motherland he knew to its new northern home.

Interestingly, as with the *Bhāgavata Sandarbha*, the authorship of the *Haribhaktivilāsa* has also been the subject of some controversy. It is sometimes ascribed to Sanatan Gosvami, sometimes to Gopal Bhatt; nonetheless, the facts of the matter seem clear. In its initial, invocatory *maṅgalācaraṇa* verse, we read that 'Gopal Bhatt is compiling it for the satisfaction of Raghunath Das, Rup and Sanatan'.[39] Furthermore, Sanatan Gosvami, in his *Digdarśinī* commentary on this verse and the one that follows, reiterates that the authorship belongs to Gopal Bhatt.[40] All manuscripts and printed editions follow suit, identifying Gopal Bhatt as its author in each of the colophons that appear at the end of the twenty *vilāsa*s (enjoyments, that is, individual chapters) that compose the work.[41]

It is an enormous text. All I can do here is give some small taste of the subjects it covers. The first vilāsa talks about the characteristics of gurus and disciples and explains the glories of mantras. The second deals with a disciple's initiation ceremony. The third speaks about the morning duties of the initiated one. In the fourth vilāsa Gopal Bhatt moves in the direction of temple worship, but he relates temple practices to the temple-like body of the devotee. He offers an elaborate description of the temple as a mandala, then describes how its emblem, the *nāman* or tilak, should be applied to the individual Vaishnava as a forehead designation. The Caitanyite tilak is but a copy of the Sri Vaishnava nāman that can be seen in the temple of Srirangam!

In the fifth and sixth vilāsas, procedures used in worshipping images in a temple setting are prescribed. Here the *rasik* in Gopal Bhatt—his aesthetic side—is in full bloom. He describes how rāslīlā, dance, *kīrtan*, *bhog* (cuisine), and *śṛṇgār* (decorations of the deity) are all to be performed, along with methods of temple decoration, the art of fashioning flower houses, and the application of *sānjhī* (sand-painting) decorations on the temple's floor. All of these display significant traces of the Srirangam tradition into which Gopal Bhatt was born, albeit mediated through the Jagannath traditions that mattered so deeply to Chaitanya. A textual basis for many of these traditions is to be found in *Bhāgavata Purāṇa* 11.27.30–5, where Ḳrishna teaches Uddhav about the life of a devotee. In other instances, however, Gopal Bhatt provides his own distinctive views, as, for instance, in regard to worshiping the Lord in the form of various *śālagrām* stones, a subject to which he devotes considerable attention. Śālagrāms are found at the origin of the Gandaki River in Nepal and are believed to be self-manifest forms of Vishnu. Here is a sample of what he says:

> The amount of enjoyment Nārāyaṇ gets from the worship of the *śālagrām* is immense. He is not so pleased even dwelling with Lakṣmī in his own abode. In the *kaliyuga* those who worship the *śālagrām* with devotion

> with various kinds of offerings such as food, flowers, incense, lamp, sandal-paste, music, and the reading of holy texts live happily in Krishna's abode (*dhām*) for millennia. Those who have *darśan* of a *śālagrām*, who pay their respects to it, bathe it, and worship it—these attain the virtues that come with infinite gifts of cows. It is rare for humans to worship the deity self-manifest from the *śālagrām* stone. In the age of Kali it does not happen without the presence of virtue on the part of the worshipper.[42]

In these very interesting chapters, so formative for the worship traditions of Vrindavan, Gopal Bhatt goes on to speak of the benefits that accrue from the offering of dress and jewellery and flowers to the deity—the latter in various forms including the 'flower bungalow' (*phūl banglā*). He also describes the merit that comes from offering an *ārati* lamp or a row of such lamps, or from giving food, music, or dance in a temple setting. The reading of such texts as the Bhagavad Gītā, the *Viṣṇusahasranāma*, and the Purāṇas before the deity is also mentioned.[43] The recitation of these thousand names of Vishnu during the worship of Sri Krishna causes one to attain the same store of virtues that would follow as a result of reading all the Vedas. Reading the Viṣṇusahasranāma may also compensate for deficiencies that may appear in one's devotional life, such as the failure to recite a certain mantra or perform a particular ritual.[44]

The seventh through the eleventh vilāsas go into considerable detail about types of flowers that should be used, different āratis that can be performed, various *namaskāras* (salutations) that are possible, and the entire round of daily routines. Chapter 10 focuses on *satsang*, that is, the various forms of Vaishnava association, and devotes considerable attention to the many ways in which the *Bhāgavata Purāṇa* should serve as the ultimate standard of Vaishnava practice and interpretation. In the twelfth and thirteenth chapters, *ekādaśī*, the auspicious eleventh day of each fortnight, is glorified with elaborate regulations prescribed for fasting. The fourteenth, fifteenth, and sixteenth vilāsas move on from there to list the annual festivals, giving details about how they should be celebrated. Interestingly, in the context of the Shiva–Vishnu chasm that developed at Kanchipuram, we find Gopal Bhatt spending quite some time elaborating what should be done on Shivaratri. The *Bhāgavata Purāṇa* declares that Shiva is a Vaishnava par excellence.[45] In that spirit, Gopal Bhatt says that 'while observing the *vrata* on Shivaratri is definitely not mandatory, nonetheless for the sake of a Vaishnava's good conduct I write about it here. Even

Vaishnavas should always keep [the Shivaratri vrata] for the love of Sri Krishna.'[46]

In the seventeenth vilāsa, we are given *puraścaraṇa* rituals, that is, directions for mastering a mantra. The eighteenth vilāsa follows with details about the different *mūrtis* (images, idols) of the Vaishnava theogony. In the nineteenth vilāsa the consecration rituals for mūrtis and temples are elaborated, and in the twentieth and last vilāsa, Gopal Bhatt gives details about ways of building a new temple or conserving an old one. He associates greater virtue with the preserving and conserving of old structures than he does with the building of something new.

Conclusion

Even on the basis of this short description of the contents and emphases of Gopal Bhatt's two major works, it must be evident that they are separated by a considerable span. In the *Ṣaṭ-Sandarbha* or *Bhāgavata Sandarbha* one has high philosophy, while the *Haribhaktivilāsa* reveals a devoted liturgical sensibility that seems to operate at another level altogether. In the *Ṣaṭ-Sandarbha*, there is a powerful evocation of a theological position that develops in relation to the ontological primacy of Radha and Krishna in relationship to one another; in the *Haribhaktivilāsa*, by contrast, there is no direct mention of Radha, as if one were reading the ritual reflections of a broadly knowledgeable but still clearly focused Sri Vaishnava. Yet the weight of tradition and the explicit witness of the manuscripts themselves force us to conclude that these two masterpieces issued from the mind of a single person.

How then to explain the distance between these two comprehensive and admirable but very different texts? In part, it follows from the fact that they were intended to serve quite different purposes. Both are mature works, but of different kinds. The one was a treatise on theology. The other was a text falling in the smṛti genre—a manual of Vaishnava lifestyle and in that way an important tool for the newly emerging Vaishnava community across north India.

Yet we should be aware of another operative factor as well. I have described the *Bhāgavata Sandarbha* and the *Haribhaktivilāsa* as Gopal Bhatt's first and second acts of service respectively, but in doing so I did not mean to imply a chronological sequence. Chronologically, in fact, we have every reason to believe that the order was reversed, with the *Haribhaktivilāsa* coming first. We suspect this because the *Haribhaktivilāsa*, for all its many citations of other works, does not draw upon the writings of other gosvāmīs, with the single exception of Rup Gosvami's *Laghubhāgavatāmṛtam*. Even there we see an oddity: the four *ślokas* Gopal Bhatt says he is quoting from the *Laghubhāgavatāmṛtam* do not appear in any manuscript mentioned in published editions of that text. Did he perhaps know an earlier version than the one that was later to become standard?

As its dedicatory verse makes clear, Gopal Bhatt does indeed expect four of the other gosvāmīs to read the *Haribhaktivilāsa*, but he does not seem to have worked in consort with them in the way that emerges in the *Bhāgavata Sandarbha*. There Gopal Bhatt seems fully cognizant of epistemological, metaphysical, and spiritual matters that were being discussed in the nascent sampradāy and enters the same broad field where the other gosvāmīs laboured. He joins them in making use of a shared language of philosophical discourse—Navya Nyāya with respect to method and Vedānta with respect to content and purpose. As in their works, so too in the *Bhāgavata Sandarbha*, Radha is well established. Hence, it comes as no surprise when, at the end of the *Bhakti* and *Prīti Sandarbhas*, Gopal Bhatt refers his readers to the writings of Rup and Sanatan Gosvami for further details on anything that he was unable to explore in the *Bhāgavata Sandarbha*. From all of this we get the sense that the *Bhāgavata Sandarbha* is a later work than the *Haribhaktivilāsa*, participating much more fully in the discourse that came to be preferred as the sampradāy, expanding its philosophical and theological corpus. One may well ask whether the physical proximity of the other gosvāmīs had something to do with shaping the distance between the *Haribhaktivilāsa* and the *Bhāgavata Sandarbha* itself. As time passed, did Gopal Bhatt become more like the others—all of whom, like Chaitanya, hailed from eastern India?

Whatever we decide in answer to this question, even to ask it makes us aware of a facet of Gopal Bhatt's life that we have not yet discussed: This pilgrim from south to north did not go straight from Srirangam to Braj. Instead, an element of indirection was involved. The biographical traditions to which we are heirs report that in sending Gopal Bhatt to participate in the construction of the new Vrindavan on the banks of the Yamuna, Chaitanya admonished him first to visit another river—the Gandaki River in far-off Nepal. There he should gather śālagrām stones from its banks, directed Chaitanya, and only then should he proceed to Braj. Just as one might expect, therefore, Gopal Bhatt makes mention of the Gandaki in the lengthy section of the fifth vilāsa, where he discusses the veneration of śālagrām stones. Then, in the year 1542, a signal event occurred. One of those śālagrāms, the one that became the principal object of Gopal Bhatt's devotion, generated from itself a fully imagistic form and became the deity known as the deity Rādhāramaṇjī, whom my ancestors, extended family, and I have had the privilege of serving ever since that day.

Hence, there were two great events that mediated between south and north in Gopal Bhatt's life—first, his journey to the Gandaki in search of śālagrāms and, second, the transformation of his own principal śālagrām into another form altogether. We do not know whether the *Haribhaktivilāsa* might have been composed before the latter of these two events, while the *Bhāgavata Sandarbha* might have come later, yet it is tempting to think this might be so. After all, Rādhāramaṇjī is not mentioned in the *Haribhaktivilāsa*, for all its attention to śālagrāms; and Radha, whose presence is implicit in the image of Rādhāramaṇjī, comes to figure only in the *Bhāgavata Sandarbha*. Still, as we have said, an element of mystery remains. What exactly did Gopal Bhatt's service to Rādhāramaṇjī have to do with his two great acts of literary service, the *Haribhaktivilāsa* and the *Bhāgavata Sandarbha*? So far, it is hard to say. All we know for sure is that the journey of bhakti from south to north as symbolized in the life of Gopal Bhatt was both ritually and conceptually a mediated journey, and that in both respects, the impact of Chaitanya Mahaprabhu was great.

Notes

1. 'Jitavara gati bhaṅgir-nāṭya-saṅgīta-raṅgī
Tanubhṛta-janu-cittānanda-vardhis-sudhīśaḥ
Carita sukha vilāsas-citracāturya-bhāṣaḥ
Parama-patitamīśaḥ pātu gopālabhaṭṭaḥ'
(Kavi Karṇapūra Gopālabhaṭṭa Aṣṭakam, verse 4, Barahanagar Granth Mandir MS #1354/30, quoted in Biman Bihari Majumdar, *Sri caitanya caritera upadana* [Calcutta: Calcutta University, 1959], 2nd edition, 166).

2. An earlier version of this chapter was delivered as the fourth Dennis Hudson Memorial Lecture in Chennai, 2012.

3. Bhāgavata Māhātmya 1.48–50. One portion of this passage has often been misunderstood. One should not translate *jīrṇa* as 'withered', 'decayed', or 'old' while forgetting other meanings such as 'ancient' (tradition) and 'digested'. See Monier-Williams, *A Sanskrit-English Dictionary: Etymologically*

and Philologically Arranged with Special Reference to Cognate Indo-European Languages (New Delhi: Oriental Publishers, 1960).

4. Friedhelm Hardy, 'Mādhavendra Purī: A Link between Bengal Vaiṣṇavism and South Indian Bhakti', *Journal of the Royal Asiatic Society*, no. 1 (1974): 23–41.

5. *Caitanya Caritamrta, Madhyalīlā*, Chapter 8.

6. 'dvijavarakulacandro bhaṭṭavaṃśapradīpaḥ' (*Gopālabhaṭṭāṣṭakam*, v. 1).

7. *Caitanya caritāmṛtam mahākāvyam* of Kavi Karṇapūra, ed. Haridasa Sastri (Vrindavan: Srigadadharagaurahari Press, 1983).

8. 'itihāsaḥ purāṇañ ca pañcamo vedam ucyate' (*Bhāgavata Purāṇa*, 1.4.20); also 'itihāsa purāṇāni pañcamaṃ vedam' (*Bhāgavata Purāṇa*, 3.12.39).

9. 'sarva vedānta sāram hi śrīmad bhāgavatam iṣyate ...'(*Bhāgavata Purāṇa*, 12.13.15).

10. 'arthoyam brahmasūtrāṇam, bhāratārtha vinirṇayaḥ' (*Garuḍa Purāṇa*, quoted in *Tattva Sandarbha*, anu.11, p. 6).

11. 'śrīmadbhāgavatam śāstraṁ kalau kīreṇa bhāṣitaḥ' (*Bhāgavata Māhātmya*, 1.11).

12. Śrīnātha Cakravartī, *Caitanya mata mañjūṣā* (Vrindavan: Haridasa Sarma, 1955), v. 1, p. 1.

13. Jīva Gosvāmī, *Bhāgavata Sandarbha* (including *Tattva Sandarbha, Bhagavata Sandarbha, Paramātma Sandarbha*, and *Śrīkṛṣṇa Sandarbha* in volume 1; *Bhakti Sandarbha* and *Prīti sandarbha* in volume 2), ed. Puridasa (Vrindavan: Haridasa Sarma, 1951).

14. A fairly good summary of these sandarbhas is found in S. K. De, *Early History of the Vaisnava Faith and Movement in Bengal: from Sanskrit and Bengali Sources* (Calcutta: Firma K. L. Mukhopadhya, 1961).

15. *Jīvakaḥ: jīva + kan* suffix, *anukampāyām kan*. The 'kan' suffix is used in the sense of 'for one's pleasure' or 'permission'.

16. *Tattva Sandarbha*, vv. 3, 4, and 5, p. 1

17. Jīva Gosvāmī, *Sarvasamvādinī*, ed. Puridasa (Vrindavan: Haridasa Sharma, 1953).

18. *Krama Sandarbha*, ed. Puridasa (Vrindavan: Haridasa Sharma, 1952).

19. Gosvāmī, *Krama Sandarbha*, verse 3, 4, p. 1.

20. Stuart Mark Elkman, *Jīva Gosvāmin's Tattvasandarbha: A Study on the Philosophical and Sectarian Development of the Gauḍīya Vaiṣṇava Movement* (New Delhi: Motilal Banarsidass, 1986), pp. 25–49. 'granthasya purātanatvam, sva pariṣkṛtatvañcāha—kopīti. Tadbāndhavaḥ—tayoḥ—rūpa sanātanayor bandhuḥ—Gopāla Bhaṭṭa ityarthaḥ' (Baladev Vidyābhūṣan's commentary on *Tattva sandarbha*, verse 4). Refer to *Tattva Sandarbha, with Ṭīkā of Baladeva Vidyabhusana*, ed. and trans. into Bengali by Nityasvarupa Brahmachari and Krishna Chandra Goswami (Kalikata [Kolkata]: Shachindra Mohan Ghose, Chaitanyabda 443 [1929]), 8.

21. Subject-wise list of manuscripts prepared by Jiv Gosvami that is to be found in the collection of Rādhādāmodara temple in Vrindavan. Granthasūcī (Rādhādāmodara Mandira) MS serial number 13298, accession number 5428, *A Catalogue of Sanskrit Manuscripts in the Vrindavan Research Institute*, Part IV, compiled by V. B. Gosvami, eds. R. D. Gupta and R. C. Sharma (Vrindavan: Vrindaban Research Institute, 1985), 478–9.

22. 'tasya-bhaṭṭasya ādyam-purātanam granthanālekham' (Baladeva on *Tattva Sandarbha*, v. 5).

23. Narahari Cakravarti, *Bhaktiratnākara*, ed. Navīnakṛṣṇa Paravidyālaṁkāra (n.p.: Sundarananda Vidyavinoda, Gaudiya Mission, 1940 [in preface]), taranga 5, vv. 1659–60, p. 182

24. 'śrīmad-īśvara-rūpeṇa rasāmṛta-kṛtā-kṛtā, stavamālānujīvena jīvena samagṛhyate' (Rupa Gosvami, *Stavamala*, ed. Puridasa [Aloya, Meymensingh.: Sacinatha Rayachaudhuri, 1946], v. 1, p. 1).

25. 'vadanti tat-tatvavidas-tatvam yaj-jñānam-advayam' (*Bhāgavata Purāṇa*, 1.2.11).

26. 'satyam jñānam anantam brahma' (*Taittirīya Upaniṣad*, 2.1.1).

27. 'athaivam-advaya-jñānalakṣaṇam tat-tattvam sāmānyato lakṣayitvā punar-upāsakayogyatā-vaiśiṣṭyena prakaṭita-nijasattā-viśeṣam viśeṣato nirūpayati' (*Bhagavata Sandarbha*, anu.1 p. 1).

28. For this understanding and analysis, I am deeply indebted to the writings of Professor T.R.V. Murti. See 'Knowing, Feeling and Willing as functions of Consciousness' in *Studies in Indian Thought, Collected Papers of Prof. T. R. V. Murti*, ed. Harold G. Coward (New Delhi: Motilal Banarasidass, 1983), 17–32.

29. 'vivicya vyalikhat grantham likhitād vṛddha-vaiṣṇavaiḥ (*Tattva Sandarbha*, v. 2, p. 1). Also see *Tattva Sandarbha*, anu. 14–15, p. 9

30. 'śraddhām bhāgavate śāstre, anindāmanyatra eva hi' (*Bhāgavata Purāṇa*, 11.3.26).

31. *Ujjvalanīlamaṇi, Śriharipriyā Prakaraṇa*, vv. 11–42, pp. 17–23.

32. See Margaret Case, ed., *Govindadeva: A Dialogue in Stone*, 161, 185, 206, 245. Jāhnavā Devī, the wife of Nityānanda, also sent an image of Radha to be installed along with Gopināth in Vrindavan. See *Bhaktiratnākara* of Narahari Chakravarti alias Ghanashyamdas, ed. Navinakrishna Vidyalankar (Kolkata: Gaudiya Mission, 1940), in preface, *tarang* 13, verses 66–81, pp. 617–18.

33. See *Bhaktirasāmṛtasindhu, paścima vibhāga*, 5th *laharī*, 111–14.

34. 'Krishnera jateka khelā, sarvottama naralīlā, naravapu tāṁhāra svarūpa' (*Caitanya Caritāmṛta*, madhya 21.83, p. 674.

35. 'ramyā kācid-upāsanā vrajavadhūvargeṇa yā kalpitā ' (*Caitanya mata mañjūṣā*, v. 1, p.1).

36. See Jīv Gosvāmī, *ṭīkā* on *Brahma Samhitā*, ed. by Haridasa Sastri (Vrindavan: Srigadadhargaurahari Press, 1981), verses 10, 34–55, pp. 45, 65–92.

37. *Kṛṣṇakarṇāmṛta* of Līlāśuka Vilvamaṅgala, ed. S. K. De, University of Dacca Oriental Publication Series, no. 5 (Dacca: Dacca University, 1938).

38. Rūp Gosvāmī, *Stavamālā*, ed. Puridasa (Aloya, Meyemensingh: Śacīnātha Rāyachaudhurī, 1946).

39. Gopāla Bhaṭṭa Gosvāmī, *Śrī Haribhaktivilāsa* (Meymensingh: Sacinatha Rayachauduri, 1946), v. 1.2, p. 2

40. 'śrīgopālabhaṭṭasyāpi tādṛktvam boddhavyam' (v.2). 'yā śrīgopālabhaṭṭasya prema bhaktis-tasyavilāsata ullāsāt' (v. 3, p. 2)

41. 'iti śrīgopālabhaṭṭa vilikhite śrīmadbhagavadbhaktivilāse ... vilāsaḥ'

42. Gopāla Bhaṭṭa Gosvāmī, *Haribhaktivilāsa*, ed. Puridasa (Meymensingh: Sachinath Rayachaudhuri, 1946), vilāsa 5, vv. 368, 375, 384, 408, pp. 131–3.

43. *Haribhaktivilasa*, vilāsa 6, vv. 190–238, pp. 152–4.

44. *Haribhaktivilasa*, vilāsa 6, vv. 192, 194, p. 152.

45. *Bhāgavata Purāṇa* 12.13.16

46. *Haribhaktivilāsa*, vilāsa 14, vv. 186, 187. p. 451.

Bibliography

Banke Bihari Saukhyasen. *Śrīguṇamañjarī prem-pratimā (Śrī Śrī Rādhāramaṇa Prādurbhāva)*, edited by Srikrishnacaitanya Gosvami. Lucknow: Mukundbihari, VS 1992.

Bhāgavata Purāṇa. 2 volumes. Gorakhpur: Gita Press, VS 2067.

Brahma Saṁhitā (pañcamo'dhyāyaḥ), with commentary by Jīva Gosvāmī, edited by Haridasa Sastri. Vrindavan: Srigadadhargaurahari Press, 1981.

Cakravartī, Narahari, a.k.a. Ghanaśyāma Dāsa. *Bhaktiratnākara*, edited by Navīnakṛṣṇa Paravidyālaṅkāra. N.p.: Sundarananda Vidyavinoda, Gaudiya Mission, 1940.

Cakravartī, Śrīnātha. *Caitanya mata mañjūṣā*. Vrindavan: Haridasa Sarma, 1955.

Caitanya caritāmṛtam mahākāvyam of Kavi Karṇapūra, edited by Haridasa Sastri. Vrindavan: Srigadadharagaurahari Press, 1983.

Caitanya Caritāmṛta of Kṛṣṇadāsa Kavirāja, translated and edited by Edward C. Dimock, Jr, and Tony K. Stewart. Harvard Oriental Series 56. Cambridge: Department of Sanskrit and Indian Studies, Harvard University, 1999.

Gosvāmī, Gaur Krishna. *Śrīgopāla bhaṭṭ gosvāmī*. Vrindavan: Anil Kumar Gosvami, 1985.

Gosvāmī, Gopāla Bhaṭṭa. *Haribhaktivilāsa*, edited by Puridasa. Aloya, Myemensingh: Śacīnātha Rāyachaudhurī, 1946.

Gosvāmī, Jīva. *Bhāgavata Sandarbha* (including *Tattva Sandarbha, Bhagavata Sandarbha, Paramātma Sandarbha*, and *Śrīkṛṣna Sandarbha* in volume 1; *Bhakti Sandarbha* and *Prīti Sandarbha* in volume 2), edited by Puridasa. Vrindavan: Haridasa Sarma, 1951.

———. *Granthasūcī (Rādhādāmodaramandira)* dated VS 1654 (1597 CE). In V. B. Goswami, R.D. Gupta, and R.C. Sharma, eds. *A Catalogue of Sanskrit*

Manuscripts in the Vrindaban Research Institute, Part IV. Vrindavan: Vrindavan Research Institute, 1985, 478–9.

———. *Krama Sandarbha*, edited by Puridasa. Vrindavan: Haridasa Sarma, 1952.

———. *Sarvasaṃvādinī*, edited by Puridasa. Vrindavan: Haridasa Sarma, 1953.

———. *Tattva Sandarbha* with the commentary of Baladeva Vidyābhūṣaṇa. Benipatti (Darbhanga): Srijivasevasangha, n.d.

Gosvami, Manas Kumar. *Govind Darshan*. Jaipur: Thikana Mandir Shri Govind Dev Ji, 2004.

Gosvami, Nabhaji. *Bhaktamāl* with the *Bhaktirasabodhinī* commentary of Priyadasa and the *Bhaktisudhāsvāda Tilak* of Sitaramsharan Bhagavanprasad Rupakala. Lucknow: Tejkumar Press, 1969.

Gosvāmī, Rūpa. *Bhaktirasāmṛtasindhu*, edited by Puridasa. Aloya, Myemensingh: Śacīnātha Rāyachaudhurī, 1946.

———. *Stavamālā*, edited by Puridasa. Aloya, Meyemensingh: Śacīnātha Rāyachaudhurī, 1946.

———. *Ujjvalanīlamaṇi* with the *Locanarocanī* commentary by Jīva Gosvāmī and the *Ānandacandrikā* commentary by Viśvanātha Cakravartī, edited by Puridasa. Vrindavan: Haridasa Sarma, 1954.

Hardy, Friedhelm. 'Mādhavêndra Purī: A Link between Bengal Vaiṣṇavism and South Indian *Bhakti*'. *Journal of the Royal Asiatic Society* (1974): 23–41.

———. *Viraha-bhakti: The Early History of Kṛṣṇa Devotion in South India*. New Delhi: Oxford University Press, 1983.

Jana, Naresh Chandra. *Vrindavaner Chhaya Gosvami*. Kolkata: Calcutta University, 1970.

Kṛṣṇakarṇāmṛta of Līlāśuka Vilvamaṅgala, edited by S. K. De. University of Dacca Oriental Publication Series, no. 5. Dacca: Dacca University, 1938.

Majumdar, Biman Bihari. *Śrī caitanya caritera upādāna*. 2nd edition. Calcutta: Calcutta University, 1959.

Monier-Williams, Monier. *A Sanskrit-English Dictionary: Etymologically and Philologically Arranged with Special Reference to Cognate Indo-European Languages*. New Delhi: Oriental Publishers, 1960.

Parīk, Nandkiśor. *Śrīgovind Gāthā*. Jaipur: Subodh Sahitya Sadan, 2003.

Rosen, Steven. *Six Goswamis of Vrindavan*. New revised edition. Vrindavan: Ras Bihari Lal and Sons, 2002.

18

SWAPNA SHARMA

Gadadhar Bhatt and His Family

Facilitators of the Song of *Bhakti* in Vrindavan

The contribution of the six *gosvāmīs* who were close associates of Chaitanya Mahaprabhu to the rejuvenation of Braj-Vrindavan is well known.[1] Yet there were many other devotees, scholars, and saints who played important roles in reconstructing the lost Braj and its culture. Gadādhar Bhaṭṭ and his family are among these lesser known facilitators of *bhakti* song in Braj. Gadadhar (1515–1610 ?) was probably the first in his family to move to Vrindavan from Telangana. Some records in the Vidya Bhavan at Kankrauli mention that he was a Brahmin from Telangana and that his native place is called Vellanadu.[2] He came to Vrindavan in the first part of the sixteenth century at the invitation of Jiv Gosvami, the youngest of the six gosvāmīs. At that time, Jiv was serving as the leader of the Chaitanya Sampradāy.

Apparently, Gadadhar was already writing beautiful bhakti *pads* in Brajbhasha. According to Priyadas, it was the language of his famous pad 'sakhī hoṅ syāma ranga rangī' (Friend, I am dyed in the colour of the Dark One)[3] that drew the attention of Jiv Gosvami to Gadadhar Bhatt in the first place, inspiring him to invite Gadadhar to come and live in Vrindavan.[4] It seems that Jiv could see the spark of true devotion and dedication in Gadadhar and noted his Brajbhasha skills, and, therefore, invited him to join the group with a purpose. In Gadadhar's time, there were hardly any other poets in the Chaitanya Sampradāy who composed poetry in Brajbhasha. Thus, he added a new dimension to the community's religious expression.

Although, as in the case of most other poets of the early modern period, it is difficult to trace the exact year of Gadadhar's birth and death, a testamentary document of Jiv Gosvami provides written evidence of Gadadhar's close and trusted relationship with Jiv, while also providing evidence of Gadadhar's presence in Vrindavan during the period when it was written. This document is available in the Vrindavan Shodh Sansthan as MS 79-A-B. It contains a codicil in Gadadhar Bhatt's handwriting, which was necessary because Jiv was unable to write or sign his own testament at that point in time. Gadadhar puts his signature on this document, which is dated Samvat 1665 (1608 CE).[5] Obviously, this document demonstrates a close and trusting relationship between Jiv and Gadadhar, suggesting that it was Jiv who introduced Gadadhar to religious and philosophical aspects of the *sampradāy*, as is also asserted in the Bengali *Bhaktamāl* of Laldas.[6] Priyadas tells the same story in his commentary on Nabhaji's *Bhaktamāl.*[7]

Gadhadhar's command of Brajbhasha encourages us to ask whether he might have been resident somewhere else in north India before coming to Vrindavan. At this time, Vallabhacharya and several others had already migrated from the south to the north and were settled in Banaras and various other places. Contemporary scholars within Gadadhar's own family, however—principally Achyut Bhatt and Janardan Bhatt, who are presently living in Vrindavan—have no specific information about the migration of their famous ancestor to the north. What they do affirm, however, is that according to oral family tradition there were two branches of Bhatts, who lived respectively in Vellanadu (which means a village drowned in water) and in Murkinadu (a village lost in fire), both located in present-day Andhra Pradesh. Gadadhar Bhatt's family belonged to Vellanadu, but after a natural disaster, perhaps indeed a flood, they moved to a place called Hanumat Puram, which is also somewhere in Andhra. As to what happened then, no further information is available from any source.

The family believes that although Gadadhar Bhatt was the first to come to Vrindavan from Andhra Pradesh, his family had been in contact with north Indian culture for quite some time. They argue that at the time, writing devotional poetry to Krishna in Brajbhasha was very popular in literary circles in the south. Even in Kerala and in Hyderabad, they say, some forms of Braj literature existed in that period.[8] It is true that the interaction between south and north was becoming very strong on the religious front during this period, so that writing verses in Brajbhasha does not prove that Gadadhar had already been living in north India. That too remains a possibility, however, since many other families were migrating from the south to the north at that time. If this was also the case for Gadadhar or his family, we would have to imagine Jiv's letter as having been addressed to him at some northern location in which he had already taken up residence.

The earliest written evidence of Gadadhar Bhatt's existence and the earliest estimate of his characteristics are to be found in the *Bhaktamāl* of Nabhaji, composed around 1600. Nabhaji tells about the great qualities of Gadadhar Bhatt and the attractive way in which he exposited the *Bhāgavata Purāṇa* through the medium of his *bhāgavat kathā* (literally, 'telling the *Bhāgavata*') discourses. Nabhaji's report reads as follows:

gunanikara gadādhara bhaṭṭa ati sabahina kau lāgau sukhada
sajjana suhṛda suśīla bacana āraja pratipālaya
nirmatsara niḥkāma kṛpā karuṇā kau ālaya
ananya bhajana dṛḍh karani dharyau bapu bhaktana kājai
parama dharama kau setu vidati vṛndāvana gājai
bhāgauta sudhā baraṣai badana kāhū kau nāhina dukhada
gunanikara gadādhara bhaṭṭa ati sabahina kau lāgai[9]

Gadadhar Bhatt possessed a cluster of praiseworthy qualities,
  liked by one and all.
Gentle and generous, he took his orders
  from those who were realized beings.
Having no ill feelings or worldly desires,
  he was a very abode of compassion.
His devotion was unswerving,
  thus showing the path to other devotees.
This made him well known in Vrindavan
  as a bridge to the ultimate good.
The nectar of *bhāgavat kathā* showered from his mouth,
  not unpleasant to anyone.
Gadadhar Bhatt possessed a cluster of praiseworthy qualities,
  liked by one and all.

In this single *chappay*, Nabhaji succeeds in drawing a wonderful picture of Gadadhar's pleasant personality, his generous and respectful attitude towards others, and his reputation as facilitator of dharma in Vrindavan. Through the nectar of his *Bhāgavata* discourses, he helped people to choose the right path of dharma; thus, he became famous as a bridge to *param dharma*, the ultimate in religious realization. His gentle and generous behaviour and compassionate nature taught others a lesson of humanity, which is the first and foremost dharma for humankind in general.

This information is supplemented in eight poems by Priyadas in his famous *Bhaktirasabodhinī* commentary on Nabhaji's *Bhaktamāl*. He elaborates upon almost every quality mentioned by Nabhaji in the chappay quoted above. In telling the story of Gadadhar's arrival in Vrindavan, for example, he illustrates his habit of taking orders from the realized ones—in Nabha's words, *vacanāraj pratipālai*. Priyadas tells us that it was while performing morning duties at a well that Gadhadhar received the letter of invitation from Jiv Gosvami, bidding him come to Vrindavan. Its result was that Gadadhar departed from that very spot.[10] Similarly, another of Priyadas's stories fills out Nabha's description of Gadadhar's compassion. In this tale, we hear that a thief once came to Gadadhar's house. After collecting many items, the thief managed to assemble a burden so heavy that he was unable to lift it and take it away. At this point, Gadadhar stepped in and offered to help lift the bundle. This act of compassion changed the thief's heart forever and caused him to become Gadadhar's disciple.[11] After this fashion, each of the eight poems given by Priyadas elaborates on a different quality of Gadadhar as briefly mentioned by Nabhaji.

Priyadas, a Chaitanyite, was not the only religious poet who admired Gadadhar. Other poets—Dhruvdas (ca. VS 1630–1700 = 1573–1643 CE) and Bhagvatrasik (1592–1662),[12] both of whom belonged to the Rādhāvallabh Sampradāy, as well as the Nimbarki poets Nagaridas[13] and Chacha Vrindavandas[14]—were also eloquent in their praise of Gadadhar's ecstatic devotion and his impressive style of bhāgavat kathā.

These qualities—poetic talent and scholarship and an amazing facility in bhāgavat kathā—were not limited to Gadadhar Bhatt alone, but have continued to be transmitted and cultivated by his family down to the present day. The lineage also gave birth to a number of fine poets: Rasikottans, a Sanskrit poet who composed the *Premapattana*; Vallabharasik, a Brajbhasha poet; and Govardhan Bhatt, who wrote the Sanskrit works entitled *Madhukelivallī*, *Rūpasanātana Stotra*, and *Rādhākuṇḍastava*. But it is in the realm of the *Bhāgavata* that the family attained its greatest renown. Govardhan Nandkumar and Mannu Lal Bhatt, for example, have especially enriched the Braj tradition through their charismatic bhāgavat kathās, which have had the power to change people's hearts. Many stories found in various Bhaktamāls and Sant Caritāvalīs speak about the impact of such kathās on those who heard them. Even today, the Bhatt family maintains the old classic style of narrating the *Bhāgavata Purāṇa*. They do so without frills or glamour, and they refuse to make it a business.

The *Sundar Śyām Vilās* and *Vṛndāvan Prakāśamālā* are two texts that praise Govardhan Bhatt's way of expressing and revealing the secrets of the *Bhāgavata*. The *Sundar Śyām Vilās* offers the following portrait of Govardhan Bhatt, a member of Gadadhar Bhatt's family who carried forth its virtues:

saba bhaktana ke saratāja, ananya bhakta śrīvṛndāvana ke
śrī govardhana jī mahārāja, hari ke sukhadāyaka jana jana ke
tinakī kathā jagata sata jānai, hari ke sukhadāyak jan janke
lākha beri dhani dhani kahiye, taba govardhana nāma ju lahiye
tinakī kathā tana tana likhāta, jo kaū sunai magana hvai jāta
ukta juktf hari rasa kī kīnhīṁ, aisī kathā kahūṁ śravana na kīnhī
chāṁḍī vṛndāvana kahūṁ na jānau, lākhi kulākh samakari jānau
binake prema kī upamā nahīṁ, vṛndāvana rasa jānyau tinahīṁ[15]

A crown among devotees, singularly devoted to Shri Vrindavan,
Shri Govardhanji Maharaj provided Hari's happiness to one and all.
The world believes his *kathā* to be true.
They all call him the embodiment of Hari's ideal devotee.
Hundreds of thousands of blessings may be uttered,
but only one man deserves the name of Govardhan.
He wrote his kathā on many hearts. Whoever listened was entranced.
His way of telling the stories of Hari *rasa* was unique. It never had been heard before.
He never would leave Vrindavan. To him neither wealth nor poverty mattered.
His love for Vrindavan was incomparable. He truly knew Vrindavan's nectar.

Similar sentiments are echoed in the *Vṛndāvan Prakāśamālā* about another member of Gadadhar's lineage:

tākc āgc bhīma siṁha jūkī kuṁja sukha puṁja
tāmeṁ latā beli druma jhūmi-jhūmi chāvai haiṁ

rasika samāja saba jāṁcana kau āvai tahāṁ
govardhana bhaṭṭa jahāṁ raṁga jhara lāvai haiṁ
candra cakora jaise sabana kī ḍora aisai
kṛṣṇa kathā kaha hīya sabake sirāvai haiṁ
tinake anaṁta guṇa kahe kahā āvai haiṁ
ve ati hī nigūḍha rūpa prakaṭa dikhāvai haiṁ[16]

After that one comes to Bhim Singh Kunj, a place where happiness abounds.
Inside it is spread with creepers, vines and trees that gently sway to and fro.
Religious devotees (or passionate people) come there to seek
The uninterrupted color (of bhakti) that Shri Govardhan Bhatt has to shower.
Thus he serves as the moon does to *cakor* birds, attracting them as if by pulling a string.
He tells Krishna's story and he fills their hearts with ecstasy.
How can his countless qualities be told? He reveals the secret-most form (of that rasa).

As we can see from such attestations, the Bhatts of Vrindavan maintained the legacy of bhāgavat kathā that Gadadhar Bhatt was the first to establish there. By contrast, however, there is hardly any information about his predecessors. The only source we have is what the present-day members of the Bhatt family report—stories about their ancestors that they heard from their parents and grandparents. They told me that most probably their family belonged to Śrī Sampradāy before Gadadhar Bhatt's initiation into the Gauḍīya/Chaitanya Sampradāy. Accordingly, to this day, their family deities are Lakshmi and Narayana. Jiv Gosvami was responsible for teaching Gadadhar the doctrines of religion and philosophy that belong to the Chaitanya tradition, and it was he who instructed Gadadhar to take initiation (*dīkṣā*) from Raghunath Bhatt. Raghunath Bhatt is the member of the famous six gosvāmīs whose skill in bhāgavat kathā is remembered. It was Raghunath Bhatt who passed on the tradition to Gadadhar, says his family. After Raghunath Bhatt's demise, Gadhadhar Bhatt took over his practice of giving bhāgavat kathā at the Govindadev, Gopinath, Madanamohan, and Radharaman temples in Vrindavan, and this tradition has been maintained to the present day. Thus, as Nabhaji said about Gadadhar, these Bhatts 'uphold the words' (*vacanāraj pratipālai*) of the *Bhāgavata*.

Over time Gadhadhar Bhatt's family, although grounded in the Chaitanyite system, have freely interacted with Vallabhaite leaders and their families, with whom they shared geographical, ethnological, and linguistic commonality. Even more important, they shared the huge arena of Krishna bhakti. This interaction with Vallabhites and *dakṣinātya ācār paddhati*, that is, the south Indian priestly liturgical tradition, importantly influenced their tradition and lifestyle. Despite accepting the culture and language of Braj, they maintained their old southern tradition in many ways. Even after living in Braj for centuries, they continue to marry within their own community, not mixing much with the broader local population. All their marriage rituals are southern.

The Vrindavan Bhatts are related to both Vallabhites and Rāmānujī families. The Vrindavan Bhatts have married freely with the Vallabhite Bhatts, which has created a dialogical enrichment of certain Chaitanyite rituals that they practice, including *bhog sevā* (cuisine), *rāg sevā* (*samāj*, that is, their traditions of musical practice), and their traditions of daily practice (*nitya sevā*, encompassing *poṣak*, *śṛngār*, and *sajāvat* aspects, that is, nurturing, adornment, and decoration) and of observing annual festivals (*utsav sevā*). It claims that their interaction with Vallabhite traditions and the southern ācār paddhati has made their tradition unique. It is a symbol of the religious harmony that can exist between two traditions.

The ācār paddhati of Shrinathji has for countless years remained the model for the Bhatts. They have tried to follow the rules of purity (*aparas*) of Shrinathji as much as they could, says Achyut Bhatt, one of the present scholars of the family. He also believes that Shrinathji's ācār paddhati is influenced by Śrī Jagannāthjī. The temple maintained in Gadadhar Bhatt's family home follows the Shrinathji tradition to some extent, but not completely. Some aspects of its practices in ornamenting the deity betray a southern influence, for example, *kaṭākṣ* (the shaping of the eyes), *cimbuk sṛngār* (the chin decoration), *nak besar* (the pearl in the nose), and so on. Bhog, the set of food offerings that defines its practice of dietary service, is also influenced by Shrinathji. Various north Indian dishes, however, are also included in the bhog menu along with southern dishes, especially in regard to the preparation of different types of rice. The styles in which the deities are dressed are influenced by canons of Mughal practice, Achyut Bhatt observes, but in the Bhatt temple a distinctive Rajasthani influence can also be seen.

The Bhattji temple samāj betrays the mixed influences of Vallabhite, Haridasi, and Radhavallabhi melodic practices, yet it has its own style of changing ragas during a single composition even though the beats *(tāl)* remain the same. The Bhatt temple is also famous for its wonderful *sānjhī kalā*, the application of designs and images on the floor using a cowdung paste base. Sanjhī worship, a tradition centred in Punjab, is also a part of Braj culture. Here is yet another example showing how Bhatt tradition exemplifies a dialogue between various religious and cultural traditions.

To conclude, let me say that I agree with Nabhaji, who called Gadadhar a *param dharam kau setu*, a bridge to the ultimate. Yet Gadadhar and his family were like a bridge in many other ways as well. By composing beautiful verses and giving *Bhāgavata* discourses in Brajbhasha, they tried to make spiritual and religious matters accessible to everyone. For example, Gadadhar Bhatt beautifully summarized the description of Vrindavan as a *yogapīṭh* (seat for the divine couple Radha and Krishna) in a long Brajbhasha poem called *Yogapīṭh Varṇan* or *Dhyān Līlā*. This poem, written in *rolā* and *chaupaī* metres, explains the concept of *mānasī upāsanā*, that is, esoteric spiritual discipline. In the course of doing so, it paints a beautiful picture of the Vrindavan that exists in the hearts of devotees—Gadadhar's readers. In composing this poem, Gadadhar recreates the spiritual space of Vrindavan by expanding on ideas set out by Rup Gosvami in his *Smaraṇamangalastotram* and by Krishnadas Kaviraj in his *Govindalīlāmṛtam*.

The Chaitanya tradition accepts Shri Krishna of Braj as the object worthy of worship (*ārādhya*) whose home (*dhām*) is Vrindavan; the best method of worshiping this Supreme Being is the one practised by *gopis*. The scriptural authority in this regard is provided by the *Bhāgavata Purāṇa*, where loving service (*prem bhakti*) is understood to be the ultimate goal of human life (*puruṣārtha*). The Bhatt family loyally follows this tradition established by Chaitanya, yet their poetry and bhāgavat kathā have simultaneously helped to bring different traditions together, as have their liturgical practices. Rup Gosvami, in his *Bhaktirasāmṛtasindhu*, explains that the *vaidhi bhakti* he enjoins—bhakti by the book, so to speak—is the very same thing as what is called *maryādā bhakti* by other Vaishnavas. Similarly, the *rāgānugā bhakti* he recommends, its spontaneous counterpart, is exactly the same as what others (specifically Vallabhacharya) call *puṣṭi bhakti*. Thus, Rup displays a doctrinal and theoretical intertextuality between the Chaitanyite tradition and the Vallabhite in explicit terms. One can see this identity come to life even more pointedly, however, in the ritual and liturgical practices seen in the Shri Radha Madanmohan temple maintained by Gadadhar Bhatt's family.

The early modern saints, devotees, and builders of Braj-Vrindavan came from different directions and distant lands to offer their best to rejuvenate the *līlā dhām* of their lord, the sacred place where he had played and still plays today. Those who came from the south doubtless had different reasons for doing so, but in choosing Braj as the place to settle they had a common purpose—to express their love and devotion for Krishna. They did not want to miss the opportunity to perform *nām* and *dhām sevā* for Krishna—the practice of venerating his name by continuously chanting it and honouring his abode by inhabiting the place where he himself had lived. In doing so they brought to bear the best materials provided by their individual pasts, producing in north Indian Braj a cultural mixture that took into account the south and Bengal, thereby making it unique and attractive.

In the general revival of Braj-Vrindavan as the theatre of Krishna līlā against the background of the bhakti movement, Gadadhar Bhatt's family played a special role as facilitators of the song of bhakti in Vrindavan. Expert in the art of synthesis, they were able to combine the Braj culture they adopted with sensibilities and practices that reflected their own southern roots. They showed us that one can keep adopting and editing and modifying things at all levels of one's life regardless of religion, culture, and language, without losing one's dignity and roots. Any culture, religion, or community that can do this will continue singing and dancing for centuries, just as the Bhatt family has done.

Notes

1. The so-called six gosvāmīs were Sanatan, Rup, and Jiv Goswami, as well as Raghunath Das, Raghunath Bhatt, and Gopal Bhatt.

2. See Naresh Chandra Bansal, *Caitanya sampradāy: siddhānt aur sāhitya* (Agra: Vinod Pustak Bhaṇḍār, 1980), 293–8. The original Kankrauli documents are no longer available. Bansal has seen a copy, but does not say where.

3. Gadādhar Bhaṭṭ, *Śrī Gadādhar Bhaṭṭ jī kī vāṇī*, comp. Krishnadas Baba (Vrindavan: Radheshyam Bookseller, VS 2015 [1958 CE], 2nd edition), pad 34, 23.

4. Rūpkalā, 'Sitārāmśaraṇ' Bhagavān Prasād, *Śrī Bhaktamāl* (Lucknow: Tejkumār Press, 1977 [1914], 6th edition), 786.

5. Tarapada Mukherjee and J. C. Wright, 'An Early Testamentary Document in Sanskrit', *Bulletin of the School of Oriental and African Studies* 42, no. 2 (1979): 297.

6. Durgā Prasād Laharī, ed., *Śrī Bhaktamāl* (Calcutta: Natavar Chakravarti, Bangavasi Press, Bengali 1312 [1906 CE]), 285–309.

7. Laharī, *Śrī Bhaktamāl, ṭīkā* 662, *kavitt* 181, 788.

8. Interview with family members (Athakambha, Vrindavan, 26 June 2013).

9. Laharī, *Śrī Bhaktamāl, chappay* 660, p. 786.

10. Rūpkalā, *Śrī Bhaktamāl*, 786.

11. Rūpkalā, *Śrī Bhaktamāl*, ṭīkā 181, kavitt 176, 791.

12. Bhagavatrasik, *Bhagavatrasikjī kī vānī* (Vrindavan: Surendranath, VS 1995 [1938 CE], 4th edition), 54.

13. Kiśorīlāl Gupta, ed., *Nāgarīdās Granthāvalī* (Kashi: Nagari Pracharini Sabha, VS 2022[1965 CE]), 69.

14. Bābā Viśveśvar Śaran, ed., *Bhaktiras phuṭkar prasang* (Vrindavan: Braj Seva Samiti, 1965), 265.

15. At present I am unable to provide a print citation for these verses, which are well known in the family's oral tradition.

16. Hit Candralāl, *Vṛndāvan prakāśamālā, parikramā ke itihās kī pratham vāṇī*, ed. Lalita Prasad Purohit (Vrindavan: Nagar Kishor Prakashan, 1989), 26

Bibliography

Bansal, Naresh Chandra. *Caitanya sampradāy: siddhānt aur sāhitya*. Agra: Vinod Pustak Bhaṇḍār, 1980.

Bhagavatrasik. *Bhagavatrasikjī kī Vānī*, 4th ed. Vrindavan: Surendranath, VS 1995 [1938 CE].

Bhaṭṭ, Gadādhar. *Śrī Gadādhar Bhaṭṭjī kī vāṇī*, 2nd ed, compiled by Krishnadas Baba. Vrindavan: Radheshyam Bookseller, VS 2015 [1958 CE].

Dhruvadās, *Bhaktnāmāvalī*. Vrindavan: Hit Sāhitya Prakāśan, VS 2053 [1996 CE].

Bābā Viśveśvar Śaran, ed. *Bhaktiras phuṭkar prasang*. Vrindavan: Braj Seva Samiti, 1965.

Gupta, Kiśorīlāl, ed. *Nāgarīdās Granthāvalī*, vol. 2. Kashi: Nagari Pracharini Sabha, VS 2022 [1965 CE].

Hit Candralāl, *Vṛndāvan prakāśamālā, parikramā ke itihās kī pratham vāṇī*, edited by Lalita Prasad Purohit. Vrindavan: Nagar Kishor Prakashan, 1989.

Laharī, Durgā Prasād, ed. *Śrī Bhaktamāl*. Calcutta: Natavar Chakravarti, Bangavasi Press, Bengali 1312 [1906 CE].

Mukherjee, Tarapada and J. C. Wright. 'An Early Testamentary Document in Sanskrit'. *Bulletin of the School of Oriental and African Studies* 42, no. 2 (1979): 297–320.

'Rūpkalā', 'Sītārāmśaraṇ' Bhagavān Prasād. *Śrī Bhaktamāl*, 6th ed. Lucknow: Tejkumar Press, 1977 [1914].

Vṛndāvan Prakāśamālā. Bibliographical information unavailable.

19

JOHN STRATTON HAWLEY

Bhaṭṭs in Braj

Forty years ago Shrivatsa Goswami was even younger than he is today, but he was already a master of hospitality. Thanks to Shrivatsa and his family, I took up residence in the temple compound of Śrī Rādhāramaṇjī in Vrindavan and became the beneficiary of the library resources of the Śrī Caitanya Prem Sansthān, the *rāslīlā* productions it sponsored, and, most important of all, hours of conversation with Shrivatsa himself. But who was to be my principal teacher as I launched into my Surdas project in a formal way? Shrivatsa thought there could be no one better than Krishna Chaitanya Bhaṭṭ, the humane and hilarious scholar whose ancient house was to be found in the Bhaṭṭjī kī Galī, Aṭhkhambhā, in the centre of the old town.

Why did Bhaṭṭjī seem just right for the job? First and foremost, because of his scholarship and teaching abilities, both of which were renowned. Second, because of his musicianship: his energetic yet devotedly traditional performances of bhakti *sangīt* in his family temple were famous in Vrindavan's *rasik* circles.[1] Finally, I suspect, Shrivatsa was mindful of Bhaṭṭjī's family ties to the Vallabh Sampradāy, who have historically played a special role as custodians of the Surdas tradition. For centuries the Telangana Bhaṭṭ family of whom Krishna Chaitanya Bhaṭṭ was the scion—the family that traces its ancestry to Gadādhar Bhaṭṭ, as explained by Swapna Sharma in the immediately preceding chapter—had sought marriage partners for their sons among the Telangana Bhaṭṭs who stand at the centre of the Puṣṭimārg by virtue of their blood connection to Vallabh Bhaṭṭ, that is, Vallabhācārya. This made them quite unusual in a town whose sectarian affiliations are not by and large Vallabhite. A portrait of Chaitanya and Nityānand in ecstatic dance does grace an important apse of the family's temple space, but musically and by long tradition of intermarriage, the ties between Bhaṭṭjī's family and the Vallabh *kul*, who have often seemed the Gauḍīyas' rivals, are strong.

Where then do Krishna Chaitanya Bhaṭṭ and his family stand with respect to *sampradāy*, that great organizing rubric in the traditional religious life of modern-day Braj? Somewhere anomalous, it seems—somewhere uncertain. Yet historically speaking, they clearly stand near the ancient centre of Vrindavan's religious life. The respect in which they and their religious traditions are held makes that obvious, and so, to be frank, does their real estate.

Perhaps it is the rubric of sampradāy, now so self-evidently normative, that is actually producing the anomaly. If so, here is a proposal: What would we learn if we were to turn things on their head and see the Bhaṭṭ identity as the primary key to the organization upon which, historically, the great sampradāys of the region came to be built? Perhaps, by focusing on the entrepreneurial Bhaṭṭs from the south who were so crucial to 'discovering' and resettling Braj in the sixteenth century—focusing on them as a group—we might learn something about their shared impetus that is lost as soon as we sort by sampradāy. It is striking, after all, that so many Bhaṭṭs were prominently involved—not just Gopāl Bhaṭṭ and Gadādhar Bhaṭṭ, about whom we learn in neighbouring pages of this volume, but Śrī Bhaṭṭ, Keśav Bhaṭṭ Kāśmīrī, Nārāyaṇ Bhaṭṭ, and, last but not least, Vallabh Bhaṭṭ, that is, Vallabhācārya. What's in a name, as Shakespeare asked? And why did these Bhaṭṭs come to settle in Braj when they did?[2]

Identifying the Southern Bhaṭṭs of Braj

Consider, for example, the figure of Nimbārka. If one reads the standard account of how the sampradāys of Braj came into being, one meets Nimbārka's name at the head of the roster of Krishna *bhakta*s who arrived in Braj and established an enduring sectarian presence there. This standard is well represented in Prabhudayāl Mītal's celebrated *Braj ke dharma-sampradāyoṅ kā itihās*, published in 1968. According to Mītal, Nimbārka made his appearance in Braj at the conclusion of what he calls the early medieval period (*pūrva madhya kāl*), that is, just before the onset of Mughal rule.[3] Mītal tells us that Nimbārka made his residence in Nīmgāoṅ, near Mount Govardhan, a place that takes its name simultaneously from his and from the great *nīm* tree that grows there. Mītal then goes on to list the names of three other prominent figures who inherited Nimbārka's mantle before the time of Akbar: Gāngal Bhaṭṭācārya, Keśav Kāśmīrī Bhaṭṭ, and Śrī Bhaṭṭ. These four Nimbārkī mahants comprise almost half of Mītal's pre-Mughal list. Only one other figure dating to this period—Vallabhācārya—joins them in taking a clear place within the framework articulated by the idea of the four sampradāys.

From our point of view it must be observed that, with the single exception of Nimbārka himself, these men are Bhaṭṭs, one and all. But we must also note a series of difficulties that are embedded in Mītal's reconstruction of Nimbārkī sectarian history. To begin with, nothing in the work most reliably attributed to Nimbārka, the *Vedāntaparijātasaurabha* (The Fragrance of the Heavenly Tree of Vedānta), which was conceived as his commentary on the *Brahma Sūtras*, betrays a specifically Krishnaite orientation. This text does not even cite the *Bhāgavata Purāṇa*, which may be an indication of its early date but may also signal the lack of a theistic orientation that would align its author comfortably into the Vaishnava frame proclaimed by the idea of the four sampradāys. Evidently, that came later. Moreover, skipping ahead to the Braj aspects of the story, there is no real reason to associate the nīm tree that appears in the name of Nīmgāoṅ with the nīm that figures prominently in the story of how Nimbārka (or Nimāditya) got his name, the one that Priyādās reports.[4] What is critical is the turn to Radha among some of the Bhaṭṭs who claimed Nimbārka as their guru—the remainder of Mītal's list—but again, that came much later. There is nothing in the writings that can best be attributed to Nimbārka himself that show any awareness of her.[5]

A similar tale would have to be told about the community's establishment at Dhruv Ṭilā on Viśrām Ghāṭ in Mathura. Again, there is no reason to associate this place with Nimbārka himself. Its proprietors are able to trace their family's presence there only as far back as the sixteenth century.[6] Of course, that date is extremely significant from our point of view, as is the fact that this sanctuary is located in Mathura, for it is there that one can trace the bulk of the older religious activity that occurred in the Braj region, as against what happened in the newly 'colonized' rural parts of the area. Very likely we should think of the Nimbārkī presence on Viśrām Ghāṭ as following from the arrival in the course of the early sixteenth century of Keśav Kāśmīrī Bhaṭṭ, the important Nimbārkī ascetic whose *samādhi* lies a short distance away.[7]

Later, as Vrindavan flourished, Nimbārkī theology turned distinctively to Radha and the order established a major site in Vrindavan—the Śrījī temple (ca. 1821), which remains a major site of worship today. As the name would seem to imply, though it also refers to Śrī = Lakṣmī = Rādhā, this temple is closely associated in memory with the figure of Śrī Bhaṭṭ, one of whose poems is included in the middle section of the Fatehpur anthology of 1582.[8] Vrindavan's most highly respected Nimbārkī scholar, Vrindavan Bihari, affirms the four-sampradāy model, yet so far as I have been able to discover, there is no Nimbārkī text of any considerable age that attests it. All we have is the unchallenged conviction that Keśav Kāśmīrī Bhaṭṭ hailed from a Telangana family which, in turn, is said to have been connected to that of Nimbārka himself. So far so good, but I do not yet know exactly what to make of the fact that the family represented at the Dhruv Ṭīlā site where his samādhi lies traces its lineage not to the south but to a Gauḍ Brahmin heritage in the north.[9]

Of course, the matter of southern origins is very significant for our concerns, and this is not the only place where there is a strong suggestion of its importance in generating the great transformations that occurred in Braj sometime around the turn of the sixteenth century. In this volume Shrivatsa Goswami discusses the figure of Gopāl Bhaṭṭ, whom Chaitanya is said to have inspired to depart for Braj when he met him as a young man at Srirangam, and who belonged to the priestly family of that great temple. He represents quite a different connection to the milieu of Rāmānuja than is suggested by the Rāmānandīs' claims, although it is important to observe that Gopāl Bhaṭṭ, like Rāghavānand and Rāmānand, remained celibate. And there is no question about his impact on the ritual life of Vrindavan-style Vaishnavism through his *Haribhaktivilāsa*, even if he himself never became the householder whom those ritual prescriptions, enshrined at the temple of Rādhāramaṇjī and honoured elsewhere, would require for temple service.

A similarly great impact on the emerging Vaishnava culture of Braj can be traced to another immigrant whose family had roots in the deep south—Nārāyaṇ Bhaṭṭ, the author of the *Vrajabhaktivilāsa*

(Devotional Enjoyments of Braj), a massive work completed in 1552, and quite a different person from the Banarsi patriarch who bore the same name. A late-seventeenth-century biography written by one of this Nārāyaṇ's descendents, Jānakīprasād Bhaṭṭ, reports that Nārāyaṇ Bhaṭṭ's father hailed from Madurai, the city whose name is the Tamil equivalent of Mathura and whose mythology connects it pointedly to its northern prototype.[10] According to this same account, however, and also according to the *Vrajotsavacandrikā* (Luminous Array of Festivals in Braj), a work reportedly written by Narayan himself, Nārāyaṇ Bhaṭṭ was born in 1531 on the banks of the Godavari, the great river that rises in the western Deccan and flows eastward through the Telugu country before emptying into the Bay of Bengal.[11] A pattern of gradual northward migration is implied. Nārāyaṇ Bhaṭṭ is said to have settled in the region around Mount Govardhan in 1545, apparently joining the ascetics from eastern India who had by then encamped at Rādhākuṇḍ—or, to use the local name, Arīṭh.

The *Vrajabhaktivilāsa* is a remarkable treatise, cataloguing every conceivable forest, grove, or ford in the Braj countryside, connecting each with a deity or character in the life of Krishna, and instructing potential visitors about the mantra to be uttered at each place and the time that would be optimal for offering such an utterance. It is an encyclopedic work—the longest ever composed about the sacred geography of Braj—and it reads, in the words of Alan Entwistle, 'not so much as a description of actual circumstances, but as a prospectus for a full reclamation of Braj, making use of any existing objects, however trivial, and inventing the rest'.[12] The *Vrajabhaktivilāsa* takes Mathura as its basic point of origin, yet its special focus is further west. Vrindavan is not especially featured, but there may be a connection with the followers of Chaitanya, as Nārāyaṇ Bhaṭṭ's several-year stay in Rādhākuṇḍ seems to imply. If so, however, such a fact could not be deduced from the description of Nārāyaṇ Bhaṭṭ that is offered by Nabhādās, who goes to some lengths to depict him as a *smārta*, someone who strives to keep the entire fabric of traditional Brahmanical learning intact.[13] Nor is a Chaitanyite orientation evident in the *Vrajabhaktivilāsa* itself. Nābhādās positions his *chappay* on Nārāyaṇ Bhaṭṭ after the one on Kamalākar Bhaṭṭ, a Mādhvite, and before the one that depicts Rūp and Sanātan. One might interpret this order as indicating a hinge between sects, but I think it is easier to read in terms of caste and perhaps regional affiliation. After all, if we were to believe that Nābhādās understood Nārāyaṇ Bhaṭṭ as being a member of the Chaitanyite fold—a pupil of Kṛṣṇadās Brahmacārī, who was in turn an initiate of Sanātan Gosvāmī, as Gauḍīya tradition asserts, then it would seem odd that Nābhā should devote a chappay to Sanātan's pupil's pupil before he got to Sanātan himself.

It is easy enough to understand how a work like the *Vrajabhaktivilāsa* might have been composed by a newcomer to Braj rather than a native. Here would have been someone who could still see the forest for the trees—and indeed, forests become the principal organizing rubric for this massive work, although specific banyans are also featured. Yet although there seems no doubt about Nārāyaṇ Bhaṭṭ's having been an outsider, it is much harder to locate him clearly within any sampradāy rubric and thereby imagine a sect-based orientation that might have brought him to Braj. Unlike Gopāl Bhaṭṭ and the six *gosvāmīs*, Kṛṣṇadās Kavirāj and the early Chaitanyite biographers never propose such a thing. Much about Nārāyaṇ Bhaṭṭ remains mysterious. He wrote in Sanskrit and may well have been a speaker of Telugu and Tamil, but as to the means of his livelihood or the exact motivation for his immigration to Braj, at present it seems impossible to say.

Other southerners were also active in Braj in the first half of the sixteenth century. Rūp and Sanātan Gosvāmī, younger and older brothers who had a major impact on the building of Braj, also belonged to the south in a certain sense. If Nārāyaṇ Bhaṭṭ's relation to the Chaitanyite project that began to unfold in Braj in the first half of the sixteenth century is somewhat indistinct, that is hardly so with Rūp and Sanātan, and in part for that reason we are heir to much more specific information about their southern roots. We learn from the writings of Jīv Gosvāmī, nephew to Rūp and Sanātan, that they all belonged to a family that traced its origins to the Deccan. There is an element of confusion in Jīv's genealogical report, since he seems to claim that the earliest ancestor whom he lists, one Sarvajña Jagatguru, himself 'ruled as a king in the land of Karnāṭa'—that is, Karnataka—but it seems clear that the man to whom he was actually referring was not the king himself but rather, as the title suggests, his guru. As we learn elsewhere in Jīv's writing, this man's name was Viśveśvara Kavicandra and he served as court poet (again, the *kavi* in his name gives it away) to King Siṃhabhūpāla, who controlled a region in the Nalgonda district of modern Telangana, not far south of Hyderabad, in the last two decades of the fourteenth century.[14]

Yet much had happened in the six generations that separated Rūp and Sanātan from Viśveśvara. Their branch of the family had long since settled in Bengal, probably coming by way of Orissa (Odisha), and within Bengal, Rūp and Sanātan had themselves been itinerant. After being educated at Navadvīp, they settled at Rāmakelī, near Gauḍ, and took up service in the court of Husain Shāh, who from Gauḍ ruled an area that extended across most of what we today would call Bengal. Clearly, Rūp and Sanātan preserved the high levels of training that their Brahmanical past implied, yet by serving a Muslim ruler they effectively become *kāyasths*, a literate scribal community with mixed-caste associations, as certain others openly called them.[15] It was Chaitanya who reinscribed their Brahmin identities upon them by giving them the names Rūp and Sanātan. When he first encountered them, we are told, they were known to him respectively as Dabīr Khās and Sākar Mallik, and these names may actually not have been personal names but the titles by which these men were known at the Shahi court of Gauḍ. Sākar Mallik is 'honoured sir' and Dabīr Khās is 'private secretary'—that is, to the Shah. In Chaitanyite remembrance, Sanātan sometimes gets this title too.[16]

No doubt these roles made Rūp and Sanātan effective interlocutors with counterparts in the Mughal and Surī courts, but their particular standing at Gauḍ, exalted as it was, may also have encouraged them to move elsewhere—to a place where they could reclaim a fuller measure of their Brahmin-ness. Of course, there may have been other motives as well. They may have wanted to dissociate themselves from a campaign on Puri that Husain Shāh was then considering. But these brothers' sense of having compromised themselves comes through at several points on their biographies, particularly as counterpoint to their efforts not to lose contact with Karnataka Brahmin families like their own.[17] In the *Bhaktiratnākara* it is said that they resettled a group of Karnataka Brahmins in Bhaṭṭabāṭī, near Gauḍ.[18] The name is certainly worth noting. Whatever exactly was in the minds of Rūp and Sanātan, it seems clear that by moving to Braj they were able to don the mantle of their Brahmin-ness—their Bhaṭṭ-ness—anew, and did so in an environment where just about everything was being made new at the same time.

The Haritrayī and Vallabh

What made Braj Braj? What made Vrindavan Vrindavan? In a certain sense, we are apt never to know for certain, but it is tolerably clear that it did not happen organically, from the inside out. Rather, the

Krishna bhaktas who moved to the area in the course of the sixteenth century played a major role in heightening—if not actually creating—the sense of identity that went with being resident there. By contrast to the examples we have given so far, however, it is important to appreciate that by no means all of these immigrants to Braj were southerners—even southerners whose routes to Braj were as indirect as those of Rūp, Sanātan, and somewhat less markedly Gopal Bhaṭṭ. Quite a number of the most significant bhaktas remembered as having made their way to Braj at this time owed their origins to places that were quite definitely on the northern side of the Vindhyas.

Three fine examples of immigrants who came from nearer by can be found in a trio of poets and musicians who were much later to be described as the Haritrayī, 'Hari's three': Haridās, Hit Harivaṃś, and Harirāmvyās. The designation Haritrayī is late, but the associations linking these three are old.[19] This is probably reflected in the fact that Nābhādās treats them sequentially in his *Bhaktamāl* (§§85–7), although the names themselves may have been a factor, since they all begin with 'Hari'. The first two members of this trio, all of whom settled in Vrindavan in the course of the sixteenth century, are said to have established followings that could suitably be called sampradāys, although the relation of these communities to the overarching four-sampradāy rubric is problematic. The last of the Haritrayī, however, is different. He seems to have allowed no ongoing succession to be established in his name—no sampradāy—and was deeply suspicious of any such enterprise. This is the poet and hagiographer Harirāmvyās. Heidi Pauwels has made the case that he is especially interesting for our story precisely because a whole group of his poems document sets of associations between bhakti heroes who settled in Braj that are quite different from what later *sāmpradāyik* reckonings have led us to expect. Furthermore, Harirāmvyās seems to treasure his ties with Haridās and Hit Harivaṃś in a way that has nothing to do with sectarian boundaries—as if they constituted a common group of rasiks and that was that. One feels a certain distance from the Bhaṭṭ southerners, even though Harirāmvyās is fully respectful of them, and as Pauwels has clearly shown, efforts to situate Vyās himself as a member of the Nimbārkī lineage were almost certainly cooked up after the fact.

So the rasik world of Vrindavan was not entirely a Bhaṭṭ creation, and neither was that of Braj on a larger scale. Still, the Bhaṭṭs' influence was evidently substantial, and we have not yet considered the southern Bhaṭṭ whom many would take as being *primus inter pares*: Vallabhācārya. Gauḍīyas such as Kavikarṇapūra and Kṛṣṇadās Kavirāj call him Vallabh Bhaṭṭ.[20] Here the major question, however, has not to do with his status as a Bhaṭṭ but with his status as a Brajbāsī. Vallabh was content to make his lifelong home not in Braj but in Aḍel, a village located on the southern bank of the Ganges just after the Yamuna joins it at the great confluence in Allahabad or, as it was called in Vallabh's time, Prayāg. If Vallabh journeyed to Braj, it was on pilgrimage, not to establish a home or colony of followers, a sāmpradāyik beachhead. That came later, at the initiative of his son Viṭṭhalnāth (1515–1585?), and very likely in response to political changes. The Mughals had returned to power, displacing the Afghans, and Akbar was at the helm of state. It was then, apparently, that Viṭṭhalnāth decided to set up a residence in Gokul, on the east bank of the Yamuna across the river and slightly upstream from Mathura; a Mughal decree (*farmān*) acknowledging this fact appears in 1577.[21] As for the well-known contest over the ritual management of the temple on Mount Govardhan, it is unclear whether that happened shortly after Vallabh's death or, much more likely, in the early years of Akbar's rule. In any case there is nothing to suggest that tales of Vallabh's interest in Govardhan and Gokul, as reported in the *vārtās*, were anything more than expressions of the community's desire to connect sites it later regarded as their spiritual home with the founder–preceptor himself. It is easier to believe the Mughal account, as recorded in the farmāns of 1577, 1581, and subsequent years. There it is said that the emperor granted land and cattle-grazing rights to Viṭṭhalnāth (or, as he is called, Viṭṭhaldās and Viṭṭhalrāy), who in turn blessed the emperor with his prayers, as if in accord with the standard *duniyā-vilāyat* system. If such a farmān could be procured, it suggests by implication that Viṭṭhalnāth and his representatives would also have been free to move and thrive along the imperial highways, especially the great one that led to Gujarat. Perhaps the funds used to buy the property in Gokul, in fact, were recruited on preaching tours to Gujarat by Viṭṭhalnāth or Kṛṣṇadās.

Vallabh, however, was a contemporary of Chaitanya and Keśav Kāśmīrī Bhaṭṭ. He certainly had serious theological purposes, but it is far less clear that he was actively trying to build a sampradāy in institutional ways. When Vallabh speaks of *brahmasambandh* (bonding with Brahman) in the short treatise called *Siddhāntarahasyam* (The Secret of Our Doctrine), he does not seem to be authorizing the ritual that would later become the distinctive mark of membership in the Puṣṭimārgī Sampradāy, but rather putting forward a mental regimen of unalloyed devotion that had been communicated to him by Krishna himself.[22] It initiates a process of 'becoming Brahman' (*brahmatātataḥ*, 5.8), not becoming a Vallabhite. Doubtless the eight-syllable mantra that later came to be transmitted from guru to disciple in the brahmasambandh ceremony—*śrī kṛṣṇa śaraṇam mama* (Lord Krishna is my refuge)—was important to Vallabh (6.9), but it is telling that another formula of the same length matters at least as much: *kṛṣṇa eva gatir mama* (Krishna alone is my goal). Vallabh gives over almost the entirety of one of his short treatises to this formula (9.1–9), which he connects to the core concept of refuge as well (*śaraṇam, āśraya*, 9.10–11). Again, no ritual dimension seems to be implied, and in this case the sampradāy did not supply one later, so far as I know.

In a similar vein we find Vallabh far more ambivalent about the value of householdership than would be suggested by the way in which the sampradāy named after him championed that form of life. In two of his pithy treatises, Vallabh does indeed struggle with the obstacles that a life of renunciant wandering can pose to cultivating an awareness of Krishna's freely given grace (11.7, 14.2–6), but he is also attuned to the difficulties that a householder's life can throw in one's spiritual path (11.2–3, 11.8) and recommends a measure of travel on that account (11.8). All this strongly suggests that the sampradāy took on its distinctive forms after the death of Vallabh, not before, despite the manner in which the community has come to understand its own early history.[23] Evidently it was Viṭṭhalnāth who made the Vallabh Sampradāy a sampradāy, not his father, Vallabh, or his elder brother, Gopīnāth.

As for Vallabh, I think it would be better to think of him as inhabiting a world of theological disputation and self-conscious practice that situated him as a member of the larger Vaishnava Bhaṭṭ community into which he was born. When Vallabh decided, in the last days of his life, to return to Banaras, the place where he had spent his youth, it was probably not just for ritual reasons—*kāśīvās* at the moment of death—but because it returned him to the place where, more than any other, the Bhaṭṭs of the south had chosen to gather in north India. His progeny, however, as they became firmly ensconced both in Braj and farther west, found it natural to intermarry with other Telangana Bhaṭṭs such as the forebears of my teacher, Krishna Chaitanya Bhaṭṭ.

Concluding Questions

As we emerge from this survey of Bhaṭṭs in sixteenth-century Braj, two principal questions remain. The first generalizes from where we have just arrived: Were the Bhaṭṭs who had so much to do with making Braj the Braj we recognize as Braj today a closely knit group or a looser confederation? Were they conscious of being Bhaṭṭs together in the rigorous way that pertained to those who assembled at the *muktimaṇḍapa* of the Viśveśvar temple in Kāśī in the seventeenth century? If by this we have in mind the sort of collocation that could issue corporate legal decisions, then evidently not. But if we mean that they were conscious of one another's Sanskrit writings and that they shared a developing consensus about proper ritual practice, then in a number of instances the answer would have to be 'yes'. Rūp Gosvāmī straightforwardly aligns his discussion of *vaidhī bhakti* with Vallabh's concept of the *maryādāmārga*, and similarly associates his own concept of *rāgānugā bhakti* with what Vallabh calls the *puṣṭimārga*—the first pair of terms referring to closely structured or ethical religiosity, the latter pair referring to its more enthusiastic, unbounded counterpart.[24] Later, by the time Kṛṣṇadās Kavirāj wrote his *Caitanyacaritāmṛta*—he finished it by 1615—things had apparently soured from the Gauḍīya side, but theological similarities remain.[25] On the ritual side of things, it is notable that when Gopāl Bhaṭṭ writes his *Haribhaktivilāsa*, he makes liberal reference to the ritual manual *Kramadīpikā* of Keśav, who is normally understood to be the same person as the Nīmbarkī acharya Keśav Kāśmīrī Bhaṭṭ.[26] And one has broad agreement about the observance of an eight-watch (*aṣṭayām*) ritual schedule celebrating a day in the life of Krishna Gopāl and the use of Brajbhāṣā lyrics in the course of doing so. Was such an awareness of shared Braj practice also a sense of shared Bhaṭṭ practice—perhaps a new and self-consciously liberal form of Bhaṭṭ practice made possible by the conviction of being 'close to the source' in some new, Renaissance-type way? After all, there they were in Krishna's own country—in Braj.

The second question has to do with motivation: Why did these southern Brahmins, these Bhaṭṭs, establish themselves in Braj when they did? Heretofore, this question has usually been answered in terms of individual inspiration: the revolutionary vision of Chaitanya, the competing but equally self-conscious vision of Vallabh, the retroactively constructed Radha-centred vision of Nimbārka, the distinctively geographical project of Nārāyaṇ Bhaṭṭ. Once we see that the critical agents of these visions were all Bhaṭṭs, however, and once we begin to look more closely for interrelationships between them, the matter of vision and motivation may take on a somewhat different colour. Later perceptions of the visions these 'founders' had for Braj may have been more fundamentally shaped by the experience of those who came after them than we have yet realized—a partitioning and crystallization according to sampradāy that may not accurately reflect what the founders experienced in the sixteenth century itself, when they would all have been newcomers together. This was not entirely a Bhaṭṭ-centred Braj consciousness. The Haritrayī show that clearly. Yet the crucial work of the Bhaṭṭs who first perceived Braj from elsewhere and who settled there for the long haul seems impossible to deny.

Was their liturgical institution-building an after-effect of being settled in Braj or somehow related to the motives that brought them there in the first place? This, I think, remains a mystery. One thing, however, is sure. By the time we arrive at the end of the sixteenth century, the stability and expansiveness of the Mughal state had made their presence in Braj seem both natural and divinely ordained. Whatever their origins, whoever their relatives, whatever their gestures to the south or by contrast to the self-conscious, newly built Braj world that had Krishna as its single point of orientation, when it came to what Sheldon Pollock has so pointedly called 'the world of men', these Bhaṭṭs were Mughal Bhaṭṭs.

Notes

1. Takako Tanaka, 'The Samāj-gāyan Tradition: Transmitting a Musico-Religious System in North India', in *Music and Society in South Asia*, ed. Yoshitaka Terada (Osaka: National Museum of Ethnology, 2008), 87–101.

2. The issue of naming is doubtless a significant one: the term 'Bhaṭṭ', with its several regional variants, has considerable currency among Brahmins. For present purposes I accept it simply as a term of use in the period we are discussing, yet keeping alive the question of whether that very use may sometimes serve as a way to assert Brahmin-ness at a level that rides above finer-grained designations of locality and endogamy. In this regard, for a somewhat later period and a different cosmopolitan setting, see Rosalind O'Hanlon, 'Letters Home: Banaras Pandits and the Maratha Regions in Early Modern India', *Modern Asian Studies* 44, no.2 (2010) and 'Speaking from Śiva's Temple: Banaras Scholar Households and the Brahman "Ecumene" of Mughal India', in *Religious Cultures in Early Modern India: New Perspectives*, ed.

Rosalind O'Hanlon and David Washbrook (London: Routledge, 2011), 174–211; also James Benson, 'Śaṃkarabhaṭṭa's Family Chronicle: The *Gādhivaṃśavarṇana*', in *The Pandit: Traditional Scholarship in India*, ed. Alex Michaels (New Delhi: Manohar, 2001), 105–18.

3. Prabhudayal Mītal, *Braj ke dharma-sampradāyoṅ kā itihās* (New Delhi: National Publishing House, 1968), 187; cf. Prabhudayal Mītal, *Braj kā sāṃskṛtik itihās* (New Delhi: Rājkamal Prakāśan, 1966), part 2, 150.

4. 'Rūpkalā', 'Sitārāmśaraṇ' Bhagavān Prasād, *Śrī Bhaktamāl* (Lucknow: Tejkumār Press, 1969 [1910]), 259, *kavitt* 135.

5. A crucial document in this transformation is the *Mahāvāṇī* of Harivyāsdev, whom Mītal estimates to have lived from about 1550–1630, and for whom we have an entry in the *Bhaktamāl* of Nabhādās (*Bhaktamāl: Pāṭhānuśīlan evam Vivecan*, ed. Narendra Jhā [Patna: Anupam Prakāśan, 1978], §74). This work provides a Nimbārkī analogue to the devotional theology that had been worked out by the great Gauḍīya theorists, and probably is dependent upon them. See Alan W. Entwistle, *Braj: Centre of Krishna Pilgrimage* (Groningen: Egbert Forsten, 1987), 171; Mītal, *Braj ke dharma-sampradāyoṅ kā itihās*, 347–8. It is noteworthy that Harivyāsdev and his predecessor at Dhruv Ṭilā are remembered as having been Gauḍ Brahmins, rather than claiming Telangana roots after the fashion of Keśav Kāśmīrī Bhaṭṭ: unlike him, they were presumably northerners.

6. Catherine Clémentin-Ojha, 'La Renaissance du Nimbārkasampradāya au XVIe siècle: Contribution à l'étude d'une secte kṛṣṇaïte', *Journal Asiatique* 278, nos 3–4 (1990): 334–5.

7. Clémentin-Ojha, 'La Renaissance', 339, 342. This contrasts with the fourteenth-century dating often given within the Nimbārka Sampradāy, but accords with the fact that Rāghavdās offers only names in the order's genealogy of mahants until he comes to Keśav Kāśmīrī Bhaṭṭ and his successors, whom he describes substantively (Agar Chand Nahta, ed., *Rāghavdās kṛt bhaktamāl* [Jodhpur: Rajasthan Oriental Research Institute, 1965], §244ff.). The fourteenth-century date has been effectively challenged by Prabhudayāl Mītal because it cannot be reconciled with the independent accounts that appear in Vallabhite and Chaitanyite sources stating that their gurus encountered Keśav Kāśmīrī (Mītal, *Braj ke dharma-sampradāyoṅ kā itihās*, 191–6); the encounter with Chaitanya is also reported by Priyādās.

8. Gopal Narayan Bahura and Kenneth E. Bryant, eds, *Pad Sūrdāsjī kā/ The Padas of Sūrdās* (Jaipur: Maharaja Sawai Man Singh II Museum, 1982 [1984]), 160.

9. Clémentin-Ojha, 'La Renaissance', 343; cf. Frederic Salmon Growse, *Mathurá: A District Memoir*, 3rd ed. revised and abridged (Allahabad: North-Western Provinces and Oudh Government Press, 1883 [1874]), 147.

10. D. Dennis Hudson, *Krishna's Mandala: Bhagavata Religion and Beyond*, ed. John Stratton Hawley (New Delhi: Oxford University Press, 2009), 12, 70–4.

11. Entwistle, *Braj*, 149, who refers to Nārāyaṇ Bhaṭṭ's *Vrajotsavacandrikā*, 228–30, and Jānakīprasād's *Nārāyaṇabhaṭṭacaritāmṛta* 1.45–54.

12. Entwistle, *Braj*, 253.

13. 'jñāna samārata paccha ko nāhina kou khaṅḍana biyau' (Jhā, *Bhaktamāl*, §83, vol. 2, 31; cf. Rūpkalā, *Śrī Bhaktamāl* [chappay 442], 589.

14. Neal Delmonico, 'Rūpa Gosvāmin: His Life, Family, and Early Vraja Commentators', *Journal of Vaishnava Studies* 1, no. 2 (1993): 147–9.

15. Parīkh, ed., *Caurāsī vaiṣṇavan kī vārtā*, *Kṛṣṇadās kī vārtā*, *prasang* 2, 536, trans. Richard Barz, *The Bhakti Sect of Vallabhācārya* (Faridabad: Thomson Press, 1976), 218; cf. Heidi R. M. Pauwels, *In Praise of Holy Men: Hagiographic Poems by and about Harirām Vyās* (Groningen: Egbert Forsten, 2002), 151–2.

16. *Caitanyacaritāmṛta* 2.1.165, 2.1.174 , trans. Edward C. Dimock, Jr, and Tony K. Stewart, *Caitanya Caritāmṛta of Kṛṣṇadās Kavirāj: A Translation and Commentary* (Cambridge: Harvard Oriental Series, 1999), 346; Delmonico, 'Rūpa Gosvāmin', 137n21, who credits Nareścandra Jānā, *Vṛndāvaner chaya gosvāmī* (Calcutta: Calcutta University, 1970), 37.

17. *Caitanyacaritāmṛta* 2.1.179: 'We are of low *jāti* ... keep low companions ... do low work' (Dimock, Jr, and Stewart, 346). Further, *mleccha-jāti*, and so on (2.1.183), 347.

18. Narahari Cakravartī, *Bhaktiratnākara* 1.592–4, trans. Kuśakranthadāsa, *Bhakti-ratnākara: The Jewel-filled Ocean of Devotional Service* (Brindavan: Ras Biharilal and Sons, 2006), 53–4.

19. Pauwels, *In Praise of Holy Men*, 140–7. Pauwels attributes the coining of the term itself to Vāsudev Gosvāmī, *Bhakta kavi vyāsjī* (Mathura: Agravāl Press, 1952), 14–18. See also Heidi R. M. Pauwels, 'Hagiography and Community Formation: The Case of a Lost Community of Sixteenth-Century Vrindāvan', *Journal of Hindu Studies* 3, no. 1 (2010): 53–90, and 'Imagining Religious Communities in the Sixteenth Century: Harirām Vyās and the Haritrayī', *International Journal of Hindu Studies* 13, no. 2 (2009): 143–61.

20. Rebecca Jane Manring, 'Kavikarṇapūra's *Gauragaṇoddeśadīpikā* (An Elucidation Regarding the Associates of Caitanya): A Translation and Preliminary Edition', MA thesis, University of Washington, 1989, §115, 141, and *Caitanyacaritāmṛta* 3.7.3, 3.7.13, and so on.

21. Krishnalal Mohanlal Jhaveri, *Imperial Farmans (A.D. 1577 to A.D. 1805) Granted to the Ancestors of His Holiness the Tilakayat Maharaj Farmān* (Bombay: New Printing House, ca. 1928), 1; cf. farmān 2, dated 1581.

22. The *Siddhāntarahasyam* is the fifth treatise to appear with an English translation in James Redington, S. J., *The Grace of Lord Krishna: The Sixteen Verse-Treatises (Ṣoḍaśagranthāḥ) of Vallabhacharya* (New Delhi: Sri Satguru Publications, 2000). The verse in question is 5.2, 64. All other references in this paragraph pertain to the *Ṣoḍaśagranthāḥ*.

23. Charlotte Vaudeville reports it as 'a well-known fact that it is to Viṭṭhalnāth that the sect founded by Vallabhācārya owes its present body of

doctrines as well as its rituals and organization' (Vaudeville, 'The Govardhan Myth in Northern India', *Indo-Iranian Journal* 22 (1980): 1–45, reprinted in *Myths, Saints and Legends in Medieval India*, ed. Vasudha Dalmia, 72–139 [Delhi: Oxford University Press, 1996], 16). I would put the matter even more strongly, questioning what is meant by the word 'founded'.

24. Premlatā Śarmā, ed. and trans., *Śrī Śrī Rūpagosvāmiprabhupādapraṇītaḥ Śrī Śrī Bhaktirasāmṛtasindhuḥ* (New Delhi: Indira Gandhi National Centre for the Arts, 1998), 1.2.269 , 102, and 1.2.309, 112.

25. Monika Horstmann and Anand Mishra, 'Vaiṣṇava Sampradāys on the Importance of Ritual: A Comparison of the Two Contemporaneous Approaches by Viṭṭhalanātha and Jīva Gosvāmī', in *Bhakti beyond the Forest* (New Delhi: Manohar, 2013).

26. Puridās, ed., *Haribhaktivilāsa* (Mymensiṃh: Śacīnāth Raicaudhurī, 1946), 1.39, 1.78, 1.214, 5.171, 5.174, 6.42, 8.110, and 17.5.

Bibliography

Bahura, Gopal Narayan and Kenneth E. Bryant, eds. *Pad Sūrdāsjī kā/The Padas of Sūrdās*. Jaipur: Maharaja Sawai Man Singh II Museum, 1982 [1984].

Barz, Richard. *The Bhakti Sect of Vallabhācārya*. Faridabad: Thomson Press, 1976.

Benson, James. 'Śaṃkarabhaṭṭa's Family Chronicle: The *Gādhivaṃśavarṇana*'. In *The Pandit: Traditional Scholarship in India*, edited by Alex Michaels. New Delhi: Manohar, 2001, 105–18.

Clémentin-Ojha, Catherine. 'La Renaissance du Nimbārkasampradāya au XVIe siècle: Contribution à l'étude d'une secte kṛṣṇaite'. *Journal Asiatique* 278, no. 3–4 (1990): 328–76.

Delmonico, Neal. 'Rūpa Gosvāmin: His Life, Family, and Early Vraja Commentators'. *Journal of Vaishnava Studies* 1, no. 2 (1993): 133–57.

Dimock, Edward C., Jr, and Tony K. Stewart. *Caitanya Caritāmṛta of Kṛṣṇadās Kavirāj: A Translation and Commentary*. Cambridge: Harvard Oriental Series, 1999.

Entwistle, Alan W. *Braj: Centre of Krishna Pilgrimage*. Groningen: Egbert Forsten, 1987.

Gosvāmī, Vāsudev. *Bhakta kavi vyāsjī*. Mathura: Agravāl Press, 1952.

Growse, Frederic Salmon. *Mathurá: A District Memoir*, 3rd edition, revised and abridged. Allahabad: North-Western Provinces and Oudh Government Press, 1883 [1874].

Horstmann, Monika and Anand Mishra. 'Vaiṣṇava Sampradāyas on the Importance of Ritual: A Comparison of the Two Contemporaneous Approaches by Viṭṭhalanātha and Jīva Gosvāmī'. In *Bhakti beyond the Forest: Current Research on Early Modern Religious Literatures in North

India 2003–2009, edited by Imre Bangha. New Delhi, Manohar, 2013, 155–76.

Hudson, D. Dennis. *Krishna's Mandala: Bhagavata Religion and Beyond*, edited by John Stratton Hawley. New Delhi: Oxford University Press, 2009.

Jānā, Nareścandra. *Vṛndāvaner chaya gosvāmī*. Calcutta: Calcutta University, 1970.

Jhā, Narendra, ed. *Bhaktamāl: pāṭhānuśīlan evam vivecan*. Patna: Anupam Prakāśan, 1978.

Jhaveri, Krishnalal Mohanlal. *Imperial Farmans (A.D. 1577 to A.D. 1805) Granted to the Ancestors of His Holiness the Tilakayat Maharaj*. Bombay: New Printing House, ca. 1928.

Kuśakranthadāsa, trans. *Bhakti-Ratnākara: The Jewel-Filled Ocean of Devotional Service*. Brindavan: Ras Biharilal and Sons, 2006.

Manring, Rebecca Jane. 'Kavikarṇapūra's *Gauragaṇoddeśadīpikā* (An Elucidation Regarding the Associates of Caitanya): A Translation and Preliminary Edition'. MA thesis, University of Washington, 1989.

Mītal, Prabhudayāl. *Braj kā sāṃskṛtik itihās*. New Delhi: Rājkamal Prakāśan, 1966.

———. *Brajke dharma-sampradāyoṅ kā itihās*. New Delhi: National Publishing House, 1968.

Nahta, Agar Chand, ed. *Rāghavdās kṛt bhaktamāl*. Jodhpur: Rajasthan Oriental Research Institute, 1965.

Pauwels, Heidi R. M. *In Praise of Holy Men: Hagiographic Poems by and about Harirām Vyās*. Groningen: Egbert Forsten, 2002.

———. 'Imagining Religious Communities in the Sixteenth Century: Harirām Vyās and the Haritrayī'. *International Journal of Hindu Studies* 13, no. 2 (2009): 143–61.

———. 'Hagiography and Community Formation: The Case of a Lost Community of Sixteenth-Century Vrindāvan'. *Journal of Hindu Studies* 3, no. 1 (2010): 53–90.

O'Hanlon, Rosalind. 'Letters Home: Banaras Pandits and the Maratha Regions in Early Modern India'. *Modern Asian Studies* 44, no. 2 (2010): 201–40.

———. 'Speaking from Śiva's Temple: Banaras Scholar Households and the Brahman "Ecumene" of Mughal India'. In *Religious Cultures in Early Modern India: New Perspectives*, edited by Rosalind O'Hanlon and David Washbrook. London: Routledge, 2011, 174–211.

Puridās, ed. *Haribhaktivilāsa*. Mymensiṃh: Śacīnāth Raicaudhurī, 1946.

Redington, James, S. J. *The Grace of Lord Krishna: The Sixteenth Verse-Treatises (Ṣoḍaśagranthāḥ) of Vallabhacharya*. New Delhi: Sri Satguru Publications, 2000.

'Rūpkalā', 'Sitārāmśaraṇ' Bhagavān Prasād. *Śrī Bhaktamāl*. Lucknow: Tejkumār Press, 1969 [1910].

Śarmā, Premlatā, ed. and trans. (into Hindi), *Rūpagosvāmiprabhupāda-praṇītaḥ Śrī Śrī Bhaktirasāmṛtasindhuḥ*. New Delhi: Indira Gandhi National Centre for the Arts, 1998.

Tanaka, Takako. 'The Samāj-gāyan Tradition: Transmitting a Musico-Religious System in North India'. In *Music and Society in South Asia*, edited by Yoshitaka Terada. Osaka: National Museum of Ethnology, 2008, 87–101.

Vaudeville, Charlotte. 'The Govardhan Myth in Northern India'. *Indo-Iranian Journal* 22 (1980): 1–45; reprinted in *Myths, Saints and Legends in Medieval India*, edited by Vasudha Dalmia. New Delhi: Oxford University Press, 1996, 72–139.

20

REMBERT LUTJEHARMS*

'Why Do We Still Sift the Husk-Like *Upaniṣads*?'

Revisiting Vedānta in Early Chaitanya Vaishnava Theology

The title of this chapter is derived from a poem by Raghupati Upadhyaya, a Bihari Brahmin who met Shri Chaitanya in Allahabad, where he recited some of his verses to Chaitanya's great satisfaction. That the question is asked by a Vaishnava is significant. The two great, established Vaishnava traditions at the time—those of Ramanuja and Madhva—were thoroughly Vedāntic. The *vedānta* (conclusion of the Vedas) expressed in the *Upaniṣads* is the foundation for their theology, and their traditions' thought develops primarily in commentaries on these and related texts, such as the *Brahma-sūtras* (a study of the *Upaniṣads*) and the *Bhagavad-gītā* (understood as the *Upaniṣad* of the 'fifth Veda', that is, the *Mahābhārata*).

As Ravi Gupta has shown in his excellent study of Jiva Gosvami,[1] the early Chaitanya Vaishnava tradition also belongs within this rubric. Although the school initially does not produce commentaries on either the *Brahma-sūtras* or any of the principal *Upaniṣads*, there is nevertheless a strong engagement with Vedānta in general and the *Upaniṣads* in particular. Before moving to Vrindavan, Jiva Gosvami studied in Varanasi, the Vedānta capital of the north, and his deep familiarity with Vedānta is evident throughout his works. Jiva quotes the *Upaniṣads* regularly in his *Bhāgavata-sandarbha*, and incorporates a brief commentary on the first four sūtras of the *Brahma-sūtras* (a *catuḥ-sūtrī-ṭīkā*) in his *Paramātma-sandarbha*. Moreover, in the *Sarva-saṃvādinī*, an appendix to the *Sandarbhas*, he engages at greater length with most of the Upaniṣadic passages that are central to Vedānta, as well as entire sections of the *Brahma-sūtras*.[2]

We could thus argue that the new Vaishnava tradition emerging by the inspiration of Chaitanya in Bengal and Vrindavan is a continuation of the older Vaishnava traditions, and sees itself in relation to the Vedic revelation in a similar way as those southern traditions did. But, as I will argue in this chapter, this is only one side of the picture. As Raghupati Upadhyaya's question indicates, this engagement with Vedānta was not a given. Why should they align themselves with Vedānta? Why should they still look to the *Upaniṣads* for theology? How central is Vedānta really to Chaitanya Vaishnava thought?

We can discern two seemingly conflicting views of the role of Vedānta and of the importance of studying the *Upaniṣads*. On the one hand, there is a close engagement with Vedānta, particularly but not exclusively in the writings of Jiva Gosvami. On the other hand—elsewhere—there is an explicit rejection of Vedānta and the *Upaniṣads*, or at least an indifference to them. In what follows I will argue that these two attitudes towards Vedānta are related, and where the Chaitanya tradition expresses its indifference to Vedānta, it does so precisely on the basis of an engagement with Vedānta, which builds extensively on the thoughts of older Vedāntists. Vedānta is thus both a means to link the fledgling Chaitanya Vaishnava tradition with the past, and a means to set itself apart from the very same traditions that constitute it.

The focus of this chapter is a work that might seem to have very little to say about Vedānta. I will look at the *Padyāvalī* ('A String of Verses'), an anthology of Sanskrit poetry compiled by Rupa Gosvami, the most influential theologian of the school. The work consists of 388 verses, of which 34 verses are Rupa Gosvami's own compositions (which makes him the most prominent author in the work) and a large portion are composed by well-known contemporaries or immediate predecessors of Rupa—Chaitanya himself (22, 31, 32, 71, 74, 93, 94, 324, 337), Ishvara Puri (18, 62, 75), Madhavendra Puri (79, 96, 104, 286, 330), Raghupati Upadhyaya (82, 87, 97, 98, 126, 300), Sarvabhauma Bhattacharya (72, 73, 90, 91, 99, 100, 133), Ramananda

Raya (13, 14), Gopala Bhatta (38), Raghunathadasa (131, 331), and so on. There are also a few lesser-known contemporaries—Shrigarbha Kavindra (84), Vanivilasa (315), Ciranjiva (157), Kesavacchatrin (153), and so on. In addition, the anthology also contains many verses of pre-Chaitanya authors, whose sentiment and theology (at least as represented in the verses quoted) Rupa obviously appreciated. Thus, Shridhara Svami is quoted (28, 43), as is Lakshmidhara (16, 29, 33, 34), the author of the *Bhagavan-nāma-kaumudī*, as well as Vishnu Puri (9, 10), the author of the *Bhakti-ratnāvalī*. Apart from these well-known authors, who had considerable influence on the development of early Gauḍīya theology, Rupa brings together a number of authors otherwise unknown to us, several of whom are *sannyāsīs*. A certain Yadavendra Puri is quoted twice (42, 76); figures bearing the name Madhava Sarasvati (57), Avilamba Sarasvati (385), and Vira Sarasvati (368) are cited once each. All these are Vaishnava authors, but the anthology does not stop there. The later sections of the book contain several verses by Amaru (223, 229, 231, 237, 314), Govardhana (190, 242, 303, 374), Bhavabhuti (325, 326), and various authors known from earlier, non-religious anthologies of Sanskrit court poetry.

The *Padyāvalī* is a carefully constructed anthology. It does more than merely string together examples of good poetry. It creates with these verses a new narrative. The work consists of two parts: the first is on the nature of devotion, while the second part describes Krishna's play in Vrindavan. This second part is by far the longer of the two. In over 260 verses (as opposed to 118 verses for the first part) Rupa first briefly describes Vrindavan, Krishna's parents, and his childhood play, and then devotes the majority of the work to Krishna's sports with the *gopīs* (in over 220 verses). What sets the *Padyāvalī* apart from other Sanskrit anthologies is that Rupa does not merely organize the verses by topic, but organizes these topics and the individual verses arrayed within the topic in such a way that they form a new narrative, a new poem. By doing so, each verse of the *Padyāvalī* has thus, in a sense, two authors: the poet who originally composed the verse, and Rupa himself who composes the anthology and gives these verses a new context, and by that a new meaning. This is particularly obvious with the secular verses he culled from older anthologies: nearly all of them occur in this second section of the *Padyāvalī*, where the context turns these 'impersonal' secular verses into devotional poetry.[3]

This is equally true for the first half of the work, which is the focus of this chapter. It opens with several short *māhātmyas*, sections extolling the greatness of Krishna and devotional practices such as meditation, chanting Krishna's name, listening to narrations of Krishna's play, and so on. The focus then shifts away from the practice of devotion onto Krishna's devotees. In a series of sections, Rupa aims to illustrate the nature of a Vaishnava's inner life and disposition. There are sections he labels 'the devotees' expressions of humility', 'the firm faith of devotees', 'the devotees' prayer of longing', 'the eagerness of devotees', and 'contempt for liberation'.

These sections (among the longest in the entire anthology) are significant because they reflect the self-understanding, not just of Rupa, but of the community to which he belongs. Rupa evidently collects verses that are well loved by devotees who were his contemporaries. Thus, the anthology does not just contain many verses composed or beloved by them; it is also meant for them, as Rupa writes in the first verse.[4] These sections of the anthology thus particularly reflect his associates' understanding of what it means to be a devotee of Krishna, and by organizing these verses into sections, Rupa teaches the aspiring devotee—someone new to the community—how he or she should approach the practice of Krishna devotion.

So, what does Rupa teach us about Vedānta? I will start with a verse by Sarvabhauma Bhattacharya, once one of the greatest Vedāntists of his day:

> na vayaṃ kavayo na tārkikā
> na ca vedānta-nitānta-pāragāḥ
> na ca vādi-nivārakāḥ paraṃ
> kapaṭābhīra-kiśora-kiṅkarāḥ
>
> We are no poets, no logicians.
> We have not crossed
>   the vast ocean of Vedānta,
> and we definitely do not win debates.
> We are servants
>   of a cheating cowherd boy.
>
> —Sarvabhauma Bhattacharya, *Padyāvalī* 72

Many of Sārvabhauma's poems in the *Padyāvalī* show a strong dislike of intellectual endeavours and a staunch devotion to Krishna that seems to disregard reason.[5] Particularly with a person like him, it is terribly difficult not to read these verses as autobiographical. Sarvabhauma was a well-respected elderly scholar who had spent his entire life researching, teaching, debating, and writing,[6] when a young *sannyāsī* named Krishna Chaitanya happened to visit his home town, Puri. Concerned that this attractive sannyāsī might not be able to maintain his vows, he decided to instruct him in Vedānta to strengthen his resolve for renunciation. And so Sarvabhauma Bhattacharya began to teach Chaitanya what he himself had studied his entire life.

When his new student finally admits that he does not think too highly of what Sarvabhauma had been teaching him for an entire week, the teaching turns into a debate, and at some point, somehow, devotion to Krishna dawns in Bhattacharya's heart. At this, Sarvabhauma comes to realize he is the servant not just of God but of Krishna, the mischievous cowherd boy of Vrindavan who roams the woods and dances with the cowherd girls. Now, swept away by his religious emotions, he casts aside his books, loses his interest in philosophical thought, and, having been at last defeated in debate—by such a junior, no less!—ceases being the dry, stern philosopher he had been his entire life.[7]

For all the autobiographical echoes, it is difficult to read Sarvabhauma's verses as merely the reflections of a philosopher who has discovered God in his old age: he gives voice to a well-known broader theme. The basic structure of the verse we have quoted—juxtaposing devotion to Krishna with a more intellectual path—is very common in the *Padyāvalī*. Consider for comparative purposes the following verse, which Rupa attributes to an unknown sannyāsī named Yadavendra Puri:

> rasaṃ praśaṃsantu kavitā-niṣṭhā
> brahmāmṛtaṃ veda-śiro-niviṣṭhāḥ
> vayaṃ tu guñjā-kalitāvataṃsaṃ
> gṛhīta-vaṃśaṃ kam api śrayāmaḥ
>
> Skilled poets may praise *rasa*,
> those rapt in the *Upaniṣads*
>   the immortal bliss of Brahman.
>
> But we seek refuge in someone
>   who wears earrings of *guñjā* berries,
>   who holds a flute.
>
> —Yadavendra Puri, *Padyāvalī* 76

All these verses—of which many are part of the section on the devotee's firm faith or resoluteness (*niṣṭhā*)—have a similar structure.

The first element often relates to Vedānta, and particularly an Advaita understanding of Vedānta. In Yadavendra Puri's verse, we have in this regard a poet who praises *rasa* (the blissful experience that a poem embodies and/or communicates) and Vedāntists who study the *Upaniṣads*, thereby praising the bliss of Brahman. Then we have a second element, which presents a contrast to such figures. In the poem at hand, it is the poet himself who worships a certain 'someone' (*kam api*) who seems rather rustic. He is not the majestic Vishnu or the otherworldly ascetic Shiva, but a person whose ornaments consist of common foliage—he wears earrings, made not of jewels but of berries from the *guñjā* (Indian liquorice) tree. Clearly Krishna is here seen as distinct from Brahman, and not the object of those who study the *Upaniṣads*. The *Upaniṣads*, Yadavendra Puri implies, do not teach us about Kṛṣṇa—or at least, do not *explicitly* teach about Krishna—but about Brahman and its bliss.

This may seem obvious to us—Krishna is not a prominent character in the *Upaniṣads*. He is only mentioned in passing in the *Chāndogya* (3.17.6),[8] but is not the subject of the principal *Upaniṣads*, which is Brahman, the imperishable, which, in the language of the *Muṇḍaka* (1.1.6), 'cannot be seen, cannot be grasped, is without color, without sight or hearing, without hands or feet'.[9] But this is a radical claim for the older, southern schools of Vedānta, and for several canonical Vaishnava texts, where Krishna, generally seen as a manifestation of Narayana, is repeatedly identified with Brahman. Indeed that Narayana is Brahman is the cornerstone of Vaishnava Vedānta, as centuries of Vaishnavas have argued. 'In the scripture of the [*Bhagavad-*] *Gītā*', Yamunacarya states, 'Narayaṇa is declared to be the Supreme Brahman'.[10] Ramanuja writes in his introduction to the *Gītā* that 'the Lord of Shri ... whose nature consists only of infinite perception and bliss which differentiates him from all other beings, the great ocean of innumerable auspicious attributes, such as knowledge, strength, sovereignty, vigor, power, and splendor, which he all possesses naturally, infinitely, and in abundance, ... is the Supreme Brahman, the Supreme Person, Narayana'.[11] Indeed, as Yamuna indicates, Vaishnava scriptures themselves repeatedly make this claim. In the Gītā, for example, Arjuna declares that Krishna is 'the Supreme Brahman, the Supreme abode'. 'All the sages, Devarsi Narada, as well as Asita, Devala and Vyasa declared this', Arjuna continues, 'and now you yourself tell me this'.[12] The *Taittirīya-nārāyaṇa Upaniṣad* (13.4) similarly declares, 'Narayana is the highest Brahman.

Narayana is the highest truth. Narayana is the highest light. Narayana is the highest self.'[13]

In other words, the earlier Vaishnava traditions all declared Brahman to be Narayana, a personal deity with 'an ocean of innumerable auspicious attributes', as Ramanuja repeatedly puts it. It is this deity that is the subject of the *Upaniṣads*—he is the *aupaniṣadaṃ puruṣam*, 'the person known by the *Upaniṣads*' (*Bṛhad-āraṇyaka Upaniṣad* 3.9.26).[14]

Yadavendra Puri, however, disagrees. Like Sarvabhauma, he does not care for the *Upaniṣad*s or Brahman, but for the young boy who roams Vrinda's woods and wears guñjā berries on his ears. This contrast between the *Upaniṣads* and Krishna, though unusual, is found in several verses of the *Padyāvalī*, and thus suggests that this idea resonated strongly with Rupa. Indeed, if there is any doubt as to what Rupa, the architect of a complex theology of religious emotions, really thinks of the *Upaniṣads*, the following verse, which he attributes to none other than Vyāsa, is abundantly clear:[15]

> śrutam apy aupaniṣadaṃ dūre hari-kathāmṛtāt
> yan na santi dravac-citta-kampāśru-pulakādayaḥ
>
> Upaniṣadic discourse
> is nothing like the nectar
> of narrations about Hari
> —it does not melt the mind
> or make you shiver
> or lead to tears or
> bristled hair.
>
> —Bhagavad Vyasa, *Padyāvalī* 39

Brahman

To better understand this new way in which the *Upaniṣad*s are viewed, I will explore two concepts that are central to Vedāntic discourse: the nature of Brahman and the nature of liberation (*mokṣa*). Let us begin with two verses from the *Padyāvalī* by Raghupati Upadhyaya, the poet whose verses Chaitanya so loved.

> kaṃ prati kathayitum īśe
> samprati ko vā pratītim āyātu
> go-pati-tanayā-kuñje
> gopa-vadhūṭī-viṭaṃ brahma

Whom can I tell?
Who will believe me now?
The pleasure seeker
with the young cowgirl
in the bushes
on the Sun's daughter's banks
is Brahman.

—Raghupati Upadhyaya, *Padyāvalī* 98

śrutayaḥ palāla-kalpāḥ
kim iha vayaṃ sāmpratam cinumaḥ
ahriyata puraiva nayanair
ābhīrībhiḥ paraṃ brahma

Why do we here still sift the
husk-like *Upaniṣads*?
Earlier the cowgirls caught
the Supreme Brahman
with a glance.

—Raghupati Upadhyaya, *Padyāvalī* 97

The inclusion of Raghupati's verses in this collection is significant, as these are some of the very few verses where Krishna is identified as Brahman.[16] But even in these two verses that identification is seen as problematic. Who indeed would believe Raghupati when he says that the person who is playing with young girls in the bushes is the Brahman the *Upaniṣads* describe as the self-satisfied foundation of all existence? Never mind, he quickly adds. This is indeed the Supreme Brahman taught in the *Upaniṣads*, but the question is: Why should we bother studying the *Upaniṣads* to find him? Why should we patiently sift them like dry, empty husks in the hope of finding some grain of truth about Krishna, when the cowherd girls of Vṛndāvana have already caught him?

Most of the other authors collected in the *Padyāvalī*, however, are not so eager to identify Brahman with Krishna. Consider, for example, the following verse by Ishvara Puri, Chaitanya's own guru:

dhanyānāṃ hṛdi bhāsatāṃ giri-vara-pratyagra-kuñjaukasāṃ
satyānanda-rasaṃ vikāra-vibhava-vyāvṛttam antar-mahaḥ
asmākaṃ kila vallavī-rati-raso vṛndāṭavī-lālaso
gopaḥ ko'pi mahendra-nīla-ruciraś citte muhuḥ krīḍatu

May an inner light,
the very essence of bliss
freed from the power of change
glow in the hearts of the fortunate
who have made the blooming groves
of the best of hills their home.
May a herder of cows
continually play in our hearts,
longing for the gardens of Vrinda,
relishing the cowgirls' love,
lustrous like sapphire.

—Ishvara Puri, *Padyāvalī* 75

Or the following, by Kaviratna, an unknown poet:

dhyānātītaṃ kim api paramaṃ ye tu jānanti tattvaṃ
teṣām āstāṃ hṛdaya-kuhare śuddha-cin-mātra ātmā
asmākaṃ tu prakṛti-madhuraḥ smera-vaktrāravindo
megha-śyāmaḥ kanaka-paridhiḥ paṅkajākṣo'yam ātmā

In the hollow of the hearts
of those who discern some ultimate truth
beyond meditation
may the self abide—
nothing but mere consciousness—
while in ours
may this charming self remain,
with lotus eyes and smiling lotus face,
dark as a cloud,
clothed in gold.

—Kaviratna, *Padyāvalī* 75

And finally, this beautiful verse of Shridhara Svami, the renowned commentator on the *Bhāgavata*:

sadā sarvatrāste nanu vimalam ādyaṃ tava padaṃ
tathāpy ekaṃ stokaṃ na hi bhava-taroḥ patram abhinat
kṣaṇaṃ jihvāgra-sthaṃ tava tu bhagavan-nāma nikhilaṃ
sa-mūlaṃ saṃsāraṃ kaṣati katarat sevyam anayoḥ

It is true:
your primordial splendor
exists undefiled
in all places, at all times,

yet it has not torn
even a single small leaf
from the tree of life.
But your blessed name
for a mere moment
standing on the tip of my tongue
obliterates the endless stream of rebirth.
Which of these two shall I serve?

—Shridhara Svami, *Padyāvalī* 28

These verses do not talk of Brahman, at least not explicitly. But they do all have the same format we have already encountered in Yadavendra's verse: we meet Krishna (or his name), who is contrasted with other conceptions of the Absolute, most of which have a rather Advaitic ring. The self that is 'nothing but mere consciousness' (*śuddha-cin-mātra ātmā*) in Kaviratna's verse; Ishvara Puri's 'inner light, the very essence of bliss, freed from the power of change' (*satyānanda-rasaṃ vikāra-vibhava-vyāvṛttam antar-mahaḥ*); or the 'primordial splendour' that Shridhara talks about, which exists untouched by matter 'in all places, at all times' (*sadā sarvatrāste nanu vimalam ādyaṃ tava padam*)—they all seem apt descriptions of an Advaitin's conception of Brahman, which is then sharply contrasted with the beauty and charm of Krishna.

If we assume that Rupa approved of the doctrines taught in all the verses he cites, it follows that he must argue Krishna both to be the supreme Brahman (as Raghupati declares) and yet different from it (as the other poets suggest).[17] And indeed he does. In his *Laghu-bhāgavatāmṛta*, a study on the nature of God, Rupa addresses this very issue:

> But why do you claim that Mukunda is superior to Brahman, since it is well-known that Brahman and the Lord are one? Repeatedly it is said in the scriptures that the Supreme Lord (*bhagavān*) is one only, and is known by the terms 'person' (*puruṣa*), 'Supreme Self' (*paramātmā*), 'Brahman', and 'perception' (*jñāna*). Thus the *Skānda* [*Purāṇa*] says, 'The Supreme Lord is called the Supreme Self by the *yogīs* of the eightfold path, Brahman by those immersed in the *Upaniṣads*, and perception by the gnostic *yogīs*.' Similarly, the first book [of the *Bhāgavata*] (1.2.11) states, 'Those who know the truth call that truth, which is non-dual perception, "Brahman", "Supreme Self" and "Supreme Lord"'.
>
> What has been said is true. Now listen to Kapila's teaching in the third book [*Bhāgavata* 3.32.33]: 'Just as a single object that has many

> attributes is perceived differently by each individual sensory faculty, so is the Supreme Lord [perceived differently] by the paths [ordained by] scripture.'
>
> To summarize: In the blessed Lord exist various forms, which become manifest to their worshipers in accordance with their worship. Just as an object like milk always possesses attributes like color and taste, and this single object is perceived [differently] by the various sensory faculties—it is white to the eyes, sweet to the tongue—so the Supreme Lord, though one, is perceived variously by [different forms of] worship. Just as only the tongue can perceive its sweetness, and no other [sensory faculty], and just as the eyes and the other senses grasp [only] their own object, so do all other forms of worship that depend on the external senses [only perceive part of God's attributes]. But devotion, which depends on consciousness, can perceive all these objects. Thus it is said in the best scriptures that Krishna is higher than this Brahman nature, because he possesses an abundance of attributes, such as sweetness.[18]

The passage is revealing: these different terms—'Brahman', 'Puruṣa', 'Paramātmā', and 'Bhagavān'—are no longer just different names to refer to the same absolute reality, as older Vaishnavas, represented here in the *pūrva-pakṣa*, might have argued, but rather names that denote the different ways in which that same reality is realized by practitioners of different paths.

Jiva develops this notion much further in the *Bhagavat-sandarbha*. Using *Bhāgavata* 1.2.11 (which Rupa's pūrva-pakṣa invokes) as a key to understand the nature of God, Jiva makes a distinction between Bhagavān, the personal deity of the earlier Vaishnava schools, and Brahman, the impersonal, abstract *nirviśeṣa* Brahman of the Advaitins—'existence that is pure awareness'.[19] This latter is perceived by the best ascetics (*parama-haṃsa*), who have no interest even in the bliss of Brahmā and who have attained oneness (*tādātmya*) by their spiritual practice, but who cannot accept God's nature and His many potencies and thus perceive God 'generally' (*sāmānyataḥ*).[20] These two aspects of God are distinct, he argues, yet part of the same 'non-dual perception' (*advaya-jñāna*), as the *Bhāgavata* verse states, and thereby non-different. The implications of this view for Vedānta in the Chaitanya tradition are very significant: since Brahman and Bhagavān are two aspects of the same non-dual truth, each of these terms can refer to the other, as Ravi Gupta has remarked.[21] This allows early Chaitanya Vaishnava authors to interpret the *Upaniṣads*' descriptions of Brahman as referring to a deity with infinite attributes, and thereby to build on the teachings of the southern Vaishnavas, while at the same time to incorporate Advaita notions of Brahman, and thereby, to some extent, integrate these two rival systems of Vedānta. But this strategy also makes it possible for them to distance themselves from Brahman and Vedānta in general, and see the *Upaniṣad*s as texts teaching about an attributeless principle, as we have seen in the above-mentioned verses. Jiva's friend Krishnadasa, for example, does just this at the beginning of the *Caitanya-caritāmṛta*, when he talks of 'the nondual Brahman [taught in] the *Upaniṣad*s' and clearly distinguishes that from 'the Lord (*bhagavān*) who is complete with the six powers'.[22]

What is striking in this attitude, however, is that the Advaitin view is not denied, but dismissed. Authors such as Rupa or Jiva do not argue that the Advaitins have failed to grasp what Brahman really is, but rather that they do not care about the nature of the realization that follows from this perception or the type of worship they should foster in its wake. Unlike Ramanuja or Madhva, they do not feel the need to argue that Brahman or the Ātmā is a person and possesses unlimited attributes, and that only this view is in accordance with what the *Upaniṣad*s teach. Rather, they concede that those who want Brahman can perfectly well have it, as long as Krishna's devotees by the same token can have *him*!

Liberation

The way in which Brahman is understood in the earlier Vedānta schools determines naturally the way liberation, the state of union with Brahman, is understood. While for Shankara liberation is attained by realizing one's nature as the self (*ātmā*) which as pure consciousness is non-different from Brahman, and is thereby 'becoming Brahman',[23] both Ramanuja and Madhva have insisted that since Brahman is a person, the state of liberation is necessarily a state of union with that person that does not imply abrogating the individuality of both God and the human self. Just as no attributeless Brahman exists, so can there be no non-dual state of liberation where all individuality disappears. This is particularly well expressed in poetic form by Nammalvar:

> If they should merge,
> That's really good:
> if the two that'll never meet

should meet
then this human thing
will become our lord,
the Dark One
with the sacred bird
on his banner—
as if that's possible.
It will always be itself.
There are yogis
who mistake fantasy
for true release
and run around
in circles
in the world
of what is and what was
and what will be.
It takes all kinds.[24]

'As if that's possible!' For Shrivaishnavas such as Ramanuja, liberation means reaching Shriman Narayana's divine abode, Vaikuṇṭha, where one is in union with Him. The self, as a small part (*śeṣa*) of the whole (*śeṣī*), can never become God, but after liberation it attains 'sameness' with God, in the sense that such a self attains his purity and experiences his bliss.[25]

Madhva agrees to some extent with Ramanuja, except that he argues that not all liberated selves experience the same bliss. Even in the state of liberation there is a hierarchy of beings, based on their proximity to God and the degree of bliss they experience.[26] Depending on their degree of devotion, some may attain the abode of God (*sālokya*), some may attain proximity to God (*sāmīpya*), some may obtain a form similar to that of God (*sārūpya*), whereas others may attain a union with God in His divine realm (*yoga* or *sāyujya*) quite similar to what Ramanuja understood.[27]

In his magnum opus, the *Rahasya-traya-sāra* ('The Essence of the Three Mysteries'), Vedanta Deshika responds to Madhva's views, and, in the course of doing so, reiterates the traditional Shrivaishnava teachings on liberation:

> Some living beings attain ... the privilege of living in the same world as Vishnu (*sālokya*), some individual selves attain proximity to the presence of Vishnu (*sāmīpya*); some attain forms similar to that of Vishnu (*sārūpya*); these, too, are sometimes called liberated in a figurative sense (*upacāra*), since they are very near the ultimate goal [though they

> are not actually liberated]. This idea is set forth in the following verse: 'Some live in the worlds of Vishnu; others approach very near to Viṣṇu; others, again, acquire forms resembling Vishnu's; yet others attain union (*sāyujya*) with Vishnu. This, alone, is called liberation.'[28]
>
> This verse declares that only union (*sāyujya*) in the highest realm is [actual] liberation.... Sāyujya refers to the relationship between two who are united in communion (*sayuk*). One might be in union with another, although only in the common enjoyment of a certain pleasure. Here, in regard to the liberated self, the object of enjoyment is Brahman with his modes (*prakāra*). Since Brahman and the liberated self both commune with each other in the enjoyment of that bliss, the liberated self is said to be in union [with Brahman].[29]

Madhusudhana Sarasvati, a prominent Advaitin of the sixteenth century, agrees with Vedanta Deshika's critique of Madhva's idea of liberation, and also considers sāyujya the only true form of liberation. For him, however, sāyujya refers not to a state in which the self and God share the same experience of bliss, but rather to liberation as Shankara understands it.[30]

In several verses of the *Padyāvalī*, poets stress that they do not long or pray for liberation. This is nothing new: such sentiments can be found in the poetry of many Shrivaishnava teachers. But what is very new is the motivation that seems to lie behind such prayers. The Vaishnavas from the south would not ask for liberation either because they felt unqualified to ask for it; or because their worship of the Lord was not motivated by such a self-centred desire as liberation; or because they wished to praise an image installed in a particular temple here on earth that they could not conceive of abandoning. When some of the poets collected in the *Padyāvalī* state that they do not want liberation, however, they seem to do so with a different motivation. Take, for instance, this verse of Yadavendra Puri:

> nanda-nandana-kaiśora-
> līlāmṛta-mahāmbudhau
> nimagnānāṃ kim asmākaṃ
> nirvāṇa-lavaṇāmbhasā
>
> We drown
> in an ambrosial sea
> of Nandanandana's youthful play.
> What are the salty waters
> of liberation to us?[31]
>
> —Yadavendra Puri, *Padyāvalī* 42

Or the following verse of Sarvabhauma Bhattacharya:

bhavantu tatra janmāni
yatra te muralī-kalaḥ
karṇapeyatvam āyāti
kiṃ me nirvāṇa-vārttayā

May I ever be born
there where my ears can drink
the soft, mellifluous call of your flute.
Why talk to me of extinguishing
my existence?

—Sarvabhauma Bhattacharya, *Padyāvalī* 91

Both verses draw a contrast between, on the one hand, the joy experienced through devotion and intimacy with Krishna, and, on the other, the unpleasant dullness of liberation—which in both verses is called *nirvāṇa*, perhaps to suggest Buddhist notions of emptiness. This seems odd from a Shrivaishnava point of view: how are these two opposed?

Towards the end of the first part of the *Padyāvalī*, Rupa has a section called 'contempt for liberation' (*mokṣānādaraḥ*). It is a short section—there are only four verses—but a surprising one, and one that illustrates very clearly how Rupa differs from Vedanta Deshika. Take the first verse, for example:

bhaktiḥ sevā bhagavato
muktis tat-pada-laṅghanam
ko mūḍho dāsatāṃ prāpya
prābhavaṃ padam icchati

Devotion is service to the Lord.
Liberation is going beyond his feet.
What fool, having obtained servitude,
desires a position of majesty?

—Shivamauni, *Padyāvalī* 110

Here liberation is not the union with God through devotion in God's own realm, beyond this world, as earlier Vaishnavas saw it, but rather the opposite of devotion! To be liberated means to step over or abandon the feet of God to the position of power (*prābhava*) that is liberation.[32] For Rupa, thus, liberation has come to mean what the Advaitins say it means.

Another verse in this section makes this contempt for liberation even more vivid:

kā tvaṃ muktir upāgatāsmi bhavatī kasmād akasmād iha
śrī-kṛṣṇa-smaraṇena deva bhavato dāsī-padaṃ prāpitā
dūre tiṣṭha manāg anāgasi kathaṃ kuryād anāryaṃ mayi
tvad-gandhān nija-nāma-candana-rasālepasya lopo bhavet

Who are you?
    I am Liberation,
    and am at your service.
Why have you come here,
unannounced?
    Your remembrance of Shri Krishna,
    Sir, has made me
    your servant.
Begone!
I am nearly sinless. Why
would you dishonour me?
Your smell
could overwhelm
the sandal perfume
that is mine
from the name of the Lord.

—Anonymous, *Padyāvalī* 113

Both Rupa and Jiva accept five types of liberation—adding *sārṣṭi*, possessing the same majesty as God, to Madhva's list, on the authority of the *Bhāgavata*[33]—and admit that these different types of liberation do not contradict devotion if they are accepted for 'service and love' rather than for personal 'pleasure and power'. That is, all except sāyujya, which those that wish to serve the Lord quite simply reject![34] Rupa and Jiva understand sāyujya to consist of a union of the self and God, not in the sense that Madhva or Vedanta Deshika interpret this, but more along the lines of Madhusudhana Sarasvati. In sāyujya liberation, Jiva explains, the self either 'enters into the blessed body of the Lord'[35] or merges 'into Brahman',[36] and is thus unable to serve God in that state.[37]

Jiva defines liberation as a realization (*sākṣāt-kāra*) of the Lord's own form (*svarūpa*).[38] Therefore, if one of the five forms of liberation is superior to all others, it would not be sāyujya, but *samīpya*, being in the presence of God, since that is the only type of liberation in which God manifests himself in person to the devotee, whereas he generally only manifests himself internally in the other forms of liberation.[39] But since God does not manifest himself in his fullness to one who is without love or devotion, Jiva argues, such devotional love is what causes true liberation. This devotion or love (variously called *bhakti*, *prīti* or *prema*) is therefore the highest goal of human life (*parama-puruṣārtha*), and not liberation.[40]

Jiva's argument may seem pedantic, particularly since his description of this devotional love comes very close to Vedanta Deshika's concept of sāyujya liberation. According to Jiva, love of God is a form of God's potency of bliss (*hlādinī-śakti*), which allows God to experience his own bliss and make others experience it too. The devotee and God are united in that common experience of bliss and through that experience become non-different from each other[41]—which is precisely the way Vedanta Deshika describes liberation! Why then does Jiva go to such trouble to present his view of liberation as if it were a clear alternative? He seems partly motivated to do so to give a place in his theology to the Advaitin's notion of liberation, and partly to include the concept of 'living liberation' (*jīvan-mukti*), a concept that many southern Vaishnavas rejected but that the Advaitins supported.[42] His main motivation, of course, seems to be to distinguish devotion from liberation, and to make devotion independent and its own goal, but he needs to do so precisely because he has reinterpreted liberation to include concepts of liberation that earlier Vaishnavas such as Vedanta Deshika had rejected.

Despite Jiva's reinterpretations of the concept of liberation to suit Rupa's theology of devotion, the concept of liberation is often primarily conceived of in Advaitic terms and rejected for that very reason, as the verses from the *Padyāvalī* illustrate.[43] This attitude towards liberation is illustrated well by an incident recorded in the *Caitanya-caritāmṛta* (2.6.259ff.).[44] One day, shortly after he embraced the path of devotion to Krishna, Sarvabhauma Bhattacharya visits Chaitanya. He offers his respects to his new master, and begins to recite a verse from the *Bhāgavata* (10.14.8), but changes the ending: 'One who lives, seeking your compassion and undergoing the fruits of his own actions, offering obeisance to you with mind, speech and body, is eligible to inherit devotion (*bhakti*).' Chaitanya quickly responds: 'The verse actually reads *mukti-pade*, but you have changed it to *bhakti-pade*. Why?' Bhattacharya, with firm faith in his newly found devotion to Krishna, replies:

> The fruit of liberation is not equal to devotion; it is merely the punishment for those who are averse to devotion to the Lord. He who does

> not accept Krishna's form as real and who blasphemes him or quarrels with him is punished for these acts by the liberation of merging with Brahman. But he who engages in devotion does not obtain this result. There are five kinds of liberation: *sālokya, sāmīpya, sārūpya, sārṣṭi,* and sāyujya. If there is a means to serve [God], a devotee may accept the four beginning with sālokya. But even hearing of sāyujya causes hatred and fear for a devotee. He may desire to go to hell, but will not accept *sāyujya.*

Chaitanya, however, offers a different reading of the verse: 'The words *mukti-pada*', he says, 'refer to the Lord himself. He at whose feet is found liberation is *mukti-pada*.... Since the word can refer to Krishna, why would you change the verse?'

Sarvabhauma Bhattacharya's response is quite telling. He says:

> I could not give that reading to the verse. Although the meaning you have given can be derived from this word, I can still not utter it because of its double meaning. Even though the word *mukti* has five meanings [the five types of liberation], its conventional meaning [*rūḍhi-vṛtti*] is still the notion of merging [with Brahman]. To say the word *mukti* brings hatred and fear to my heart, but when I say the word *bhakti* my heart fills with joy.

Hearing this, Chaitanya laughs and embraces his new disciple. Krishnadasa, the author of the text, delights in Sarvabhauma's staunch devotion, and completes the section by saying that 'Bhattacharya who read and taught *māyā-vāda* now blossomed forth in such speech by the grace of Chaitanya!' In other words, the meaning that the word *mukti* had acquired was reason enough for Sarvabhauma to reject the word and edit the prayers of the *Bhāgavata*. Though other meanings could be given to the word, the Advaitins had ruined it for him. Just as with the notion of Brahman, here too the Advaitins' understanding of the term has prevailed, and the poets of the *Padyāvalī* and the early Chaitanya Vaishnava theologians have made room for it, shifting their attention elsewhere.

Where Does This All Come From?

What caused this shift in the perception of Vedānta? Why do these Vaishnava poets of the *Padyāvalī* seem to throw in the towel and let the Advaitins win the centuries-old debate on the nature of Brahman and liberation?

The attitude towards Brahman and liberation exhibited in the verses of the *Padyāvalī* is not entirely unheard of in Sanskrit literature, and there are some important precedents in the amorous, secular Sanskrit poetry composed at royal courts. Such works often contain verses that are similar in style to those we have seen above. Part of their power comes precisely from their juxtaposition of an otherworldly, emotionless Vedānta with impetuous, passionate, wildly corporeal love. As must be immediately apparent, contrasts of just this sort resemble what we find in the *Padyāvalī*. I will offer only two examples here, but more could easily be given. The first is from the *Āryā-saptaśatī* (70) of Govardhana, a work which Rupa cites several times in the *Padyāvalī*:[45]

asatī kulajā dhīrā prauḍhā prativeśinī yadāsaktim
kurute sarasā ca tadā brahmānandaṃ tṛṇaṃ manye

If the girl next door,
noble but unchaste,
resolute, bold, and passionate,
would only become attached to me,
then I'd think the bliss of Brahman
straw.

In a famous verse from the *Śṛṅgāra-tilaka* (24) attributed to Kalidasa, liberation is described and dismissed in a way that resembles the sentiments of the Vaishnava authors of the *Padyāvalī*. The translator is W. S. Merwin:

avidita-sukha-dukhaṃ nirguṇaṃ vastu kiñcit
jaḍa-matir iha kaścin mokṣha ity ācacakṣe
mama tu mataṃ anaṅga-smera-tāruṇya-ghūrṇan
mada-kala-madirākṣī nīvimokṣo hi mokṣaḥ

Some in this world insist
that a certain whatever-it-is
that has no taste of
joy or sorrow
no qualities
is Release
they are fools
to my mind her
body unfurling
with joy of being young

flowering out of love
her eyes floating as with wine and
words wandering with love
then the undoing of the knot
of her sari
that
is Release.[46]

The poets of the *Padyāvalī* were clearly familiar with the court poetry, and it is, therefore, no surprise we find the strongest dismissals of the *Upaniṣads*, Vedānta, Brahman, and liberation in poetic works such as the *Padyāvalī* rather than the tradition's theological works.

But whereas such literary tropes are obviously borrowed from amorous court poetry, we need to turn elsewhere to find possible theological influences. The most important, and most obvious, of these is undoubtedly the *Bhāgavata Purāṇa*. Both Rupa and Jiva ground their entire theological system in the *Bhāgavata*, and cite the text repeatedly to support their theological claims, including their views on Brahman and liberation. Though the *Bhāgavata* is not unambiguous in its views on these two topics and lends itself often to alternative interpretations, we do find the seeds of early Chaitanya Vaishnava theology in this text. The *Bhāgavata* frequently refers to the triad Brahman–Paramātmā–Bhagavān, and often they can easily be interpreted as having the same referent (as indeed Rupa's pūrva-pakṣa did with *Bhāgavata* 1.2.11),[47] but at times the text suggests that, though these terms have the same referent, they nevertheless articulate distinct aspects of it, as when the text clearly distinguishes between 'Narayana ... who is indicated by the word "Bhagavān" and the "attributeless Brahman"'.[48] The *Bhāgavata* too makes a distinction between liberation and devotion,[49] and rejects the five forms of liberation—including an Advaitic 'oneness' (*ekatva*) or sāyujya[50]—if they are devoid of the possibility to attend the divine,[51] and states that a devotee should, therefore, never desire union with God.[52] The *Bhāgavata* is a notoriously difficult text, and though it teaches a clear theism and is uncompromisingly devotional in its outlook, its theological language is nevertheless often profoundly Advaitic, as Daniel Sheridan has highlighted,[53] and it is probably this mixture of monistic discourse and devotional theism that contributed to the revisioning of Vedānta among early Chaitanya Vaishnavas.

The Advaita influence goes beyond the *Bhāgavata*, however. It is remarkable how many Advaitin *daśanāmī* sannyāsīs[54] surround Chaitanya: there is his own guru, Ishvara Puri, and his guru's guru,

Madhavendra Puri, as well as Chaitanya's sannyāsa-guru, Keshava Bharati, and Ranga Puri, a disciple of Madhavendra whom Chaitanya met in Pandharpur.[55] Once Chaitanya settles in Puri, several others join him, such as Paramananda Puri, Brahmananda Bharati, Damodara Svarupa (said to be a disciple of one Chaitanyananda), and Shankarananda Sarasvati.[56] Kavikarnapura lists nine additional sannyāsīs who 'played with the Lord Gaurahari', but about whom very little is known: Nrisimhananda Tirtha, Satyananda Bharati, Nrisimha Tirtha, Chidananda Tirtha, Jagannatha Tirtha, Vasudeva Tirtha, Rama Tirtha, Purushottama Tirtha, Garuda Avadhuta, and Gopendra Ashrama.[57] Early Gauḍīya texts also list other sannyāsīs as important influences or predecessors of Chaitanya: Brahmananda Puri, Krishnananda Puri, Sukhananda Puri, and Vishnu Puri.[58] It is difficult to determine exactly what the religious affiliations of these sannyāsīs were. They are praised in the biographies of Chaitanya as staunch Vaishnavas, yet their sannyāsa identified them as Advaitins too.[59]

What exactly does it mean to be an Advaitin, and particularly a sannyāsī initiated in an Advaita lineage in this first half of the second millennium? The rise of Shrivaishnava and Mādhva Vedānta and their constant debates with the rival school of Advaita Vedānta have profoundly altered the latter's development. Though it is quite clear that Shankara had Vaishnava leanings,[60] when Vaishnava Vedānta began to flourish in earnest, some Advaitins, at least, seemed to take more and more of it in. We see this already in the eleventh century in Krishnamishra Yatī's *Prabodha-candrodaya*, an allegorical drama teaching Advaita Vedānta. The play reads entirely like a Vaishnava work, until one comes to the final act. Its heroine is Vishnu-bhakti, who subdues everyone and reigns supreme; only in the final (rather anticlimactic) act does she retreat when Wisdom (*Prabodha*) appears. While Krishnamishra still subordinates Vaishnava devotion to monistic wisdom, over the centuries much more of Vaishnava theology is adopted by Advaitin theologians. This is perhaps most clearly demonstrated in the works of Shridhara Svami, who pays respect to Shankara in his writings and who might have been the abbot of an Advaita monastery in Orissa.[61] His teachings are often so incompatible with traditional Advaita Vedānta that Jiva claims he was a Vaishnava trying to convert his fellow Advaitins.[62] Shridhara's continuous emphasis on devotion (bhakti) being the only means to liberation; his insistence that this is not a particular form of knowledge (jñāna), as other Advaitins might argue, but superior to it;[63] and his ambivalent but, at times, very Vaishnava views of the nature of God only reinforce the point.

As mentioned before, there are a number of such sannyāsīs among the poets of the *Padyāvalī*. Were these Advaitins, or Vaishnavas, or both? It is hard to tell, but it seems likely that there was a strong influence on the poets of the *Padyāvalī* from the 'Vaishnava' Advaita Vedānta that developed in the centuries prior to Chaitanya. Were they once Vedāntic Advaitins initiated into Advaitin ascetic lineages who 'converted' later in life to devotional Vaishnavism? Such conversion narratives are indeed frequently found in Chaitanya Vaishnava texts and even in the *Bhāgavata*, the tradition's principal sacred text. Shuka, the speaker of the *Bhāgavata*, is said to have been 'established in transcendence (*nairguṇya*)', but, when hearing about the attributes of Krishna, he gave this up and pursued devotion.[64] Similarly, the four Kumaras, when encountering God in person, were moved with devotion, even though they were previously 'devoted to the imperishable [Brahman]'.[65] Several early Chaitanya Vaishnava authors consider Bilvamangala, the author of the *Kṛṣṇa-karṇāmṛta*, to have been an Advaitin who was lured to the path of devotion by Krishna himself,[66] and a few of Chaitanya's associates followed a similar religious journey. We have already seen Sarvabhauma Bhattacharya's conversion, but Brahmananda Bharati is said to have had a similar experience,[67] as is Prakashananda Sarasvati.[68] Perhaps some of these poets, such as Yadavendra Puri, were so dismissive of Brahman and liberation, and Vedānta as a whole, because they had a change of heart similar to but not necessarily as sudden as that of someone like Sarvabhauma Bhattacharya. So then, can we trace the firm dismissal of Vedānta in the *Padyāvalī* to these poets' own religious experiences, which theologians such as Rupa and Jiva then tried to accommodate and explain in their own theology?

Whatever the exact causes for this redirection of Vaishnava theology, the consistent attempt to make space for the experiences of the Advaitins among early Chaitanya Vaishnava theologians seems particularly remarkable when considered alongside the tradition's fierce opposition to Shankara's *māyā-vāda*, but as I have attempted to show in this chapter, these two attitudes are harmonized in the new Vedānta that Rupa and Jiva articulate, which allowed the Chaitanya Vaishnavas to engage as Vaishnavas with Vedānta, but also to relinquish Vedānta to the Advaitins, who are conceded the right to claim all its terminology—such as Brahman and mokṣa—as their own.

Vedānta is no longer the choice discourse for the Krishna-centred Vaishnavism of Chaitanya, at least not as expressed in the *Upaniṣads*. The *Purāṇas* take central stage, and particularly the *Bhāgavata*, which is not just seen as the best *Purāṇa*, but also as a commentary on the *Brahma-sūtras* and thus as the Vedāntic text par excellence.[69] Their Vaishnava colleagues from the south might have seen this as an admission of defeat, but this inclusive theology of Chaitanya's devotees is the outcome of a centuries-long interaction and rapprochement between Advaita Vedānta and Vaishnavism. It meant that even the experience of the Vaishnava's great opponents could now be seen as a limited, but valid, experience of the cunning cowherd boy of Braj.

Notes

* I am very grateful for the insightful comments and suggestions I received from the late Professor M. Narasimhachary, Dr Sanjukta Gupta-Gombrich, and Professor John Stratton Hawley.

1. Ravi Gupta, *Caitanya Vaiṣṇava Vedānta of Jīva Gosvāmī: When Knowledge Meets Devotion* (Abingdon: Routledge, 2007).

2. Jiva also acknowledges his indebtedness to Ramanuja and Madhva, as well as other Vaishnava authors, in Jiva Gosvami, *Tattva-sandarbha*, ed. Haridasa Shastri (Vrindavan: Shri Gadadhara-Gaurahari Press, 1983), para 27. In this chapter, I focus on the Chaitanya Vaishnavas from Mathura, but the same attitudes towards Vedānta can be found in those from Bengal, particularly in the writings of Kavikarnapura and his guru, Shrinatha Chakravarti. For more on their views of Vedānta, see chapter 2 of my forthcoming book *Splendour of Speech: The Theology of Kavikarṇapūra's Poetics* (Oxford University Press).

3. Rupa can easily do so because such verses are 'impersonal', as Daniel Ingalls once remarked. See Daniel Ingalls, *Anthology of Sanskrit Court Poetry: Vidyākara's 'Subhāṣitaratnakoṣa'* (Cambridge: Harvard University Press, 1965), 22–9. Nevertheless, Rupa does edit a few of those secular verses to suit the devotional theme of his anthology. See, for example, Rupa Gosvami, *Padyāvalī*, ed. Sushil Kumar De (Dacca: University of Dacca, 1934), vv. 190, 219, 281, 284, 303.

4. 'padyāvalī viracitā rasikair mukunda-sambandha-bandhura-padā pramodormi-sindhuḥ ramyā samasta-tamasāṃ damanī krameṇa saṃgṛhyate kṛti-kadambaka-kautukāya' (*Padyāvalī* 1).

5. See *Padyāvalī* 73, 99.

6. For more on Sarvabhauma's works, see Dinesh Chandra Bhattacharyya, 'Vāsudeva Sārvabhauma', *The Indian Historical Quarterly* 16, no. 1 (1940): 58–69.

7. *Caitanya-caritāmṛta* 2.6.

8. 'Tad dhaitad ghorāṅgirasaḥ kṛṣṇāya devakī-putrāyoktvovāca' (*Chāndogya* 3.17.6).

9. Translation by Patrick Olivelle (Olivelle, trans., *Upaniṣads* [Oxford: Oxford University Press, 1996], 268).

10. 'Nārāyaṇaḥ paraṃ brahma gītā-śāstre samīritaḥ' (Yamuna, *Gītārtha-saṅgraha*, in *The Bhagavad-gītā with Eleven Commentaries*, ed. G.S. Sadhale [New Delhi: Parimal Publications, 1992], v. 1).

11. Ramanuja's *Gītā-bhāṣya*, ed. and trans. Svami Adidevananda (Madras: Sri Ramakrishna Math, n.d.) v. 1.1.

12. 'Paraṃ brahma param dhāma [...] āhus tvām ṛṣayaḥ sarve devarṣir nāradas tathā asito devalo vyāsaḥ svayaṃ caiva bravīṣi me' (*Gītā* 10.12–13).

13. 'Nārāyaṇaḥ paraṃ brahma tattvaṃ nārāyaṇaḥ paraḥ, nārāyaṇaḥ paro jyotir ātmā nārāyaṇaḥ paraḥ' (*Taittirīya-nārāyaṇa* 13.4).

14. See Madhva, *Brahma-sūtra-bhāṣya*, ed. K. T. Pandurangi (Bangalore: Dvaita Vedanta Studies and Research Foundation, 1997–2002), v. 1.1.3.

15. As if considering that even Vyasa himself is not a strong enough authority, Jiva, who cites the verse in *Bhakti-sandarbha* 69, says it was 'sung by the Lord who descended to deliver the *kali-yuga*' (*ata eva gītaṃ kali-yuga-pāvanāvatāreṇa śrī-bhagavatā—śrutam apy aupaniṣadaṃ ... iti*), which is a common epitaph for Chaitanya.

16. Kaviratna also identifies Krishna with Brahman when he declares that his mind 'only bathes itself in/pure Brahman/the splendor of a cloud/ with motionless lightning/on Kālindī's forest banks/caught by the vine of a milkmaid's arm' (*kālindī-vana-sīmani sthira-taḍin-megha-dyutau kevalaṃ/ śuddhe brahmaṇi vallavī-bhuja-latā-baddhe mano dhāvati, Padyāvalī* 78). For another example of this, see *Padyāvalī* 317 (quoting *Sāhitya-darpaṇa* 6.314). All the other verses in the collection that identify Krishna with Brahman are Raghupati Upadhyaya's.

17. Kaviratna does seem to hold that view: in verse 78, he identifies Krishna with Brahman, but in verse 75, he makes a distinction between an Advaitic notion of the *ātmā* (often used as synonymous with Brahman in Vedāntic discourse) and Krishna.

18. Rupa Gosvami, *Laghu-Bhāgavatāmṛta*, ed. Bhaktivilasa Tirtha (Mayapura: Shri Chaitanya Maṭha, 1995), vv. 1.5.194–205.

19. 'Yasya brahmeti saṃjñāṃ kvacid api nigame yāti cin-mātra-sattāpi' (*Tattva-sandarbha* 8).

20. 'Tad ekam evākhaṇḍānanda-svarūpaṃ tattvaṃ thūtkṛta-pārameṣṭhyādikānanda-samudayānāṃ paramahaṃsānāṃ sādhana-vaśāt tādātmyam āpanne, satyām api tadīya-svarūpa-śakti-vaicitryāṃ, tad-grahaṇāsāmarthye cetasi yathā sāmānyato lakṣitaṃ, tathaiva sphurad vā, tadvad evāvivikta-śakti-śaktimattā-bhedatayā pratipadyamānaṃ vā

brahmeti śabdyate' (Jiva Gosvami, *Bhagavat-sandarbha*, ed. Haridasa Shastri [Vrindavan: Shri Gadadhara-Gaurahari Press, 1984], v. 1).

21. See Gupta, *Caitanya Vaiṣṇava Vedānta*, 32–9.

22. *Caitanya-caritāmṛta* 1.1.3. The six powers (*ṣaḍ-aiśvārya*) are mentioned in a famous passage from the *Viṣṇu Purāṇa* (6.5.73–5), which Jiva comments on in *Bhagavat-sandarbha* 1. Perhaps the strongest dismissal of an unqualified Brahman, as understood in Advaita Vedānta, is found in the writings of Raghava Pandita, a south Indian Brahmin who had settled at the foot of Govardhan and became a friend of Raghunathadasa Gosvami. In his *Śrī-kṛṣṇa-bhakti-ratna-prakāśa*, ed. Puridasa Mahashaya (Vrindavan: Haridasa Sharma, 1954), he contrasts various alternatives to devotion to Krishna, and in the second chapter (2.11) brings up *brahmopāsanā*, the worship of Brahman.

> 'Likewise, what is the point of worshiping Brahman?' he asks. 'Brahman too is void (*śūnya*). By worshiping the void, one gains emptiness. As the *śruti* states: 'Whatever one's meditation is like, the perfection one attains is likewise.' So what is the point of worshiping something that is void? Let it be cheated by the sweet liquor of the nectar of the love for the lotus feet of Shri Krishnachandra, whose nature is the eternal, imperishable joy of the highest bliss!
>
> Tathaiva brahmopāsanena kim? brahmāpi śūnyam. Śūnyopāsanena śūnyatvaṁ prāpnoti. Yathāśrutiḥ—yādṛśī bhāvanā yasya siddhir bhavati tādṛśī iti śūnyopāsanena kim? Nityākṣaya-paramānanda-sukha-svarūpa-śrī-kṛṣṇa-candra-caraṇāravinda-premāmṛta-madhu-pānena vañcitaḥ syāt.

The Buddhist reading of Brahman as being *śūnya* is not so surprising, given that the Vaishnavas have long held that Shankara is really a Vedāntic Buddhist!

23. *Brahma-bhāvaś ca mokṣaḥ* (Shankara, *Brahma-Sūtra Bhāṣya*, ed. V. Sadanand [Chennai: Samata Books, 1999], v. 1.1.4). See also his commentary on *Brahma-sūtra* 4.4.4.

24. *Tiruvāymoli* 8.8.9. From A.K. Ramanujan, *Hymns for the Drowning* (New Delhi: Penguin Books India, 1993).

25. See Ramanuja's commentary on *Brahma-sūtras* 4.4.4.

26. See chapters 56 and 57 of B.N.K. Sharma, *The Philosophy of Śrī Madhvācārya* (New Delhi, Motilal Banarsidass, 1991), for a full analysis (and defence) of this view.

27. Madhva on *Brahma-sūtras* 4.4.19. As far as I understood, Madhva is arguing that all four of these can be obtained in Śvetadvīpa, Vishnu's realm within this world, but there seems to be disagreement within the Mādhva tradition about this. See Sharma, *The Brahmasūtras and their Principal Commentaries: A Critical Exposition* (New Delhi: Munshiram Manoharlal, 1986), 803–4.

28. In Shrivaishnava circles, this verse is generally attributed to the *Bhāgavata*, but it is not found there.

29. Vedanta Deshika, *Rahasya-traya-sāra*, trans. M.R. Rajagopala Aiyangar (Kubakonam: Agnihothram Ramanuja Thathachariar, 1956), chapter 22. Translation based on this edition.

30. Madhusudhana Sarasvati, *Advaita-siddhi*, ed. N.S. Ananta Krishna Sastri (Bombay: Nirnaya-Sagar Press, 1915), 894–5.

31. See *Padyāvalī* 42. It is very tempting to see in this a reference to the salty water that Uddālaka uses to teach his son about Brahman in *Chāndogya* 6.13.

32. Many verses in the *Padyāvalī* talk of liberation as being a state of ultimate dominion, or talk of the wealth and splendour of liberation, for example, *mokṣa-sāmrājya-lakṣmī* (12), *mukti-lakṣmī* (45), *mokṣa-lakṣmī* (102), *svārājya* (18).

33. See *Bhāgavata* 3.29.13, cited in Rupa Gosvami, *Bhakti-rasāmṛta-sindhu*, with commentaries of Jiva Gosvami, Mukundadasa, and Vishvanatha Chakravarti, ed. Haridasa Dasa (Navadvip: Haribola Kuṭīra, 1961), 1.2.28. Jiva defines it as follows: 'sārṣṭis tatraiva samānaiśvaryam api bhavatīti' (*Prīti-sandarbha* 10).

34. 'Sukhaiśvaryottarā seyaṃ prema-sevottarety api sālokyādir dvidhā tatra nādyā sevā-juṣaṃ matā' (*Bhakti-rasāmṛta-sindhu* 1.2.56).

35. 'Sāyujyaṃ keṣāṃcit bhagavac-chrī-vigraha eva praveśo bhavatīti' (*Prīti-sandarbha* 10).

36. See Jiva on *Bhakti-rasāmṛta-sindhu* 1.2.56: 'tac ceśvare brahmaṇi ca sāyujyaṃ jñeyam.' See also his commentary on *Bhakti-rasāmṛta-sindhu* 1.2.27: 'ekātmatāṃ brahma-sāyujyaṃ bhagavat-sāyujyam api.'

37. See Jiva on *Bhakti-rasāmṛta-sindhu* 1.2.56.

38. See *Prīti-sandarbha* 1, 7.

39. *Prīti-sandarbha* 10 ('tatra sālokya-sārṣṭi-sārūpya-mātre prāyo'ntaḥ-karaṇa-sākṣātkāraḥ, sāmīpye prāyo bahiḥ, sāyujye cāntara eva'), and 16 ('sālokyādiṣu ca sāmīpyasyādhikyaṃ bahiḥ sākṣātkāramayatvāt tasyaiva hy ādhikyaṃ darśitam').

40. *Prīti-sandarbha* 1. See also Shrinatha Chakravarti, *Caitanya-mata-mañjuṣā*, ed. Haridasa Dasa (Navadvip: Haribola Kuṭīra, 1952), v. 0.1, and Krishnadasa's *Caitanya-caritāmṛta* 1.7.84–5, 2.9.261, 2.19.164, 2.20.125, 2.23.101, 3.7.24. Jiva comments in *Bhakti-sandarbha* 233, that if one considers liberation to be the only goal of human life, one's devotion is not transcendental and pure, but conditioned by the material mode of goodness (*sattva*).

41. *Prīti-sandarbha* 65. Moreover, Jiva argues in *Prīti-sandarbha* 1, that if the principal aim of human life is defined as the cessation of suffering, the attainment of happiness, and the realization of God—as liberation is often conceived—love for God must be considered the principal aim of human life, as it accomplishes these three aims to the highest degree.

42. If liberation is defined as 'seeing God', it is easier to argue that liberation can be attained in this world. Jiva talks of *jīvan-mukti* in *Prīti-sandarbha* 1, and *Bhakti-sandarbha* 111. Rupa defines it in *Bhakti-rasāmṛta-sindhu* 1.2.187. Ramanuja rejects the concept in his commentary on *Brahma-sūtra* 1.1.4, and Vedanta Deshika refutes it (see, for example, S.M. Srinivasa Chari, *Fundamentals of Viśiṣṭādvaita Vedānta: A Study Based on Vedānta Deśika's Tattva-Muktā-Kalāpa* [New Delhi: Motilal Banarsidass, 1987], 310–16). Madhva's position is a little more complex. Though he argues against Shankara's notion of jīvan-mukti, he does accept the concept. See Daniel Sheridan, 'Direct Knowledge of God and Living Liberation in the Religious Thought of Madhva', in *Living Liberation in Hindu Thought*, ed. Andrew Fort and Patricia Mumme (Albany, State University of New York Press, 1996), 91–112, and Mesquita, *The Concept of Liberation While Still Alive in the Philosophy of Madhva* (New Delhi: Aditya Prakashan, 2007).

43. See also *Bhakti-sandarbha* 132.

44. The story is also told in Kavikarnapura's *Caitanya-caritāmṛta-mahākāvya* 12.89*ff.*

45. *Padyāvalī* 190, 242, 303, 374.

46. W.S. Merwin and J. Moussaieff Masson, trans., *Sanskrit Love Poetry* (New York: Columbia University Press, 1977), 166–7.

47. See, for example, *Bhāgavata Purāṇa*, with Sanskrit commentary *Bhāvārtha-bodhinī* of Shridhara Svami, ed. J.L. Shastri (New Delhi: Motilal Banarsidass, 1999), 1.2.11, 3.28.41, 3.29.36, 3.32.26, 5.7.7, 5.16.3, 6.2.41, 6.9.42, 7.5.41, 7.10.10, and 10.28.6.

48. *Bhāgavata* 11.15.16–17, 12.6.39.

49. *Bhāgavata* 5.6.18.

50. *Bhāgavata* 7.1.14, 20: Shishupala is said to attain to attain sāyujya 'in the Lord, Vasudeva' (*vāsudeve bhagavati sāyujyaṃ*, 14), and later, it is clarified that he merged into Krishna (*layam īyatuḥ*, 20).

51. 'Sālokya-sārṣṭi-sāmīpya-sārūpyaikatvam apy utadīyamānaṃ na gṛhṇanti vinā mat-sevanaṃ janāḥ' (*Bhāgavata* 3.29.13).

52. *Bhāgavata* 3.25.34.

53. Daniel Sheridan, *The Advaitic Theism of the Bhāgavata Purāṇa* (New Delhi: Motilal Banarsidass, 1986).

54. It is very doubtful that these different sannyāsīs were called 'daśanāmī' in Chaitanya's time, for as Matthew Clark has demonstrated the daśanāmī orders, as they are known now, were only formed in the seventeenth century (see Matthew Clark, *The Daśanāmi-Saṃnyāsīs: The Integration of Ascetic Lineages into an Order* [Leiden: Brill, 2006]). There existed, however, several distinct Advaitin sannyāsa orders in Chaitanya's time (see *Caitanya-caritāmṛta* 2.6.70–2), which later were grouped together and called 'daśanāmī', and, though anachronistic, I use that term to refer to them, for convenience's sake.

55. *Caitanya-caritāmṛta* 2.9.285–303.

56. For Shankarananda Sarasvati, see *Caitanya-caritāmṛta* 3.6.288.

57. Kavikarnapura, *Gaura-gaṇoddeśa-dīpikā*, in *Grantha-ratna-pañcakam*, ed. Krishnadasa Baba (Kusumasarovara: Krishnadasa Baba, 1953), vv. 99–101. See *Caitanya-caritāmṛta* 1.10.114.

58. See *Caitanya-caritāmṛta* 1.9.13–15 and Kavikarnapura, *Gaura-gaṇoddeśa-dīpikā*, 24.

59. See, for example, Act 4 of Kavikarnapura's *Caitanya-candrodaya-nāṭaka*, ed. Ramchandra Mishra (Varanasi: Chowkhamba Sanskrit Series Office, 1966), where after his sannyāsa initiation Chaitanya is repeatedly identified as an Advaitin. Both Chaitanya and Damodara Svarupa renounce their sacred thread and *śikhā* when they became sannyāsīs, which is an Advaitin practice, normally not followed by Vaishnava renouncers (see Vrindavanadasa, *Caitanya-bhāgavata*, ed. Bhakti Kevala Audulomi Maharaja [Calcutta: Gauḍīya Mission, 1961], vv. 2.26.132, 161–80 and *Caitanya-caritāmṛta* 2.10.108).

60. See Paul Hacker, 'Relations of Early Advaitins to Vaiṣṇavism', *Wiener Zeitschrift für die Kunde Süd- und Ostasiens* 9 (1965): 147–54.

61. See Ananta Ch. Sukla, *Śrīdhara Svāmī: A Medieval Philosopher of Religion* (New Delhi: Sahitya Akademi, 2010), 13–22.

62. See *Tattva-sandarbha* 27.

63. See particularly the conclusion to his *Bhagavad-gītā* commentary.

64. See *Bhāgavata* 2.1.9 and 1.7.8–11. *Bhāgavata* 1.7.10 figures prominently in early Chaitanya Vaishnava works. See *Caitanya-caritāmṛta* 2.6.184ff. and 2.24.

65. See *Bhāgavata* 3.15.43ff.

66. See *Bhakti-rasāmṛta-sindhu* 3.1.44; *Caitanya-caritāmṛta* 2.10.177–8; and *Caitanya-candrodaya-nāṭaka* 8.22. The verse, attributed to Bilvamangala, is not found in the *Kṛṣṇa-karṇāmṛta*.

67. See *Caitanya-caritāmṛta* 2.10.175.

68. See Jan Brzezinski, 'Prabodhananda Sarasvati: From Benares to Braj', *Bulletin of the School of Oriental and African Studies, University of London* 55, no. 1 (1992): 52–75.

A conversion might also explain why a deeply emotional devotee like Madhavendra Puri would have a disciple that seems so staunchly Advaitic like Ramacandra Puri: Ramacandra Puri is said to have been present when Madhavendra Puri was on his death bed. When Madhavendra cried out in separation from Krishna, Ramacandra rebuked him, telling him to remember Brahman and be absorbed in the bliss of Brahman, which seems a rather odd comment for a Vaishnava! The story is told in *Caitanya-caritāmṛta* 3.8.

69. *Tattva-sandarbha* 21; *Caitanya-caritāmṛta* 2.25.98–100, 142–6.

Bibliography

Primary Sources

Bhāgavata Purāṇa, with Sanskrit commentary *Bhāvārtha-bodhinī* of Shridhara Svami, edited by J.L. Shastri. New Delhi: Motilal Banarsidass, 1999.

Govardhana. *Seven Hundred Elegant Verses* (*Ārya-saptaśatī*), edited and translated by Friedhelm Hardy. New York: New York University Press and JJC Foundation, 2009.

Jiva Gosvami. *Sarva-saṃvādinī*, edited by Baba Krishnadasa. Kusumasarovara: Krishnadasa Baba, 1964.

———. *Tattva-sandarbha*, edited by Haridasa Shastri. Vrindavan: Shri Gadadhara-Gaurahari Press, 1983.

———. *Paramātma-sandarbha*, edited by Haridasa Shastri. Vrindavan: Shri Gadadhara-Gaurahari Press, 1983.

———. *Bhagavat-sandarbha*, edited by Haridasa Shastri. Vrindavan: Shri Gadadhara-Gaurahari Press, 1984.

———. *Bhakti-sandarbha*, edited by Haridasa Shastri. Vrindavan: Shri Gadadhara-Gaurahari Press, 1986.

———. *Prīti-sandarbha*, edited by Haridasa Shastri. Vrindavan: Shri Gadadhara-Gaurahari Press, 1986.

Kavikarnapura. *Gaura-gaṇoddeśa-dīpikā*. In *Grantha-ratna-pañcakam*, edited by Krishnadasa Baba. Kusumasarovara: Krishnadasa Baba, 1953.

———. *Caitanya-candrodaya-nāṭaka*, edited by Ramchandra Mishra. Varanasi: Chowkhamba Sanskrit Series Office, 1966.

———. *Kṛṣṇa-caitanya-caritāmṛta-mahā-kāvyam*, edited by Haridasa Shastri. Vṛndāvana: Śrī Gadādhara-gaurahari Press, 1983.

Krishnadasa Kaviraja. *Caitanya-caritāmṛta*, edited by Bhakti Kevala Audulomi Maharaj. Calcutta: Gauḍīya Mission, 1957.

Madhusudhana Sarasvati. *Advaita-siddhi*, edited by N. S. Ananta Krishna Sastri. Bombay: Nirnaya-sagar Press, 1915.

Madhva. *Brahma-sūtra-bhāṣya*, edited by K. T. Pandurangi. Bangalore: Dvaita Vedanta Studies and Research Foundation, 1997–2002.

Mahā-nārāyaṇa Upaniṣad (*Taittirīya-nārāyaṇa Upaniṣad*), edited and translated by Svami Vimalananda. Madras: Sri Ramakrishna Math, 1968.

Raghava Pandita. *Śrī-kṛṣṇa-bhakti-ratna-prakāśa*, edited by Puridasa Mahashaya. Vrindavan: Haridasa Sharma, 1954.

Ramanuja. *Gītā-bhāṣya*, edited and translated by Svami Adidevananda. Madras: Sri Ramakrishna Math, n.d.

———. *Śrībhāṣya: Śārīraka-mīmāṃsa-bhāṣya*, edited by M. A. Lakshmitathachar. Melkote: The Academy of Sanskrit Research, 1985–1991.

Rupa Gosvami. *Padyāvalī*, edited by Sushil Kumar De. Dacca: University of Dacca, 1934.

———. *Bhakti-rasāmṛta-sindhu*, with commentaries of Jiva Gosvami, Mukundadasa and Vishvanatha Chakravarti, edited by Haridasa Dasa. Navadvip: Haribola Kuṭīra, 1961.

———. *Laghu-bhāgavatāmṛta*, edited by Bhaktivilasa Tirtha. Mayapura: Shri Chaitanya Maṭha, 1995.

Shankara. *Brahma-sūtra-bhāṣya*, edited by V. Sadanand. Chennai: Samata Books, 1999.

Shrinatha Chakravarti. *Caitanya-mata-mañjuṣā*, edited by Haridasa Dasa. Navadvip: Haribola Kuṭīra, 1952.

Upaniṣads, translated by Patrick Olivelle. Oxford: Oxford University Press, 1996.

Vedanta Deshika. *Rahasya-traya-sāra*, translated by M.R. Rajagopala Aiyangar. Kubakonam: Agnihothram Ramanuja Thathachariar, 1956.

Vrindavanadasa. *Caitanya-bhāgavata*, edited by Bhakti Kevala Audulomi Maharaja. Calcutta: Gauḍīya Mission, 1961.

Yamuna. *Gītārtha-saṅgraha*. In G.S. Sadhale (ed.), *The Bhagavad-gītā with Eleven Commentaries*. New Delhi: Parimal Publications, 1992.

Secondary Sources

Bhattacharyya, Dinesh Chandra. 'Vāsudeva Sārvabhauma'. *The Indian Historical Quarterly* 16, no. 1 (1940): 58–69.

Brzezinski, Jan. 'Prabodhananda Sarasvati: From Benares to Braj'. *Bulletin of the School of Oriental and African Studies, University of London* 55, no. 1 (1992): 52–75.

Chari, S.M. Srinivasa. *Fundamentals of Viśiṣṭādvaita Vedānta: A Study Based on Vedānta Deśika's Tattva-Muktā-Kalāpa*. New Delhi: Motilal Banarsidass, 1987.

Clark, Matthew. *The Daśanāmi-Saṃnyāsīs: The Integration of Ascetic Lineages into an Order*. Leiden: Brill, 2006.

Gupta, Ravi. *The Caitanya Vaiṣṇava Vedānta of Jīva Gosvāmī: When Knowledge Meets Devotion*. Abingdon: Routledge, 2007.

Hacker, Paul. 'Relations of Early Advaitins to Vaiṣṇavism'. *Wiener Zeitschrift für die Kunde Süd- und Ostasiens* 9 (1965): 147–54.

Ingalls, Daniel. *An Anthology of Sanskrit Court Poetry: Vidyākara's 'Subhāṣitaratnakoṣa'*. Cambridge: Harvard University Press, 1965.

Merwin, W.S. and J. Moussaieff Masson. *Sanskrit Love Poetry*. New York: Columbia University Press, 1977.

Mesquita, Roque, *The Concept of Liberation While Still Alive in the Philosophy of Madhva*. New Delhi: Aditya Prakashan, 2007.

Ramanujan, A. K. *Hymns for the Drowning*. New Delhi: Penguin Books India, 1993.

Sharma, B.K. *The Brahmasūtras and Their Principal Commentaries: A Critical Exposition*. New Delhi: Munshiram Manoharlal, 1986.

———. *The Philosophy of Śrī Madhvācārya*. New Delhi: Motilal Banarsidass, 1991.

Sheridan, Daniel. *The Advaitic Theism of the Bhāgavata Purāṇa*. New Delhi: Motilal Banarsidass, 1986.

———. 'Direct Knowledge of God and Living Liberation in the Religious Thought of Madhva'. In *Living Liberation in Hindu Thought*, edited by Andrew Fort and Patricia Mumme. Albany: State University of New York Press, 1996, 91–112.

Sukla, Ananta Charan. *Śrīdhara Svāmī: A Medieval Philosopher of Religion*. New Delhi: Sahitya Akademi, 2010.

21

EMILIA BACHRACH

Religious Reading and Everyday Lives

At 5.30 on a humid June evening in Ahmedabad city, a three-hour-long session of reading and discussing religious literature specific to the Vallabh Sampraday begins with the performance of a *dhoḷ* (hymn) by the nineteenth-century Gujarati poet, Dayaram.

> Taking a vow, I bow daily to the pollen-dust of my Guru's lotus feet;
> Remover of sorrow, Treasure of joy, Giver of the fruit of devotion and love.
> Here I describe by name those eighty-four great devotees
> Who fulfilled the purpose of Shri Vallabh, Shri Vitthal, and Lord Krishna.[1]

The above lines, which commence Dayaram's praise poem called the *Caurāsī Dhoḷ* (84 Dhol), are sung at the start of each meeting held by a reading group that gathers weekly in the home of Kashmira Sharma[2]—a practising doctor of obstetrics and gynecology in her early sixties, a committed follower of the Vallabh Sampraday, and an avid reader of sectarian literature. The rest of the dhoḷ offers the names and signifying qualities of eighty-four devotees who are remembered for their devotional attributes and for having been most dear to Vallabhacharya (1479–1531), the popular Vaishnava theologian after whom the sect in his name was established. As well as being celebrated in song, these eighty-four devotees are remembered in numerous ways: their likenesses are painted on temple walls and their life stories are recounted in text, film, *pravacan* (sermon), theatrical performance, and on Internet forums. However, the most common way of engaging with the memory of these eighty-four devotees is through reading their hagiographies in *satsaṅg*—that is, in the company of fellow devotees.

Hagiographies of these eighty-four devotees are enshrined in a text called the *Caurāsī vaiṣṇavankī vārtā* (Accounts of 84 Vaishnavas, hereafter *84VV*), which is closely associated with another text called the *Do sau bāvan vaiṣṇavan kī vārtā* (Accounts of 252 Vaishnavas, hereafter *252VV*).[3] Just as the *84VV* gives accounts of devotees initiated into the *sampradāy* by Vallabhacharya, the *252VV* contains narratives of devotees initiated by Vitthalnath (1515–1585), Vallabhacharya's son and successor. According to tradition, both texts were originally based on oral accounts of Vitthalnath's son Gokulnath (1551–1640), and redacted and commented on by Gokulnath's grand-nephew Hariray (1591–1716).[4] Originally composed in Brajbhasha (old Hindi) prose with frequent citations from Sanskrit treatises and Brajbhasha verse, contemporary versions of the texts are often translated into Gujarati, the language spoken by a majority of those who follow the Vallabh Sampraday today.

Previous scholarship on the *84VV* and *252VV* has often focused on how the hagiographies reveal the Vallabh Sampraday's struggle to articulate itself as a distinct sectarian community in the early modern period.[5] While the *vārtās* (accounts) are a valuable source for understanding the community's early representation of itself, the *84VV* and *252VV* do much more than report sectarian views of history: they are also devotional and didactic texts with an aesthetically distinct way of articulating theology, devotional practice, and religious identity through intertextually rich narratives of the devotees' lives. Interpretations of the texts, however, are far from uniform, and vārtā satsaṅgs invariably become spaces in which contemporary readers negotiate what is considered to be socially and devotionally normative.

By considering the lived contexts in which the vārtās continue to be read and discussed, my ethnographic work in Ahmedabad invites us to rethink the ways in which the vārtās have been characterized, and to take seriously the devotional and didactic function of the narratives. To what extent do the protagonists of the *84VV* and *252VV*, their qualities and their behaviour, continue to influence the ways in which devotees and sectarian leaders construct religious and social ideals and practices? What is considered to be normative for whom and when, and how does the context of vārtā satsaṅg help to negotiate sectarian belonging? In addressing these questions, we will be invited to reconsider how reading functions and what it means to read religiously.

* * *

The Vallabh Sampraday promotes a philosophical system called *śuddhādvait* (pure non-dualism) and a devotional and ritual system called the *puṣṭimārg* (the path of nourishment).[6] Central to the teachings of Vallabhacharya, Vitthalnath, and their successors, and still primary for members of the sect today, are the following prescriptions: singular devotion to Krishna as the Supreme Being; the practice of *sevā* (ritualized worship or 'service')[7] of Krishna *svarūp*s (essential forms), often referred to as Thakurji, in the devotees' homes; the rejection of traditional forms of renunciation in one's spiritual path (that is, the mandate to lead a householder's life); and a formal initiation into the sect, called the *brahmasambandh*,[8] which is to be performed by a direct male descendent of Vallabhacharya. A majority of Vallabhacharya's living descendents (commonly known as the Vallabh Kul, or Vallabh Dynasty)[9] and their disciples are based in or have direct ties to western India, especially Gujarat. Today many lay followers hail from upper-middle-class communities of urban Gujarat as well as from the city of Mumbai.

While the contemporary demographic of devotees is fairly homogenous in terms of caste and class, protagonists of the 84 *VV* and 252 *VV* represent a range of socio-economic and religious groups from early modern South Asia. Readers will encounter Brahmins, Muslims, merchants, farmers, thieves, kings, queens, prostitutes, warriors, and widows.[10] In addition to presenting the social diversity of early followers, the texts also emphasize the diversity of human emotions and behaviours. Though some characters exhibit conventional qualities of humility, patience, and unwavering faith in Krishna's divine grace, others are irascible,[11] vain, tactless, or even violently aggressive. What brings these diverse characters together are the ways in which they struggle to make sense of the sectarian prescriptions outlined above as they develop their relationships with Krishna, their gurus (Vallabhacharya and Vitthalnath), and fellow devotees.

In order to give further coherence to the narratives of the sampradāy's lauded yet imperfect devotees, a Brajbhasha commentary attributed to Hariray, called the *Bhāvprakāś* (an illumination of the text's *bhāv*, or 'intention'), was added to these vārtā texts.[12] One of the commentary's functions is to anticipate and quell readers' doubts about correct sectarian conduct. For example, when one vārtā tells how a devotee, Virbai, is told by her Thakurji to carry on with sevā even though she is in a state of impurity due to childbirth, the *Bhāvprakāś* is quick to justify the character's behaviour. Do not misunderstand, the commentary tells us. 'Since Virbai was much-loved by Thakurji' and was given permission by the deity to carry on with sevā, her actions were neither 'wicked nor impure'.[13] The *Bhāvprakāś* is not, however, the final word on the vārtās. Rather, as the following case studies demonstrate, the dialogue between text and commentary, by pointing implicitly to questions that might be asked of the document as a whole, invites readers to participate in this discussion. Modern-day devotees have the chance to enter into a vivid and sometimes even argumentative relationship with the vārtās as they negotiate between what the narratives are perceived to teach and their own lived realities.

* * *

A theme central to *84VV* and *252VV* narratives, and one of the most widely debated issues for readers of the texts today, is the perceived challenge of harmonizing familial and social life with commitments to the sectarian community and the performance of sevā. This was the topic of discussion on the same humid June evening that I recorded the women of Kashmira's satsaṅg singing Dayaram's *Caurāsī Dhoḷ*.

Once the satsaṅg is initiated with the performance of the dhoḷ, the thirteen women gathered in Kashmira's living room open their respective copies of the *Coryāsī vaiṣṇavonī vārtāo*—a Gujarati translation of the *84VV*.[14] Kashmira, who began hosting her satsaṅg twelve years ago in celebration of the birth of her guru's son, signals to a woman named Dipa, seated to her left, to begin reading aloud to the group. The *prasaṅg* (episode) that Dipa reads comes from the vārtā concerning

Purushottamdas and his wife, two Kṣatriya devotees from Agra. We may summarize the episode as follows:

> When Purushottamdas and his wife meet Shri Acharyaji [Vallabhacharya] they prostrate themselves and ask for initiation. Shri Acharyaji initiates the couple, giving man and wife *mālās* (religious necklaces) to wear around their necks as marks of their new Vaishnava identities. However, when Purushottamdas asks to perform sevā, Shri Acharyaji tells the couple that their mothers are *asurījīv* (wicked souls), and so they must wait some time before beginning sevā. Indeed, when the couple's mothers discover that their children are wearing mālās they become upset, thinking: 'our children have become ascetics!' Purushottamdas explains that wearing the mālās does not mean that they have become ascetics and that the mothers may still share the family home. 'However', Purushottamdas clarifies, 'unless you also receive initiation from Shri Acharyaji, we will not accept food and water from your hands'. Hearing this, the mothers become enraged: 'Do you wish to disgrace us and our community? We might as well die!' Indeed, during the night the mothers drown themselves in the household well. After completing the last rites, the couple goes to Shri Acharyaji who tells them that now they can perform sevā.[15]

When Dipa finishes reading the account, Kashmira initiates discussion by asserting that the vārtā 'intimately describes the anguish' experienced when families of Vaishnavas do not understand the '*puṣṭi* lifestyle'.[16] Kashmira continues:

> But I was also deluded once, I was also thinking that my husband and in-laws must be some sort of ascetics! They wouldn't even let me in the kitchen after marriage until they had taken me to get initiation. Even after my initiation, I was completely ignorant: I didn't know anything, not even how to say *Jai Shri Krishna* [the standard greeting for most members of the Vallabh Sampraday].

Kashmira explains that while, at first, she neither understood nor felt compelled to follow the religious observances of her husband's family, it was natural in her position as new *bahū* (daughter-in-law) to appease her spouse and in-laws. 'Don't misunderstand', Kashmira says adamantly, 'I am not saying that you should force your bahūs to become Vaishnavas! I naturally felt compelled to follow along ... and before long', Kashmira says, placing her hands to her heart, 'I had replaced the *Hanumān Cālīsā* [a non-*Puṣṭimārgī* poem about Hanuman as the ideal devotee of Lord Ram] with the *Yamunāṣṭakam*!' At this point, Kashmira launches into the first verse of the *Yamunāṣṭakam*,

Vallabhacharya's Sanskrit praise poem about the river goddess Yamuna and her singular devotion to Lord Krishna. 'But let's return to Purushottamdas and his wife', Kashmira says, wrapping up her own observations:

> The reason Shri Acharyaji called their mothers wicked was that they tried to take away the mālās. But according to me, they were merely ignorant. Sisters: Shri Acharyaji would never permit us to disrespect our mothers and fathers.... We are not to understand from this account that we are permitted to remove ourselves from our families ... even if they are, as I was once, ignorant of the '*puṣṭi* lifestyle'. As long as Thakurji doesn't suffer we must show some patience.

Kashmira concludes with a quotation from the *Vivekadhairyāśraya*, another of Vallabhacharya's sixteen short Sanskrit treatises, which takes its place alongside the *Yamunāṣṭakam* in a collection called the *Ṣoḍaśagrantha*. The verse Kashmira quotes is frequently cited in many versions of the *84VV*:

> pratīkāro yaddṛcchātaḥ siddhaścennāgrahī bhavet
> bhāryādīnāṁ tathānyeṣāmasataścākramaṁ sahte.

> But if a remedy of [one's suffering] should chance to occur, one should not stubbornly insist [on continuing to suffer]. One should, however, patiently endure the wrongs committed [against oneself] by wife and children, household, and others.[17]

Hearing this, the other women nod in agreement, clearly impressed with Kashmira's ability to recall and recite the Sanskrit verse with seeming ease.

Kashmira finally opens the floor for whatever further reflections, questions, and discussion may be stimulated by the reading of Purushottamdas's vārtā. During the next hour, many women share personal experiences and reactions. Dipa describes how she is the only practising devotee in her family and frequently experiences criticism from her husband and two teenaged boys, who do not follow the widely recognized food restrictions of the Vallabh Sampraday. Such restrictions include routine and seasonal fasting, as well as maintaining a pure vegetarian diet and only accepting food that has first been offered to one's personal household Krishna svarūp (the consecrated food offering is then taken by the devotee as *mahāprasād*). These prescriptions preclude some observant members of the sect from eating in other peoples' homes or in restaurants—leisure activities that are otherwise considered common for many upper-middle-class residents of Ahmedabad. 'But I don't complain,' Dipa continues, 'I make the food that my family asks for and then ritually purify myself. It is not suitable behaviour for a Vaishnava to make complaints.'

This brief account of Kashmira's satsaṅg reveals some of the ways in which readers weave the vārtās into the everyday fabric of family dynamics, social exchanges, religious thought, and ritual practice. In this context, the hagiographies' protagonists are perceived to be vividly real figures whose experiences directly resonate with the lived realities of contemporary devotees. Just as Purushottamdas and his wife are shown to struggle with explaining their new faith commitments to uninitiated family members, satsaṅg members discuss the challenges they experienced in learning to balance sectarian prescriptions and what is often referred to as *kautumbik mūlyo* ('family values': The Gujarati phrase is likely a calque of the English phrase 'family values'), that is, familial and social obligations.[18] Moreover, domestic stability and the successful performance of sevā are considered to be mutually exclusive. 'If Thakurji is unhappy, the Vaishnava is unhappy; and if the Vaishnava is unhappy, then Thakurji cannot endure it', one of my interlocutors explained to me in a private interview.[19]

These kinds of intimate devotional relationships between a devotee and his or her household deity are central to many of the hagiographies and continue to be articulated both by individual devotees and in public religious discourse. As one contemporary vārtā commentator writes:

> Thakurji will slowly begin to take shape according to you and will begin to identify with each and every member of your family. God's involvement will increase as he becomes a family member, becoming interwoven into your family's *kathā* (tale). [The *Bhaktivardhinī* states:] *gṛhe sthitvā svadharmataḥ* ... [20]

The brief excerpt quoted from Vallabhacharya's *Bhaktivardhinī*, a treatise also found in the *Ṣoḍaśagrantha*, means 'remain a householder and follow one's own *dharma*'. The larger context for this citation is Vallabhacharya's instruction to remain, whenever possible, a householder: while everything should be 'dedicated' (*samarpit*) to Krishna, the devotee is not encouraged to live removed from the social world.[21] The vārtā of Purushottamdas and his wife playfully engages with this sectarian value when the two 'wicked' mothers mistake their children's new Vaishnava identities, represented by the mālās, for a choice to leave their particular caste community and shun their families. Purushottamdas and his wife are, of course, not to be taken as ascetics, and their attempt to explain this to their indignant mothers is highlighted in the narrative. While the rather histrionic end to the two mothers is found to be somewhat objectionable to Kashmira and her satsaṅg members ('Vallabhacharya would never permit us to disrespect our mothers and fathers', Kashmira told her group), reading Purushottamdas's narrative opened the floor for discussion and negotiation on the matter of how Puṣṭimārgīs should negotiate the tension between being devotional caretakers for Thakurji on the one hand, and mothers, daughters, wives, and so on, on the other.

* * *

Across the city from Kashmira's home, another satsaṅg gathering further articulates the issue of harmonizing sectarian commitments and kautumbik mūlyo. This group is led by a female descendent of Vallabhacharya named Raja Betiji. Some of my informants claim to prefer satsaṅg groups that are led by figures such as Raja Betiji because there 'advice' can be given by an established source of religious authority. Others, however, prefer lay leadership, and precisely because of this authority's absence. According to Raja Betiji, reading the vārtās in her satsaṅg indeed gives the devotees an opportunity to learn about 'correct' sevā practices and to ask questions about sectarian principles. She also believes, however, that discussing the vārtās can lead to what she calls in English 'healthy *puṣṭi* debate'.

One such debate in Raja Betiji's satsaṅg sprang from reading the vārtā of Damodardas Sambhalvale, a figure from the *84VV* who was said to have lived in the town of Kanauj, in today's Uttar Pradesh.[22] In one episode, Vallabhacharya asks his disciple Damodardas if there is anything that he desires. Damodardas replies: 'Aside from your grace, there is nothing that I desire.' Vallabhacharya then tells his disciple: 'Ask your wife if she desires anything.' When Damodardas's wife says that she wishes to have a son, Vallabhacharya tells her: 'a son will come'. Several days later, Damodardas's wife becomes pregnant. However, to confirm her pregnancy, she consults a fortune teller.[23] 'Yes,' the fortune teller reassures the mother-to-be: 'a son will come'. When Damodardas again meets with his guru, Vallabhacharya tells him: By consulting someone other than myself on this matter, your wife has committed the offence of *anyāśray* (taking refuge in another)![24] Before departing for his home in Adel, Vallabhacharya tells Damodardas: 'There will still be a son, but he will be a *mlecch* (a vile outsider or non-believer).'[25] When Damodardas's wife hears what has been prophesied, she stops performing sevā for fear that she will pollute her Thakurji and tells her mother: 'If I do have such a son, take him away from me immediately. I never want to see his face!' At this point in the version of the vārtā that Raja Betiji is reading, the narrative pauses for Hariray's explanatory comment, which states that 'there is no greater perversion than taking refuge in another. It is just like the woman who loses all her *dharma* by leaving her husband to be with another man'.[26]

When Raja Betiji finishes reading, a woman named Surekha expresses the following sentiment:

> I don't even speak to anyone who isn't Vaishnava.... The woman comes for the trash, I leave it for her to take, but I don't even look at her. I buy my vegetables from a Vaishnava only.... I come here, to Raja's satsaṅg, but otherwise, I keep so few social relations. Now, imagine how Damodardas's wife must have been feeling—giving birth to a mlecch!

Around the room, several people are shaking their heads and clicking their tongues in agreement, but most make faces of disapproval. 'You surely have firm faith, Surekhaben', Raja Betiji says, 'but your situation in life allows you to take so much time for your sevā'. Surekha fidgets in her chair. Raja Betiji smiles at Surekha and then indicates that another woman named Lila may have something to share with the group. Lila, a middle-aged teacher at a government school, often confronts the sharp-tongued Surekha in weekly satsaṅg. Just as Kashmira had emphasized in her commentary on the vārtā of Purushottamdas, Lila explains that she cannot comprehend how Vallabhacharya would endorse turning away family members—especially children. On the matter of anyāśray, she states that indeed 'Damodardas's wife had no reason to consult the fortune-teller'. It was her *aparādh* (transgression) to do so. Yet Lila goes on to explain that she does not endorse the kinds of exclusive sectarian behaviour that prohibit interactions with 'others'. 'I know I have firm faith', she says, 'but this I cannot endure.'

Lila's commentary reflects her own life situation and is a corrective to the statement given by Surekha. In a private interview, Lila explained her particular familial circumstances. Like Dipa from Kashmira's satsaṅg, Lila struggles with family members who are not adherents of the Vallabh Sampraday. Her son, who lives in Florida, is not only openly apathetic about the 'puṣṭi lifestyle', but is also married to a German woman who, as Lila explains, 'understands nothing about Indian culture—let alone sevā and Thakurji. She also eats meat in the house and feeds it to the kids. It is a difficult thing for me and it gives me sorrow.' Regardless, Lila has a close relationship with family: 'It's my task to bear the burden, not theirs', she explains. 'But the problem is this: when I go to Florida to visit them how can I bring my Thakurji?' Instead of bringing her Krishna svarūp with her when she travels to visit family in the United States, as many Gujarat-based devotees frequently do, Lila entrusts a close friend to care for the deity. 'Shoba takes my Thakurji when I'm in Jacksonville, but allows me to sing to him on the phone each night. In Ahmedabad it's morning and he's just waking up.' Lila's sentiment beautifully expresses the devotion and love she has for her personal deity as well as her ability to effectively negotiate between satisfying both familial commitments and what she considers to be her obligations in caring for her Thakurji.

Lila's personal account and the exchanges from Raja Betiji's satsaṅg further highlight the distinct ways in which vārtā reading function. As we observed in the example from Kashmira's group, reading the hagiographies provides a platform for the intimate sharing of devotees' everyday experiences and the ways in which these experiences follow or challenge certain models for sectarian thought and practice. The example of Raja Betiji's group also indicates that devotees do not necessarily have predictable or uniformly shared reactions to the vārtās. Rather, readers are actively engaged in negotiating between what the narratives are perceived to teach and their own individual interpretations. Paul Ricoeur speaks to this phenomenon when he describes how all active readers naturally 'appropriate' texts as they seek to interpret and make sense of them: 'interpretation brings together, equalizes, renders contemporary and similar, thus genuinely making one's own what was initially alien'.[27] This type of engagement, however, is reminiscent of certain structures in Hariray's *Bhāvprakāś*: just as the commentary raises doubts and glosses the actions of vārtā characters in terms of siddhānt (doctrine), contemporary readers also entertain questions—not only questions about the vārtās themselves, but also questions that challenge interpretations heard from fellow devotees and established religious authorities.[28]

A telling example of this feature of satsaṅg arose during a meeting held by Goswami Tilak Bava,[29] Raja Betiji's nephew, who also holds weekly vārtā readings at his family's temple, the Goswami Haveli.[30]

The discussion in question focused on issues of purity and pollution during sevā and was triggered by the Tilak Bava's reading of the account of a devotee named Virbai, whose vārtā was briefly discussed earlier. Here is a summary of the episode that Tilak Bava read aloud:

> When Virbai gave birth to a son she was distressed because, due to her impure state, she could not perform sevā. 'Who will awaken Shri Thakurji?' she thought to herself. After several days she began to cry over the matter and felt great *viraha* (anguish of separation from Krishna): 'What shall I do?' Then Shri Thakurji spoke to her: 'So what if there isn't anyone else to wake me? You alone should wake me!' Surprised, Virbai replied: 'Maharaj! I've fallen into a *aghornarak* (fearsome hell). How can I touch you?' Then Shri Thakurji told Virbai that she could return to sevā: 'Bathe and put on fresh *kāch* (garments). I will not have anyone else perform my sevā. This is my order, there will be no transgression.'[31]

After reading the episode, Tilak Bava begins by offering a simple gloss: 'Our Virbai was such a dedicated devotee ... that Shri Thakurji said, "don't cry like this, perform my sevā. It is no transgression."' However, Tilak Bava quickly goes on to comment on the broader theme of ritual purity and the ways in which devotees should dress when performing sevā. 'See, Shri Thakurji told Virbai: wear your kāch, that is, *sāṛī*.[32] Today the situation is such that so many ladies are wearing ... what do you say, those things called "maxi" (a woman's nightgown). They don't put on the sāṛī and according to me ... this is not right.' At this point Tilak Bava's wife, Goswami Vrajbhamini, who often joins her husband and their congregation for vārtā readings, interjects: 'But isn't it okay if the maxi that a lady uses is only used during sevā?' Goswami Vrajbhamini goes on to explain that many women tell her that they prefer such maxi garments to the sāṛī even while observing all normative measures of ritual purity. 'Because of this', she continues, 'I tell them that it is acceptable.' Tilak Bava grimaces: 'A sevā maxi!' The discussion soon spreads into the crowd of nearly seventy devotees:

> Of course ladies must wear a sāṛī in sevā—we can't be so lazy!
> If ladies wear sāṛī, then men must wear *dhotī*!
> My daughter doesn't even know how to tie a sāṛī—let alone do sevā!

While the issue of how to perform and prepare oneself properly for sevā is a sincere and serious matter, the debate sparked by Virbai's vārtā is also light-hearted and filled with laughter. One teenage boy makes a face like Tilak Bava and repeats his guru's complaint: 'sevā maxi!', and then bursts into laughter. The discussion is finally brought to a close and Tilak Bava returns to the reading—but not before he and his wife come to the conclusion that the appropriate clothing to wear in sevā depends on the devotee's individual relationship with his or her guru and with Thakurji.

The element of humour, just as it arose during the Virbai discussion, often finds its way into vārtā satsaṅg—particularly when devotees draw attention to seeming incongruences between elements of modern life and the ritual practice of sevā. During satsaṅg at a different temple, I recorded a similar conversation in which one participant joked about ordering Thakurji a pizza rather than preparing him more traditional food offerings, such as milk-based sweets. While many found the comment immediately humourous ('Who would be so lazy!?'), others seriously questioned why Thakurji could not be fed such food items ('Isn't He supposed to eat what we eat? Isn't He a part of the family?'). Like the debate about sartorial propriety during sevā, the debate about whether or not to feed Thakurji pizza yet again points to the kind of questioning that occurs when devotees discuss the relationship between textual models and real-life practices. Humour during satsaṅg reveals a certain sense of intimacy between devotees and their religious leaders and also helps to facilitate the kinds of serious questions and negotiations that are so integral to vārtā readings.

In conversations about the various features of vārtā satsaṅg, both devotees and members of the Vallabh Kul expressed the view that questioning the texts is key to religious learning and to the cultivation of sectarian identity. As Shyam Manohar Goswami, a prominent member of the Vallabh Kul, said during a recent inspirational talk: 'What's the use of being like a bird in a cage? One has to leave that cage and engage in discussion—this is how you learn.'[33] Similarly, another Goswami told me: 'We [members of the Vallabh Kul] should also emphasize the importance of reading and learning in this way. If you seek to know more and strengthen your devotion, then it is okay to even have religious debate with your guru. These are positive Vaishnava qualities ... we can see such behavior modeled by characters from both the *84VV* and *252VV*.'[34] Yet, Tilak Bava reminds us that not every devotee will question in the same way: 'Every devotee will find his own stream that will lead him to that ocean [of the *puṣṭimārg*]. It depends on one's guru, own nature, life circumstance, but ultimately it is all God's grace [*bhagvānnī kṛpā*].'[35] These sentiments point to the special role that vārtā satsaṅgs have in structuring the lives of members of the Vallabh Sampraday, but they also suggest that religious reading functions more broadly as a distinct practice. As for the modelling of behaviour, that seems the particular province of hagiography.[36]

* * *

In his acclaimed book *The Final Word: The Caitanya Caritāmṛta and the Grammar of Religious Tradition,* Tony K. Stewart writes that hagiographies do more than interact with other texts: they 'also depend on and interact with the cultural texts that constitute the rules of social conduct, logical argument, systematic theology, ritual practice'.[37] Further, he suggests, the act of composing hagiography is a 'religious act'. When the author of a hagiography indicates that he/she has written about his/her guru—or of lauded devotees—we should accept that this statement is reflective of the author's own experiences. In this way, the 'history' that such texts proclaim is not so much that of the guru, but 'that of the religious imagination of the community gathered around him'.[38] While the case studies presented in this chapter focus on the connection that hagiographies have to contemporary life experiences rather than on the aspects of hagiography that fundamentally relate to history and memory, Stewart's comment on the religious imagination that sacred biography represents is key to understanding the institution of vārtā satsaṅg. If writing a hagiography is a religious act, then clearly reading and discussing one is as well. This practice is not only visible in the contemporary context; it can also be internal to hagiographic texts themselves. In both the *Caritāmṛta* and the *84VV* and *252VV*, we see images of satsaṅg—of devotional performance, group reading, and discussion—as a practice that both confirms and recreates religious imagination.

Paul J. Griffiths has suggested that reading 'religiously' shapes one's role as an interpreter, and that religious readers' primary aim is to come closer to texts—even if by challenging and questioning them.[39] Linda Hess, in her work on the practice of raising doubts (*śaṅkā*) about the Rāmāyaṇ, eloquently describes this aspect of religious reading:

> The questioning process is not just a means of getting answers. Those who question are already assumed to be lovers, and the process enacts the love that exists. It is a way of lingering in the text, enjoying *satsang*, savoring the endless possibilities of wisdom and pleasure that text and community afford.[40]

The context of vārtā satsaṅg similarly reminds us of these distinct features of religious reading. Here reading is inherently a collective and performative act that inspires group dialogue and debate. This way of reading is also a natural extension of the vārtā genre itself. The vārtās, along with Hariray's Bhāvprakāś commentaries, are inherently dialogical texts, which themselves seek to interpret and validate sectarian doctrine through narrative examples of devotees' lives.

Further, as vārtā readers repeatedly pointed out, satsaṅg also provides a space in which to cultivate *bhāv*, or the 'devotional mood', which allows people to strengthen their relationships with one another and with Thakurji. This network of relationships, as Robert Orsi has argued, is naturally a defining feature of any religious tradition. Religion, Orsi writes, is not only a 'medium for explaining, understanding, and modeling reality', it is also a 'network of relationships between heaven and earth involving humans of all ages and many different sacred figures together'.[41] These relationships have 'all the complexities—all the hopes, evasions, love, fear, denial, projections, misunderstandings, and so on—of relationships between humans'.[42] Above all else the hagiographies offer a template for discussing, negotiating, and strengthening these complex relationships.

The context of vārtā satsaṅg has shown that religious readers not only read with the ambition to 'come closer to texts', but also with the aim of becoming hagiographers in their own right—retelling and questioning well-known narratives in light of everyday experiences and personal convictions. Recognizing this aspect of vārtā satsaṅg reveals the inherent plurality of scriptural interpretation and moral discourse.[43] While textual prescriptions and sectarian leaders continue to assert their authority, vārtā readings demonstrate that negotiations of normative behavior are fluid—situated in particular socio-historical moments and influenced by intersubjective relationships, both human and divine.

Notes

1. All translations are my own unless otherwise indicated. I thank Goswami Anandabava for graciously assisting me in my translation of the *Caurāsī Dhoḷ*. All mistakes are my own. My translation is based on a reading group's oral performance on 22 June 2012 in Ahmedabad.

2. With the exception of public figures, all individuals who have been cited or referred to in this chapter have been given pseudonyms to protect their

identity (this is in accordance with the IRB approval for my ethnographic research).

3. Part of a larger canon of *Vārtā Sāhitya* (Account Literature), the *84VV* and *252VV* are among the most widely circulated texts in the contemporary sectarian community. Since they first became available in print during the late nineteenth century, countless versions of the *84VV* and *252VV* (which differ to varying degrees) have been produced in Brajbhasha, modern Hindi, and Gujarati. While readers in Ahmedabad use many different versions, the most popular versions are based on Brajbhasha publications of the texts edited by Dvarakadas Parikh (Parikh's first editions of the *84VV* and *252VV* were first published in 1948 and 1952 respectively). The 2009 and 2011 versions of the hagiographies that I refer to in this chapter are nearly identical to these first editions, but with slightly different paratext (for example, notes, topical essays, and study guides). According to Parikh's editorial notes (from the 2011 publication), seven manuscripts were consulted for his edition of the *84VV*—the oldest with a colophon bearing the date of VS 1752 (Dvarkadas Parikh, ed., *Caurāsī vaiṣṇavankī vārtā: tīn janmakī līlā bhāvnā vālīsahit* [Vaishnava Mitra Mandal Sarvananik Nyas: Indore, 2011], 13). Parikh does not give the details of manuscripts used for his edition of the *252VV*. For further issues with dating and manuscripts, see Hariharnath Tandan, *Vārtā sāhitya: ek vṛhat adhyayan* (Aligarh: Bharat Prakasan Mandir, 1960), 103–5; Shandip Saha, 'A Community of Grace: The Social and Theological World of the Puṣṭi MārgaVārtā Literature', *Bulletin of School of Oriental and African Studies* 69, no. 2 (2006): 231n22.

4. Dates given according to tradition.

5. For example: Saha, 'A Community of Grace'; Vasudha Dalmia, 'Forging Community: The Guru in a Seventeenth-Century Vaiṣṇava Hagiography', in *Charisma and Canon*, ed. Vasudha Dalmia, Angelika Malinar, and Martin Christof (Oxford: Oxford University Press, 2001); Charlotte Vaudeville, *Myths, Saints and Legends in Medieval India* (New Delhi: Oxford University Press, 1996); and Frederick Smith, 'Dark Matter in Vārtāland: On the Enterprise of History in Early Puṣṭimārga Discourse', *The Journal of Hindu Studies* 2, no. 1 (2009).

6. The standard introductory text on sectarian theology is Richard Barz, *The Bhakti Sect of Vallabhācārya* (New Delhi: Munshiram Manoharlal, 1992).

7. 'Sevā' refers not only to the ritual worship of Krishna svarūps in devotees' private homes, but also to a range of actions including the preparation of food items and ritual decorations for temple deities, attending to the needs of one's guru and his family, and the giving of *dān* (donations).

8. The initiation is intended to clear the soul of imperfections (*doṣas*) so that the devotee becomes worthy of a relationship with Krishna. See Barz, *The Bhakti Sect of Vallabhācārya*, 18–20.

9. While the terms of religious authority in the Vallabh Sampraday are complex and contested, there are seven commonly recognized lineages of the

Vallabh Kul. For details, see Barz, *The Bhakti Sect of Vallabhācārya*, 54–5. Male members of the Vallabh Kul are respectfully referred to as *bāvā*, *gosvāmī*, or *mahārāj*. Their female counterparts—their wives (*bahūjīs*) and unmarried daughters (*beṭījīs*)—are also considered to be members of the Vallabh Kul. Married beṭījīs and their descendents are still revered, but are generally considered to be members of the Vallabh *parivār* (the family of Vallabhacharya).

10. While some figures from the vārtās have names recognizable beyond the sectarian context, such as the sixteenth-century poet Surdas, most will not be found outside of the tradition.

11. See Richard Barz, 'Kṛṣṇadās Adhikārī: An Irascible Devotee's Approach to the Divine', in *Bhakti Studies*, ed. G. Baily (New Delhi: Sterling, 1992).

12. I have addressed the complexities of this commentary elsewhere. See Emilia Bachrach, 'Justifying Religious Authority: The Function of Hariray's Bhavprakash Commentary in the *Caurasi Vaishnavan ki Varta*' (paper presented at the 38th Annual Conference on South Asia, Madison Wisconsin, October 2009). For a brief study on the differences between the two recensions of the *84VV* (with and without the commentary), see Rousseva-Sokolva, 'Sainthood Revisited: Two Printed Versions of the Lives of the Eighty-Four Vaishnavas by Gokulnāth', in *Bhakti beyond the Forest: Current Research of Early Modern Literatures in North India, 2003–2009*, ed. Imre Bangha (New Delhi: Manohar Publishers, 2012), 83–97.

13. Parikh, *Caurāsīi vaiṣṇavan kī vārtā*, 339–44.

14. Rameshbhai V. Parikh, trans., Goswami Shri Vagish Kumar, ed., '*Coryāsī vaiṣṇavonī vārtāo: tūm bīn tattva kachu nahī jagmeṃ (84 bhagavadīyatatvavicār)*', in *Puṣṭimārgīya patrācār: Śuddhādvait sevābhūṣaṇ* (Baroda: Shri Vakpati Foundation, 2002), 291–558.

15. My translated synopsis of what was being read aloud in Gujarati comes from Parikh, '*Coryāsī vaiṣṇavonī vārtāo*', 399.

16. All translated dialogue was originally spoken in Gujarati unless otherwise noted. Code-switching (between Gujarati, Hindi, and English) is common.

17. James Redington, trans., *The Grace of Lord Krishna: The Sixteen Verse-Treatises of Vallabhacharya* (New Delhi: Sri Satguru Publications, 2000), 96.

18. The ease with which devotees identify with and critique vārtā protagonists appears to be distinc when compared to certain western hagiographical traditions. In her study of medieval Christian women's religiosity, Caroline Walker Bynum notes:

> Indeed, medieval hagiographers pointed out repeatedly that saints are not even primarily 'models' for ordinary mortals; the saints are far too dangerous for that. Like Christ himself, they could not and should not be imitated in their full extravagance and power. Rather (so their admirers say), they

should be loved, venerated, and meditated upon as moments in which the other that is God breaks through into the mundane world, saturating it with meaning' (Caroline Walker Bynum, *Holy Feast and Holy Fast: The Religious Significance of Food to Medieval Women* [Berkeley: University of California Press, 1987], 7).

While Vallabhacharya and his kul are not to be imitated (they are divine in their own right and, as Bynum notes, too 'full of extravagance and power'), the vārtās' protagonists are not in the same category and are both open to criticism and potentially imitable.

19. Interview with female interlocutor in Ahmedabad (3 March 2012).

20. In the Vaishnava context the word 'kathā' also refers to ritualized recitations and exegesis of the *Bhāgavata Purāṇa*. Kathā can also be used interchangeably with the term satsaṅg, referring more generally to contexts in which devotees read and discuss religious literature together. Bhupendra Bhatiya, *Ṣoḍaśgranthāgat upadeś ane tem-nī 28 vārtāo (Bhāg 2)* (Rajkot: Purvi Press, 2008), 13.

21. Vallabhacharya's position on the matter of asceticism is also evident in another treatise from the *Ṣoḍaśagranthāḥ*, the *Saṃnyāsanirṇaya* (A Consideration of Renunciation). Further on this text, see Fredrick M. Smith, '*Saṃnyāsanirṇaya*: A Śuddhādvaita Text on Renunciation by Vallabhācārya', *Journal of Vaishnava Studies* 1, no. 4 (1993): 135–56.

22. The vārtā is being read aloud from Parikh, '*Coryāsī vaiṣṇavonī vārtāo*', 131–2.

23. I have used the term 'fortune teller' to translate the Gujarati word *teliyorājā*. The term is explained as 'a Tantrik who bathes in oil, or puts on clothes dripping with oil and pretends to tell future events by looking into the oil': P.G. Deshpande, *Gujarātī-Angrejī koś* (Ahmedabad: University Granthnimarn Board, 2002), 459.

24. It should be emphasized that the actions of Damodardas's wife are determined to result in anyāśray not because she consulted a fortune-teller as such, but rather because she consulted *any* person other than her own guru. Hariray discussed the dangers of anyāśray in detail in his *Baḍe sikṣāpatra* (a text he also refers to when discussing anyāśray in his *Bhāvprakāś*). The vārtās' emphasis on the term is also addressed in John S. Hawley, 'The Four *Sampradāyas*: Ordering the Religious Past in Mughal North India', *South Asian History and Culture* 2, no. 2 (2011): 169.

25. The word used is 'mlecch', which can be translated as 'barbarian; non-Aryan; non-Indian' or 'base; sinful; non-believing' (R.S. McGregor, *Oxford Hindi-English Dictionary* [New Delhi: Oxford University Press, 1993], 839). The *Shabdsāgar* defines the term as follows: 'manuṣyoṃ kī jātiyoṃ [*sic*, for jātiyaṃ] jinmeṃ varṇaśram dharm na ho'. The term is generally used in the vārtās to refer to Muslim characters along with another term *yavan*, which can mean:

'Greek, an Ionian' or 'a foreigner (by origin); a Muslim; a European; a barbarian' (McGregor, *Oxford Hindi-English Dictionary*, 839). In most instances the term is inherently pejorative, but not all to the same degree. Contemporary translators have interpreted the word in several ways—sometimes glossing or replacing it with the more ambiguous *adharmī* (immoral) and sometimes even explicitly stating that the term does *not* refer to Muslims.

26. Parikh, *Coryāsī vaiṣṇavannī vārtāo*, 333.

27. Paul Ricoeur, *From Text to Action: Essays in Hermeneutics*, vol. 2 (Evanston: Northwestern University Press, 1986), 119.

28. Because satsaṅg participants from these first two case studies are predominantly women (several men regularly join Raja Betiji's group), the experiences shared during discussion clearly reflect gendered concerns. While I know of no exclusively male satsaṅgs, many reading groups consist of both men and women. My forthcoming dissertation, 'The Living Tradition of Hagiography in the Vallabh Sect of Contemporary Gujarat', addresses the various demographics of religious readers in the sampradāy and gendered readings of the vārtās specifically.

29. Tilak Bava or Tilak Goswami also goes by Madhusudanlal. His father Vrajnath Maharaj currently presides over the Goswami Haveli—a role that Tilak Goswami will inherit.

30. I recorded this reading session on 1 December 2011.

31. Tilak Bava reads from Parikh's 2011 edited version of the text (pages 339–44).

32. The word 'kāch' is defined as '*dhotī*, esp. the end of the dhotī tucked in at the waist behind' (McGregor, *Oxford Hindi-English Dictionary*, 186). Sumit Sharma (a member of the Vallabh Kul who is also well read in *Vārtā sāhitya*) confirmed that here kāch refers to a sāṛī tied in a 'dhotī style' as per the mentioneddefinition (personal communication, 31 March 2012).

33. This *pravacan* was given in Mumbai in February, 2013. I accessed the recorded lecture on 1 March 2013: http://72.167.35.235/ongoing/fal_seminar_2013/01_upkaram/

34. Personal communication, 21 February 2012.

35. Personal communication, 16 October 2012.

36. For further scholarship on the function of hagiography in South Asia and beyond, see John S. Hawley, ed., *Saints and Virtues* (Berkeley: University of California Press, 1987); Rupert Snell and Winand M. Callewaert, eds, *According to Tradition: Hagiographical Writing in India* (Wiesbaden: Harrassowitz, 1994); Karen G. Ruffle, *Gender, Sainthood, and Everyday Practice in South Asian Shi'ism* (Chapel Hill: University of North Caroline Press, 2011); and Tony K. Stewart, *The Final Word: The Caitanya Caritāmṛta and the Grammar of Religious Tradition* (New York: Oxford University Press, 2010).

37. Stewart, *The Final Word*, 15.

38. Stewart, *The Final Word*, 16.

39. Paul Griffiths, *Religious Reading: The Place of Reading in the Practice of Religion* (New York: Oxford University Press, 1999), 42–3.

40. Linda Hess, 'Lovers' Doubts: Questioning the Tulsi *Rāmāyaṇ*', in *Questioning Ramayanas: A South Asian Tradition*, ed. Paula Richman (Berkeley: University of California Press, 2001), 28.

41. Robert Orsi, *Between Heaven and Earth: The Religious Worlds People Make and the Scholars Who Study Them* (Princeton: Princeton University Press, 2005), 2.

42. Orsi, *Between Heaven and Earth*, 2.

43. For an ethnographic monograph dedicated to the plurality of moral discourse, see Leela Prasad, *The Poetics of Conduct: Oral Narrative and Moral Being in a South Indian Town* (New York: Columbia University Press, 2006).

Bibliography

Hindi

Parikh, Dvarkadas, ed. *Caurāsī vaiṣṇavan kī vārtā: tīn janma kī līlā bhāvnā vālī sahit*. Indore: Vaishnava Mitra Mandal Sarvananik Nyas, 2011.

———. *Do sau bāvan vaiṣṇavan kī vārtā: tīn janma kī līlā bhāvnā vālīsahit*. Indore: Vaishnava Mitra Mandal Sarvananik Nyas, 2009.

Tandan, Hariharnath. *Vārtā sāhitya: ek vṛhat adhyayan*. Aligarh: Bharat Prakasan Mandir, 1960.

Gujarati

Bhatiya, Bhupendra. *Ṣoḍaśgranthāgat upadeś ane temnī 28 vārtāo (bhāg 2)*. Rajkot: Purvi Press, 2008.

Deshpande, P.G. *Gujarātī-Angrejī koś*. Ahmedabad: University Granth-nimarn Board, 2002.

Parikh, Rameshbhai V., trans. 'Coryāsī vaiṣṇavonī vārtāo: tūm bīn tattva kachu nahī jagmeṃ (84 bhagavadīyatatvavicār)', edited by Goswami Shri Vagish Kumar. In *Puṣṭimārgīya patrācār: śuddhādvait sevābhūṣaṇ*. Baroda: Shri Vakpati Foundation, 2002.

English

Arney, Paul. 'The *Bade Shikshapatra*: A Vallabhite Guide to the Worship of Krishna's Divine Images'. In *Krishna: A Sourcebook*, edited by Edwin F. Bryant. Oxford: Oxford University Press, 2007.

Bachrach, Emilia, 'Justifying Religious Authority: The Function of Hariray's Bhavprakash Commentary in the *Caurasi Vaishnavan ki Varta*' (paper presented at the 38th Annual Conference on South Asia, Madison Wisconsin, October 2009).

Barz, Richard. *The Bhakti Sect of Vallabhācārya*. New Delhi: Munshiram Manoharlal, 1992a.

———. 'Kṛṣṇadās Adhikārī: An Irascible Devotee's Approach to the Divine'. In *Bhakti Studies*, edited by G. Baily. New Delhi: Sterling, 1992b.

Bynum, Caroline Walker. *Holy Feast and Holy Fast: The Religious Significance of Food to Medieval Women*. Berkeley: University of California Press, 1987.

Dalmia, Vasudha. 'Forging Community: The Guru in a Seventeenth-Century Vaiṣṇava Hagiography'. In *Charisma and Canon*, edited by Vasudha Dalmia, Angelika Malinar, and Martin Christof. Oxford: Oxford University Press, 2001.

Galina, Rousseva-Sokolva. 'Sainthood Revisited: Two Printed Versions of the Lives of the Eighty-Four Vaishnavas by Gokulnāth'. In *Bhakti beyond the Forest: Current Research of Early Modern Literatures in North India, 2003–2009*, edited by Imre Bangha. New Delhi: Manohar Publishers, 2012.

Griffiths, Paul. *Religious Reading: The Place of Reading in the Practice of Religion*. New York: Oxford University Press, 1999.

Hawley, John S. 'The Four *Sampradāyas*: Ordering the Religious Past in Mughal North India'. *South Asian History* 2, no. 2 (2011): 160–83.

———, ed. *Saints and Virtues*. Berkeley: University of California Press, 1987.

Hess, Linda. 'Lovers' Doubts: Questioning the Tulsi *Rāmāyaṇ*'. In *Questioning Ramayanas: A South Asian Tradition*, edited by Paula Richman. Berkeley: University of California Press, 2001.

McGregor, R.S. *Oxford Hindi-English Dictionary*. New Delhi: Oxford University Press, 1993.

Orsi, Robert. *Between Heaven and Earth: The Religious Worlds People Make and the Scholars Who Study Them*. Princeton: Princeton University Press, 2005.

Prasad, Leela. *The Poetics of Conduct Oral Narrative and Moral Being in a South Indian Town*. New York: Columbia University Press, 2006.

Redington, James D., trans. *The Grace of Lord Krishna: The Sixteen Verse-Treatises of Vallabhacharya*. New Delhi: Sri Satguru Publications, 2000.

Ricoeur, Paul. *From Text to Action: Essays in Hermeneutics*. Vol. 2. Evanston: Northwestern University Press, 1986.

Ruffle, Karen G. *Gender, Sainthood, and Everyday Practice in South Asian Shi'ism*. Chapel Hill: University of North Caroline Press, 2011.

Saha, Shandip. 'A Community of Grace: The Social and Theological World of the Puṣṭi MārgaVārtā Literature'. *Bulletin of School of Oriental and African Studies* 69, no. 2 (2006): 225–42.

———. 'The Movement of *Bhakti* along a North-West Axis: Tracing the History of the Puṣṭimārg between the Sixteenth and Nineteenth Centuries'. *International Journal of Hindu Studies* 11, no. 3 (2008): 299–318.

Snell, Rupert and Winand M. Callewaert, eds. *According to Tradition: Hagiographical Writing in India*. Wiesbaden: Harrassowitz, 1994.

Smith, Frederick M. 'Dark Matter in Vārtāland: On the Enterprise of History in Early Puṣṭimārga Discourse'. *The Journal of Hindu Studies* 2 (2009): 27–47

———. 'The Saṃnyāsanirṇaya: A Śuddhādvaita Text on Renunciation by Vallabhācārya'. *Journal of Vaishnava Studies* 1, no. 4 (1993): 135–56.

Stewart, Tony K. *The Final Word: The Caitanya Caritāmṛta and the Grammar of Religious Tradition*. New York: Oxford University Press, 2010.

Vaudeville, Charlotte. *Myths, Saints and Legends in Medieval India*. New Delhi: Oxford University Press, 1996.

About the Editors and Contributors

Editors

Tyler Williams is assistant professor in the Department of South Asian Languages and Civilizations at the University of Chicago, USA. His primary research and teaching areas are Hindi language and literature, South Asian religion and aesthetics, and book history. His current research projects centre on the early manuscript culture of Hindi and on merchant religious and literary culture in precolonial north India.

Anshu Malhotra is associate professor in the Department of History, University of Delhi, India. She holds a PhD from SOAS, University of London, England. She is the author of *Piro and the Gulabdasis: Gender, Sect and Society in Punjab* (2017) and *Gender, Caste and Religious Identities: Restructuring Class in Colonial Punjab* (2002). She has co-edited *Punjab Reconsidered: History, Culture and Practice* (2012) and *Speaking of the Self: Gender, Performance and Autobiography in South Asia* (2015).

John Stratton Hawley—informally, Jack—is Claire Tow Professor of Religion at Barnard College, Columbia University, New York, USA. His most recent books on India's *bhakti* traditions are *A Storm of Songs: India and the Idea of the Bhakti Movement* (2015), *Sur's Ocean* (with Kenneth

Bryant, 2015), and a poem-by-poem commentary called *Into Sur's Ocean* (2016).

Contributors

Emilia Bachrach is assistant professor of religion and gender, sexuality, and feminist studies at Oberlin College, Ohio, USA. Her research currently focuses on the reception of early modern Brajbhasha *bhakti* literature in contemporary Gujarat, and, more broadly, on gendered practices of religious reading and devotional performance in modern India. She is currently completing a book project called *Religious Reading and Everyday Lives in Pushtimargi Hinduism.*

Imre Bangha is associate professor of Hindi at the University of Oxford, UK. He studied Indology in Budapest, Hungary, and holds a PhD in Hindi from Visva-Bharati University, Santiniketan, West Bengal, India. His publications include English, Hindi, and Hungarian books and articles on literature in Brajbhasha and other forms of early Hindi, with special focus on the poetic works of Anandghan, Thakur, Vishnudas, Tulsidas, Kabir, and Bajid as well as on Nāgarī Rekhtā literature.

Allison Busch is associate professor of Hindi and Indian literature at Columbia University in the city of New York, USA. She specializes in classical Hindi (Brajbhasha) poetry and Mughal period court culture. Her current research projects include various explorations of Hindi historical poetry from the Mughal period and a collaborative book, with art historian Molly Aitken, on the interface of Brajbhasha with early modern visual culture.

Stefania Cavaliere is assistant professor of Hindi language and literature in the Department of Asian, African and Mediterranean Studies, University of Naples, L'Orientale, Italy. Her research investigates court poetry in Hindi from the sixteenth and seventeenth centuries, Indian aesthetics, and parallel translations of allegorical texts belonging to the *Prabodhacandrodaya* tradition. Her most recent publications in this area (among others) include 'Eating and Fasting to Liberate the Mind. Some Remarks on the Theme of Food in Keśavdās's *Vijñānagītā*' (in *A World of Nourishment: Reflections on Food in Indian Culture*, 2016).

Shreekant Kumar Chandan has taught at the University of Delhi, India, and is now working as an independent research scholar. His research centres on the literary and political culture of the early modern period, in particular on sources of Mughal history in the vernacular.

John E. Cort is professor of Asian and comparative religions at Denison University, Ohio, USA. His research focuses on the ritual, devotional, and literary cultures of the Jains of western India, and combines historical research with fieldwork on contemporary issues and practices. He is the author of *Jains in the World: Religious Values and Ideology in India* (2001) and *Framing the Jina: Narratives of Icons and Idols in Jain History* (2010), as well as several dozen articles.

Arthur Dudney is a Leverhulme Early Career Fellow at the University of Cambridge, UK. He is author of *Delhi: Pages from a Forgotten History* (2015). His current project, 'Making Persianate People', considers how literary Persian was taught in the vast region where it had cultural currency but was not a mother tongue. Previously he was a Mellon Postdoctoral Fellow at the University of Oxford, UK. He received his PhD from Columbia University, New York, USA, in 2013.

Shrivatsa Goswami comes from a family of spiritual leaders and scholars at Sri Radharaman Mandir, Vrindavan, India. He often serves as a spokesman for Hinduism at interreligious forums within India and around the world, and has delivered the Hibbert Lectures at Oxford. Goswami is the author, with Jack Hawley, of *At Play with Krishna* (1981) and he has been deeply involved in the publication of a number of scholarly volumes, including *Govindadeva: A Dialogue in Stone* (ed. Margaret H. Case, 1996). His regular lectures on the *Bhagavad Gita* and the *Bhagavata Purana* have a devoted following. He is also founder–director of the Sri Caitanya Prema Samsthana, a Vrindavan-based institution that plays host to scholars from around the world.

Rembert Lutjeharms is a research fellow and librarian at the Oxford Centre for Hindu Studies, University of Oxford, UK, and a tutor in Hinduism at the Faculty of Theology and Religion of the University of Oxford. The main subject of his research is the early intellectual history of the Caitanya Vaishnava tradition. He is also an editor of the *Journal of Hindu Studies.*

Hiroko Nagasaki, PhD, is associate professor at Osaka University, Japan. Her main research area is early Hindi devotional literature and

Hindi *chand śāstra* (metrics). She is the editor of *Indian and Persian Prosody and Recitation* (2012), has written articles about Hindi *bhakti* literature, and has translated poetry by Tulsidas, Rahim, and Raskhan, as well as the hagiography of Tulsidas (*Mūl gosāīṃ carit*) into Japanese.

Luther Obrock is assistant professor in South Asian religions at the University of Toronto, Canada. He focuses on the religious, political, and intellectual history of Sanskrit literature in medieval South Asia. His research centres on Indic conceptions of politics and religion in the centuries surrounding the stabilization of Islamic states in the subcontinent, particularly in premodern Kashmir.

Heidi R. M. Pauwels is professor in the Department of Asian Languages and Literature at the University of Washington in Seattle, USA. She teaches Sanskrit and Modern and Old Hindi language and literature, and courses on Hinduism. Her publications include various articles in scholarly journals and conference proceedings as well as two monographs on sixteenth-century *bhakti*. Her book *Cultural Exchange in Eighteenth-Century India: Poetry and Paintings from Kishangarh* has recently been published. She is currently working on a Guggenheim project on the mobilization of myth and hagiography in the works of Savant Singh of Kishangarh.

William R. Pinch is professor of history and environmental studies at Wesleyan University, Connecticut, USA, and associate editor of the journal *History and Theory*. His publications include *Peasants and Monks in British India* (1996), *Warrior Ascetics and Indian Empires* (2006), *Speaking of Peasants: Essays in Indian History and Politics in Honor of Walter Hauser* (2008), and *History and Theory in a Global Frame* (2015).

Dalpat Rajpurohit is a lecturer of Hindi–Urdu at Columbia University, New York, USA. He has published essays in the Hindi journals *Ālocanā* and *Sammelan Patrikā*, in *Bhakti beyond the Forest* (2013), and in *Swaminarayan Hinduism* (2016). He has also published on issues of classical Hindi literature in the Hindi national daily *Jansattā*. Together with William Pinch and Allison Busch, he is preparing a translation of two eighteenth-century historical poems in Brajbhasha.

Teiji Sakata is professor emeritus of Takushoku University, Tokyo, Japan. He has also taught at Tokyo University of Foreign Studies and has served as the director of the Institute for Research in the Humanities in Japan since 2005. Among his many publications, the most recent include. *The Historical Development of the Bhakti Movement in India, Theory and Practice* (ed., 2011), *Hindi Folktales* (1999), and *Imaging India Imaging Japan: A Chronicle of Reflections on Mutual Literature* (edited with Unita Sachisdanand, 2004). Sakata has done extensive research on medieval Hindi literature and folk literature.

Swapna Sharma is senior lector in Hindi at Yale University, USA. Before joining Yale, he taught at the University of Chicago, USA, and the University of Leipzig, Saxony, Germany. Among her many publications, the most recent include the *Dictionary of Bhakti: North Indian Text into Khariboli Hindi and English* (with Winand M. Callewaert, 2009) and *Gadadhar Bhaṭṭ Paramparā: Siddhānt Aur Sāhitya* (2008).

Raman P. Sinha is associate professor in the Centre of Indian Languages, Jawaharlal Nehru University, New Delhi, India. His research centres on Hindi literature, translation, and art and culture. His recent publications include *Ramcaritmānas: Pāṭh, Līlā, Citra, Saṅgīt* (2011) and *Śaṁśer Kā Saṁsār* (2013).

Jaroslav Strnad is senior research fellow at the Oriental Institute, Czech Academy of Sciences, Prague, and lecturer in the Department of South and Central Asian Studies, Faculty of Arts, Charles University, Prague. His research focuses on Old Hindi dialects and literature in the context of the political, economic, and cultural history of medieval and early modern India. Recent contributions include *Morphology and Syntax of Old Hindī: Edition and Analysis of One Hundred Kabīr Vānī Poems from Rājasthān* (2013).

Samuel Wright is former assistant professor in the School of Historical Studies, Nalanda University, Bihar, India. His research focuses on the intellectual history of early modern and early colonial South Asia in conversation with the cultural and political history of premodern Bengal. His research addresses the political culture of local polities in Bengal; connections between intellectual and social debates in Varanasi; Sanskrit and Bengali literary interactions; and theories of property in early modern Bengal. He is currently completing a book-length project on the intellectual history of logic (*nyāya*) in early modern India.

Index